The Careers Book

Be your own boss

Editors:
KLAUS BOEHM AND
JENNY LEES-SPALDING

Jobs Editor: Jane Shaw
Careers Editor: Pam North
Business Editor: Andrew Ferguson

PAPERMAC

First published as *The Alternative Careers Book* in 1988

This edition published in 1989 by
PAPERMAC
a division of Macmillan Publishers Limited
4 Little Essex Street London WC2R 3LF
and Basingstoke

Associated companies in Auckland, Delhi, Dublin, Gaborone, Hamburg, Harare,
Hong Kong, Johannesburg, Kuala Lumpur, Lagos, Manzini, Melbourne, Mexico
City, Nairobi, New York, Singapore and Tokyo

ISBN 0–333–48261–1

A CIP catalogue record for this book is available from the British Library

Typeset by Wearside Tradespools, Fulwell, Sunderland

Printed and bound by Richard Clay Ltd, Bungay, Suffolk

Contents

Foreword

Do you want to spend your life jumping through a progression of hoops just as you did at school and may still be doing at polytechnic or university? Do you secretly aspire to be Head of School, only this time in the wider world of work, securely located on the 21st floor of your World HQ? If this is the sort of life you want, the *Careers Book* is not for you; stick to conventional careers literature.

But if you want to work towards becoming your own boss you'll get little help from conventional careers literature. Not to put too fine a point on it, you'll probably find it's constipated and boringly unattuned to the rich multitude of jobs outside bureaucracies. Much of it is focused on the bureaucratic aspects of occupations: how to work in the crown prosecution service rather than as a solicitor in private practice; how to become an assistant hotel manager by the time you are 40 rather than how to run your own hotel; how to become a corporate executive, not how to run your own business, even in this age of enterprise.

Perhaps this state of affairs can be put down to inertia. It's certainly a lot less trouble to regurgitate employers' recruitment literature than to prepare the material oneself. But the uneasy suspicion remains that it ain't necessarily so; that it's a reflection of obsolete social values; that the proliferators of careers literature, almost by definition bureaucrats themselves, think that independent professionals are a little too independent; that the creative worlds of the arts, literature, music, film and video and the wonderful range of crafts are simply not quite nice; and that, as the taste of the nation changes, the splendid expansion of specialist farming, and the sharp end of marketing, sales promotion, public relations and direct selling are not quite the thing for those with trained minds. As for the practitioners of alternative medicine, are they not quite possibly quacks? Certainly psychologists, counsellors and independent careers consultants who work as their own boss (instead of knuckling down to the public service) must be so. If you take the trouble to read the weightier careers tomes (or national newspaper careers supplements) you'll end up with the impression that the only jobs that count are those within a bureaucracy.

You'll also notice that the world of work, as portrayed in this literature is astonishingly funless. Question: Does this correspond with reality as you observe it? Do you suppose that the proliferators of conventional careers literature have ever been to a pub, a restaurant, a wine bar? Have they ever rented a holiday cottage, attended a wedding, a sporting occasion or a private viewing? Have they ever considered travelling, visiting an historic house, windsurfing or reading a book? Does it occur to them that the economy thrives because people get off their backsides and do something they actually like doing? It's not the funlessness alone, it's as if entrepreneurial energy simply didn't exist; that export/import businesses, commodity dealing, specialist retailing, property development, timeshare ownership and being a landlord were on a different planet.

Meanwhile in the real world attitudes are rapidly changing. Whatever you think of Mrs Thatcher, you'll have to agree that the economic and social position of the non-bureaucrat has notably improved in the last ten years. Nevertheless the UK still has the smallest small firm sector of any advanced industrial economy, for which conventional careers literature has to accept its share of the blame. Its prejudice against those whose ambition it is to stand on their own two feet has done nothing at all to help.

There is one huge advantage to working for yourself, not recognised by the conventional careers literature: we've called it mix and match. The literature maintains an astonishing adherence to the unitary notion of graduate jobs ie that graduates should do one single job for the duration of their working lives. This preposterous notion makes little sense for the 90s (it's probably never made much). Musicians have always mixed a variety of jobs (performing, teaching, counselling, fixing . . .) and it's beginning to catch on in lots of other areas. Working for yourself you can do this and the *Careers Book* gives some possibilities under each job profile for you to think about – MP and solicitor, farmer and holiday accommodation owner; actor and scriptwriter – once you start talking to people who are their own boss, you realise how widespread it is. So keep your mind open. Not only does mixing and matching allow you to use different skills and put yourself under different pressures (counsellor and cabinet maker) but makes it easier to switch jobs in mid-career, change the mix of jobs, sell a business but keep the second job going during the launch of another. Flexibility!

But that's not the only advantage to being your own boss. You can decide how quickly you want your career to develop. You don't have to prove yourself on a dreary, externally imposed ladder of traineeships and under-assistant-junior executiveships. You may want to concentrate on other things for a few months, spend time writing, travelling, playing with your children or designing your garden. You can set your own pace and decide what your job is; no-one else is going to thrust a job description at you. You can do what you want to do and pay others to do the rest.

So, if you are attracted to a career that does not shackle you to employers for the rest of your working life, you're going to have to think things out for yourself. Talk to your careers advisers and enlist their help but you won't be able to just reach for the bumph in the careers library. You'll have to research the jobs information you need and talk to people actually doing the job. And you're going to have to get a strategy. You'll find in many cases that you'll have to begin by working for someone else before springboarding and becoming your own boss. Nobody can think all this out for you; it's your life, not theirs. The *Careers Book* should help you begin to develop a personal strategy but remember that in the end, it's up to you to get up, find out for yourself and get on with it.

We are very grateful for the help we have received in producing this book from a wide range of people. Our special thanks go to Gill Drake, to Bryan Reading for the cartoons and to the many people who have helped in the preparation of the job profiles –

ARMITAGE, Aileen: Novelist
BARKER, Noel: Singer – Classical/Operatic
BARNES, Hilary: Foreign Correspondent; Newsletter Publisher
BEARN, E.M.: Dentist
BESCH, Anthony: Opera Producer or Director
BICKERSTETH, Jane: Printmaker
BILLEN, Stephanie: Production Team (Film)
BLOODWORTH, Colin: Timeshare; Holiday Accommodation; Import/
  Export Broker
BODGENER, Beste: Picture Restoring
BONCZYK, Philip: Caterer
BOWDAGE, Ruth: Picture Framer

BRIGGS, Stephen: Cabinet Maker
BROOKES, Anna: Fashion Clothes
CAIRNS, David: Music Critic
CAMPBELL, Alan: Greyhound Trainer; Media Space Sales; Advertising
  Agent
CARR, Antonia: Hypnotherapist
CATTO, A.G.: Chiropodist
CHADWICK, Anna-Mei: Contemporary Art Gallery Owner
CHADWICK, Brian: Publican; Restaurateur; Wine Merchant
CORBETT, Nigel of Summer Lodge: Hotel Keeper
CROUCH, Colin: Thatcher
CUMING, Hugh: Kennel and Cattery
CURTIS, P.J.: Chiropractor
DALAMORE, Robert: Reflexologist
DEAN, Lee: Stage Designer
DEWHURST, Barbara: Dealer in Small Antiques
DILL, Rosanne: Property Manager
DOGGART, W.L.: Embalmer
DUNWOODY, Dr John: GP (NHS)
EDWARDES, Phil: Healer
EVANS, Deborah: Various
EYNON, Mark: Festival Director
FORD, Kevin: Caterer
FOSTER, Charlotte: Various
GELLER, Maurice: Various
GIBBS, Michael: Bookseller
GILBERT, John: Jobbing Printer
GODDARD, Anthony: Wine Grower
GRAINGER, Ashley: Direct Marketing
GREGORY, Jane: Literary Agent
GUBBAY, Raymond: Impresario
HANKIN, Christine: Music Instrument Retailer
HARCUS, James, of Gordon Dadd: Solicitor
HAYNES, Judith: Child/Educational Psychologist
HONEYMAN, Louise: Orchestral Fixer
HOPKINS, Brian: Dental Technician
HUGGINS Haulage: Haulier
JOHNSON, Anne: Various
JOHNSON, Brian: List Broker; Garden Gnome Maker
JONES, Robin: Chemical Engineering Consultant
KAWALL, Kieron: Dancer

KAY, Andrew: Criminal
KIDD-HEWITT, Jan: Insurance Broker
KING, Chris: Film Director
KOREN, Anna: Graphologist
LANGFORD, Philip: Pop Group Sound Engineer
LINDLEY, John, of Activ Sports: Specialist Sports Shop; Windsurfing
  School
LEE, Lilly: Calligrapher
LEA, Liz: Gardener
LEES-SPALDING, Tim: Post Office; Village Shopkeeper
LIVINGSTONE-LEARMONTH: Various
LONERGAN, B.: Osteopath
LOWDELL, Paul: Instrument Repairer
LOWRY, Stephen: Actuary
McCAUSLAND, Tina: Acupuncturist
McCULLOCH, Andrew: TV Scriptwriter
MANSELL, Ros: Silversmithing
MARINE, R.P.: Sailing School
MARSTON, Ray: Wigmaking
MATTHEWS, David: Composer = Classical
MEINHARD, Tom: Marketing Consultant
MELLUISH, Sarah of Cameo Events Organisation: Events Organiser
MILMAN, David: Musicians' Answering and Booking Service
MILLS, Simon: Tourist Guide
MILLS, Steve: Street Entertainer
MOORE, John: Fashion Shoe Maker
NEWMAN, Edward: Leatherwork
OLIVER, John: Bookseller; Sales Agent
ORME, David: Magazine Publishing
OULTRAM, Kenn: Kennels and Cattery
PARKER, Jim: Composer and Arranger
PARKIN, Lynd: Direct Marketing
PEARSON, Esther: Knitwear Designer
PERRY, Ted: Record Company
PHELAN, Brian: Private Investigator
PICKETT, Maggie: Music Therapist
PRICE, Fiona of Fiona Price and Partners Ltd: Independent Financial
  Adviser
RANGER, Helen: Concert Agent
RANGER, John: Piano Tuner
REISS-McCULLOCH, Amanda: Theatrical Agent; Dress Agent

RENNIE, Mike: Music Copyist
REYNOLDS, J.G.: House Convertor
RICHARDSON, N.W.: Shipbroker
RIGBY, Penny: Magazine Publishing
ROBINSON, Sarah: Nanny Agency
RUSSELL, Peter: Driving Instructor
SANDYS-RENTON, David: Publican; Brewer
SANDYS-RENTON, Harriet: Inventor
SANDYS-RENTON, Tim: Sculptor
SHEERMAN, Barry: MP
SMITH, Ainsley: Optician
SMITH, Catherine: Various
SOLON, Jackie: Various
STEELE-PERKINS, Crispian: Instrumental Soloist
STEVENSON BROTHERS: Toymaker
STORCH, Christopher: Hi-Fi Shop Owner
STRICKLAND, John: Cleaning Contractor
STROMAN, Scott: Jazz Musician/Singer
THOROGOOD, John: Estate Agent
TOMKINS, Robert: Plumbing and Heating Engineer
TOMLINSON, James: Typesetting; Wordprocessing
TOOKEY, Fleur: Glass Design/Making
WARHURST, Fiona: Film
WESTRAY, Katharine: Costume Designer
WHEELER, F.: Coal Merchant
WHITE, Malcolm: Graphic Designer
WILLIAMSON, Malcolm: Alexander Technique
WILTSHIRE TRACKLEMENTS: Specialist Food Manufacturer
WOODMAN, Peter: Landlord
WOODMAN, Trevor: Carpenter
YOUNG, John: Funeral Director
and many others who prefer to remain anonymous.

Klaus Boehm and Jenny Lees-Spalding
London
January 1989

How To Use The Book

How To Use The Book

The *Careers Book* is a guidebook not a definitive map. It is intended for undergraduates, sixth formers and those in employment wishing to become their own boss. It is deliberately impressionistic; personal not generalised; a snapshot of reality in one situation not an attempt to produce material for an MPhil in occupational studies. Use it for what it is – a means of narrowing down your options so that you can begin to create your own shortlist.

The book is divided into a number of sections so that you can get a strategy and start your shortlisting from different starting points.

Abbreviations This gives the meanings of some of the more common of the thousands of ghastly abbreviations you may meet.

How To Go About It – Careers A–Z This gives some of the information you might consider before choosing which career best suits you. It's alphabetically arranged.

How To Go About It – Business A–Z Information on starting up in business (and any job where you work for yourself is a business, whether you are an accountant or an actor). Again this is alphabetically arranged.

A–Z Jobs More than 260 profiles of jobs where you can be your own boss, based on real people. Browse through and see what interests you. Beware of comparing one job profile with another. Sources and contributors were asked to provide insights, not measurable data; in particular the financial and training information is often personal and impressionistic. The book makes no attempt to cover jobs in employment – thus the piece on solicitors does not cover work in the crown prosecution service or local authorities; the profile on publican does not cover pub managers, employed by the brewery.

Each profile contains an 'At A Glance' box, which has the key information about the job, followed by a description of the job. The 'At A Glance' box gives you information on

Qualifications/Training This tells you if you need to do a course, leading to a certificate, to do the job.

Licence For some jobs (eg Publican) you are legally required to hold a licence; for others (eg Architect) it is a professional requirement; for a few (eg actor), it is necessary to have a union card. This section is only concerned with personal licences; it is not concerned with any need to register your activities with any local or government depart- . ment, seek planning permission etc.

Experience/Springboard   For many jobs, you need to have worked in the business to gain experience or contacts or both. This section tells you whether this is required or recommended. Some training courses include some work experience, eg barristers must serve as a pupil before qualifying, and this is not included here. If the answer is 'no' it means you can (or must) go straight into the job as freelance, self employed or as a professional partner.

Mid-career entry   Some jobs you must start when you are older (consultants, psychoanalyst); others are almost exclusively young people's jobs; others are particularly suitable for mid-career job changes.

Entry costs   How much you need to start. This always excludes the cost of your own home. The costs may be lower than we've indicated if you have some of the start-up kit already eg it need cost you nothing to become a jazz singer if you already have a telephone and a record player.

Income bracket   Low means up to £12,000 per annum; medium is broadly £12,000–£25,000; and high, more than £25,000. The bracket given is the norm eg actor is given as low because that is the case for the majority. But even as an actor, *you* can strike lucky and be a tax exile. Good Luck!

Town/Country   Where you usually need to locate the business.

Travel   Whether you need to travel as part of the job.

Exit sale   If the answer is 'yes', it means you may be able to sell the business for more than you put in.

Work at home   You can in some – hopeless in others. The answer is no if you only happen to live above the shop.

Enquiries   Where you can get more information about the job.

Mix and match   Almost all jobs can be combined with others to a greater or lesser extent. The list given under each job is to give you ideas, not a blueprint for your life. You obviously can't do a job requiring travel with another where total accessibility is important; you can't run a shop with another job which requires 18-hour working days; you probably won't want to do more than one three year training course. But there is still plenty of scope – and if you have a partner or you are large enough to have employees, the scope is greater still. The mix and match lists are of different sorts: jobs you can sensibly do at the same time e.g. MP and novelist; jobs to keep you going while you start up a business or between jobs (actors); lines into which you can diversify when you are successful (racehorse owner, landlord etc.).

Job Spotter   Taking yourself as the starting point, you may know, for example, you want to work in the country, or work using your writing skills. If that's so you could start with the Job Spotter – there are lists of jobs under some 20 headings.

Special Features Index   The key information on all the jobs in the book is here, in compact form so you can glance down eg the column on entry costs and see what jobs to look up with the fortune you have amassed or money you think you could con out of the bank. For explanations of the headings, see explanations of the 'At A Glance' box under A–Z JOBS above.

Addresses   Addresses of those organisations mentioned in the text in small capitals eg EQUITY.

Bibliography   This gives details of the books and trade mags given in the text in italics eg *Farmers Weekly*.

Index   Use it!

Once you have a strategy and a shortlist, follow it up with further reading and interrogate your careers adviser. Then, most important, find out about the jobs and their difficulties. Find people doing those jobs and *talk to them*.

We would like to have suggestions for information you would like to see in the next edition of this book. Please write to the editors at the publisher's address.

Abbreviations

The job world is peppered with abbreviations. Here are some which you may come across.

ABTA	Association of British Travel Agents
ACTT	Association of Cinematograph, Television and Allied Technicians
ACU	Auto Cycle Union
AFAEP	Association of Fashion, Advertising and Editorial Photographers
AFBD	Association of Futures Brokers and Dealers
AGCAS	All Graduate Careers Advisory Service
AMCA	Amateur Motor Cycle Association
APRS	Association of Professional Recording Studios
ASM	Assistant Stage Manager
BABA	British Artist Blacksmiths' Association
BBC	British Broadcasting Corporation
BIBA	British Insurance Brokers' Association
BIE	British Institute of Embalmers
BIPP	British Institute of Professional Photography
BMA	British Medical Association
BTEC	Business and Technician Education Council
CAM	Communications, Advertising and Marketing
CAMRA	Campaign for Real Ale
CHE	College of Higher Education
CII	Chartered Insurance Institute
COIC	Careers and Occupational Information Centre
CoSIRA	Council for Small Industries in Rural Areas
CRAC	Careers Research and Advisory Centre
CSU	Central Services Unit (of AGCAS)
CV	Curriculum Vitae
DE	Department of Employment
DES	Department of Education and Science
DHSS	Department of Health and Social Security
DIY	Do It Yourself
DJ	Disc Jockey
DOE	Department of the Environment
DOG	Directory of Graduate Appointments
DTI	Department of Trade and Industry
EC	European Community

ET	Employment Training
FDR	First Destination Return
FE	Further Education
FIMBRA	Financial Intermediaries Managers and Brokers Regulatory Association
GCE	General Certificate of Education
GCSE	General Certificate of Secondary Education
GBP	Great British Public
GO	Graduate Opportunities
GP	General Practitioner
HE	Higher Education
HGV	Heavy Goods Vehicle
HMSO	Her Majesty's Stationery Office
IBM	International Business Machines
IEE	Institution of Electrical Engineers
IMRO	Investment Managers' Regulatory Organisation
IPM	Institute of Personnel Management
ISM	International Society of Musicians
ITB/TB	Industrial Training Board/Training Board
ITDG	Intermediate Technology Development Group
ITV	Independent Television
LAUTRO	Life Assurance and Unit Trust Regulatory Organisation
LEA	Local Education Authority
LGSM	Licentiate of the Guildhall School of Music
LRAM	Licentiate of the Royal Academy of Music
LRCM	Licentiate of the Royal College of Music
LTCM	Licentiate of Trinity College of Music
MOT	Ministry of Transport
MP	Member of Parliament
MSc	Master of Science
MSC	Manpower Services Commission
NATTA	Network for Alternative Technology and Technology Assessment
NFPDC	National Federation of Painting and Decorating Contractors
NFSE	National Federation of Self-Employed and Small Businesses
NFU	National Farmers' Union
NGA	National Graphical Association
NHS	National Health Service

NICIEC	National Inspection Council for Electrical Installation Contracting
NME	New Musical Express
NMFB & AEA	National Master Farriers, Blacksmiths & Agricultural Engineering Association
NUJ	National Union of Journalists
OND	Ordinary National Diploma
PC	Personal Computer
PCAS	Polytechnic Central Admissions System
PER	Professional and Executive Registry
PGCE	Post Graduate Certificate of Education
PR	Public Relations
RAD	Royal Academy of Dancing
RCVS	Royal College of Veterinary Surgeons
RHS	Royal Horticultural Society
RICS	Royal Institution of Chartered Surveyors
RSA	Royal Society of Arts
RSC	Royal Shakespeare Company
ROGET	Register of Graduate Employment and Training
RYA	Royal Yachting Association
SAE	Stamped Addressed Envelope
SDP	Social Democratic Party
SE	Stock Exchange
SIAD	Society of Industrial Artists and Designers
SIB	Security and Investments Board
SOGAT	Society of Graphic and Allied Trades
SRN	State Registered Nurse
SRO	Self Regulatory Organisation
TA	Training Agency
TSA	The Securities Association
TSB	Trustee Savings Bank
UCCA	University Central Council for Admissions
VAT	Value Added Tax
YES	Youth Enterprise Scheme

How to go about it

Careers   A-Z

How To Go About It
Careers A–Z

Ageism

'Graduates required, under 25'; 'Likely age of successful candidate: 24–27'.

When you see ads like this, you realise that in some occupations there is bias against the over-30s never mind the over-50s.

Mature graduates often have to fight harder to get jobs: a recent survey of City Poly graduates showed that although older graduates got better degrees, they were less likely to be employed than younger graduates.

Many jobs in this book are well suited to the victims of ageism. There is really no substitute for experience and a well-developed network of contacts.

Alternative Technology

The development of a highly industrialised society has lead certain groups and individuals to look at new work structures and power sources and to set up enterprises which are less destructive of the world's resources than conventional industry.

On a small scale, self-sufficiency may be the aim, but there are also communes, companies and research establishments who devote their work to alternative technology. *Resurgence*, a bi-monthly publication, covers green politics, conservation and the environment as well as alternative technology. The CENTRE FOR ALTERNATIVE TECHNOLOGY in North Wales, and its offshoot, the URBAN CENTRE FOR ALTERNATIVE TECHNOLOGY in Bristol provide training, practical research and demonstrations. The Open University's Faculty of Technology also has a good reputation in the field, and was where NATTA (the Network for Alternative Technology and Technology Assessment) started; NATTA publishes a useful newsletter. ITDG (the Intermediate Technology Development Group) is mainly concerned with the appropriate development of technology in underdeveloped countries.

Alternative Work

'Alternative work' means different things to different people. It could mean:

- Involvement with 'clean' products (re-cycled, non-nuclear, and in

no way connected with animal testing, oppressive or fascist regimes, exploitation, apartheid or weapons technology);
■ Working for non-commercial, non-profit based companies;
■ Working for charities;
■ Working for pressure groups – which is now often big business;
■ Being involved in a co-operative or commune;

Some universities and polys run Alternative Work Fairs for those interested in 'clean' work. Contact the careers advisory service or Students' Union at York, Newcastle and Liverpool.

Application Forms

For most students, filling in application forms is a pain in the prover-bials. Tough. Most bureaucracies use them to find out more about you, your qualifications and your experience. They vary in shape, size and complexity and to complete them fully and to do yourself justice takes many hours of work. Once you have sorted out the relevant informa-tion each one becomes much easier to complete. But beware of completing them mechanically. Each form is a peculiar medium of communication with a handful of identifiable bureaucrats, just as an examination paper is a method of communicating with one or two known examiners. Use the application form as an opportunity to sell yourself – your skills, abilities, achievements, interests, motivation and attitude to work. (Remember that you can only communicate with the employer if you fill in the form LEGIBLY.)

There are many courses, leaflets and even videos available on this dreary skill. Ask your careers adviser.

Application Game

The thing about applying for jobs is to concentrate on selling yourself to your employer. It's just like any other form of selling: not every consumer wants to buy a green tie with pink spots, not every employer wants someone just like you. But you cannot begin the game until you have been noticed, which means getting shortlisted. Concentrate on getting shortlisted.

Get your formula established – decide on your strong points.

Present them: by putting them in the appropriate box on the

THE APPLICATION GAME

application form, or including them in your CV.

Decide what the selector wants: trained selectors will have a clear idea of the skills, knowledge and attitudes that they are looking for – they may even have a checklist of them, against which evidence of your skills, as shown on the application form, are assessed.

Answer the questions: few employers are going to be interested in someone who skirts a question, or has unexplained gaps in their employment record. And when it comes to questions about general interests, for example, employers are not really bothered about how large your stamp collection is or how many different sports you watch on television – they look at what your interests say about you and your ability. If propping up the bar and going to the cinema are your main pastimes, then this may indicate that you are sociable and enjoy passive cultural activities. But if you can say that you run a social club, arranging a varied annual programme and have doubled the membership in the last six months, the prospective employer can conclude that you are someone who can organise, plan ahead and achieve results.

Put across your experience: even if the work you have done so far does not seem relevant to the new job, some aspects may be useful – for example if you have had to work under pressure or deal directly with the public, then you have developed skills which can be transferred and developed in the new job.

Try to get offered this job, even if you are pretty sure that you do not want it. You can always turn it down.

Aptitude Tests

You probably know (or think you know) where your natural abilities lie, but your view will have been influenced by many factors: general interests, parents' and teachers' advice, motivation, abilities of your peer groups at school and college.

Aptitude tests are used mainly to test prospective employees of major organisations, as part of their selection procedure. At the simplest level they involve tests of manual dexterity and clerical data handling. At the graduate recruitment level they include:

Verbal reasoning: This is to test your ability to distinguish levels of information, make reasoned answers and evaluate a situation in a logical way. Analogies are often used (puppy is to dog as kitten is to – – –); or statements are made and you are asked to make appropriate deductions based on the information given.

Numerical reasoning: Some tests simply ask you to select the next number in a series – 3, 9, 27, ... to show you have the ability to manipulate numerical information, or you may be given sheets of data and asked to interpret and present information drawn from them.

Diagrammatic reasoning and spatial visualisation: This involves the ability to judge shapes and sizes and to visualise the relationship of objects to each other.

Remember when taking aptitude tests that they are demanding – you're not supposed to finish, as they are testing your speed and accuracy at the same time. You can practise tests to help improve your score and assess your aptitudes; the AGCAS/Saville and Holdsworth Management/Computer Aptitude tests are available through all university and polytechnic and some college careers services. Eysenck's books *Know your own IQ* and *Check your own IQ* have some examples that you can practise. Before taking a test, throw away your calculator for a week and think figures; aptitude testers seem to think there are merits in being able to do long multiplication in your head.

Psychological/motivational testing: This gets to the basics of what sort of work you're most suited for and will enjoy. You may want to have yourself tested to make sure you are making the right career decisions, or you may find that you want to employ someone, and would like to check their abilities. You can get this done by professional agencies – check the Yellow Pages under Career advice. Watch out for high charges. College careers centres can sometimes provide the service free.

You can't always rely on the results; remember they are produced by computers (or people who think like computers). There is the apocryphal case of the person who was told their aptitudes pointed to a career in the church. The computer had not asked what sex she was, or whether she believed in God.

Assessment Centres

If you go into bureaucratic employment before launching into an alternative career you may be sent to an assessment centre as part of the selection procedure. Selection interviews are notoriously poor on predicting behaviour in the job. Assessment centres provide observable evidence on how people perform in a variety of situations over a longer period of time. They enable selectors to see how you behave in a group situation and how well you accomplish particular tasks.

They normally last 1–3 days, at a hotel or management centre. They often include aptitude and personality tests as well as

- Further interviews
- Group exercises, including mock meetings, and committees, and business games, either with or without a leader
- Work situation exercises (eg testing how you would deal with a typical 'in-tray' given a specified time to decide on immediate or deferred action; a drafting test, in which you are asked to draft replies to tricky letters about a particular situation)
- Presentations, in which you may be asked to choose a particular topic and present it to a given group of people (or you are given a topic to prepare such as a press conference about industrial relations in your company).

Biodata

Trends come and go in recruitment and selection, and this relatively new approach to application forms appears to be increasing. It is a computerised method of preselection, based on the information provided on the application form. Factual information such as the number and grades of 'O' and 'A' levels is marked, together with manner of approach to study, outlook on life, sociability and so on. Questions are usually presented on a form, where you tick the relevant box, so that results can be fed into a computer and analysed. It's worth bearing in mind that there is little point in 'cheating' on these forms – they are not always looking for the straight 'A' grades and sensible 'time-planned' approach to exam studies.

Blockers

Blockers which stop you getting on may be real or apparent:
Real: too little money
too little time
no premises
no support from others
no constructive ideas
no creative inspiration
no confidence
no ability to organise
no success with selling
no negotiating skills
Apparent: the belief that these real blockers can't be overcome

Work out ways of getting around blockers: eg borrow money, learn to manage your time, ask for help – people might not know you feel a lack of support, identify your strengths and if necessary employ someone else to do the things you can't do, or take a relevant training course.

Career Choice

When choosing a career, there are thousands upon thousands of different jobs you could consider, but only five points to investigate:

- **You** – your skills, aptitudes, interests and values
- **The occupational area** – find out about types of work within the field
- **The job** – what will you actually be doing all day?
- **Who you will be working for** – (employers if you are spending some time in conventional employment; clients in other cases) who they are, what they want and whether you want to work for them
- **The job market** – if you can understand how it operates, you're half way to a job.

Career Development Loans

A new Government-backed scheme enabling you to borrow up to £5000 to finance fees and living expenses. You can train in your own career or make a mid-career change of direction. It's run by three banks: Barclays Bank, the Clydesdale Bank and the Co-operative Bank. Enquiries to any of them – you do not need to be one of their customers.

Careers Advice

The main source of formal careers advice is through the careers advisory service at your school, college, polytechnic or university. You may still be able to use their services once you've left, too. You can also get information at libraries, Job Centres and Adult Education Centres. There are private advisers if you can afford to pay.

The problem with careers advisers is that they are such a mixed bunch you are taking pot luck when you consult them. Some advisers have no training at all – and, if they are new to the job, no experience other than their previous jobs. If they have been in the same job for 20 years, their knowledge of the working world could be more limited than yours. Other advisers could be well trained and have wide experience of different jobs themselves. Their experience of how different students' careers have progressed and knowledge of the job market puts them in a better position to point you in the right direction.

The other problem you may come up against is that some careers advisers do things by the book, and can be very prescriptive in what they advise: 'You've got a degree in mathematics, you're not up to university teaching, so why don't you do a teaching certificate so you can teach maths at secondary school?' This type of advice may suit some people, but if you're reading this book, it's probably not the sort of advice you're looking for. To make the best of your time, do a bit of research and preparation before going for a careers interview. It's not the adviser's responsibility to set you on the road to a career. It's your's.

Before the careers interview identify clearly what you want from the session. If you have no idea what you want to do you can't expect to come away with a career planned in detail. Don't expect the careers adviser to do all the work. Read up about various different jobs and occupations and start to analyse your skills and interests. Find out how the careers information room is organised, so that you can use it to your best advantage. Try some of the careers choice computer-assisted-questionnaires available at your careers centre (Gradscope, Cascaid). They can generate some job ideas and set you thinking about where your talents lie.

During the interview remember that it is a two-way process. If advisers are going to be helpful, you must build up a rapport with them. If you don't feel this is possible, you may be able to work with another adviser at the centre, so check out the interview booking procedures and find out as much as you can about the personnel.

Careers interviews usually start with the adviser finding out about your ideas. These are far more important than anything they can suggest – after all, they only met you five minutes ago.

After the interview follow up the ideas. Go back, even if you didn't feel the interview was particularly helpful. There's no point in just writing off any advice you were given: tell them, so they can look at further ways of helping you. And if the adviser has suggested some careers which you hadn't thought of you need time to chew the ideas over – you can't decide your whole future on the basis of only one interview.

Careers advice after college You may be able to go for a careers advisory interview at your old college as an ex-student (particularly if you are a recent graduate). There is a Mutual Aid System, whereby ex-students can get interviews at colleges closer to home, but since careers advisers' first loyalties are to current students, you will be unlikely to get an interview through this system at busy times. There is usually no restriction on using the careers centre's library, so check opening hours, and use the information service. Local authorities may run education advice centres, but they tend to focus on courses rather than careers.

Careers Guidance (Private)

Private careers guidance companies are even more of a mixed bag than the services at institutions, and they charge hefty fees. Before consulting one, find out what they offer, what they specialise in, how much they charge and what guarantees they offer. Typical charges for 3–4 hours, including interest inventories, tests and discussion are £150–£300. Some centres charge up to £3,000 so check very carefully what is included and what services are offered. The Yellow Pages list advice centres in your area.

CAREERS INFORMATION

Careers Information

Beware. Most careers information is written and published by bureaucrats with the aim of selling you the proposition that you too should become a bureaucrat; it's usually disseminated uncritically by careers officers. Careers directories and encyclopaedias derive much of their content from the same sources. If you happen to want to make your way up a bureaucratic ladder to (say) Air Chief Marshal, Chairman of ICI, or Permanent Secretary at the Ministry of Agriculture this is fine. It's also OK if you have less ambitious bureaucratic aspirations, eg to lead a modestly prestigious and not unrewarded life in a secure job with the prospect of an adequate occupational pension when you retire. Some graduates want just that; many do not. For those who want to become their own boss, conventional careers information may seem worse than useless. If you are one of them, the simple message for you is find out for yourself. Nobody can do it for you. Read *The Careers Book*; talk to people in the jobs you have shortlisted. Try working (at any level) in the area that interests you, even for a few weeks in the vacation. Meanwhile do NOT ostracise your careers service – USE IT to help you further your own career.

Charm

Charm will get you a lot of jobs, and out of a lot of tricky situations. It is also a great asset in dealing with staff and getting the best out of people.

You needn't go as far as going to Charm School, but there always seem to be new books on executive manners and charm. Try browsing in a business bookshop.

Clean Work

Clean work is (apparently) defined as that which does not in any way adversely affect other inhabitants of the planet (except perhaps those whose views you don't agree with). It will probably involve working with alternative technology, but if you are going to be really dedicated to clean work you will have to investigate things very carefully – some fanatics wouldn't even consider travelling to work by bus, as that would be contributing to pollution.

Communication Skills

Communication is a two-way process. Getting your message across is vital in any job: skills may be oral or written, informational or persuasive. You must also be able to extrapolate the right information from communications addressed to you.

Oral skills As well as the gift of the gab, these involve other interpersonal relationships and body language, which may affect how information is perceived and received by the audience. You may need to develop skills in the following areas:

asserting yourself
public speaking
lecturing
teaching
debating
presenting
persuading
chatting/small talk
conversing
telephone manner
interviewing

On the receiving end, you may need to be good at:
listening
reflecting
responding
questioning
clarifying
summarising

Written skills You may not need to be able to write exquisite prose, but you may need to be able to present relevant information in written documents.

Can you write:
   letters
   memos
   quotes
   reports
   essays
   project proposals
   business plans
   CVs
   publicity material (selling copy)
   press releases?

On the receiving end can you:
   analyse
   synthesise
   collect
   collate
   classify
   evaluate
   summarise?

If you haven't got all the skills you think you need, you can take Industrial Society courses, read books, or employ someone to do the work for you.

Visual/spatial skills Another field of communication skills you may need to develop is visual communication: if you are a trained designer, your course will have included work on illustration and presentation, which are often essential in putting your message across. Recognising the importance of the visual message is vital in successful advertising and publicity. You may need professional help from a graphic designer to produce your publicity material.

Company Information

If you're a graduate looking for work with a bureaucracy as a spring-board before going solo, you'll need to find out as much about prospective employers as possible. Sources include: the free directories, such as ROGET, DOG or GET, which provide thumbnail sketches of major graduate recruiters, the type of organisation, what jobs they have available for graduates and the geographical areas they cover; ROGET also provides very useful job descriptions from which you can identify the main tasks in the various work areas; more detailed information is usually given by each company in its own graduate recruitment brochures, available from careers services or by direct application to the company concerned; some companies/organisations produce videos, organise presentations to final year students, or run work experience programmes and may organise open days where you can go along and see what they have to offer.

Once you are in business you need to know about other companies in the field – possible competitors, suppliers or purchasers of your goods and services – what size they are, whether they could put business your way, how healthy their turnover is. This type of information is available in trade directories (Mintel, Extel, Market information) in trade and reference libraries (eg CITY BUSINESS LIBRARY).

Trade magazines keep you abreast of personnel changes, new developments and trade gossip. You can also find out a good deal from the information companies supply at COMPANIES REGISTRATION OFFICE.

Compartmentalising Your Life

If you want to lead an entirely separate job life and personal life, then bureaucratic jobs are for you. If you are your own boss, there are various degrees of possible compartmentalisation. An actor in the third year of a walk-on part in a television soap opera may be able to separate work and play; a resident owner of a country hotel cannot. Those with young families may not want their life compartmentalised – but beware of working with small children under your feet without adequate childcare arrangements. Either your work or your children are likely to suffer.

If you let your work get into the way of your family life you may find that stress and tension build up and you have nothing but problems, instead of the support you need. Compartmentalise your time and your space, and you might find working for yourself a lot easier.

If you are based at home, you have the advantage that you don't have to travel to a place of work but at the same time you require self discipline. This works in two ways. If you're a workaholic, you will have to draw the line and STOP when it's time to – or you'll go stale. On the other hand, you may be the type of person who gets diverted and would rather spring-clean the cellar than sit down to send out invoices (in which case, don't work at home).

Constraints

You may have real constraints to contend with – you may be handi-capped, have a young family to look after or be responsible for the well-being of an ancient granny. Be realistic when choosing your job.

If you're in a wheelchair, for example, you would probably find it hard to manage as a GP but you could well be a successful solicitor.

CONSULTANCY

Consultancy

When you've worked in a field for some years, the knowledge you acquire becomes useful to others in the field. So you can take off on your own into consultancy work. This can be combined with other jobs – if you're an architect, for example, you may find yourself working as a consultant to a large firm or government organisation, while at the same time you do some teaching work, or take on some private refurbishment projects. Fees to consultants are usually massive com-pared to fees for more mundane work. There is a definite trend towards a reduction in the number of permanent jobs in many fields, and an increase in the use of consultants for specific tasks.

Creative Skills

You are likely to need creative skills and you should analyse these. Are you the sort of person who can dream up new ideas (for products and services)? Are you able to work on your own without supervision? Can you take a sketchy idea and see it through to fruition?

In many jobs working on your own, these skills are essential. With or without creative skills you will have to rely on hard work to bring in the income, but without creative skills you will have to work that much harder.

CV

A CV (curriculum vitae) is your way of presenting yourself to prospective employers or clients. It is essential that you put across basic information: your name, address, telephone number, age, experience and educational details. You can also add information on personal interests, special skills, and the names of people who can provide references for you (academic, as employers, or personal).

The way in which you present the information is all part of the CV game. If in doubt, get help.

CV GAME

CV Game

Presentation: is all important. Beg, borrow or steal the use of a typewriter (or word processor) to produce a perfect typescript and a clear layout. If all else fails, go to a typing agency and pay for someone to type it properly. Never send photocopies of CVs: employers want to feel that you have chosen the advertised job because you are particularly suited to it – not that you are applying for everything.

Tailoring the CV: It is important to tailor each CV to suit the job you are applying for: emphasise experience in a related field, even if it was only a holiday job. For example, if you had a temporary job working as a typist for a travel agent, it is worth mentioning if you are applying for a job as a courier but not necessarily if you are applying for a job as a cookery writer. You may need very many versions of your CV, to send with different job applications.

Creating a CV: If you are a full-time student, your work experience may be minimal, but look out for vacation jobs to embellish your CV, however lowly or poorly paid. If you can't find paid work, consider voluntary work, so that you can demonstrate some work experience on your CV.

Chronological or reverse chronological order? The more experience you have, the less relevant early jobs in your career will be to a prospective employer. Usually, for the first two or three jobs after graduation it is best to arrange your CV in chronological order. As you gain more experience, start your CV with the most recent jobs you have done. By the time you are 30 you no longer need to list exam grades (unless you are particularly proud of them).

Covering letter: Remember that while the CV will be accompanied by a covering letter it should **always** speak for itself. Keep the covering letter to a single page. It should explain where you saw the advertisement and why you feel you are particularly interested/suited to the job.

Disability

Remember that physical disabilities need not prevent you working as your own boss. And new technology now makes it easier to work with only the aid of a computer terminal and a telephone line.

Consult your careers advisers, and also read *Employment for Disabled People*, which includes a chapter on running your own business, which outlines information available and gives some inspiring examples of disabled entrepreneurs.

Driving Licence

Get one. Keep it. The younger you are when you take your test, the more naturally it will come to you and the fewer lessons you will need.

The experts reckon on one lesson for every year of your life. So take your test as soon as you can.

Entrepreneurial Skills

If you want to be your own boss, entrepreneurial skills always help. Initiative, confidence, energy, persuasiveness, tact, salesmanship, reliability, ability to work under pressure, efficiency – the list is a challenging one, but these are the qualities you need to be a successful entrepreneur.

Equal Opportunities

If you are a member of a disadvantaged group (racial minority, women etc) working for yourself may be a way of doing the sort of job you want. Don't forget you still have to contend with the attitudes of the public you deal with, even if you can avoid prejudice in your workplace. But don't see your ethnic background as an insuperable disadvantage – it gives you access to some markets that are closed to others. Marginality is often the drive to get you going: how do you think M & S started? A number of agencies can help eg Paul Bozel Foundation, BBDA.

If you are employing staff, all jobs advertised must be open to all racial groups. Only the smallest of employers are exempt from equal opportunities legislation.

Experience

In some jobs there is no real substitute for experience: you can go on doing courses and reading books, but until you actually get on with it out in the field you won't really get to know the business. Getting a job in the traditional job market is one of the best ways of gaining experience – and it's a useful springboard to setting up on your own. As a student or after graduation you can find out more about how specific organisations work by getting temporary, part-time or full-career training post employment. But beware of getting sucked into permanent employment.

Family Commitment

Family commitment to your job is often vital. This is quite unlike many bureaucratic jobs, where the bureaucrat's family knows little or nothing about the job that pays the bills. All they see is the company car and the company dinner-dance, the company pay-slip, the company pension, and increasingly, the company's redundancy cheque. On the whole it's all they need to see. Not so if you are your own boss. The levels of family commitment will depend on the job but in general if you cannot rely on the commitment of your immediate family join a bureaucracy. Family help can also play a vital part: look at the success of the Asian families in the newstrade and corner shop.

FAMILY TRADITION

Family Tradition

Some families have a tradition of self-employment and it's easier to cope with the risks and uneven income if you've been brought up with it. Other families don't – if yours hasn't don't worry – why not be the first?

If your family has a traditional line of business, you will be in with a flying start. You will have instant contacts and experience derived from older generations. You will be able to reduce a lot of the initial risks. It may seem like a cop out to join the family profession or the family firm, but you could also regard it as a challenge: look at the way it works and improve upon it.

But if you have strong views which don't match those of your parents, you may be in for a stormy relationship. You pays your penny . . .

Freelancing

There is increasing scope for freelance work, from the area in which it originated (mercenaries) to the area in which the term is most commonly applied (journalism).

Most freelancers train in employment first. Many start to take on extra, part-time jobs (moonlighting) before using the contacts they have developed to set up on their own. Many freelance because the idea of working for themselves appeals; also to earn more for the same work. But remember you have to organise your own tax, NI and accounts before earning any income, and seek work while producing the goods.

For some jobs you may find *The Freelance Alternative: Working for Yourself* is also useful.

Graduate Destination List

If you want to know what all last year's graduates ended up doing after six months you can find out. Some are employed, some are in training, some are unemployed. Ask your careers adviser to show you a copy of First Destination Return (FDR) if you are interested in:
1 how many graduates you are competing with
2 what graduates have done in the past
3 the network of contacts provided by the firms/organisations/colleges your ex-colleagues have joined.

Handling Information

Computers have revolutionised this. For many jobs at least a word-processor is a must. Take a course in word processing (or a short-term job in a company where word processors are used). Teaching yourself computing is a time-consuming business, so if you have the option, do a course while you are at college.

If you're hell-bent on living without high tech you could get a filofax or a card index or at least keep those backs of envelopes in good order. Be methodical.

Interviewing Game

Preparation: When you go for an interview of any kind, make sure you've got a clear idea of what you want to get out of it. Bring with you anything you think the interviewer may be interested in (eg qualification certificates for a job interview; bank statements and accounts for a financial interview).

Think about any likely questions so you are one step ahead.

Prepare a list of the questions that you genuinely want to ask, to satisfy yourself about the job/loan scheme/product involved.

Presentation: Whatever your attitude to outward appearances, there is plenty of evidence to show that first impressions count. Clean, appropriate clothes and a minimum of nervous habits are all positive assets. Make eye contact (but don't stare). While you don't want to look like a stuffed dummy, interviewers will be put off by wild gesticulations, fidgeting and nose-picking.

Tactics: There are professional tutors in interview techniques, whose services are aimed at business people and spokespeople who are in a position to be called on at short notice for radio and TV interviews, and their media techniques have some general application if you are your own boss.

Here are some of the tactics they teach:

- **The message:** On the way to the interview, get an envelope out of your briefcase, make a list of the points you want to put across.
- **The no-go areas:** On the other side of the envelope, make a list of the points you don't want to come across: consider ways of avoiding (not evading) issues. Don't let the interviewer see your envelope.
- **Delaying and diversionary tactics:** If you're stumped by a question, think on your feet (or backside). In the meantime, cause a diversion by taking a sip of water, having a coughing fit, or saying 'Now that's a very interesting question, but before I answer it could I just add one or two points about the last matter we were discussing . . .'. Also you don't have to answer the question as given – eg 'The real question is . . .'. A further diversionary tactic is to pick up on one of the words in the question and deflect with your prepared answer which will now include the 'picked' word.
- **Be honest:** If the interviewer persists, and you don't know the answer to the question, tell them you weren't prepared for that one, but will go away and check your facts. People are impressed by honesty. If you are presented with information which contradicts

your story, politely thank the interviewer for pointing this out, and explain you would like to look into the matter further before commenting.

■ **After the interview:** If you are the interviewer, follow up with a letter. For a job interview this may be a straight letter of rejection or a letter offering the post; or if a different type of interview, send a letter summarising the main points made and decisions reached. If you are the interviewee, wait a week, then ring up to see what the outcome of the interview was. Don't be too pushy – if you haven't heard anything it may be because the interviewer is still making a decision and doesn't want to be harrassed. On the other hand, they may have forgotten about you, and in this case the odd phone call can produce results.

Job Hunting

If you are looking for a job in employment as a springboard to being your own boss, here are the main sources of information about vacancies:

CSU: CSU vacancy lists are available at all graduate careers advisory services (AGCAS). The forward list, available from October to March, gives vacancies starting the following summer; and the current list has immediately available jobs. Start to pick the forward list up during your last year at college and use the current lists nearer the time you graduate and whilst still job hunting.

Careers office: Your careers office may also have its own list of vacancies, either with local firms, or with firms with a special link with your college.

Trade publications: These are widely used for jobs in specialised areas. Some publications are more useful than others. It's worth consulting trade magazines regularly at your local library both to keep you informed of job vacancies and to widen your knowledge of the industry. See also *Finding Job Vacancies*, a booklet on where to find vacancies in chosen areas.

National and local papers: Most newspapers advertise particular types of jobs on particular days: find out which days your area comes up in which paper, and make sure you get to see it.

Professional bodies and trade associations: Many professional bodies and trade associations produce lists of vacancies.

Vacancy directories: Your careers office will have directories such as

ROGET, DOG, GET and so on, which list major organisations and may be worth consulting.

PER: Produces *Graduate Post* and *Executive Post* which list jobs and training opportunities: available from job centres and careers services or contact PER.

Milk round programme: Your careers service will organise open days and interviews towards the end of the academic year.

Recruitment fairs: These are increasing not only during summer but are now held in some places at other times. Check with careers offices for details.

Jobcentres: Don't forget your local Jobcentres.

Speculative applications: There's nothing to stop you writing to organisations to offer your services. If you don't have any links with firms in your field, consult business directories, professional year books or 'The Financial Times Top 1,000 Firms'. If firms are successful they're likely to have more vacancies. Write to the personnel manager of larger companies, the managing director of small ones. Many companies need extra help at busy times of the year, or when staff are on holiday, so you may at least find you get a short term job which will tide you over and give you an insight into how firms work.

Networking: Once you've got contacts in the field, networking is the most helpful source of jobs. Ask everyone you know if there is anything going, write to companies you have worked for in the past and keep your ear to the ground.

Job Information

Get as much as you can. Read *The Careers Book*. If the jobs you are interested in are covered in other directories, read them too – eg *Equal Opportunities = a Careers Guide; COIC Annual Careers Guide; Occupations 88; Career Encyclopaedia*.

Job Sharing

Formal job-sharing is where two or more part-timers share a job. For example, some education authorities will employ two teachers to share one job. This gives the job sharers a regular income, plus time to go out and do their own thing – perhaps a part-time course, voluntary work, look after their families or start out to become their own boss.

If you want to be your own boss but don't want to take the plunge all at once, why not suggest such a scheme to your employer, particularly if you have a possible job-sharer lined up.

Life Skills

A certain *joi de vivre* is one of the greatest assets in the employment game. Life may seem to be about getting by, getting on or getting ahead, but it should also be about getting what you want and value.

Life skills are about understanding, communicating and working with others. You need to understand yourself before you can understand how you relate to other people and other organisations.

You
- Know yourself:
  - your identity
  - strengths
  - weaknesses
  - abilities
  - knowledge
  - values
- Develop and use your confidence
- Develop your skills:
  - Interviewing
  - Selling
  - Negotiating
  - Interpersonal
  - Social
  - Communications skills

You in relation to other people
- Start to identify other people's skills, aptitudes, attitudes and needs
- Learn how to motivate, lead and develop other people – read management books on motivation and leadership
- Develop and practise your planning, organising and entrepreneurial skills

You in relation to other organisations and systems
- Learn how systems operate
- Identify key people in an organisation
- Learn how to use systems to your advantage
- Use your management skills to manipulate the systems

Life Style Choices

Conventional career planning often forgets about life styles. To a large extent, in choosing your job you choose your lifestyle. Do you want to grow strong local roots? Join the jetset? Develop an exquisite judgment of the wines of the Côte d'Or? Work 18 hours a day? Drive a battered Land Rover or a snappy new Porsche? As your own boss nobody is going to be able to dictate to you. The thickness of your office carpet, which lavatory you use, or what car you drive will be your decision, not some senior bureaucrat's. Nevertheless, within the job you have chosen, constraints of behaviour, dress and business manners will remain.

Luck

Have you got it? If not, you can offset the deficiency by joining a bureaucracy, but do not start out on your own.

Management Skills

Courses
Some management skills can be taught, but fewer than are sometimes claimed in the more glossy management education prospectuses. Before signing on a course check that the syllabus matches your job requirements. Local enterprise centres may have details of local courses. (Fees can be part of a training package offered by the Training Agency or Department of Employment.)

Text books
Skim read general management textbooks – see your local or college library – then identify the area of knowledge you need to develop.

Management training
Most graduate level jobs offered by major organisations for new graduates in the milkround/recruitment fairs are part of that company's management training scheme. One option is to get a job with a major organisation and learn about management through their training schemes; then move on to be your own boss.

Manual Skills

You may have been shunted into an academic education, when in fact your manual skills are your greatest asset. Don't be afraid to let go and move on if you feel that your interests are different to your educational qualifications. You can do evening classes to polish up your skills – and everyone knows that plumbers get paid more than teachers these days.

Mix and Match

It's important to remember you can mix and match jobs – as your own boss you can do two or more jobs in parallel and are often well advised to do so. Barristers are often MPs; MPs may write bestsellers; most writers do almost anything else while waiting for royalties and some playwrights are barristers. Don't be frightened of apparently bizarre career mixes. One of the country's best known opera directors is also a medical researcher who trained as a doctor; one successful restaurateur and wine merchant (mix and match again) is a professional musician. Really, anything is possible.

Moonlighting

It is possible to do a full-time job, and to take on extra work by the light of the moon. It's exhausting but gives you useful experience.

It can give you the chance to hold on to one main job whilst experimenting in a new area of work to gain experience.

It also gives you the opportunity to 'test the water' and find out how much business will come your way if you do go it alone.

BE WARNED Some companies' terms of employment prohibit you from taking on extra work without permission and the Inland Revenue has 'Moonlighting squads' whose aim is to check up that moonlighters pay tax. You also run the risk of getting so exhausted that you don't do yourself justice anywhere.

Numerical Skills

Numerical skills are the ability to calculate, manipulate and interpret numbers together with an understanding of basic statistical approaches. Such skills are often equated with maths – but don't think you're not numerate just because you did miserably at maths 'O' level. Geometry and algebra have little to do with the sort of skills you need in most business careers.

Life will be easier if you are:

- quick at arithmetic or adept with the calculator
- accurate
- figure-minded

Part-time Work

Part-time work is growing. In 1951, part-time workers accounted for 4% of the labour force; in 1987, it was 20%.

This is mainly due to the increased numbers of working women, but there is speculation that the time is coming when the majority of people working in Britain will be part-timers, many with more than one job.

But beware – part-time workers have few of the benefits organised for full-time employees. They are often lower paid, do not get paid holidays or sick pay and take longer to qualify for the same state benefits.

But there are good reasons for working part-time:

- to give you time to develop another job where you are your own boss;
- to complete studies on a part-time basis, or to take extra courses to further your career;
- to give you free time to pursue leisure or family activities.

Personal Circumstances

Your personal circumstances help to determine what you can do – eg if you haven't got any money, start small. If you've got a dependent family, don't take risks that'll make them suffer. Make sure you're doing something you enjoy. NB Having a lot of money may be a hindrance if you're worried about losing it all.

Personal Qualities

Before taking the plunge try some self-analysis. Jot down the answers to the following questions:

What type of person do you think you are?

How would your best friend describe you?
How would your family describe you?
How would your colleagues describe you?
What would your worst enemy say about you?
When you've decided on a shortlist of jobs, write down the attributes you believe those jobs need. Do they match?

You may find life more pleasant if you get on with the people around you, but the qualities you look for in a friend aren't necessarily those needed to get on.

Personality Tests

These can be a useful way of identifying your qualities (ask your careers service). They tend to have been devised by big firms as part of their selection procedure so an acceptable profile in a personality test may not be a prerequisite for success as your own boss.

For example a recent survey of sacked or redundant managers found them to be intelligent, imaginative, conscientious, calm and independent thinkers. However, they were also found to be less manipulative, too trusting and didn't plot and scheme enough. Being good at your job and interested in excellence is not enough in bureaucracies; you need to be good at the power game as well. If you don't want to play other people's power games, why not set your own rules and go it alone.

Professional Qualifications

Degrees in themselves do not normally licence you to practise a profession. A professional qualification is also necessary. The list below gives enquiry points from which details of the qualifications necessary for practice are available. You will also be told how long professional qualifications take and what exemptions your degree will give you.

Accountants
(Certified): Association of Certified Accountants, 29 Lincoln's Inn Fields, London WC2A 3EE (01-242 6855); **(Chartered):** Institute of Chartered Accountants, PO Box 433, Chartered Accountants Hall, Moorgate Place, London EC2P 2BJ (01-628 7060); **(Scotland):** Institute of Chartered Accountants of Scotland, 27 Queen Street, Edinburgh (031-225 5673); **(Cost and Management):** Institute of Cost and Management Accountants, 63 Portland Place, London W1N 4AB (01-637 4710); **(Public Finance):** Chartered Institute of Public Finance and

Accountancy, 3 Robert Street, London WC1 (01-930 3456)

Acoustics
Institute of Acoustics, 25 Chamber Street, Edinburgh EH1 1HU (031-225 2143)

Actuaries
Institute of Actuaries, Staple Inn Hall, High Holborn, London WC1V 7QJ (01-242 0106)

Advocates
(Scotland): Faculty of Advocates, Advocates Library, Parliament House, Edinburgh (031-226 5071)

Air Pilots, Engineers & Navigators
Guild of Air Pilots and Navigators, 30 Eccleston Street, London SW1 (01-730 0471)

Architects
Royal Institute of British Architects, 66 Portland Place, London W1N 4AD (01-580 5533); Royal Incorporation of Architects in Scotland, 15 Rutland Square, Edinburgh EH1 2BF (031-229 7205)

Barristers
(England and Wales): Council of Legal Education, 4 Grays Inn Place, London WC1R 5DX (01-405 4635); **(Northern Ireland):** Council of Legal Education (Northern Ireland), Institute of Professional Studies, Queen's University, Belfast BT7 1NN

Dentists
General Dental Council, 37 Wimpole Street, London W1M 8DQ (01-486 2171)

Dietitians
Council for Professions Supplementary to Medicine, Park House, 184 Kennington Park Road, London SE11 4BU (01-582 0866)

Doctors
General Medical Council, 44 Hallam Street, London W1N 6AE (01-580 7642)

Engineers
Fellowship of Engineering Institutions, 2 Little Smith Street, London SW1P 3DL (01-799 2688)

Mathematics
Institute of Mathematics and its Applications, St Ives House, St Ives Road, Maidenhead, Berks SL6 1RB

Navy, Merchant
Department of Transport (Marine Division), Sunley House, 90–93 High Holborn, London WC1V 6LP (01-253 9393)

Nurses
(England and Wales): General Nursing Council for England and Wales,

23 Portland Place, London W1N 3AS (01-637 7181); **(Northern Ireland):** Northern Ireland Council for Nurses and Midwives, 216 Belmont Road, Belfast BT4 2AT; **(Scotland):** General Nursing Council for Scotland, 5 Darnaway Street, Edinburgh EH3 6DP

Physiotherapists
Chartered Society for Physiotherapy, 14 Bedford Row, London WC1R 4ED (01-242 1941)

Radiographers
College of Radiographers, 14 Upper Wimpole Street, London W1M 8BN (01-935 5726)

Social Workers
Central Council for Education and Training in Social Work, Derbyshire House, St Chad's Street, London WC1H 8AD (01-278 2455)

Solicitors
(England and Wales): Law Society, 113 Chancery Lane, London WC2A 1PL (01-242 1222); **(Northern Ireland):** Council of Legal Education, Institute of Professional Legal Studies, Queen's University, Belfast BT7 1NN; **(Scotland):** Law Society of Scotland, Law Society's Hall, 26 Drumsburgh Gardens, Edinburgh EH3 7YR

Speech Therapists
College of Speech Therapists, Harold Pastor House, 6 Lechmere Road, London NW2 5BU (01-459 8521)

Surveyors
(Chartered): Royal Institution of Chartered Surveyors, 12 Great George Street, Parliament Square, London SW1P 3AD; **(Quantity):** Royal Institution of Chartered Surveyors (address as above)

Teachers
Department of Education and Science, Elizabeth House, York Road, London SE1 7PH (01-934 9000)

Town Planners
Royal Town Planning Institute, 26 Portland Place, London W1N 4BE (01-636 9107)

Transport
Chartered Institute of Transport, 80 Portland Place, London W1N 4DT (01-636 9952)

Veterinary Surgeons
Royal College of Veterinary Surgeons, 32 Belgrave Square, London SW1X 8PQ (01-235 4971)

If, as a prospective employer, you want to check up on the relevance of an applicant's qualifications, you can find out more from the NATIONAL COUNCIL FOR VOCATIONAL QUALIFICATIONS.

Qualifications

There are legal requirements for many professions (eg solicitors). Appropriate qualifications (in anything from embalming to midwifery) increase public confidence while membership of professional associations will get you into the network.

However, in other cases, people who are their own boss can worry less about qualifications than those looking for employment. You just need to be able to make it work.

Race

Although the Commission for Racial Equality has expressed concern about possible bias within certain professional bodies, racial discrimination is less of a problem if you're your own boss. Your career prospects are less vulnerable to the whims and prejudices of somebody else.

Recruitment Fairs

Go to recruitment fairs if you're looking for a suitable employer to give you the appropriate experience before becoming your own boss. Graduate recruitment fairs are usually held after finals or at Christmas in various locations about the country. Keep in touch with your careers centre for details.

Other recruitment fairs are also held to attract experienced staff in shortage areas such as computing – national press and trade press give details.

CVs and shin pads are essential equipment.

Refugees

THE BRITISH REFUGEE COUNCIL has an enterprise training unit, which offers advice, support and training courses on self-employment. Refugees can also obtain general careers advice from the British Refugee Council.

Science and Technology Students

Those reading for science and technology degrees who want to become their own boss have special problems if they want to remain within their discipline. Most science and technology jobs are bureaucratic jobs because only large bureaucracies can afford the equipment and the R & D budgets. Even university research is being concentrated in large bureaucracies. Pressures from politicians, the media, careers advisers and your own teachers to become a science/technology bureaucrat is insidious. But consider your own interests first. Remember it's your life not theirs. Ask yourself if your interest in your subject and its practical applications is sufficient to outweigh your ambition to be your own boss, and make sure you know what is going on in your own science park.

Self-employment

If you are self-employed, you are not alone: a recent survey indicated that 11% of the working population work for themselves, and there is still an upward trend. The NATIONAL FEDERATION OF THE SELF EMPLOYED was set up to promote and protect the interests of the self-employed. Their leaflet 'Be your own boss' is useful, as is *Working for Yourself*.

Sex

Research has shown that sex discrimination is alive and well, but often at a hidden level.

Working for yourself may be a good route round residual prejudice. However, women still have to tackle additional constraints arising out of, eg childcare responsibilities.

Springboarding

Beware! For many jobs in this book you will need to 'Springboard'. That is, you will need first to succumb to employment (very often within a bureaucracy) for a period as a necessary/advisable step to working for yourself. This is self-evident in the case of most professions, eg accountancy, architecture and the law, where it is an integral part of the process of qualifying and obtaining a licence to practise. In many other jobs it is essential in order to acquire sufficient expertise, business know-how and job contacts before setting up on your own, eg consultancy. So, if your strategy is to become your own boss the first thing paradoxically may be to get a job. Tough. But at least you will be able to start up with your job networks in place.

Stress

Some people perform well under pressure, but research shows that people under stress do not perform well.

Stress is not necessarily caused by overwork, but by setting unrealistic targets and attempting the impossible. There are also external stress factors, including: bereavement, divorce, moving house, having children.

To avoid suffering under stress:

- Have realistic plans and goals.
- Talk over problems – a fresh view often helps.
- If you're totally stuck, do something else.

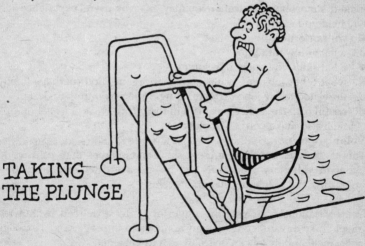

TAKING
THE PLUNGE

Taking the Plunge

There are two ways of doing this:

- Diving board: all-or-nothing approach – often used by the most successful entrepreneurs: (essential in retailing, for example).

■ The steps: easing yourself in through moonlighting or part-time working, until you've built up the contacts and workload you need for the deep end.

Unemployment

If you're working for yourself you must be prepared to keep the wolf from the door when work is not coming in. You may be able to rely on your savings, but you may have to look at other forms of work to keep you going. Typical casual jobs taken up by 'resting' actors include promotional work at exhibitions, secretarial work, gardening, cleaning, bar work. You must be prepared to 'mix and match' so that, if your main aims are in a highly competitive or seasonal field, you can fall back on other work, eg drive a mini-cab or hearse, babysit.

Vacations (while a student)

Work
Even the most boring vacation job may give you useful experience and will help you identify:
■ your priorities
■ what you want to do
■ what skills you enjoy developing
■ what other jobs are available in that organisation (perhaps totally unrelated to the job you were doing, from accounting to design)
■ useful contacts to keep up with in the future.
  It will also make your CV look better.
Voluntary work
This is likely to develop different skills and abilities than paid work. Often in voluntary work you will be given greater responsibilities, organising and managing staff and events.
Travel
Long vacations give you the opportunity for extended, unhurried travel. Take advantage of foreign holidays to improve your language skills, meet and make contacts abroad and get a tan.
Vacation courses
Many firms and organisations run vacation courses, for example, CRAC runs Insight into Management; Insight into Retailing; Insight into Entrepreneurship. They are often well run, cheap, and many national

firms sponsor their young managers to help run them. Organisations may offer participants an automatic first interview for a job. Develop contacts made at such courses as part of your networking.

WORK FAMILIARISATION

Work Familiarisation Events

Many organisations offer introduction days and work familiarisation events (eg Marks and Spencer, Unilever, Police and Armed Services). Treat them as free seminars and use them:

- to improve your knowledge of organisations
- to improve your knowledge of bureaucratic practice
- to help decide if you want to join their bureaucracies
- to make contacts for the future.

Ask your careers adviser to tell you what is available.

You

Here are five questions to ask yourself:

Q1 What do you want out of life:
    A   to get by or
    B   to get ahead

Q2 Do you always want to work:
    A   for somebody or
    B   for yourself

Q3 Do you value:
    A   stability or
    B   can you cope with and enjoy uncertainty

Q4 Do you:
    A   enjoy routine and being part of a machine
    B   prefer to see the job through
Q5 Can you:
    A   quite happily give and take orders from someone else
    B   prefer to be in charge

If the answers are mainly **A**s, you will probably be happier in a bureaucracy.

If the answers are mainly **B**s, you should probably be aiming for a top job in a bureaucracy or being your own boss.

Running your own business is one of the best places to find out about and develop yourself. Some books that help with this are *Think and Grow Rich*, *Pathfinder* and *Breakthrough*.

How to go about it

Business   A-Z

How To Go About It
Business A–Z

Accessibility

Whatever type of work you go for, people have got to be able to get in touch with you.

Phones are the most direct method of contact, and here you have several options. If you can't be by your office phone all the time you could get an answerphone (a phone which gives out and takes recorded messages); a bleep (a gadget you carry round which bleeps when people are trying to reach you – you then find the nearest phone and ring the answering service to find out what the message is); a paging system (your pocket gadget has a digital display which gives you a short message); or a cellular telephone (operates like an ordinary phone, but is portable – if you can carry the batteries it needs). A car phone, although expensive, means that you can run a mobile office if you need one. Find out more about all these in Yellow Pages (telephone answering machines and telephone answering services) or from British Telecom. A radio phone extension to your household or office line may be useful – eg if you run a small plant nursery, and spend a lot of time in the potting shed, or if you let holiday cottages and spend time away from your office while you are cleaning them. Message taking services can also be a smart answer.

A smart address is another useful asset: you probably won't be able to afford an office in Central London, but you can get your mail sent to one. Check the entries in the Yellow Pages under Accommodation agencies – business. Many agencies offer more than just an address and mail service: they provide office space and have telex and fax machines, photocopiers, secretarial services and so on.

If you want something cheaper, and anonymous, a PO Box number may be best: ask the post office.

Accounting and Bookkeeping

Boring – boring – but without it, you sink.

First rule: get a good accountant. To find one, you're best off asking people you know who already have one. Initially you may be better off with a small firm/self employed accountant who lives in your world. Only if you are thinking of raising venture/development capital do you need one of the big six accounting firms to get you past bankers for whom 'meaningful cash flow' is only 'meaningful' if authenticated by one of the great firms!

ACCOUNTING & BOOK KEEPING

Get a system

Develop a system for incoming and outgoing invoices. You must keep careful records to check your business is profitable. Make sure you know a bit about basic bookkeeping and talk to your accountant before you start, to ensure your records make good accounting sense.

Note all expenses when they occur: simply keep receipts and put them in a box. It's easy to forget things and lose track. Keep a notebook with a list of unreceipted expenses (fares, drinks with contacts) and GET IN THE HABIT of checking it daily.

Pay by credit card where possible: this gives you up to six weeks free credit, and provides a monthly record of payments made with names and dates. Pay credit card bills when they are due: there are cheaper sources of finance if you want to borrow.

Try asking for part-payment for a job in advance: to cover paint and wallpaper, if you are a decorator or an advance on royalty if you are an author. Demand interim payments if the job is a long one. The quicker you send out your invoices, the sooner they'll get paid. Conversely the slower you pay your bills the more money you will have in your own bank.

Big companies often have gigantic accounts departments who take a long time to pay and have their own systems which don't lend themselves to eg partial payment in advance. Get clear at the outset what their system is and make it work for you.

All invoices must show: your name and address and preferably phone number; your VAT number if you have one; the date; who the customer or client is; what the invoice is for (goods, services – some customers demand detailed information); any order number you or the customer has. Make sure your system includes all this automatically, and also chases up unpaid invoices every month. If customers and clients are not forthcoming with the cash, consider employing a debt collecting agency – addresses from the NATIONAL ASSOCIATION OF TRADE PROTECTION SOCIETIES. Never part with your file copy of an invoice.

You will find *Working for Yourself* useful; also some business courses.

Advertising

Get your name known to the people who need you.

The most basic form of advertising is a business card: leave them in likely places, slip them through the front door of private households, hand them out at exhibitions – whatever is relevant to your job.

Other forms of advertising depend on your job: an entry in the Yellow Pages and Thompson's Directory are most useful, and local papers are effective for advertising your services if you are a small company in the building industry, for example. In certain professions (eg medical and legal) there are tight restrictions on advertising, so check with the appropriate professional body.

Placing an advertisement costs anything from 25p per week for a notice in the local newsagent to £25,000 for a colour spread in a national magazine. Outlets to consider are trade press listings, local business directories, poster sites (including hoardings, buses and tubes, taxis, any public places), leaflet drops (some services are provided by the post office), mail shots (based on mailing lists purchased from agencies), exhibitions (from art school graduation shows to major international exhibitions in your field). On top of the cost of placing the ad, there is the cost of producing it – negligible for a notice in the small ads in a paper, phenomenal for a snazzy ad with snappy copy put together by a top advertising agency.

Before placing an ad think about: (a) your target market: if you know what publications they are likely to read, what sort of tastes they have and what sort of budget they have for your goods or services, this will not only help you tailor your output to suit them, it will point the direction for advertising outlets as well; (b) your unique selling proposition – what is special or unique about your product or services, and why people/companies might prefer to do business with you.

Any ad has got to answer the questions: who are you, what are you offering, when, where, why and how can people purchase your goods or services or find out more?

If you can offer any special discounts or freebies, this may help to attract people to you – the important thing is to give people the idea that you provide value for money and are unique in your field.

Consider the more direct face to face approaches first.

Short business courses normally cover some advertising. Special courses are also run by CAM, The Communication, Advertising and Marketing Education Foundation. Or you can read *Spending Advertising Money, The Fundamentals of Advertising*.

Advice – General

Never take advice uncritically. Listen carefully, then decide what you will do. It's your life and you can only live it your way. Don't boggle your mind by reading too much before you get started: the most important thing is knowing who to go to when you've got a particular problem. You'll find that most books and courses say much the same thing – sift through them and just buy a couple of books which are relevant to your particular needs. Consult your local (Thompson) directory for help in your area. There are government run Small Firms Services, which come under the control of the Department of Trade and Industry (dial 100 and ask for Freefone Enterprise). If you're in a New Town or Development Area, there will be extra advice and assistance. Rural companies may get free advice from COSIRA, the Council for Small Industries in Rural Areas. The NATIONAL FEDERATION OF SELF EMPLOYED AND SMALL BUSINESSES produces a very useful leaflet. For young entrepreneurs (teens and early twenties) there are several government or charity sponsored organisations: LIVEWIRE, for under 26s who want to start their own business or be self-employed and YOUNG ENTERPRISE. Some design consultants (eg BASS RILEY) offer free design advice to the under 24s.

Keep up with new developments by reading the financial pages and weekly supplements in the national press. Most of all, don't forget to ask – friends, family, colleagues – for advice. They may not know the answer, but they might know someone who does.

Bankruptcy

One of the side effects of an increase in small businesses has been an increase in the number of bankruptcies.

If your outgoings are greater than your incomings, the people you owe money to can go to court and petition for bankruptcy. If you still don't pay up, a licensed insolvency practitioner will move in to sort out your assets and pay your debts.

Some creditors have a greater claim than others: for example, people like the taxman, the Customs and Excise (if you pay VAT) and secured creditors.

The main lesson to be learned from the bankruptcy of others is that it is usually a muddled approach to financial management or half-hearted marketing, rather than a failure in the underlying business, which gets you into deep water. Keep your plans and books orderly, and you can pull out before it is too late. If it happens to you, don't be put off trying again – you'd be surprised at who has gone bankrupt en route to wild success.

Begging/Borrowing/Stealing

Begging can produce help. Begging letters to benevolent companies for any spare scrap paper or redundant office equipment often produce results – start at the top by contacting the Managing Director – their names are listed in *Kompass*, a directory available in reference libraries. Some organisations and companies have bursaries and charitable funds available to individuals with particular needs. For example, if you want to set up a company designing educational toys, you could contact charities concerned with child welfare, major retailing companies who might want to expand into the toy market and chemical companies who are looking for new markets for their plastics or paints might be able to help. Sponsorship of this nature could be a free source of funds.

Stealing Not recommended. But some forms of stealing are socially acceptable: collecting materials and equipment when businesses close down; scouring skips (technically the contents are the property of the skip hire firm); investigating the rubbish thrown out from shops and offices – for example, many clothes shops discard clothes hangers after use, and there's no harm in asking if you can have them.

Time stealing is difficult to detect: if you're not busy at work, it is impossible for anyone to stop you thinking about private projects. Einstein wrote his book in his employer's time, and many an office worker has used the office typewriter for doing private work in the lunch hour.

Borrowing equipment is cheaper than hiring: for example, you may be able to borrow cameras or studio space from a photographer friend; or borrow help from your spouse or family in producing an advertisement for a trade magazine; or borrow time from friends who are happy to help you get started – they might service your van, or give you advice on people to approach with ideas for new products.

Borrowing money is often vital for business. On the whole, banks and institutions prefer lending large rather than small amounts of money because it takes them just as much time to manage a loan/investment of £5,000 as it does to manage £500,000.

Banks are primarily responsible to their shareholders, not to you their customer. Even if they may seem ridiculously worried about granting loans to what you know is your excellent business, persevere. They are in business to lend *you* money. If you're approaching a bank manager, go armed with a watertight case for needing a loan, and suggestions for how you are going to repay it. Ask for more than you think you'll need (but not more than you can afford) – you don't want to waste time working out another case for more money, and the bank manager may offer a smaller loan than you ask for. Remember that bank managers are often perverse: they only like to lend you money when you do not need it, and the way to cope with that is to get your cash flow worked out and walk into the bank when you look most flush with cash and fix up the borrowing arrangement from a position of strength.

See Finance below.

Budget

Your budget is the amount of money which has to be spent to achieve your targets (your expenditure), balanced against the amount you expect to make on sales and services (your income). Professionals will project an annual budget, breaking it down into monthly figures: you may just think in terms of 'I must earn another couple of grand before Christmas, so I can buy a new computer', but if you haven't a budget plan with monthly figures as targets and guides you won't know how well things are going. One way of reducing the risk of overspending is to allow for 12 months expenditure and only 10 months of income in your calculations.

The monthly budget should list estimates of income and outgoings, both fixed – rent, rates, loan repayments, insurance etc – and variable – costs of materials, day-to-day expenses. Armed with these lists you can juggle the bills to ensure the best cashflow: try to withhold payment on certain bills until your invoices have been paid. Remember that one cause of disaster in small businesses is not lack of profit, but lack of liquidity (or cashflow): if there isn't the cash to cover immediate, short term outgoings, you may be forced out of business even though your business idea is sound.

By drawing up a budget which works, you can convince the banks that you can look after their money and are creditworthy. And if the figures aren't reaching the planned targets, you can take appropriate action – pick up small jobs to fill the gaps, or sell off something to see you through the hard times until the big jobs pay off.

Your bank may offer courses or leaflets and advice on setting up a business – they don't want your enterprise to go down the tubes any more than you do. And for high powered advice the major accountancy firms provide information in the form of private consultancy, leaflets, books and courses. There are seminars for enterprising graduates, for example those run by the SCOTTISH ENTERPRISE FOUNDATION, GRADUATE ENTERPRISE IN WALES, GRADUATE INTO ENTERPRISE and the GRADUATE ENTERPRISE PROGRAMME.

Bumf

Business bumf proliferates, and departments of business studies, central and local government, accountants, newsletter and paperback publishers are all guilty. There's far too much of it about in the Enterprise Era. Don't let yourself be swamped by it – bin it.

Bureaucratic Benefits

If you do intend to springboard, take advantage of the benefits provided most readily to bureaucrats by the financial services industry. For instance, try to
- get credit cards: gold cards in particular offer sufficient unsecured credit to get many small businesses off the ground (at a cost!).
- arrange a good line of credit/borrowing facility with your bank while you still have a regular monthly salary.

- get adequate health insurance: health is a key to success as your own boss and ill-health the cause of many failures.
- get a personal pension plan (avoid employers' pension schemes like the plague): personal pension plans can sometimes be used as collateral or to buy premises for your new business if you make sure before you begin that such uses are written into the rubric of the plan.
- get a mortgage for as large a house as you can afford in an area which will be fashionable by the time you need to sell it.
- get a second mortgage on your house so that you can buy a second property, eg a cottage in the country – you can use this as collateral when financing your new enterprise without hazarding your prime residence.

Business Courses

There are plenty of courses at evening classes and colleges as well as seminars run by local business enterprise agencies. These are only worth attending if the presenters run their own businesses. Check their credentials first. Check with your local library for courses near you. Also locally, you may find that your local Chamber of Trade and Commerce runs occasional courses or seminars and you can find out about your local enterprise agency from BUSINESS IN THE COMMUNITY. There are also courses sponsored by the TA and graduates are welcome on these. You can find out more about them from career services and from the TRAINING AGENCY.

Professional bodies (eg the INSTITUTE OF MARKETING, the BUILDING EMPLOYERS' CONFEDERATION) often employ information officers and advisers whose services are free (or cheap) for members. Professional bodies may also run courses and some specialist small training firms (eg the BREAKTHROUGH CENTRE) run on-going programmes and work-shops.

Capital Needs/Entry Cost

These vary enormously from job to job. Each of our job profiles gives a very rough indication of the entry cost, excluding your own personal costs of qualifying, training and living. For some jobs you need to get your hands on prestige premises, expensive equipment, valuable stocks or have access to large sums of money to demonstrate 'capital sufficiency'.

Do not despair – loads of others just need a battered van, a telephone in your home or use of somebody's garage as a workshop. You can get a rough idea of what you can do with the amount of capital/borrowing that you would feel comfortable in investing in your job – from £1.00 to £1,000,000 – from the *Special Features Index*.

Choosing Your Own Clients and Suppliers

Concentrating effort is the name of the game. While good, straightforward clients who know what they want, tell you what that is and then pay you for it quickly, are easy to deal with, the unproductive parts of your business can take up a lot of time. Clients who pull out at the last minute after hours of discussions and suppliers who fail to come up with what they promised are the main culprits here. These rules should help cut down on time wasting:

1 Work only for people/companies who will pay you
2 If in doubt, take a substantial deposit
3 If they object to this, you're right to have asked
4 Don't part with any money until you're sure you know what you're getting.
5 Don't put all your eggs in one basket. Make sure you've got enough clients and suppliers to ensure that even if one or two get into financial trouble, *you* won't.

Conferences

The main aim of most conferences is to make money for the conference organiser. Your aim in attending should be to stimulate your own ideas about your industry, profession or field of study. You can use them to make and develop contacts, to meet recruiters if you are looking for traditional employment and potential clients if you're self-employed. They can be expensive to attend throughout; part-time attendance may be all you need to make contacts (there are often special rates for full-time students). If you can't attend, write for conference details and copies of the proceedings. Conference attendance lists provide a useful source of information on companies and personnel.

Contacts

Your contacts are your lifeline to many forms of alternative employment, particularly when you are setting up on your own. You need a well established network of clients and suppliers, and to keep a record of it.

Journalists pinched the idea of a complete contacts book from the army and the church: Filofax originally produced their diaries-cum-address-books-cum-information-sources-cum-notebooks for these groups. Now the journalist's most valuable tool has been taken up by other professions. Whenever you meet someone, or read about someone who you feel might be helpful, **write it down**. Include friends, friends of friends, organisations listed in directories, work colleagues, contacts you have made in traditional employment and so on. Write down as much information as you can spare the room for. Where appropriate, make a note of when and how you came across the name.

Co-ops

A co-operative is a formal agreement between a group of people working together. It may involve a group of workers getting together to buy the company they work for, or a group of people with similar or interdependent skills getting together to market those skills. It is particularly appealing to those in alternative employment, since you can set your own terms and adapt the conditions of the agreement to meet your needs.

The CO-OPERATIVE DEVELOPMENT AGENCY (CDA) provides advice on setting up and financing a co-op, encourages the setting up of local agencies, and will put you in touch with local agencies. As a co-op, you may be able to get a grant or loan from a local authority, or specialist agency (eg agencies which specialise in providing advice and training for ethnic groups).

Decision-making Strategies

Decide quickly (but not hastily). Change your decisions slowly.

Making the right decisions is an essential part of being your own boss. You cannot pass the buck like the vast majority of bureaucrats.

The first point is that the decisions must be MADE – not put off for a couple of days. Problems which need a decision rarely go away, and you'll only have to make the decision in a week's time.

So how do you make the decision? Here are some well-established strategies.

Strategy 1: Arbitrary: toss a coin.

Strategy 2: Toss a coin and analyse your reaction. This helps you to identify your feelings about an arbitrary decision. Once your feelings are clearly exposed you can start to analyse the information available, which should be the basis of your decision making.

Strategy 3: The rational approach. Start to identify the facts, and project the consequences of different courses of action.

- List all the facts, as you know them;
- list all the difficulties and problems associated with each fact;
- list all your options, however bizarre;
- weigh up the likelihood of achieving each option and give it a percentage score;
- list what you have to give up if you pursue a particular action (the opportunity cost) and analyse how much it matters to you;
- look for any compromises that might be possible;
- identify a priority/preference scale and place the options in order;
- choose between the more certain and riskier options.

Review the situation: if it's a major decision, sleep on it and take a fresh look at your options in the morning. If you haven't time for that, just go through the options again, make sure you've considered all the possibilities, consult colleagues to see if they can see any alternatives you have not considered and look again at the likelihood of success for each course of action. If all else fails, go back to strategy 1.

Then make your decision AND ACT ON IT!

Displacement Activity

Classic examples of displacement activity are sharpening pencils or worrying about tax, VAT and NI instead of getting on with the business. Don't worry, almost everyone does it. The key is to know when you are doing it so that you can make sure you begin to get on with the job as soon as its over.

Divorce

There is plenty of it around, but recent research indicates that the self-employed are no more likely to suffer marital breakdown than anyone else. If your business is jointly owned, divorce could have dire consequences. It could pole-axe the entire enterprise. So draw up a written agreement at the start, and seek legal advice if things start to go wrong. Know who owns what within the business.

Employing Others

Employing others immediately involves you in office politics, office socialising and office administration. Whether they are casual labour, part-timers, full-timers or freelancers, once you start employing others your headaches begin. You're not just responsible for making a success of your life, you're responsible for the livelihood of others as well. Likewise, the success of your business is no longer entirely dependent on you.

Delegating effectively can be very difficult, particularly in a new business which has always been your baby. You should also accept that employees are unlikely to work as hard for your business as you will. One business owner reckoned it took three employees to do the work of one owner.

Once you've realised you need someone, decide what you want them to do, and make sure both you and they are clear on the terms and conditions of employment, and their job description (even if it's just 'general dogsbody').

Get professional advice on:
- Contracts of employment
- National Insurance contributions
- PAYE, income tax
- Statutory sick pay
- Unfair dismissal
- Redundancy
- Sex/Race Discrimination

Business courses can help a lot.

Find out more from the leaflets published by the Department of Employment, at your local office and read the *One Minute Manager*.

Equipment

In some fields of work, good equipment is vital. When you're setting up, you may be able to borrow, you may have to hire (keep a close eye on the amount you are spending on hire fees) or buy secondhand. There soon comes a point when you are better off borrowing the capital to buy equipment new. Always build an allowance for replacement of equipment into your budget. You'll never make money if your word processor is always broken or you're always mending the car. The same applies of course to one's telephone service but regrettably that's not in your control. BT can easily wreck your business for you if you let it.

EXHAUSTION

Exhaustion

When you're working for yourself, it is easy not to notice how long and hard you're working. The result can be that you exhaust yourself, which is counterproductive. If you're working on your own, you need to force yourself to take proper breaks. It is a matter which only you can determine in the light of your job and your own stamina. Research shows that most small businessmen work more than 50 hours a week.

Exhibitions and Trade Fairs

Vital sources of information and contacts if you are your own boss. Try to get to any that are relevant – in the UK or overseas – even if only for a few hours. They are advertised in trade publications. Entry fees are not usually prohibitive although fees to exhibitors often are.

You will not only see what the competition is up to, you will be able to meet suppliers, pick up trade and find out more about the structure and future trends of the trade.

The catalogues from these exhibitions are full of useful information, so get hold of any that are relevant. (Some of the major exhibitions in Birmingham arrange for their catalogues to be on sale at Euston Station – useful if you're London based and can't afford the train fare or the time.)

Exit Sale

Once established, you can often sell all or part of the expectation of the future income from your job, usually as a capital sum. This is obviously so in the case of businesses that are not entirely dependent on your own unique contribution as a craftsman or expert, eg an established magazine; less so where the income derives from intangible rights eg performing rights, copyright, film rights; and less obvious still when you're simply selling good will eg many professional practices. In some jobs you are prohibited from making an exit sale at all, eg NHS doctor, where you can sell the surgery but not the practice. But there are quite a lot of jobs where you can be your own boss and still, like a bureaucrat, find that your income ceases when you stop working. Working out the permutations of earned income, pensions and capital in financial terms is a highly technical matter on which it is almost certainly necessary to take proper advice. But Nigel Lawson is trying hard to equalise the tax treatment of income and capital so that the advantage of taking a capital sum against collecting income in the future is less clear cut in tax terms. It is worth thinking about exit sales before you start; if you decide that you want to work towards an exit sale consult your accountant and solicitor before taking the plunge.

Finance

Loans, grants, bursaries, sponsorship, family capital, redundancy payments – all these have been used to start up businesses. It's important to do your sums before you start: work out how much finance you will need, then decide which is the most appropriate source. If you are thinking of setting up a small, soft toy making business, for example, your local bank manager should be able to lend you the few hundred pounds you need to get started. On the other hand, if you want to go into property development you may need to approach the big city financiers. Anything is possible; they are in business to lend *you* money, not do you a favour. Today you no longer need to distinguish between being simply rich and poor; it is a matter of who is creditworthy and who is not. Make sure you are. Most accountants should be able to suggest who to approach where.

Beware. Sales are the only real source of finance. The rest comes from borrowing/using other people's money to provide working capital and to get your business off the ground. But the injection of other people's money often has entirely the opposite effect because many people find it easier and more palatable to seek further 'injections' of other people's money than to get on with the job of selling their products or services. That route only leads to failure.

Finance Checklist

Places you could look at if you need to use other people's money include:

Banks The major source of borrowing. During the recent push by the NatWest Bank to attract small businesses which needed finance, they achieved a 31% share of small business start-up financing. You don't necessarily have to be a customer of the bank you approach. All banks produce literature on obtaining finance. Even if you don't need any capital to start with, it is worth talking to your bank manager to arrange a loan and/or overdraft facilities in case you have cash flow problems: they'd rather know about possible problems before you start. Make sure you are talking to a manager who has authority to make the arrangements you want, otherwise you may be fobbed off because he does not want to lose face by telling you he's too junior.

Local Authority Grants There are many schemes administered by local authorities which may be useful. Local enterprise agencies are listed in the *Directory of Enterprise Agencies and Community Action Programmes*.

EAS Grants Under the Enterprise Allowance scheme, grants of £40 per week are available from the Employment Service, Department of Employment, for a period of 52 weeks while your business gets under way. To qualify, you must work a minimum of 36 hours per week and must apply for the grant before you start trading. The grant continues to be paid for a four week holiday and up to 8 weeks sick leave. Apply via your local Jobcentre.

Under 30s There are several schemes which are specifically designed to help young people setting up businesses. The *Prince's Youth Business Trust* will provide loans of up to £3,000 and bursaries for young unemployed people who want to start up their own businesses, or loans, training grants and ongoing support for new or expanding businesses. *Livewire* give awards for promising business ideas.

The *Shell Enterprise Loan Fund* makes loans to 18–30 year olds who want to set up a new business, live in Greater London and have some resources themselves. *Legal and General's Young Entrepreneurs' Scheme* lends money to 16–25 year olds.

Small Firms Loan Guarantee Scheme This is a government backed loan scheme, with the loan being arranged through a bank. The government provides a guarantee for 70% of the total loan agreed. It may be for property purchase, extending premises, purchasing business assets, setting up costs and/or working capital. The maximum you can borrow under such schemes is £75,000, over 2–5 years, at a cost of one–two percent over the base rate.

Start Up Schemes Banks through The Business Expansion Scheme (previously called the Business Start Up Scheme) arrange special loans with tax incentives for investors in established and small, unquoted companies.

Government Finance There are cash grants and special loan schemes for companies in development areas. Further information from the Department of Trade and Industry.

EEC Money Loans may be available for up to 50% of capital costs at reduced rates from the European Investment Bank. Your local bank or Enterprise Agency should be able to tell you whether you are eligible.

The City Many financial institutions and big companies have money to invest in start-ups and venture capital. Consult the list published each year (available in libraries) called Development and Venture Capital, reproduced in the *Investor's Chronicle* and also in *Working for Yourself*. Look up *Crawford's City Directory*, the best source book. The Bank of England also produces a useful guide – *Money for Business*.

Other sources you may consider:

There are local co-operatives offering a variety of loans, advice, support and shared back-up facilities (childcare, photocopying) – eg *Bootstraps* – currently in Hackney but planning to expand.

If you're creating jobs in a mining area or in a British Steel Opportunity Area you may be eligible for a bank loan from BRITISH COAL ENTERPRISE or BSC INDUSTRY, and if you can offer a job with training to a school-leaver you might be able to use the YTS scheme.

Private Loans If you are borrowing money from friends and relatives, draw up a proper agreement, listing the terms of repayment and rate of interest so that there is no misunderstanding. Consult a solicitor. Business courses guide you round many of the pitfalls.

A book to put you into the right frame of mind is *Think and Grow Rich*.

Financial Control

A prior condition of success is financial control. Take instructions from banks and accountants (all of which may sound deadly boring) and follow it. Do not attempt to devise your own original approach; install a well-tried, foolproof financial control system. Many failures are not business failures but are simply attributable to lack of financial control.

Franchising

In franchising owners of businesses allow others (franchisees) to market their products or services under their own nationally promoted name. The franchisor sets standards; the franchisee sets up with reduced risks. There are three basic types of franchise:

Job franchise Usually in service industries. Training is supplied by the franchisor. You buy the equipment. Examples: Dyno-rod services; Scotchcare; car tuning and carpet cleaning.

Business format franchise Usually in retailing. Examples: Prontoprint; Avis rent-a-car; Sketchley dry cleaning; The Body Shop; Holland and Barrett.

Investment franchise These cost a lot. Examples: hotels (Holiday Inn) and milk distribution (Northern Dairies).

For more information read *Working for Yourself*. Also the BRITISH FRANCHISE ASSOCIATION produces background information sheets, a checklist of questions to ask a franchisor (also available in the Department of Industry's Small Firms Advice Service booklet no. 3), and many other services.

Getting Started

Thinking about getting started is fun. The trick is to keep it that way through all the frustrations and often long hours of planning and actually getting going. First get clear what's fun for you.

Then find the people who'll pay you to have fun. That's your business.

What's your TRIP? – Talents, Resources, Intentions, Passions. List them all. Ask friends and elders how they see you.

Above all, the way you are defines the special style which will make you stand out. Maybe your greatest asset is a smile.

In business you're either different or you're dead. Vive la différence! Before you firm up on an idea, check there is a market for it, enough people crying out for it and prepared to pay a sensible price.

Once this is clear, planning becomes easy because you know precisely what you're offering and who to. The plan clarifies how it will work. Once you can see that, your confidence will grow and you'll feel like investing time, money and energy in it. Others who you approach for funding will also be able to see what you're on about and share your enthusiasm.

Having got your steam up, don't get carried away. This is the point to deal with the detail. Focus on detail too soon and you'll drown. Ignore it altogether and you'll also go under. Just keep it in perspective. A useful book on this is the *Greatest Little Business Book*.

Then involve people in your vision and get cracking. You can do all this on your own, but if you want to get there in months rather than years, tap into clubs and workshops for the self-employed eg; BREAK-THROUGH CENTRE, TRAINING AGENCY etc and check out your plans with the local Enterprise Agency. This gets you into the world of the self-employed, tapping into the energy and ideas of people who've done it thousands of times already.

A book that takes you through this is *Breakthrough*.

Getting Things Done

You won't get anywhere if you procrastinate. Getting things done is as easy as

A   for action
B   for belief
C   for commitment.

If you're the sort of person who tends to leave things until it's too late, working for yourself might not be the right thing for you. However, you can change if motivated. Write down what has to be done and when. Then check it every morning before you start work.

Make sure you're doing things that are worthwhile, not just trivia. Do the really important tasks first.

Growth Planning

Creating a new business needs different skills to those needed in the day to day running of an established business. People who are good at setting up may find it difficult to keep things going so they should:
1 find a structure that works easily
2 keep the business interesting for themselves.

Health

You're all right!

A survey by the Small Business Research Trust showed that, in spite of the long hours and extra stresses of self-employment and running small businesses, you are likely to be healthier than your counterparts in employment.

Remember reliability is essential to your good name. You can't have frequent days off sick, and you won't get any sick pay. Many self-employed people take out health insurance to protect their income, (although some major insurance companies charge women half as much again as men – the insurers seem to think they're a bad risk).

Smoking, alcohol, over-eating and anxiety are the main causes of ill health so deal with them positively NOW. You can try worry beads.

Hustling

Learn to hustle. Hustling as a strategy involves:
■ asking for favours
■ asking people to do things for you
■ asking for advice

Ask colleagues, family, friends, colleges and companies for help and advice. Use your contacts and develop new ones. Keep trying, keep pushing. People can only say no; usually they feel guilty and come up with the goods.

Insurance

Make sure you are properly insured. Depending on your job, you will almost certainly need to insure your premises and equipment. You may also want to insure your income. You may also need public liability insurance, professional indemnity, partner or key man insurance, insurance to cover accidental injury, vehicle insurance, fidelity insurance (or bonding) and so on. Some professional institutes and trade associations run special schemes.

Whatever your job you have to pay national insurance for yourself and any employees. But that will only guarantee a minimum pension, so find out about life insurance and pension schemes *before* you get old and grey.

Interpersonal Skills

Interpersonal skills are important when you're your own boss. You'll have no big company image to hide behind. You'll need good relations with customers, clients and suppliers – you can't just leave it to the sales department. Try reading *The Psychology of Interpersonal Behaviour*.

INTERVIEWING SKILLS

Interviewing Skills

When you're your own boss, you need to be able to ask the right questions: listen, establish rapport, respond appropriately. Whether the interview is in the form of a meeting, for example with a prospective supplier, or interviewing an assistant you must decide what information you are looking for and work out a strategy for getting it.

Prepare for the interview by finding out all you can about the other party. Read the letter of application; ring referees; or it may involve looking into the background of a company to find out how big an operation it is, what other clients it has and so on. Use your contacts.

For job interviews, decide what qualities you are looking for and organise the interview so that the interviewee can demonstrate them. If you want someone who can perform under pressure, you may want to take a formal approach. If you are looking for an easy-going, accurate typist, hold an informal interview, and give them a typing test.

Interviews

An interview is simply a conversation with a purpose:
- your job interview with recruiters
- a job interview you conduct with a prospective employee
- a financial interview with a bank, accountant
- an interview about the possibilities of going into business with an enterprise agency or grant giving body.

For all interviews, plan ahead, identify all the topics you want covered, and make sure they are covered in the interview. You do not normally get a second chance. Think what objections or difficult questions might come up (eg 'Didn't your last business go bust?') and prepare answers.

Isolation

Research into the problems facing people moving from large organisations into their own businesses at mid-career established that most of their problems were psychological rather than practical and administrative. They were made brutally aware of the true cost of much of their job support services – offices, tea-ladies, photocopiers and telephones – all of which they had taken for granted in their sheltered, organisational environment. As a result, they experienced greater anxiety and need for reassurance. Their real problem was isolation – isolation from colleagues, mutual support, organisational beanfeasts and people with whom to share professional worries.

As this is the most common single complaint of people starting up on their own it's worth thinking about before you jump at mid-career and worth considering before you become your own boss. Get into the small business world. Look at clubs and workshops for the self-employed, eg the BREAKTHROUGH CENTRE.

Keeping in Business

People who provide workshops and consultancy for new businesses (eg the BREAKTHROUGH CENTRE) assert that new businesses often seem to run out of money and energy 22 months after they first set up. Whatever the precise timing, very many people are exhausted and overwhelmed by the business they've created within a couple of years and may need help to survive what is akin to nervous exhaustion. Lots of people underestimate the time it takes to set up – allow at least three years and make sure that you'll have enough to live on over this time.

Getting the right amount of money into a business is not as simple as it sounds. If you have too much you may not be able to afford to service the loan/capital; if you have too little you may strangle the business at birth. With a modest loan/capital base you need a good overdraft facility which will allow you to borrow more money as your business expands and you can afford to pay more interest. If you start small and build up from a sound base it's difficult for the business to get out of financial control. If you start off with a hell of a lot of other people's money and no business base you're likely to find all you succeed at selling is shares in your business right up to the point at which it collapses.

Start small and let the business grow slowly. This needs commitment and patience but gives you time to learn more about how to run your business. You can get things to happen with very little outlay by subcontracting (say) manufacturing, sales etc.

Limited Companies

It may be to your advantage to turn yourself into a limited company. If your business is a private limited company, it means that the shareholders are not responsible for the company debts in the case of bankruptcy (unless the company has been trading fraudulently). Read *Working for Yourself*. Your accountant will tell you if you should do this

– then get your solicitor to set it up. Don't try it yourself unless this is your patch. There are disadvantages to going limited and in many crucial ways it does not even limit your risk. Many people, however, find it easier to handle their suppliers and clients as a limited company than as a sole trader. COMPANIES HOUSE has a centre in London and one in Cardiff.

Location – Office and Home

When you are your own boss, you can choose where you work. You can work at home, thus avoiding time spent travelling to work. On the other hand you may need to be able to visit customers and clients easily, so an office close to their's cuts down travelling time during working hours. Consider also your business address; a solicitor may be more plausible at a High Street address than 'Primrose Cottage', for example.

If you are setting up a venture where you are dependent on the public at large coming to you, location is very important. For example, a clothes shop or picture gallery would have to be very special to attract people to come out of their way. Groups of like retail outlets have tended to develop (eg clothes shops in Bond Street) and are developing all the time, so watch out for new trends. For instance, if there is a group of photographers together, they will all want equipment suppliers and photo lab facilities nearby; useful if that's what you are offering.

Many people use their homes to fund new ventures – either selling up and moving to a cheaper area, or selling their home and using the profits to buy a property which will provide both income and housing (eg hotel or old people's home). You may need to increase your mortgage when starting up.

As long as you don't make a nuisance of yourself or have a lot of visitors, it is usually all right to work from home as far as local authorities are concerned. However, officially, and if you ask them, they are likely to say No. Don't.

Market Research

Before taking the plunge look carefully at the market to ensure there is an adequate demand for the goods or services you plan to produce.

- You can start in a simple way by asking friends and contacts what they think of your ideas.
- You can look at others in the field to see how they are trading.
- You can ask groups of potential customers if they would be interested (eg ask local shoppers if they would visit your proposed coffee shop).
- You can call in a professional market research company to advise you.
- You can run your own 'pilot' launch to help you develop your product or service before getting too committed to something that needs changing.
- Some major reference libraries stock copies of published market research reports eg tourist authorities data.

The *Small Business Guide* is a good but, now, long in the tooth guide to sources of market and other information. For a more expansive view of trends in the world have a look at *Megatrends* and the *Third Wave*.

Marketing

Finding, getting and keeping more customers so you can live – ie the essence of business. Selling is one of the primary tools of marketing.

Books to read: *Marketing*, *Marketing for Small Firms* and *Breakthrough*.

Mortgages

A domestic mortgage can be a useful source of long-term borrowing for your job. Or you can take out a second mortgage on your home, especially if it has increased in value.

It's essential to go into this with your eyes open: consult your accountant, bank manager, building society, financial consultants, and mortgage brokers to get the best deal. Most building societies only give mortgages to self-employed people on the basis of three years' trading figures. So it's almost always worth getting your first or second mortgage fixed up before starting out.

Motivation

Motivation is one of the keys to success. You've got to motivate yourself first, then motivate others. For some, it's simply a question of sitting at their office desk with a picture of their children in front of them, to remind them that they need a good income to provide for their family. But everyone has their own reasons for wanting to be success-ful. Identify your reasons for wanting to do something, and you'll find it easier to be enthusiastic and confident.

Names – Business

Your business name is what hits people first and first impressions count. You can trade under your own name but in some fields a catchy, memorable tag is an asset.

Once you've decided on a name, you can make it official in a variety of ways.

- The department of Trade and Industry have a free pamphlet, 'Business names – guidance notes'.
- If you buy an off-the-shelf company you can apply to change the name for £10 through the REGISTRAR OF COMPANIES.
- You can trade under a name that is different from the official company name, but you must disclose the names of the owners and the registered office address.
- You can register your trading name with the Trade Marks Registry at the Patents Office, as well as your trade mark or logo (the emblem you use at the top of your stationery and on your products). This is usually more complicated than it sounds and you probably need a patent agent to get anywhere.

National Insurance

When you're self-employed, you have to arrange this yourself. Phone the DHSS on freephone 0800 666555 for advice.

Negotiating Skills

Before you can negotiate, you've got to get round a table. Whatever type of negotiations you want to enter into, there are some basic points to remember.

- Talk to the person who has the power to make decisions.

- Find a point of mutual interest or benefit and emphasise it.
- Be flexible in your approach.
- Listen to what the other person has to say – negotiations are two-sided by their very nature.
- Start by asking for the maximum (or offering the minimum) to give yourself room to manoeuvre.
- Identify the other person's point of view, and use it to your advantage.

The aim is not to crucify the other guy; the aim is for you both to feel you have won.

Useful reading: *Managing Negotiations*; *The Skills of Negotiating*.

NETWORKING

Networking

What used to be called the Old Boy network is now known as networking or using your contacts. Who you know counts, especially when you are setting up on your own.

Partnership

There are few restrictions on setting up a partnership. An important point is that all members are equally liable for the partnership's debts, even if clandestinely entered into by one partner. Also for each and every partner's tax liability from the income of that partnership. Liability for hefty tax bills, can arise from your partners' muddle as well as from their dishonesty.

Before entering into a partnership make sure you know your partners well: their strengths as well as their weaknesses and find someone who complements your own.

Have a written partnership agreement stating what will happen when (rather than if) the partnership ends.

Further reading: *Professional partnerships – Facing the future*; *Working for yourself – The Daily Telegraph guide to Self-Employment*.

Pensions

Personal pensions are the most tax-effective method of savings and also a useful form of collateral for financing your job. Avoid other employers' (other than your own!) company pension schemes like the plague unless you think you will be able to publish a *Spycatcher* to replace the income when the employer's scheme lets you down on retirement.

Unless you are a pensions expert, get advice.

Premises

Whatever you do you have to have somewhere to do it.

There are various alternatives: work at home; lease or buy business premises; share premises through local authority schemes, co-ops etc.

Before deciding remember:

- Working at home may be the cheapest and easiest option, but if your neighbours complain you'll have to move or close;
- Your lease, deeds or local authority restrictions may prevent trading from home;
- If you are renting business premises, check planning restrictions with your local planning officer, and get the fire department to look it over before taking it on;
- Never sign a lease without consulting a solicitor;
- Read *How to choose business premises*;
- Consult your local Enterprise Agencies.

Presentations

These range from a simple meeting where you present your ideas to a prospective client, to a full-blown advertising agency presentation, or presenting new business plans to your bank or other sources of finance. A professional approach is essential; scrappy ideas, badly presented do not win contracts – and winning contracts is what presentations are about.

Some marketing courses and more general courses on communication and presentation skills may help – ask your local careers service.

PRICING

Pricing

If you're selling goods or services, you'll need a pricing policy. Charge too little and you won't be able to meet your costs; too much and customers will go elsewhere. Do a bit of market research to find out what competitors offer and how much they charge.

The correct price is what the market will stand. Simple 'cost plus' pricing is a bit of a blunt instrument. You won't always have to be the cheapest.

Publicity

It can be good or bad; free or paid for. On the whole, you'll have to pay for it if you want to control it.

Many professions have strict rules on publicity and some allow none at all. Anyone else has a wide choice:

- Advertisements (newspapers, local radio, shop windows, hoardings)
- Press releases
- Taking a stand at an exhibition
- Giving talks/demonstrations
- Writing and broadcasting
- Sponsorship
- Competitions
- Direct mail and leaflet drops
- A clearly identifiable logo
- Free trials; free samples; free bags and badges; free information packs.

Once you are established, the main publicity is the product or service itself.

Self-presentation

Remember there are two forms of presentation: you in person, and you on paper. You must get the right image across.

- **Personal presentation:** If you don't feel up to scratch, take courses in public speaking, presentations, interviewing, negotiating and selling, preferably when you are a student or trainee, and can take advantage of cheap rates or company training schemes.
- **Written presentation:** This covers CVs, application forms, business cards and letter heads, brochures, price lists, reports. Take note of how the competition presents itself and make yours better.

The more professional the presentation, the more convincing you will appear to prospective purchasers of goods and services. Courses are available, and there are plenty of books on the subject – consult your local library.

Selling

Selling is the main way you present your product or service to people you feel will want it. To be a whizz at selling:

1 Believe in it yourself (most salesmen don't).
2 See who will benefit (most products don't have benefits).

3 Present it to people who need it (not just to everyone regardless).
4 Help them buy (don't ram it down their throats).

Two good books on selling are *How to Win Customers* and the *One Minute Sales Person*.

Initially the main problem (if you have decided not to springboard) may be that nobody knows you from Adam and you lack respectability and credibility. To overcome this:

1 Start with people you do know.
2 Drop names, piggy-back (do subcontracted work for) established traders.
3 Tap into the people who influence sales.
4 Use commission sales agents already known in your market.

Before you set up, you should know the names of at least 10 clients (for service businesses) or 100 customers (for shops) who will actually buy, rather than promise to.

Sickness

If you work for yourself you don't get paid if you're too ill to work. That means you can probably afford a couple of colds a year but what happens if you get glandular fever? You can insure yourself so that you still have an income if you're ill. This is easier to do when you're working for someone else in what an insurance company thinks is a safe job. Sickness insurance is vastly more expensive for women – and it is expensive for anyone to insure a decent income. Look at the figures carefully, and think about your personal circumstances (if you've a family and a large mortgage, it's probably worth it).

Social Skills

Social skills are your ability to handle cutlery, glasses, formal invitations and other people. They form part of self presentation: affability, good conversation and charm are attractive and can be your passport to success; picking your nose when you visit your bank manager is unlikely to help you.

SOCIAL SKILLS

Sole Trading

Sole trading is not what fishmongers do (necessarily), it is the term given to a one-person business. There is little to stop anyone setting up as a sole trader. You must:

- Inform the tax inspector (or get your accountant to do so)
- Look into the need to register a business name
- Be aware that if the business fails you will be liable for all the debts of the business

THE NATIONAL FEDERATION OF SELF-EMPLOYED AND SMALL BUSINESSES LTD aims to promote the interests of the sole trader and has good literature.

Tax

Tax evasion is illegal. Tax planning isn't. Indeed, it is a substantial industry in its own right. If you are working for yourself, your tax bill may well be lower, since you will be able to offset certain costs including your car against your tax. If you work from home, you may be able to count a certain proportion of your heating and lighting bill as business expenses. Obviously, there are certain expenses which are purely business – stationery, materials, reference books and so on. Get an accountant to sort it all out. Make sure the Inland Revenue is aware of your tax status. Keep a careful note of all business expenses, plus receipts where possible. It's very boring but saves you lots of money. If you have turned yourself into a company, you will be liable for corporation tax. If you are registered for VAT, you may have to pay that too. Make sure you anticipate large tax bills and have a good accountant.

Thinking Skills

You can develop your thinking skills, particularly if you have worked mindlessly as a bureaucrat for some time. Here are some approaches:

- Develop your lateral thinking by reading *The five day course in thinking*.
- Develop problem solving techniques with systematic problem analysis: Select, Define, Record, Examine, Develop, Implement and Monitor progress. Alternatively (or as well) use the questions What, How, Why, When?
- Brainstorming (think tanks). Get a group of people together to focus on a situation or problem: everyone must present their ideas with a minimum of criticism, so that you can draw together areas of similarity, common associations and so on. It is essential to record all the ideas.

Time Management

Two valid approaches:

'Never leave till tomorrow that which you can do today.' (Benjamin Franklin)

'I like work; it fascinates me. I can sit and look at it for hours. I love to keep it by me.' (Jerome K. Jerome)

Many people have some of the qualities needed for success as their own boss (self-motivation, risk-taking), but it is clever use of time that is often the essential ingredient for success.

Essential for success

- Identify your goals, both immediate and long term
- Decide when you work best: (up with the larks or burning the midnight oil)
- Analyse what you actually do with your time
- List what you have to do, with any deadlines
- Anticipate how much time a particular project ought to take
- Use a diary or a planner
- Review your achievements
- Delegate where it's time and cost effective

- Tie up loose ends as you go along
- Plan breaks and time off

But don't

- Spend too much time analysing, planning, and over-accounting.
- Stick by your plans doggedly if the situation changes.
- Be too perfectionist.

Watch out for time wasters

The telephone: is this chat necessary for business? Plan your calls and know what points you want to cover.

Paperwork: read priority post first; learn how to write business letters, develop standard phrases and formats.

Meetings: don't attend too many, or the wrong sort of meetings.

Decisions: learn how to make the right ones.

Plans: inform others and stick to them.

Systems: develop systems to deal with common tasks (eg invoicing). Develop good filing systems and stick to them.

Tidiness: saves time looking for things (so does filing).

Unfinished business: finish it.

Time management is particularly important when working at home with a family. Physical boundaries (a room set aside) will help you manage your time better.

VAT

If your annual turnover (ie your charges for goods or services) is more than the VAT minimum (the figure often changes at the time of the budget) you must register for Value Added Tax with the CUSTOMS AND EXCISE and you can register even if it is not that high. Consult your accountant. VAT is an involved tax. You have to pay 15% of the value of your outputs, but can offset against that any VAT which you have been charged by your suppliers. VAT is deadly boring, but it has advantages. First, when you are starting up, you are likely to be spending money faster than you are earning it. This means that the VAT man pays you, not you the VAT man, which can be quite important to your cash flow. Second, it forces you to keep proper accounts. (The VAT man can launch a dawn raid and inspect your books at any time.) What's more, you have to keep all the paperwork for five years, so buy a vat.

Other reasons for registering are
– It makes you look bigger than you are.

– Your business is zero-rated.
– You're selling mainly to people who can claim back VAT.

Being VAT registered isn't as complicated as a lot of people think – you'll need an extra column in your accounts book and you have to fill in four more forms a year and that's it!

Talk to your local VAT inspector – contrary to popular belief they're usually delightful people!

Wills

Make one and take advice. If you've got a business and you die intestate you can easily leave your partners and family with nothing.

> Make sure you read the How To Go About It: Careers A–Z even if you have already decided on your job. Much of it applies to running your own business and you may be employing others, reading CVs and conducting interviews so it is worth knowing something about their side of the interview desk.

A-Z Jobs

A–Z Jobs

Accountant

At a Glance

Qualifications/Training	Yes	*Income bracket*	Medium–High
Licence	Yes, to audit	*Town/Country*	Town
Experience/Springboard	Necessary	*Travel*	Local
Mid-career entry	Possible	*Exit sale*	Yes
Entry costs	£20,000	*Work at home*	Possible

Mix and match Possible. You could think about: Company doctor, Journalist, MP, Holiday accommodation owner, Cabaret performer . . .

Enquiries Institute of Chartered Accountants, Chartered Association of Certified Accountants

If you are happy doing people's bookkeeping, you need no qualifications but a way with figures. If you want to do more, you will need to be a qualified accountant. By law, only a chartered or certified accountant can audit company accounts.

To become a chartered accountant, you need to take out a training contract with a firm of chartered accountants. This training period lasts 3 years for graduates and 4 for non-graduates who have passed an accountancy foundation course. During this time you have to pass professional exams – fewer if your degree was in accountancy but don't be over-swayed by that. Maths graduates are most likely to pass the professional exams first time round; Oxbridge graduates and those with good A-levels are more likely than others. Training as a certified accountant is similar except your training contract can be in relevant work in industry or the public service. Older entrants, who are changing career, are welcomed. Don't expect to enjoy the training. Your responsibility and work satisfaction increases with your experience.

Two years after qualification, and with the sponsorship of a partner for whom you work, you can ask the INSTITUTE OF CHARTERED ACCOUNTANTS or CHARTERED ASSOCIATION OF CERTIFIED ACCOUNTANTS for authority to be a partner or set up on your own. In practice, most wait longer. To be a partner in an existing firm normally involves working for the firm and proving yourself first. You usually contribute towards the firm's working capital when you are made a partner, and may be asked to pay towards its goodwill. Your profit share usually increases to parity with other partners over a period of years.

As a sole practitioner, either start on your own or buy an established practice – through practice brokers or adverts in *Accountancy Age*,

Accountancy or the *Certified Accountant*. If you are working on your own from home you should aim to turnover at least £25,000 in the first year and will need at least £20,000 to get going, apart from buying the practice. You will, in due course, want to hire staff and buy a computer. It is not recommended that more than 15% of your fee income is from one client.

Most small firms provide general accounting services but a few are more specialised and other firms refer specialist problems to them. Within some rules, advertising is allowed. There are no restrictions on where you set up but certified accountants cannot join partnerships of chartered accountants. Mixed partnerships with other professionals are spoken about but not smiled upon yet.

The workload peaks during the first half of the year as most companies have a December or March year end. The job gives you good insight into other industries and working practices. You need to be numerate and accurate; auditing needs tact and integrity and you should get on with people. To succeed, you should have the ability to establish what is actually happening beneath the figures and then work out the most favourable way of dealing with it.

You will need *Tax Intelligence*; once you have bought this you will be sent updates.

Actor

At a Glance

Qualifications/Training	Recommended	*Income bracket*	Low
Licence	Union card essential	*Town/Country*	Town
Experience/Springboard	No	*Travel*	Yes
Mid-career entry	Unlikely	*Exit sale*	No
Entry costs	£100	*Work at home*	No

Mix and match   Often essential.   You could think about: Puppeteer, Cabaret performer, Street entertainer, Scriptwriter, Novelist, Illustrator, Theatrical agent, Mini-cab driver, Bartender, Market research interviewer, Window cleaner . . .
Enquiries   Equity

According to the UK actors' union EQUITY, at any one time more than eighty per cent of its 35,000 members will be without work. And that's after going through the whole business of getting an Equity Card. Acting is surely one of the last great closed shops, and union membership is essential. To control the entry of newcomers and protect existing members, most branches of the profession operate a quota system; so a provincial repertory company might have an annual allotment for two new actors and two stage management staff, who are employed with provisional membership. It's because these allotments are so limited that people are moved to take up anything from fire-eating to striptease as a means of getting into the profession.

To get provisional membership in the field of 'variety', whether you're a pub-theatre group, comedian or 'exotic dancer' you have basically to show a number of contracts at professional rates. Once you've got your provisional card you need a total of thirty weeks' Equity-recognised work – mercifully, not consecutive – to qualify for full membership. Not everything counts – check with Equity.

In certain specialised areas like opera or ballet you can get full membership as soon as you are accepted for a company and a similar system is planned for the theatre. This means a company can hire graduates of accredited drama schools (get a list from the NATIONAL COUNCIL FOR DRAMA TRAINING) as full members – and it won't eat into their allowance of provisional cards.

The whole question of drama school is a moot one. It's generally regarded as an important process – even if you reject a lot of what you learn – and it gives you a chance to perform. It's a lengthy and an expensive business – it could cost you as much as £1000 a term, though scholarships or LEA grants may be available (but grants for drama students are discretionary, even on an approved course). While drama school doesn't automatically lead to an Equity card, it is a great help in finding an agent, another essential ingredient. By no stretch of the imagination does having an agent guarantee you work, but it's difficult even to get auditions without someone to represent you – open auditions are very much the exception, especially in film and TV. But don't undervalue 'work training' if drama school is not your scene.

Acting is not a career that lends itself to precise planning – there's so much luck and chance involved. At the start of your career, aim for as much and as diverse experience as possible. Setting up a pub group or some profit-sharing production at the further reaches of the Fringe will hardly make your fortune but it will keep you working, practising your art, and it can provide you with some very worthwhile exposure.

The financial side is no more predictable. You could work for years on £5,000 pa – and count yourself lucky – then hit a smash soap, to earn twenty times that. To give some idea of the range of rewards, the Equity minimum rates for theatre work hover around the £130–160-a-week mark, depending on size, location and so on. Big success could lead to a percentage of the gross, so that a handful of stars might take a few thousand pounds a week, say, on the West End stage – by contrast with the National Theatre and the RSC where, almost without exception, nobody gets more than £400. The BBC television minimum rate, for anything more than a walk-on role, is £250 a time; the independent television companies generally pay rather better. The star of an average ITV sitcom would probably get £4–5000 an episode, while the star of big hourly TV drama might earn three times that. The real money of course is in films, but you could be a long time in the wilderness before anyone offers you 1 million dollars a movie plus a share of profits.

Apart from the fundamental problems of survival on no guaranteed income, you'll have some essential expenses to take care of (most you can write off against tax – should you ever earn enough to pay any). You'll need some publicity shots done, photos for agents and so on, which could run to about £150; travel expenses; clothes for auditions (if you're auditioning for the part of a glamour puss, say, you'll make a better impression turning up in something chic). You may also have to find extra money for various classes.

Whether or not you're drama-school trained, a voice coach is definitely advisable – you have to learn to use your voice properly or you can lose it, especially if you're going to work in the theatre. Singing lessons are a worthwhile investment, even if you're not planning to follow a musical route; they are a big help with general technique – breathing, projection and so on. By the same token, dance classes won't hurt either, especially when you're starting out – it will all make you more employable, as well as helping you keep in shape.

An actor's life can be peculiarly demanding. That is not to say it can't be fun, but it can certainly take a toll on your personal life. Experience suggests that it is not conducive to lasting relationships. The hours can be preposterous. Filming always starts at some unearthly hour in the morning; the theatre ends late at night. In words of one thespian, 'when you're out of work you're miserable, when you're working you're exhausted, when you finish a job you're sure you'll never work again – but if you can't take a joke you shouldn't have joined the profession.'

Contacts is a vital publication with the names and numbers of agents, management, studios etc – everything you need to know. From the same stable comes the casting directory, *Spotlight*, which serves the same function for actors, so you must be in it – everybody is. It costs you around £60 for a year, for a photograph and a half page entry.

The *Stage* is not the greatest read but it is very useful, particularly for jobs, auditions and so on; and get *The Author's Handbook*.

Actuary

At a Glance

Qualifications/Training	Essential	*Income bracket*	High
Licence	Yes	*Town/Country*	Town
Experience/Springboard	Essential	*Travel*	Yes
Mid-career entry	Possible	*Exit sale*	Possible
Entry costs	£2,000+	*Work at home*	Yes

Mix and match Possible. You could think about: Journalist, Newsletter publisher, Oyster farmer . . .

Enquiries Institute of Actuaries, Faculty of Actuaries

Actuaries are problem solvers concerned with forecasting and with assessing future effects of (usually) financial decisions. It's a small profession (there are about 2,000 qualified actuaries in the UK) and the bulk – 60% – are employed in the insurance industry where actuaries use their specialist knowledge and training to formulate and implement pension, life assurance and insurance policies and schemes. A few actuaries are employed by the government, as watchdogs for life assurance companies or as advisers on DHSS benefits and pensions. Deregulation and expansion of the financial services industry have increased the demand for actuaries and the opportunities for small actuarial companies to act as consultants on a wide range of financial matters are expanding. Many companies who do not employ an actuary on their staff, seek advice on company pensions, employee benefits, investment and business consultancy; those with in-house actuaries need second opinions and the specialist advice an independent can give them.

To satisfy the statutory definition of actuary, you must be a Fellow of the INSTITUTE OF ACTUARIES (IA) or, in Scotland, the FACULTY OF ACTUARIES (FA), before you can practise. This requires at least four years' practical training with an approved employer (usually, but not always, an insurance company or firm of actuaries); your careers services can help you to find one. During this time you are a student member of the IA or FA and you'll have to pass the 10 subjects of the qualifying exam – exemptions from some papers are possible. Teaching is done by correspondence course and tutorial. Employers give study leave to exam candidates and there's no formal limit to the number of times you can retake exams; it's rare to pass them all in less than 4–5 years. Most recent entrants to the profession are graduates and you're recommended to get a degree in maths, economics or statistics. Actuaries have to be numerate (good maths A-level), pay great attention to detail and be good at explaining what they're doing and why to people who don't understand. Assessing the best policies to adopt needs flair. There are no hard and fast rules or procedures to follow and this isn't a job for anyone who wants only to crunch figures all day. Set up costs aren't great; you don't need an office because you can visit clients at their's. You'll need a telephone, a wordprocessor/computer, a desk and some stationery. Most actuaries are in the south east, Edinburgh or Glasgow. You don't need to follow them but you must be close to the institutions that use actuaries ie close to a commercial centre.

Actuaries are well paid – in employment in London you can expect £25,000 pa on qualifying rising to £40,000+ over the next ten years. As an independent with the experience you need before you set up alone, you'll be able to get a lot more.

The usual way of setting up is to springboard from a large company once you've had some experience and have collected enough clients to live on. You can operate as a sole proprietor, in partnership or as a limited company. Seek out the owners of small businesses with their own self-administered pension schemes; larger firms will want help as their needs change through growth and restructuring; insurance companies also need independent actuaries and some work is available through sub-contracting (bear this in mind when you're springboarding and keep your employer on your side). Remember that pension scheme valuations are only needed once every three years (unlike company audits) so make sure you've got enough clients to keep you going. Advertise in accountancy and personnel management magazines and in the *Financial Times*; good editorial in any of these is better than a paid ad. Useful organisations (as well as the Institute/Faculty of Actuaries) are the ASSOCIATION OF PENSION TRUSTEES, the ASSOCIATION OF CONSULTING ACTUARIES, the SOCIETY OF PENSION CONSULTANTS and the PENSIONS MANAGEMENT INSTITUTE.

The people you're likely to see are finance directors and chief executives; accountants for some of your smaller clients. About a third of your time will be spent in management and administration; correspondence, reports and discussions with colleagues. The rest of the time you'll be with clients or working on their cases; setting contributory rates for pensions, advising on how to respond to new financial legislation, evaluating life assurance schemes, acting as consultants on investments etc. To a degree the work is seasonal – life assurance valuations after a December 31 year end must be in by the end of June (Department of Trade and Industry rule); pension scheme work tends to bunch around April 5. Other factors are new accounting standards regulations, financial legislation and company takeovers, all of which increase the demand for actuaries. The IA and FA publish useful leaflets.

Acupuncturist

At a Glance			
Qualifications/Training	Yes	*Income bracket*	Low–Medium
Licence	Recommended	*Town/Country*	Town
Experience/Springboard	Yes	*Travel*	No
Mid-career entry	Possible	*Exit sale*	No
Entry costs	£1,000	*Work at home*	Yes
Mix and match Yes. You could think about: Doctor, Artist, Journalist . . .			
Enquiries Acupuncture Association			

Acupuncturists treat the cause and symptoms of illness by inserting special needles into specific locations of the patient's body. These needles alter the flow of energy within the body causing chemical changes and so facilitating the healing process. To practise you must study this form of medicine. You can do this at a number of colleges eg the BRITISH COLLEGE OF ACUPUNCTURE or at the COLLEGE OF TRADITIONAL CHINESE ACUPUNCTURE. Each is associated with an association or register.

You need a compassionate, sensitive personality, to be dedicated and to possess some counselling skills. The career prospects vary across the country.

It's a good idea to start by working in a mixed clinic, with other kinds of complementary medical practitioners. This makes referrals easy and helps in setting up a network of useful contacts such as physiotherapists and those doing therapeutic massage. Make sure your name is on a

ACUPUNCTURIST

Register of Acupuncturists, join the ACUPUNCTURE ASSOCIATION and take out the good insurance they provide. After 3–4 years it is safe to start a practice of your own. This can be in your own home if you live near public transport and have parking facilities. You can treat 2 or 3 patients at the same time, in separate cubicles, if you have enough space.

You will need hot and cold running water, separate loo, needles, an autoclave (£200), telephone, answerphone, filing cabinet and stationery, say £1000 in all. Your premises must be inspected and licensed by your local authority. You can start by charging £12 an hour, rising to £25.

This is a satisfying job as you are independent, can organise your own hours, see your patients improve and continually learn something new. Patients tend to disappear during the summer holiday season and after Christmas when they are short of cash.

As translations of more Chinese medical books become available in this country, the practice of acupuncture is widening. It's also possible now to do a postgraduate course in Chinese herbal medicine.

Advertising Agent

At a Glance

Qualifications/Training	Useful	*Income bracket*	Medium
Licence	No	*Town/Country*	Town
Experience/Springboard	Essential	*Travel*	Possible
Mid-career entry	Unlikely	*Exit sale*	Yes
Entry costs	£5,000	*Work at home*	Unlikely

Mix and match   Yes.   You could think about: Marketing consultant, Public relations consultant, Direct marketing agent, Illustrator . . .

Enquiries   Communications, Advertising and Marketing Foundation

Advertising agents promote their clients' products and increase their sales by telling people about them. They do this by launching advertising campaigns, in which they play two key roles: creating advertisements; and buying media space or time in which to display them. Campaigns are of varying intensity, depending on how much clients want to spend and how desperate they are for coverage. Regular clients are called accounts; account handling is the third, and one of the most important, aspects of advertising. Advertising on TV, radio, the press and cinema is called above the line advertising. Agents also arrange advertising outside the media (brochures, mail shots, giveaways etc) which is called below the line advertising. Below the line tends to be one-off jobs and clients don't always have agency accounts as they usually do for above the line. To run a successful agency you have to exploit any opportunities of extending the client's market and find gaps in their current supply of advertising above or below the line.

You don't need any formal qualifications but you can take the COMMUNICATIONS, ADVERTISING AND MARKETING FOUNDATION (CAMF) exams by post or at some local colleges (further details from CAMF). This will give you a certificate and a good grounding in advertising but is of little practical use when you're finding work. Experience is essential and a small agency is particularly good for this because it gives an overview of the whole business rather than limiting you to one department as you may be in a larger one. Advertisers need to be good at self presentation and promotion. You'll have to build up your clients' confidence in your ability and trustworthiness: self confidence is a great help because clients tend to know very little about advertising. Anything that *you* don't know you can soon find out. You need to be able to write and to have ideas for the creative side of advertising;

understanding and manipulating people will make it easier to create successful adverts and to handle accounts.

You'll need an office to operate from with a telephone and a typewriter/word processor. Thereafter, your only expenses are running the office. Even though most agencies sub-contract a lot of work to freelancers, cash flow doesn't cause problems because suppliers' bills are sent directly to the client. Occasionally (especially for below the line) you may have to pay up front (eg for a brochure) and it's worth having credit insurance in case any of your clients go bankrupt before they've paid their bills. Most media space and time buying is done by special companies – you'll need to lodge bonds of about £50,000 if you want to do this yourself. You charge commission (usually about 17%) on everything that your clients spend on a campaign. For producing one-off below the line services you can charge a fixed fee. Obviously the more advertising you create the more money you'll make. Some campaigns cost millions of pounds.

Clients come through personal contact and knowing something about a specific business. You can't advertise, although, during your early days, you can approach potential clients with your ideas. You may be able to poach some from wherever you're getting experience, especially if you've been account handling. Other useful people to know are possible subcontractors eg writers, artists, designers, planners, printers and radio, TV and video production companies. It's a good idea to set up with somebody else whose skills and specialisation complement yours eg somebody creative if you're good at handling accounts. On the whole, there is a wider range of advertising opportunity in large cities and the south-east but some small local agencies survive on accounts from local businesses who have little interest in advertising and who are willing to pay for it to be handled by somebody else.

Read *Ogilvy on Advertising* and subscribe to all or some of *Campaign*, *Marketing Week* and *Media Week*.

Advertising Photographer

At a Glance

Qualifications/Training	Recommended	*Income bracket*	Medium–High
Licence	No	*Town/Country*	Town
Experience/Springboard	Recommended	*Travel*	Yes
Mid-career entry	Possible	*Exit sale*	No
Entry costs	£6,000	*Work at home*	No

Mix and match   Yes.   You could think about: Photojournalist, Picture researcher, Editorial photographer, Wood carver . . .

Enquiries   British Institute of Professional Photography, Association of Fashion Advertising and Editorial Photographers

This is where the real money is in the photographic field. A top photographer, shooting say a Benson and Hedges ad, can charge £1,500 per day – and will charge for the days spent setting up the shoot as well as the actual studio work. Suggested rates are set by the professional association, the ASSOCIATION OF FASHION, ADVERTISING AND EDITORIAL PHOTOGRAPHERS (AFAEP).

As with all photographic jobs, you must be meticulous, and have top technical skills. Commissions come from advertising agencies and most work is in central London. In most cases you will work closely with the creative director from the agency, and if you're working for a top agency, no expense will be spared in getting things right down to the last detail. You may find yourself constantly bowing to their wishes, but some creative directors appreciate your comments on the shoot. Sometimes, you may even be able to create work for yourself by coming up with new ideas for ads in a current series – then you can charge extra fees for the concept, as well as the actual shooting involved.

Most advertising photographers have an art school training, but generally learn more about the business through assisting experienced photographers. Vocational courses at art school are recognised by the BRITISH INSTITUTE OF PROFESSIONAL PHOTOGRAPHY. Cultivate contacts working in advertising agencies, get to know other photographers and get your name known as widely as possible. You will probably have to do a lot of legwork, showing your folio to creative directors.

Creative Review will keep you up to date with design developments in the advertising field; *Marketing and Campaign* will keep you informed about which agencies are handling which products. The *Creative Handbook* is a useful annually revised handbook. Get your name in it.

You can start out by hiring studios and equipment (AFAEP will help), but most successful advertising photographers will have their own studios or share facilities with other photographers. You will certainly want to buy your own cameras and a range of lights as soon as you can afford to. The total bill for equipment when setting up will be several thousand pounds. Overheads include studio facilities, repairs, processing, motor-bike messengers, a well-stocked drinks cupboard and an allowance for entertaining clients at lunch.

Alexander Technique Teacher

At a Glance

Qualifications/Training	Yes	Income bracket	Low–Medium
Licence	No	Town/Country	Town
Experience/Springboard	Recommended	Travel	None
Mid-career entry	Possible	Exit sale	No
Entry costs	£500	Work at home	Yes

Mix and match   Possible.   You could think about: Antique furniture restorer, Newsletter publisher . . .

Enquiries   Society of Teachers of Alexander Technique

Teachers of this technique advise their clients on how to use their own bodies more effectively through better balance and co-ordination to give greater efficiency, release more energy and thus improve their mental and emotional wellbeing.

To receive training, it's necessary to have a good all-round education and be between 20 and 40 to enter a school recognised by the SOCIETY OF TEACHERS OF ALEXANDER TECHNIQUE. You can take one lesson a week for a year to make sure that this is what you want to do before doing the 3-year full time course. You need to be interested in people, be a good communicator, dextrous and sensitive because you are handling and must be able to sense what is going on inside a body. Many problems derive from mental and emotional stress and tension and the teacher must be aware of this.

It is best to go alone after a period of supervised probation following qualification. Many parts of the country have no Alexander teachers so you should be able to succeed. It is useful to join the SOCIETY OF TEACHERS OF ALEXANDER TECHNIQUE. You can advertise discreetly; you can let GPs know of your existence as they are useful and can send you many referrals. You need a ground floor room, possibly in your own home, and a treatment table costing £120. You also need a phone. answerphone, filing cabinet and chair. You can charge from £8 to £15 per ½hr.

You tend to work outside normal working hours to fit in with clients. The advantage of this job is that you have the freedom to plan your own day and the pleasure of seeing clients get better. The disadvantages are that your income fluctuates, clients disappear in the summer and after Christmas, and you must be careful if working at home that the job is kept separate from family life. You can do another job at the same time if you organise yourself.

Useful books are *Alexander Technique, Body Learning, Alexander Principle* and *Use of Self*.

Antique Furniture Restorer

At a Glance

Qualifications/Training	Recommended	Income bracket	Low–Medium
Licence	No	Town/Country	Either
Experience/Springboard	Recommended	Travel	Local
Mid-career entry	Yes	Exit sale	No
Entry costs	£5,000	Work at home	Possible

Mix and match   Yes.   You could think about: Dealer in antiques, Wood carver, Furniture maker, Man with a van . . .
Enquiries   British Antique Furniture Restorers Association

This has become highly scientific – techniques are being updated constantly – and requires an aptitude for woodwork and a love of antiques. It is extremely labour intensive – you may have to work for weeks on the same piece. There will always be a demand for your skills, but you need total commitment and self-discipline to succeed. It can be a very rewarding but solitary and sometimes frustrating occupation.

You will need to take a suitable course – the Conservation Department at the VICTORIA AND ALBERT MUSEUM has information, as does the BRITISH ANTIQUE FURNITURE RESTORERS ASSOCIATION, or local education authorities. The mecca is WEST DEAN COLLEGE. You can help pay for your course by taking on commissions while you are training. Some experienced restorers will take on apprentices. You can specialise (eg gilding, french polishing).

Tools cost approximately £1500 (vice £80; bandsaw £500; kit for polishing, colouring, staining £100+). You also need a van to transport pieces between client and workshop. Some commissions incur a high outlay on materials, eg veneering (£500). Repairs may involve buying 'breakers', (eg a mahogany wardrobe) for suitable material (up to £1000). Find suppliers through *Woodworker*.

Many restorers prefer to share a workshop for financial reasons and general working methods – better discipline, shared expertise, new techniques. Initially you may be better off taking smaller commissions. Frequently a seemingly uncomplicated job can involve far more detailed restoration once taken to pieces – take this into account when giving estimates. It may be better to complete at a break-even price but near the estimate. Likewise if the job takes less time, reduce the price and gain goodwill.

You will need to advertise – local papers, *Antiques Trade Gazette*. Approach local antique dealers – a useful source of steady work – but be aware that they will not give you any credit, so unless you are prepared to work for just the trade, do your own promotion. The ideal is to find, restore and sell your own pieces, but it's risky unless you're experienced in all these fields.

Architect

At a Glance

Qualifications/Training	Essential	*Income bracket*	Medium–High
Licence	Yes	*Town/Country*	Town
Experience/Springboard	Yes	*Travel*	Yes
Mid-career entry	Unlikely	*Exit sale*	Yes
Entry costs	£2,000+	*Work at home*	Possible

Mix and match Possible. You could think about: Property developer, Holiday accommodation owner, Artist, Garden gnome maker . . .

Enquiries Royal Institute of British Architects

Architects design buildings and supervise their erection. This involves producing plans that are aesthetically acceptable and technically feasible; obtaining planning permission; contracting builders; working with surveyors and engineers and keeping an eye on building in progress by visiting the site regularly. Most of the work done by architects in private practice is for houses and offices; there are some opportunities in private sector health and education buildings, but most hospitals and schools are designed by employees of local authorities or the government. The demand for architects fluctuates. Recently big clients have included property developers who are converting old buildings. Some firms become specialists – often in the type of building for which they were first commissioned while others prefer, if possible, to keep their options open.

An architect, like a doctor, is a member of a registered profession and must be a member of the ARCHITECTS' REGISTRATION COUNCIL OF THE UK (ARCUK). This means passing the ROYAL INSTITUTE OF BRITISH ARCHITECTS (RIBA) exams (usually done over a five year course at an RIBA recognised school of architecture), and having two years of practical training with an ARCUK registered firm. Most newly qualified architects first join an established practice and, unless you've got some capital and win a competition, or have a friend/relative to commission you, it is difficult to start up alone immediately after training: perhaps dangerous too without some experience in an established office. As an alternative to setting up alone you may choose to stay with an existing firm and hope to graduate as a partner (probably after several years as an associate). In many cases this will bring a more interesting range of work than could be expected in the earlier years of a new firm. As well as being creative and practical, in order to design attractive buildings that suit their function and surroundings, architects need to be good at presenting themselves and their ideas – this is a competitive profession.

Set up and running costs depend largely on your ambitions and location. You could operate from home or a very small office with that minimum of equipment you would have had as a student, and a telephone. Early commissions are likely to be small: designing extensions and inserting new kitchens for example. Once you've broken into the market for bigger projects, you'll need to increase capital for a proper office and a staff of assistants and secretaries. A bank loan may be available if you can prove the validity of the commission. Architects are paid in stages and, as some projects can take several years to complete, you may have cash flow problems, especially when the size of the project necessitates a team of assistants. For a large finished building design there may be thousands of drawings, completed by a team of many architects. They must be paid – perhaps before your own fees arrive.

Some commissions come through competitions, often for showpiece buildings, banks, parts of large developments etc that will bring publicity and, possibly, further contracts. Winning a competition can get your own practice started, as long as you make the most of the publicity and manage to get further commissions to follow. If you don't win, you won't be paid for the work you've done or had done by employees. Architects usually get about 6% of the costs of new buildings and a higher percentage for alterations. A mandatory fee scale is, however, no longer allowed and fees are negotiable – sometimes in competition with other architects. In your early days the traditional sources of work include friends and relations and anyone else you can interest in your work. Architects depend on establishing a reputation because the majority of clients don't need their services regularly and go to someone they've heard something about. This also means that architects who do well as associates for another firm may have difficulty when they set up alone. On the other hand, the firm you've left may well pass on small jobs to help you on your way. It is hard and taxing work with most time spent in the office. But site visits and the nature of the work make it a stimulating career.

Read *Starting up in Practice*.

Art Historian/Critic

At a Glance

Qualifications/Training	Recommended	*Income bracket*	Low–Medium
Licence	No	*Town/Country*	Either
Experience/Springboard	Essential	*Travel*	Yes
Mid-career entry	Yes	*Exit sale*	No
Entry costs	Nil	*Work at home*	Yes

Mix and match Yes. You could think about: Journalist, Dealer in antiques, Artist, Picture restorer, Contemporary art gallery owner, Art dealer . . .

Enquiries Art Colleges or auction houses

As well as writing art books, self employed art historians can be reviewers, journalists, authors, cataloguers, researchers, lecturers or exhibition organisers who have proved themselves especially knowledgeable in some field. This may be Rembrandt etchings or Andy

Warhol. Your expertise will become known and required but it may take years to build up and, to succeed, you must be 100% immersed in your career. The going is tough at the bottom, hawking your knowledge around the art journals, newspapers, local radio; once successful, however, you will be fêted. The usual way in is through a good History of Art degree. You will need languages – German, French and Italian but also Latin and Greek for medieval studies. The COURTAULD INSTITUTE has a reputation that will take you one step closer to success; short courses are offered by specialists like Sotheby's and Christie's. Once you've got a degree, you'll need experience in the field to build both your knowledge and contacts. This can be through working for a public or private gallery, teaching, working at an auction house – anywhere you'll be in touch with works of art and art experts. While you're doing this, you can start submitting your work to likely publications. The *essential* qualifications are talent and a good eye. You must enjoy forming and defending opinions; for this you need to know what you're talking about; one loudly voiced argument from you that proves to be wrong could blow your career. Starting up costs are minimal and you work from home (which needs to be near a cultural centre). You should have a second source of income for at least ten years. Finding a toe-hold can be luck, but you will not become known unless you are prepared to sell yourself. Very few art journals (*Arts Review, The Artist, Burlington, Apollo, Antique Collector*), or newspapers, have large budgets for sending their reviewers around the country. Offer to cover an exhibition in Manchester/Liverpool/Cardiff (or better still abroad while on holiday). Try reviewing books; they may pay very little (sometimes just the book) but keep at it as the articles will follow (approx £100 per 2,000 words) and it's the readership you're out to impress. Museums, galleries, academics all read these magazines and once your name is known you can get involved in exhibitions or lecturing. Try local radio stations which need experts on exhibitions or paintings that need saving for the nation. Very often you will be required at short notice, so make sure it's your telephone number that they can find. It can be a stressful life, you're staking your career every time you open your mouth but, as long as you've got the necessary knowledge and interest, it's a rewarding and enjoyable way of living.

Artist

At a Glance

Qualifications/Training	Recommended	*Income bracket*	Low
Licence	No	*Town/Country*	Either
Experience/Springboard	No	*Travel*	Possible
Mid-career entry	Yes	*Exit sale*	No
Entry costs	£500	*Work at home*	Yes

Mix and match   Yes.   You could think about: Illustrator, Art historian, Art dealer, Picture restorer, Artists' agent, Mini-cab driver . . .

Enquiries   Royal Society of Painters in Watercolours, Royal Society of Painter-Etchers and Engravers, Art colleges

Artists make money from creating and selling works of art. You'll need a lot of talent and drive to succeed, and, in the early days at least, will almost certainly have to mix and match being an artist with other work. For anyone with artistic flair, it's a wonderful way of making money while surrounding yourself with whatever pleases you most – plants, Mediterranean landscapes, nudes, animals. . . . You don't need any formal qualifications but a degree course at a good art school is an excellent way of learning some basic techniques, choosing your favourite media, practising and developing your own style and building up contacts. You may want to study further abroad, eg, at the BRITISH SCHOOL IN ROME or in the USA through the BRITISH COUNCIL. Most artists concentrate on one or two media – water colours, etchings,

ARTIST

lithographs, oils, murals . . . – few, however, work exclusively in one without experimenting in others at some point in their career. There are various specialist societies like the ROYAL SOCIETY OF PAINTERS IN WATERCOLOURS and the ROYAL SOCIETY OF PAINTER-ETCHERS AND EN-GRAVERS.

Set up costs depend on the media you're going to use. Brushes cost about £35 each (and you may need up to 30 or 40), an easel costs £200. You may need carrying cases for your paints, portfolios for your work, paper, pencils, canvas. You can buy second hand equipment through the *Artist*. Other expenses may include having plates cut for etchings or transporting yourself and equipment to places you want to paint. It may be difficult to make much money. In the early days, you'll probably have to do something else to keep the wolf from the door. Ideally you want something you can fit around your art rather than something that demands your presence in an office for 8 hours a day.

You'll have to create things that people will buy; this doesn't necessarily mean prostituting your art but it does mean working hard to find your particular market and being prepared to accept that this market may be very small. To find buyers, your work must be seen; art college graduation exhibitions are a good first step. Try to get local libraries, theatres and restaurants to show some of your work and tramp around art galleries with your portfolio. Some galleries specialise in the work of young artists; look out for galleries where your work would fit in particularly well with what they usually sell. Galleries take up to 50% commission and most want framed pictures, but they have excellent contacts amongst art buyers and critics. In addition to selling and showing completed works you may be able to get some commis-sions, eg, for portraits. There are several ways of supplementing your income, most of these are easier to get into once you've started to establish your reputation – the ARTS COUNCIL gives advice and spon-sorship on exhibitions. You can lecture, teach, become an artist in residence or an art therapist. There are opportunities in commercial art, painting murals for interior designers or illustrating books, a good way of getting wide coverage for your work. There are also competitions. As long as you're not too worried about owning a BMW by the time you're 25, you can have a wonderful life as an artist; there are plenty of biographies that tell you what's entailed.

Artists' Agent

At a Glance

Qualifications/Training	No	*Income bracket*	Low
Licence	No	*Town/Country*	Town
Experience/Springboard	Helpful	*Travel*	Local
Mid-career entry	Yes	*Exit sale*	Possible
Entry costs	£5,000	*Work at home*	Not recommended

Mix and match   Yes.   You could think about: Contemporary art gallery owner, Illustrator, Art dealer . . .

Enquiries   Artists' Agents

Commercial artists – whether they are illustrators for books and magazines, advertising or marketing – often need an agent to do the donkey work.

If you've got a good background in design (you needn't have technical skills), and an understanding of printing techniques (so that you can talk to the art editors and advertising agents intelligently) you can start up your own business. Agents usually work for another agency to start with, and build up a close relationship with several artists, then 'poach' the illustrators they like to work with, and build up their own stable of artists.

Most agents specialise in a particular field, such as illustrating practical step-by-step features, or producing illustrations for romantic fiction. Or you may be an agent for a range of illustrators, so that whatever the commission, you have the contacts to fulfil it. The technical knowledge can be picked up at art school, if you do an option in printing or book design. The selling skills come naturally to some people, or you can pick them up while working for another agent.

As well as a fair knowledge of printing, you must be outgoing and get on easily with people. You will have to be clued up about accounting and be able to cope with 'cold calling' (plenty of small talk when you are showing folios to people whom you have had no previous contact with).

The *Creative Handbook* is revised annually, and lists agencies, artists, photographers and so on. You must get yourself (and your artists) listed in it. You may even find it worth taking a full colour page ad to promote yourself.

Your income comes from the commissions: art editors and directors will commission you and pay you once the finished artwork has been accepted – you will have to pay the artists, taking your own cut on the way.

For a professional image, you will need an office (or at least an office address) in the centre of town (preferably London), complete with telephone line and receptionist (or answering machine). You will also need to employ an accountant to deal with finances and the Revenue (not to mention the bank manager).

Junior jobs in the field are advertised in the design magazine of the moment (*Creative Review*, *Design* or *Blueprint*). Artists' agents will also recruit assistants and illustrators direct from art college – the finals show can be all-important.

Assistant Film Director

At a Glance

Qualifications/Training	No	*Income bracket*	Low–Medium
Licence	Union card	*Town/Country*	Town
Experience/Springboard	Yes	*Travel*	Yes
Mid-career entry	No	*Exit sale*	No
Entry costs	£500	*Work at home*	No

Mix and match Limited. You could think about: Mini-cab driver, Market research interviewer, Bartender . . .

Enquiries ACTT

The assistant director handles the director's practical needs, including planning the schedule for the day's shooting on set or location, drawing up call-sheets and working with the production manager on the equipment required for the shoot. They are also go-betweens for the producer and director. Depending on the scale of the film, there may be more than one assistant director (called 1st, 2nd and 3rd etc in decreasing order of seniority). The 2nd and 3rd assistants have more to do with the nitty gritty of getting equipment and cast on set on time, as well as general organisation while filming.

The film industry is difficult to get into. There are no formal qualifications but you need an ACTT union membership card for most jobs. A qualification from an ACTT accredited school is useful for background experience, credibility, contacts and because it makes you eligible for an unemployed ACTT card (first step to getting the real thing). The best way in is via a production company as receptionist/

secretary/runner so that you can get an inside view of filming and build up some contacts before you start to freelance. Get to as many shoots as possible so that you're seen and can be on site should any extra help be needed. Offer your services to anyone likely to use them. Ultimately it's a case of pushing; nag producers, they may hate you but at least they'll remember you and may pass you on to somebody else who can use you. Investigate the Jobfit scheme from ACTT, which gives you on the job training and experience through temporary junior positions with various production companies.

When you set up you'll need a telephone and an answering machine; better still register with a booking service who will handle all your calls while you're away. As you become better known, it's worth getting an agent who can hustle and negotiate for you. The ACTT sets minimum rates of pay (£150–300 per week). These are regarded as low throughout the industry and you can get more. Commercials and promos usually pay a higher rate because the bookings you get for them are for shorter lengths of time than for feature or documentary films.

Assistant directors have to be indefatigable and are at the heart of the film making process, liaising between the production office and the director. They are usually the first to know when something goes wrong. Their responsibility is to ensure that no shooting time is wasted. This is a close knit world where good reputations are hard-earned but easy to lose.

Money into Light gives an account of what goes into making a film.

Barrister/Advocate

At a Glance

Qualifications/Training	Essential	*Income bracket*	Medium–High
Licence	Yes	*Town/Country*	Town
Experience/Springboard	No	*Travel*	Yes
Mid-career entry	Unlikely	*Exit sale*	No
Entry costs	£2,000+	*Work at home*	No

Mix and match Possible. You could think about: MP, Novelist, Property developer, Journalist, Puppeteer . . .

Enquiries Council of Legal Education, General Council of the Bar

Barristers in England, Ireland and Wales, and advocates in Scotland present cases in court, dressed in wigs and gowns. They also provide legal advice. Barristers cannot be directly contacted by lay clients but are engaged by solicitors on their behalf. Superior court cases must be presented by barristers although this monopoly is under threat. They tend to have specialised knowledge of legislation and precedent in an area of the law, and are consulted for their opinion and advice by solicitors whose knowledge is far more general. The work can be broadly divided into criminal and commercial law; roughly speaking, criminal barristers spend more time in court than commercial ones whose main role is as consultants. Advocates do not specialise. Greater amounts of money can be made in commercial work but it takes longer to assimilate the specialist knowledge involved. After 15–20 years of successful practice barristers may apply to the Lord Chancellor as prospective Queen's Counsel. Only the very best (judged on earnings and ability) will make this grade and they handle only the most important cases.

Whatever area they go into, barristers have to have a good short term memory, be able to grasp situations and information quickly and to remain emotionally detached. In addition they need flair, the ability to think logically and excellent communication skills in order to present cases in court convincingly and in such a way as to be comprehensible to both the judge and the jury. Steeped in tradition, women are beginning to get in but there aren't many ethnic minority barristers or barristers with working class parents around and contacts are very useful.

Qualifying as a barrister requires a law degree or another degree and a law diploma, a year's study leading up to the Bar exam, eating 12 dinners at your inn, being called to the bar (if you pass the exam) and serving pupillage for a year. Pupils are attached to barrister pupil masters and are not usually paid during their pupillage unless they win a scholarship or are involved in a case as some pupils are later in their pupillage. Successful completion of this does not guarantee employment. In Scotland you do 21 months with a solicitor after your LLB degree and diploma, then 'devil' for nine months with a member of the bar.

Barristers are self employed but are obliged by the Bar Council to work from a set of chambers (rented from the Inns of Court in London and Scotland) and have a clerk to administer their work. Sets, usually of between 15 and 30 barristers, share a clerk and junior clerks and may pass work to one another but are in no sense partnerships. On finishing pupillage you must find a tenancy at a set of chambers (either criminal or commercial depending on the field you're in). There are far fewer of these than of pupillages; about 200–300 as against 700, they tend to go to pupils of the set or through contacts. While you're looking for a tenancy you may be able to stay on with your pupil master and take on work from there; this helps to build up useful contacts for when you move to your own chambers. Although new sets of chambers can be set up with the consent of the circuit leader outside London, the Bar Committee in London, it is extremely unlikely that a group of young barristers will be allowed to do so because they will lack the necessary experience to operate chambers successfully.

It's financially difficult at first. The £200 or so you'll need for a wig and gown (essential for court appearances) is minimal compared to the cash flow problems caused by being paid only on completion of a brief and having to pay rent (based on income), travel and other expenses in the meantime. Initially you'll spend a lot of time handling parts of cases

CRIMINAL BARRISTER

for other barristers; solicitors brief a barrister but are not usually averse to the case being handled by another barrister from the same set of chambers. You may also get some research and consultancy work. By appearing in court for others you will be noticed and solicitors will start to bring work to you. It takes roughly 3–5 years to become established (commercial takes longer than criminal) and if you're successful you can be selective about which cases you take. A lot of work comes from Legal Aid which operates on a taxi rank system: if it's your turn you have to take the case unless you can pass it on to someone else in your chambers.

Legal aid fees are set nationally; private fees are negotiated between the clerk of the chambers and the solicitor. On average you could be earning between £10,000 and £25,000 a year (sometimes a lot more) but this depends on a lot of factors. Some barristers choose to represent only the defence, fewer the prosecution, most represent either – clerks encourage this because the more flexible the chambers, the more work they will get.

Even criminal barristers will usually spend far more time in the preparation of cases than on their presentation. Court work is unpredictable, cases can go on for far longer than predicted or be cancelled at very short notice. You may find yourself under great pressure to prepare for a case in a short time and you must expect to work long and irregular hours. Sometimes you may have very little to do, on other occasions you'll be scheduled to appear in two different courts at the same time, (pass on one to someone else in chambers). Court work is physically and mentally demanding. Most of the time you will deal with other members of the legal profession, but you'll meet your clients, often in prison if you're a criminal specialist and have to be able to overcome any aversion or sympathy that you may feel.

Further information from the COUNCIL OF LEGAL EDUCATION and the SENATE OF THE INNS OF COURT AND THE BAR. See also *Counsel*, the magazine of the Senate of the Inns of Court and the Bar.

Bartender

At a Glance

Qualifications/Training	No	Income bracket	Low
Licence	No	Town/Country	Either
Experience/Springboard	No	Travel	No
Mid-career entry	Yes	Exit sale	No
Entry costs	Nil	Work at home	No

Mix and match Yes. You could think about: Actor, Musician, Novelist, Minicab driver, Painter/decorator . . .

Enquiries Pubs, wine bars, hotels

Bartenders work in pubs, wine bars or cocktail bars, mixing and serving drinks. Most establishments employ part-time, casual labour as well as full-time employees. Rates set by breweries are pitifully low – around £2 per hour. A session (say 5.30–11.30) pays as little as £12–15; but if you work in a cocktail bar you can make a healthy living as you will pick up tips as well as an inflated hourly wage reflecting unsocial hours. Most establishments will also provide meals.

If you want to run your own business, then you could set yourself up as a freelance cocktail mixer, providing drinks at private parties. The main problem is getting round the licensing laws: you cannot actually sell drinks without a license, but you can arrange for the hosts to buy drink on a sale or return basis through your wholesaler – you deliver and serve the drink. You will need some basic equipment – tables, cloths and glasses – you provide the garnish – lemon, cherries, ice, paper parasols and so on. You will need transport, and to promote yourself you should have a cocktail menu printed, and business cards. The best promotion is by word of mouth, and you can also advertise your services in local papers, society magazines and so on. It may also be worth going into partnership with someone who does food for parties, so you can give a complete party service.

One of the great advantages of working as a bartender is that you meet people all the time. If you are aiming to get into a particular career, you can use your hours behind the bar to great advantage, if you choose the right drinking hole. If you want to get into advertising, choose an 'in' cocktail bar, close to one or more major advertising agencies. If theatre is your area, go for jobs in pubs and clubs in theatreland.

The bartenders' bible is the *Savoy Cocktail Book* with recipes for all the traditional mixes. There are several other cocktail books on the market.

Beauty Consultant

At a Glance

Qualifications/Training	Recommended	*Income bracket*	Low–Medium
Licence	No	*Town/Country*	Town
Experience/Springboard	Recommended	*Travel*	Local
Mid-career entry	Possible	*Exit sale*	No
Entry costs	£2,000	*Work at home*	Possible

Mix and match Possible. You could think about: Make-up artist, Hairdresser, Knitwear designer, Yoga teacher . . .

Enquiries Beauty houses or beauty parlours

A beauty consultant normally starts by working for one of the beauty houses. Their job is to offer advice and instruction on that company's products, normally for a salary plus commission. This is quite distinct from beauty therapists who usually complete Diploma courses at recognised schools not just in the make-up and beauty courses the consultants take, but in the intricacies of waxing, electrolysis, hair removal, etc. Such training is then usually followed by entry to a beauty parlour specialising in beauty 'problems', rather than the speculative buying indulged in by Ms Average who just wants 'to look like Madonna or Kelly Emberg'.

Anyone branching out on their own will normally have followed one of these routes. Freelance opportunities exist, generally for beauty advisers who are prepared to visit clients in their own homes.

Good reputations travel fast, and you need to be patient, informative, instructive – as well as ready to make up people who need a facelift or a paper bag over the head. For the impatient, or anyone too inexperienced to gain entry directly to a beauty house or beauty parlour, one option could be to try one of the agencies which supply the beauty houses with temporary staff to give extra cover for promotions, Christmas, etc. These will give a 2/3 day cramming course on several houses' products and then hire out staff for short periods, thus providing minimal experience.

Most good companies will not employ people under 21, which fixes the lowest point of entry, unless you have something special to offer such as languages or training at a recognised beauty therapy school. Race, and perhaps surprisingly, sex, offer no barrier, as many female customers find it appealing to have a man giving them time and attention. Nevertheless, most men would find it intimidating to work in such an unquestionably female environment.

There is no world so bitchy as the beauty consultant, few others where one's appearance is analysed every hour by customers and fellow consultants, and where one is open to such personal criticism. You'll need patience to compromise between what the customer actually needs and what she says she needs, and strong legs, as you need to stand for long hours, sometimes virtually all day. Delicate flowers tend to wilt very quickly in this over-heated atmosphere.

The main requirements are an obvious desire to enter the beauty world, plus willingness or proven ability to deal with the public. Good grooming, self assurance and an interesting personality will cross almost all bridges. Driving licences and similar extra strings to one's bow are useful but not essential.

A consultant starting work in London might expect to earn £130 a week, less for the provinces, although this will depend upon how many customers you can pack into a working day.

Any magazines on beauty and health care are useful.

Beekeeper

At a Glance			
Qualifications/Training	Available	Income bracket	Low
Licence	No	Town/Country	Country
Experience/Springboard	Useful	Travel	Local
Mid-career entry	Yes	Exit sale	Yes
Entry costs	£5,000	Work at home	Yes
Mix and match	Yes. You could think about: Farmer, Gardener/garden designer, Book publisher, Inventor . . .		
Enquiries	Bee Farmers Association		

Successful bee-keeping needs complete dedication. The active season starts slowly in March, faster in April, with May to August being the busiest months, dealing with swarming and harvest. Bees should be fed with winter stores by mid-September, when they hibernate. You must check bees for swarming about every nine days from mid-May to mid-July when the main honey flow ends.

The site of your apiary is vital. You need good nectar-producing flora like white clover, limes, sycamore, apples, oil seed rape, rosebay willow herb, blackberries etc. The site should be sunny; have protection from the weather particularly from the north and east; be snug, warm and airy; be easily accessible to transport and not too close to other people. If you are close to heather moors, it is possible to get another crop of honey from mid-August to mid-September; it will also provide the bees with 2/3 of their winter stores, so making the transport cost and site rental worthwhile.

Very few people have succeeded in making a living by bees alone. The average yearly yield per commercial hive for flower honey (as opposed to heather) is about 30lbs. But in 1985 and 1986 it was only 20lbs and 50% of bees perished in the cold winter of 1985–86.

There are no legal requirements for setting up a bee farm. A tiny piece of ground is needed to accommodate 10–15 hives; don't put too many in one location or you reach saturation point and get nothing. Equipment is expensive but it is frequently possible to buy bees and hives advertised locally for £50–60 from someone giving up. You can sometimes pick up a swarm for nothing. Some can be easy and some suicidal. You need a bee-proof shed for storing equipment and extracting; also a veil, gloves, smoker, hive tools, overalls, feeders, ripener and extractor (sometimes you can borrow one from an association). Your main expenses are sugar, transport and honey jars (in the event of having some honey to sell).

You can join your local county bee-keeper's association which exist in most parts of the country. These have regular meetings and practical demonstrations during the summer. Many counties have bee-keeping instructors who run courses. Once you are commercial, you can join the BEE FARMERS ASSOCIATION. There are two journals – Beecraft and the British Bee Journal.

You can sell honey in grocers' shops; but it is less likely to get lost among the jars of marmalade and chutney in cafés, pubs and garden centres.

It is useful to have an assistant (who won't bolt) who can use the smoker while you examine a hive and who can help you lift supers (honey boxes) on and off hives as they can become very heavy. It is sometimes possible to obtain a pollination fee for say taking your bees to the fruit orchards of Kent or fields of beans.

You can only bee-keep in reasonable weather which makes the planning of a social life impossible. The job can be very rewarding at times and heartbreaking at others and sometimes very painful. You must be in an area with suitable flora; keep diseases under control; do not let your bees swarm out; rid yourself of any useless queen heading your hive; and be sure not to let your bees starve – if you fail on any of these counts, you will get nothing and there will be some more cheap bees for sale.

Bespoke Furniture Maker/Designer

At a Glance

Qualifications/Training	Recommended	Income bracket	Low–Medium
Licence	No	Town/Country	Either
Experience/Springboard	Recommended	Travel	Local
Mid-career entry	Yes	Exit sale	No
Entry costs	£10,000+	Work at home	Yes

Mix and match   Yes.   You could think about: Cabinet maker, Wood carver, Tree surgeon, Sculptor . . .

Enquiries   Design Council, Craft Council

In spite of the ready availability of mass produced furniture, people and businesses are still prepared to pay for handmade furniture. It's possible to make a living from making pieces of furniture to order or in small batches but you'll need a lot of skill – it's time consuming, materials are expensive and you're unlikely to make a fortune. However, you can set up a furniture making business if either you've got the necessary dedication and good business sense, or you're an entrepreneur and can employ others to design and make the furniture. Craftsmen are notoriously short of business acumen and many of the best furniture makers prefer to work for other people. You won't need any formal qualifications but you do need to be taught how to make furniture. This includes design and construction (you'll have to know how materials react to being treated in certain ways); wood, stone, leather, glass, metal and plastics; drawing, technical drawing and model making. The traditional way of doing this used to be through a five-year apprenticeship; now you can do a course at eg the JOHN MAKEPEACE SCHOOL FOR CRAFTSMEN IN WOOD, the LONDON COLLEGE OF FURNITURE or RYCOTEWOOD COLLEGE. You may be able to find a private teacher or to pay an existing workshop to train you. Before setting up on your own get as much experience as possible; you'll have to know how long a job is likely to take and what to do if anything goes wrong.

BESPOKE
FURNITURE
MAKER/DESIGNER.

You'll also have to be good at dealing with people and coping with their demands. Good courses will include something on managing the business. (If you're in doubt about doing this yourself get someone else in – many furniture makers fail because they don't understand how to run a business.)

Setting up costs a lot. You'll probably have had to pay for your training (this can be as much as £5,000). Then you need premises which, although they can be in cheaper rural areas, must be big enough to store large bits of wood and machinery. You'll also need a large car or van for transporting wood and furniture. Essential machinery and hand tools cost about £5,000 and can be added to as you expand (businesses with high turnovers need about £50–100,000 worth of equipment). Setting up with other furniture makers and sharing equipment cuts costs. Especially in the early days, you'll have to pay quite a lot for advertising (brochures, cards, advertisement in the local press). Customers are charged by job so make sure you're able to work quickly enough to earn something over the cost of materials and that you're adept enough not to have to do the same job several times over because something's gone wrong. You can regard yourself as doing quite well if you're making about £10–12 per hour. The CRAFTS COUNCIL and the RURAL DEVELOPMENT COMMISSION can tell you about any grants or loans that are available. Banks aren't always very helpful; they like to see a clear cut business plan and, unless you've got a well established range, the profits of furniture making are unpredictable.

Work comes from mail shots, good editorial in magazines or newspapers, exhibitions (starting with ones at college), and building up a good reputation. Useful contacts are interior designers and architects, galleries and shops and anyone who can help you to track down the right bits of wood or leather. As well as making furniture for individuals or (in small batches) for shops, you may be able to get work making office furniture or shop fitting. For either of these it is essential that the job is finished in time – businesses are not indulgent to craftsmen and word will travel fast if you fail to come up with the goods on time. If you need extra help and can give some training you may find people prepared to pay you for allowing them to work for you. You can augment your income by teaching or through design consultancy by providing manufacturers with designs for furniture that will be made up by cheaper overseas labour. The DESIGN COUNCIL keeps a list of approved designers for manufacturers to call on so get onto that. Days can be long especially if you've got a deadline and something goes wrong, but the better the reputation you establish the freer you are to pick and choose what you do and when you do it.

Book Designer

At a Glance

Qualifications/Training	Recommended	Income bracket	Low–Medium
Licence	No	Town/Country	Town preferably
Experience/Springboard	Recommended	Travel	Local
Mid-career entry	Doubtful	Exit sale	No
Entry costs	£1,000+	Work at home	Yes

Mix and match Yes. You could think about: Book packager, Magazine designer, Greyhound trainer, Potter, Illustrator . . .
Enquiries   Art Colleges, Publishers

Increasingly, book publishing companies are using freelancers, both to edit and design books. So there are plenty of openings for working freelance, if you have the experience and the contacts. Illustrated book design is by far the most interesting to most people.

For most freelance illustrated book designers, the job starts with a book manuscript being sent by an editor or managing editor. The style of the book will usually have been set by an in-house designer or art director, so there are 'dummy' layouts (which were used for early publicity). The designer then has to follow the style which has been set, and the direction of the editor, to fit copy, tables, illustrations and so on into the set number of pages. After producing a rough mini-plan of the book, showing what goes on what page, the designer will 'mark up' the copy. This involves indicating on each page of the typescript, what typeface, type size and column width the typesetter should use. The next stage is usually galley proofs, which are read by an editor, laid out on the appropriate pages with the appropriate pictures traced in by the designer, and the whole thing thoroughly checked.

The printer will then produce page proofs, and the colour house (a different branch of printing) will make up colour proofs: moment of truth time for the designer – does it all fit? The designer must be able to visualise how his rough layouts will look when the book is finally printed, as there is usually no budget for major alterations once the colour proofs have been produced.

Book designers, like magazine designers, usually start with an art school training, then go on to work for a book publishing company to gain experience and contacts before going freelance. (Alternatively, they may stay within the company, as an art director determining the look of the whole range of the company's books.) There are also openings for design consultants who will advise publishing companies on various matters, such as choosing the right typefaces and other ways of making their books more attractive.

To set up on your own, you can start in a room of your own house, equipped with drawing board, Grant projector (for blowing up pictures), light box (for examining transparencies and checking colour proofs against page text proofs), and a wide selection of stationery. Some designers find it better to work from an office near the centre of London, either on their own or in partnership with other designers and editors. This makes communication with the publishers easier, and means that you are easily available for rush jobs (in publishing, everything tends to end up as a rush job!). If you are in this situation, you may find that you actually form a packaging company with other designers and editors, producing books up to either typescript and layout stage or completed page and colour proof stage to sell to publishing houses.

Book designers may also diversify into magazine design, which is closely related in many ways, but is more often an in-house job. Traditionally, book designers belong to the NATIONAL UNION OF JOURNALISTS and the NATIONAL GRAPHICAL ASSOCIATION. Jobs are advertised in the creative and media pages of the quality national press, the *Bookseller*, and sometimes *Campaign*. You will find *Editing and Design* useful.

Book Editor

At a Glance

Qualifications/Training	Available	*Income bracket*	Low–Medium
Licence	No	*Town/Country*	Town preferably
Experience/Springboard	Almost essential	*Travel*	No
Mid-career entry	Possible	*Exit sale*	No
Entry costs	£1,000	*Work at home*	Yes

Mix and match   Yes. You could think about: Book packager, Newsletter publisher, Journalist . . .

Enquiries   Publishers, Book House Training Centre

A book editor's job involves reading the typescript of a book, and ensuring it is accurate, correctly spelled and punctuated before it is sent to the printer. It will then be set by the printer and returned in the form of 'galley' proofs which have to be read again to check for mistakes. In some cases, book editors will also have to structure the book, insert cross references where necessary, write introductory passages, or virtually re-write the text (particularly with practical books).

As the industry is becoming computerised, it is useful to be familiar with word processing aspects of computing.

Some book editing is done totally by full-time employees. But freelancers may frequently be used either 'in-house' or working from their own office or home. Most editors have degrees, often in English, though the actual subject is not usually considered important. Typing qualifications are useful, though not essential. However, a great many editors come to the profession through working first as a secretary for a firm of publishers, or in a related field. Traditionally, editors are members of the NATIONAL UNION OF JOURNALISTS (book branch).

It is essential that you can read quickly and thoroughly, and have a

BOOK EDITOR

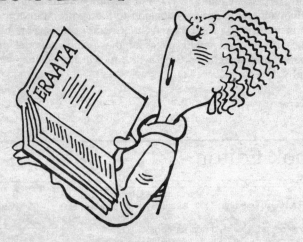

complete grasp of English. You also need to be able to visualise, from an author's draft, how the book will 'feel' when complete. For books on practical subjects, skills in devising and checking illustrations are also necessary. All these come through experience, which is normally gained while working full-time for a publisher. After some years, many editors feel confident enough to go freelance, often specialising in particular fields (medical, interior design etc). It is essential to keep in touch with contacts made while a full-time employee, and to keep a note of names of senior editors at different publishing houses, so that you can circulate a CV and tout for work whenever necessary. You can also consult the *Writers' and Artists' Yearbook* and look out for advertisements in the press (the *Bookseller, Publishing News* and media pages in the *Guardian* and the *Independent*).

Setting up as a book editor is not expensive: a good typewriter is useful but more useful is a word processor, which costs no more than an electric typewriter. You will also need a certain amount of stationery (including plenty of large envelopes) and office furniture, including a desk and filing cabinets. A good range of reference books is useful, particularly if you specialise in one particular field. But a good local library may suffice.

Apart from stationery, and a few 'social' drinks with former colleagues to keep up with developments, there are few expenses. If you find you are working to tight deadlines, accounts with a motor-bike messenger service and British Rail's Red Star service (if you live out of London) may be useful.

Successful editors are able to choose to do books they find particularly interesting and you can work hours to suit yourself (although you must attend meetings with senior editors, authors and so on). It is a fairly sedentary job.

Most freelancers charge on a daily basis, £50–£100 per day, although senior editors will try to offer a price for the whole job, to make their budgeting easier.

Get more information from BOOK HOUSE TRAINING CENTRE.

Bookkeeper

At a Glance

Qualifications/Training	Available	Income bracket	Low–Medium
Licence	No	Town/Country	Either
Experience/Springboard	Recommended	Travel	Some
Mid-career entry	Yes	Exit sale	No
Entry costs	£2,000	Work at home	Yes
Mix and match	Excellent. You could think about: Word processor, Musicians answering and booking service, Snail farmer . . .		
Enquiries	Local accountants and bookkeepers		

If you're good with figures and enjoy keeping accounts, you'll find plenty of people and businesses who will pay you to prepare their accounts for bank managers and auditors, leaving them free to concentrate on other things. You can operate from anywhere near shops and offices and can work as much and when you like. This makes bookkeeping a good option for people who want to mix and match with something else. You don't need any formal qualifications to be a bookkeeper but you'll have to know what you're doing. You should know about VAT (if you need any help with a particular case contact the department of CUSTOMS AND EXCISE – contrary to popular belief, they can be helpful and would far rather you got it right first time than left them with a muddle to sort out later on). You'll also need an accounting system you can use; to know how to present accounts, draw up graphs and make reasonably accurate forecasts. It's inadvisable to set up on your own without having had some experience; say in an insurance office, sales or accounts department or in some position (eg Sales rep) where you're accountable for money. There's a useful basic book called *Teach Yourself Bookkeeping* which will fill in any small gaps in your information. From experience you'll learn to see certain patterns in your clients' cashflows. Bookkeepers have to be logical, accurate, honest and patient, so that they can cope with other people's lack of these qualities.

Essential equipment is a computer with appropriate software, a telephone and an answering machine. You may also need a car to get to your clients and to transport bags and boxes of their bills and receipts. Bookkeepers provide the stationery for the accounts they make, so get supplies of files, account ledgers and graph paper from stationery wholesalers. Learn how to judge the amount of time a job is going to take, charge by the hour and give an indication of how long you think the job is going to take. The number of clients you need depends on the workloads that each generates. 6 or 7 can make you a living. Approach small local businesses and one man bands. The best way of doing this is through a mail shot; the Post Office offers one of 1000 free to new businesses so use this and the *Yellow Pages*. Put up adverts in shop windows; advertising in the local press may bring you nothing but offers from rival publications to place further adverts. Once you're established, you'll get more clients by word of mouth and clients tend to stick with you once you've established a system with them.

Clients are liable to call on you at the last minute, when the VAT man is breathing down their necks and they're in danger of being liable for non-payment surcharges. They'll hand you carrier bags full of receipts and bills which you have to put in order. Most clients need your services once a month or once a quarter, they may also want help with cash flow forecasts to present to their bank managers or building societies. Do these cautiously; don't be too specific in forecasting or you risk being sued and always put in a disclaimer.

Clients may want to see you at a specific time but once you've picked up their stuff the hours you work are up to you. Allow yourself more time to do a job than you expect to need – it's better to hang on to finished work for a day or two than to be late with a job. You can easily build holidays into your schedule as long as you take into account clients' VAT deadlines and arrange to get the work done at a different time.

Book Packager

At a Glance

Qualifications/Training	Available	*Income bracket*	Medium
Licence	No	*Town/Country*	Either
Experience/Springboard	Essential	*Travel*	Possible
Mid-career entry	Likely	*Exit sale*	Yes
Entry costs	£5–10,000	*Work at home*	Possible

Mix and match   Yes.   You could think about: Book designer, Book editor, Book publisher, Trout farmer, Football commentator . . .

Enquiries   Book House Training Centre

Book packaging involves conceiving, writing (or commissioning), illustrating and designing a book, so that, apart from paying you for this package or pre-production costs, the publisher has only to manage and carry the production and sales costs (typesetting, colour separating, printing, marketing and distributing). Sometimes publishers manage typesetting as well as pre-production costs. Packagers as a breed concentrate on supplying packages that reflect their own strengths, expertise and interests rather than supplying goods to publishers' precise specifications.

Book packaging companies are usually set up by groups of experienced publishing people – perhaps an editor and a designer working together. The only premises needed are an office with a couple of desks and a drawing board, plus the usual filing cabinets and light box. Use of a photocopying machine is also an asset – often good facilities are available at local business centres.

Little capital is needed. What is at risk is largely your time – time spent on projects which may not find a publisher. Other direct costs are dependent on the type of book you are producing – whether highly illustrated, technically complex with lots of tables and graphs or a relatively simple narrative. Plenty of contacts in the publishing world are vital, the market is becoming slightly overloaded, so there is more risk involved than say five years ago. Several book packagers have gone under recently. A couple of good signed contracts with reputable publishing houses to show the bank manager are more important than vast amounts of investment capital.

Packagers are paid partly in advance, partly on completion, and more rarely, partly on sales performance. But there are very many different packaging arrangements and packagers' contracts usually contain tailor-made clauses, within a standard package contract, for each specific title under contract.

The *Bookseller* is by far the most useful publication for book packagers. It is full of information on what books are being launched, which publishers are doing well, what other packagers are doing and, importantly, news about promotions and new appointments within the industry, to keep your contacts book up to date.

The BOOK HOUSE TRAINING CENTRE has useful information.

Book Publisher

At a Glance

Qualifications/Training	Available	*Income bracket*	Low–High
Licence	No	*Town/Country*	Town
Experience/Springboard	Essential	*Travel*	Yes
Mid-career entry	Possible	*Exit sale*	Yes
Entry costs	£20,000	*Work at home*	Yes

Mix and match   Possible.   You could think about: Book editor, Novelist, Beekeeper, Greyhound trainer . . .

Enquiries   Book House Training Centre

Book publishers are businessmen who trade in (1) books and (2) rights – paperback rights, film rights, serial rights, electronic publishing rights, foreign language rights. Many book publishers only publish hardcover editions and sell the paperback publishing rights to specialist paperback houses such as Pan or Penguin. While there is a worldwide English language book market, many publishers begin by publishing their own editions in the UK only, selling the right to publish in key overseas markets (such as Australia, Canada or the US) to local publishers whose distribution and sales arrangements are already in place. It is possible, technically, to enter the world market by publishing only one title.

The job falls neatly into two unequal components. First investment – 10% of the job at the most. It requires flair, the ability to make specific choices on the basis of little experience and much intuition: (1) what books to publish, (2) what niche to occupy in the worldwide English language market, (3) what parts of your business are best run hands-on and what you can safely delegate to suppliers (eg printers). Secondly, managing that investment – 90% of the work is managing authors, data, sources, manuscripts, typesetters, paper buyers, printers and binders, rights, sales, advertising sales, relationships with booksellers, book promotion, reviews, distribution, cash and currency (pound v dollar) etc. Without flair, do not attempt to set up on your own. The giant publishers are littered with managers masquerading as publishers who command sufficient resources to beat you at your own game. You can acquire the management skills inside or outside the industry. Some obviously successful publishers have moved into the industry, but within publishing specific technical skills can be acquired from courses run by BOOK HOUSE TRAINING CENTRE or you can take postgraduate courses at for instance the LONDON COLLEGE OF PRINTING, OXFORD POLYTECHNIC or WATFORD COLLEGE. It is almost certainly worth working for an established publisher for a few years, to acquire some know-how. Get in at any level – secretary, VDU operator, salesman, editor – and then look around for further openings. Once in, you can begin to assess whether you are likely to have the necessary flair. By visiting the warehouse, you will also discover the only fact of publishing life worth committing to memory: it's easy to publish books but enormously difficult to sell them.

All you need to set up as a publisher is notepaper, a telephone, a typewriter (or preferably word processor) and the finance to carry one or two projects through to profitability. Later you may require more sophisticated finance, for instance the injection of venture capital, plus whatever you need to live on until your cash flow becomes positive, together with a good bank manager who understands your business plan and a printer and typesetter willing to extend generous credit terms (as they often are to small new publishers). Keep overheads to a minimum. Successful new publishing houses often began in a spare room. Use good quality restaurants to do business with those who need to be impressed. Avoid employing staff as long as you can. One reason why it is relatively easy to set up as a publisher is that the industry boasts a host of sophisticated suppliers eager to sell their services to you. They do their job excellently and to time – writers, book designers, illustrators, editors, printers, warehouses, advertising and PR agencies, direct mail specialists and freelance sales forces. Many can be located through the *Creative Directory*, the *Writers' and Artists' Yearbook* or *The Writer's Handbook*. Make sure you read the intensely narcissistic trade press (the *Bookseller*, *Publishing News*) but do not let it put you off. The definitive text on the business is still Sir Stanley Unwin's the *Truth about Publishing*; the most entertaining and informative introduction to the business is *Bluff Your Way in Publishing*.

Because you are dealing with a very wide variety of busy suppliers, your life to begin with will leave little time for anything but your business. Do not set up as a publisher if you want to segment your life into work and play.

Bookie

At a Glance

Qualifications/Training	Available	*Income bracket*	Highly variable
Licence	Yes	*Town/Country*	Town or on-course
Experience/Springboard	Essential	*Travel*	Yes (on-course)
Mid-career entry	Yes	*Exit sale*	Possible
Entry costs	£1000 (on-course)	*Work at home*	No

Mix and match   Possible.   You could think about: Mini-cab driver, Market research interviewer, Painter/decorator . . .

Enquiries   Gaming Board of Great Britain, National Association of Bookmakers, Horserace Totalisator Board

Turf accountants offer odds and accept bets on the results of sporting or other events. They usually work in a shop, supervising cashiers who take money and record the time of the bet and are responsible for settling winning bets, balancing cash and keeping records. Some fix odds and travel to race courses. Betting and gambling are a small but significant part of the leisure industry – which is strictly regulated by the GAMING BOARD OF GREAT BRITAIN whose intention is to limit gambling rather than to encourage it (although new legislation makes betting shops arguably more pleasurable places). There is a living to be made from betting and gaming – despite the intention to limit gaming there will always be people who wish to place bets and the industry is there to cater for them.

Start by working for someone else (no formal qualifications required). The big 4 betting chains give on-job training and have training schools. You can also contact the GAMING BOARD OF GREAT BRITAIN; NATIONAL ASSOCIATION OF BOOKMAKERS; or HORSERACE TOTALISATOR BOARD. The calculations involved can be quite complex viz in the case of multiple bets with doubles, trebles and accumulators. You have to know the rules, be good with figures (lightning settling centreing on percentage), fractions and anything to do with bet calculation; happy with, or used to handling money, and sure you don't infringe any regulations. You yourself will need honesty, a careful calm nature, attention to detail, numerical ability, the ability to manage people, quick thinking, good organising ability; and most important you will need to know how to handle people who are trying to cheat you.

On-course you need to hold a permit (renewable each year) and operate under national rules. There's a lot of driving, courses being scattered all over the country and you're out there in all weathers (usually dreadful). You live by pitting your judgement against that of others, which is exciting. You can lose a lot of money but make it as well. You don't need a lot of money to set up (if you're on-course all you need is an umbrella, a blackboard and a carrying voice). You do need to know a lot about 'form' – how horses or dogs are likely to perform – as this is how you make your living.

Anyone considering working in this industry must be prepared for unsocial hours – betting shops are open six days a week with Saturday being the busiest day (and who knows what will happen with Sundays). Betting shops are regulated by law – though not as strictly as casinos or other gaming establishments and are not quite the God-forsaken places they used to be – now allowed to sell light refreshments and to install TV (offering live televised coverage). The opening hours are 10–6 every day except Sunday (currently) and Christmas – Boxing Day is a busy racing day. Also some evenings (summer for horses; dogs, especially on-course). Work is pressurised at times and can involve people who are being awkward or aggressive. Conditions are noisy and crowded (not for people who can't bear cigarette smoke).

Bookseller

At a Glance

Qualifications/Training	Available	Income bracket	Medium
Licence	Booksellers Association	Town/Country	Town
Experience/Springboard	Recommended	Travel	None
Mid-career entry	Yes	Exit sale	Yes
Entry costs	£20,000	Work at home	No
Mix and match	Possible. You could think about: Novelist, Artist, Word processor . . .		
Enquiries	Booksellers Association		

Although many small booksellers are being bought out by large chains, local shops in the right areas can still survive and increased public spending on books is predicted. However, bear in mind that about 50%

of the British population don't read a book a year; choose a fairly middle class area to set up in. To sell books you will need to know a lot about them (both classics and new titles) so that you can advise customers. Bookshop owners need a lot of enthusiasm to put up with long hours and bookkeeping. Also patience and the ability to think laterally in order to cope with vague or difficult customers. Hard retailing skills are just as necessary as a great love of books.

The BOOKSELLERS ASSOCIATION has courses on how to run your own bookshop and publishes a guide to starting and running a bookshop. But it is probably more useful to work in a bookshop for a while. This gives an idea of pitfalls and problems and of how the business is run as well as helping to broaden your knowledge of books. It would be useful to read *Book Retailing in the 1990s*. To set up you need premises (costs vary), or a year's rent for one, with shelving, some sort of cash register and, preferably, a micro-fiche of British Books in Print (£500). The Booksellers' Association recommend that you start off with about £25–30,000 of stock (although other sources suggest that you can get away with about half as much). You get this from a wholesaler who will send you a general selection to begin with until you get a better idea of what books to concentrate on and may offer extended credit (6 weeks). After that you get most of your stock from publishers' reps having advertised in the trade press to ask them to visit. Not all will come straight away. You must register, and remain registered, with the Booksellers Association to be supplied by publishers.

It's important to establish a good credit rating so that you can open accounts with them (2 trade references and a banker). The net book agreement (currently under threat) sets the retail price of books. This means that you aren't free to make special offers to your customers; however, you're less likely to lose out to larger booksellers who can buy in bulk. Publishers usually give 35% trade discount which means that booksellers' mark up is substantially less than that of other retail outlets. In addition publishers' credit terms (they demand very quick settling of accounts) mean that some of your stock will remain unsold long after you have paid for it.

The Booksellers' Association suggests that a complete turnover of stock 4 or 5 times a year is the minimum required to survive. It takes about 3 years to become established and you are very unlikely to get rich; the trade as a whole suffers from low profits and subsequent lack of funds for developing, marketing etc. Bear in mind that about 40% of annual book sales are made in the 6–8 weeks before Christmas.

Booksellers have to sell what their public wants which may mean stocking books that you hate (although about 50% of booksellers refuse to stock war books). There are obvious risks in being overtly political or specialised unless you choose your area very carefully, and you are bound to face criticism at some time for the books you do or don't stock.

Brewer

At a Glance

Qualifications/Training	Available	*Income bracket*	Low–High
Licence	Yes	*Town/Country*	Either
Experience/Springboard	Essential	*Travel*	No
Mid-career entry	Likely	*Exit sale*	Excellent
Entry costs	£60,000+++	*Work at home*	Yes

Mix and match Possible. You could think about: Publican, Farmer, Wine merchant, Property developer . . .

Enquiries Brewers Society

Brewing's rather more complicated than the rubric on the side of a can of home brew material would have you believe. First step is to work out what you want to brew – ale, strong or weak, lager, stout, etc. It's relatively easy to brew traditional ale but it requires more complicated equipment (filters and refrigeration) to brew lager. 10 years ago lager represented under 30% of the beer market – today it's 50% and rising – inexorably squeezing out ale and the ale brewer. This is not a business for bucolic amateurs. The next step is to work out who will buy what you're going to produce. It's easier if you have your own pub – preferably in an area of population density or by a big main road.

The beer must be good, healthy and palatable – and you'll have to be a good, hygienic brewer. Some experience, apprenticeship or education in brewing is essential. Good quality materials must be bought, recipes created and adapted to suit your drinkers' palates. Care must be taken in the brewing process to avoid any spoilage and, hence, off-flavour. You're subject to all the usual hygiene, safety and other regulations covering food factories – ie white coats and no smoking. Brewing hygiene and sterility are vital – and very costly if they are less than perfect, rendering your product undrinkable. The fact that you're brewing for sale rather than personal consumption only, makes you eligible for excise tax, calculated on the potential strength of the beer before it starts fermenting. The strength is calculated on the original gravity (or OG) of the liquid before fermentation starts. From this point onwards, the liquid becomes valuable; every drop wasted effectively increases the tax rate on the rest of the brew and it's difficult to get the excise tax back on any beer which subsequently becomes unsellable. Depending on the strength, excise tax can be between £50 and £70 per barrel of 36 gallons (288 pints). On top of this, you have to keep detailed records for the excise man who will visit you frequently, sometimes at unlikely hours to make sure you aren't cheating. Many pubs have large outhouses which could be used as breweries. If you could build a brew-pub, you would save on transport because you don't need a lorry to cart all those barrels about. In this case, you should think of spending some £650,000 – a good pub (not the best) £600,000+; and a mini-brewery £50,000.

If you aren't going to get your own pub or want to sell your beer to other pubs, you'll have to buy barrels (no, you can't nick anyone else's). An 18 gallon beer barrel costs almost £70 – for a 10 barrel a week brewery, you might need about 100 casks. You'll also need to buy the raw materials. You can use either traditional malt and hops in which case you'll need a mill and associated equipment for extracting the fermentable sugars. Alternatively, you can use syrups and concentrates which are made from the same raw materials, require less kit to use but cost more. Malt comes from maltsters, hops from hop merchants (most are based in the south east) and syrups from corn merchants.

About 60–70% of pubs are tied to a particular brewery: either because they are owned by one (and there's no way that they are allowed to sell anyone else's brew); or they are so-called free houses, which have been loaned money in exchange for their agreement to sell the brewer's beer. This makes 60% of the market, in effect, closed to you. Not surprisingly this 60% represents the bigger, high volume pubs leaving you with the smaller ones.

The only glimmer of hope lies in the deliberation of the Monopolies Commission, currently examining the brewing industry. If it insists on the divestment of pubs from the breweries – there could be openings for the small man. On balance though, the big brewers are more than likely to find a way of keeping the small man out and certainly of keeping him small.

Further information on the industry from the BREWERS SOCIETY and on suppliers from the ALLIED BREWERY TRADERS ASSOCIATION.

Butcher

At a Glance

Qualifications/Training	Available	*Income bracket*	Medium
Licence	No	*Town/Country*	Town/Village
Experience/Springboard	Essential	*Travel*	Local
Mid-career entry	Possible	*Exit sale*	Yes
Entry costs	£20,000	*Work at home*	No

Mix and match   Limited.   You could think about: Caterer, Journalist, Potter . . .

Enquiries   Local butchers

Not a glamorous job and one that is very male dominated. Butchers have to know a lot about meat and perhaps more about their public ('often patronising, demanding or irritatingly vague about what they want'). Fierce competition with supermarkets has meant small butchers are experimenting with specialist meats eg additive free, game etc. You need to know your market well and be prepared to provide extra services such as delivery.

You must be strong enough to carry large bits of meat around. Otherwise there are no qualifications necessary (although courses are available at many local colleges). You do need some experience of working in a butcher's to get an idea of what it's like and to learn some of the techniques of meat chopping, preparing and storing. Go for a small butcher, not a large chain or a supermarket.

Establishing a new shop will mean getting compliance from the local Public Health Authority who may stipulate the type of display, flooring, and refrigeration (essential). You should expect to spend up to £20,000 to equip your shop and provide cleavers etc in addition to the cost of the shop itself. Credit is difficult to get at the start and many people find that banks do not understand food retailing.

Join any local traders' association (eg the LONDON RETAIL MEAT TRADERS ASSOCIATION) which will provide ladies' nights and public liability insurance in case you cause an outbreak of salmonella.

You should aim to turnover your stock completely at least every 10–14 days. Meat keeps for a long time but its looks deteriorate and it becomes difficult to sell. Surplus stock can be turned into sausages, pies etc. There is no sale or return and you should expect to sell less in summer when people eat less meat (particularly red meat).

Some ordering of stock can be done by telephone and you can order direct from the slaughter houses. Many butchers prefer to go to the market (at least until they have found a supplier whom they can trust completely) but this means an early start (from 5am); once the meat is in the shop, you need to hang it and chop it as well as serve the customers. A good assistant is essential, but difficult to find since the pay and image of the job are both poor.

Cabaret Performer

At a Glance

Qualifications/Training	Recommended	Income bracket	Low–High
Licence	No	Town/Country	Town
Experience/Springboard	No	Travel	Yes
Mid-career entry	Possible	Exit sale	No
Entry costs	£2,000	Work at home	No

Mix and match   Probably essential.   You could think about: Actor, Puppeteer, Jazz musician, Dancer, Stockbroker, Typesetter . . .

Enquiries   Cabaret bookers, theatrical agents

Cabaret performers entertain people in clubs, pubs and theatres. There's a massive range of ways of doing this: telling jokes, doing magic tricks, singing, stripping, dancing, juggling. There are two main types of cabaret venue (called circuits). The mainline circuit is nation-wide and includes working men's and political clubs and holiday resorts. Alternative cabaret circuits are more local; London's the best place for these but there are opportunities in other towns especially during festivals and carnivals (eg the EDINBURGH FRINGE FESTIVAL). Alternative cabaret venues include pubs and alternative theatres such as the COMEDY STORE in Leicester Square. You can work both circuits as long as you have material that suits both traditional mainline cabaret and the experimental alternative. You can work as many nights as you want, making this a good job to mix and match with others. You should be prepared to do a lot of travelling between venues and some low or even unpaid work when you're starting out.

There are no essential formal qualifications but you'll need a skill that people will enjoy watching. You could do a short (1–2 year) course in various basic stage skills; contact your local adult or further education college for details. This might help you to stand up in front of an audience and perform but it won't give you any material for the show; for that you need your own ideas. Creating an act which works is largely a matter of trial and error; you won't be given many opportunities for experimenting on the cabaret circuit so get some experience of live audiences in children's theatre, at parties or doing street entertainment. Cabaret performers have to be sensitive to audience response and quick witted enough to develop their show to suit each audience (there's a certain amount of patronising in this). You mustn't mind being heckled as long as you can usually get the better of the hecklers. You'll have to be good at late nights, energetic and dedicated enough to go on with the show no matter how ill you feel – missing a booking is breaking an unwritten law of cabaret. It's hard work and tiring but very rewarding.

Apart from any equipment you need for the show, you also need a telephone and answering machine and a car is useful when you're touring. As a group, entertainers have to pay more for things like pension plans and insurance (house insurance premiums can be up to 50% more expensive than for other people). On the mainline circuit you can expect to get from £45–50 for 25 minutes up to about £5,000 if you're very famous. This varies and many bookers want a free trial unless they've seen you at one of the top places. Cabaret bookers (usually the managers of clubs or pubs or the organisers of special events) have budgets which don't allow much leeway; it's up to you to decide whether or not a job's worth taking. Always ask for expenses; most will pay. Alternative cabaret varies even more than this. New performers have a chance to perform for nothing; sometimes the night's takings are shared amongst performers – not lucrative if the audience was small. Otherwise rates are set in the same way as for mainline cabaret, although they tend to pay less.

You get work by being seen: start off with talent shows and open (unbooked) spots in alternative cabaret. You can sometimes get work from bookers who haven't seen you if you're good at selling yourself. Get some agents; there's no limit to the number you can have and each has a slightly different speciality. They charge commission but should provide work for you. Establish a personality – your own will do unless you find it easier to pretend you're someone else when you're performing. Never accept work that doesn't suit you; bookers often don't know exactly what they want so you should be able to tell them. Alternative cabaret is expected to be socially and politically sound (ie no racism or sexism); mainline isn't always.

Wednesday–Sunday are the busiest days of the week and in the early days when you want to accept any booking that comes, taking time off to suit you can be a problem. Cabaret bookings are often made up to a year in advance. There's plenty to do when you aren't performing or rehearsing; letters and confirmations to write, researching new material from books or by working out ways of getting the final result you want, writing and experimenting with new material. Keep in touch with cabaret contacts. It's a closeknit world and there are opportunities for travel: work on cruise liners, at holiday camps and resorts. Don't publicise your new ideas too widely though unless you want to see someone else perform them first.

Cabinet Maker

At a Glance

Qualifications/Training	Recommended	Income bracket	Low
Licence	No	Town/Country	Either
Experience/Springboard	Recommended	Travel	No
Mid-career entry	Yes	Exit sale	No
Entry costs	£500+	Work at home	Yes

Mix and match Yes. You could think about: Bespoke furniture maker/ designer, Wood carver, Picture framer, Antique furniture restorer, Counsellor . . .

Enquiries Local cabinet makers

The term cabinet-maker implies a greater degree of skill than furniture-maker; as well as making furniture cabinet makers make ornate boxes and other things. You can make simple furniture like children's bookshelves, or get involved in marquetry and elaborate dove-tailing, or modern design. The choice is wide. With a gift for skilled wood working, perhaps gained at school, coupled with an interest in the craft, anyone can set up as a furniture maker with greater or lesser quality of workmanship. It is possible to improve as you go along and perhaps end up as a master cabinet maker.

There are endless DIY manuals about to help you improve your skills, and magazines like *Practical Woodworking* and *Woodworker*. Four books by Krenov, including *A Cabinet Maker's Notebook* are inspiring. Best of all is being an apprentice to an expert craftsman to really learn and improve your techniques.

You need a good solid workbench and some fine hand-tools; machine tools and a table saw are useful. You can do wood-turning for which you need a lathe; but you can start with little and build up. You can operate in a garage or a cellar to begin with, and buy second hand (though second hand tools tend to be collectors' items). Seasoned wood is easily available and advertised in the back of woodworking magazines. You can work part-time teaching woodworking at colleges so that you can go on making a living while getting established.

Your first orders will probably come from friends who have seen your work, but you can put advertisements in local papers. Repair work is always needed for antique furniture, and you can do this privately or for antique dealers. It might lead on to a commission for a new piece.

Calligrapher

At a Glance

Qualifications/Training	Necessary	Income bracket	Low
Licence	No	Town/Country	Town preferably
Experience/Springboard	Good idea	Travel	No
Mid-career entry	Possible	Exit sale	No
Entry costs	£200	Work at home	Yes

Mix and match Yes. You could think about: Illustrator, Graphic designer, Artist, Book designer, Interior designer . . .
Enquiries Crafts Council, Society of Scribes and Illuminators

Traditionally, calligraphy is the art of beautiful writing combined with illustration techniques, mainly in connection with books. More modern calligraphers, particularly in America, use calligraphy as an art form in its own right, sometimes marrying calligraphy and typography. Calligraphy is now used commercially in advertising, packaging and posters. Classic techniques are still needed eg illumination, heraldic art, gilding, burnishing, and work related to manuscripts and books. Specialist maps, family trees and botanical illustration are commissioned. The bread-and-butter side of the business is writing certificates, cards, invitations and place names: some commissions are for very traditional work with rule-bound formation of letters; others are for something modern/artistic.

You need to do a calligraphy course for at least two years (although there are hopes of a degree course soon). You can apply for a CRAFTS COUNCIL grant. You can attach yourself to a master calligrapher as an apprentice for a couple of months. A spell in America often opens up your ideas. The CRAFTS COUNCIL may give you a workshop grant so you have a base to work from; in which case it will promote your work to prove that you are a good investment. You do not need a lot of space, just enough for a leaning drawing board, pens and inks. But beware of your posture while you spend hours writing in one position and take plenty of exercise to off-set potential physical problems.

Survival is hard until you have made enough contacts and gained a reputation. You can do certificates, place names, or invitations, or perhaps teach in the local art college, to keep you ticking over, while taking your portfolio to design groups, or advertisers or commercial groups to persuade them of your ideas. Your first orders may come from friends and it snowballs as your work is seen. You can then move on to business cards, letter-heading, packaging, book jackets, logos, shop signs, record sleeves if you are good. To appeal to the fashion or record industries your work should be in the modern idiom. Try entering competitions and get your work into exhibitions. Advertise your services in magazines, but only in those relevant to your own specialism.

The *Scribe* is the journal of the SOCIETY OF SCRIBES AND ILLUMINATORS and is full of information about forthcoming exhibitions, lectures and articles.

Camera Person

At a Glance

Qualifications/Training	Recommended	*Income bracket*	Low–Medium
Licence	Union card necessary	*Town/Country*	Town
Experience/Springboard	No	*Travel*	Lots
Mid-career entry	Unlikely	*Exit sale*	No
Entry costs	£500+	*Work at home*	No
Mix and match	Limited. You could think about: Photographer, Mini-cab driver, Film director . . .		
Enquiries	ACTT		

The camera crew shoot the film so that it recreates the director's artistic intentions on the screen. The top job here is the lighting camera person, sometimes called the cinematographer or director of photography. Unless the crew is very small, the lighting camera person does not usually handle the camera but is concerned with creating the lighting, camera angles, close ups and other techniques that will achieve the effect the director wants. Years of experience on the job are required to gain necessary creative expertise. Camera operators control the camera and ensure that the shot is exactly what is wanted. They are assisted by layers of assistants with various different responsibilities for focussing the lens, loading the film, moving the camera on its rigging, building rig for special shots etc.

The best way of getting the initial know-how to operate the camera is through an ACTT recognised course. This will also make it far easier to get hold of ACTT union membership, essential for most jobs in the film industry. After that it's a case of getting a foot in the door at whatever level you can; building up a portfolio of stills or a show reel helps here. Establish contact with as many film people as possible, and try to get onto film shoots – you can do this initially by working for a production company as a general assistant or runner. Alternatively some of the big equipment companies run training schemes or need general helpers

CAMERA CREW

from time to time. Once you've got the contacts you can hustle for work by offering your services to other camera people as extra assistants, grip, etc. You'll need technical know-how and talent tempered with the ability to work to other people's ideas rather than being free to exercise your own creativity. To actually get into this field in the first place you'll need great persistence and determination.

Because of the vast range of sophisticated and expensive equipment available, film production companies usually rent rather than own camera equipment. You'll need a telephone and an answering machine; better still, register with a booking service who will handle all your calls while you're away. As you become better known, it's worth getting an agent who can hustle for you and negotiate rates. The ACTT sets minimum wages – which are normally well below the going rate; ranging from about £90 for an assistant to £600 for lighting camera. Because bookings for commercials and promos are for far shorter lengths of time you usually get paid more per week for them than for longer feature film bookings.

The director/producer will appoint a lighting camera person and usually leaves it to them to appoint operators and assistants. This leads to the establishment of freelance teams and you may find yourself doing quite a lot of work with the same people. Work snowballs: every shoot you go to will remind someone about you and may lead to more. The film world is a very close knit industry, word travels fast and reputations are easily ruined if you make a mistake. Life can be unpredictable and you may find yourself with a broken camera or dealing with a thunderstorm in the middle of a crucial take.

Read *Money into Light* for further information.

Caravan Site Owner

At a Glance

Qualifications/Training	No	*Income bracket*	Medium
Licence	No	*Town/Country*	Country
Experience/Springboard	No	*Travel*	No
Mid-career entry	Good	*Exit sale*	Yes
Entry costs	£125,000	*Work at home*	Yes

Mix and match   Excellent. You could think about: Trout farmer, Publican, Farmer, Holiday accommodation owner, Opening to the public, Import/export broker . . .

Enquiries   British Holidays and Home Parks Association

Running a caravan site is a convenient way of combining home and work in a (hopefully) pleasant country setting. Most operators of fairly small sites will do all the work themselves. Larger sites will have managers, cleaning staff and groundsmen.

The first thing to do is to find a site. It is generally better to buy an existing site than to consider buying land and hoping to get planning permission for a site; most local authorities in beauty spots seem to think there are enough sites in their area already.

It is worth joining the BRITISH HOLIDAYS AND HOME PARKS ASSOCIATION (formerly the National Federation of Site Operators) as a prospective operator. Their journal carries advertisements for sites which are on the market. You can also try estate agents in the area you are interested in.

A small, viable site, including a house, would cost in the region of £200,000. On this you can expect to earn about £20,000 per annum. This may not sound like a particularly good return but if the house alone is worth £75,000 this is actually a return of £20,000 on capital outlay of £125,000. On a small site there is no need to employ much extra labour: on a site of up to about 60 pitches, a couple, plus a part-timer in the high season, can cope quite adequately. However, there are opportunities for expansion in setting up a shop on the site and providing extra facilities for the campers.

Caravan site operators usually start to advertise by getting their details into one of the guides produced by the local tourist information office, and other guides produced by various camping and caravanning clubs. On a larger scale, they can advertise in one of the 20 or so magazines which specialise in the field.

Besides the administration involved in taking bookings and collecting fees, the main work is cleaning and maintaining the site. Larger sites will have part- or full-time cleaning staff and groundsmen. During the winter months there will be long-term maintenance, such as repairing or rebuilding toilet blocks and other facilities, or laying on power and water to different parts of the site.

Each site has planning permission for a set number of touring caravans (and tents in some cases) and a set number of permanently parked holiday homes. To increase the size you will need to apply for planning permission.

Careers Adviser

At a Glance

Qualifications/Training	Recommended	*Income bracket*	Medium–High
Licence	No	*Town/Country*	Town
Experience/Springboard	Usual	*Travel*	Local
Mid-career entry	Yes	*Exit sale*	Possible
Entry costs	£2,000	*Work at home*	Possible

Mix and match Yes. You could think about: Counsellor, Conference organiser, Headhunter . . .

Enquiries AGCAS, Careers Advisers

There is a massive and largely unrecognised need for independent careers advisers to help, among others, new graduates and school leavers, the recently redundant or people who are stuck in a rut. While careers advisers are found at virtually all schools, universities and polytechnics, they are usually only able to see their immediate client group. This means that many people who would benefit from advice and counselling aimed specifically at them, are unable to obtain advice and hence they form a strong market for the independent careers adviser to exploit.

You need a lot of determination to succeed as an independent. Many people still regard seeking careers advice as a sign of failure and resent paying for it. Half the battle for independent careers advisers lies in convincing people that it *is* worth paying for help in making one of the most important decisions of their lives.

To provide this sort of analytical counselling you need a wide range of knowledge and know-how. Not only do you need to know a lot about careers and the practicalities of job hunting (CV writing for example), you also need to know a lot about people. Springboarding from employment in the public or private sector (ie as a careers adviser for schools or university or working for a management consultancy) is a good way of building up a network of contacts and information sources to keep you in touch with developments in the careers market. To become a careers adviser in schools you'll need to do a year's postgraduate course in careers guidance (not necessary for work in higher education).

One of the more useful short courses for people who want to set up on their own and provide more analytical advice, is that run by the UNIVERSITY OF LONDON, DEPARTMENT OF EXTRA-MURAL STUDIES. You should also have a background in psychology or counselling; you need to be able to recognise the difficulties your clients have in certain areas and to help them overcome these. Careers advisers need to be interested in and good with people, analytical and imaginative enough to suggest suitable careers.

To set up you need an office, a telephone, a filing system and a typewriter or computer. You also need a basic library of careers books: CRAC publishes a wide range of careers materials; there's a useful book called *Equal Opportunities* and the AGCAS series as well, of course, as *The Careers Book*. Having ready access to current job vacancies isn't necessarily worth the expense as long as you can point clients in the direction of likely sources of work: recruitment consultants, the relevant sections of the daily press and employment agencies. Ideally you should charge an hourly counselling fee of about £35. However, many clients are used to the idea of careers advice coming in the form of a tangible package with written assessments and advice. Charges for this range from £300 to £3,000 but you'll have to supply a lot of backup support at the upper end of this range – some of the larger consultancies, for example, provide clients with a temporary office and secretarial backup for several months of job hunting.

You need a steady flow of clients; this is an area where people expect quick results and aren't going to go on paying for your services if they don't get them. Advertise in the educational and careers press (*Executive Post*, *Graduate Post*) and in other publications aimed at job hunters (*DOG* and *ROGET* for example). Try also the job pages of the national press. Others come through referral, you may be able to convince school/university careers officers to recommend you to anyone they can't help themselves. Clients are likely to be pretty desperate when they seek your advice and it's important that you find out as much as you can about them and follow up your analysis and counselling with practical advice on self-presentation, how to go about finding a job, interview technique etc. Helping people to overcome the blockers that prevent them from succeeding is immensely rewarding.

Carpenter

At a Glance

Qualifications/Training	Recommended	Income bracket	Low
Licence	No	Town/Country	Either
Experience/Springboard	Recommended	Travel	Local
Mid-career entry	Possible	Exit sale	No
Entry costs	£2,000	Work at home	No

Mix and match   Possible.   You could think about: Wood carver, Cabinet maker, Man with a van, Stage technician carpenter, Physiotherapist . . .

Enquiries   Carpenters, Construction Industry Training Board, Guild of Master Craftsmen

Carpenters do woodwork on buildings – either constructing new buildings or maintaining old ones. That means constructing door and window frames, putting in floor and skirting boards and building shelves and cupboards. On the whole you'll do more varied and interesting work by working for yourself. There is almost always a demand for carpenters to do smaller jobs for private customers or larger ones under sub-contract to building and construction companies. Formal qualifications aren't essential; you should start by working for someone else as a way of learning the trade. For the best training work as an apprentice, but it's not always easy to get an apprenticeship. It will take between 3 and 5 years to become competent. Use this time to learn as much as possible, never be afraid to ask for advice or help from experienced colleagues and build up a network of other people in the construction industry which will be useful in the future. It helps if you've got a working knowledge of other areas of construction. You'll also need to be good with people, patient with their lack of knowledge of what's possible and as reliable as possible at timing and pricing jobs.

To set up you need the tools you'll already have collected while you were learning: hammers, saws, chisels, planes etc. You also need a van and some ladders. An answering machine helps to ensure that you don't lose new work while you're out. Additional expenses are advertising, dropping cards through letter boxes and putting ads in the local press; stationery, letter heads for quotes, invoice books, business cards. You may need money/credit for materials which you might have to buy in advance before the client pays you. Make sure that you've got a good supplier of wood, screws and nails. Charges are based on materials plus time (allow for unforeseen problems and consider things like awkward sites and difficult access). The better you are and the more experience you have the more you can charge; remember you also have to pay for insurance and public liability insurance. You give potential clients an estimate and some indication of when the job will be completed. They'll expect these to be pretty accurate if they give you the job, but most are reasonable if you've had to do more work or take longer because of unforeseen contingencies.

First jobs may come through friends or relations while you're still in employment. Once you're confident enough to work for yourself other work comes through advertisements and word of mouth. Respond to potential clients quickly. Always view a job and, when you're calculating how long the job will take, take into account anything you think could possibly go wrong. Giving verbal quotes is a very bad idea, take measurements and notes and calculate your estimate at home. For some jobs you may want to employ an assistant who'll need to be paid. It's important to establish a reputation for being prompt and reliable and tidying up after every job is a good way of keeping clients happy and ready to recommend you.

Although you may have some lean times in the early days, you stand to make more by working for yourself in the long run. Make sure that you book some time off and that all your jobs are finished before you go away.

Caterer

At a Glance

Qualifications/Training	Useful	Income bracket	Low–Medium
Licence	No	Town/Country	Town or nearby
Experience/Springboard	Useful	Travel	Local
Mid-career entry	Yes	Exit sale	Possible
Entry costs	£2,500+	Work at home	Yes

Mix and match   Yes.   You could think about: Publican, Restaurateur, Wine bar owner, Specialist food manufacturer, Artists' agent . . .

Enquiries   Local caterers

Caterers can opt for directors' lunches, providing a fairly regular service to offices, or they can specialise in party food and service and perhaps equipment hire (candlesticks and ashtrays) and service (waitresses etc). What you decide to do will depend largely on experience and opportunities. Although there are overlaps between the two, on the whole cooking for a handful of offices provides more regular, secure work than parties which are far more subject to seasonal demands. Whichever you do there is a lot of competition so perserverance is essential.

There are no hard and fast rules about experience and qualifications although you may find a formal qualification such as cordon bleu a useful way into directors' lunches. Some business knowledge is essential especially when you're setting up and need to decide on menus and pricing and to make cash flow predictions. You'll need cooking flair (to turn out large quantities of sellable food; mistakes cost a lot) and enough enthusiasm to carry you through shopping and paperwork. Expect to spend at least 50% of your time on this.

You can share the responsibilities by setting up with a partner whose skills or interests complement yours. Image is important – develop one that suits your speciality and clientele; you'll meet clients before you cook for them and first impressions count for a lot.

To set up you need a typewriter, telephone, answering machine, freezer, cooking utensils and stationery, including business cards. A car or van is also useful but can be hired until you feel secure enough to make the necessary financial outlay. Most clients will provide a kitchen to do most of the work in but you'll do a lot of cooking at home building up stocks of regular basics. You need insurance against accidentally poisoning your clients or damaging their property (through fire for instance). Try to find an understanding bank manager (not easy) to finance initial expenses.

Cash flow problems are rife. Supplies have to be bought well in advance of receiving payment. Insisting on a deposit and payment of invoices within 15 days helps but the accounts departments of large companies aren't geared to cope with this. You'll also have to pay casual serving staff; pay them more than the usual rate to build up a willing workforce (one caterer reports paying more for a night's serving than he pays himself in a week). If you overspend in one area, cut back in another; don't expect to reach more than subsistence level in less than 2 years. Try the Enterprise Allowance Scheme for the first year or find some flexible temporary work. Base your charges on the competition. Most caterers offer menus at a price per head (between about £5 for cocktail party food, to about £25 for dinner) and charge extra for corkage if the client provides the wine. You can also offer service and hire of cutlery, plates etc – provide these through a hire company many of which open accounts for established companies.

Clients are businesses (publishers, galleries, promoters etc) and established (often middle aged or overseas) business people. There is also a market in wedding and christening party catering. You can probably start off with friends and contacts. Choosing a specialist or unusual cuisine will get you noticed. You may have to compromise and do some diplomatic convincing to fit into the market, but don't lose sight of what you want to do. This is seasonal work with surprises – January is not quiet. You can use quiet times to replenish stocks, and drum up more customers through demonstrations, arranging advertising and visiting potential clients. Catering involves hours of cooking alone. You have to make a lot of effort to maintain a high enough profile and to build up trade contacts. *Caterer and Hotel Keeper* is good background reading but not specifically aimed at small catering companies.

Chamber Group Director

At a Glance

Qualifications/Training	Essential	Income bracket	Low
Licence	Union card necessary	Town/Country	Town
Experience/Springboard	Vital	Travel	Lots
Mid-career entry	Yes	Exit sale	No
Entry costs	£5,000	Work at home	No

Mix and match   Yes.   You could think about: Orchestral musician, Orchestral fixer, Music teacher, Classical composer, Counsellor, Man with a van . . .

Enquiries   Incorporated Society of Musicians

A group's director recruits the musicians, organises, promotes and finds engagements for them. Chamber music work is part time with little financial reward unless your group is outstanding, has won an international competition or acquired a job as quartet-in-residence at a university.

You can train, and meet other musicians, at music college; or you can do a postgraduate year at music college after university to reach the necessary technical standard. Most chamber musicians teach, coach and work as freelance orchestral players. Join the MUSICIANS' UNION.

Before setting up, you will need a room where the group can rehearse without disturbing the neighbours, £2,000 for publicity brochures, stationery and postage. Obtain lists of promoters. Write to them and to the diminishing number of members of the NATIONAL FEDERATION OF MUSIC SOCIETIES large or rich enough to employ you. Use one of the labelling services advertised in the *Musician*. Get a good accountant; keep receipts of everything.

You will need a typewriter or word processor, telephone, answering machine and diary service. Canvass the musical grapevine before fixing your group's rates. Allow for a management fee for yourself and sufficient for overheads as well as musicians' fees. If you join the INCORPORATED SOCIETY OF MUSICIANS, their legal service can provide a contract with protection from cancellation, ruthless and dishonest promoters. It can also chase up unpaid fees. Music, music stands, dresses for female musicians, bags/suitcases will cost a further £1,000. A car is useful; if you hire a van, include the cost in your fee.

Good national press notices are important so invest £1,000 in a concert preferably in London, eg at the Wigmore Hall. Aim to fill the hall with friends and relations to cover its hire and advertising costs. A concert manager will charge £250 and should persuade the critics to attend. Use every bit of influence to persuade the Arts editors to send someone. Avoid a Friday night or weekend booking when they are out of town.

Having received good reviews, print brochures with the group's photograph. Send these with sample programmes and press notices to anyone who might engage you. Approach BBC Radio 3 for an audition although they like proof of a number of concerts to show you are a permanent ensemble.

Agents prefer full time string quartets which are more economic, but try and get a recommendation to others on the continent. You must believe in your group, overflow with enthusiasm and energy. You should also be a good communicator and be able to cope with rejection. There should be a clear understanding with members of your group that having agreed to work with the group, they do not disappear to do another gig. You need to be calm, patient, logical, resilient and diplomatic with them – you will be at the mercy of their private lives and moods. An owner/administrator of a chamber orchestra deals direct with impresarios and borough entertainment/arts officers. Chamber music improves your standard of playing but is demanding. The job is stressful, artistically creative and satisfying; it provides greater freedom of expression than other musical work. The future is gloomy unless you have a really good original idea or approach when you will be saleable if you can become a workaholic for 3 years.

Chemical Engineering Consultant

At a Glance

Qualifications/Training	Essential	*Income bracket*	Medium–High
Licence	No	*Town/Country*	Town
Experience/Springboard	Essential	*Travel*	Yes
Mid-career entry	Yes	*Exit sale*	Possible
Entry costs	£8,000+	*Work at home*	Not recommended

Mix and match   Yes.   You could think about: Newsletter publisher, Landlord, Musical instrument repairer . . .

Enquiries   Institution of Chemical Engineers, Consultant Chemical Engineers Bureau

Chemical engineers are concerned with processes such as the production of solids, liquids and gases in bulk, approximately 5% of practising chemical engineers are self-employed or work as consultants in the chemical, food, pharmaceutical and steel industries. As a consultant you act as an adviser or help formulating projects. Much of the work concerns improving productivity of existing plant, rather than starting from scratch.

A degree in chemical engineering is essential. You will need also to gain experience in a large company, working as part of a team, before going solo. Verbal and written communication skills are important for explaining your plans to the uninitiated; also imagination, salesmanship and the ability to solve problems. Your time in employment should be used to develop a range of contacts so personal recommendations will result in consultancy contracts from large companies. Attend trade fairs and conferences to be seen and become known.

To set up on your own, you will need capital to acquire or rent premises and purchase drawing equipment, microcomputer, a vehicle, telephone, answering machine or service and secretarial help; also, most importantly, sufficient funds to tide-over the first 4–6 months in business.

You will spend a lot of time visiting sites and selling your services; three quarters of your time might be spent on real chemical engineering and the remainder on administration and sales. You may want to join the CONSULTANT CHEMICAL ENGINEERS BUREAU which was set up by a number of small consultants and publishes a directory. You will need to read the *Chemical Engineer*, published by the INSTITUTION OF CHEMICAL ENGINEERS, which will also provide further information. You will also find useful *Inside the Technical Consultancy Business* and the *Standard Handbook of Consulting Engineering Practice*.

This is a 'feast and famine' occupation: a balance between work flow and income is not easy to achieve. Contracts can last several months, ranging from local farms to multi-million pound schemes. You may be searching for your next contract, or working a 50-hour week to meet a deadline.

Any advance you make must involve increasingly lucrative contracts. Expansion will be difficult because highly-skilled professionals may earn more in large firms. Opportunities for working abroad, particularly in developing countries are good, and increasing. At home, opportunities are increasing as large firms cut back on their own engineering and training staff.

Child/Educational Psychologist

At a Glance

Qualifications/Training	Essential	*Income bracket*	Medium
Licence	Recommended	*Town/Country*	Town
Experience/Springboard	Essential	*Travel*	Local
Mid-career entry	Possible	*Exit sale*	Possible
Entry costs	£1,500	*Work at home*	Yes

Mix and match   Possible.   You could think about: Psychologist, Careers adviser, Counsellor, Musician . . .

Enquiries Association of Educational Psychologists, British Psychological Society

Child and educational psychologists help children to overcome social, emotional and learning problems. Clients are families – child psychologists work with both children and parents, assessing and providing follow up counselling and advice. The Warnock Report suggested that about 20% of children up to the age of 19 would benefit from access to a psychologist; currently only a very small proportion of this 20% are given any help and those that are, have usually been referred by their local authority education or health departments. Most child psychologists work for local authorities, operating within tight budgets. This means that a lot of children slip through the net unless their problems are making them a nuisance to others. Many children regarded as passing through difficult or unhappy phases could be helped but aren't, not least because of parents' and schools' reluctance to admit that the child has the sort of problem a psychologist could alleviate. But this seems to be changing gradually.

Although there is a clear need for independent child and educational psychologists to work with children in both the independent and maintained sectors, the move to independence from employment is slow. Gaining professional recognition almost certainly necessitates springboarding from local authority employment both to acquire sufficient experience and an essential network of contacts.

The BRITISH PSYCHOLOGICAL SOCIETY has recently introduced the registration of psychologists and, although this isn't yet a legal requirement, you're advised to register as a chartered psychologist before attempting to set up on your own. To become a chartered educational psychologist you need a degree in psychology, a post-graduate educational psychology qualification, a teaching qualification, at least 2–3 years of teaching experience and at least 3 years as a psychologist working under supervision. As an independent you'll need a lot more experience; you've got to have the courage of your convictions. In addition, the longer you've been at the job, the easier it is not to become too emotionally involved in cases and, even more important, you need good networks. Networks work in two ways, firstly, professional referrals from psychiatrists, teachers, children's organisations and GPs from whom you obtain your clients. It's useful having colleagues who have regular contact with schools and local authorities or to remain partially involved yourself in an employed position. Child psychologists work with children and parents and they themselves must be well rounded people, lively, agile and fit.

You can work from home as long as you're accessible to clients and have an amenable consulting room. You also need a typewriter and a phone (answering machines should be used as little as possible). As soon as you can afford it, employ a secretary to type reports, answer the phone and receive clients; suitable secretaries aren't easy to find but make a great difference, you shouldn't be interrupted in the middle of a consultation. Compared to other professions which have similar lengths of training, psychology is undervalued; this is reflected in the rates that you can charge, currently about £50 an hour in London – remember that's for the consultation only and you'll have to do some follow up work on each meeting as well as the writing of a detailed and often lengthy report.

New clients do not only come from referrals, but from satisfied clients: people are only likely to talk to you about their problems if they can see that you are being professional about your work. As an independent you need an additional commitment to break into a completely new market, starting off by educating parents and teachers to accept your services as valuable rather than a sign of failure on their part. Visit schools and tell teachers what you do and how you can help a wide range of children; design and teach training courses for teachers which will help them to recognise and deal with some of the minor problems they are most likely to come across.

Child psychologists see children from a wide range of ages and backgrounds and with very various problems. As an independent you're freer to expand the help you can give and aren't restricted to dealing with only those few cases a local authority regards as being severe enough to warrant psychological help. You're as likely to be working with children who are gifted as with children who seem to be slow learners. As well as children with severe and deep rooted emotional problems, you'll see children who only need some encouragement to overcome what's bothering them.

Read *Careers in Psychology* for further information. As well as the British Psychological Society investigate the ASSOCIATION OF EDUCATIONAL PSYCHOLOGISTS although they tend to be of more use to those in employment than to the self-employed.

Child Minder

At a Glance

Qualifications/Training	No	*Income bracket*	Low
Licence	Yes	*Town/Country*	Town/Village
Experience/Springboard	Yes	*Travel*	None
Mid-career entry	Yes	*Exit sale*	No
Entry costs	Nil	*Work at home*	Yes
Mix and match Limited. You could think about: Typist, Upholsterer, Novelist, Artist . . .			
Enquiries National Childminding Association			

This is an ideal job for someone who loves children, probably has some of their own, and wants to spend as much time at home as possible.

However, it is not lucrative, you can't take much time off, and you have to keep cheerful even when you don't feel it.

Most child minders look after other people's children while their parents are at work. Hours can be long (perhaps 8.00–6.30) if the child's parents do a full working day and have to travel a long way. However, you can fit in your own daily chores (cooking, cleaning and washing) around the children you look after. It can also be very enjoyable, taking children to local parks, and watching their development day by day.

Child minders have to be registered with the local council. There is a Catch 22: you cannot take on children unless you are registered, and you cannot register unless you have been looking after children for some time. Mothers who have worked in infant schools and nurseries find it fairly easy to register, and other people get round the problem by looking after children for friends or relatives before taking on strangers' children.

You don't need any special equipment or any capital, but your life will be easier if you have an automatic washing machine, suitable (ie washable) flooring in the rooms where the children will be, and space to store toys. Assistance from the local authority varies, but it is often possible to borrow high chairs and double buggies when necessary.

The number of children you are allowed to look after, and therefore the amount you can earn, is strictly controlled by law and supervised by the local authority: usually you are not allowed more than one child under the age of one, and not more than three children altogether. You will be lucky to earn £100 per week. You will not be paid if you take a holiday, although the children's parents should continue to pay you if they are away (it helps if you can all take holidays at the same time). It is essential to agree on terms and draw up a contract before taking on a child.

Local authorities will supply your name to people who come to them looking for a child minder, but you can also advertise in local newsagents. If you build up a good reputation word will soon spread, and since most children stay for three or four years if possible, you should not have difficulty finding children to look after.

The NATIONAL CHILDMINDING ASSOCIATION produces advisory leaflets and draft contracts for childminders and parents. There is a chapter on childminding in *Working Mother – a Practical Handbook*.

China Restorer

At a Glance

Qualifications/Training	Recommended	*Income bracket*	Low
Licence	No	*Town/Country*	Town preferably
Experience/Springboard	Recommended	*Travel*	Local
Mid-career entry	Possible	*Exit sale*	No
Entry costs	£1,000	*Work at home*	Yes

Mix and match   Good. You could think about: Picture restorer, Potter, Art historian/critic, Beekeeper . . .

Enquiries   West Dean College

There's more to this than shoving some superglue on to detached cup handles or tea pot spouts. The pieces that are sent to a professional china (and porcelain) restorer are likely to be old and fairly valuable; the work they will need ranges from re-joining a simple break to rebuilding bits that have been broken off and lost. Restored antiques are less valuable than perfect originals but look better and are worth more than obviously broken ones so, as long as you can do a good job and are in an area where there are enough antiques (in both shops and houses), you can make a living from restoring china. You can work at this when it suits you, which makes it something that can be combined with another job.

You'll have to be able to mend broken china; mix clay to the right consistency for replacing missing parts; model and paint missing bits so that they fit in as well as possible with the rest of the piece. There aren't many places where you can learn all of this on the job but you can do a course in ceramic conservation and restoration at WEST DEAN COLLEGE. This lasts 1–3 years and you'll get a diploma at the end. As well as being artistic enough to be able to recreate broken china, you have to be incredibly dexterous for this job. Not only is the work you're doing extremely fiddly, anyone who's remotely clumsy stands a pretty good chance of destroying whatever it is they're meant to be mending. You'll have to be diplomatic with clients, many of whom will have little idea of what's involved in the job they're asking you to do.

You'll need a studio to work in. This can be a room in your house but, while you're deciding which one, remember it'll soon start to smell strongly of glue. You'll need a table to work at and some sort of kiln. Kilns can be bought second hand from a variety of sources from about £300. You need access to some very expensive books (eg the *Royal Doulton Figures*) which will show you what a broken piece of china

ought to look like. You'll also need a supply of ceramic paints, glue and clays. Take out all risks insurance to cover your clients' pieces while they're in your charge. Charges are based on the amount of time you expect to take on a job; get good at judging this accurately and don't undervalue. Agree the price with the client before you start a job. Allow plenty of time to get a job done, it's better to be early than late; this also allows you to take on emergency jobs at short notice without messing up your schedule (you can charge a higher rate for rush jobs). Most china restorers are in London so, if you aren't, local antique dealers will be delighted to find you and will have plenty of work. Some may want to make a piece look more valuable than it really is; it's up to you what you do but if you forge a manufacturer's mark you're breaking the law. It's worth advertising in antique shops and the antique press (trade and collectors') as some people may want a damaged antique restored straight away, especially if they're shipping it overseas. British china restorers have a good reputation worldwide. Other clients are anyone who has some china they value. Some jobs are far more troublesome than others. You may have to do a lot of research to find how to restore something to as close to its original as possible. Others need long hours to get something mended before its owner gets back from holiday, for example. Your own holidays needn't be a problem once you've established a good enough reputation to have people prepared to wait longer than usual for jobs to be done.

Chiropodist

At a Glance

Qualifications/Training	Vital	*Income bracket*	Medium–High
Licence	Yes	*Town/Country*	Town
Experience/Springboard	Recommended	*Travel*	Local, possibly
Mid-career entry	Possible	*Exit sale*	No
Entry costs	£5,000	*Work at home*	Possible
Mix and match	Possible. You could think about: Journalist, Cabinet maker . . .		
Enquiries	Society of Chiropodists		

Chiropodists specialise in illness or discomfort of the lower leg and foot. They can give medical aid ranging from cutting the toe nails of the elderly to minor surgery. To be State Registered you need to take one of the 12 recognised chiropody courses. These are held at NHS teaching hospitals, further education colleges or the LONDON FOOT HOSPITAL – you can get a list from the SOCIETY OF CHIROPODISTS.

You need manual dexterity, as you handle a knife a lot of the time; a liking for people; a sense of humour and excellent communicating skills. You will be dealing with all kinds of people – children, geriatrics, and the physically and mentally handicapped.

There is a shortage of good chiropodists. There is no union but join the SOCIETY OF CHIROPODISTS which holds lectures, meetings and has its own magazine, the *Chiropodist*. Make sure you are covered by malpractice insurance and have a good accountant.

Once qualified, it's best to do some regular part-time sessions for the NHS or industry until you have built up enough clients for your practice, as you cannot advertise. Circularise your local doctors and put yourself into the local Yellow Pages and Thompsons. You can treat patients on NHS or privately.

You can use a room in your home but it must be on the ground floor and near public transport. You will need planning permission to use your house as a clinic. You can share premises with other professionals, such as dentists, so saving on overheads. You need hot and cold running water, a separate loo, an operator's chair (£100), a patient's

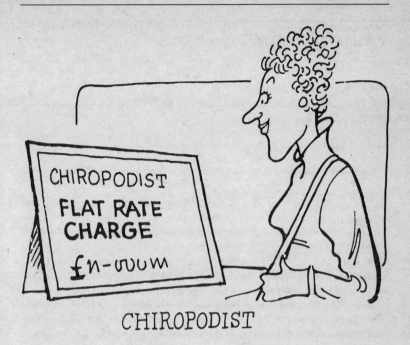

CHIROPODIST

chair (£2,000), an autoclave (£1,200) – essential since the advent of AIDS. Apart from the premises, this will cost a total of £4,000–5,000.

Depending on the area you work in, you can expect to start with an income of £10,000 and if you work in a fashionable place this can rise to £50,000. The average is £25,000–30,000 per annum.

You can vary your hours of work to suit yourself and take a holiday when you feel like it. This makes it ideal for women with families. You can do home visits if you wish. However you can develop a bad back or chest from bending over all day. Useful information is found at the SOCIETY OF CHIROPODISTS.

Chiropractor

At a Glance

Qualifications/Training	Essential	Income bracket	Medium–High
Licence	No	Town/Country	Town
Experience/Springboard	Yes	Travel	No
Mid-career entry	Unlikely	Exit sale	No
Entry costs	£9,000	Work at home	Possible

Mix and match   Limited.   You could think about: Dealer in antiques, Musician . . .

Enquiries   British Chiropractic Association

A chiropractor is a specialist in the treatment of spinal pain syndrome by using manipulation rather than drugs.

You need 3 A-levels, including science subjects, to gain admission to the ANGLO EUROPEAN COLLEGE OF CHIROPRACTIC. The 4-year course leads to a doctorate in chiropractics which is recognised in the USA, Australia, New Zealand, Canada and Denmark. It has yet to be officially recognised by the DHSS in the UK. Soon you will need to have worked as an assistant to another experienced chiropractor to qualify. For the time being, you would be wise to anticipate this. There is no union but the professional body to join is the BRITISH CHIROPRACTIC ASSOCIATION, which has its own malpractice insurance scheme which is vital.

You need an open personality, good communication skills, energy, sensitivity and a strong belief in your particular calling – very important when it lacks the recognition of the establishment.

You need £9,000 capital, in addition to premises, to set up in a ground floor consulting room near public transport and a car park if possible. This can be in your own house but you must have planning permission to use it as a clinic. You need a treatment table, phone, answerphone, filing cabinet, typewriter and X-ray and developing equipment. (The new electro-magnetic resonance scanning and other imaging techniques will be better than X-rays). A receptionist will cost £8,000 per annum.

You can work any hours but usually 9.00am to 7.00pm with a movable lunch hour so patients can come out of normal working hours. Your income to start with is usually between £12,000 to £15,000 per annum rising to £25,000 upwards. There is a shortage of chiropractors, but you must be situated where people can or will pay for treatment as it is not available on the NHS.

If you enjoy helping people you will get a big buzz from this job but you must be prepared to see patients after hours, or at the weekends in an emergency, which can interfere with your family/social life. If you do sessions at a clinic with other kinds of primary care medical practitioners, it is possible to work part time.

You can get more information from the BRITISH CHIROPRACTIC ASSOCIATION, read their journal *Contact* (and that of the American Association), the *Lancet*, the *British Medical Journal* and *Bone and Joint Surgery* magazine.

Classical Composer

At a Glance

Qualifications/Training	Recommended	Income bracket	Low
Licence	No	Town/Country	Either
Experience/Springboard	Recommended	Travel	Possible
Mid-career entry	Possible	Exit sale	Yes
Entry costs	£1,000	Work at home	Yes

Mix and match Essential. You could think about: Music copyist, Music teacher, Light music composer, Conductor, Musician, Festival director, Music critic, Book editor . . .
Enquiries Association of Professional Composers, Composers Guild

A classical composer writes serious music to be performed by 'straight' musicians in concert halls and opera houses. You must be born with the unusual ability to hear music going on inside your head and want to write it down. To do this and to understand the problems of performing, study other people's compositions and learn to play an instrument, preferably piano. It is not necessary to attend music college or university; but this will put you in touch with other musicians and composers and provide mutual support when you want your works to be performed. Being a gofer for a good composer will encourage you to overcome practical difficulties and gain inspiration. You need this, along with talent, persistence, optimism, courage and luck. If you have all these and become accustomed to rejection, eventually you will succeed. You must believe in your talent.

Few composers can live on performing rights. You will probably always need another job such as teaching, copying, arranging, freelance editing or journalism (like Berlioz). Writing for films full time is lucrative but dangerous to the composer trying to write music which will stand the test of time.

You need a small piano or synthesiser, a quiet room where you will not disturb the neighbours, manuscript paper, pencils and a rubber.

Join the SOCIETY FOR THE PROMOTION OF NEW MUSIC and hope that they will accept one of your works and give it a performance. If this attracts good notices in the national press you may be approached by a publisher. Send scores to the BBC Radio 3. Be sociable and get to know as many performing musicians as possible. They may commission a work from you and the more performances they give the better for your reputation. You are paid on a rate set by the ARTS COUNCIL or GUILD OF COMPOSERS, by the minute and number of instruments. Only composers like Britten make £100,000 pa.

It is marvellous to write music enjoyed by performers and audience but also nerve-racking and exciting; it's also depressing to have a work refused or experience a bad performance. You can set your own working hours; a daily routine suits most composers. Try not to compose and arrange on the same day; they don't mix well. The one-time bias against female composers is changing. Travel will come once you are successful and are asked to attend premiers. You are vulnerable to cuts in government grants to the Arts Council unless you have other good commercial connections.

The ASSOCIATION OF PROFESSIONAL COMPOSERS is useful. Read a good book on orchestration (eg *Orchestration* by Walter Piston) and the *British Music Year Book*.

Classical/Operatic Singer

At a Glance

Qualifications/Training	Recommended	*Income bracket*	Low
Licence	Equity for opera chorus	*Town/Country*	Town
Experience/Springboard	No	*Travel*	Yes
Mid-career entry	Unlikely	*Exit sale*	No
Entry costs	£500+	*Work at home*	No

Mix and match Essential. You could think about: Music teacher, Book editor, Word processor, Photographer, Market research interviewer, Bartender, Minicab driver . . .

Enquiries Incorporated Society of Musicians

This person sings a classical repertoire in concerts/recitals, groups, oratorios and in opera companies. To be successful you need a reasonably good voice, an accurate ear, sense of rhythm, pleasant appearance (weight for a man, good figure for a woman), firm build, stamina for the long hours and travelling, self-discipline for the training and persistence. A solid family background which produces good self-esteem is important as the voice reflects personality, and an extrovert one helps. Above all you must have the rare ability to communicate emotion to an audience. A good singing teacher is vital. O and A levels are not necessary but a knowledge of French, German and Italian is useful, and how to pronounce them correctly is very important. Going to music college is not essential, but the advantages are good contacts and giving free performances to agents and opera companies.

To satisfy your bank manager, get a job which is not too physically tiring. When you and your teacher feel you have the necessary technical grounding, enter a music festival or vocal competition to gain experience of public exposure. Approach the YOUNG CONCERT ARTISTS' TRUST, the ISM (INCORPORATED SOCIETY OF MUSICIANS) Young Artists' Recital at the Wigmore Hall, or apply to an opera company or the conductor(s) of amateur choral societies for an audition. If you are lucky enough to join the chorus of an opera company, you must join EQUITY. Your contract will be short or long, depending on the company, and earnings will be about £170 a week. With this experience you can cover for the principal singers' understudies, and possibly have the opportunity of going on one night unexpectedly.

Get a fixed address where you can practise without disturbing the neighbours, a telephone and answering machine or service. You will need about £500 to cover singing lessons, coaching, publicity and postage. You do not need an agent to start with.

There is no sex or race bias and the number of coloured singers in the UK is increasing. The hours are long, lonely and unsocial and you will need to fill in the time spent hanging around by knitting, doing crossword puzzles etc. Family life will be disrupted by the travelling, often abroad and sometimes for weeks at a time. Air travel can cause dehydration of the voice. Rehearsals, costume fittings and work with repetiteurs are demanding. In spite of the exhaustion of constantly working with new people in strange places you still have to give a first class performance, and there's often a party afterwards.

The job is marvellous if you enjoy communicating with others and cannot bear to do anything else. Losing your voice is a hazard and you should have alternative work to call on.

Consult *Careers in Music*, *British Music Year Book*, *Competitions for Singers*, the *Federation of International Competitions* and *Career Guide for Young American Singers*.

Cleaner

At a Glance

Qualifications/Training	No	*Income bracket*	Low
Licence	No	*Town/Country*	Town/Village
Experience/Springboard	No	*Travel*	Local
Mid-career entry	Yes	*Exit sale*	No
Entry costs	Nil	*Work at home*	No

Mix and match Yes. You could think about: Cleaning contractor, Holiday accommodation owner, Nurse, Yoga teacher, Property manager . . .

Enquiries Local agencies

Cleaning other people's homes is not everyone's idea of fun and it's no soft option. The advantages are that you don't need any qualifications, there's no capital outlay and the taxman doesn't get a look in. Nearly all cleaners are female but male cleaners have a good reputation, novelty value and a certain cachet, so they won't find themselves short of work.

The most important personal qualities are honesty (dishonest cleaners don't last long, they almost certainly get found out); discretion (Mrs Bloggs won't thank you if you tell her next door neighbour what/who you found in her fridge/bathroom cabinet/bed); a pleasant outgoing personality (a lot of employers find their relationship with their cleaner difficult because they know they'd find the job demeaning, so they're grateful if you don't make them feel guilty/lazy/mean); dependability and good time keeping (everyone likes to rely on the same time every week, rain or shine); and pride in a job well done (clean every hour as if you're expecting the Queen to lunch and the grapevine will keep you in as much work as you want).

There's more to cleaning than just flicking a duster around as every housewife knows. Many cleaners find it useful to work for a while as eg a domestic in the health service – where you'll be shown the ropes by helpful colleagues and demanding supervisors. You can start working privately for a few people in your spare time, then go freelance when you've built up enough clients to risk leaving your job.

There's a shortage of good cleaners and people are crying out for them, so it won't take you long to fill your week. The best way of doing this is by word of mouth and personal recommendation, so once you've made yourself indispensable as Mrs Bloggs's 'treasure' you'll be inundated with applications for your services. Look too for advertisements in local newspapers and newsagents' windows.

The money varies according to area, but generally it's between £2 and £4 an hour. Some employers feel so guilty/generous/anxious not to lose their cleaner that they are quite happy to pay travelling expenses plus the usual rate for an annual holiday (usually two weeks). Cleaners are nearly always paid in cash and no questions asked. If overwhelming honesty gets the better of you, you can pay your own national insurance contributions and be taxed as a self-employed person as long as you have several employers.

Really ambitious cleaners could hit the big time by setting up their own cleaning agency or specialist cleaning firm. You need to have a telephone and, preferably, office premises – not necessarily plush but, above all, clean – and some kind of reliable transport. Get an insight into how these agencies operate by working for one yourself for a while. Then, if old Aunt Fanny dies and your boat comes in, you'll know where to begin.

Cleaning Contractor

At a Glance

Qualifications/Training	No	Income bracket	Medium
Licence	No	Town/Country	Town
Experience/Springboard	No	Travel	Local
Mid-career entry	Yes	Exit sale	Possible
Entry costs	£3,000+	Work at home	Not recommended

Mix and match   Possible.   You could think about: Cleaner, Nanny and babysitting agent, Magazine publisher, Property manager, Wigmaker . . .

Enquiries   Local cleaning contractors

Cleaning contractors provide cleaning services for their clients. Much of their time is spent recruiting cleaning staff and scheduling staff and jobs. In some parts of the country (eg the South East) there is a high demand for domestic help. The service of cleaning contractors is especially useful for busy people who do not have time to find their own reliable cleaners. There are opportunities in office cleaning but, on the whole, this is highly competitive and tends to operate in different areas.

There are no formal qualifications. It's essential that you're good with people; you'll have to discuss, with interest, the cleaning needs of your clients and to cope with staff. You should also have some idea yourself of how to clean so that you can provide reasonable quotations to prospective clients. (You may prefer to sub-contract jobs like upholstery cleaning to specialist firms – see *Cleaning* and *Cleaning Business News* for addresses.) Cleaning staff can't always work outside their regular, set hours so you may have problems juggling the work force around to fulfil these needs and should be prepared to do a spot of cleaning yourself from time to time. Image is important both for you and the staff. Clients may have preconceived ideas and prejudices which you'll have to indulge if you want their business.

Recruit staff initially via ads in local papers and shop windows. Your accountant will insist that your staff is on the books and you may find that many cleaners, used to working in the black economy, are reluctant to commit themselves to this. Once you've got some staff they may introduce their friends to you but even then you'll spend a lot of time interviewing and recruiting. Cleaners don't want to spend a lot of time and money getting to work so operate in a mixed area where staff can walk to work. Other problems here are in reliability (many cleaners have commitments to family etc and will not always be available). Employ people you can trust (they will have access to your clients' houses), and who will maintain high standards of cleaning. Ensure this by getting references and employing them for a supervised trial clean before taking them on. Employing staff means paperwork, so be prepared for that.

Business comes from ads and articles in local papers, Yellow Pages, leaflet drops and word of mouth. As well as private clients who want regular cleaning, a lot of work comes from letting agencies and one-off jobs (spring cleans etc). There is more money to be made from these, and a one-off may lead to a contract, but they are often at very short notice.

You'll need an office to operate from and to store some equipment in, a phone and an answering machine; also a car or van for ferrying staff to distant, lucrative one-offs. Have cards printed. On the whole clients will supply their own materials and equipment but having backups is useful. As well as employer's liability insurance you'll have to be insured against damage to clients' property (depending on the area this could mean up to £1 million worth of cover); broken ornaments may cost a lot and lost keys mean having to replace the locks. Expect to pay your staff slightly above the normal rate to ensure a reliable workforce (about £3.50 per hour in London). You can charge about £6 and upwards per hour for regular contracts but profits on spring cleans etc are a lot higher. Clients will expect excellent service for this.

Although the cleaning gets done during the day you may have to see new clients in the evening. You'll also have to cope with crises such as cleaners refusing to work in filthy houses and clients who have managed to live in squalor noticing any speck of dust left by a cleaner. As well as operating to a strict schedule for much of the time, you'll have to deal with last minute extra jobs.

Coal Merchant

At a Glance

Qualifications/Training	Recommended	Income bracket	Low–Medium
Licence	Yes, if new	Town/Country	Either
Experience/Springboard	Recommended	Travel	Local
Mid-career entry	Possible	Exit sale	Yes
Entry costs	£5,000	Work at home	Possible

Mix and match   Possible.   You could think about: Haulier, Man with a van, Tree surgeon, Jazz musician/singer . . .

Enquiries   Coal Merchants' Federation, Solid Fuel Advisory Service, Approved Coal Merchants' Scheme

Coal merchants can operate from coal yards, buying supplies and storing them until they're sold. Otherwise they can act as a sort of delivery service between large suppliers and customers – charging more for the coal than they paid for it.

To set up a new coal merchant's business, you need to be a member of the APPROVED COAL MERCHANTS' SCHEME before suppliers will deal with you. This involves demonstrating a knowledge of fuel (there are about 15 different sorts) and the trade. You will also need to know suppliers who are willing to supply you once you've joined. One way of learning is through apprenticing yourself to a good coal merchant, preferably not too close to where you hope to set up in business. You can also take a certificate of professional competence, details from the APPROVED COAL MERCHANTS' SCHEME who will recommend a course if they don't think you know enough about coal. You'll need a HGV licence (course and exam cost about £500) and an operator's licence from the MOT if you propose to operate a lorry over 7.5 tons. Another useful organisation is the COAL MERCHANTS' FEDERATION who run courses through the SOLID FUEL ADVISORY SERVICE. You need to be au fait with accounts, VAT etc or hire someone who is and who could perhaps take orders as well.

To set up in business you need premises, a yard and some arrangement for taking orders while you're out delivering. To convert your garden into a coal yard, you need planning permission and the neighbours are unlikely to be enthusiastic. You also need sacks, gloves, aprons and a good weighing machine (£200) and a lorry or two (handy when one is undergoing its bi-monthly MOT). Second hand lorries cost about £2,000 rising to about £17,000 new. You collect the coal from Concentration Depots or in bulk from wholesalers near the pits (cheaper but reluctant to give credit). Besides insuring against the normal things, you need public liability insurance and professional indemnity insurance in case somebody's stove explodes because you've supplied the wrong coal.

It is very hard and dirty work and not recommended for those with bad backs or folie de grandeur.

Company Doctor

At a Glance

Qualifications/Training	No	Income bracket	Low–High
Licence	No	Town/Country	Town
Experience/Springboard	Essential	Travel	Yes
Mid-career entry	Essential	Exit sale	No
Entry costs	Nil	Work at home	No

Mix and match   Yes. You could think about: Accountant, Marketing consultant, Timeshare holiday accommodation owner, Racehorse owner . . .

Enquiries   Management Consultants Association, Large accountancy firms

Failing companies may call on outside help to try to save themselves from imminent collapse. The people who are called upon, company doctors, are meant to diagnose the problems, come up with a remedy and implement it. They are at the top end of management consultancy and their expertise is such that they are usually called upon only by quoted companies and often when drastic action is needed. Demand for company doctors has increased over the past twenty years; while long established companies find that their old ways are no longer successful, there has been a rash of new companies who find that they are unable to maintain their, often quickly won, success. Even in the face of the 1986 Insolvency Act which combines the role of receiver with that of company doctor, company doctors are unlikely to disappear; there will always be companies prepared to call on expert help to avoid collapse rather than waiting for collapse before being doctored.

Essential qualifications are credibility and connections. Success depends to a large extent on restoring internal and external faith in an ailing company. This means raising money from sources which may have been pouring money into the company for years and introducing changes that won't always be popular with those they affect. You'll need to be so highly thought of that the right people are prepared to listen to you even when you're backing something they think's a loser. Contacts are also essential when you're saving a company and need to call on more expertise either as a second opinion or to take on an executive role in the client company to put your suggestions into effect. Most company doctors are over fifty with a lifetime in industry or business behind them and an impressive track record as managing directors. They have to know virtually all there is to know about how companies operate – management, accounting systems, marketing. Most will continue to hold directorships or chairmanships but will be free enough of other commitments to be able to throw themselves into fulltime rescue when needed.

Company doctors need to be analytical and to combine some of the generalities learned through experience with the specifics observed about a particular company before focusing on the problems. You must be entrepreneurial enough to see the potential for success even in a company that's floundering and willing to accept the formidable challenge this presents. The work often involves making sweeping changes to the structure of a company or redirecting its main activities (leading a company whose turnover was principally in eg chemicals, on to other areas). At other times companies need to be shown how to make the best of assets they already have; to build up previously underdeveloped areas. It can take years to lead a company on to success and needs patience and determination coupled with the ability to cope with only partial success or even failure. Company doctors often find that the root of the problems faced by client companies lies in the management; the first job is often to appoint new executive and financial management and weed out some of the old so, in spite of the great things your presence may herald, don't expect to be greeted with cries of welcome by everyone at client companies.

There are no set up costs but you shouldn't depend on a regular income from company doctoring; companies don't get into financial trouble to order. On the other hand, you don't have to pay for advertising, because all the people who are interested in company doctors will know who to call on. The fees you charge can be enormous; you're charging for expertise, experience and connections, and the work you do, in the long run, could be worth millions to clients. Client companies are likely to have reached the limits of their credit and to have no more bank support. Sometimes the bank will have called the doctor in advance, at other times it may be management consultants who realise a problem is extremely serious before it has exploded. Once called in, you can expect to be working full-time for several months; starting with a period of intense activity, liaising with the present management finding out what's gone wrong and what can be made to go right; working out how to alleviate the immediate problem (this usually means getting hold of some more money and investors, working out a new finance system and, often, appointing a new finance director) before moving on to the more positive role of establishing conditions that will prevent the same thing from happening again as soon as you've gone. There will be times when you have to drop everything and put in some long hours but most of the time your role is that of expert consultant. Company doctors and their assistants tend to have direct day-to-day contact with the company. They're saving for at least 3–12 months, followed by a watchdog period during which they are on call should they be needed. Although there are failures, there are great rewards when the company you have rescued from the brink of disaster goes on to great things. There is a MANAGEMENT CONSULTANTS ASSOCIATION; many accountancy firms have corporate rescue teams; banks, eg HAMBROS, have intensive care units and INVESTORS IN INDUSTRY has a special management unit.

Computer Consultant

At a Glance

Qualifications/Training	Available	*Income bracket*	Medium–High
Licence	No	*Town/Country*	Town
Experience/Springboard	Vital	*Travel*	Local
Mid-career entry	Usual	*Exit sale*	No
Entry costs	£8,000+	*Work at home*	Yes

Mix and match   Yes.   You could think about: Computer hardware engineer, Computer software author, Media converter, Fish curer and smoker, Timeshare holiday accommodation owner . . .

Enquiries   British Computer Society

This job provides the bridge between computer hardware and software dealers who sell standard products, and their customers whose needs are anything but standard. Business computing is a growth area and consultancy provides an essential service at its current stage of development. Consultants specialise in particular systems, but the current boom area is in business microcomputers – IBM PCs and compatible computers.

Most customers are business or professional people who need someone to interpret their computer needs and set up a working system. Normally, you can expect to spend some time getting to know clients' business and discussing their needs prior to recommending the purchase of a suitable system and overseeing its installation. To be a good consultant – there are plenty of bad ones – you need a sound practical knowledge of business computer hardware and software plus an all-round understanding of how a variety of businesses operate.

Some consultants specialise and work as part of a team, but if you go it alone you need many skills. At minimum you should be familiar with a wide range of software and have practical programming experience in the main industry-standard databases, spreadsheets, word processors, accounts and integrated packages. You should also be familiar with a range of computers, printers and other peripherals, and on top of this you'll need a working knowledge of accountancy and business practice, plus good communication skills. Contacts with computer dealers are useful but not essential and tend to develop naturally.

Having said all that, there are no formal qualifications and people set up consultancy practices from many different backgrounds. Some start by working in a dealership and gain experience by providing a service linked to the dealer's sales. Others work from within the computer department of a larger company until branching out on their own.

You won't need much in the way of space – a small office, a telephone and answering machine is enough to get started – but you will need computers, peripherals and a wide range of software. If you work in the industry for a while you should be able to acquire much of what you need cheaply. But if you buy at retail prices, budget a minimum of £3,000 for hardware, and probably as much again for software. Fees vary widely, depending on the type of client as well as the quality of your work, but expect to receive from £100 to £300 per day, and to have the possibility of long slack periods.

You can advertise your services in the specialist press, but the most worthwhile jobs come by word of mouth and personal recommendation. It helps to be listened to if you are personable and look convincing in a business suit (or female equivalent).

There are many consumer computer magazines but the more serious are: *MicroScope*; *Computing*; *PC User*; *PC Week* and *Systems International*. Most of these are controlled circulation and free to legitimate business readers. The BRITISH COMPUTER SOCIETY runs courses and has useful information.

Computer Hardware Engineer

At a Glance

Qualifications/Training	Necessary	*Income bracket*	Medium
Licence	No	*Town/Country*	Town
Experience/Springboard	Recommended	*Travel*	Local
Mid-career entry	Yes	*Exit sale*	No
Entry costs	£5,000+	*Work at home*	Possible

Mix and match Possible. You could think about: Computer consultant, Motorcycle racer, Disco owner/DJ, Import/export broker . . .

Enquiries British Computer Society

Most computer engineers' jobs involve repairing or modifying the basic machine. Although computers are inherently reliable, they and their printers or other peripherals do break down from time to time, and need mending. And some users need special modifications to suit their own requirements – anything from a simple job like making a special head, through to constructing a special interface. The other main opening for hardware engineers is development of new hardware add-ons, which can still be done on a small scale and a manageable budget. Manufacture and marketing on any scale takes substantial resources, however, and if you have perfected a new expansion card for a PC, say, you may be better off taking it to a company who has established manufacturing and distribution chains – rather than setting yourself up as a cottage industry manufacturing and selling direct. If the idea and the product are good enough, you can reasonably ask for an advance on setting up the deal, and a royalty on sales of the product – although if it is unlikely to sell in large numbers, you may prefer a cash sum.

Repairs may seem to offer more regular work, but many repair jobs – particularly on new business machines – are handled through service contracts. These usually guarantee the owner a quick response and fixed terms in return for an annual fee, usually linked into their dealership. The service company employ their own service agents and demand standard qualifications. But openings exist for private enterprise to fill the gaps left by service contracts. Generally, these comprise the cheaper machines, ones which don't have a large enough dealer network to have negotiated service arrangements, and secondhand equipment.

There are two ways to approach such business. One is to establish friendly links with local dealers. If they are small, they may themselves need the occasional bit of wiring modification done or special circuit made up that they cannot do themselves. They may also be prepared to refer business to you from customers who need this kind of work. The alternative is to advertise, but this may prove expensive compared to the amount of business you can expect to handle as a single operator. You need practical qualifications for the job and a relevant course in computer or electronic engineering is desirable. As a sole operator, you don't need a particularly large workshop, but you'll need to be able to store bits and pieces and customers' equipment. Transport capable of moving you and machines around is desirable, although ways can be found around this if it is a problem. You need standard electronic test and repair equipment, plus a range of components or spares for the type of machines you intend to work on. You should also think about the consequences of failing to fix, worse still, damaging someone's equipment: it may be worth obtaining professional indemnity insurance against this contingency. Get information from the BRITISH COMPUTER SOCIETY; there are many computer magazines eg *MicroScope*, *Computing*, *PC User*, *PC Week* and *Systems International*. Also read the *PC Year Book*.

Computer Software Author

At a Glance

Qualifications/Training	Usual	*Income bracket*	Medium
Licence	No	*Town/Country*	Town or nearby
Experience/Springboard	Recommended	*Travel*	Local
Mid-career entry	Possible	*Exit sale*	No
Entry costs	£2,000+	*Work at home*	Possible

Mix and match   Possible.   You could think about: Computer consultant, Media
    converter, Word processor, Book editor, Kennel/cattery owner . . .

Enquiries   British Computer Society

Software isn't what it used to be in the days when millionaire teenage
whizzkids seemed to make the headlines every week for writing a
best-selling game. Things have quietened down since then, and generally programs don't sell in such epic numbers nor are they so often the
work of one inspired enthusiast. Software publishing has settled down
to become perhaps closer to book publishing than record publishing.

The market splits into two – entertainment and business software.
Major business packages nowadays are almost invariably the work of a
team who each contribute different skills, and involve a lengthy
development period. And selling such a program successfully generally
calls for massive production, documentation and user support. Having
said that, there are still some examples of programs written by small
independent groups that have found a niche.

Perhaps the most rewarding field (though not necessarily financially
so) is in specialist, so-called 'vertical market' applications. If you have
specialist knowledge of the needs of a particular business and can write
a program to meet them, your market is easily defined. Such software is
often written using a standard applications package (dBase III, for
example), or it may use a programming language (a surprising number
use BASIC).

Typically, such software costs a substantial amount – £1,000 or more
is not uncommon, in addition to any basic software required to run it.
In some cases the software was developed for a single user who will
have helped to meet the costs, and if it can then be sold on, there may
well be potential for profit. Because it sells to a small specialist market,
it is unnecessary to provide extensive packaging and so on, since sales
will be very much on a personal, consultative basis. But it will be
difficult to find a field which is not already well tapped, and many
programs fail to sell in substantial numbers. For examples of the kind of

things on offer, see the back pages of *Micro Decision* (which lists the numbers sold against each package) or the listings in the *PC Year Book*. Advertising such software tends to have easy avenues through the trade press, exhibitions, etc.

Entertainment software – games, music and graphics packages etc – is possibly less demanding than the business market. But the field is flooded with many competing products and success still tends to mean professional attention to marketing. Software houses are much more hard-bitten than they once were, and although they are always on the look out for a new product, it will have to offer something special.

In either business or entertainment software, if you do succeed in interesting a software house, expect your royalty to reflect the size of the program – whether it needs heavy investment in packaging, documentation etc – in other words how much work they will have to put into it.

Of the host of computer magazines, the more serious are *MicroScope*, *Computing*, *PC User*, *PC Week* and *Systems International*. Contact the BRITISH COMPUTER SOCIETY.

Concert Agent

At a Glance

Qualifications/Training	Recommended	*Income bracket*	Low–Medium
Licence	Yes	*Town/Country*	Town
Experience/Springboard	Essential	*Travel*	Yes
Mid-career entry	Possible	*Exit sale*	Possible
Entry costs	£5,000	*Work at home*	Yes

Mix and match Possible. You could think about: Impresario, Orchestral fixer, Festival director, Musician, Music publisher, Word processor . . .

Enquiries British Association of Concert Agents

The agent or manager procures engagements for a few chosen performing musicians/singers and also organises individual concerts, usually recitals. Ideally you should have musical interests and secretarial skills and have completed either a Business Studies or Arts Administration course (eg City University). You need to be able to recognise talent and predict what promoters will like; and you must possess patience, persistence, iron determination and diplomacy when dealing with artists and promoters.

Five years' experience of working in different fields of arts administration is essential for contacts and making mistakes in a safe environment. In order to go it alone, you will then need at least £5,000 capital. You can work from one room at home with a supply of stationery, a typewriter or word processor, telephone, answering machine or service and, after several years, a computer and telex. You will also need a good accountant.

It's a good idea to join the BRITISH ASSOCIATION OF CONCERT AGENTS and apply to your local council for a licence to register as an agent. You can charge 12½% commission fee on an artist's concert fee and £250 for organising a Wigmore Hall recital. This will involve arranging publicity and encouraging critics to attend. You cannot expect to make a decent living for 3–5 years so it is necessary to have other employment as well, or an earning partner but the sky can be the limit for a successful international agent. You will attend your concerts, in addition to working office hours. If you want to chat up promoters you will have to travel. Female agents feel they are not taken as seriously as their male counterparts.

CONCERT AGENT

PROMPT   AGENT

The disadvantages of the job are that it disrupts social life and unless you strike lucky with a genius of a client, you will find it difficult to become rich: artists' fees are low; concert organisation in the UK is badly funded; the music agent is the victim of Arts Council and government arts policies, or lack of them. The advantages are the interesting people you meet, the flexible hours and the satisfaction of making concerts happen.

Useful books are *British Music Year Book*, the *British Association of*

Concert Agents list of artists directory, the Musicians' Handbook, the National Federation of Music Societies Handbook and the Incorporated Society of Musicians Arts Festival Book.

Conductor

At a Glance

Qualifications/Training	Recommended	Income bracket	Low–High
Licence	No	Town/Country	Town
Experience/Springboard	Yes	Travel	Endless
Mid-career entry	Possible	Exit sale	No
Entry costs	£2,000	Work at home	No

Mix and match   Yes.   You could think about: Musician, Classical/light music composer, Music teacher, Instrumental soloist, Music copyist, Music critic, Repetiteur/accompanist/coach . . .

Enquiries   Music Colleges

To become a conductor you need an excellent sense of rhythm, a quick intelligence, confidence, courage and determination. Going to music college or university is useful for skills – keyboard ones are very helpful – and for contacts. It is not necessary to have a degree in music but being able to play an instrument and/or sing is a distinct advantage.

Most important, apart from being able to hear music from a score before it is played, and to memorise it, is the ability to communicate with other people – musicians, directors, designers, concert promoters and sponsors. To speak several languages is an advantage, as is diplomacy and the imagination to inspire other artists, and to sell yourself and your ideas. Career prospects are grim unless you have personality, talent, luck and money.

To get started, try to join a number of good quality amateur musical organisations. Conduct local choir(s)/orchestra(s) and if at college, form your own orchestra/choir/opera group. Persuade well-established musicians to come and see or hear your work so that it becomes known and you either win an international competition, get appointed assistant conductor or repetiteur in an opera house, or are given the opportunity to conduct a professional orchestra. It helps to have a private income or a sponsor. If you can persuade the critics of the national press to attend one of your concerts and their judgment is

CONDUCTOR

encouraging you may begin to get more engagements.

There is no union you need to join, but it is helpful to know as many influential people as possible. It is a good plan to have a job either playing, teaching or editing music as you will have no income for several years. You will require a room with a piano, telephone and answering machine or service, and a working husband/wife/partner to help with income for the first 10 years. You can become successful either under 30 or over 45 – in between it is necessary just to keep struggling.

Income will start at £12 an hour for a repetiteur. At the top, income can be £400,000 per annum plus royalties on recordings etc (up to £50,000).

The disadvantages of this career are its lack of work security and depression at having to work with poor orchestras and thus being unable to express oneself. The hours are very long: often starting early in the morning learning or studying scores; travelling to a rehearsal anywhere in the UK; rehearsing all day; followed by an evening concert or meetings with organisers and artistes.

There seem to be few female or coloured conductors in the UK, perhaps because they are not seen as dominant leaders – the quality expected of conductors.

Try and live near the local public library so *Grove's Dictionary of Music*, a book on orchestral timings, and the *BBC Index* are to hand. And read *Music and Musicians*.

Conference Organiser

At a Glance

Qualifications/Training	No	*Income bracket*	Medium–High
Licence	No	*Town/Country*	Town
Experience/Springboard	Essential	*Travel*	Yes
Mid-career entry	Yes	*Exit sale*	Possible
Entry costs	£5,000++	*Work at home*	Yes

Mix and match   Yes.   You could think about: Public relations consultant, Events organiser, List broker, Opening to the public, Hotel keeper . . .

Enquiries   Conference organisers, PR agencies

Business and professional conferences and seminars are thriving – an industry in which professional conference organisers can flourish. Conference organisers act either as principals (taking the financial risk and managing the entire event) or as suppliers of an administrative conference service – running the event directly on behalf of clients or indirectly on contract to the client's PR agency. At the same time, hotels, local authorities, schools, universities, polytechnics and colleges are clamouring for people who will buy their services and hire their amenities. If you have an idea for a conference which people will pay for and the wherewithal to make it worthwhile for them to do so, you can organise your own conference and make money. Usually, the people you book conference accommodation from provide food, refreshments and often hire of equipment. It's up to you to do everything else: organise travel, decide who will speak when, choose a suitable centre and, above all, publicise the conference. You must have some idea of what's involved before you launch out and you need contacts among the people who are likely to attend or contribute towards your conference. Go to a few conferences yourself (see the *Conference Blue Book*) to get an idea of the sort of scheduling you'll have to do; what you can lay on by way of spin-offs (eg books and videos) and as entertainment; ways of encouraging sponsorship from businesses and organisations. Hotel and catering experience (especially if it includes working at large conference hotels and centres) is useful for this especially if you're going to specialise in internal company conferences for clients who can lay on their own speakers and who aren't dependent on external publicity for attendance.

People go to conferences to listen to speakers rather than for free pens and the chance to see London or Cannes by night. That means knowing people who are prominent in major interest groups. Likely areas for this are in higher education or within professional bodies; if you're involved in either of these they may be enthusiastic about your organising a conference under their auspices. Anyone with PR, journalism or marketing experience may have built up a network of suitable speakers and interested participants. You need phenomenal organisational skills coupled with the flair to come up with interesting ideas and the imagination and attention to detail necessary to turn those ideas into successful and enjoyable conferences.

You're going to need some money to start out with. As well as publicising your conference in suitable trade, professional and consumer press or by mailings (lists for which have to be bought, if you don't have your own), you need to book a centre and pay a deposit. Although you can make a provisional booking well in advance without paying a deposit, it's unlikely that you'll be able to whip up enough interest in time to avoid having to finalise the booking (usually about 9 months in advance) before you're sure you've got a full contingent. During very quiet times, you can sometimes negotiate with a centre willing to take a provisional booking rather than nothing at all. Students halls of residence are a lot cheaper (but a lot less comfortable) than hotels and you'll probably get free use of projectors and videos as well (hotels often charge £100+ for this). Conference rates are usually less than normal hotel rates but rooms can cost up to £150 per night with an additional minimum charge of £35 per person per day for food and drinks. The food supplied by hotels at conferences isn't usually the best the kitchens can offer. On top of accommodation costs are the costs of speakers and extras like buses from the station/airport to the centre. You may be able to raise some sponsorship from professional institutions or companies which will use the conference for their own publicity (eg giving commemorative presents). You must be sure you'll be able to charge enough to cover your expenses and make a profit. Don't forget the months of work you've put in when you're calculating how much you want for each day of the conference. Conferences aimed at business may draw a lot of participants whose employers pay the fees; people are more aware of how much a conference costs to attend when they have to pay it themselves. A day's conference including food but no accommodation raises about £75 per participant. It can take 2–3 years of liaising to get speakers and participants to be at the same place at the same time. If you're short of a speaker, PR consultants may be able to provide one from their clients. Schedule everything (including time to cope with the shortage of lavatories in halls of residence; conferences cause constipation). You must meet deadlines. That means

having contingency plans for virtually everything: speakers may be ill
at the last minute so have reserves on hand; coaches break down or fail
to turn up; crises are normal.

Contemporary Art Gallery Owner

At a Glance

Qualifications/Training	No	*Income bracket*	Medium
Licence	No	*Town/Country*	Town
Experience/Springboard	Recommended	*Travel*	No
Mid-career entry	Yes	*Exit sale*	Yes
Entry costs	£20,000+	*Work at home*	No

Mix and match Yes. You could think about: Art historian/critic, Journalist,
   Public relations consultant, Artist . . .

Enquiries Local galleries

Contemporary art galleries are market places for the works of living
artists. Gallery owners sometimes buy works of art outright from artists
but the majority sell on behalf of artists for a commission. Selling
affordable art (anything under about £2,000) is much like many other
kinds of specialist retailing; you've got to know both your market and
your supplier, to be flexible enough to move with both and inspired
enough to develop them. A lot of people are eager to buy the works of
living undiscovered artists either in the hope that they may be making
an investment or because they like the pictures. You may not stand to
make millions on the sale of one painting but neither do you have to
make massive capital outlays in order to get your stock in the first place.

  You don't need any formal qualifications but a knowledge of the art
world is essential; you have to know which artists to use and to have an
idea of how much they should be charging for their work. You should
also be able to talk about art authoritatively to customers and so you
need some idea of the different techniques used as well as some
knowledge of art history. Working in someone else's gallery is a good
way of finding out what you're taking on. Other useful experience (and
a good source of contacts) is working on an art magazine or journal.
Keep up with what's going on by visiting galleries and reading *Galleries*,
Arts Review, *Burlington* etc. You'll need to know how to organise,
promote and put up exhibitions; to have excellent organisational skills,

to keep punctilious records and to be good at dealing with people, whether they are artists unhappy with the way you're displaying their work or demanding customers. You may want to consider having a partner – someone who can advise on the business side of selling art for example. Some of your artists may be registered for VAT so make sure you know about this. Unlike a shop, where stock is displayed until it is sold and deliveries are made whenever they're needed, art galleries operate by mounting exhibitions of the work of one or more artists and releasing the pictures to clients at the end of an exhibition. Shows last about 3–6 weeks and are planned up to 2 years in advance to give the artist time to build up a collection. You have a complete change of stock at the end of every exhibition. Draw up a contract with each artist, stipulating the number of works to be shown and their agreement not to mount any other one-man exhibitions in local galleries in the meantime. Keep a careful log of what the artist brings in and takes out of the gallery.

You need to have the right sort of premises for an art gallery. It helps to be in an area with other galleries and you need enough wall space to hang pictures. The right premises tend to be in expensive areas – surrounded by buyers or somewhere they'll travel to. On top of this you need security and alarms (art galleries aren't popular with everyone and can be the victims of attack) and insurance to cover the art that's in your gallery. If you don't have a partner, you'll have to employ someone to look after the gallery while you're talking to artists, going to exhibitions, etc. Although you don't need to make any capital outlay on the stock itself, you do need to finance the rent, rates, insurance, security, fixtures and fittings, staff and promotion; press releases, invitations, food and wine for exhibition openings, (ultimately, however, you may be able to get some of this through sponsorship from food and wine companies). Although many artists frame their own work you might have to pay for framing of some pictures – make sure you know some good reliable framers. When you're organising an exhibition, make sure that you've got enough value on the wall to make it worth while. Although it's obviously dependent on what you're exhibiting and on how experimental you want to be – some exhibitions sell nothing. If in doubt, price works moderately; you can always increase an artist's prices if he or she sells out. At the end of the day, only good art sells. An 80% sell out is extremely good; it's safer to reckon on about 50%. You can augment your own income by selling prints and cards.

You need to find suppliers. Most established artists already have galleries which they use but there are plenty of lesser known ones desperate to show their work. You can find suitable ones through contacts and through the endless stream of artists who will drop in to the gallery in the hope you may like their work. You may need to advise the artists on how much to charge for their work; this will increase as the artist becomes better known. You'll have to know your own price bracket and may find that you've helped to price an artist out of your market. You should be able to build up a regular clientele; keep a mailing list so you can let them know when you're mounting a new exhibition. Days are long, and there's a lot of paper work keeping tabs on whose work you've got and who wants to buy what (selling the same picture twice isn't impossible if you don't keep careful records). You'll have to change exhibitions regularly, arranging for art to be collected and delivered. This is a very personal business, it's important that the artists you work with trust you (that may mean having to shell out yourself if anything gets stolen) and that customers know that you're likely to have something they like. Busy seasons are at Christmas and in early summer.

Continuity Person

At a Glance

Qualifications/Training	No	*Income bracket*	Medium
Licence	No	*Town/Country*	Town
Experience/Springboard	Yes	*Travel*	Yes
Mid-career entry	Yes	*Exit sale*	No
Entry costs	£100	*Work at home*	No

Mix and match Limited. You could think about: Typist, Market research interviewer . . .

Enquiries ACTT

In film making the continuity person is responsible for seeing that costumes, hairstyles and set designs remain consistent, especially when scenes that are to be only seconds apart on the finished film have been shot out of sequence over several days. Continuity people also keep a log of each day's work, details of each shot, dialogue timing, lenses and any other important information the film crews and editor will need.

There are no formal qualifications but you'll need to have a wide general knowledge of filming and film equipment; how using different lenses affects the shots and how to record camera and set positions. Continuity people do not usually come from film school. The most likely route in is by starting as a secretary in a production company or as a personal assistant to a producer, production manager or director. You'll probably learn more in a small company where there is overlap between different departments and roles and where there are fewer general assistants around to help out at shoots. You need to pick up as much as possible from as many areas of film production as you can. Try and get to shoots where you'll see what happens and pick up contacts who may be useful in future. Continuity people need to be observant and efficient with good eyesight and hearing and the stamina to concentrate all the time. Although they're freelance, they have to be able to work as part of a team.

Your first continuity job will probably come from knowing the right person at the right time. Set up costs are therefore virtually nil but you'll need a telephone and some business cards as work increases and your network of contacts grows. Consider registering with a booking service who will manage your diary for you while you're on the set all day. ACTT minimum rates are about £230–300 per week but you can get more than that.

Continuity people are hired for the duration of a shoot and spend the day on the set keeping an eye on what's going on and making sure that actors limp on the right leg, don't change their accents, etc and that furniture doesn't move. At the end of the day you have to record the duration of each shot, the number of shots filmed and any problems.

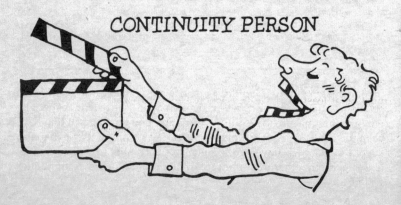

CONTINUITY PERSON

Continuity is responsible and exacting but it is not likely to help you on your way to being a producer; the experience and knowledge that you need as a continuity person takes a long time to accumulate and is far more general and broadbased than the sort of experience that you need for other areas of film production.

Conveyancer

At a Glance

Qualifications/Training	Essential	Income bracket	Medium
Licence	Yes	Town/Country	Town
Experience/Springboard	Essential	Travel	Local
Mid-career entry	Yes	Exit sale	Possible
Entry costs	£5,000	Work at home	Possible

Mix and match   Yes.   You could think about: Surveyor, Estate agent, House converter, Music teacher, Reflexologist . . .
Enquiries   Society of Licensed Conveyancers

Conveyancing is the transfer of land or property rights from one person to another. Licensed conveyancers are qualified to advise buyers and sellers and to transact the conveyance. It's a new profession created by the 1985 Administration of Justice Act; before that the monopoly on conveyancing was held by solicitors and 'certain others' (mainly barristers and public authorities). Currently there aren't many independent licensed conveyancers around (most are employed by solicitors) and there's room for more; especially with the introduction of one-stop house buying, which has encouraged close working contact between estate agents, financial advisers and conveyancers.

All conveyancers must, by law, be licensed members of the COUNCIL FOR LICENSED CONVEYANCERS (CLC). This is the profession's regulatory body, established to set standards and protect consumers especially from unqualified conveyancers practising illegally. To get a licence you must be at least 21, have passed the CLC's two part exam, have two years' practical training in employment with a supervising conveyancer or solicitor and be deemed fit and proper as a licence holder by the CLC. Register as a student with the CLC; this costs £50 and you'll need at least four GCSEs or (if you're over 25) some appropriate work experience. Six months later you're allowed to sit Part I of the exam if you're ready – details on the course and where to take it from the CLC.

CONVEYANCER

Parts I and II can be taken at the same time and you can resit any papers you fail but at least one year of training must be done after passing. If you've got suitable experience you may be exempted from the exams, the training requirement or both. To set up your own firm you need to have been licensed for at least 3 years and, if you want to practise as a limited company, your firm must be a recognised body with the Council. Conveyancing is a legal profession, you'll need to have a general knowledge of the law (tested in part I of the exam) to be able to advise clients on the legal aspects of property ownership. You must pay attention to detail and be patient with clients. House buying is considered one of the most stressful activities people indulge in and you'll probably see some very worried clients. You must also be quick and efficient – when the house market is buoyant, speedy conveyancing can make the difference between buying or losing a house. You'll need an office with a phone, an efficient filing system and computer/ word processor. A photocopier is useful and a fax will speed up communications when you're in a hurry. Charges are made by the hour. Expect an average of about £250 per job. Some conveyancers offer a very cheap £100 fixed fee but it's unlikely that you'll be able to do a very good job for that in most cases. The average charge made by solicitors is more, about £350.

There's an increase in the number of house buyers, many of whom have no experience of employing solicitors and are, therefore, more willing to call on licensed conveyancers. Many clients come through referral; develop contacts at estate agents or busy solicitors. You won't just be needed when someone is buying a house or flat; conveyancers can advise and act in cases of marital breakdown, change of use of premises, mortgages, property development, death. Although it's possible to mix and match this with other jobs, the Council for Licensed Conveyancers lays down the conditions under which you can, for example, practise as both a conveyancer and an estate agent. They are currently looking into ways of including some estate agency in the profession of licensed conveyancer; in the meantime, unless you or one of your partners is a member of the RICS (Royal Institution of Chartered Surveyors) or ISVA (Incorporated Society of Valuers and Auctioneers) you can only work alongside estate agents.

The SOCIETY OF LICENSED CONVEYANCERS aims to increase public awareness of the profession. Contact them and the CLC for further information, or read *Conveyancer and Property Lawyer*.

Corporate Video Producer

At a Glance

Qualifications/Training	Recommended	*Income bracket*	Low–High
Licence	No	*Town/Country*	Town
Experience/Springboard	Recommended	*Travel*	Essential
Mid-career entry	Possible	*Exit sale*	Possible
Entry costs	£2,000	*Work at home*	No

Mix and match Yes. You could think about: In-company trainer, Public relations consultant, Landlord, Private investigator . . .

Enquiries Independent Film, Video and Photography Association

Corporate video is the general term used for video tape or film productions made for businesses, government, or other groups, notably training bodies. They tend to be short but can be of any length and are usually made to sell a corporate image, product or service or simply to inform.

The corporate video producer's job is to co-ordinate all aspects of production from the original idea right through to delivery of the video to the client, on time and within the client's budget. Making videos is primarily a creative process but also a money-making operation, so sympathy for creative ideas, creative people and an aptitude for managerial and business matters is important.

As video producer, you'll obviously be liaising closely with your client; also with the directors, editors, cameramen, all of whom you hire. Members of the video team will look to you for decisions regarding budget, pay, as well as quite trivial matters like where to park their car on the location shoot.

There are no formal qualifications, but obviously a good understanding of video production techniques is necessary. Short introductory production courses are available (look in the *Guardian* or industry press such as *Broadcast*). Working in the industry for a while is another good way to get the necessary experience – joining one of the many corporate production companies as a runner, production assistant, researcher or secretary will teach you the basics. The corporate video market is expanding rapidly with smaller companies increasingly using video for promotions and training. It is easier to get into than film – there are no unions – and more work is available.

If you have the confidence and plenty of ideas about ways of presenting information in words and pictures, all you will need to start with is a phone and the usual business cards etc. Start by approaching local small businesses that you think would benefit from their own video; try community groups and especially local authorities which are increasingly using video.

Having completed a few low budget and simple videos you will have a show reel with which you can tout for more work. Remember that working in any creative field is notoriously difficult as people are often very unclear what it is they want until you produce it and then it may be too late. Be prepared for disappointments; you can avoid them through meticulous planning and good communication with your clients.

Producer's earnings are directly related to the budget which for a corporate video can range from a little under £1,000 to several hundred thousand pounds. How well you do will depend on your ability to find work and the type of work it is. Some videos, eg training films, can be very lucrative if there is a market for copies of the original; anywhere between £10,000 and £20,000 is reasonable.

You will have to work hard for your rewards. Days, especially shoot days, can be very long and you will experience slack periods followed by intense activity. Be prepared to bid for plenty of jobs with the probability of only a fraction coming to you.

Costume Designer

At a Glance

Qualifications/Training	Yes	*Income bracket*	Low–Medium
Licence	No	*Town/Country*	Town
Experience/Springboard	Recommended	*Travel*	Yes
Mid-career entry	Difficult	*Exit sale*	No
Entry costs	£100	*Work at home*	No

Mix and match   Limited.   You could think about: Fashion clothes/hat designer, Artist . . .

Enquiries   ACTT, Broadcasting and Entertainment Trades Alliance, Arts Council

Cutbacks have affected the entertainment industry as much as any other and work is fairly scarce. A costume designer can work in repertory theatre, television or film. It is a tough world and you have to have a vocation and a love of the business to give you the determination to succeed. This is not the job for the home lover or those with family commitments. It is hard work, with long hours, late nights, overtime and last minute crises to sort out. You might have to work through the night to meet deadlines. Your social life will revolve round the others in the production. If you are filming, you may be away from home for weeks, possibly in bad hotels.

Costume designers in repertory are very busy; they usually work out the costume requirements for two plays ahead, while sorting out the daily problems of the current play. In a small company they will probably have to act as dresser and wardrobe mistress as well. For a new production costume details have to be got right with the scenery and lighting in only two days (and probably nights).

In television there may be 12 hour recording days, plus an hour to check all the costumes before the cameras start rolling and an hour to clear up at the end. If, for example, a large ball scene is being shot, there might be hundreds of period costumes to check. You will have the help of a wardrobe staff, an assistant designer, and dressers (who also press and hang clothes up, mend, etc) and the job is to oversee the whole operation. Filming on location brings its own problems, eg small hotel space to prepare costumes and distance from suppliers. While shooting, the designer shares responsibility for continuity; keeping a continuity book and recording what each actor is wearing in every scene, down to the watch and how many buttons are undone. Then if an adjoining scene is shot days later there are no discrepancies between the scenes. A polaroid camera is essential.

Part of the costume designer's function is to be able to manage people and delegate. There is a lot of tension, it's a long day, everyone gets fraught, and tempers can get frayed. The designer is always working under pressure and has to remain calm while ironing out the perpetual small problems.

In addition there is research. You need artistic flair as well as historical knowledge to be able to interpret the scripts and the characters, working closely with the director. You need to work out the costume requirements; how many outfits are needed, cost, and the accurate clothes for a particular character in relation to class, background, and period. For a big show both costume designer and assistant will be working for several weeks before it opens, researching, ordering costumes (hiring, buying or having made), hiring wigs, buying tights and safety pins, taking the measurements of actors, and working out eg whether to double up on costumes that might get damaged in a fight scene.

COSTUME
DESIGNER

You should be a member of BETA (the BROADCASTING AND ENTERTAIN-MENT TRADES ALLIANCE) or ACTT (the ASSOCIATION OF CINEMATOGRAPH TELEVISION AND ALLIED TECHNICIANS) which work out the rates of pay and conditions.

Most designers have a Diploma in Theatre Design from an art college. After that you might get a start in repertory (usually means getting involved in all aspects of production, lighting, props, wardrobe, scene painting, stage management as well as costume design). Or you could become an assistant to a costume designer in television or films. Some people come from a fashion background. The ARTS COUNCIL offer post-graduate Theatre Design Bursaries – the winners are seconded to a theatre for a year and there are post-graduate courses run by eg Margaret Harris at the RIVERSIDE STUDIOS, HAMMERSMITH.

Further reading: The *Stage* is invaluable as a source of information. Also read *Contacts* (publication listing all the theatre companies etc) available from *Spotlight* offices.

Counsellor

At a Glance

Qualifications/Training	Essential	Income bracket	Medium
Licence	No	Town/Country	Town
Experience/Springboard	No	Travel	None
Mid-career entry	Essential	Exit sale	No
Entry costs	£500	Work at home	Yes

Mix and match   Excellent.   You could think about: Orchestral musician, Cabinet maker, Gardener/garden designer . . .
Enquiries   British Association of Counsellors

Counsellors give their clients regular periods of time when, in complete confidence, they support and help the clients work through their personal or emotional problems and discover more satisfactory ways of living and relating to others. They give their clients uncritical regard, empathy and insight and, through their psychological training and awareness, help the client to fulfil their potential as a human being.

To enter one of the many training courses (full or part time) recognised by the BRITISH ASSOCIATION OF COUNSELLORS (BAC) (RELATE have their own), you need to be over 30, and to have had a broad life experience. Educational qualifications don't matter so much as a good natural intelligence, emotional stability, intuition, common sense, sense of humour and a fascination with other people. Most important is an ability to be unjudgmental and to communicate with others. Counsellors work in educational, medical, industrial and pastoral settings. As well as learning psychological theory on your course, you have to be prepared to grow and develop emotionally which can at times be quite painful. You need to be well motivated, and on some courses receive psychotherapy (which can cost as much as £20 a session). There is a dearth of good counsellors in many areas. The BAC insist that counsellors should always be supervised by a psychotherapist or experienced counsellor at least once a month to retain a healthy, balanced view of themselves and their job.

You can start your practice in a quiet room in your home as soon as you are qualified. Let local GPs know you exist. You need a phone which you can turn off, and an answerphone and lockable filing cabinet. Make sure that you are properly insured. A session lasts 50 minutes and rates vary from £10 to £25. You can do another job at the same time and it's possible to fix clients' appointments at a mutually satisfactory time, often outside working hours. It's important to balance counselling with a rich personal life. The good part of this job is that it is never boring if you are interested in and enjoy helping people to help themselves. The bad points are that it needs enormous energy and concentration so it's quite exhausting and if you work within your home, be careful to keep your work separate from the family. There is a heavy bias towards people who are mature with plenty of life experience.

Get more information from the BRITISH ASSOCIATION OF COUNSELLORS. Also read *On Being A Counsellor* and *Individual Therapy in Britain*.

Courier Service

At a Glance

Qualifications/Training	No	*Income bracket*	Low–High
Licence	No	*Town/Country*	Town
Experience/Springboard	No	*Travel*	No
Mid-career entry	Excellent	*Exit sale*	Possible
Entry costs	£1,000+	*Work at home*	No
Mix and match Limited. You could think about: Novelist, Inventor . . .			
Enquiries Courier companies			

Couriers on foot or horseback were used to carry messages for thousands of years. Much of this job has changed with quicker transport, telephones and radios, fax, telex and computers. But couriers are still much in demand, especially in town centres where they are used to carry a variety of documents and parcels for distances of a few hundred yards to thousands of miles. Courier service companies liaise between customers and couriers who may be motor cycle messengers, bicycle messengers, van drivers, and aeroplane passengers. Their job is to get couriers to where they're needed. People use couriers either because the alternatives (eg postal service or railway) are too slow, or because they are sending something of value. This means that couriers have to be fast, reliable and trustworthy.

You don't need any formal qualifications to set up a courier service. You will, however, need to know your area of operation extremely well, not just the street names and lengths, but normal traffic conditions, one way systems and anything else that may affect journey times for your couriers. Couriers use various forms of transport – usually motorbikes, with vans for larger commissions. Even though you won't necessarily be doing much of the couriering yourself, it helps if you can drive these. In places with very heavy traffic, or for very short distances, you may also want to use bicycles. For couriering overseas, you'll have to use airports and airlines. You may get business collecting parcels and documents from your nearest airport for delivery but, if you're going to offer a full courier service overseas, you'll have to get hold of air tickets at very short notice. Most of this business is done by large companies for whom it's easier to get the necessary airline co-operation. You'll have to cope with people who are probably under pressure and in a hurry; this means being calm and organised.

To set up you'll need a telephone that has to be manned all day, and some couriers: use contacts or advertise. Couriers usually provide their own bikes or vans, but they'll need to have extra insurance cover for couriering (some companies arrange this for them). You'll need radio phones (some companies rent these to couriers) so that you don't have to be based centrally. Base your charges on local competition; couriers are paid on commission so, if you undercut too much, you won't be able to pay them properly – it's better to compete with good service. Payment is made either when the courier collects the parcel, or on account for regular customers. Most of your customers will be local businesses; you get them by advertising and coming up with the goods. Think up a name for your company that implies speed and efficiency and use your couriers as mobile bill boards. Use the Yellow Pages and leaflet drops. Once you've pleased a new customer, the chances are they'll use you again.

Criminal

At a Glance

Qualifications/Training	No	*Income bracket* Low–High
Licence	No	*Town/Country* Either
Experience/Springboard	No	*Travel* Maybe
Mid-career entry	Yes	*Exit sale* No
Entry costs	Nil	*Work at home* Possible
Mix and match . . .		
Enquiries NACRO		

If you like the idea of working in a highly charged atmosphere laden with potential overnight riches, you may want to consider a life outside the law. The hours (although they can be anti-social) are flexible and you won't have to spend much on taxes. In addition, you stand to capture the public imagination and to join the ranks of Robin Hood, Zorro, the Great Train Robbers and other legendary figures. There are many opportunities for permanent positions, especially for anyone who is an expert. Alternatively, if you prefer variety, you can float through a wide range of fields as a general hand or apprentice. Entry qualifications are virtually nil – a bit of bottle will usually suffice. In so far as any endeavour can be subverted by the darker side of the force, the criminal mind is forever busy. However, it is also predictably banal. Criminals are a rather dull bunch; a fact that belies the myth and underscores the point that true professionals are as rare in this walk of life as in any other. Perhaps more so because they are nearly impossible to find – and they never talk about their work, no matter how much they may want to boast about their successes and achievements. Set up costs can be minimal; unless you want to specialise in, for example, violent crime or safe breaking, there is no essential equipment for a life of crime. Contacts can be a great help both as sources of work and for expert advice. Finding the right contacts, however, is a difficult and risky job; maintaining their loyalty once you've found them is virtually impossible. The more people involved in a crime the thinner the proceeds have to be spread and the greater the risk of being arrested, tried, convicted and sent to prison. There are currently 50,000 Britons in UK prisons (ask NACRO). The courts dispense lumps of bird like it's lunch and sentences tend to stick. An award of over 5 years lessens your chances for first time parole (after ⅓ of the sentence); if the offence involved drugs or violence then you are likely to serve ⅔ of your sentence; use of a gun gets you at least an 8-year stretch, and stash

CRIMINAL

away or spend much of the loot and you're up to 10. Most convicted drug dealers end up in Victorian playpens devoid of basic sanitation; spend 23 hours a day banged up in dark dank cells with three furtive slop outs a day. You're likely to have had about 15 months of this between arrest and conviction – bail is far from probable. For some, spells in prison become a way of life – something to be sought out as a break from the stresses of life outside. The system seems geared towards making it easy to get back into prison once you're out. As a rough indication of how likely you are to be a successful criminal, see how many of the following points apply to you:

So far, circumstances have prevented you from succeeding in a variety of situations, eg, job, business, love, school. You are an avid gambler and the excitement of the race track appeals to you. You win almost any argument you enter. You prefer activities of a short rather than a long duration. You like people to be aware of your achievements. You can (and do) drink more alcohol than most people. You are seldom wrong. You can usually justify your actions in terms of what others have said or done to you. You like to be aware of where you stand with everyone you meet. You aren't afraid of more than casual use of soft drugs and can handle moderate amounts of hard ones. You have little time for people whose views are dissimilar to your own. You are aware that some people don't expect you to succeed in life and have set out to prove them wrong. You have a long memory for events that have displeased you.

If you answered with mostly 'yes' then avoid crime; prisons are full of people like you.

That's the down beat. Where then are the successful, professional criminals? To be one you need excruciating self-discipline, extreme emotional stability, self-motivation and intelligence. You need to be able to work coolly and efficiently without others noticing or without any public recognition of your immense abilities. If you really do have what it takes to make it in the field of crime then your prospects for success are so good that you don't belong in it – the world's your oyster anyway. So turn back to the table of contents and choose something else.

Dancer

At a Glance			
Qualifications/Training	Necessary	Income bracket	Low
Licence	No	Town/Country	Town
Experience/Springboard	No	Travel	Lots
Mid-career entry	No	Exit sale	No
Entry costs	£200	Work at home	Limited
Mix and match	Yes.	You could think about: Dance teacher, Bartender, Typist, Book editor . . .	
Enquiries	Dance Forum		

Most dancers are self employed and work under contract for companies – some accept only very short term contracts and move around a lot. Dancers tend to specialise in one field of dance (ballet, contemporary, modern, jazz etc) and different disciplines are required for each of these. Competition for jobs is stiff; most dance in the corps or chorus with few opportunities to be a principal or soloist. Not many make it to the top and the drop out rate is high. Most dancers stop performing in their late 30's or early 40's and move into choreography, teaching, administration or into something completely different. Many dancers are prone to accident and injury partly due to limited awareness of practice and training techniques especially when compared to athletes.

You'll need to train, preferably with an accredited school in your chosen field of dance – see *Dance Theatre Journal*. Ballet dancers normally start at 6 or 7 (although boys can start later – at 12 or 14). Jazz, contemporary and modern dancers usually start by the time they are 18, although some decide to train as performers later eg after taking a degree course in dance. Training is expensive and you will have to take classes even when you are unemployed just to keep in shape for auditions. You'll need an EQUITY card to have access to a lot of auditions. Sometimes 'spare' Equity cards are available for productions and these are given to any non-members whose exceptional talent the company wants to promote.

You'll need to provide your own practice clothes and shoes, which wear out quickly and are sometimes difficult to find; some companies subsidise these while you're working. Earnings are paltry: a corps member in a major company gets about £100–130 a week, £70–100 in smaller companies. Soloists get more, £160–180 per week – up to about £100,000 per annum plus the perks that come with mega-stardom. You'll need an accountant and also an agent.

A lot of work comes via agents who are told of 'closed' (Equity only) auditions when they come up. Other auditions are listed in the *Stage* or on dance studio notice boards. Contracts may be for a year, a season or for the run of a production. They are somewhat one-sided, you'll have great difficulty getting out of your commitment but companies tend to

DANCER

pay only their top performers for broken contracts; so, if a show flops, you could be out of work very quickly. If you trained with a good school or one which is attached to a dance company, it's easier to find work, also if you can sing or have other talents that may be useful on stage.

Dancing is an international area and you may be able to work abroad for a foreign company. In some countries, though, you'll have to be pretty exceptional to justify getting a work permit. Otherwise you can tour with a British company – not as glamorous as it may sound; this usually involves a lot of bus travel, living in cramped, grotty hotels and dancing in run-down theatres. You may get time to explore if you're lucky.

It is an arduous way of life requiring complete dedication and constant training and practice. Be prepared for periods of unemployment and to have to travel to find work sometimes. Injuries may prevent you from dancing but there are stories of dancers failing to recover properly from injuries and going on with broken toes and painkillers. Rheumatism and arthritis are rife among ex-dancers. Hours are long, with classes, rehearsals and performances; there is little free time and little social life outside the company. Being under contract to a company means fitting in with their requirements and whims, and it may take a long time to get the sort of role you find interesting. For some the commitment required is limiting and the sense of being a piece of company property dispiriting; in general this is harder for people who come late to dancing. There is some encouragement in the thrill dancers get from performing to an appreciative audience and from the close friendships that build up in the company.

Contact DANCE FORUM for advice and information on courses and resources for dancers.

Dance Teacher

At a Glance

Qualifications/Training	Essential	*Income bracket*	Low
Licence	No	*Town/Country*	Town
Experience/Springboard	Recommended	*Travel*	Local
Mid-career entry	Possible	*Exit sale*	No
Entry costs	£200	*Work at home*	No

Mix and match   Yes.   You could think about: Dancer, Typist, Market research interviewer . . .

Enquiries   Council for Dance Education and Training

If you're thinking of becoming a dance teacher it's probably because you're in love with dancing or because you're a professional dancer who isn't trained to do anything else. Whatever your standard as a dancer you'll certainly need some formal training to teach, as well as a thorough grounding in music notation, anatomy, etc. Whether you plan to teach spring points to tiny tots or kicksteps to troopers, to make any real headway you'll need a decent qualification. Otherwise some options will be closed to you altogether – teaching ballet to schools, for example; and if you're setting out on your own, you won't find the right openings or attract the pupils – the competition is too great.

The full works probably means a three-year, full-time course, (contact the COUNCIL FOR DANCE EDUCATION AND TRAINING for accredited colleges and courses), though shorter-term alternatives are available such as a one-year teaching certificate for professional dancers. Good courses are not by any means restricted to classical ballet but also include modern theatre dance, jazz, contemporary and other disciplines.

Many people's first move on qualifying is to join a school staff (in the UK or overseas) for a year or two to build up some form and teaching practice. If and when you're ready to go your own way, you can start by hunting around the dance centres looking for empty slots in their timetables – the better the centre, of course, the harder it will be to get in and to begin with you'll probably be offered all the worst hours.

Typically, you'll be offered a medium size room, to hold around 15 dancers, with some music facilities such as a piano and a tape player; the dance centre may offer to supply or refer you to a pianist, if you don't know one. You can use tapes but many teachers find while they're hunting for the appropriate track, the class will lose concentration completely. Some teachers think even a mediocre pianist is far better than none, others find records and tapes they know well are a better (and cheaper) solution.

The hours in this job are not too unnatural, though early evening and Saturdays tend to be busy. It can be quite tiring physically, but as a dancer you're trained for that. Brilliant dancers are not necessarily good teachers; the most important qualities are probably enthusiasm and temperament, especially working with children. You need dedication because the rewards are not great and can be a long time in coming. You could aspire eventually to work with a good school or be attached to a ballet or theatre company. If you're *very* successful you could make £15,000 pa but this is unusual.

Read *Dancing Times* and *Dance and Dancers*.

Dealer in Large Antiques

At a Glance

Qualifications/Training	Available	*Income bracket*	Low–High
Licence	No	*Town/Country*	Town/Village
Experience/Springboard	Recommended	*Travel*	Essential
Mid-career entry	Excellent	*Exit sale*	Yes
Entry costs	£10,000+++	*Work at home*	Possible

Mix and match   Yes. You could think about: Dealer in small antiques and collectibles, Man with a van, Art historian/critic, Antique furniture restorer, Book packager, Beekeeper, MP . . .

Enquiries   London and Provincial Antique Dealers' Association

Large antique dealing includes furniture, statuary and masonry like fireplaces. Antiques dealing runs the gamut from rinky-dink Bond Street showrooms to smelly junk shops or aircraft-hangar-style 'Antiques Warehouses'. Antique dealing is ostensibly a very attractive riff. No obstacles to anyone becoming a dealer – you can build it up from part-time or collecting as long as you've got enough specialist knowledge to buy and sell. To trade independently on any serious level you need knowledge of current prices and adequate capital as well as historical and artistic know-how.

To be a dealer, you have to study the market; the best way to learn is by working in the trade with a dealer or in auction rooms, coping with prices, pieces and punters. Ideally you should also get involved in selling for the complete picture. A good visual memory is a valuable asset, as is an eye for shape and colour – a good eye or informed observation connected with your visual memory, which has a great deal to do with taste. You can cultivate it to an extent and it grows with experience. Knowledge of foreign languages, especially French, German or Italian, is useful for buying and selling and you'll need to be able to bargain because prices aren't fixed.

Fine/decorative arts courses are available but they are expensive and often over-subscribed; you can read and go to lectures or evening classes. But there's no substitute for going around, looking at antiques in museums and country houses, then visiting antique shops and auction rooms where the sheer volume of things passing through gives you an idea of price and how to handle antiques. Auction room experience also helps you to build up contacts and a track record. Membership of a regulatory organisation such as the LONDON AND PROVINCIAL ANTIQUE DEALERS' ASSOCIATION gives you the necessary credibility to sell to other dealers or into the valuable American market; getting on with other dealers is important. Anonymous faces are viewed with suspicion in this business – you might have nicked your stock – so make sure that people know who you are and don't be secretive about your address and phone number. Likewise, you should trust no-one you don't know. Don't buy anything that's been stolen – if you do, you have to hand it back to the owner and risk being done for handling stolen property. You also have to contend with being robbed yourself; nicking large antiques may not be easy, but a lot of people manage it and insurance premiums are too prohibitive to make comprehensive theft cover feasible.

Your real concern must be to ensure adequate finance – first, to get the right premises (the appropriate location is vital), then to purchase, maintain and keep purchasing stock even if weeks go by without any business. If you're raising a loan, remember that banks like to see impressive credentials. For big antiques you need big premises, unless you opt to 'run', that is to buy stock and sell it straight away to other dealers. For this you'll need a van or lorry but you won't need a massive stock. Once you're known, you may be able to take things on spec although people will go off you if you keep bringing things back, unsold. You'll also have to finance getting the stock.

You may need to pay somebody else to man the shop while you go buying or use a trucking company to transport your stock (they aren't cheap). Useful contacts (as well as other dealers) include truckers, restorers and runners who scour the country for pieces that you may

ANTIQUES

not be able to find yourself. It helps if you know the tastes of dealers and customers so that you know where to try and place a specific piece.

There are two main ways of buying, either from auction houses like Christie's, or by hiking up and down the country exhausted and looking like something the cat brought in, attending auctions. In winter this means leaving before it gets light – driving for miles to a dismal sale in a cow-shed, where there's bugger all you actually want, and everybody is chasing the few pieces remotely worth having – all in the hope that you may be lucky. You have to know your place in the antiques chain. This means other people may make more money from some of your finds than you made – until you get close to the top yourself. Most of the time (about 70%), your business is going to be with other dealers who'll go on about 'what's good for the trade' when they're trying to make you drop your price. Rings of dealers conspiring to force sale prices down at auctions are illegal but beware of knockers who upset the market by buying their stock directly from (often country) houses at well below market value. You have to be good at the trading side, but more important you have to be good at buying, selling and haggling. If it irritates you, you might just as well run a shoe shop where everything is at recommended retail price – 'take it or leave it, squire'.

Dealer in Small Antiques and Collectibles

At a Glance

Qualifications/Training	Available	Income bracket	Low–High
Licence	No	Town/Country	Town/Village
Experience/Springboard	Recommended	Travel	Yes
Mid-career entry	Excellent	Exit sale	Possible
Entry costs	£500++	Work at home	No

Mix and match   Yes. You could think about: Dealer in large antiques, Art historian/critic, Picture restorer, Interior designer, Illustrator . . .

Enquiries   London and Provincial Antique Dealers' Association

You can drift into dealing. Depending on what you want to make of it, it can be as large or small a business as you like. Opportunities for selling and buying range from car boot sales to big London auction houses. If you've got a lot of energy and enthusiasm you should be able to find a niche somewhere.

There are no formal qualifications. You'll need to know your stuff whatever that is; it helps to have some basic abilities such as telling silver from plate, recognising different woods and gemstones. A lot of this comes from experience, talking to customers and colleagues, browsing in museums and auction rooms. You can deal generally in small antiques and bric-a-brac; or you can specialise in almost anything – clocks, Victorian jewellery, boxes, 1920s clothes, stamps, oriental ceramics. . . .

As well as liking old things, antique dealers should enjoy bargain hunting – success depends on getting more than you paid for things. You can't be clumsy – breakages do happen and can be financially disastrous because it's seldom worth shouldering the massive costs of insurance.

Car boot sales are an inexpensive way of starting up (a pitch costs about £5 per day) and you don't need much stock. In large towns there are regular outdoor antiques markets. These cost £5–12 per day and you can book a regular pitch there through the local authority. Antique fairs (in hotels etc) cost about £20–30 per day. Details of these from the trade press, in particular the *Antiques Trade Gazette*. Otherwise you can rent a space in a permanent covered market (especially common in London and tourist areas). This is cheaper than a shop, and also means that advertising costs can be shared and groups of traders in the market can organise a rota to man the stalls, allowing more time for buying. Rent for these varies depending on size and location (perhaps £40 a week including heating, lighting etc). Unlike some other small retailers, antique dealers flourish by being close to competition because this creates an increased antique buying traffic. Many customers buy things they like the look of rather than being serious collectors. There are exceptions especially at annual antique fairs which attract a lot of trade business. Stock comes from other dealers, auctions and people bringing things in. There is a chain of antique dealing: pieces being bought for a fiver in a flea market, going through several dealers and ending up at auction. As long as you don't mislead your customers, by selling old china as Ming dynasty, you can charge what you like. But anything that appears in a price guide will be difficult to sell for any more. Auctions provide pricing guidelines. In general, working to 100% mark up is safe – some finds will allow you to make a lot more. This tends to be a cash in hand business.

If you get your hands on pieces that are worth more than you could get from your usual market, sell them through an auction room. The value of an antique is equal to what you can sell it for; you'll learn how to tell how much that is through experience.

Keeping abreast of the trade is essential. Visit other shops and dealers to get an idea of how prices and fashions are fluctuating. Small antiques tend not to be things that people buy because they're useful and unfashionable ones are difficult to move. Of the masses of publications around, the most useful include *The Antique Dealers' and Collectors' Guide* and *Miller's Professional Antique Price Guide*. There are also a lot of specialist publications. Trade organisations include the LONDON AND PROVINCIAL ANTIQUE DEALERS' ASSOCIATION.

Dental Practice Broker

At a Glance

Qualifications/Training	Recommended	*Income bracket*	Medium
Licence	No	*Town/Country*	Town, preferably
Experience/Springboard	Useful	*Travel*	Yes
Mid-career entry	Yes	*Exit sale*	Possible
Entry costs	£5,000	*Work at home*	Possible

Mix and match Yes. You could think about: Surveyor, Estate agent, Conveyancer, Dealer in antiques, Beekeeper . . .

Enquiries Dental practice brokers

Dental practice brokers organise the sale or leasing of dental practices, premises (including attached living areas) and equipment. They also help and advise dentists who are looking for partners or partnerships to join. The work is a mixture of selling and offering specialist advice. There are opportunities for firms to deal exclusively with dental practices but most are attached to estate agents, chartered surveyors or insurance brokers.

There are no formal qualifications for dental practice brokers but to make anything of it you'll need to qualify as a surveyor through the ROYAL INSTITUTION OF CHARTERED SURVEYORS. Estate agency experience is useful – you'll have to know how to advertise and sell property. Developing the more specialist ability required to evaluate dental practices comes with time, helped by keeping an eye on dental exhibitions and catalogues. You'll need the selling ability for the property market – perseverance and persistence coupled with a convincing appearance, knowledge of values and potential problems with areas and types of building.

Actual set up costs needn't be great. You can operate from home. You'll need a telephone, business cards, office stationery and a car, your area of operation may be quite extensive and clients may want you to find a practice for them in a distant part of the country. So you'll spend a lot of time on the phone. You're likely to have cash flow problems. You're paid on commission once you've sold a practice and completion may take 6 months; you're not paid at all if you fail. That means you'll have to shoulder the costs for advertising the practice, circulating particulars, showing potential buyers around etc. Valuations and other services are charged for separately. There's a lot of work involved and returns aren't massive. Set up with enough money to keep yourself for a year.

A lot of business comes via word of mouth. Dentists are useful contacts, not only as clients but because, although you don't need to know about dentistry itself, the more you know about the needs of dentists and the running of dental practices, the better. A lot of your clients will know all about mouths but not have much idea of what's involved in running a business. Keep in touch with this network by circulating them with particulars of properties you have in your books. The wider the geographical area you cover the more business you should be able to drum up but broking practices abroad can lead to problems with currency regulations. Add to this network by advertising in the *British Dental Journal*.

You have to value the property and also the equipment and the practice. The practice is valued according to its goodwill, based on patients' records, NHS schedules and accounts. It gives only an approximation because it's affected by the reputation and popularity of the dentist. Dental practice brokers, with relevant RICS qualifications can be called on to arbitrate in disputes between dentists, to review rents and leases of practices and, rarely, as expert witnesses in court.

Dental Technician

At a Glance

Qualifications/Training	Recommended	*Income bracket*	Medium
Licence	Not yet	*Town/Country*	Town
Experience/Springboard	Essential	*Travel*	Local
Mid-career entry	Unlikely	*Exit sale*	Yes
Entry costs	£65,000	*Work at home*	Unlikely

Mix and match Limited. You could think about: Goldsmith/silversmith/ jeweller, Illustrator . . .

Enquiries National Joint Council for the Craft of Dental Technicians

Dental technicians are contracted by dentists to make false teeth, bridges, plates, braces and other dental appliances for their patients. Technicians also repair broken appliances. Most of their work is done in small laboratories usually run by themselves or in partnership with one or two other technicians.

There is no official register although the NATIONAL JOINT COUNCIL FOR THE CRAFT OF DENTAL TECHNICIANS is working on one. Most technicians take a BTEC diploma following a 4-year course and then a year's experience working in a dental laboratory. Alternatively, the traditional way in is through serving a three year apprenticeship. In either case, some experience of working for a lab is essential before you set up on your own.

This is a delicate craft, no two commissions will be alike and all have to be made by hand. You'll have to be painstaking and accurate with a good eye for colour (mistakes are bad for business). You'll also need technical knowledge of how to operate specialist equipment and how to work with a wide range of material: gold, porcelain, plastics etc.

Set up costs are massive. As well as premises, telephone etc, you need up to £50,000 worth of equipment, furnaces (about £3,000), ultrasonic cleaner, polishing lathes, casting machine etc. Materials can be bought as required from dental suppliers. The dentist is your client and will pay you for each job you do. You set the fees for private work; the NHS sets it for anything you do for them and although you can undercut their rates you can't charge any more.

Build up your clientele through contact with dentists – try an initial mailing to start. Your business will build up by word of mouth and you can advertise in the *British Dental Journal* and others if you want to expand. About 10–12 dentists should produce enough work to support a two technician partnership. You get a completion date with each job giving you about 10 working days. Most of the time you can work to a fairly regular schedule, some times are busier than others (for some reason the lead up to Christmas is one), and you may have to deal with some emergency repairs when teeth are required by the following day. Small labs serve predominantly private patients who, having opted to pay for treatment, expect particularly reliable and prompt service.

Dentist

At a Glance

Qualifications/Training	Essential	*Income bracket*	Medium–High
Licence	Yes	*Town/Country*	Town
Experience/Springboard	No	*Travel*	None
Mid-career entry	Highly unlikely	*Exit sale*	Yes
Entry costs	Highly variable	*Work at home*	Possible

Mix and match   Yes.   You could think about: Inventor, Jazz musician/singer, Landlord, Dealer in antiques . . .

Enquiries   British Dental Association

The dental profession is becoming over-subscribed and more time and effort is now spent on preventive dentistry than artistic reconstructions.

To practise as a dentist, you must by law be registered with the GENERAL DENTAL COUNCIL and to achieve this you must be trained. In the UK you can take the 4 year degree course at one of about 18 schools of dentistry (all part of universities – see *The Student Book*). You will need respectable A levels to get in, as well as having the necessary aptitude for the job, which includes manual dexterity, precision, good general health, reasonable eyesight and an understanding of the human race (the same treatment may not be applicable to the labourer with little concern for his appearance as to the model). One year trainee schemes in general practice are now being introduced. If you prefer, you can join one of the armed services and be paid to be trained.

Most dentists work in general practice and there is the choice of joining an existing practice or setting up on your own – although only the foolhardy would set up on their own the day after graduation. All practitioners are self-employed – even in the NHS, the contract is between dentist and patient for a course of treatment and ends when the treatment ends.

Practices may be wholly private or within the National Health Service, or a mixture. Private practitioners fix the fees which they charge the patient; the NHS sets out a scale of fees, part of which are recoverable by the dentist from the patient and part from the NHS. This is time consuming and there are rules and regulations covering the materials and the treatment available under the NHS. Some forms of treatment require prior approval. For 1986/87 the NHS recommended a target net income for general practitioners of £21,700. Those in private practice may be able to earn substantially more (up to twice that), depending on the local population's wealth – and of course interest in teeth.

Unlike doctors, dentists can open up shop anywhere. It's up to you to make sure you'll have some customers. To start up your own practice involves finding and equipping a surgery. The cost of premises will depend on local prices (you will need planning permission unless you use a room in your house or take over an existing practice). Equipment will cost £10,000–£30,000. Second-hand equipment is possible.

To join an existing firm, read the *British Dental Journal* (the journal of the BRITISH DENTAL ASSOCIATION), or go through dental practice brokers. There are a variety of financial arrangements: associates pay a percentage of their income to their principals; partners pay their share of the overheads or may buy a share of the practice.

Each practice will need access to a source of materials and a range of staff (dental nurses, hygienists) and facilities such as labs and X-ray equipment but these may be shared by even the most respectable West End practices. If you are in the NHS you are at liberty to buy your equipment and materials where you choose. You should assume the annual overheads for a one-man practice are between £25,000–£40,000 at 1987 prices. NHS practices are subject to inspection of the premises and scrutiny of proposed treatment plans. You are allowed to advertise discreetly.

Your hours are under your own control. There are not at the moment any anti-social hours required although the possibility may be afoot for some occasional weekend and evening cover on a rota basis within an area. You must enjoy people, although you will have the ideal method of gagging chatty patients!

Also worth reading may be the *Dentist* and *Dental Practice*.

Dietary Therapist

At a Glance

Qualifications/Training	Essential	*Income bracket*	Low–Medium
Licence	Yes from 1992	*Town/Country*	Town
Experience/Springboard	No	*Travel*	Local
Mid-career entry	Possible	*Exit sale*	No
Entry costs	£1,000	*Work at home*	Yes

Mix and match   Yes.   You could think about: Yoga teacher, Journalist, Potter . . .
Enquiries   Dietary Therapy Society

Dietary therapists prescribe diets and dietary supplements to treat and prevent illness. They may also use naturopathic techniques such as enemas and water treatments and are complementary to many other areas of alternative medicine. Dietary therapy is an holistic therapy (it aims to treat the whole person rather than merely suppressing the symptoms of disease), and may be successful in patients where years of conventional medicine has failed. It can be used to treat all sorts of health problems: mental or physical; chronic or degenerative. As the number of cases of illness increases that conventional medicine hasn't yet learnt how to deal with (for example ME), more and more people are investigating alternative medicines.

DIETARY
THERAPIST

Currently dietary therapists practice under common law, ie they need not be registered. This is set to change in 1992 and, at the moment, DTs are seeking EEC validation along with other alternative therapists. In the meantime, you're strongly advised to join the DIETARY THERAPY SOCIETY. For this you need a diploma (which can be taken by correspondence with the addition of some clinical experience) from the COLLEGE OF DIETARY THERAPY. The college also runs advanced courses for practising dietary therapists. You can do this straight after A-levels so long as you have some science background but very young therapists may have problems establishing credibility without the sort of worldliness people expect of someone who's telling them how to lead their lives. For this reason, lots of people take up dietary therapy after they've worked at other things. Dietary therapists must like and be interested in other people. They have to be good listeners and able to read between the lines of what people are saying. Many therapists have been through some health or emotional trauma themselves and so are able to understand and empathise with patients. You'll find it easier not to become too emotionally involved with your patients as time goes on. The success of dietary therapy depends on patients persevering and taking responsibility for their own health, and so you'll have to be very enthusiastic and committed about it even if it means never eating another hamburger.

You can practise from home but this may be too isolated – you want as high a profile as possible to keep up a good supply of patients. Renting a room at an alternative or natural health centre is probably the best way of doing this though it can be expensive. You'll need a telephone and answering machine, some sort of filing system and a couple of chairs. Much diagnosis can be done by iridology (the examination of the iris) and if you use this method, you'll need some eye examining equipment. It's a good idea to get some cards and leaflets printed to explain some of the basics of dietary therapy to your patients. You can get insurance (essential in case one of your patients has a very bad reaction to your prescriptions) via the DIETARY THERAPY SOCIETY.

Your first meeting with a new patient will probably last about 1½ hours because you need to get a complete history (medical, family and personal) before you're able to prescribe a diet. After that patients come back every 6–8 weeks for about 45 minutes consultation. When you're working out a scale of charges, allow for some free time between consultations – this is demanding work and you've got to give patients your full attention. London prices are around £25 for the first and £15 for subsequent consultations. You may be able to earn some money from running or working on short residential courses; cookery demonstrations; lecturing or consultancy for restaurants wanting to offer healthier options on their menus. Many patients come through referral from other patients and alternative practitioners (rarely from GPs), which is why being in a centre with others is useful. Also, although the Dietary Therapy Society code forbids you from advertising yourself, a natural health centre can and this helps to bring people in to you. Your patients will be of all ages and conditions. Some will continue to consult you for ages, others will drop out quickly when they find it impossible to keep to the diet that you prescribe – many people have difficulty accepting responsibility for their own health and expect you to make them better on your own. It can be immensely satisfying to see a chronically ill patient recover and improvements are often noticeable very quickly. During the early stages of the cleansing process that dietary therapy causes, it is possible for patients to have violent reactions while their bodies adjust so you should be on call for any emergencies. Evenings after office hours are busy times of day and spring can be a slightly busier time of year (everyone goes on self-improvement binges). Holidays need forward planning; make sure your patients know in advance. You may want to find a locum who can give a few consultations (while paying your rent); this isn't ideal because the locum will have to be very familiar with each case history before they can be much use. It's useful to know about other therapies which may help your patients; the *Journal of Alternative and Complementary Medicine* and *Here's Health* are useful sources for this and also for keeping you in touch with developments in your own field.

Direct Marketing Agent

At a Glance

Qualifications/Training	Useful	*Income bracket*	Medium–High
Licence	No	*Town/Country*	Town
Experience/Springboard	Essential	*Travel*	Yes
Mid-career entry	Yes	*Exit sale*	Possible
Entry costs	£1,000+	*Work at home*	Possible

Mix and match   Yes.   You could think about: List broker, Sales agent, Marketing consultant, Exhibition designer, Photojournalist . . .

Enquiries   British Direct Mail Producers Association

Direct marketing involves selling products and services directly to the final customer, rather than selling through wholesalers and retailers. Direct marketing agencies act as the direct marketing sales specialists for suppliers of a wide range of industrial and consumer goods and services. This is done through advertisements in the press, radio, television and specialist press and by direct mail shots or telephone sales. Direct marketing agencies often do the work of a marketing department for client companies which are too small to have their own: planning, designing and writing projects, advising on whom to contact and how, chasing up material etc. For larger companies they act as consultants, on specific products or problems. Success depends on having good ideas and the confidence to put them forward. This is an expanding industry, having doubled in size during the last 5 years (approximately £500 million spent on it per annum). Direct sales now make up 10% of Britain's retail spending and there are a lot of opportunities for small companies or partnerships particularly if they specialise.

There are no formal qualifications necessary but a marketing diploma is useful. The Post Office runs short introductory courses on direct marketing, as do other companies like FERRARY (who publish *Direct Mail Magazine*). Marketing experience is essential. At least a year spent in a fairly small marketing department gives an overview of the business (better than working for a large agency where jobs are specialised and you won't get experience of certain areas). Set up costs aren't great. You need a telephone, an answering machine, and a word processor. You don't need an office if you're prepared to visit clients or take them out. Have enough money to live on for at least six months – even if you start with a lot of work, there may be cash flow problems. Large companies are often slow to pay up and you may have to pay your suppliers before you've been paid yourself.

What you charge is based on the time and costs you expect to spend on the agreed project. Clients will use you for a specific job (rather than running advertising agency style accounts) so you need to establish a reputation to ensure a sufficient supply of work. If you do good work, you will find yourself recommended to new clients by existing ones.

Contacts are all important. Sources of work are everywhere, so carry business cards with you all the time ('You're never off duty in this business'). Useful contacts are designers, printers, mailing houses, list-brokers, telephone sales bureaux and anyone else you can sub-contract to. Using freelancers rather than full time staff gives greater flexibility and a choice of different styles as well as cutting down on overheads. Build up a portfolio which you can use in the early days to encourage new clients. Once you are better known, touting for custom must be more subtle. Get onto as many mailing lists as possible (AA, Reader's Digest) to keep you in touch with developments ('Change in style of one of the big mailing companies indicates something!'). Join the BRITISH DIRECT MAIL PRODUCERS ASSOCIATION.

It's helpful to have at least one partner whom you can use to bounce ideas off. Your area of specialisation will extend when clients return to you with work in different fields. Life revolves around your diary. Some projects are planned months in advance, others allow only days to complete. You'll spend a lot of time liaising with clients. You have to respond to clients, setting yourself workable deadlines, so an average day is a mixture of working to your schedule and fitting in any ad hoc developments.

Direct marketers need to understand their clients and their clients' customers so they can come up with ideas that the clients will like and that have the desired effect on customers. Good communication skills are essential; you need to establish trust. You have to be disciplined to work to deadlines and be prepared to work overnight and weekends if necessary. You need to be realistic and to be able to mix creativity with a business-like approach.

Useful further reading, *Marketing Week* and *Marketing*; a basic source of reference, published in association with the Royal Mail, is the *Direct Mail Handbook*.

Disco Owner/DJ

At a Glance

Qualifications/Training	No	*Income bracket*	Medium–High
Licence	No	*Town/Country*	Town
Experience/Springboard	No	*Travel*	Lots
Mid-career entry	Highly unlikely	*Exit sale*	Possible
Entry costs	£4,000	*Work at home*	No

Mix and match   Yes. You could think about: Piano tuner, Hi-fi shop owner, Light music composer, Man with a van, Mini-cab driver, Accountant . . .
Enquiries   Dealers, eg Young Disco Centre

These provide, set up and organise discos. They are responsible for amplification and lighting as well as acting as disc jockey and playing the records.

A business studies course or degree will give you an enormous advantage in this highly competitive field. Good organisational and sales skills will enable you to sell your product down the phone and deal with the public, drunk or sober. A clean driving licence is essential. Get advice on insurance, and from an accountant. Be able to present your records in a relaxed, chatty and confident manner. You will need to be diplomatic and able to prevent fights when your customers become tired and emotional.

A knowledge of music is not necessary, but the disco owner must listen regularly to BBC Radios 1 and 2 and independent stations to learn what people like, eg 'golden oldies', records of the 40s, 50s and 60s as well as recent hits.

Working hours are normally Friday through Sunday unless you work temporarily as a DJ at the HIPPODROME in Soho, or on a touring contract with the MECCA clubs. You can earn about £100 per night at the Hippodrome but since your contract with them is exclusive, you cannot also work elsewhere. Mecca pay £60 or £70 per night. Arab countries offer £350 tax free, all found, but sexual favours may be expected.

Most DJs start at £15 a night in pubs or strip clubs, or work as a roadie for a disco owner. This is good experience before starting on your own. Jobs are advertised in *Record Mirror*, *Disco International*, *Jocks* magazine, local shops, pubs and newspapers.

The cost of recording equipment, records, transport and lights is high. For your own disco you will need to invest at least £1,250 in hi-fi equipment, turntable, speakers etc (cheap electronics break down), and a large car or van. You will need a telephone, answering phone or service, and a typewriter/word processor. Get business cards printed and advertise your services in the local press and shops. If you have a large room or garage you can keep a mobile disco at home – if you can stand the smell of smoke which emanates from it.

Long drives on motorways, loading and unloading before and after a 'gig' are exhausting, so you need physical strength and stamina. Most 'gigs' last at least 4 hours; if you leave home in the late afternoon or early evening, you cannot expect to get home until the early hours of the morning. You will then have to get up at a reasonable hour to answer the telephone, take messages, and prepare for the next job. You may feel like death but must always be charming and enthusiastic towards your customer, the party giver.

Expect to spend at least £12 a week to keep up with the latest records.

It can be difficult for coloured people and women to become successful. The long hours can limit one's social life and disrupt sleep patterns. Expect to earn a maximum of £250 per night before tax, ie £500 to £750 per week, so you will never become rich though you may get addicted to the excitement of it. You can also run a separate business, eg selling or hiring equipment to other DJs. It is worth taking advice from dealers eg YOUNG DISCO CENTRE.

Dispensing Chemist

At a Glance

Qualifications/Training	Essential	*Income bracket*	Medium
Licence	Yes	*Town/Country*	Town
Experience/Springboard	Yes	*Travel*	None
Mid-career entry	Unlikely	*Exit sale*	Yes
Entry costs	£20,000	*Work at home*	No

Mix and match Limited. You could think about: Healthfood shopkeeper, Newsletter publisher, Sculptor . . .

Enquiries Society of Apothecaries, Pharmaceutical Society of Great Britain

Chemist shops primarily dispense prescriptions, but it is unlikely you'll make a living from this so you need counter stock to augment the income from this. The National Health Service is your main customer, so you'll have to fulfil more requirements than other small, independent shops. You are contracted to specific opening hours (including late nights and Sunday opening) by the local Family Practitioners Committee (FPC). Small chemists cost the NHS more so it is trying to restrict their numbers. Under a new law the FPC must give permission before a new chemist will be granted an NHS contract – without which it is difficult to survive. Also by law a pharmacist must be on the premises whenever prescriptions are dispensed or certain other items sold so, if you aren't a registered pharmacist yourself, you'll have to employ somebody who is. As well as making up and dispensing prescriptions and serving in the shop, chemists are expected to give free medical consultations to customers who don't want to bother their doctors.

Pharmacists have to register with the PHARMACEUTICAL SOCIETY OF GREAT BRITAIN which means completing a degree course in pharmacy followed by a year's practical experience. Once registered, you can set up shop alone. Chemists have to be extremely meticulous – there is no room for error in making up prescriptions. They also need lots of patience and the ability at least to appear concerned; many of their customers are ill and require fairly specialist advice.

Set up costs vary depending on size and location of premises etc. You will need somewhere to make up the prescriptions, and equipment for making them up with (scales etc); storage for drugs (refrigeration for some) and retail goods; and fixtures and fittings for the shop itself. In addition you need at least £10,000 (and, depending on the size of your clientele and the sort of drugs they need, this could be up to

£80–100,000) of prescription drug stock from a drug wholesaler; some give credit to new chemists. There are initial cash flow problems: firstly because you will have to establish what drug stock you need (easier if you take over an existing business); secondly because the NHS takes about 2 months to pay for drugs, containers and dispensing fees. Prescription charges are deducted from what the NHS pay. This means a lot of administration for pharmacists. The NHS set the rates for prescriptions.

How much counter stock and what you stock is up to you. However your customers will expect baby food, loo-paper, soap, contraceptives etc as well as non prescription drugs; or you can specialise in eg theatrical or hyper-allergenic toiletries. As well as customers who drop in for shampoo and toothpaste, you can exploit the traffic of prescription collectors by stocking supplies of cough pastilles, digestion tablets and corn plasters and it may be worth experimenting with alternative medicine such as homeopathic cures.

Further information from the SOCIETY OF APOTHECARIES and the PHARMACEUTICAL SOCIETY OF GREAT BRITAIN who publishes the *Pharmaceutical Journal*. See also *Chemist and Druggist* and *Community Pharmacy*.

Doctor (GP in the NHS)

At a Glance

Qualifications/Training	Essential	*Income bracket*	High
Licence	Yes	*Town/Country*	Town/Village
Experience/Springboard	Recommended	*Travel*	Local
Mid-career entry	Limited	*Exit sale*	Possible
Entry costs	Highly variable	*Work at home*	Possible

Mix and match   Yes.   You could think about: Homeopath, Doctor (private GP), Bookseller, Restaurateur . . .

Enquiries   Royal College of General Practitioners, British Medical Association

There are some 30,000 general practitioners in the National Health Service (NHS) who work either in partnerships or in single handed practices. There are conditions of service to which they must comply, and they can only set up where it is deemed there is a need. But they are not employed by the NHS and have considerable independence in running their own clinical practices, which are businesses in their own right with balance sheets and profit and loss accounts.

It is less the case now that doctors breed doctors – instead it is highly competitive. The long training and the difficulty of earning money during the course because the vacations are shorter means that medicine generally draws heavily from the middle, professional classes.

First you must qualify – usually five years after being accepted for medical school. London medical schools still have much of the prestige but you may not see a live patient for some time – less common in the provinces. Then you must do one year in a hospital job to get on the Medical Register before taking a one year training course in general practice. These are run by the regional health authority (details from the postgraduate dean at your medical school). It involves you being attached to a practice and doing a relevant hospital job, eg paediatrics or geriatrics; it is intended soon to include topics such as management and budgeting to help you run your practise. You will need to pick up communications skills although they are still not normally taught explicitly. Take the course in the area where you will want to work so you get known. You can apply for membership of the ROYAL COLLEGE OF GENERAL PRACTITIONERS (means another exam), though this is not necessary to practise. You can then look for a job as an assistant in a practice. Vacancies are normally advertised in the *British Medical Journal*.

Single-handed vacancies must be advertised and you are chosen by the local Family Practitioners Committee (FPC), subject to approval by the Medical Practices Committee. You may find yourself in competition from local partnerships, seeking to incorporate the practice and its list. There is no obligation on partnerships to advertise vacancies; the partners choose (and it may be their son/daughter or the current assistant) so long as it meets with the approval of the FPC. You may have to buy your way into a partnership, ie contribute to the capital value of property and equipment: 'hidden sale of goodwill' is illegal. NHS may make loans at favourable rates for the capital needed but as they are agreed nationally, they may not be much use in areas of very high property prices. Some health centres are owned by the health authority.

Unlike the private doctor, you are under an obligation to provide for cover 24 hours a day, 365 days a year. Partners usually cover for each other so there is no cost. Single-handed doctors use a locum/answering service when they aren't available. Locums (mostly doctors between jobs or waiting to find a first job) are found through commercial agencies or a bureau such as that run by the BRITISH MEDICAL ASSO-CIATION (BMA). There are also deputising services, which provide locums and deputies to see patients when the doctor is not able to. These are run by groups of doctors or commercially, on the basis of a monthly retainer plus a fee per visit. The FPC must approve the arrangements you make and the amount you use them. Most doctors have something over 2,000 patients and there is a DHSS maximum of 3,500. How you define your area is up to you, within guidelines laid down by your FPC. You can also decide your style of operation: write all of your letters to hospitals, patients' notes etc in handwriting on the spot or hire a medical secretary and dictate them. You are not allowed to advertise. Patients will hear of you by word of mouth – worth having the local chemists on your side if you need more patients. You must live within easy reach of your practice.

You are paid through a capitation fee – a fixed fee per patient per year (more for elderly patients who are likely to make more demands on their GP); areas of low population such as Highlands and Islands have special arrangements. In addition, you are paid for some other services as you provide them (maternity service, vaccination, cervical cytology and temporary and emergency treatment) and there is a mileage allowance in rural areas when you have to travel more than 3 miles. The most profitable practices are therefore those in rural areas with holiday trade, and where there are low overheads and a local population likely to make use of the chargeable services. The target income of a GP after expenses is £23–24,000; the turnover of a practice of 4 partners might be some £200,000. It is worth finding both an accountant and solicitor who specialise in general practice. Medical schools teach you little or nothing about the business side of the practice at present.

In rural communities, the local family doctor has a distinct role in the local community – more anonymous in a city practice. The setting up of the ROYAL COLLEGE OF GENERAL PRACTITIONERS has helped to make general practice more respectable; most medical schools now have an academic department of general practice and it is now the favoured option for medical students. It is rewarding, stimulating work and highly unpredictable. You must be able to get on with all sorts of people and be able to live with your inevitable mistakes. The difficulties include differentiating the ill from the not so ill; maintaining standards all the time; and knowing your own limitations. Many value the fact that there is no direct link between the amount of work you do for the patient and the amount the patient pays into the system. Others combine work in the NHS with some private work. You can also combine general practice with work in hospital clinics, work for industry (eg stress clinics) or life insurance examinations. Some GPs run book shops or restaurants. No matter, so long as you maintain your obligations to your patients.

Doctor (Private GP)

At a Glance

Qualifications/Training	Essential	*Income bracket*	High
Licence	Yes	*Town/Country*	Town
Experience/Springboard	Recommended	*Travel*	Local
Mid-career entry	Highly unlikely	*Exit sale*	Yes
Entry costs	Highly variable	*Work at home*	Possible

Mix and match Yes. You could think about: Doctor (GP in the NHS), Homeopath, MP, Novelist, Winegrower . . .

Enquiries Royal College of General Practitioners, British Medical Association

Private family doctors in general practice are paid directly by their patients. The basic medical training takes 5 or 6 years; after an extra year's training, including time spent in a practice, you can become a member of the ROYAL COLLEGE OF GENERAL PRACTITIONERS.

In private practice, you must not mind being available 24 hours a day. It is useful to be able to drive a car, and being married with children of your own helps you to understand your patients better. You also need patience and the ability to compromise between what your patients want and what you think they need. On average, you can't expect more than 50% co-operation from them and you will be forced to meet them half way. There is more to medicine than just prescribing it. You must try and understand your patients. They are paying for your time and expertise and as a private practitioner you take full responsibility.

The prospects for private practice in London are very good as it now enjoys worldwide fame as a centre of medical excellence. The rich from many countries would rather fly to London than go to their local doctor. Big cities are best for private practice; businessmen and professionals prefer to pay for quick service, when and where it is convenient to them.

It is advisable to work as an assistant in a practice for 5–10 years to gain experience and make useful contacts before going alone. It takes about 5 years to build up a practice, and can cost £30,000 to buy into an existing one. If you haven't the ready cash, it is possible to be paid half salary for the first few years.

It's necessary to join the BMA and commercially vital to arrange a protective insurance (the American hobby of suing one's doctor seems to be crossing the Atlantic as fast as AIDS). Your income to start with may be £20,000+ pa and it's possible for this to rise to £50,000 or more. Your surgery should preferably not be in your home, but close by. The costs of the practice will include a medical secretary (about £11,000 pa), rent of premises (this varies according to area), telephone, answerphone and answering service (vital) with a bleeper so you can be contacted at all times. A car phone ensures you can make calls when stuck in traffic while making domiciliary visits.

You need to find time in the day for dictating letters and telephoning, as well as holding surgeries and visiting patients (critically ill patients require 2 visits per day). Arrange a joint rota with 3 other doctors for emergency duty, say, 1 night a week and one weekend in 4.

The job's advantage is the freedom to practise good medicine, with the best referral system and technical equipment available at a few hours' notice. It's possible to give really personal attention to your patients, even to be in the operating theatre with them when they have surgery, or discuss their case with their own physician at the hospital of their choice. This is satisfying to the patient, making them feel more important than the system. There's little red tape. It's hard work, so essential to have a good hobby with which to blow off steam.

Read the *British Medical Journal*, the *Handbook* of the Royal College of General Practitioners, and use the library of the ROYAL SOCIETY OF MEDICINE.

Dress Agent

Dress agents have shops from which they sell their clients' old clothes for a proportion of the proceeds. Although there is a market for most second hand clothes their selling price means that it is usually only worthwhile dealing in good quality clothes that are in good condition. Most dress agents specialise to a degree (men or women or children's); some choose to specialise further, with say, wedding outfits or evening dress.

There are no formal qualifications but you'll have to have some idea of how to sell things, how to display the stock etc. You also have to be fairly methodical to cope with all of the paper work involved. Stock has to be labelled with the supplier's name so that you know who to pay when you've sold it. Records have to include names and addresses, date when stock was brought in and when it goes out; you'll get through a lot of cheques and will probably want to establish a system for returning/disposing of unsold clothes after a few weeks. Even more important is knowing how to price second hand clothes, which don't come into your shop with a ready made wholesale price as does stock for ordinary shops. You'll need several years of second hand clothes buying and browsing behind you.

You need suitable shop premises with good storage space because any 'new' stock has to be checked before going on sale. Nearby parking is useful; you don't necessarily want to be on a High Street because customers are prepared to travel to get to you. You may attract passing trade by being close to complementary shops and businesses (eg nursery schools if you're selling children's clothes). On top of rent or mortgage set up costs are about £2,000 to equip the shop and fund printing and initial advertising. You don't pay for stock but you may have to pay for advertising (in local shops and newspapers and by posting leaflets).

Most second hand clothes are worth about a quarter of their original value but this varies according to the condition and demand; if you're too greedy, you won't sell. It's up to you to decide how much of this you want for yourself. Bear in mind that clients sometimes grumble if they think that you're making too much; also they will be surprised at how little you expect to get for their nearly new designer clothes. Aim for a fast turnover rather than a big mark up: this attracts both buyers and sellers. Some dress agents experiment with manufacturers' end of line mark downs – this may work but equally the price range may be wrong compared to your usual stock. It will take a few months before you can see how business is going; after that you may find that you want and can afford to hire help to look after the shop from time to time. It may take you a long time though before you feel like delegating any of the more responsible jobs like pricing, which are largely a matter of judgement. Clients must trust you and it helps if, certainly to begin with, you spend some time in the shop meeting them. You'll build up a regular clientele which grows by word of mouth. The busy times for most dress agents are at the beginning of new seasons (March–May and September–November) when you have to cope with increased volumes of stuff coming in and going out while customers replace the contents of their wardrobes.

Driving Instructor

At a Glance

Qualifications/Training	Essential	*Income bracket*	Medium
Licence	Yes	*Town/Country*	Town
Experience/Springboard	Recommended	*Travel*	Local
Mid-career entry	Good	*Exit sale*	Possible
Entry costs	£10,000	*Work at home*	Yes

Mix and match Yes. You could think about: Garage owner, Courier service, Mini-cab driver, Motorcycle messenger, Disco owner . . .

Enquiries Driving Instructors' Association, National Joint Council for Driving Instructors

Most driving instructors are self-employed and work by themselves, running the business between lessons (exceptions are HGV and public service vehicle instructors, who tend to be employed by firms and training associations). Every year about 10,000 people apply to be driving instructors; about 1,000 get through. Driving instructors are meant to teach people to drive well enough to pass the Department of Transport's driving test. Instruction is given almost exclusively in the instructor's own car on ordinary roads. From time to time alternatives such as classroom teaching or using simulated machines, rather than cars, are discussed but no changes are imminent. Driving instructors are always at least 21 and you may want to wait until after you are 25 when insurance premiums are lower.

Before you can sit the instructors' exams you'll need: to have had a full British Driving Licence for at least 4 years; no (or, at the most, one very small) motoring or other convictions; and references from 2 people including your last employer. You can train on the job with a 6 months' trainee licence and sponsorship from a driving school; after you have passed the first two of the three exams you take a professional training course. Details from the NATIONAL JOINT COUNCIL OF DRIVING INSTRUCTORS or the DRIVING INSTRUCTORS ASSOCIATION. Allow about £1,000 to cover training, fees for the Department of Transport's exams and the subsequent £100 fee for registration as an approved driving instructor, for four years, when you pass.

Beware of any promises to get you through for a lot less. Working for another instructor (as either a trainee or after you are qualified) is good experience before you set up on your own. Being a good driver is essential, but the ability to teach people and adapt to their vastly differing backgrounds, intelligence, and skill is even more important. You'll need a lot of patience, and you'll have to be constantly alert without giving your pupils the impression you are terrified. Being a good judge of other people's nervousness and reactions is a big plus. 1 million driving tests are passed every year; 2 million are taken so there is a lot of instructing going on.

Apart from the costs of preparing yourself you will also need to buy a new car (capable of standing up to being driven by learners) about every 18 months. It is essential that you are successful enough to do this; many new driving instructors go bust when the first car needs replacing. Dual controls cost about £100 and insurance, £400–500 per annum. A telephone answering machine is also useful as you should be out most of the time and a large diary is vital. Because of the need for fairly rapid success you must make sure that the area you choose is going to support you. Check out the competition, investigate the age and affluence of the population etc. Many instructors now offer a door-to-door service, picking up their pupils from home for the lesson.

Where work comes from depends on where you are but, on the whole, learners prefer an instructor they know something about, so a lot will come from word of mouth. Unless you're in a very rural area, people won't expect to travel very far. As business increases you may employ other instructors (all of whom you will have to vet carefully) and set up a school. This can make you deskbound, involving added paperwork and possibly administrative staff.

Further information from the DRIVING INSTRUCTORS' ASSOCIATION who have a Hotline to answer any question. See also *Driving*, *Running Your Own Driving School* and the *Driving Instructor's Handbook*.

DRIVING INSTRUCTOR

Editorial Photographer

At a Glance

Qualifications/Training	Recommended	*Income bracket*	Medium–High
Licence	No	*Town/Country*	Town
Experience/Springboard	Recommended	*Travel*	Yes
Mid-career entry	Possible	*Exit sale*	No
Entry costs	£1,000+	*Work at home*	Possible

Mix and match   Yes.   You could think about: Advertising photographer, Photographer, Artist, Picture researcher, Tourist guide . . .

Enquiries   British Institute of Professional Photography, Association of Fashion, Advertising and Editorial Photographers

For many photographers, editorial photography offers the best balance between commercial and artistic photography. Within the field, you can specialise in fashion, home interiors, still life, travel, cookery portraits or even narrower fields such as underwater or aerial photography.

The usual training is through art school, completing a course recognised by the BRITISH INSTITUTE OF PROFESSIONAL PHOTOGRAPHY. However, many successful photographers agree that the best training is as a photographer's assistant. There are also editorial photographers who have learned the trade through working as a fashion model or a photographic stylist.

As with so many other freelance jobs, the main problem is getting yourself known to start with. You will need top class, reliable photographic equipment (cameras, lenses, lights) and most editorial photographers work from their own studios. However, to start with, and if you find you are doing a lot of work on location, you can hire studio space – perhaps from other photographers you know in studio complexes. You can also hire the equipment you need while you are starting out – though if you do hire everything you need (including a photographic assistant) you will soon find that your fees have all been swallowed up.

Fees vary according to the type of work you are doing, but most top magazines pay in the region of £400 per day: the cost of film and processing is also met, but usually few other extras. Rates are set by ASSOCIATION OF FASHION, ADVERTISING AND EDITORIAL PHOTOGRAPHERS (AFAEP), who also provide help in finding studios, assistants, stylists, lighting and so on.

The work is varied and usually interesting: most photographers build up a working relationship with a dozen or so popular publications. A typical day's work for a top magazine will involve liaising with the client (fashion editor, home or cookery editor, art editor or picture editor) to discuss the shoot, arriving at the studio to get cameras and backgrounds set up. The stylist (or appropriate editor) usually arranges for props to be delivered and books any models that are needed. Together, you will work out a programme for the day, and then the shooting begins. Sometimes there is a tight brief, and you have little opportunity for creative work: your skill is needed to create the right lighting and atmosphere for the shot. On the other hand, you may be given a free hand in deciding what props to use and what angles to shoot at. At the end of the day you will have to straighten up the studio and arrange for the processing of the film, ready for delivery the next day. And if anything goes wrong you may have to re-shoot at your own expense.

You may also work on books: for example you may find yourself booked for a two-week period, working with a freelance home economist and stylist to photograph a hundred or so dishes for a cookery book.

Top fashion photographers may find themselves in demand for foreign trips: colour magazines have to go into production well ahead of publication, so to shoot summer fashions in February you have to go abroad to find the sun. The client will arrange for travel, and a party of half a dozen or so (fashion editor, assistant, two models, yourself and your assistant) will spend a week shooting several spreads for publication later in the year.

As well as faultless technical skill and an ability to work under pressure, it helps if you are outgoing and adaptable. There is a lot of lugging around of equipment and props, and although this could be considered the assistant's job, it helps to speed up and keep relations good if everyone mucks in.

Many editorial photographers will take on a certain amount of advertising work as well: usually pay is better, but the brief is tighter.

Electrician

At a Glance

Qualifications/Training	Essential	*Income bracket*	Medium
Licence	Yes	*Town/Country*	Either
Experience/Springboard	Good idea	*Travel*	Local
Mid-career entry	Possible	*Exit sale*	No
Entry costs	£2,000	*Work at home*	No

Mix and match Yes. You could think about: Man with a van, Property manager, Disco owner, Plumber . . .

Enquiries National Inspection Council for Electrical Installation Contracting

The work of an electrician involves installation of electrical wiring in new or old buildings (homes, factories, hospitals, schools or offices) and checking, adapting or extending existing installations. Most electricians in this field, particularly if they specialise in domestic wiring, own their own businesses.

Qualifications are essential. Electricity is dangerous if it is not treated with respect. Although it is not a legal obligation in England and Wales, any electrical work should conform with the Wiring Regulations, specified by the INSTITUTION OF ELECTRICAL ENGINEERS. There are courses at colleges of further education, which can be attended on a day release basis if you work for a large company, leading to City and Guilds certificates. You can also train by getting a job with one of the local Electricity Boards. Once qualified, you will have to enrol with the NATIONAL INSPECTION COUNCIL FOR ELECTRICAL INSTALLATION CONTRACTING. They hold a roll of approved electrical installation contractors, which anyone wanting to employ an electrician can consult.

If you run your own business you can set your own rates: often you will be called out to work unsocial hours, and many people may prefer you to do work in their homes at weekends. You can expect to earn upwards of £300 per week.

When setting up you will need to buy a small van and some specialist tools (pliers, wire clippers, screwdrivers and so on). You will also need a stock of commonly used materials and components (cable, sockets, junction boxes). A couple of thousand pounds should do the trick. On domestic jobs you can usually ask for part of the payment (to cover materials) to be made on start of work, and the balance to be made up when the work is satisfactorily completed.

There are other fields of specialisation, such as in repair work on electrical appliances, which involve a greater knowledge of electronics. You may also need your own premises if repairs cannot be done on site.

Embalmer

At a Glance

Qualifications/Training	Recommended	*Income bracket*	Low–Medium
Licence	No	*Town/Country*	Either
Experience/Springboard	Recommended	*Travel*	Local
Mid-career entry	Yes	*Exit sale*	No
Entry costs	£300	*Work at home*	No

Mix and match   Yes.   You could think about: Funeral director, Kennel/cattery owner, Driving instructor, Taxidermist . . .

Enquiries   British Institute of Embalmers

Embalmers treat dead bodies to preserve them, disinfect them and present them in a viewable state for funerals. Most self-employed embalmers own undertaking companies; there are also some opportunities to work freelance by taking up contracts from funeral directors who do not offer their own embalming service. It is a predominantly male profession – only about 12% are female.

Embalming is not legally required but usually necessary in some cases, eg many airlines will not transport dead bodies without some sort of assurance that they are not infectious and funeral directors usually insist on a body being embalmed before being transported from one undertaker to another (see the *Law of Burial, Cremation and Exhumation*). Formally, you don't need any qualifications but membership of the BRITISH INSTITUTE OF EMBALMERS (BIE) is recommended. This involves a course (with an accredited teacher or school) and passing qualifying exams. It gives professional recognition and support, as well as the professional journal, *The Embalmer*.

To set up you will need at least £200–300 worth of equipment. You'll also need access to a mortuary because, although some people, especially in rural areas, like you to work from their houses, most embalming is done at the undertaker's and the body returned to the mourners if requested. You are paid through the funeral director.

Embalming involves draining out all the body fluids and injecting sterilising agents into the circulatory system (this takes about an hour), followed by any cosmetic work necessary to repair the effects of violent or unpleasant death. (See the *Principles and Practice of Embalming*.) It is not a job with universal appeal and requires knowledge of anatomy and bacteriology. Although you'll have to take a fairly scientific approach in dealing with the dead, your clients, the bereaved, will require tactful and sympathetic handling if you come into contact with them.

Your job is easier if you work as soon after death as possible; you will only know a few days in advance about a job (funerals are usually arranged to take place within a week of death). There are slight seasonal variations, the death rate is slightly higher in winter (December–March) and after a 'flu epidemic. You usually work alone, occasionally with an assistant.

You'll encounter mixed reactions to your profession. Taken far more seriously in America and Canada, embalming tends to provoke mirth or distaste in the UK although the BIE reports that this is gradually changing.

English Language School Owner

At a Glance

Qualifications/Training	Recommended	*Income bracket*	Medium
Licence	Recommended	*Town/Country*	Town
Experience/Springboard	Recommended	*Travel*	No
Mid-career entry	Yes	*Exit sale*	Yes
Entry costs	£8,000	*Work at home*	No

Mix and match Yes. You could think about: Tourist guide, Book editor, Landlord, Travel agent, Winegrower, Interpreter . . .

Enquiries British Council, ARELS-FELCO LTD

There are two basic types of private English Language Schools, teaching English as a foreign language (EFL): language schools set up in this country to teach English to foreign visitors, and schools set up in foreign countries to teach English to the local population. This is a thriving business these days.

Whichever type of school you want to set up, it is useful to start by getting some qualifications: the Royal Society of Arts sets examinations in teaching English as a foreign (or second) language (TEFL and TESL). Courses are run by some FE colleges, and may be taken on a part-time basis (you usually have to be a mature student, or have some previous academic qualification). There are also courses sponsored by the BRITISH COUNCIL which are usually short, intensive courses, and quite difficult to get on.

Once you've got the teaching qualifications, you can start to get experience: there is plenty of demand for private tutoring in English:

put notices on boards in colleges or universities. Hospitals are another area where there is some demand for tutorial English classes: qualified doctors from, say, the Indian sub-continent may have perfect knowledge of English as far as technical terms are concerned, but often need extra coaching in 'bedside manner' (discussing tummy aches with patients, and so on). It might be more constructive to get a job in an English Language School to learn the ropes.

Language schools in Britain are often set up to run during the summer period only: you can hire premises (private educational establishments during the school holidays), you will need to hire teachers, and you will have to put out a lot of publicity material – advertisements in foreign press are a good start. Other schools own their own premises – large houses, redundant school buildings and so on. The best way to attract students is to offer a complete package: lessons, assessment, examination courses (Cambridge Certificate), extra curricular activities (visits to historic sites and cultural entertainments), accommodation and travel. Accommodation is usually offered with private families on a half or full board basis. Up-market schools may provide hotel or self-catering accommodation. You may need to appoint someone to take care of these arrangements. For travel facilities, you will probably have to make special deals with travel agents. To make the most of the costs, students are usually split into two groups, each getting three hours of teaching a day, giving them time to sightsee, travel or relax the rest of the day. Teachers work two three-hour shifts a day, teaching two different groups.

Language schools should be inspected and 'recognised' by the British Council. Once you have been recognised you can join ARELS-FELCO LTD – the association of schools recognised by the British Council (Association of Recognised English Language Schools and The Federation of English Language Course Organisers – the two organisations merged). They can offer you advice and publish information leaflets. If you are setting up a school abroad, controls will depend on the legislation in the country you work in. Budgets for promotion and accommodation will be low or non-existent.

Whichever type of school you set up, word of mouth is the best form of advertising. Offer good courses and make the students feel they have achieved something, and you will be assured of a good name, and will be able to inflate your prices.

Estate Agent

At a Glance

Qualifications/Training	No	Income bracket	Low–High
Licence	No	Town/Country	Town
Experience/Springboard	Essential	Travel	Local
Mid-career entry	Yes	Exit sale	Yes
Entry costs	£10,000+	Work at home	No

Mix and match   Yes.   You could think about: Surveyor, Independent financial adviser, Property manager, Property developer, Conveyancer, Solicitor, Magazine publisher . . .

Enquiries   National Association of Estate Agents . . .

Estate agents find buyers for property on behalf of their clients (called vendors). This means agreeing an asking price with the vendor, taking measurements and details of the property, preparing particulars (with photographs if appropriate) and circulating them around applicants. Then arranging for potential buyers to view properties, showing them round yourself if necessary, and liaising between vendor, buyer, solicitors and financial sources while a property is being sold. Recently a lot of estate agent chains have been bought by banks and building societies. This, however, doesn't seem to have closed the way for new businesses to open up, especially in places like the south east when the property market is buoyant.

You don't need any formal qualifications to become an estate agent unless you want to do professional, structural surveys and valuations (in which case you must be a qualified member of the ROYAL INSTITUTION OF CHARTERED SURVEYORS). Under the Financial Services Act you need to be registered and therefore properly qualified if you want to give any financial advice (with mortgages, insurance etc). In any case, however, you will have to be able to judge accurately the market value of a property. This depends on how well it suits the market and the sort of people who buy in that area; a structurally sound house can lose value because it's decorated in the wrong taste. You will certainly need some experience of the business before setting up alone and may find it useful to join the NATIONAL ASSOCIATION OF ESTATE AGENTS, a mildly self-regulating body, membership of which sometimes inspires public confidence. Property selling is often by negotiation, so you'll need to be diplomatic and sometimes quick thinking to keep everyone happy; also good at convincing people that what you say is true.

Finding good, central premises is important. High Street sites are best or somewhere where you are easily visible so that both sellers and buyers know you're there. You'll need a telephone and somebody to answer it when you're out who can talk intelligently about the properties on your books (answering machines don't sell houses). A computer makes life easier and a typewriter and photocopier are essential for particulars. A fax is also useful if you're involved in a contract race with other agents when getting documents delivered quickly is essential. The vendor pays you commission on the sale, which will depend on your area and the amount of nearby competition. It's normally about 1¾% if you're sole agent rising to about 2½% if you're one of many, although some estate agents (not generally respected in the business) work for less. You are paid when, and if, you sell the property; in the meantime you'll have had to pay for advertising etc. Sometimes buyers pay agents a retainer for finding a suitable property.

ESTATE AGENT

You get clients by advertising. Straightforward mail drops aren't very satisfactory (people ignore them), but try local newspapers and free magazines until word of mouth and reputation take over. Some properties are sold at auctions especially if they're ready for development when property speculators step in. Others that are difficult to sell, you can share with another agent and split the commission. Useful contacts are financial sources (for help with buyers' mortgages), solicitors; also reliable damp proofers, wood worm killers etc: this is because almost always a buyer will get an independent survey done which sometimes finds a problem with the property and you will have to negotiate with the vendor to try to get it put right. Business is affected by the market (it slows down after Stock Market crashes) and by the season. January to June are busy with a drop off in July until October. December is usually quiet. That means that some days you are very busy and on others you have to look for things to do to make business. Trade press includes the *Estates Gazette*, the *Negotiator* and the *Estate Agent*.

Events Organiser

At a Glance

Qualifications/Training	No	*Income bracket*	Medium–High
Licence	No	*Town/Country*	Town
Experience/Springboard	Recommended	*Travel*	Yes
Mid-career entry	Likely	*Exit sale*	Possible
Entry costs	£3,000	*Work at home*	Partly

Mix and match   Possible. You could think about: Caterer, Public relations consultant, Artists' agent . . .

Enquiries   Events organisers, Public Relations consultants

There's a lot of demand for organisers who will help corporate and private clients arrange special events to impress customers, the media or their friends. Events organisers are particularly useful to clients who need to put on spectacular promotional or social events which they are too busy to organise themselves. You can make a living by undertaking all the organisation for anything from getting a birthday cake to the launch of a major new consumer product with a multi-million advertising and promotional budget. In addition, you can offer a wide range of personal services (secretarial, ticket finding, weddings, party decorations); the core of the work will mainly involve organising some sort of party or event. Potential private and corporate clients are, by definition, people with a lot of cash; you need to be based near them, in London, Edinburgh, Bristol or anywhere else where corporate money is freely spent on ostentatious consumption.

You don't need any formal qualifications but you need experience and contacts. You need a proven track record as a good organiser, secretarial skills and have financial experience. You also need to be good with people and have real personal flair to make people interested in using you rather than your competition. A few years in PR or sales-promotion is the most useful springboard; it'll give you a chance to learn how to organise some complex, large scale events and will also let you get to know reliable suppliers, eg caterers, the owners and managers of venues, entertainers, equipment hire companies, graphic artists and designers, secretarial services agencies. Before you start up you need to have built up a network of suppliers you can trust: if the food you supply is disgusting or the clown too drunk, it reflects badly on you.

Success depends largely on your personality: as well as being a good organiser and liaiser, you should be outgoing and friendly; good at making things happen without being too grim about it. It's a good idea to set up with a partner who has complementary skills and contacts, who will help come up with new ideas and who can share the work. Essential set up equipment is a telephone and answering machine, a photocopier, files, a word processor and stationery – presentation is important so be prepared to spend on this and your own promotional material. A fax is also useful for rushing last minute details to clients but doesn't provide good enough quality reproduction for main communications like quotes. Once you're established you may want to employ an assistant to help with the administration while you spend more time dealing directly with clients. You are paid at an hourly rate (say about £25 per hour but don't undercharge) and also charge commission on anything supplied by other people and agencies. You yourself pay suppliers with your own cash before you charge your client, for the supplies plus commission. Cash flow can be a problem. Make sure your client pays you in advance for at least 50% of the estimated final cost of the event (including your fees and what you pay to suppliers). Invoice for the rest the day after the event, chase after 15 days (clients are usually good at paying quickly but one client in financial troubles before you've been paid the balance of your account for a massive event could be serious financial trouble for you). Pay your own suppliers' invoices as late as is decently possible but remember that many of the people you use are small businesses equally dependent on prompt settlement. It's a business that badly needs a good accountant and understanding bank manager and it's probably worth investing in a short business course for yourself.

Every event you organise should be a source of more work from the satisfied client and the impressed guests. Yet more will come by word of mouth and good write-ups in magazines and newspapers. You can start off in a small way, perhaps mixing and matching meanwhile, by organising events for friends and business contacts.

Although each job will be vastly different in scale and detail the basics are similar. Meet the client and find out what's wanted and whether it's possible to provide it within their budget, put in your quote, get it accepted and go ahead. Select a shortlist of suitable venues and take the client around 2 or 3 of these before deciding, then contact suppliers and make sure that they can provide what you want on the night. You'll almost certainly be expected to attend the event itself in order to make sure everything runs smoothly, while the guests must be allowed to think that your clients have organised the whole thing themselves. Make sure you stay sober. A lot of your work will overlap with your own social life because many clients will want to see you outside office hours. At Christmas you could find yourself attending at least one of your own parties every night. Make sure you book a holiday.

Exhibition Designer

At a Glance

Qualifications/Training	Yes	*Income bracket*	Medium
Licence	No	*Town/Country*	Town
Experience/Springboard	No	*Travel*	Yes
Mid-career entry	Unlikely	*Exit sale*	No
Entry costs	£2,000	*Work at home*	No

Mix and match   Yes. You could think about: Graphic designer, Advertising photographer, Sales promoter, Stage technician carpenter, Garden gnome maker . . .

Enquiries   Art colleges and design agencies

Exhibition design involves making displays for exhibitions or shops; making film or theatre sets; setting up museum and educational displays; industrial model making. Exhibition designers are responsible for the appearance of the various stands in an exhibition, for ensuring that all fire and safety regulations are adhered to and for planning the directional flow of visitors to the exhibition. It's a good area for freelancers because few companies need full time exhibition designers.

Routes into the business are via an interior design course, or a special exhibition design course – see *Design Courses in Britain*. Good colleges have close contacts with industry and teachers tend to be practising designers. Exhibition design interrelates with a lot of other disciplines like graphics (for the notices at exhibitions or museums), crafts, photography, advertising and promotions. There are side lines for the freelancer.

To set up you'll need a telephone and design equipment. You'll also need somewhere to work but not necessarily a studio that clients will visit because most meetings are on site.

A lot of exhibition design is done under contracts which last for from 6 months to 2 years. It can be difficult finding work to begin with because of the catch 22 of having to have experience before you're taken on; the work you've done at college may help here but is unlikely to be on the large scale of many of the jobs you'll be going for. There are design agencies (usually specialist), where you can place your work when you first start.

Farmer

At a Glance

Qualifications/Training	Recommended	Income bracket	Low–High
Licence	No	Town/Country	Country
Experience/Springboard	Useful	Travel	Local
Mid-career entry	Yes	Exit sale	Yes
Entry costs	£100,000+++	Work at home	Essential

Mix and match   Excellent. You could think about: Holiday accommodation owner, Caravan site owner, Butcher, Opening to the public, MP, Accountant, Dealer in large antiques, Racehorse owner . . .

Enquiries   National Farmers' Union

If you can afford to start farming in the south of England, you can afford to retire, with prices in excess of £3,500 an acre. If you choose to start on a small scale in, say, the hills of Scotland or Wales the land is cheaper, under £1,000 an acre, but you must be foolhardy and tough. The government is currently trying to reduce production generally, while keeping people living in the countryside – so there is enthusiasm for farmers to turn their hands to other things, eg turning the cowshed into holiday flats.

You can start farming part-time, as a millionaire looking for investment or if your parent(s) are farmers who are conveniently elderly and about to retire (most modern farms cannot support two families). Starting part-time can be a good way so you can keep another source of income – eg use farm buildings for tourism, keep your existing job or you can combine farming with being a butcher or cattle dealer. Most arable farms of 80–100 acres can be managed in evenings and weekends as you can subcontract a bit if necessary (in dairy farming, this size farm will keep you busy from dawn to dusk). A farm of 300–400 acres makes a comfortable family farm ('Don't even think of getting divorced'). Anything larger, you will need to employ staff to keep you going – dairy farming will need twice as many staff as most others. On a sheep farm, for example, you should assume you need about one person per 800 sheep. When it comes to crops, it depends what you grow – one acre of grass or peas will take the same time to harvest as two acres of corn.

Most farms change hands at auctions. These are advertised in the press and with estate agents: the more modest with the local agents and *Farmers Weekly*; large ones within commuting distance of London will be with West End estate agents and advertised in *Country Life*. These can end up being run by a manager on behalf of a landlord largely involved in other things. Farms that are waterlogged all winter will be sold in summer.

You can own the freehold of a farm or be a tenant farmer. With a tenancy, the landlord (often a large institution such as an insurance company or the CHURCH COMMISSIONERS FOR ENGLAND) owns the ground and the farm buildings. However, there are 'tenants rights', whereby, if you go, the new tenant pays you a sum (agreed between the valuers you have each appointed) towards improvements you have made. You own the farm machinery and buy seed, animals etc. Tenants have little interference from their landlords, except occasionally they press for more. Many landlords encourage tenant farmers to pass on the farm to a son (or increasingly, a daughter, since the amount of physical work is relatively less these days). Heirs of the tenant who have drawn their principal source of income from working on the farm for five years are legally entitled to inherit the tenancy even against the landlord's wishes. Freehold farmers only have death duties as an impediment to passing on the farm – the higher the theoretical price of the land, the higher the duties. Once you own a farm and need to expand, you can 'share-farm'; you use land and buildings owned by someone else, you supply the seed, labour etc and the profit is divided between you both.

If you were not brought up on a farm, you will normally need a year's practical experience on a farm before being accepted for any agricultural course. You should then take a degree in agriculture or a course at a reputable agricultural college (better to stick to the straight practical course if you propose running your own farm rather than going for an agricultural management course).

Production of a number of farm products is controlled by EEC quotas. This means you buy 'at market price' from a seller, eg milk at 32p a litre, potatoes £400 an acre. This applies to eg milk, hops, sugar and potatoes. Quotas are valuable commodities and, if you don't need it yourself, there is a lively market in their sale or lease. There is not the same intervention with fruit and vegetables. Furthermore, you can cut costs by getting Jo Public to pick his own, if you are very accessible and can be highly professional – answerphone giving the current prices etc, and perhaps combine it with selling other things such as bedding plants. For apple farms, you need a good cold store to get them to the market in proper condition when there is demand. With animals, you can find a market if you go in for something different – goats, deer, or dairy sheep. And livings have been made farming garlic or leeches.

Farming is definitely big business. £60 will only buy you 100 new pullets or one very small new heifer calf. For just over £200, you can buy a large white boar or a 2 week old Charolais bull. Then, at the end of the day, you can sell a ton of potatoes for £40-100 or a fattened steer for £600. Farm equipment and machinery is notoriously expensive (£20,000 for a new tractor). But you can buy good secondhand equipment if you know what you're doing – eg £2,500 plus for a baler or £8,000 for a 5 year old combine.

The growing trend is for farmers to set up co-operatives which store and sell their produce. You can also sell to specialist dealers or in the local market. If you are big enough, you can sell direct to a major user such as a supermarket chain. This means you have to contend with their obsessive size and quality control – most farmers with eg bullocks to sell, find they are all different shapes and sizes.

There is plenty of bureaucracy and Jo Grundy-style resistance is not helpful. There are regulations governing the way you store your petrol; the logging of livestock in and out of the farm by ear numbers; the logging of crop sprays in and out; and the spraying records which must be kept (which fields they have been used on, the weather conditions and so on and so on). If you have the misfortune to get any notifiable disease on your farm, there will be more. For some, such as foot and mouth, you will get compensation although it will not stop you feeling as though you personally have leprosy. In case of accidents, eg Chernobyl, it can take the government an apparent age to decide whether or not you will get compensation. You can spend many hours alone on a tractor in this job; it is not for the gregarious. But you do need to be able to manage staff effectively and the local farmer is almost always an integral part of any rural community. You should not attempt this job if you are not very healthy – although you can get a contractor to do some of the work if you suddenly break a leg. It is still extremely hard work and it is vital that you love the work and the place you are farming. Farming is a complete way of life, since you live within the job. You must be prepared to work all the hours in the day for certain periods, depending on your product – lambing, sowing time or when the peas are ready for harvesting.

You should belong to and support the NATIONAL FARMERS' UNION. *Farmers' Weekly* is useful reading. All farmers receive a host of other farming freebies.

Farrier/Blacksmith

At a Glance

Qualifications/Training	Yes	*Income bracket*	Low–Medium
Licence	Farriers, yes	*Town/Country*	Country
Experience/Springboard	Essential	*Travel*	Local
Mid-career entry	Possible	*Exit sale*	Possible
Entry costs	£100–£30,000	*Work at home*	No

Mix and match Possible. You could think about: Man with a van, Garage owner, Snail farmer, Gardener/garden designer, Saddler/leatherworker . . .

Enquiries National Master Farriers', Blacksmiths' and Agricultural Engineering Association

Farriery and blacksmithing are separate and highly skilled crafts. Farriers work with horses but need training in blacksmithing to enable them to make shoes properly. Blacksmiths work with iron and may never have contact with horses; although traditionally blacksmiths trained in farriery may shoe horses legally if authorised by the FARRIERS' REGISTRATION COUNCIL.

Farriers have to be capable of hard work and able to handle fractious animals and owners. You undergo an apprenticeship of four years with an approved training farrier and pass the examination before becoming registered. Find a training farrier through the FARRIERS' REGISTRATION COUNCIL or advertisements in *Forge*. Apprenticeships are interspersed with periods of residential training at the HEREFORDSHIRE TECHNICAL COLLEGE where you cover oestology (bones), shoemaking theory and veterinary science. You can also enter the trade if you have trained in the Army. Once qualified a yearly registration fee is required to practise. The farrier should now be familiar with the work, and have built up contacts, confidence and business acumen. Few independent farriers can succeed without blacksmithing as a sideline. Be careful when finding a site, that you do not encroach on other farriers. Farriers may work from the back of a van (travel to hunts, shows, farms) with cold-shoeing equipment (portable anvil £40, range of shoes, nails) or hot-shoeing (gas forge £300). Many make their own anvils and tools otherwise a forge will cost £200, and anvils £70 each. A nucleus of loyal customers soon builds up, with publicity by recommendation. The work is immensely hard and the hours long but it is very satisfying.

Blacksmiths have a craft that is intellectually and aesthetically demanding. The whole field has recently expanded with contemporary design much in demand. You can train by taking a full-time degree or diploma course, usually included within art colleges' silversmithing/ metals/sculpture syllabus; (Herefordshire Technical College run a 1-year course in blacksmithing and metalwork). There are also apprenticeship/trainee schemes or you can take part-time classes. A full list can be obtained from the NATIONAL MASTER FARRIERS', BLACKSMITHS' & AGRICULTURAL ENGINEERING ASSOCIATION (NMFB&AEA) or SCOTTISH and WELSH DEVELOPMENT AGENCIES. On completing the training the smith can set up independently – many start with a homemade forge and anvil (approx £100), but more modern equipment would cost up to £30,000. Grants can be obtained from CoSIRA, Small Firms Service, Enterprise Allowance Scheme etc. Publicity will be necessary – local papers, exhibit at art and craft shows, galleries, county shows, have your own showroom adjacent to the forge. Take portfolio and samples to architects and interior designers for commissions, whether traditional or contemporary. The BRITISH ARTIST BLACKSMITHS' ASSOCIATION (BABA), supply a quarterly magazine, *British Blacksmith* and hold annual conferences. Advertisements may be placed in *Forge*, a free bi-monthly trade magazine to members of NMFB&AEA. Ornamental ironwork can be rewarding, with scope for creativity and physical work.

Fashion Clothes/Hat Designer

At a Glance

Qualifications/Training	Advisable	*Income bracket*	Low–High
Licence	No	*Town/Country*	Town
Experience/Springboard	Yes	*Travel*	Probably
Mid-career entry	Unlikely	*Exit sale*	No
Entry costs	£500	*Work at home*	Possible

Mix and match   Yes. You could think about: Illustrator, Fashion retailer, Magazine designer, Public relations consultant . . .

Enquiries   Clothing and Footwear Institute

The image of the sweat shop in the rag trade might not be very far from the truth. It is a very hard working, highly competitive and ruthless world where pressure to succeed, meet deadlines and supply on time can mount. Getting on with people is important, as are price, quality and punctual delivery. Independent designers have a choice of direction: freelance illustration for fashion magazines, freelance design work for others to make into clothes or hats or designing and producing from their own workshop; all of these can be supplemented by part-time teaching.

Fashion courses at art school provide the basic technical skills and cover everything in the design room, from design and illustration through to pattern-cutting, garment construction and some business aspects. Specific courses are available for millinery. Good colleges have close connections with the fashion industry where you can make contacts at fashion shows. If you decide to set up your own workshop and design clothes which you produce yourself for sale, you should expect to spend at least a year working in a design room to gain experience. This is almost like an apprenticeship, ie low paid and hard worked, especially before showing a collection. You'll learn about the panics and the problems.

For your workshop, you need enough space for large cutting-out tables, pressing table, dress stands, clothes rail and hanging space, an overlocking sewing machine (industrial or good domestic). You may be able to operate from home, but if you want to operate a retail outlet from the same premises you'll need a lot of space. You'll also need equipment like a yardstick, shears, scissors, set square, pins and needles. You'll need more specialist equipment for hat making, and leatherwork. For suppliers and trade information and second hand goods for sale see the *Drapers Record* and *Fashion Weekly*. For choosing fabric you can see samples at the INTERNATIONAL INSTITUTE FOR COTTON and the INTERNATIONAL WOOL SECRETARIAT and choose swatches from a wholesaler. You can also get fabric specially designed or printed by a textile designer. It is cheaper to get cloth printed abroad. Rag trade shops generally group together in one area of a town. The rate of pay for a finished full figure drawing is £100 to £150. Many designers supplement their illustration work by part-time teaching.

Freelance designing is a difficult field to get into – big companies employ their own designer. Contacts are the most important thing. You have to hawk round your portfolio to the fashion magazines and design houses. Competition for freelance fashion illustration work is so fierce that it is crucial to have a rapport with the fashion editors. Decide which part of the market you are aiming at: high, middle or low, then make and price accordingly. You'll probably specialise, for example, in fashion, casual, evening gowns, bridal, rainwear, swimwear, leatherwear or whatever. Researching the market is important: there are fashion forecast companies which show business selling trends. It is important to get some advertising or editorial about your work.

Information and addresses from the *Clothing Industry Yearbook* and the CLOTHING AND FOOTWEAR INSTITUTE.

HAT DESIGNER

Fashion Retailer

At a Glance

Qualifications/Training	Not necessary	*Income bracket*	Low–High
Licence	No	*Town/Country*	Town
Experience/Springboard	Recommended	*Travel*	Some
Mid-career entry	Yes	*Exit sale*	Excellent
Entry costs	£8,000+	*Work at home*	No

Mix and match Limited.   You could think about: Fashion clothes/hat designer, Photographer, Magazine publisher, Artist . . .

Enquiries Local fashion shops

There is a vast range of markets to choose from in fashion retailing depending on location, age and price range. Once you've chosen your market you have to move quickly to keep abreast of it. One successful outlet may lead you to opening up others (choose sites that will suit your established image). This brings a change in emphasis from acting as sole manager and spending a lot of time in the shop, to learning how to delegate responsibility and control increased stock and staff. Stock control and much other administration has been made a lot easier with the availability of computers. Sporadic discussions may one day result in relaxation of the Sunday trading laws which would have a significant effect on shop keeping.

You'll need some experience of working in a clothes shop. As well as being able to sell things, you have to know how to create an ambience for your shop, how to display goods and how to give your shop market appeal. It also helps if you have some idea of the sort of problems you may face from suppliers, unpleasant customers etc. As you expand you may find a management training course useful, or a course in running a small business. Fashion retailers need to have a good eye and an interest in clothes, they also have to enjoy serving people.

Before setting up, get a good accountant and a solicitor who can, among other things, give advice about leases and premises. For security and to enable reasonable insurance cover for your stock install a burglar alarm. You can't be insured against shoplifting which eats into profits, and so you may want to pay for a stock tagging system. It's important to build up a network of reliable suppliers. Initially, you'll find them at trade fairs or by visiting offices and showrooms (Soho is full of them). It takes time to find the right suppliers and to get used to the inevitable delays between expected and actual delivery days. Suppliers you can trust are also useful when you have to order clothes 6 months in advance for the next season – their stock should give ideas of style and colour ranges. If you're very enterprising you may branch out into manufacture yourself – this will increase your profit margins but needs a lot of organising.

The mark up on clothes is 100% or more. Gross profit percentages are reduced by shoplifting, sales, promotions and mark downs to about 44%. Aim for a complete stock turn around every 8–10 weeks. As long as you don't make too many buying mistakes, don't worry if you have to knock off about 20% to get some things moving. All stock can be sold eventually by cutting prices repeatedly and bringing out at subsequent sales. You should always have 2 sales per year in January and July, in which to clear old lines and make room for the new season's deliveries. Start with reductions of 25% or 33% depending on amount of stock left.

When you're opening up your new shop choose the site carefully; competition is good as long as you use different suppliers and you may in time have enough buying power to stop your suppliers from supplying other nearby shops. Managing a chain requires stringent stock control and the establishment of an image; you also need procedures for management, dealing with customer complaints etc. This may cramp your style a bit – a personal touch for one shop may not work for several when you don't have time to see to it yourself. Make sure that staff know what is expected of them, establish working relationships and keep tabs on what's going on. Introduce new blood, employ managers with training and experience different to yours. Once you've got several branches opening a central office is a help. You can buy from there and hold regular meetings as well as having a central address for invoices and post. Try to keep staff to a minimum to keep down overheads and create a busier, fast moving atmosphere.

Like all retailing, this is a full time job made more so by the need to change stock every season in a very volatile market. Useful trade magazines include *Fashion Weekly* and *Woman's Wear Resources*.

Fashion Shoe Maker

At a Glance

Qualifications/Training	Necessary	*Income bracket*	Low–High
Licence	No	*Town/Country*	Either
Experience/Springboard	No	*Travel*	Yes
Mid-career entry	Unlikely	*Exit sale*	No
Entry costs	£500	*Work at home*	Possible

Mix and match　Yes. You could think about: Fashion clothes/hat designer, Fashion retailer, Cabaret performer, Advertising photographer . . .

Enquiries　British Footwear Manufacturers Federation, British Clothing Industries Association

Unlike the conventional industry where people are used to producing component supplies, the fashion shoe-maker carries out most of the processes from design to production. It is possible, however, to sub-contract last-making to specialist firms to your specification.

The independent shoe designer/maker has emerged in this country as a reaction against an old fashioned, long established shoe industry which has neither the inclination nor the investment to produce new lines. People are tired of limited choices in their shoes and fashion shoe design is booming. UK designers are eagerly sought abroad – notably in Italy, but the opportunities for the designer in this country are fairly small. There is some resistance to new ideas and a certain resentment of young designers.

You can't design shoes if you don't know how to make them. There are specialist courses in the technical expertise, the design ability and business skills necessary to go it alone – eg CORDWAINERS TECHNICAL COLLEGE in London and SOUTHFIELDS COLLEGE in Leicester. The CLOTHING AND FOOTWEAR INSTITUTE has details of courses and some are listed in *Design Courses in Britain*. A more general fashion course will not enable you to actually make shoes. The industry has almost lost its apprenticeship scheme; what there is tends to concentrate on component-making rather than the whole shoe.

A fashion shoe-maker can operate in a fairly small space – you can make a pair of shoes over a last on your knees. All you need is a place to store a small amount of leather and your equipment. You need a hammer, knives, pincers, an industrial sewing machine and a roughing wheel. You can farm out some operations like last-making to specialist firms who implement your design to your specifications. If you get a big order you could consider sub-contracting to a manufacturer. Italy is a good place to go because design studios there are much smaller than their British counterparts and much more adapted to wide variation in design on their advanced machines (eg laser pattern grading, and computer control). They might produce 500 pairs of shoes a week retailing at between £80 to £150 a pair.

You have to secure commissions by hawking round your portfolio and range of sample shoes to likely outlets, eg small exclusive designer shops who may commission more. You can get a collection of shoes ready while still at college. Contacts are very important and designers will help each other. Word of mouth, fashion shows etc will get you more orders. You have to be very sure of your ambition and product and not be afraid to go out and sell.

Handmade shoes are bought for their fine workmanship, variation in design and colour, beautiful leather, handstitching, embroidery and innovation. They are therefore more expensive than other shoes and are sold at the exclusive end of the market. For the designer the aim is the product, not to save pennies. You can go in for zany products but these retail for a lot because of the work involved. You have to make sure that you charge enough for your work, currently about £85 to £100 a pair for men's fashion shoes and perhaps £120 for ladies' shoes. A one off special might cost £250. You may have cash flow problems when you've had to pay for eg shipping shoes and then have to wait weeks until delivery for the pay off. Distance creates its own problems when selling. The first year is particularly difficult until orders pick up.

Pitfalls of the business can be learned as you go along. Producing too much variation on a design theme, for instance, is expensive. One good motto is 'if it's not there they won't ask for it'. Another problem is taking too many orders and being unable to fulfil them, or taking too few and not having enough work. After a while you get the balance right.

For supplies and service, *Shoe and Leather News* and the *Shoe Trade Directory* are useful. Also contact the BRITISH FOOTWEAR MANUFACTURERS FEDERATION. The BRITISH KNITTING AND CLOTHING EXPORT COUNCIL produces a useful Yearbook and also organises exhibitions for fashion, including shoes. The BRITISH CLOTHING INDUSTRIES ASSOCIATION also has useful information and publishes a Yearbook.

Festival Director

At a Glance

Qualifications/Training	Available	*Income bracket*	Low–High
Licence	No	*Town/Country*	Town
Experience/Springboard	Essential	*Travel*	Yes
Mid-career entry	Good	*Exit sale*	No
Entry costs	£500	*Work at home*	No

Mix and match Essential. You could think about: Events organiser, Artists' agent, Contemporary art gallery owner, Chamber group director, Opera producer/director . . .

Enquiries Current festival directors

This work involves organising festivals, choosing venues and artists, raising sponsorship and subsidies from local and national sources. No particular academic qualification or arts administration course is needed, but a good general knowledge, enthusiasm, experience and love of arts and crafts is essential. Like planning a party, festival directors must be able to administrate, delegate and inspire a team. Being a good judge of people and getting on with sponsors, committees, artists and caterers is essential. The festival director must be able to empathise with the community and be able to produce a plan with which they can identify, but more imaginative than they themselves would choose. You must be able to balance your own ideas against the conflicting elements of audience appeal and the policy and finance of the city or town council.

Working as a gofer (often unpaid) at festivals can lead to contacts and a recommendation for paid administrative work; or get a job either in, or with, the arts – stage management, writing, editing, orchestral/operatic groups or with the local entertainment department. Form and run an unusual amateur dramatic/operatic venture or gallery so that you meet people and hopefully find sponsorship. Travelling and working abroad is valuable.

Get a cheap flat with a telephone or answering service and a typewriter or word processor. This job is normally part-time so you will need another to boost your income. A small festival will pay little, a large one up to £50,000. You can compete for these jobs, or be invited. Once appointed, you should visit your festival town about once a week. There is no age, race or sex bias, but you must gain experience by travelling to performances and exhibitions at home and abroad, meeting sponsors and agents. A car is not necessary. Hours are flexible but become demanding immediately before and during the event. A good way to meet lots of interesting and creative people, but not good for a conventional social life.

Film Director

At a Glance

Qualifications/Training	Available	*Income bracket*	Medium–High
Licence	Union card	*Town/Country*	Town
Experience/Springboard	Not necessary	*Travel*	Lots
Mid-career entry	Good	*Exit sale*	No
Entry costs	£250	*Work at home*	No

Mix and match   Yes.   You could think about: Journalist, Scriptwriter, Festival director, Opera producer/director, Actor, Racehorse owner . . .

Enquiries   Directors' Guild of Great Britain, ACTT

A director might work in: Features; TV drama; TV documentary and news; Commercials; Corporate films; Video promotions; or Animation.

The factor common to all these specialisations is the employment of a camera but each specialisation demands skills not necessarily required by the others. Many individual directors cross over or do a combination of the different specialisations (for instance many distinguished feature directors have started their careers either in documentaries or in television or, more latterly, in commercials). Very few manage to keep a foot in all camps.

The director's function is to put the film on the screen. They are responsible for the visualisation of the film and are present at all stages in the filming process, from the preparation of the script to the grading (the colour matching of the various shots) of the final show-print. Because they have a watching brief through all the technical areas of film production (all technicians are answerable to the director's interpretation), directors have to be jacks of all trades. This explains why many directors are recruited from the other film disciplines. Writers become directors in order to protect their original vision; lighting cameramen in order to control the editing of their material; editors in order to establish a style in the shooting; producers in order to attract the greater kudos attached to the director's function. Technical knowledge is necessary but a director need not be expert in the other disciplines – they employ the experts to do it for them. However they must know enough to be able to describe the effect they wish to achieve.

In documentaries, a journalistic background is useful to be able to sift through unrelated information and create an ordered coherent argument. In video promotion, a sense of rhythm is obligatory. In film drama, be it for theatrical or TV release, a knowledge of actors' rehearsal techniques, though not essential, is helpful in finding a common language with the actors.

Because the skills used by directors are so varied, there is no set pattern by which would-be directors get their first film. The traditional route-in was via another film discipline. In features, young aspirants joined the camera or editing department (very seldom the art department and never the sound department) and worked their way up through the grades. This was a very lengthy process and only bore fruit by chance. In TV the promotion ladder is more secure. It is still possible to work up from the floor. The 1970s saw a proliferation of film schools and university film courses and many graduates of these institutions are working as directors in features and television. Even now, however, the best way to get started is to control a project (a script or a programme idea) which aspirant film-makers can use as a lever to persuade producers or financial backers to give them the film to direct.

The most essential skills for successful directors are: charm and the ability to sell themselves; ability to manipulate and persuade others to their way of thinking; patience and dogged determination not to let the vagaries of the weather, the ever-decreasing budget and the intransigencies of actors, technicians and money-men obstruct their view of how the film should be made; unfailing optimism that someone will give them a film to direct and that they have something worthwhile to say on film.

CASTING DIRECTOR

How much you make will depend upon the area of specialisation and experience. Very few directors work for the ACTT minimum rates. Top feature directors can command fees (which are negotiated by agents) of up to 10% of the film's budget and can secure 'points' in the profits of the film. At the other end of the scale, pop promotion directors working on shoestring budgets earn very little. In TV the rates are set by union agreements with the companies. At the BBC, top rates are around £500 per week whereas in ITV companies the figure rises to £800 per week.

Many directors join the DIRECTORS' GUILD OF GREAT BRITAIN.

Film Production Person

At a Glance

Qualifications/Training	Recommended	Income bracket	Medium–High
Licence	Union card	Town/Country	Town
Experience/Springboard	Recommended	Travel	Lots
Mid-career entry	Yes	Exit sale	No
Entry costs	£500	Work at home	No
Mix and match	Limited.	You could think about: Film director, Typist, Artist ...	
Enquiries	ACTT		

These are the people who are responsible for organisation and logistics and for getting films made on time and within budget. The production team is headed by a production manager who, under the auspices of the producer, prepares pre-production budgets and the shooting schedule. Production managers are usually helped by a production assistant, primarily a secretarial job that also involves dealing with any crisis that the production manager throws at them. Depending on the size of the shoot, there may also be a production designer who is in charge of the overall design of sets and costumes and a location manager who has to find suitable locations for filming, get permission to use them, ensure they have the right facilities etc. General fetching and carrying on the set and at the studio is done by runners.

The film industry is difficult to get into. There are no essential formal qualifications but you need an ACTT union membership card for most jobs. A qualification from an ACTT accredited school is useful for background experience, credibility, contacts and because it makes you eligible for an unemployed ACTT card (first step to getting the real thing). The best way in is via a production company as receptionist/secretary/runner so that you can get an inside view of the industry and build up some contacts before moving on or starting to freelance. Get to as many shoots as possible so that you're seen and can be on site should any extra help be needed. Offer your services to any one likely to use them. Ultimately it's a case of pushing; nag producers, they may hate you but at least they'll remember you and may pass you on to somebody else who can use you. Investigate the Jobfit scheme from ACTT, which gives on the job training and experience through temporary junior positions with various production companies.

Production people need to be methodical with good organisational skills and the ability to spot and solve problems. In the earlier stages you have to be prepared to do the running for other people (hence the term 'runner').

Once you go freelance, you'll need a telephone and an answering machine; better still register with a booking service which will run your diary while you're away. As you become better known and your circle of sources of work widens, it's probably worth getting an agent who can hustle and negotiate for you. The ACTT set ludicrously out of date minimum rates for production people (£150–380 per week). On the whole you can expect to earn more than they stipulate; commercials and promos command higher rates than feature films because the length of the booking is shorter.

Production people often work in informal teams, the producer appoints the production manager who then appoints assistants, etc. This means that you may do quite a lot of work with the same people but that you are free to work with others. Every shoot you go to will increase your network of useful contacts and gives you access to industry gossip. News travels fast so try not to make mistakes.

Having worked up the production team ladder, you should have useful experience for producing or directing. Read *Money into Light* for an account of producing a film.

Fish Curer and Smoker

At a Glance

Qualifications/Training	Recommended	*Income bracket*	Low–Medium
Licence	No	*Town/Country*	Country
Experience/Springboard	Essential	*Travel*	Local
Mid-career entry	Possible	*Exit sale*	Yes
Entry costs	£10,000	*Work at home*	Yes

Mix and match Possible. You could think about: Oyster/Salmon/Trout farmer, Restaurateur, Winebar owner . . .

Enquiries National Federation of Fishmongers, Agricultural Training Board

A curer and smoker fillets, cooks and smokes fish, giving it a unique flavour and a longer shelf life. This is becoming an overcrowded profession; you should be sure you can produce goods well above average quality in order to withstand the competition. You need a hardy physique as you will be standing for long hours in unheated premises in winter. You must be dextrous so you can fillet fish, with no waste, at speed. An excellent palate is essential, as the same critical qualities as those of a good cook are needed to test the taste of the cure (which is usually based on a mixture of salt and brown sugar). The best smoking methods are unchangingly traditional so you are relatively untouched by technical developments.

The AGRICULTURAL TRAINING BOARD in Scotland runs short (2 week) courses in smoking and curing. In addition, you need at least two years working in a smokery with someone who is really skilled. Before setting up alone, do some market research. You must be prepared to spend the first year hawking fish around to find steady customers. It's useful to join the NATIONAL FEDERATION OF FISHMONGERS, who know the market and can give advice. Find a good accountant.

You need a small building with a car park, near a main road, for retail sales. The cost of buying or renting will depend on the area of the country. You must have planning permission and you will also receive the attentions of the local environmental health officer. You need drains, hot and cold water and a separate septic tank (£5,000). A modern smoking kiln which draws smoke through a fan costs £2,000. Negotiate with the local saw mill for sawdust and woodchips for burning in the kiln. You can produce up to 130 sides of smoked salmon a week with this equipment. You will start with an income of £5,000 per annum rising to £10,000–£12,000, with car and perks. This job needs constant attention to detail and is normally a 50 hour week. It involves filleting all day 9.00am until 6.00pm; putting on the cure to soak all night; then smoking for anything from 2 to 24 hours; then slicing the flesh, as many chefs are nervous of this job.

Organisations such as the SCOTTISH SMOKED SALMON ASSOCIATION are useful for giving minimum specifications.

Football Commentator

At a Glance

Qualifications/Training	Available	*Income bracket*	High
Licence	No	*Town/Country*	Town
Experience/Springboard	Essential	*Travel*	Essential
Mid-career entry	Yes	*Exit sale*	No
Entry costs	£100+	*Work at home*	No

Mix and match   Good. You could think about: Journalist, Public relations consultant, Book editor, Specialist and sports retailer, Garlic farmer . . .

Enquiries   Television companies

Television sports commentators are self-employed and work under contract to TV stations and companies (radio commentators tend to be employed). Whoever you're under contract to has first call on your time but you're free to take on other jobs such as working on books, programmes and brochures; speaking at public and private functions and working on videos. The BBC won't let you take on any direct advertising but you can still work on material for football sponsors. Television football commentators have a high profile so spin-off work is likely, while you're working and after you've retired. Contracts last for about 2–5 years and are often renewed; the only risk is if the TV station you're under contract to loses its contract from the relevant sporting body to broadcast football matches. Currently the BBC has the contract to report on FA and England matches at Wembley; ITV has the Football League.

There are no formal qualifications but you'll need experience of sports reporting. The way in is through journalism (information on journalism courses from the NATIONAL COUNCIL FOR THE TRAINING OF JOURNALISTS). You need a lot of determination; first push to be taken on by a local newspaper and, once you've some experience of football reporting, get on to local radio as a commentator. From there, if you're determined and good enough, you may get noticed and get on to TV. You need a good voice, to be quick with words, observant and quick to notice, identify and report what's happening. You must be passionate and knowledgeable about football, its history and that of the teams you're watching. Forget any flowery vocabulary you may have picked up from having to keep up a constant commentary on the radio; TV viewers are happy to have some minutes of silence from you; and they can see how beautiful the weather is and how vast the crowd. You have to add to what they can see, so specialist knowledge is essential as is the ability to concentrate on the game while still remaining in constant contact with the producer who directs the camera shots and decides which area of the field is being shown on the screen. Languages are useful when you're keeping up with what's going on abroad or commentating on a match with a foreign team.

The only equipment you need is a warm coat; a typewriter or word processor is useful while you're doing pre-match research. All technical equipment is provided by the TV company. Expenses include any books or magazines about football that you can lay your hands on. Keep up with what's going on at home from eg, *World Soccer*, *Match Weekly* and *Shoot*; read also overseas magazines like French *Onze*, and the sports pages of the national press. Contract fees roughly reflect the amount of work you're expected to put in; they range from about £35–80,000 pa. Football commentating takes up an average of 3–4 days a week during the season. There are no matches on Monday, but you could be working for any or all of the rest of the week. Fees for other work are negotiable; agents can help and are usually worth their 15–20% commission.

You need a lot of contacts to do the job properly. That means getting to know football managers and players for after match interviews; club secretaries who provide essential information about ticket allocation and crowd segregation as well as details of players' height, weight, age and biography; team physiotherapists for immediate information on any injuries during the game; commentators abroad who can tell you about visiting teams. Contacts will also get you work writing programme notes, club histories, articles for magazines and work on club videos.

Each match needs about 2–3 days of preparation. You'll probably only use a small proportion of the information you collect but before a match it's impossible to judge what you'll need on the day. By looking at the fixture list at the start of the season you'll have a pretty good idea of when you're going to be called on to commentate; expect to have about 3 weeks warning of a definite booking. Get to know the teams playing, this may involve travelling to watch them in other matches. If one of the teams is foreign, get hold of videos and try to watch a training session as soon as they reach the country. Notice who wears which number and what each player looks like. Prepare notes on each of them, you won't necessarily have all this information in front of you but writing it down helps remember it. Prepare a card of essential information on each player. Find out too, all you can about the ground and make sure you know how to pronounce all the players' names.

The hours are irregular and there's a lot of travel including visits abroad and to tournaments like the World Cup. This gives you the chance to meet other commentators and build your network. It can be stressful and sore throats are an occupational hazard.

Foreign Correspondent

At a Glance

Qualifications/Training	Available	*Income bracket*	Low–High
Licence	No	*Town/Country*	Town
Experience/Springboard	Recommended	*Travel*	Yes
Mid-career entry	Yes	*Exit sale*	No
Entry costs	£1,000	*Work at home*	Partly

Mix and match Excellent. You could think about: Newsletter publisher, Radio reporter and presenter, Novelist, Farmer, Public relations consultant . . .

Enquiries IFCA, Newspapers, BBC, Press agencies

There are three routes to becoming a foreign correspondent, a job which may sometimes be exciting (do you really want to get your legs blown off while covering the latest war?) but consists for the most part of reading foreign newspapers.

Route 1 is through the direct in-take of graduates to the BBC and REUTERS (or ASSOCIATED PRESS or other agencies) and is especially to be recommended. The on-the-job training is the best available and will open many other avenues on your way to the top.

Route 2 begins on the Wigglesworth Evening News, from which you gradually elbow your way to one of the national newspapers, BBC, ITV, *Time Magazine* or any other employer who will undertake to send you abroad.

Route 3 is to take yourself off to a city or country of your choice – some like it hot, some like it cold – and set up as a stringer. A stringer is a freelance correspondent (whether the Wigglesworth Evening News' bowling correspondent or The Times' man in Outer Mongolia) who is usually paid per line published/minute on the air and if lucky may also receive a monthly retainer and expenses.

Route 3 is best practised after some experience of Routes 1 or 2, but with luck, perseverance and good media connections it is possible to make a success of it without either. Why choose Route 3? In nine out of 10 cases, it's love that takes the unsuspecting Brit abroad without any visible means of support.

Before leaving for your destination, trawl the foreign desks in London, visit magazine editors and so on, to establish connections and credentials. Having selected your city, you will almost certainly need to supplement stringer earnings by translation (don't be romantic: only undertake business translation, as you'll starve faster if you try the literary genre), teaching English to locals or with jobs for the English/ American language programmes of the local broadcasting media. Try charming your way to menial tasks for Reuters and other agencies: the local correspondent may be only too glad of someone prepared to relieve him of the late-night results for the Asian kayak championships, and once in with a finger you may be able to insinuate an elbow.

The going is probably slightly easier if you choose a big news centre (Brussels, Paris, Bonn, Tokyo, New York), where there are more opportunities but also more people competing for them, than in small news centres, where hungry local correspondents may chew up the newcomer for dinner. In Europe life is expensive, but you may be saved by the social security network. In some Far East centres (no personal experience) it is said that one can live quite nicely even on the pitiful rates which such as the Grauniad pays its stringers.

The rewards and style of life for the successful foreign correspondent are attractive, although the hours are long and unpredictable (which tends to upset co-habitants). You may meet The Great, sometimes face to face, more often with 500 other correspondents. You will eat and live well, and may influence the policy of nations. But don't underestimate the slog of getting established via bread-and-butter reporting (rape, mayhem, sports results).

Equipment: a portable computer is now essential. Forget typewriters. Get yourself, for example, a Tandy 200 with a communications programme from IFCA (International Foreign Correspondents Association) which will enable you to communicate with virtually all UK daily newspapers at the touch of a button – singly or collectively, as a kind of one-man news agency.

Franchisee

At a Glance

Qualifications/Training	Franchisor's	Income bracket	Low–High
Licence	No	Town/Country	Town usually
Experience/Springboard	Useful	Travel	Varies
Mid-career entry	Good	Exit sale	Yes
Entry costs	£5,000+++	Work at home	No

Mix and match   Depends on business.   You could think about: Restaurateur, Cleaning contractor, Fashion retailer . . .

Enquiries   British Franchise Association, Franchise Development Services

Operating a franchise lies somewhere between starting up your own business from scratch and managing an outlet of somebody else's.

Franchisees buy the rights to sell certain products or services from a franchisor. There are franchises for a wide range of services and goods, eg cleaning services, fast food outlets and sock shops. In exchange for paying an annual royalty to the franchisor, franchisees get initial training and advice with establishing and running their business and subsequent support and help as it develops. They also benefit from the reputation, marketing and experience of the franchisor but are restricted to running their business to the company format. Originally an American idea, the franchise industry is growing in Britain and now accounts for about £3 billion in annual sales and nearly 150,000 jobs. A handful of disreputable franchisors helped to give the concept a shaky reputation but this is improving, partly due to regulation of franchisors on the part of the BRITISH FRANCHISE ASSOCIATION, the FRANCHISE DEVELOPMENT SERVICES and also to greater media coverage of what's involved.

There are no formal qualifications but you may have to face some sort of vetting procedure from the franchisor to assure them that you suit their product. What they're looking for varies. Experience in a related field (eg catering for pizza franchises) is useful but not necessary; in general franchisors are far more interested in proof of your ability to run a successful business and commercial experience is more useful. Franchisors know what they want to sell and how they want to sell it, (they will usually train you in their ways and techniques) and you may find you don't have a lot of opportunity to experiment: innovative ideas are not usually greeted enthusiastically – what may work for your outlet wouldn't at others and any risks you take could reflect badly on the whole company if they didn't succeed. Good franchisors, however, meet their franchisees regularly which gives you a chance to put forward any suggestions and some franchisees have found that, once they're established, the regular income they derive from the franchise allows them to set up their own separate businesses. You will have to be good at selling your product, capable of coping with customers and managing staff and prepared to work long hours.

A franchise will cost you from £5,000–400,000. Banks are usually quite willing to lend about 65% of this. For this you should get a ready-made business with necessary premises, equipment and initial materials plus advice about selection of staff etc. After that you will pay them an annual royalty of 4–10%. Generally speaking, you'll be selling a product with an established image, reputation and market; this means that franchises are relatively safe ventures (statistics show a 4% failure rate for the first 2 years as against 35% for other new businesses). On the other hand, your autonomy is limited and thus your potential to cash in on successful experimentation. Profits are regulated because the company will probably provide the goods at their own price and set the selling price.

Franchisors help with a lot of the customer finding and attracting that new businesses need, through centralised advertising, marketing and market research. You can augment this with your own local campaign. You'll have to find a franchise that you can afford and are interested in. Do a lot of research before committing yourself, check out the company's financial standing and management structure. Talk to other franchisees to find out what support you have and how easy it is to succeed within the company's price and management structure. You can get help from the BRITISH FRANCHISE ASSOCIATION and FRANCHISE DEVELOPMENT SERVICES and read *How to Evaluate a Franchise*. Other useful reading is *Franchise World* and the *Franchise Magazine*.

Funeral Director

At a Glance

Qualifications/Training	Recommended	*Income bracket*	Low–Medium
Licence	No	*Town/Country*	Town
Experience/Springboard	Useful	*Travel*	Local
Mid-career entry	Good idea	*Exit sale*	Yes
Entry costs	£50,000+	*Work at home*	No

Mix and match Limited. You could think about: Embalmer, Garage owner, Jazz musician/singer . . .

Enquiries National Association of Funeral Directors, British Institute of Embalmers

Although anybody can arrange a funeral, most people prefer to call on the professional help of a funeral director, also called undertakers, to take care of the corpse from death until burial or cremation and to make all the necessary arrangements. Exactly what this entails varies a lot – compare *What to do When Someone Dies* to the *American Way of Death*. Basic undertaking includes obtaining death certificates; providing a coffin and pallbearers; providing an embalming service and placing newspaper announcements if required; arranging the burial or cremation and transport of body and mourners to the funeral. Many funeral directors are small family businesses employing casual help at funerals.

The recent emergence of body disposal units, which will remove a body from the place of death and dispose of it without ceremony, has posed a cheap alternative though it doesn't threaten traditional funeral directors at present.

In Britain there are no necessary qualifications or licences, which has led to the occasional cowboy undertaker setting up with no experience. But you are well recommended to obtain a diploma from the NATIONAL ASSOCIATION OF FUNERAL DIRECTORS and, if you're going to do your own embalming, join the BRITISH INSTITUTE OF EMBALMERS. Working for another undertaker is useful experience. Your clients, the bereaved, will need sympathetic and gentle handling, but you'll have to maintain a fairly detached outlook and not become emotionally involved with other people's death. On the whole age is a help. A mature appearance is somehow regarded as more appropriate, and undertaking attracts people who are retiring from other areas. You will need the organisational abilities necessary for arranging funerals without hitches and a non-squeamish attitude towards dead bodies.

There are no laws specifically covering the storage of corpses but check with your local council to make sure that you don't fall foul of local health regulations – you will almost certainly want to install refrigeration. Premises should have a reception area, a preparation room and possibly a small chapel for body viewing. Suitable cars cost about £15,000 each second hand, and a second hand hearse is about £22,000; you should also have a basic supply of coffins which can be furnished according to client demand. Allow at least £50,000 for set up costs. You need at least one full time member of staff for reception and telephone answering especially when you're at funerals, and a network of casual pallbearers, hearse drivers etc. You pay all the necessary fees on behalf of your clients, billing them for the whole funeral (between about £300 and £800), later.

Public opinion prevents you from going in for overt advertising so your premises have to be discreetly obvious. Clients will come to you because you are the local funeral director or because of personal recommendation (particularly from a doctor) or family tradition. It's better not to set up too close to other funeral directors. In addition to funerals, undertakers are sometimes called on to exhume bodies and some have body removing contracts with the police, eg to remove any dead body found in the local river; these do not include contracts for arranging funerals.

Clients usually contact you after a death although initial discussions may have taken place when it became imminent. There is about 10 hours work per funeral spread out over 3 to 8 days. There are no legal controls over when bodies are buried, but conventionally all are disposed of within 2 years of death; modern embalming techniques do not preserve bodies longer than this. Special arrangements have to be made with the MINISTRY OF AGRICULTURE for burial at sea. You will find yourself rather busier in the winter than the summer.

Futures Broker

At a Glance			
Qualifications/Training	No	Income bracket	High
Licence	Yes	Town/Country	Town
Experience/Springboard	Essential	Travel	No
Mid-career entry	Yes	Exit sale	Possible
Entry costs	£20,000	Work at home	Possible

Mix and match   Yes.   You could think about: List broker, Accountant, Insurance broker, Greyhound trainer . . .
Enquiries   AFBD

There are four commodity exchanges in London: metal, energy, grain and feeds and softs (coffee, sugar, cocoa and tea) where commodities are sold by producers and bought by processors through intermediary brokers and traders. The prices of commodities vary day by day making long term financial planning difficult for buyers and sellers alike and the notion of commodity futures arose to provide a way for both to hedge against price fluctuations. A future is a contract which allows a commodity to be bought and sold in advance of delivery, at today's price. Between the day on which the future is issued and delivery this contract can be bought and sold many times in response to moves in the market. Every commodity exchange has a futures department where this trading is done. For example, should a buyer think that the price of the grain they're contracted to buy is going to fall, they will sell the future as quickly as possible and buy another one when the price has dropped. This keeps the market liquid (which it wouldn't be if everything was bought and sold in advance) by allowing buyers and sellers to hedge against any swing that would otherwise lumber them with buying or selling at a price that is very different from the current prices on delivery day. Futures trading is normally done through

commodity brokers (who also advise clients on when and what to buy
and sell) by instructing their trading representatives on the exchange
floor on when to act. Unlike commodity markets, the futures market is
available to the public and much of the dealing is on behalf of private or
institutional speculators, not the ultimate buyers and sellers of the
commodity.

You must be a member of the AFBD (the Association of Futures
Brokers and Dealers), which means proving your suitability in financial
standing, integrity, ability to advise clients and experience. There are
no hard and fast rules but experience of financial institutions and
considerable knowledge of and expertise in the market are essential.
This is best gained through a traineeship from another broker, getting
experience of each of the areas of commodity broking and trading
including working on an exchange floor for a while. Throughout this
time you'll be working as part of a team so the ability to work well with
others is essential. A background in economics or maths is useful;
understanding of geology or agriculture can also help when you're
dealing in a market based on natural or agricultural resources. Commodity brokers must be intelligent, analytical and very interested; you
have to keep in touch with any political or natural event which could
affect the market. You'll also have to take a certain amount of flak; it's a
high risk area where your advice may lose a client a lot of money.

It's not a cheap job to get into. As a broker you don't need to put up
the £10–144,000 needed for a seat on the exchange because you can
trade through locals or another larger commodity firm. But you will
need at least as much as this before AFBD will register you. This is to
back up the traders you use (in case they lose vast sums in a crash for
example) and so that you can afford a few short term losses on the way
to long term gains. You'll need an office and administrative staff,
equipped with telephones, typewriters and filing systems and, most
important, with an information system from a specialist news agency
(eg REUTERS) which will cost you about £10,000 a year. This is essential
because you must have ready access to far more detailed and up to the
minute information on current events and the market than the general
press is likely to be able to provide; you also need it for pricing. You'll
also need telex and direct links with other broking and trading firms
and with your own representatives on the exchange floor. Other
expenses include paying for outside consultancy and research and
AFBD fees, currently £500 for initial membership plus an annual
subscription of £875. Money comes from the commissions you charge
clients on deals; commissions charged to clients who generate large

volumes of business is at a lower rate than commission charged to smaller private clients. The futures markets are used by speculators, investors managing their own portfolios, investors using the services of a fund manager, and institutions using the commodity markets to offset against their risks on cash markets. Starting out as a small brokerage you're likely to attract more private clients than institutions. You can generate business through carefully placed advertisements but these cost a lot and you may prefer to use direct mail or the services of introducing brokers (also members of AFBD who recommend your services to clients).

This is an unpredictable, high stress job but there's the potential for great rewards if you're good (and lucky) enough. Hours are long to take in American trading hours making the working day stretch from 9am to 10pm if you want or if the market's particularly busy. Read the national and financial press for background, look out for useful newsletters and develop contacts who can feed you the right information.

Current events play a very important role in the state of the market so books on the subject give only a general background to what it's like or how it's done. To start with, try the *GNI Guide to Traded Options*, *Trading in Oil Futures* (the same principles apply to all futures), commodity and financial yearbooks, *Controlling Interest Rate Risk* and the brochures produced by broking companies for their private clients.

Garage Owner

At a Glance

Qualifications/Training	Recommended	*Income bracket*	Low–Medium
Licence	Yes, (MOT)	*Town/Country*	Town/Village
Experience/Springboard	Yes	*Travel*	No
Mid-career entry	Yes	*Exit sale*	Yes
Entry costs	£1,000+++	*Work at home*	No

Mix and match   Limited.   You could think about: Man with a van, Motorcycle Dealer or Racer . . .

Enquiries   Road Transport Industry Training Board

The motor trade is popularly believed to be full of dishonest people. This means that, no matter how law abiding you are, once you own a garage you'll be regularly visited by official bodies (eg various offices of the local authority), watching what you're doing and demanding to look at your books. Your customers will also be extra-vigilant and ready to assume the worst. If you thought that a spot of second-hand car dealing was a good cover for any less legitimate activity – forget it.

Garages can do all or some of vehicle servicing: MOT tests; repairs, including crash repairs and panel beating; car and van hire; new and second-hand dealing; selling petrol. If you're going to sell vehicles with hire purchase arrangements you'll need a standard credit brokers licence from the OFFICE OF FAIR TRADING; this costs about £300. For MOT tests you need a licence from the DEPARTMENT OF TRANSPORT. Unless you're taking over premises that are already used as a garage you will need planning permission. Otherwise to open up your own garage you don't need any formal qualifications but you'll need a lot of mechanical experience and contacts in the trade. You may have built these up through your own interest in car maintenance and practising on any old wrecks you can get your hands on. Any work in the trade is extremely useful; you'll have to know where to get spare parts as quickly and cheaply as possible so cultivate any contacts you make. The best experience is by working at another garage for a while. For this you probably will need to have some sort of City and Guilds, BTEC (or SCOTVEC) qualification or a motor manufacturer's own certificate of competence (contact the ROAD TRANSPORT INDUSTRY TRAINING BOARD. Once cars have been repaired or serviced, you have to give them a road test so you'll have to be licensed to drive any of the vehicles you're repairing. To open your own garage you'll have to be a very good mechanic, quick at picking up new skills and techniques as there are new developments all the time and manufacturers change their models frequently. Although some garages specialise in one make of car, you have more flexibility if you are able to repair and maintain any make. You'll also have to be diplomatic in your handling of customers, many of whom have little idea of what's involved in repairing their car, find life difficult without it and think you may be cheating them anyway.

You could start off in a small way, mending people's cars in their own garages or streets. Ultimately, you need suitable premises with some sort of office, storage space for parts and equipment and as much off-street parking as possible, in an area where there's room for a few extra cars to be parked during the day. You *could* start out with a box of tools and a telephone but you really need more than that to set up properly; electronic diagnostic equipment, exhaust gas analysers and vehicle hoists. Some of this is available second-hand. You also need insurance against theft of customers' cars belongings or damage and faulty repairs even though it's expensive and you may never need to use it. To begin with you might manage everything on your own or with a partner, but having somebody in the office as a receptionist and to help with the paperwork will stop you from spending half your time wiping oil off your hands on the way to the phone. Finding mechanics can be a case of trial and error. Although the qualifications mentioned above may have helped you to find a job, you'll soon find that they don't necessarily guarantee any great mechanical skill or initiative. The NATIONAL JOINT COUNCIL FOR THE MOTOR VEHICLE RETAIL AND REPAIR INDUSTRY sets minimum rates of pay for garage mechanics; expect to pay at least £110+ per week.

The charges you make are based on the spare parts needed and the number of man-hours taken (you set the rate for this, taking into account overheads, your own salary and the competition; you don't have to undercut as long as you can provide a consistently good service). You can get parts from manufacturers' own agents as you need them; for some old cars you may need to make or adapt your own spare parts and for a few foreign cars, less commonly used spare parts have to be ordered from abroad. The longer it takes to get a part the more impatient your customers will become so find a dealer you trust and who can come up with the goods quickly. Customers may want you to quote for a job in advance. This is risky unless you are absolutely sure you know what's involved; things can easily go wrong and you may end up spending far longer on the job than you anticipated. Once you've got a strong enough reputation you shouldn't need to quote in advance.

Work comes from your being known in the area. There is more work in towns but there is also room for garages in many rural areas. You may want to do some advertising to begin with. Mechanics have to be good at diagnosing cars' problems: if you get it wrong the first time it'll cost the customer more; if you get it very wrong it'll cost you – MOTOR AGENTS' ASSOCIATION policy is that you re-do or pay someone else to re-do any repairs that go wrong because of faulty parts or mechanics' mistakes. As well as repairs and MOT services, all cars are given regular services when they've reached certain mileages, these vary from manufacturer to manufacturer. Leasing companies are a steady source of work although they have fixed pricing. Doing your own car/van rental can be risky if you end up spending more on getting a car cleaned than you make from hiring it.

Working days are unpredictable, people bring their cars in at any time and may expect you to repair them on the spot – be wary of doing this, it may not be as simple a job as they or you think. Garage owners report that one of the greatest hazards is incessant telephone enquiries from customers asking when their car will be ready – the unpredictability of the work means you may have been working through a backlog or dealing with the results of a crash when they brought their car in for its service. It is easy to work 52 weeks a year so be forceful about taking holidays and time off. Rewards lie in the satisfaction of getting a battered heap back onto the road in full working order; frustrations, in finding that your hours of work have failed to do so.

Useful trade press, most of it free, includes *Garage and Transport*, *Car and Accessory Trader*, *Autotrade* and *Garage Equipment*.

Garden Gnome Maker

At a Glance

Qualifications/Training	No	*Income bracket*	Low
Licence	No	*Town/Country*	Either
Experience/Springboard	No	*Travel*	Local
Mid-career entry	Yes	*Exit sale*	No
Entry costs	£500	*Work at home*	Yes

Mix and match   Essential.   You could think about: Gardener/garden designer, Toymaker, Listbroker, Chiropractor . . .

Enquiries   Local garden centres and craft shops

All you need for this is a suitably shaped mould, which will cost about £5–6 from a craft shop, a bag of cement and sand (about £6.50 from a builders' merchant), some suitable paints and a car. Then go into production, mix the cement, make the gnomes and paint them. You can probably make about 40 a day.

As well as the ability to mix cement to the right consistency, an imaginative attitude to the use of colour is useful. However what is essential is the ability to sell. You need to operate in the right sort of area or be prepared to experiment in the hope that you may find a gnome that has widespread appeal.

Sell them through local garden craft shops, garden produce auctions or by advertising. Unless your gnomes are specialist ones you should probably sell them for less than the usual price. You may find that you have to be fairly persistent.

Gardener/Garden Designer

At a Glance

Qualifications/Training	Recommended	*Income bracket*	Low
Licence	No	*Town/Country*	Either
Experience/Springboard	Useful	*Travel*	Local
Mid-career entry	Yes	*Exit sale*	No
Entry costs	£600+	*Work at home*	No

Mix and match   Yes. You could think about: Landscape designer, Property manager, Man with a van, Osteopath, Typist . . .

Enquiries   Institute of Horticulture

A living is to be made from helping other people to design, redesign or maintain their gardens. These can be small town gardens or rural estates, but on a smaller scale than projects tackled by landscape architects. The popularity of garden design is growing, helped by the media (eg The Observer Garden Competition), the increase in house ownership and people simply getting fed up with the boring rectangle at the back of the house.

Many clients prefer a mixture of garden design and maintenance which makes for a job requiring flair but with regular work. You can drop the maintenance side as commissions for design come in, offering a service of layouts and planting plans either by post, or to a client in person.

This is a flexible business: you can operate in the town or the country, at home or abroad, and there is a great variety in scope and scale. You can sub-contract or include in your business clearing, paving, fencing, wall building, tree-felling and tree-surgery, turfing and so on. If you are designing only, acting as a mediator between your client and your sub-contractors, you need a room with a telephone and drawing board. You don't need to be involved with planning departments or architects unless you decide to include conservatories in your business. Once the garden is established you can maintain it yourself or leave it to your client.

Resources depend on the extent of the business. An answerphone will prevent you losing further business when you are on site. Order turf, paving stones, fertilisers and other bulky items for each job as and when you need them, and get them delivered direct; then you do not need storage space, except to house basics like wheelbarrow, secateurs, spades, forks and perhaps a few garden chemicals. You will need a car. Decide how much you are worth and charge per day or per hour;

charging per job is always risky in case the job takes longer than you expect. Your rate can go up as you acquire more commissions and become more experienced. As a small business you won't be able to buy in bulk, but get to know your suppliers and they may give you small discounts for regular supplies. If you sub-contract operations, try and ensure you have the money secured from your client before paying your sub-contractors; but don't risk spoiling good relations by with-holding payment for too long.

Once you have your first commissions, the business snowballs by word of mouth. You can advertise in the local press and the Yellow Pages; *Thompson's Local Directory* is free. In an advertisement, letters after your name create a good impression, for example NCH (the National Certificate in Horticulture) or OND (the Ordinary National Diploma). Obviously you need a basic horticultural knowledge. Quali-fications can be acquired on various courses: see the Department of Education and Science's booklet *Agriculture, Horticulture and Forestry (Choose your Course)*, or ask the INSTITUTE OF HORTICULTURE. Many private courses are advertised at the back of magazines such as the *National Trust Magazine* and the *Garden*; the ROYAL HORTICULTURAL SOCIETY runs courses and has many useful publications.

GARDEN DESIGN

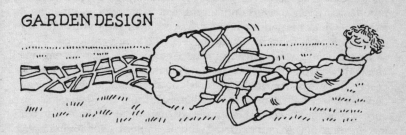

You will need to be able to get on with people and be fairly persuasive when the client wants something you know will not work; the ability to imagine what the garden will look like when it has grown to full size; an eye for colour and detail; some talent for drawing; an interest in and knowledge of horticulture; and some key reference books. You may need to know about methods of construction; you should sub-contract heavy work such as paving if your back or constitution is not strong.

Other helpful publications are *Horticulture Week* and *Landscape Design* which is the journal of the LANDSCAPE INSTITUTE. For herbs, contact the HERB SOCIETY.

Garlic Farmer

At a Glance

Qualifications/Training	Useful	*Income bracket*	Medium
Licence	No	*Town/Country*	Country
Experience/Springboard	Useful	*Travel*	Some
Mid-career entry	Yes	*Exit sale*	Excellent
Entry costs	£50,000+	*Work at home*	Yes

Mix and match   Yes. You could think about: Farmer, Import/export broker, Holiday accommodation owner, Restaurateur, Shopkeeper . . .

Enquiries   Ministry of Agriculture, Garlic farmers

Garlic isn't the easiest of crops to grow in the UK but if you've got a few spare acres in the south of England, it makes a change from wheat, rape and potatoes. Garlic consumption has gone up dramatically recently, so if you persevere and get your garlic crop going you'll be able to sell it. But it's not a quick way to a million, and there's no Common Market support to bail out British garlic farmers or help you over the first few years.

There are no formal garlic farming qualifications but you should know something about agriculture; a farming background is very useful. Visit garlic growers on the continent before you set up on your own. They may be amused at the idea of a British garlic farmer (all the better to impress them the following year with your bumper crop) but, as well as giving you some idea of what's involved, they will provide you with seed for your own crops and with their own garlic to tide your customers over when British garlic is out of season. As well as being good with plants, you need some selling skills, patience and perseverance. It's advisable not to be completely dependent on garlic for your income; tie it in with other farming (another minority crop for example) which you can sell to the same customers.

To produce garlic on a commercial scale you need about 50 acres of land. You also need storage sheds for the crops and a good supply of seasonal labour. Harvest is in late summer; garlic needs to be picked and sorted by hand so you'll need up to 80 extra workers. You may also need help with planting. Large chain stores want produce that is of uniform size and colour; you can sell the rest of your crop to small local greengrocers and delicatessens. Customers want a regular supply so when you don't have any of your own garlic, import some from abroad and wholesale it.

The MINISTRY OF AGRICULTURE may help but garlic is still very much of an alternative, minority crop.

Glass Designer and Maker

At a Glance

Qualifications/Training	Recommended	Income bracket	Low
Licence	No	Town/Country	Either
Experience/Springboard	Useful	Travel	Some
Mid-career entry	Possible	Exit sale	No
Entry costs	£50,000	Work at home	Possible

Mix and match Limited. You could think about: Goldsmith/Silversmith/ Jeweller, Potter, Beekeeper . . .

Enquiries   Glass Manufacturers' Federation

Embarking on a glass-making business is a total commitment because of the equipment and premises needed. You need all the equipment (£10,000 plus) immediately you start. The kiln runs day and night, and you must produce enough work to run it continuously. You need premises large enough to house the kiln, electric furnaces and an annealing oven, with enough space to move around both comfortably and safely. The kiln must have a special ventilation duct (again expensive) to remove to the outside the lead oxide fumes created by melting glass. Setting up a studio will mean visits from fire prevention officers and if you set up a company with employees, a factory inspector. For electric furnaces (used for blowing, pressing and casting) you need three-phase electrics, which is also expensive. The size of the annealing oven depends on the size of the kiln. Other equipment will depend on what processes you use: electric or gas kilns for fusing, bending and enamelling; cutting, engraving and intaglio lathes for conventional decoration of glass; and if you are adding metal (such as silver) or wood to glass, you will also need the relevant special tools and silversmithing facilities.

The premises you choose must be big enough to house all these things plus craftsmen's benches. You need space to store a supply of cullet (broken glass) or batch (mixed glass whose fumes are more hazardous). If you are not on mains gas, you will also need somewhere safe to store a supply of bottled gas. Because blowing glass is very hot work, you have to be able to create lots of draughts for the workers (but not on the actual glass or it will crack). A gallery area where you could display your finished work for sale is an advantage. Smaller items needed are blowing irons, wooden blocks for forming, colours, and clothes that do not catch in things.

Training for the studio glass-maker can be gained at art college, followed by an apprenticeship in a workshop like the GLASSHOUSE in London (which has a Workshop Training Grant from the CRAFTS COUNCIL). Some studios in Sweden, Finland and America also offer training. Czechoslovakia is a centre for glass; in the UK Stourbridge, Edinburgh, Sunderland and West Surrey are centres. Factory work is not useful to the studio designer/maker.

Tools and colours for glass-making come mainly from Germany. A lot of glass is sold to Germany, America, and – recently – to Japan. Trade Fairs (for example in Berne, Belgium, Germany and New York) operate but are very expensive if you are just starting up.

The only specific glass design magazine is *Neues Glas* (published in Germany), although general crafts magazines are sometimes useful.

You may find it helpful to contact the GLASS MANUFACTURERS' FEDERATION.

Glazier

At a Glance

Qualifications/Training	Recommended	Income bracket	Low
Licence	No	Town/Country	Town
Experience/Springboard	Essential	Travel	Local
Mid-career entry	Possible	Exit sale	Possible
Entry costs	£5,000+	Work at home	No

Mix and match Yes. You could think about: House builder, Dealer in small antiques and collectibles, Man with a van, Disco owner/DJ . . .
Enquiries Construction Industry Training Board

Glazing is a semi-skilled trade, and glaziers fall into several different categories. At the most basic level, a glazier probably combines his work with other semi-skilled jobs, working as a handyman, repairing domestic broken windows. More specialised tradesmen will provide a

24 hour service supplying and fitting plate glass for emergency repairs to shop windows. Glaziers may also specialise in building site work, supplying and fitting glass in new buildings. They may also own their own shops, concentrating on supplying different types of glass, and employing a driver and handyman to deliver and fit glass.

Most glaziers will need a specially adapted van to carry sheets of glass safely, but beyond that the only special tools needed are for cutting the glass.

A related field of specialisation is in fitting complete windows. Several large companies promote replacement, double-glazed windows and employ salesmen and fitters, often on a freelance basis. However, with the continued interest in period features in traditional homes, there is plenty of demand for traditional style windows, put together by carpenters, and glazed with ordinary glass.

Or you can fit specially tailored double glazing known as sealed units. If you are going into this field you will have to widen your skills, or employ others to take care of making good, plastering and painting after the replacement windows have been fitted.

Qualifications are those set by the CONSTRUCTION INDUSTRY TRAINING BOARD. Courses lead to City and Guilds certificates. As with most jobs in the building trade, one of the best ways to learn the work is to get a job with a busy glazing firm. Wages will be low, but once you have learned the necessary skills, you can start doing odd jobs at evenings or weekends, and gradually build up a business. Once you have set up on your own, you will need to promote yourself in the yellow pages and local press.

Goldsmith/Silversmith/Jeweller

At a Glance

Qualifications/Training	Recommended	*Income bracket*	Low–Medium
Licence	No	*Town/Country*	Town
Experience/Springboard	No	*Travel*	Yes
Mid-career entry	Possible	*Exit sale*	No
Entry costs	£2,500	*Work at home*	Yes

Mix and match   Yes. You could think about: Fashion clothes/hat designer, Dealer in small antiques and collectibles, Man with a van, Contemporary art gallery owner . . .

Enquiries   ADAR, Goldsmiths' Company

It's a small, highly competitive craft industry, with outlets concentrated (apart from the tourist routes) in a few centres such as London, Cardiff, Glasgow, Basle and Tokyo. Vocational degrees, diplomas or certificates are no guarantee of success. Most who are independent are designers or designer/craftsmen although some independent craftworkers act as out-workers for established companies. Specialisation is usual. Fashion and jewellery are more rapidly lucrative. In gold and silversmithing, working in precious metals or stones, objets d'art or trophies, it's slower to get established but rewards are greater, especially at the top. Contacts invaluable – trade fairs and competitions the way to get your name known and get to the top. You need persistence to get commissions or work as well as making what people will buy.

The most usual way to start is to take a degree or diploma course (details from the ADAR) and then start on your own – the better courses give some basic grounding in running a business. Less usually, you can, at 16, take a pre-apprenticeship course at an art college, followed by a 4 year apprenticeship. A very small number of successful designers are self-taught, or have taken short or part-time courses (eg courses leading to the GEMMOLOGICAL ASSOCIATION exams). But to succeed untrained you must be both good and lucky.

To start up on your own you'll have to equip yourself with tools, publicity, materials and premises. You need more tools for silversmithing than for jewellery. The cost of materials will depend on what you will make – feathers and plastics are obviously cheaper than gold (prices quoted in the newspaper). Some grants are available (Craft Council, local councils etc). Use all your contacts to reduce your costs – any college mates who can do art work for your publicity? You can try sharing costs through joint workshops or co-operatives – which give moral as well as financial support. Look out for second hand equipment in the *Retail Jeweller* (the trade bible). Some shops such as Hyper Hyper rent out units and manage publicity – but at a price. Others use markets one or two days a week. In the early stages it usually pays to combine your own work with other sources of income; teaching or selling others' work along with your own (out-working for an established company is possible but you will need a specialist skill such as pearl stringing). Your time is largely under your own control, so it's possible to mix and match.

Your biggest early problem is to get known. Use all your contacts, get known and *sell*. If you are going to make a real name for yourself, you should exhibit at all the trade fairs (eg London, Basle, Tokyo) and enter the competitions (eg Platinum Award sponsored by Ayrton Metals and De Beers in alternate years; annual competitions run by the GOLD-SMITHS' COMPANY). Competitions are advertised in the trade mags: *Retail Jeweller*, *Goldsmith's Gazette* and *Design Magazine*. Winning is worth a lot. Exhibit where you can – libraries, boutiques, galleries. Send photos to magazines and slides to designer groups promoting new designers. Wear your own jewellery to parties; write, phone, visit, hawk your samples/portfolio around. Be organised; keep a record of people you have met, and which shops you have visited. Take commissions and don't be too proud to do repairs which might result in further work.

Knowing your market and what it will pay is important – the English, for example, prefer 'safe' jewellery when they are spending a lot of money – the Americans often prefer something more showy. In fashion jewellery, the more different the better. There is always a small market for objets d'art which can pay for its exclusive taste. There is some published market research. One study identified silver items which sell and the price range; it established that way-out design doesn't sell and the most popular item singled out was a silver mounted nightcap decanter. Need we say more?

Graphic Designer

At a Glance

Qualifications/Training	Recommended	*Income bracket*	Low–High
Licence	No	*Town/Country*	Town
Experience/Springboard	No	*Travel*	Local
Mid-career entry	Unlikely	*Exit sale*	No
Entry costs	£1,000	*Work at home*	Possible

Mix and match   Yes. You could think about: Book packager, Magazine publisher, Illustrator, Artist, Greyhound trainer, Wood carver, Mini-cab driver . . .

Enquiries   Design Council, Chartered Society of Designers

Graphic designers are concerned with creating and projecting images for products, services and companies and with marketing, advertising and sales promotion. Much use of freelance graphic designers is made in design studios, publishing houses, advertising agencies, television companies and the film and video industries. Graphic designers usually specialise – eg in illustration, computer graphics, typography, poster design, book design, packaging, print-making, corporate image, photography and reprographics, animation, audio-visual.

Most graphic design work is in London and other big cities like Bristol, Birmingham and Manchester, because the big budget businesses are centred there. To begin with graphic designers often back up their income with part-time teaching; a lot is available in London.

Graphic designers usually start by attending a graphic design course (see *Design Courses in Britain*). During the last year of the course they usually choose which direction they want to work in: eg towards design groups or advertising agencies or publishing. There are no general graphic design agencies but the DESIGN COUNCIL recommends graphic designers. It is worth getting vetted by the Design Council because it is useful to be on their lists (divided into particular expertise). You can also advertise in *Creative Review, Design Week, Direction, Marketing Week* or *Marketing*. Join the Chartered Society of Designers.

You'll need a phone and some business cards as well as equipment such as drawing boards, pens and pencils. You can set yourself up as a graphic designer straight from college if you have managed to acquire the right contacts and have talent and persistence. To set up as a design consultant it probably takes about ten years to get enough experience before you can form a group with confidence and have enough contacts, although some people leave the ROYAL COLLEGE OF ART and set up as consultants straight away. Develop a portfolio while you're at college and show it to contacts and potential clients. A leading designer can earn more than £100,000 a year.

The designer's role is to supply ideas. Clients may approach you thinking they know what they want. But it's up to you to interpret their ideas, help to think them through, find the solution and then commission illustrators, photographers, typesetters to produce the necessary work. You can present your design solution as a 'rough' which is then further discussed, amendments made, until the final design is arrived at. For example, a company might come to you wanting a new brochure, but you can tell them that what they really need is a whole re-think of their image – perhaps a new logo, letter-heading, reception area, and sign above the premises, which create a new corporate identity for the public. This process applies whether you are dealing with corporate image, the selling power of consumer products, books or whatever. It is a world of deadlines and panics, and you have to be able to cope with that. It is very fast-moving and exciting and pretty ruthless.

GRAPHIC DESIGNER

Graphologist

At a Glance

Qualifications/Training	Recommended	*Income bracket*	Low–Medium
Licence	No	*Town/Country*	Either
Experience/Springboard	Essential	*Travel*	Possible
Mid-career entry	Possible	*Exit sale*	No
Entry costs	£1,000	*Work at home*	Yes

Mix and match Yes. You could think about: Careers consultant, Private investigator, Headhunter, Psychologist . . .

Enquiries Graphology Centre

Graphologists can tell a lot about other people by looking at their handwriting. To a skilled eye, a specimen of writing can show how healthy the writer is, or how logical, reliable, punctual, self-controlled, systematic, garrulous, sensitive to beauty or emotionally stable. It can also indicate attitudes to a range of situations and even pregnancy at a very early stage. A new and undeveloped area, graphologists are already being used by many large employers to assess the personalities and suitability of job applicants or candidates for promotion.

To become a graphologist you should serve an apprenticeship with a qualified graphologist. If you think you may have the gift, read the *Secret Self: A Comprehensive Guide to Handwriting Analysis* to vindicate your instinct. To succeed you'll have to be good with people and have a very good eye and attention to detail. Extensive psychological knowledge is needed and the ability to convince clients of your ability is extremely important. Your credentials are those people whose writing you have diagnosed correctly.

The only set up costs are for advertising. Try the local press or newsagents for private clients, otherwise the trade and professional publications likely to be read by the management of large companies. Fees depend on the depth of analysis required: base these roughly on the amount of time and expertise involved; with experience and a reputation you could be getting up to about £35 an hour on some jobs, starting with about £5 for a very quick, basic assessment of suitability as an applicant for a job.

Private clients are people who want to know, for example, what sort of career they may be suited to or what particular skills (especially interpersonal ones) they have which could be developed. Employers are a very good source for volumes of work. They may want assessments of reliability for jobs involving the handling of money for example; on intelligence; ability to cope under stress; management or executive potential; mental and physical fitness etc. Employers like handwriting analysis because it's unobtrusive and doesn't overtly invade the candidate's privacy by asking specific questions. Handwriting can be judged as a whole as well as in separate components (width of margins, spaces between words) so any inconsistencies adopted by a writer who wants to create a certain impression can be ironed out. Forensic graphology is beginning to take off; you'll need to do some further training for this and anyone appearing in court as an expert witness needs a well established background, knowledge and experience.

You can work the hours you choose, as long as you get things done by deadline and are prepared to do some quick turnover work when an employer wants to weed out unsuitable job applicants as quickly as possible. Although Britain seems to be lagging behind many other countries in using graphologists as reliable sources of information about people, things are changing so persevere.

Further information from the GRAPHOLOGY CENTRE.

Greyhound Trainer

At a Glance

Qualifications/Training	No	Income bracket	Low
Licence	Yes	Town/Country	Country
Experience/Springboard	Recommended	Travel	Yes
Mid-career entry	Possible	Exit sale	No
Entry costs	£5,000	Work at home	Yes

Mix and match   Yes. You could think about: Man with a van, Kennel/Cattery owner, Farmer, Book designer, Picture framer . . .

Enquiries   Greyhound Stud Book, National Greyhound Racing Club

Greyhound trainers look after and train racing and coursing dogs for their owners. They have contracts with race tracks to supply dogs for races and are responsible for feeding the dogs and keeping them fit to run – dogs with bad track records can expect, at best, to be demoted to household pets. Greyhound racing is getting a lot of media coverage, due partly to increased middle class interest in the sport and this has broadened the market of dog owners that trainers can provide service for.

Trainers have to be licensed by the GREYHOUND STUD BOOK (for coursing) or to have a professional trainer's licence from the NATIONAL GREYHOUND RACING CLUB (NGRC) for racing. The most useful experience is as a kennel maid/lad for somebody else. You need to like dogs and to have friends who can put up with your smelling of dogs all the time. Training coursing dogs is quite straightforward. A trained greyhound is one who runs when it's in a race; most dogs do instinctively and if they don't, there isn't much that the trainer can do. You will need to know how to feed and exercise dogs so that they are in top form.

You'll need kennels to keep the dogs in and somewhere to exercise them; this means being somewhere fairly rural. You'll also need some way of getting the dogs from kennel to racetrack. You're paid a weekly fee by each owner (about £20 per week) and a retainer from racetrack owners who contract you to supply dogs for each race. Owning greyhounds is for fun rather than a serious way of making money, but there are prizes for the owners of winning dogs and they like to see their animals run as often as possible. Track owners and bookies also like to see a lot of dogs running. The NGRC does not allow trainers to augment their incomes by using their knowledge of the dogs to gamble, nor to slow down dogs (by giving them water before a race for example) nor speed them up.

You'll need contacts among dog owners who don't want to train their dogs themselves, vets who will come out in an emergency and can advise about how to look after racing dogs and track owners who want supplies of dogs for their races. Bookies are also very useful because they often have influence over which dogs should run. You need to be there most of the time because dogs need daily attention; holidays can be difficult if you don't have anyone to take over while you're away.

Ground Worker

At a Glance

Qualifications/Training	No	*Income bracket*	Low
Licence	No	*Town/Country*	Either
Experience/Springboard	Recommended	*Travel*	Local
Mid-career entry	Possible	*Exit sale*	No
Entry costs	£5,000+	*Work at home*	No

Mix and match   Yes.   You could think about: House builder, House converter, Man with a van, Solicitor . . .

Enquiries   Local builders

Ground work is the term given to the work done on a building site before the actual building starts. The work is usually done by un- or semi-skilled builders' labourers: site developers may employ a firm of sub-contractors to do the work, or employ labour on a casual basis, depending on the scale of the job in hand.

The work may just involve clearing and levelling the site, or sub-contractors may undertake digging trenches, laying drains and foundations, and sometimes concreting and laying drives. The work continues in all but the worst weather conditions.

If you want to work in this field on more than just a casual basis, you will have to invest in a JCB (an earth mover/excavator) which you may be able to buy secondhand for something in the region of £5,000. Or you could specialise in one aspect of the work – such as drain laying or drive building.

Guardian ad Litem

At a Glance

Qualifications/Training	Essential	*Income bracket*	Low–Medium
Licence	No	*Town/Country*	Either
Experience/Springboard	Essential	*Travel*	Local
Mid-career entry	Vital	*Exit sale*	No
Entry costs	Nil	*Work at home*	Partly

Mix and match Yes   *You could think about:* Social worker, Journalist, Jazz musician/singer . . .

Enquiries   Children's Legal Centre, IRCHIN

If you are a qualified social worker with considerable experience of social work in the child care field, you can apply to a local authority to join its panel of Guardians ad Litem (Curators ad Litem in Scotland) and Reporting Officers. If a court needs an independent report on a child (in the case of say a dispute between the parents and the local authority social services department) a guardian may be appointed from the panel. The reports may be needed in, for instance, care proceedings in the magistrates court, adoption applications in the county court or for children who are wards of court in the High Court – and if either party appeals, you can end up in the Appeal Court or even the House of Lords.

You must have undertaken the usual social work training – a course leading to the Certificate of Qualification in Social Work (CQSW) and at least 2 years' experience. Then 5–10 years specialising in children is recommended (and a good range – fostering, psychiatric, residential etc). This means you are unlikely to be under 35. Once you have the confidence to go it alone, you can apply to local authorities before you resign from your conventional employment.

In adoption cases, where the mother consents, you act as a Reporting Officer, discovering whether the natural mother truly understands the implications of her child being adopted. If she does not agree, and in all other cases, you act as Guardian ad Litem. Here you are formally the guardian of the child in the case so you will need to get to know the child very well. You must be able to communicate with children quickly (a well-stocked box of toys helps) and be able to relate to parents and school teachers as well as other social workers. Your report will recommend what kind of order is in the child's best interests – which can be far from easy ('I want to go home but I want it to be nice again').

Cases can last up to 6 months (though this is undesirable). At the end of each case, you have to withdraw – both from the child and the people with whom you have worked closely while preparing your report. This can be a problem and is part of what can make the job isolated and lonely. You can discuss cases with other guardians and the child's solicitor who, in most cases, you are responsible for appointing (unless the court appointed the solicitor before the guardian). But you are not working with a team or within an established departmental policy – you are wholly dependent upon your own judgement.

The local authority social workers can be given a rough ride in court; but the Guardians ad Litem, although often subjected to tough cross examination, can be sure their views will be respected by the court itself. You need to have a sound understanding of the law relating to children, and to be able to defend your views in open court. Not for the weak minded. You need compassion and toughness.

An hourly fee for independent social work is fixed by the LAW SOCIETY but in some areas this is not paid to guardians in full. Some courts are more likely than others to use their panels but most guardians find work from 2 to 3 panels keeps them going; if you work for 3 or 4 you may get more variety – perhaps rural and urban communities and their different problems.

There is no national support group although the CHILDREN'S LEGAL CENTRE will keep you in touch with what is happening in the field and publishes *Childright*. Also the IRCHIN (INDEPENDENT REPRESENTATION FOR CHILDREN IN NEED) is a useful organisation for guardians. You will need to read *Adoption and Fostering* as well as general social work mags such as *Community Care* and *Social Work Today*. You can also usefully read two DHSS leaflets, *Guide for Guardians ad Litem in Juvenile Courts* and *Guide for Guardians ad Litem in Adoption Proceedings*.

Hairdresser

At a Glance

Qualifications/Training	Recommended	*Income bracket*	Low–Medium
Licence	No	*Town/Country*	Town
Experience/Springboard	Recommended	*Travel*	Maybe local
Mid-career entry	Possible	*Exit sale*	Yes
Entry costs	£8,000+	*Work at home*	No
Mix and match	Possible. You could think about: Beauty consultant, Make up artist, Wig maker, Interior designer . . .		
Enquiries	Local hairdressers and colleges		

As a barber or hairdresser, you'll have to know how to wash, cut and style hair. Traditional barbers whose clients are men, may not go in for much perming or dyeing, but they do have to be able to shave their customers. Many hairdressers are now unisex.

You'll need some sort of training, through a course or better still an apprenticeship. Private hairdressing schools are expensive (£3,000–4,000 for an 8 month course) but their diplomas often have prestige. Within the trade, the LONDON COLLEGE OF FASHION is among the most highly thought of but there are good courses at a number of FE colleges which lead to City and Guilds certificates. On the whole, though, you need salon experience through an apprenticeship or traineeship with day release or night school courses. It will take about five years to acquire the experience and standard of a top stylist and that's the stage at which you should open your own salon. Hairdresser's need to be dextrous, with an eye for what suits whom and good communication and understanding skills.

Itinerant hairdressers who visit their clients at home, are increasingly popular especially if they are prepared to call during the evening or at weekends. If you're going to operate like that, and cut down on overheads, you need a car to carry you and your equipment (scissors, combs and materials) around in. Alternatively, you can work in a hotel or club and pay them commission on what you earn. Working on a ship is well paid as long as you don't mind long, hard hours. Otherwise, a 10 seater salon in the city centre, costs about £20,000 to decorate and equip with heating, chairs, mirrors etc (about £8,000 in the provinces). Costs of buying or renting property are on top of this. You can raise the money through a bank loan. Most salons now are open plan. You'll need staff to help with the cutting, shampooing, drying, reservations etc. Junior staff are often easy to find especially if you offer some sort of training. For the others, use your own network and the *Hairdresser's Journal International*. You want well qualified staff who work on commission; most hairdressers want to open their own salons so you may find keeping staff difficult. Base your charges on location, overheads and local competition. Neighbouring hairdressers, unless they're aiming at very different markets, usually agree to charge similar rates. You can add to your hairdressing income by having sun beds (if you have the space), selling jewellery or introducing a manicurist or beautician to the salon on commission.

Clients come through word of mouth or because you're local. When you first open, make sure you bring some clients with you – tell as many as possible, but keep quiet to your employers though. Hairdressing can be hard work and, at times, you will have to cope with disasters (clients hating what you've done or asking for miracles) but it does allow you to be creative and experimental.

Haulier

At a Glance

Qualifications/Training	Recommended	*Income bracket*	Low–High
Licence	Yes	*Town/Country*	Either
Experience/Springboard	Not necessary	*Travel*	Yes
Mid-career entry	Possible	*Exit sale*	Yes
Entry costs	£40,000+	*Work at home*	Partly

Mix and match Yes. You could think about: Garage owner, Snail farmer, Winegrower, Coal merchant, Dealer in large antiques . . .

Enquiries   Freight Transport Association

Hauliers arrange the transport of goods by road for their clients who are manufacturers and producers. This means providing lorries and drivers and delivering to anywhere in the UK, also in Europe if you get the necessary licence. It's a business which is fraught with regulations and you must know what you're doing; if you break any of the conditions laid down by the Department of Transport you risk losing your licence and being forced to close immediately. For anyone who enjoys long distance lorry driving, it's a good way of making a living; you can operate on any scale from a one owner-driver business where you do all the driving yourself in your own vehicle, to owning a fleet of, say, 50 lorries and employing others to do most of the driving. You could mix and match this with something like specialist food manufacturer, making deliveries for other people while you don't need your lorry yourself. You need a standard (or standard international if you're going to work abroad) goods vehicle operator's licence from the DEPARTMENT OF TRANSPORT. This means you or a partner having a Certificate of Professional Competence for which you'll have to pass exams. There are residential, non-residential and correspondence courses to prepare you for these exams; the ROYAL SOCIETY OF ARTS (Orpington office) can tell you about courses. In addition you have to show that you are a fit person to hold a licence; that your drivers will keep the rules governing working hours and records; that you will ensure your vehicles are not overloaded and that you have facilities and financial resources to keep them properly serviced. You'll also have to have environmentally acceptable off-street parking for your vehicles while they aren't on the road. Before getting a licence you'll have had to advertise in your local paper, inviting any objections or comments on your business. Your licence permits you to operate the optimum number of vehicles that your facilities could support which means you can vary the size of your fleet within that limit. You're only charged for the vehicles you operate (currently £100 each), not for the maximum number for which you are licensed. Your operator's licence has to be renewed every 5 years.

If you're going to do any driving yourself, you'll need to have a Heavy Goods Vehicle (HGV) driver's licence, also from the Department of Transport; once you've got one you'll be a very skilled lorry driver. In addition it's very helpful to be a qualified mechanic. To comply with the licence requirements you have to show that you have servicing facilities. You can contract with a local garage for this but it costs a lot because lorries need to be serviced every 5 or 6 weeks and may also need emergency repairs at anti-social hours. Hauliers need to be punctilious and patient about regulations and you'll need great organisational skills to make the business succeed and avoid having too many empty lorries on or off the road. As well as being good with lorries, you must be good with people to find suitable drivers and a ready supply of clients.

Each of your vehicles must also be licensed and have its own registration plate stipulating its maximum full weight. Vehicle licences are renewable every year at which point your vehicle is checked by the Department of Transport. If you buy a second hand lorry in the middle of its licensing period, it needs an extra check when you take it over.

A new lorry tractor (the bit at the front) costs about £40,000, a trailer costs £12,000 (£20,000 if refrigerated). As an owner/driver you can just buy the tractor and work for people who have their own trailers. In addition you need off-street parking for the lorry and sufficient funds to keep it serviced. If you're out on the road yourself, you'll need a cordless phone to keep in touch with sources of work; you also need an office (this can be at home) and a phone with an answering machine.

You aren't allowed to use freelance drivers so, if you become an employer, you must ensure that you've got enough work to make it worthwhile. Find staff by advertising in the local paper, there are usually plenty of drivers around but few stay at the same job for very long. You are held responsible for drivers and vehicles while they're on the road, even if you haven't seen either for days and aren't there when the lorry is being loaded. All lorries are fitted with tachographs which record their every move to ensure that drivers keep to legal working hours and speed limits. The tachographs are checked every two years and you're in trouble if one of yours is found to have exceeded this legal limit. The police keep a close eye on lorries to make sure that they're in good condition while they're on the road.

You need to find clients to give you regular work which matches your schedules; when you send a lorry from A to B you want it to return full. You'll have to cold call to start with and it can take a while to build up a clientele of people who know you. It helps to be able to provide a wide range of containers, eg for hazardous chemicals or for large industrial plant. You're responsible for carrying the right goods and weights in the right vehicles. You can find work from agencies. Some handle a lot of one-off trailers full, these are very useful for owner/drivers who can collect at short notice from, eg, the port. Others handle backloads for hauliers. Beware, these can lose you money; they usually don't pay much believing that you'll take a pittance rather than go home empty, and you may end up losing a day waiting while the agent's client loads your lorry. If you're working overseas, your clients are responsible for any import/customs requirements but it's your time, not the clients', that is wasted at the borders/ports if they haven't complied with the regulations. Keep in touch by reading the *Commercial Motor*. Further information from the FREIGHT TRANSPORT ASSOCIATION and the ROAD HAULAGE ASSOCIATION.

Headhunter

At a Glance

Qualifications/Training	No	*Income bracket*	Medium–High
Licence	Yes	*Town/Country*	Town
Experience/Springboard	Essential	*Travel*	Yes
Mid-career entry	Likely	*Exit sale*	Possible
Entry costs	£10,000+	*Work at home*	Unlikely

Mix and match Possible. You could think about: Careers adviser, Marketing consultant, Accountant, Graphologist . . .

Enquiries British Institute of Management, Employment Consultants Institute

Also called recruiters or executive searchers, headhunters identify suitable people for their clients (employers), who are looking outside their own organisation for key staff – top management and executive staff. Headhunters themselves can specialise, for example, in finding senior banking staff, or they can be generalists helping a wide range of clients fill a variety of top positions. It's a job set to develop as the demand for high calibre personnel increases; economics and competition make it more important than ever that firms and businesses have the right person in the right role so more and more employers are using the services of a headhunter to achieve this. Headhunters are well placed to supply this service because of their objectivity, their access to top personnel and ability to discuss opportunities without revealing the name of their client.

Some big recruitment companies offer management training which can be a useful springboard but isn't necessarily the best way into the business. Successful headhunters depend more on personal networks and flair than on professional testing methods to fit people to jobs. To succeed you should have personal credibility, well developed contacts, experience, and a good track record. The best way of gaining these is to work for another headhunter with experience within the industry in which you plan to hunt heads (absolutely essential if you're planning to specialise). Many successful head hunting businesses are started by 2 or 3 people who pool their resources, experience and contacts. Some teams of headhunters stem from accountancy and management consultancy firms; people from both will normally have good business contacts and experience and are used to seeking new blood when helping to develop businesses. Clients must believe that you can find the right person. Candidates must believe that what you're telling them about a possibly anonymous client, is worth listening to and, more important, following up. You need to be outgoing, confident and to know what you're talking about.

Although you should keep files on high calibre people you know are looking for a career move, headhunters are not dependent on job searchers seeking them out. Many of the people you're looking for won't have advertised that they're looking for another job and some of them won't be unless the job is sold to them. That means having a lot of information about a lot of people. You'll need up-to-date press reports on who's doing what; a library full of relevant Who's Whos and professional directories; a word processor/computer; files and a telephone. You'll also need at least one researcher/assistant who works with you (including going to client meetings) while you're tracking candidates down. Above all you need excellent contacts who can point you in the right direction for likely candidates; who are likely to use your services themselves or to refer others to you. Networks like this are built up in a variety of ways; some date back to school or university; others are people you've met since, through your career or socially. Very often clients invite several headhunters to bid for a job. When this happens you put in a proposal outlining your approach to filling the vacancy having taken into account the client's needs.

Fees are usually paid in 3 instalments irrespective of delivery – first instalment on acceptance of the contract make sure your fee structure is clear. The charges headhunters make are usually based on the salary for the position they are helping to fill. Headhunters make roughly the same as other employment consultants; they are paid more per assignment but have a more detailed, painstaking approach. After the initial client meeting, and the acceptance of your proposal, you usually have three months to complete the job. During this time you'll have follow up meetings with the client. You may be expected to advise on suitable remuneration for the position you're filling and, at the level at which headhunters are involved, this is usually high. You can advertise discreetly for candidates, (in trade publications, the *Financial Times*, etc) but this is normally a last resort to be used only if your research and network of contacts fails. In some cases you may only track down one candidate, which doesn't matter so long as it's the right person. In others you may carry out the initial interviews and in-depth reporting in order to present clients with a shortlist of a few possibles after which you can either step down and leave it to the client to make the final decision, or continue to advise and attend interviews. There may be occasions when you can't fulfil a commission. This can't happen too often if you want to stay in business. Successful headhunters depend on their reputation and, while one high profile success can make you, credibility is rapidly lost if you don't deliver the goods.

Further information from the BRITISH INSTITUTE OF MANAGEMENT and the EMPLOYMENT CONSULTANTS INSTITUTE.

Healer

At a Glance

Qualifications/Training	No	*Income bracket*	Low–Medium
Licence	No	*Town/Country*	Town
Experience/Springboard	No	*Travel*	Local
Mid-career entry	Yes	*Exit sale*	No
Entry costs	£2,000	*Work at home*	Possible

Mix and match Yes. You could think about: List broker, Sculptor, Nursing home owner, Trout farmer . . .

Enquiries   College of Psychic Studies

Healers in terms of this job profile are defined as people used by 'God', 'the Creator', or 'the Power of Love' as an instrument through which patients are cured of their physical or emotional ills. This is achieved either by the laying on of hands, or the healer's hands being held near the body of the patient.

Healers should be convinced that their ability to make people better

HEALER

is a gift, and that they themselves are just ordinary and imperfect human beings. It is also necessary that they believe and feel strongly that this reality is only part of a much longer spiritual life which began long before conception and will continue after death.

You should be interested in people and possess intuition, sensitivity and belief in some kind of higher spiritual power. It is not necessary, however, to belong to any organised religion, religious body or society.

Healers' career prospects depend wholly on their results; if they can heal they will always have plenty of patients. As soon as you have faith in your gift and believe you are fulfilling God's desire, you can set up on your own.

You need a quiet, warm, ground floor room, if possible near public transport and with parking facilities. It should contain 2 easy chairs and a stool. You will need a telephone and receptionist to make appointments if you are busy. The average fee is £15 per hour and you can organise your day to suit yourself.

There is tremendous satisfaction and fulfilment in this job, but you must be careful to keep your work separate from family life if you are using a consulting room in your home. It's possible to do this job part time; you may need to travel to visit patients who cannot get to your consulting room.

The most useful sources of information are any books you can find in the public library on faith healing; and any literature, the more eclectic the better, which will broaden your awareness about man in relation to the unseen spiritual world. The COLLEGE OF PSYCHIC STUDIES has an excellent library.

Healthfood Shopkeeper

At a Glance

Qualifications/Training	No	*Income bracket*	Low–Medium
Licence	No	*Town/Country*	Town
Experience/Springboard	Useful	*Travel*	No
Mid-career entry	Good	*Exit sale*	Good
Entry costs	£5,000+	*Work at home*	No

Mix and match   Possible.   You could think about: Restaurateur, Homeopath, Specialist food manufacturer, Potter . . .

Enquiries   National Association of Shopkeepers

If you go into this business you must decide what market you are catering for. Are you going to deal in pills and potions? Are your basic foodstuffs going to be priced below the local supermarket? How health/ecology conscious are your prospective customers? Will you stock books? Will you get involved in the community by supporting local groups or sticking notices in your window? In a nutshell are you for lentils and beans or evening primrose oil? These two sides can be combined successfully but it is unwise to attempt this at the beginning. If you decide to go for the wholefood side think about wholesaling as well as retailing. Hospitals, other shops, cafés, restaurants, even burger bars could be wholesale customers, but you have to go out and find them or attract them through your retail business.

To start up you will need £5,000 for initial stock and retail premises (situation is important but not as much as for many shops as less passing trade is involved). Transport, owned or hired, is essential for collecting from your suppliers and delivering to your customers. You will need good management skills. Wholefood sales are labour intensive as bagging up sacks into smaller packages is necessary (you may need to employ a full time helper to do this). You may like to sell home baked snacks/bread and will need someone to cook these.

All food selling is a risky business as foodstuffs have a limited shelf life and can be subject to infestations. You will also have trouble persuading wholefood suppliers to supply the correct amount when you want it. This area of retailing is expanding fast thanks to better health education and a higher standard of living. Homeopathic cures are particularly on the increase – partly due to some disillusionment with traditional medicine and partly some American influence. Despite this growth you are highly unlikely to become a millionaire but should make a comfortable living. If you do choose to get involved in community projects and have a feel for their needs, experience has shown that the rewards are personal rather than material.

Hi-Fi Shop Owner

At a Glance

Qualifications/Training	No	Income bracket	Low–High
Licence	Yes for HP	Town/Country	Town
Experience/Springboard	Essential	Travel	No
Mid-career entry	Yes	Exit sale	Excellent
Entry costs	£12,000	Work at home	No

Mix and match Possible. You could think about: Disco owner/DJ, Music/Instrument retailer, Newsletter publisher . . .

Enquiries   Hi-Fi shop owners

There's a growing market for good quality sound systems; recent developments in hi-fi equipment have made people more willing than ever to spend a lot on CD, record and tape players. The ready availability of cheap equipment means that anyone entering the market will have to compete with high street shops and the cut prices they can offer with their large turnover. But if you're a good judge of hi-fi, you can build up a reputation for providing only the best at the more specialist end of the market. On the whole that will mean dealing in systems of £350 upwards and components of £100+.

Essential qualifications are a wide knowledge of what's available and what it sounds like, an excellent business sense and good selling skills. The best previous experience is working in someone else's hi-fi shop for at least a year, best in a fairly small one with a wide range of equipment. This will let you learn about the different components of hi-fi and give you some idea of the quality of various manufacturers' equipment so that you can start to develop your judgement of what's best. It will also put you in touch with suppliers' agents who may supply you in the future and with the hi-fi network which will help keep you in touch with future developments. That's apart from giving you some idea of what to expect when you're selling hi-fi, how to deal with customers and what the pitfalls are. But working in an established shop will not show you what it's like when you first start. You must be very interested in what you sell and it's unlikely that you'll enter this field unless you like music – much of the job involves listening to it. It's advisable to set up with a partner who can share the responsibility and who may concentrate on the accounts while you do the selling or vice versa.

Premises must be close to your customers, just off a main shopping street is ideal; probably not the cheapest you can find but it's worth getting the right shop to avoid expensive moves later (if you start off in the wrong place you may never be able to afford to move). Expensive hi-fi doesn't depend solely on passing trade (casual customers can waste a lot of time) but less specialist dealers may send customers to you and people don't travel far to buy hi-fi. Being near a business centre is useful for regular customers. You don't need masses of space for display or storage but must have an amenable demonstration room where people can listen to the equipment. To insure your premises you must have an alarm system. The telephone is essential; it's your link with prospective customers. To start with you don't need a lot of stock: about £8,000 worth will give you a full range as long as your suppliers are reasonably fast. The amount of stock you hold will increase to several tens of thousands as you grow and widen your market. Providing a free delivery and installation service is good for customer relations so having a van saves taxi bills. You can get a warehouse for holding stocks of best sellers when you're more established and turnover is higher. This saves you from moving to a larger shop but there are quite a lot of hidden costs in time and phone bills for communications. You'll soon have to employ help in the shop; find people with an interest in music and good product knowledge which will help you as well as the customers. Profit margins are approximately 30% of turnover – good accounting is essential so that you know how much of this actually ends up in your pocket.

Buying an entire hi-fi system at once can cost a lot and many shops offer hire purchase to customers. If you want to do this you need to have the protection of a credit company such as Lombard Tricity or North British Credit. You'll need a Consumer Credit Licence (costing about £40), available from the licensing branch of the OFFICE OF FAIR TRADING. If you decide to deal in second-hand equipment, or to operate a system of part exchange, make sure that you know how much it's worth to you before you buy it from the customer. To work out how much to pay for it, deduct your usual profit margin from this.

Initial business comes from advertising; word of mouth and reputation take over so your advertising budget should shrink quite quickly starting from about 5% of turnover in the early days. A spin off from advertising is the good editorial you may get from publications you've advertised in. Get to know your competition; not only may they refer customers to you but suppliers will be reluctant to supply you if they think that doing so will upset any local stockist they already supply. Suppliers teach you to instal equipment and also operate a one year parts and labour guarantee. For a specialist shop this isn't enough (customers won't like it if thousands of pounds worth of equipment packs up after eighteen months because of a manufacturer's fault which wasn't obvious until then). You may want to extend the guarantee to two years for your customers. Some (not all) suppliers will do the same; when they don't, it'll be up to you to pay for repairs on any unsatisfactory equipment you sell. Using British suppliers (or the British subsidiaries of foreign manufacturers) speeds up delivery time and eases communication considerably. You must keep up with developments: read the hi-fi press, *What Hi-Fi*, *Hi-Fi News* and *Hi-Fi Choice* and get to know which reviewers or equipment are best. Don't be tempted to stock anything that isn't up to standard just because it completes a range; success depends on establishing a reputation for selling only the best. Customers will come back if you provide a good service and if you're obviously well informed without being daunting. You have to listen to them and make sure you know what they want; don't contradict them if they want to buy something you wouldn't specifically recommend for them (another reason for being sure of everything you stock). They'll also come back to upgrade their equipment so make sure that you always have something rather better and more expensive for them to buy. As with any shop, hazards are shop lifting (against which there is no insurance) and unsellable stock. There's label snobbery in hi-fi too so only stock unknown names if you're sure that you can sell them.

High Street Photographer

At a Glance

Qualifications/Training	Recommended	Income bracket	Medium
Licence	No	Town/Country	Town
Experience/Springboard	Yes	Travel	Local
Mid-career entry	Possible	Exit sale	Yes
Entry costs	£10,000	Work at home	No

Mix and match   Possible.   You could think about: Advertising photographer, Photographer, Wedding shop owner, Contemporary art gallery owner ...

Enquiries   British Institute of Professional Photography

If you want to work as a photographer in a small town, the most likely opening is in a high street practice. Many of the commissions may be repetitive (weddings and bar-mitzvahs) and a large part of your business is likely to be in individual or family portraits. Another, less publicised, source of income is the less pleasant business of photographing people with injuries, to be used as evidence in court cases or insurance claims. You'll need to be able to be discreet when necessary (no-one likes a pushy wedding photographer) and bring out the best in people (the gift of the gab can be helpful in getting subjects to relax). You'll also have to be able to charm children – and their doting parents. If you want to work for yourself, the best bet is to set up your own practice.

Training usually involves a spell at art school (vocational courses are recognised by the BRITISH INSTITUTE OF PROFESSIONAL PHOTOGRAPHY), and then an 'apprenticeship' working for a high street practice. To set up you may start in a small way, working from home and advertising your services in the local press, or you may raise the necessary capital to take over an existing practice, or lease premises to set up on your own.

You will need reliable equipment, and good processing facilities – some practices do their own processing, others send film to labs for developing and printing.

You may also find you are commissioned to do some commercial photography, for local industries, property companies or advertising agencies, for example. You will not be able to charge the same rate as commercial (advertising) photographers in the centre of London, but you should be able to negotiate fees which are more substantial than usual.

The *Photographer* is published for the BIPP, and is a useful way of keeping in touch with developments in the photographic field, and it carries a good range of advertisements for equipment.

Hire Shop Owner

At a Glance			
Qualifications/Training	No	Income bracket	Low–Medium
Licence	No	Town/Country	Town
Experience/Springboard	Useful	Travel	No
Mid-career entry	Yes	Exit sale	Yes
Entry costs	Highly variable	Work at home	No
Mix and match	Limited. You could think about: Garage owner, Shopkeeper, Sub-postmaster . . .		
Enquiries	Local hire shops		

Hire shops own equipment and derive their income by charging people for borrowing it. There's a massive range of things that people would rather hire than buy: office equipment, cement mixers, sports equipment, televisions etc. Some things can merely be collected from the shop by the customer – eg cutlery, others need to be delivered because they are too large for most customers to be able to transport – eg skips; and others need some additional service – eg public address systems to be wired up.

In general, hiring doesn't require any qualification but you may need some specialist knowledge of what you're hiring – portable lavatories need to be plumbed into septic tanks, keyboards need to be tuned. Some experience in a field related to whatever you're hiring is useful; it'll give you an insight into some of the less obvious needs of your market and customers may want advice about which model to hire. Contacts you build up will be potential customers. You'll have to be meticulous to handle all the administrative paper work and to be good at coping with customers.

Set up costs vary a lot – obviously the value of what you're supplying affects this. Then there are premises and storage. If you're hiring carpet cleaners, your customers won't necessarily want to inspect a choice, you'll only need somewhere to store them and you can handle most bookings over the telephone. You may need to supply transport for the equipment if it's very large. Some hire businesses can be entirely run by one person; for others, eg marquees, you'll need help, often casual, to erect or install. As the business grows you'll probably want help with administration. Useful contacts, as well as people who may want to hire from you, include people who can lend you a hand from time to time and anybody who can repair and maintain equipment quickly.

Base charges on your overheads and the demand for your service. Hired goods tend to wear out more quickly than your own; they have a lot more use and aren't always treated well. Charge a deposit on anything breakable or stealable and check everything for damage as it's returned; some things, eg clothes, have to be cleaned between each hire. Make sure that you know where each item is – this will mean having customers' names and addresses, and for things like videos where you have a lot of customers and a lot of transactions it may be worth operating a membership system – issuing cards to customers and sending them regular bills.

Keep an eye on the trade press and add new equipment to your range as it becomes available and as you can afford it. For some things like cars or skis you may be able to sell off your stock from time to time when it is no longer hireable.

Publications for the hire market, *Hire News* and *Hireman*, tend to concentrate on the hire of plant and equipment.

Holiday Accommodation Owner

At a Glance

Qualifications/Training	No	Income bracket	Low–High
Licence	No	Town/Country	Either
Experience/Springboard	Not necessary	Travel	Possible
Mid-career entry	Good	Exit sale	Excellent
Entry costs	Highly variable	Work at home	No
Mix and match	Yes.	You could think about: Timeshare holiday accommodation owner, Village shopkeeper, Farmer, Import/export broker, Accountant . . .	
Enquiries	Tourist boards and other owners and agencies		

This can involve managing a single cottage or a block of holiday flats: in rural Wales or round Victoria station. It is well suited as a family business. Unless you happen upon the premises before you start, it is highly capital intensive. The banks are generally cautious about the holiday business and you should expect to put up 50% of the money yourself. Some grants from the relevant tourist board may be possible depending on their own cash flow and how keen they are to get tourists into the area.

You should think carefully about the size of the operation. A single cottage in your village may provide pocket money for you as well as headaches; a block of eg 20 flats will be more cost effective. If you stay below the VAT threshold your prices will be more competitive.

There are other considerations: the situation, whether to be beside the beach or near good salmon fishing; standard of accommodation, jacuzzis all round or just the basics; whether to stay open all year or just in the peak season; parking space for cars, boats or even caravans; whether to encourage singles/couples or families with children in which case you need somewhere for them to play, washing machines and relatively indestructible furnishings.

What you will charge will depend upon these conditions – and the prevailing weather expectations. The more you require payment in advance the fewer the risks of bad debts – though some areas of the country are worse than others for this. If you are well equipped, willing to help and reasonably priced, you can expect a number of recommendations and repeat bookings. This helps in reducing advertising costs. Where you advertise will depend upon your chosen market – the *Lady*, the *Times* or the post office window. There are a number of agencies and the tourist boards are very likely to help.

Whatever the size of your operation, your holidaymakers will need to be able to get hold of someone when they lose their key or the tap leaks, even if it is only a telephone number. You will also need to consider booking people in and out and cleaning on change-over day. If you have more than about a dozen units, you will probably need someone present most of the time although you may be able to bribe eg a local shopkeeper to cover in emergencies.

The cost of setting up will depend on the cost of local property, the standard of your furnishings and the cost of local labour if necessary. You need good insurance.

You can regard this as an investment and pay others to manage the business on a day to day basis. If you do everything yourself you should be practical and resourceful in dealing with emergencies. As with all jobs associated with the tourist industry, you are a worker in a world of holidaymakers and your clients will expect everything to be perfect.

Homeopath

At a Glance

Qualifications/Training	Essential	*Income bracket*	Medium
Licence	Yes from 1992	*Town/Country*	Town
Experience/Springboard	Recommended	*Travel*	No
Mid-career entry	Yes	*Exit sale*	No
Entry costs	£5,000	*Work at home*	Yes

Mix and match Yes. You could think about: Doctor, Journalist, Dispensing chemist, Illustrator, Music teacher . . .

Enquiries Society of Homeopaths

Homeopaths try to cure illnesses ranging from colds to AIDS suffered by patients of any age or background, but using very different methods from conventional doctors. Homeopathy takes an holistic approach to curing disease, treating the whole patient rather than the symptoms. Not everyone will have the same response to an illness or to a cure; before any treatment is prescribed, the homeopath tries to find out as much as possible about the constitution of the patient as well as the history of the specific illness and its symptoms. In addition, the remedies used by homeopaths are quite different from those used in conventional medicine. Homeopathy stimulates the body's powers of healing itself by prescribing minute amounts of substances that in a healthy person would provoke the symptoms that are being treated. Currently, there is a shortage of homeopathic practitioners as the demand for alternative medicines increases in response to the growing number of illnesses and complaints with which conventional medicine has yet to devise ways of dealing.

Currently, you don't need to be registered to practise as a homeopath. This is set to change over the next few years, and when it does, it is expected that professional prescribing will be restricted to registered practitioners. In the mean time, you're recommended to get proper qualifications before you start. There are two ways of qualifying as a homeopathic practitioner. As a registered doctor it is possible to become a homeopath by doing a course through the FACULTY OF HOMEOPATHY. Although this allows you to call on your conventional training as well as homeopathy, there are disadvantages; the approaches of both are so different that much conventional medical training has to be unlearned before you can practise homeopathy with complete conviction. (Homeopathic hospitals are staffed by members of the Faculty of Homeopathy, the only branch of alternative medicine recognised by the NHS.)

The alternative is to do a course at one of several colleges that are associated with the SOCIETY OF HOMEOPATHS. These last for 4 years, 3 of theory and one of clinical training. You don't need any special qualifications to get onto them and they're taught at weekends with a lot of home study. If you can't get an LEA grant it will cost you about £3,000 in tuition fees. When you pass the course you become a provisional member of the Society of Homeopaths for two years during which you can practise while undertaking in-service training. After that, as long as you're at least 25, you're a fully registered member, although continued in-service training is expected. Members of the Society of Homeopaths are not allowed to work for the NHS. Many people come to homeopathy from other careers. It helps if you're mature enough to cope with some of the very great emotional stresses and strains of dealing with the sick. Patients die and leave friends and relations who need continuing support. Even those who aren't seriously ill can be distressed and distressing. You must be dedicated (and you will be if you've got through the course which is very gruelling), be interested in health and healing and good with people.

Set up costs aren't great as long as you've got somewhere to practise from. This can be in your own home but renting a room in a natural or alternative health centre is a good way of getting more widely known by patients and other practitioners. Apart from that you need basic stationery and books. This could all cost as little as £200 but a computer with some special software will make life a lot easier and costs about £4,000. The software you need works out suggested prescriptions from what you tell it about particular cases and the *materia medica* that you are using – this can save hours of complicated calculations. Because of the amount of information you need to collect about each patient, first consultations usually last about an hour and a half; subsequently they'll be about half an hour. Most homeopaths are in private practice and charge patients per consultation; London homeopaths charge about £35 for the first consultation and £20 subsequently. Many operate a sliding scale, charging less for children, the elderly or those on low incomes. Annual earnings range from £10–20,000 with £12–15,000 being about the norm.

Once you've seen a patient, you have to work out and write the prescription which you either dispense yourself from stocks obtained from a pharmacy or send to a specialist homeopathic pharmacy. Because there aren't many of these around, most operate mail order systems. For the prescriptions you make up yourself you'll need a dispensing licence if you're going to charge but most practitioners avoid this by including the remedies in the basic consultation fee. Homeopathic remedies are inexpensive so this won't cost you much and saves time having to deal with a pharmacy for each prescription. Most patients will come to you (they have to pay extra for a home call) but some need home or hospital visits. Occasionally, you may need to get a patient into hospital as a precaution in case they need emergency surgery. Very rarely will you be called out on an emergency but you need to be on call all of the time unless you can make some arrangement with another homeopath. As long as you can afford it and have a locum, you can have holidays whenever you like.

Although some patients will come to you as a last resort after all else has failed (currently many people with AIDS use homeopaths), there is an increasing number of people who are deciding not to use orthodox medicine and are turning to homeopathy for its own sake for themselves and their children.

For further reading, see the *Science of Homeopathy* and *Homeopathy, Medicine for the 21st Century*. The SOCIETY OF HOMEOPATHS, associate membership of which is open to all, publishes a Register of Practitioners, a Journal and a Newsletter.

Hotel Keeper

At a Glance

Qualifications/Training	Recommended	*Income bracket*	Low–High
Licence	Yes for alcohol	*Town/Country*	Either
Experience/Springboard	Recommended	*Travel*	Local
Mid-career entry	Ideal	*Exit sale*	Excellent
Entry costs	£150,000++	*Work at home*	Yes

Mix and match   Possible.   You could think about: Restaurateur, Caterer, Holiday accommodation owner, Wine merchant, Farmer, Windsurfing school owner . . .

Enquiries   Tourist boards, Hotel and Catering Training Board

Anyone considering a career in the hotel business should think very carefully before going ahead; enjoying a stay in a hotel is very different from doing the entertaining yourself, seven days a week from 7.30 until late. Living over the shop, as is usually the case, may be tax efficient but you never get away from the problems – no front door to shut the world away! This career is a way of life, its great joy is that a considerable degree of success can be achieved without a lot of training.

There are all sorts of formal courses in hotel management – at catering or FE college or degree courses at a poly or university. Check with the HOTEL AND CATERING TRAINING BOARD. But someone striking out on their own usually relies upon a short intensive course at a cookery school such as CORDON BLEU or LEITHS which gives enough appropriate cookery experience; and the WINE AND SPIRIT EDUCATION TRUST runs excellent courses on the drinks side of the business at a variety of levels of sophistication. One way of getting the knowledge you'll need if you want to avoid costly mistakes is through working for a good hotel as a general assistant (badly paid and long hours) for at least a year. Find one similar to the sort of hotel that you want to set up but more up-market. Staying in hotels (buying the product), is also essential research for anyone who hasn't been properly trained, and is something that you won't have much time for once you've set up yourself. If you want to serve wine and have a bar, you need a residential liquor licence, and for non-residential diners a restaurant licence. You can get these as long as you're considered suitable and as long as the building complies with certain regulations. It's more difficult to get a full on-licence that lets you serve booze without food. You need a fire certificate if 6 or more people are to be accommodated. The Health Officer can walk in at any time to assure himself that the premises comply with regulations and if you're converting other property into an hotel, you'll need to get planning permission.

Think clearly about the market you're aiming for before you set up, as chopping and changing is bad for business. Affinity with your guests allows you to compete with large, impersonal but well-financed chains because of the friendlier atmosphere you can build up. There is a vast range of hotels from which to choose. One of the basic considerations is whether to cater for principally business visitors (in which case you'll most likely be in a town, serving bed, breakfast and, possibly, dinner from Monday to Thursday), or for people on holiday (when you'll most likely be in the country or at a tourist centre, and will have busier weekends than weeks). On the whole, business hotels need to emphasise efficient and professional service while people on weekend breaks are more impressed by your personality and the hotel's character. Rural hotels may be more pleasant to live in but tend to take longer to become established, require more travelling on your part to market and provide slower capital growth on your investment. Staff may also be difficult to find and may need accommodation/transport home when you do find them.

You can buy a going concern (agents or look in the *Morning Advertiser*). This may be good value if it is well done up but has been badly run. However, if you do this you may inherit an unwanted reputation or clientele that are hard to lose. Never underestimate the cost in time and money of a garden, therapeutic though it may be. Hotels aren't cheap, they start at about £150,000 and a modest sized hotel in a good trading position can cost £500,000. (Buying a house and converting it won't cost much less.) However, people are prepared to pay for comfort and good food, and you can make a living although running costs cut what look like massive gross profits very quickly. Unless you've got a lot of working capital, you'll have to do most of the work yourself; consider a partner, 'two owners can do the work of 6 employees'.

For your first clients, contact local hotels and pubs for their turn-aways and local businesses for their visitors. Advertising is expensive and can prove to be bad value if you haven't done enough research. The English and the Regional Tourist Boards have useful publications as does the BRITISH HOTELS, RESTAURANTS AND CATERERS' ASSOCIATION. Get onto your local large town's accommodation register and, once you're good enough, try and get into guides like *Egon Ronay*, the *Good Hotel*, the *Good Food*, *Michelin*, *Ashley Courtenay*, the AA, and the RAC.

Running a hotel demands total commitment to the job which is, above all, about caring for people, both guests and staff. This makes it unsuitable for people with young families. The long and unsocial hours, with meals grabbed whenever they can be fitted in, requires a strong constitution. The main advantage is that success lies mainly in the hands of your own ability as a host and your own sound financial judgement.

House Converter

At a Glance

Qualifications/Training	Available	*Income bracket*	Low–High
Licence	No	*Town/Country*	Either
Experience/Springboard	Essential	*Travel*	Local
Mid-career entry	Yes	*Exit sale*	Possible
Entry costs	£30,000++	*Work at home*	Possible

Mix and match   Yes. You could think about: New house builder, Property developer, Surveyor, Property manager, Estate agent, Landlord . . .

Enquiries   Local estate agents

This entails buying up a single property, renovating or converting it and selling it again. It is not advisable to do this on your own home unless you and your family are able to cope with enormous disruptions in your domestic arrangements. It requires a rising house market, so is therefore more likely to succeed in the south of England or near other main centres.

You can make more money out of buying a house and converting it into a number of smaller units than simply renovating. You may lose friends if you acquire a reputation for buying up all the run-down cottages in the area, doing them up to a high standard and selling them as second homes.

Banks, by and large, understand lending money against bricks and mortar so are likely to be reasonably helpful; even so, they will only lend ⅔ of the sum and that on your own collateral. They need a well-presented package rather than a cigarette packet sketch. The amount which you will need to start off, and the profits you can make, will both depend upon local property prices and how much you can do yourself. Unless you are working in an area with exceptionally high property prices there is probably little profit to be had unless you can do the bulk of the work yourself, sub-contracting only the specialised work; on the other hand, it is quicker to subcontract all the work and co-ordinate it yourself. You need to know your contractors will work fast for you. To remain liquid you must be able to turn the property round quickly. If you're developing listed buildings or properties with preservation orders your plans may need to be passed by eg the VICTORIAN SOCIETY who will take time. Even planning permission and building regulations can slow you up, depending on the local authority and this needs to be considered when you are selecting properties. If you're operating as a business, you're subject to corporation tax or income tax; if it's a side line, to capital gains tax.

There are no formal qualifications except the eye for a property with potential; if you're in doubt about the structure, consult a surveyor before buying. If you are not a competent builder yourself, you should be able to communicate effectively with your contractors; local authority officials will always be part of your life and you should be able to live with them too. Your money needs to be tied up for as little time as possible, so the work needs to be carefully scheduled, eg not trying to change the roof of a house in January or put a seaside property on the market in November.

Hypnotherapist

At a Glance

Qualifications/Training	Yes	Income bracket	Low–Medium
Licence	No	Town/Country	Town
Experience/Springboard	No	Travel	No
Mid-career entry	Recommended	Exit sale	No
Entry costs	£1,000	Work at home	Possible

Mix and match Excellent. You could think about: Counsellor, Music teacher, Market research interviewer, Knitwear designer . . .
Enquiries Hypnotherapists

A hypnotherapist treats conditions, controlled by the sub-conscious, through the use of hypnosis. The best qualification for hypnotherapy is the experience of life, and it's therefore not a good choice for the very young person. It's not usually regarded as a full-time career on its own because it doesn't always guarantee enough money to live on. For these reasons, it is often practised by retired people and by those – usually women – who have some other form of income.

Hypnotherapy bears very little relation to the popular image of hypnosis as portrayed on the television. A hypnotherapist cannot – and would not want to – make a client do or say something against his or her will. The mind is a very powerful tool, and the hypnotherapist knows how to communicate with it at both conscious and subconscious levels.

The accepted formal qualification is a course in psychotherapy and hypnosis at one of the specialist colleges, like the UK TRAINING COLLEGE

OF HYPNOTHERAPY AND COUNSELLING (this holds weekend and evening courses in central London, Bristol, Edinburgh and Dublin). Training takes three years and costs around £1,000 a year, but some of this can be recouped by going into practice once you've completed the first year. There are other hypnotherapy schools and training centres, many of which advertise in magazines, such as *Here's Health* and the *Journal of Alternative and Complementary Medicine*. Good books to read if you're interested in taking up hypnotherapy are *Hypnosis: Guide for Patients and Practitioners*; *Hypnosis*; and *Hypnosis: A Gateway to Better Health*.

It's useful to have experienced personal problems yourself and to have worked through them with the help of therapy. This will give you a good grasp of what it's all about and a healthy conviction that it can indeed work. The most important quality of all is an interest in people. You've got to be a good listener, to be highly sensitive and, above all, to care. There's no point in going into it for the money alone.

All you really need is a comfortable chair or couch, a telephone and, ideally, an answering machine which enables you to pull out the plug during a session so that the telephone doesn't disturb you. Some hypnotherapists use tapes, in which case you'll need a couple of inexpensive tape recorders perhaps costing £40 or so.

Hypnotherapy is not yet as popular a form of therapy, as, say, osteopathy, though it has the approval of many orthodox practitioners and is fast gaining ground. But it is not always easy to set yourself up in practice. Depending on where you live, you could start by charging around £15 an hour; £20 is about average. Once you're established, with good contacts and good publicity, you might be able to earn as much as £40 an hour, though this is not common.

Most hypnotherapists see five or six clients a day, and work only three days a week. It can be a draining process and some therapists feel that many more than that would be not only exhausting for the therapist but unfair on the clients. A few see up to 60 clients in a week, though that's far from usual. A lot of experienced hypnotherapists like to devote some of their time to teaching and to sharing some of their expertise with others.

The surest way of getting work is by recommendation. Advertising in local papers can work but word of mouth is the best way, particularly through any sympathetic local doctor. Application and perseverance are the key factors. You won't see many clients at Christmas or in the summer holidays but expect a sudden influx of clients if there's something about hypnotherapy on the television or in the press.

Illustrator

At a Glance

Qualifications/Training	Recommended	*Income bracket*	Low–Medium
Licence	No	*Town/Country*	Town
Experience/Springboard	No	*Travel*	Some
Mid-career entry	Unlikely	*Exit sale*	No
Entry costs	£50	*Work at home*	Yes

Mix and match   Good.   You could think about: Artist, Graphic designer, Artists' agent, Book packager, Greyhound trainer . . .

Enquiries   Art colleges

Illustrating books and magazines is one of the most attractive careers for those who would like to make their name as artists in their own right, but want to take on commissions to ensure an income.

The work can involve long hours and tight deadlines, with periods of inactivity. Commissions come from book or magazine art editors or designers and range from imaginative book jacket illustrations to painstaking technical drawings of buildings or machinery. Most illustrators specialise in a particular field and build up a 'stable' of clients. Successful illustrators can set their own fees, but in most cases, income works out to about £250–£500 per week.

A foundation course at art school, followed by a vocational course which includes options in printing, layout and design and illustration are the usual qualifications. If you want to go straight into freelance work, you will then have to put together a portfolio of work and start the long, weary business of selling yourself to the right people – the commissioning editors and designers who can give you work.

You will have to set up a studio, with a drawing board and storage space for materials. You may need some special equipment, such as a light box, a compressor for an airbrush, a Grant machine, and you may also need accounts with artists' suppliers, printing companies (if you are producing annotated artwork) and motorbike messengers.

To be successful, you need to be outgoing, able to sell yourself and your work, fast, accurate and imaginative. You may have to work from a minimal brief – some book jacket illustrators have no more than a set of proofs to work from – or you may be given complicated instructions which must be followed to the last detail. If you want to specialise in cartoon illustrations you will have to be quick witted – the work doesn't usually pay enough for it to be worth your while pondering in depth over each image.

Illustrators may be members of the NATIONAL GRAPHICAL ASSOCIATION, the CHARTERED SOCIETY OF DESIGNERS or even (on newspapers) the NATIONAL UNION OF JOURNALISTS.

Import/Export Broker

At a Glance

Qualifications/Training	No	*Income bracket*	Medium–High
Licence	No	*Town/Country*	Either
Experience/Springboard	Essential	*Travel*	Possible
Mid-career entry	Excellent	*Exit sale*	Yes
Entry costs	Bank credit	*Work at home*	Possible

Mix and match   Yes.   You could think about: UK correspondent for overseas media, Foreign correspondent, Property developer, Shipbroker, Accountant, Holiday accommodation owner . . .

Enquiries   British Overseas Trade Board

You can import and export an enormous variety of products and services – legally – between two industrialised countries, between the Warsaw Pact and the West, and of course between the Third World and the industrialised North. Carpets, floodlighting, fruit and vegetables, oil industry supplies, books, print, machine tools . . . You can switch from product to product but the key to this job is to establish market knowhow and a personal niche.

In this business, networks are all. If you have those, the only other musts are a telephone and access to a telex, fax or electronic mail. There are no essential qualifications and you do not need to be authorised by anybody to act as an import/export broker. You need to involve your own capital only until you start receiving income, apart from the cost of setting up an office. Banks finance thousands of transactions every week, using standard documentation and insurance, including government guarantees where appropriate – they usually want 23–30% cover before opening a letter of credit. There is little personal risk so long as you stick to recognised well-established UK banks and ensure that business is conducted on terms of confirmed letters of credit for every transaction. A good relationship with a bank manager is important for speed and efficiency and because you'll need credit standing while you wait for payments to come through.

You can usefully team up with someone whose networks complement your own – and if you specialise in importing from or exporting to a particular country, a reliable and trustworthy local partner or agent and/or supplier is vital for distribution and quality control. You can work from a rustic cottage while renting a busy-sounding metropolitan address, complete with telephone number and telex, if that suits you. They will ring through telephone messages and telexes and forward your mail. You can start up with access to either demand or supply although starting with demand is easier.

Because of the need for networks, it is especially suited to people in mid-career – particularly those leaving an industry with good contacts in it. If you know that you want to set up as a broker in a particular industry, it often pays to take a job first to establish your networks. You can do as much or as little work as you need; you will have to work odd hours if you are dealing with countries in very different time zones.

The job involves introducing suppliers and purchasers. You can let them worry about customs, shipping, and red tape but it's worth your while making sure that they have all the right permits otherwise the goods won't get through the relevant customs, they'll lose the deal and you your commission. All you have to worry about is getting the price right. Remember that the market may be very competitive and that to gain a foothold you should be prepared to keep the margin for commission very low. Keep an open mind – people have succeeded in exporting flowers to Holland and snow ploughs to the Middle East but importers and exporters can lose a lot if they can't sell; in addition to shipping costs, VAT and customs duty are irredeemable and paid on nearly all imports.

Further information from the BRITISH OVERSEAS TRADE BOARD or through *Export*.

Impresario

Impresarios engage an orchestra, opera or dance company and take financial responsibility for their performance. The most important skill is an ability to work quickly and accurately with figures. An accountancy training is helpful but not essential. No academic or practical musical training is necessary. The local library can help you acquire the good general knowledge of music and musicians which is necessary. Ideal qualities are a phlegmatic temperament, patience, diplomacy and an organising ability. Physical and psychological stamina are required to withstand high levels of anxiety while waiting to see if your inspired idea for a concert series will attract the public or leave you financially drained. Confidence in your own judgement is vital.

Start by working as a gofer for an impresario and read the files. When you have acquired contacts and feel sufficiently confident to work alone, you need a room, telephone and typewriter. A computer and more sophisticated office equipment will make life easier when you can afford it. You do not have to join a union. Useful books are the *British Music Year Book*, the *British Association of Concert Agents list of artists*, *Grove's Dictionary of Music* and any record catalogues you can find.

Begin by approaching local authorities about promoting concerts jointly. Circularise artists about acting as their agent. For the first 2 years or so, earnings will be low, rising to £50,000 when you are established. Working hours will be irregular, up to 18 per day if you have to attend an evening performance. Allow some thinking time each day to create and develop your ideas. The job is lonely and you will be responsible for taking painful decisions and working in an area of high financial risk. There will be some travelling though a car is not essential. You meet interesting people and have the satisfaction of making things happen. The job is never boring.

In-Company Trainer

At a Glance

Qualifications/Training	Recommended	*Income bracket*	Medium–High
Licence	No	*Town/Country*	Town
Experience/Springboard	Essential	*Travel*	Yes
Mid-career entry	Essential	*Exit sale*	Possible
Entry costs	£20,000+	*Work at home*	Not recommended

Mix and match Yes. You could think about: Marketing consultant, Computer consultant, Picture restorer, Gardener/garden designer, Journalist . . .

Enquiries In-company trainers

There is growing demand for independent in-company trainers who will train other people's employees to do anything from answer the phone to manage a multi-national. Although many large companies have their own training departments, many prefer to augment their own resources with outside help especially in specialist fields. In addition an increasing number of smaller companies don't want a permanent training staff themselves but find that they need to provide some sort of training from time to time. Independent trainers also provide courses for the public in, for example, time management, sales techniques or marketing.

Client companies won't hand over their staff training to someone they know nothing about. You need credibility and contacts to set up on your own and, although some people get there earlier, you're unlikely to have collected enough of either until you're at least 40. In the meantime, there are 2 main routes you could follow. The first is through working in industry to management level and building up training experience in, say, personnel, sales or in the training department itself. The second is the academic route where, via a second degree (preferably an MBA), you are employed to teach but meanwhile develop contacts in industry and workable training programmes before springboarding. This second route is more prevalent in the USA, where links between industry and higher education are stronger. Some trainers start after they have written a fantastically well received specialist book and using it as the flagship for a programme of training courses which they teach themselves or delegate.

In-company trainers need to be at the forefront of training, able to identify new areas where there's a training need, and analytical enough to develop training programmes which succeed in filling those gaps. Communication skills and the patience to deal with trainees of a vast range of ability are also necessary. Essential equipment for setting up is an office and a manned telephone. You'll certainly need a car and should set up near a commercial or industrial centre. Training generates a lot of paper work (hand outs for the training programmes etc) so a typewriter and a photocopier (or a word processor) are essential. In addition, although you can hire them, you're advised to have your own flip charts, projector and video equipment. You don't need your own training premises; they are expensive to maintain and anyway clients usually provide their own. If they don't or if you're running a course for the public you can hire college or university accommodation during the holidays or simply book into a hotel or conference centre. You can expect to spend £20–30,000 pa on mailing and administration.

Because training is intensive and hard work (you're talking to an audience all day), you shouldn't plan to do more than about 3 days a week actually training people. Set your fees accordingly. Start off by quoting your upper limit so that you can let yourself be bargained down. Some clients have fixed prices in which case you must decide whether the job's worth taking. If you're planning a course for the public you'll have to base your prices on competition and the number of people you expect to attend. You may develop a series of off the peg courses and this can work but many clients will want modifications to suit their own needs. It is most important for your business that you find out as much as you can about the organisational structure of the company whose employees you're training – you are, in effect, an intruder in a client's sub-culture when you're working there.

As an in-company trainer you may not need many different company clients as long as those you do have have large enough staffs. You won't need to advertise. You'll find that clients approach you through your network of contacts, and that people moving to another company will use you again there.

Clients will usually give you about two months' notice when they're going to need you; occasionally they may call on you in an emergency at only 2–3 weeks' notice. After a preliminary meeting to discuss the nature of the course, and to agree the structure and fees, you design and write handouts and other training material, inspect premises and hire the equipment you'll need if the client cannot provide it. The busy season is from September–April when companies are more likely to have new staff. Holiday times are quieter.

Independent Financial Adviser

At a Glance

Qualifications/Training	Not yet	Income bracket	Medium–High
Licence	Yes	Town/Country	Town
Experience/Springboard	Essential	Travel	Local
Mid-career entry	Yes	Exit sale	Possible
Entry costs	£12,000+	Work at home	No

Mix and match   Yes.   You could think about: Stockbroker, Insurance broker, Futures broker, Disco owner/DJ, Timeshare holiday accommodation owner, Novelist . . .

Enquiries   FIMBRA

These are the people who help private clients get the most from their money by advising them on financial products and services. Financial products and services come from companies operating investment schemes, pension plans and life assurance policies; financial advisers are intermediaries between companies and clients. You can if you want work as an agent for one of these companies (eg FPS or the MI GROUP) but this restricts you to their products only.

Independent financial advisers may use any of the wide range of products on the market. This means that while each transaction requires wide familiarity with the market and probably spending more time selecting what to advise, you have great flexibility. Clients usually prefer your impartiality and it's easier for you to extend your range of activities by offering (and charging for) a more general financial advisory service that doesn't always end with buying a financial product or policy. Demand for independent financial advising is increasing, partly due to recent changes in financial regulations but also on account of increased public awareness of financial services in general. Many people, including investors, home owners, the self-employed and small businesses, want help with financial decisions and accountants and bank managers don't usually have a direct involvement in financial planning.

You must be authorised by a self regulatory body before you set up on your own. For independent financial advisers this is virtually always FIMBRA (FINANCIAL INTERMEDIARIES, MANAGERS AND BROKERS ASSOCIATION). This means showing you're right and proper. Exactly what this entails depends on the nature of the business you're going to carry out; roughly speaking you'll need at least 2 years' relevant experience to be registered as an individual able to deal directly with the public in an

advisory capacity. As a company registered under the Financial Services Act, you must be solvent and trustworthy (no chance if you've got
a criminal record). FIMBRA judges each case individually and can take
five months or more to accept you into membership. A financial adviser
needs to be creative and imaginative, with the experience and judgement to choose the best from a wide range and the ability to put
proposals into effect quickly. Seeing options is even more important
than being a wizard figure juggler. This is very much a people industry,
communication skills are important – clients must always understand
what you're recommending and see you as someone whose judgement
they can trust. To set up you need an office which is easily accessible to
clients, many of whom will want to see you outside normal office hours
– at lunchtime and in the evening. As well as equipping yourself with a
calculator, telephone, typewriter and filing cabinets (or, better, a
computer) make sure that your office has a suitably professional image.
Very rapidly, you'll need to employ someone to answer the phone and
type letters. Setting up as a partnership lets you share overheads. Much
of your income will come in commission from the companies whose
products you are selling. Some companies offer massive commission,
tempting, but long term success depends on happy customers rather
than a temporarily healthy bank balance. In addition, at the beginning
of 1990 it will become law for financial advisers to disclose to their
clients full details of the commission paid on any of the transactions
you're recommending, so the days of hefty commissions may be
limited. Partly in response to this and partly in a move to increase the
overall professionalism of the business, some financial advisers now
charge clients consultation fees or charge fees in addition to receiving
commissions when business is placed, as it may not be appropriate to
do business with a client at every client meeting.

A lot of clients come through recommendation. Start off with people
you know augmented by some advertising and PR. Seminars telling
people about what you do and how you could help them also boost
business. Try to target a selected market (eg self-employed, doctors,
teachers) and become known as a specialist in that field, this may also
help to increase the amount of media coverage and interest you
generate. At your first meeting with new clients you must collect
exhaustive information about them and their finances. This helps you
to see a wider range of options than the client may have realised
existed. On the strength of this information you can make some general
recommendations before selecting which products are best and transacting their purchase. It is important to keep in regular touch with

clients, (six months to a year) to ensure they are aware of any charges in financial legislation that may affect them (pension changes for example) and make sure that you keep up with their changing financial position. It can be a very time consuming job, there's a lot of follow up work for every meeting. Make sure that you book time off to avoid getting bogged down.

Read *Money Management* and *Marketing Week* to keep abreast with what's going on.

Instrumental Soloist

At a Glance

Qualifications/Training	Essential	*Income bracket*	Low–High
Licence	No	*Town/Country*	Town
Experience/Springboard	No	*Travel*	Lots
Mid-career entry	Unlikely	*Exit sale*	No
Entry costs	£2,000+	*Work at home*	No

Mix and match   Probably essential.   You could think about: Orchestral musician, Music teacher, Conductor, Chamber group director, Counsellor, Photographer . . .

Enquiries   Musicians Union

This is someone who gives solo recitals and plays with orchestras. You need an aggressive agent, some talent, plenty of confidence and the will to succeed. Most important of all, you need a really good teacher – ask around amongst professional instrumentalists who play your particular instrument. Going to music college is not essential but it's more fun than private tuition. University will provide a wider view of life so long as you have regular lessons; a sport or a hobby will avoid an obsessional preoccupation with the instrument and provide the necessary balance. You must be independent and healthy. It's a lonely and tiring life with long hours of rehearsal, often in hotel bedrooms before a concert. Foreign languages are useful if you work internationally. Always look smart, organise yourself, answer letters and telephone calls promptly; it's all good PR. Learn to speak fluently to your audience, concert promoters and the media. The ideal soloist is an extrovert with charm, always amenable (temperamental tantrums are out of date) and more interested in music than self. The punters can spot someone on an ego trip.

You will need a really good instrument, telephone, somewhere quiet to practise (and avoid disturbing neighbours), cassette recorder for making demo tapes and taking timings for conductors, metronome and electronic tuner: concert pitch varies in different countries. Always have a good accountant and join the MUSICIANS' UNION. You need access to the *British Music Year Book* and *Grove's Dictionary of Music*.

It's important that your name gets known and stays known; so try and win a national or international competition. Solo engagements alone may not provide a living: you are always likely to need to supplement by orchestral work or teaching and adjudicating. Starting fee is £70 per concert but once you're successful, you can make £80-£100,000 pa.

Specialise in a certain style or period of music; make a name in that before expanding. Make sure your name is constantly in the press, on radio or TV. If you have £10,000 to spare you can hire an orchestra, conductor and hall for a concert in which you play concertos and invite agents and critics from the national press. You can make a recording the same way, as long as a good record company can be persuaded to accept and distribute it.

You are independent and free of organisational ties in this life but must be able to cope with loneliness and professional jealousy – a phenomenon of success. Constant travelling will interfere with your marriage and social life so your partner needs other interests. Maintaining your high standard of performance becomes difficult as you get older: you tire more easily.

Insurance Broker

At a Glance

Qualifications/Training	Essential	*Income bracket*	Low–High
Licence	Yes	*Town/Country*	Town
Experience/Springboard	Essential	*Travel*	Local
Mid-career entry	Good	*Exit sale*	Yes
Entry costs	£1,000	*Work at home*	Possible

Mix and match   Possible.   You could think about: Estate agent, Conveyancer, List broker, Newsletter publisher . . .
Enquiries   British Insurance Brokers' Association

Insurance brokers are agents for insurance companies and under-writers; their clients are people or businesses who want insurance cover and advice on how to get the best and most appropriate cover. The amount of work and the sums of money that are involved in this varies a lot from insuring a second hand car to providing the full range of cover required by a large manufacturing or retailing company. By and large, the bulk of your business will depend on where you are and the size of your firm. Smaller firms tend to look after smaller policies leaving most large scale business and industrial firms to larger brokers, most of which are in London. Having discussed the client's needs the broker has to decide which insurance company or companies can provide the best deal. For example, to insure a house and contents you may want to use different companies to provide cover for the building, the contents and individual valuable items in the house. The broker then liaises and negotiates with the company to provide cover and acts on behalf of the client on any subsequent claims. Brokers who are members of Lloyds deal directly with underwriters, otherwise, the insurance company does.

As a broker you have to register with the INSURANCE BROKERS' REGISTRATION COUNCIL (IBRC). To qualify for that you need 5 years' experience or 3 years' experience and associateship with the CHARTERED INSURANCE INSTITUTE (this means passing exams – the BRITISH INSURANCE BROKERS ASSOCIATION can tell you how to train for these, usually by day release, evening class or correspondence course). You'll also have to present accounts regularly to the IBRC and satisfy them of your solvency. If you're going to handle life assurance you also have to be a member of LAUTRO or FIMBRA. Accountancy experience is a useful background. Brokers need to know a lot about insurance, to have sound financial sense and good communication skills so that they can negotiate effectively with companies and cope with clients. In many cases clients will be parting with a lot of money under your guidance so it's important that they should trust you.

To set up you need a telephone and a typewriter. Answering machines don't inspire confidence or cope with enquiries. You'll need some letterheads and a rubber stamp (so that insurance companies know your clients' policy application forms come from you and pay you commission). Reduce the risk of mistakes by organising an efficient logging system with records of daily incoming and outgoing post and money. You'll have to apply to underwriters to be their agent and they will probably want to have a reference from your bank. The more experience you have and the better known you are within the industry the easier this will be to arrange. Some underwriters will only grant agencies to brokers who sell a minimum annual premium on their behalf; this is usually quite low (about £5,000) but it has to be kept up. You're paid commission by the underwriter; this is usually 10% of the premiums you generate for them.

A lot of clients come via word of mouth or advertising. One of the characteristics of a small brokerage is that they can get to know their clients better. Most of the work has to be done during office hours when insurance companies are open. This means a lot of time on the phone finding the best policies, reminding clients to fill in their forms, confirming premiums and policies etc. Make sure that you always quote the right premium to clients because you're responsible for any mistakes you make. Underwriters and companies will keep you informed of rate changes and will give a quotation for each premium.

This is a competitive business and although the bulk of your clients will stay with you for most of their cover some areas are unpredictable (eg car insurance) because people change their policies frequently.

The CHARTERED INSURANCE INSTITUTE publishes the *Insurance Journal* which gives news of what's going on in the industry.

Interior Designer

At a Glance

Qualifications/Training	Recommended	*Income bracket*	Low–High
Licence	No	*Town/Country*	Mostly town
Experience/Springboard	No	*Travel*	Local
Mid-career entry	Yes	*Exit sale*	No
Entry costs	£5,000++	*Work at home*	Possible

Mix and match Yes. You could think about: Antique furniture restorer, Upholsterer, Exhibition designer, Events organiser, House converter . . .

Enquiries Local interior designers

Interior design is an expanding field. Many people having successfully 'designed' their own homes, are motivated to develop this into a career that calls for flair, professionalism and extremely hard work. It is not something that can be dabbled at if you want a thriving business. Formal training may not be necessary but you'll need a reliable team of builder/plumber/electrician/decorator/carpet layer/track fitter (and that's just the start!).

You can train through specialist courses of 1 year to a few weeks, weekends or day/evening classes. A feel for cloth and precision cutting is helpful until you can afford outworkers. A sound business sense is needed (bookkeeping essential), a love of interiors and a willingness to constantly learn. Small commissions can be undertaken from home. If you're ambitious you'll soon find you want to buy or rent premises. The right location will bring passing trade. Publicity, if needed other than through recommendations, should be in local magazines and papers.

The initial cost of setting up at home is approximately £300, then you'll need probably several hundred pattern books, which cost £30–60 each. The trade is very clannish; find a friendly trade rep, get taken seriously. Go to trade fairs, keep abreast of latest fashions through showroom open days, seminars, make contacts. Try designing fabric manufacturers' showrooms and trade stands (good publicity and own stand very expensive). Keep trade fair catalogues for future reference. Many manufacturers require an initial order of £250.

It is most important that you take a 50% deposit (or more) before ordering fabric, wallpaper, fittings. You will undoubtedly learn from your mistakes. A difficult customer can prolong payment on any pretext to reduce the final bill. It may be necessary to use a debt-collecting agency. Print your conditions clearly on the back of estimates. Outworkers will become necessary; the best tend to approach

INTERIOR DESIGNER

you, or train your own. Watch that they don't pass on trade secrets to competitors. Collect a stable of individual craftsmen: ceramics (lamps, tiles), textiles (reflect a theme), artists (stencilling, wall murals). All will give you an individual style and prompt commissions.

It is possible to specialise, in fabrics (curtains, loose covers, cushions, lampshades etc). Stock a range of haberdashery (brings in customers). Beware of opposition and individuals questioning with no intention of giving commission and only cribbing ideas.

Only 50% of estimates will result in commissions; there will be disappointments and frustrations, but it is enormously stimulating and rewarding.

Interpreter

At a Glance

Qualifications/Training	Essential	*Income bracket*	Medium–High
Licence	Recommended	*Town/Country*	Town
Experience/Springboard	Necessary	*Travel*	Yes
Mid-career entry	Yes	*Exit sale*	No
Entry costs	£500+	*Work at home*	No

Mix and match   Yes.   You could think about: Tourist guide, Solicitor, Novelist, Import/export broker . . .

Enquiries   Institute of Interpreters, Association Internationale des Interpretes de Conferences

At international conferences and meetings where the participants do not have a common language, interpreters translate simultaneously from one language into another so that everyone can follow what is going on. Although it's an international profession, it is also very small; the ASSOCIATION INTERNATIONALE DES INTERPRETES DES CONFERENCES (AIIC) has only about 2,000 members worldwide, about 100 of which are based in the UK. This is unlikely to change dramatically but demand will probably increase rather than decrease thanks to political developments in the EC (1992), Russia (glasnost) and China, coupled with greater business links with the Middle and Far East. In the UK the centre for interpreters is London although about 50% of UK based work is out of London and there's far more regular work abroad in cities where international organisations have their HQs. If you want to make interpreting your main source of income you'll have to do a lot of travelling. With careful planning it's possible to mix and match your interpreting schedule with other work at home or overseas. As a freelance interpreter you should be a member of AIIC and this means doing a course at an interpreting school (details from their Geneva headquarters indicate which are the best schools). There are 9 main schools in Europe and the States (in the UK most go to the POLYTECHNIC OF CENTRAL LONDON SCHOOL OF LANGUAGES); courses are usually short (about 6 months) and intense. To be accepted on a course you should have a degree (not necessarily in languages) and proficiency in an appropriate language combination. English, French and Spanish are the most commonly used, with some Russian. A useful combination is what will get you work. That means having excellent French and English plus at least one other mainstream EC language (eg Spanish or German), Russian or Arabic, plus a less common (often EC) language such as Danish or Greek. Interpreters divide languages into three groups: group A is the mother tongue into which they do most interpreting; group B is the language or languages other than mother tongue into which they may do some interpreting and group C is the languages from which they interpret. Most people have some work experience before they go to interpreting school in their late 20s. This usually, but not always, involves languages or living abroad; teaching, couriering, working for a multi-national. Follow up this course with on the job training from a major organisation such as the EC or the UN which employ full time interpreters as well as using freelance backup. To become a full member of AIIC you must be nominated by 3 existing members as a candidate and do 200 days of work that is vouched for by members with the same language combination as your own. As well as a facility with languages, interpreters need to be able to react quickly and spontaneously. You have to be able to communicate the speaker's ideas rather than giving a verbatim translation of what is being said and this, unlike translating where you tend to work alone and to have longer to check on the exact meaning of words, has to be done almost immediately. To do this requires wide general knowledge and under-standing of people's motivations and it's for this reason that you're recommended not to come straight to interpreting from university or polytechnic; also to have lived for a while in at least the country of your major language. Interpreters don't necessarily do a lot of written translating.

Essential set up equipment is membership of AIIC which publishes a list of its members. You also need a phone and an answering machine but the complicated equipment needed to connect you in your inter-preting booth with your listeners is provided by the conference organisers and the organisations you're working for. There are open-ings for interpreters in courts, the community and in business but these are often filled by language speakers within firms and organisations. The bulk of freelance interpreting work comes via the AIIC and will be for conferences and meetings or for organisations like the UN and the EC. That means that the main centres for interpreters are in Paris, Geneva, Strasbourg, Brussels and New York and you have to be able to travel to find work. Other sources of work are in smaller business or professional conferences in the UK (less often overseas as home grown interpreters are more often used for this) and, occasionally, for televi-sion; this is still a fairly unexploited area in the UK where TV viewers aren't always very interested in what foreigners have to say. The AIIC sets rates (officially these are minimum although few interpreters command fees that are far in excess of this minimum, unless they're working for TV) and daily expenses which are calculated to suit local prices. Travel costs are also charged.

When you're taken on for a job, you'll be paid for its duration regardless of how many hours' work you actually do; very often armies of stand-by interpreters will be called on to cover the possibility of several simultaneous multi-lingual meetings which do not necessarily occur. On these occasions there's a lot of hanging around which is a good way of meeting other interpreters; you'll also have plenty of chance to chat to whoever you're sharing your interpreting booth with, between bouts of interpreting; so the ability to get on with people is essential. Interpreters are taken on in teams to cover all the necessary language combinations. There are about 4 or 5 recruiting interpreters in London and they are the people to cultivate. To begin with it's difficult to get enough work but once you've had one good meeting where you did a terrific job this changes. It's a small world with a fast moving grapevine, which can be very useful, but also makes it difficult to live down a bad meeting. Interpreting is very stressful. There's often a lot of long haul travelling involved, sometimes at fairly short notice and, when you're on a job you have to concentrate very hard because what you're communicating to your listeners is usually important.

The busy times are May/June and September/October when most of the conferences take place. January/February and July/August are a lot quieter but you should be able to make enough at other times to tide you over. Interpreters tend to take a long time to retire (irritatingly long for new blood) and, once you've got a good enough name, you can choose to do as many or as few jobs as you like. Contact also the INSTITUTE OF LINGUISTS for further information.

Inventor

At a Glance

Qualifications/Training	No	Income bracket	Low–High
Licence	No	Town/Country	Either
Experience/Springboard	Probably	Travel	Yes
Mid-career entry	Probably	Exit sale	Yes
Entry costs	Highly variable	Work at home	Possible

Mix and match   Probably essential.   You could think about: Electrician, Computer consultant, Dentist, Bespoke furniture maker/designer, Garage owner ...

Enquiries   Institute of Patenteers and Inventors

The British are superb at coming up with inventions, but notoriously bad at getting them onto the commercial market, a view upheld, interestingly enough, by the Japanese Ministry of International Trade. British inventions are hard to sell to UK manufacturers so very many British inventions are first developed and marketed overseas. Thus the path of the ordinary British inventor is difficult and can be long, expensive and dispiriting. But it is possible to make a lot of money out of inventing if you make sure that you take the right steps.

The first step is to protect your idea which involves the Patent Office. If you go direct to the PATENT OFFICE the initial application costs £20 giving you limited protection by just logging your idea. But this level of protection is far from adequate, and as a patent application is a complex legal and technical document, and useless if drawn up incompetently, most inventors do not apply directly but go through a patent agent (list obtainable from CHARTERED INSTITUTE OF PATENT AGENTS).

Once your patent application has been filed, you have 12 months to pursue it or let it lapse. The whole process up to obtaining a full patent is not cheap and although fees vary from patent agent to patent agent, a UK patent costs somewhere in the region of £1,000. If a European or other foreign patent is necessary the cost automatically rises. US, European and Japanese patents currently cost between £1,000–£1,500 on top of any existing UK patents. Even a full patent will not always protect you against the huge financial, legal and technical resources of a large company which deliberately takes advantage of your commercial or legal inexperience.

Marketing is the key to the successful exploitation of your invention. Traditionally inventors look to their patent agents but many are not qualified to help. There is nothing to stop you taking your brainchild to manufacturers and this can be very successful in spite of the many pitfalls. But remember, you are not the only budding inventor. Manufacturers often find it difficult to see the individual merits of different inventions, many of which purport to do the same thing, so your presentation is of the utmost importance and it is not much use inventing something highly technical if you do not have the technical know-how to put your dream into practice or to prove that it works and is cost effective, or even worth the expense of making a prototype. You also need thorough research into unit costs to make your idea more interesting to manufacturers.

There is rarely harm in getting publicity for your invention when it has been fully patented. If the idea is specialist you can try the specialist trade magazines. For more general publicity there is the national press, eg the Innovation Page of the *Sunday Times*, but it's not easy to get featured. There are also innovation exhibitions, eg the TECHMART EXHIBITION, and competitions like the PRINCE OF WALES' AWARD for innovation.

Once you have found a manufacturer to produce your idea your next problem is the licensing agreement. Like the original patent it's a complex legal document under which you give the manufacturer the rights to produce your idea while you retain the patent rights. Most licensing agreements involve an up-front payment and fixed royalties for the inventor. See that your agreements are not biased in favour of the manufacturer, who normally has much more legal muscle than you do.

It's a good idea to work closely with an Inventions Agency or Inventions Sales company, using their commercial experience to help you with marketing, presentation and licensing. The best known Inventions Agency is a British London-based company, INVENTALINK, which has a national network of associates. You are charged a fee at the beginning and they take a percentage of your royalties. Some research based companies (eg BP) have venture departments which look out for new ideas. Government Enterprise Agencies are able to give you help and advice; a useful address is the INSTITUTE OF PATENTEES AND INVENTORS; a useful book is *A Better Mousetrap* by Peter Bissel, published by Wordbase Publications.

Investment Manager

At a Glance

Qualifications/Training	Recommended	Income bracket	Medium–High
Licence	Yes	Town/Country	Town
Experience/Springboard	Yes	Travel	No
Mid-career entry	Yes	Exit sale	Yes
Entry costs	£50,000+	Work at home	No

Mix and match Possible. You could think about: Stockbroker, Solicitor, Accountant, Direct marketing agent, Newsletter publisher . . .

Enquiries   IMRO, FIMBRA

Investment managers advise on and manage sums of money (portfolios) on behalf of their clients who are private investors, pension funds, trusts and charity trusts. The aim is to make this money earn more by investing it; there is a variety of ways in which this can be done. Investment managers have to decide which is the most appropriate for the client's objectives. They operate as agents, with no direct access to or control over their client's funds. For a small firm this can be a difficult area to break into – your best bet is to woo the small investor (some of the larger managing firms only deal with investments of £100,000 or more). To succeed, you'll need credentials, experience and capital.

Under the Financial Services Act investment management is regulated by a number of self-regulated bodies. All investment management companies now have to be registered with IMRO (Investment Managers Regulatory Organisation) or FIMBRA (Financial Intermediaries Managers and Brokers Regulatory Association). This means proving that you are 'fit and proper' before you set up. At the moment you'll need about 5 years' 'appropriate experience' (with another registered investment management company), a good past record and financial stability.

If you want to issue your own unit trust (and you probably will if you're managing for lots of small investors and don't want to go on putting money into other peoples') you should talk to the UNIT TRUST ASSOCIATION. You and your board will need to have a lot of financial experience and a paid up share capital of at least £50,000.

Before you're allowed to give investment advice you have to pass the Stock Exchange Registered Representative's Exam. Any history of fraudulent practice reduces dramatically your likelihood of acceptance.

You'll also have to convince them that your back office facilities comply with SE rules.

A qualification in accountancy or law or experience with a stockbroker or merchant bank is useful both for credibility and for what you'll learn. Small companies may give a wide range of experience because they aren't split into departments the way that large ones are. Large ones, however, may offer more structured training and a large well known company gives you more credibility. You'll need to know about financial and political trends, and enough about industry and technological developments to be able to give good investment advice. You must be good at getting on with existing and potential clients. This can be a precarious business where the more you know and the wider your range of interests the better. One of the advantages that a small non-specialist firm of investment managers has is that it can call on a variety of expert advisers including stockbrokers, merchant bankers, company and financial analysts and other investment managers. Use your contacts to keep in touch and co-opt anyone with kudos (economists, stockbrokers etc) onto your board if you can.

You'll need enough money to set up and run an office which is equipped and staffed to allow you to comply with SE regulations (eg all bargains must be reported to them within up to 15 minutes). You'll also need administrative and reception staff; clients don't like telephone-answering machines. The chances are that you'll be managing sums of money that are far greater than your own capital; although it's rare for clients to sue their investment managers, you should have professional indemnity insurance and fidelity bonding for your staff. Your income comes from acceptance fees from new clients; regular fees based on a percentage of the clients' portfolio capital; dealing charges on all transactions; and you may earn commission on some transactions. Some forms of investment (unit trusts for example) pay an additional commission (from the client's 'front load premium'); this will give you a quick income but at your client's expense.

Your first clients can come from friends and personal contacts. Small investors (with funds of as little as £7–8,000 are likely to bring you more business by word of mouth; but any losses they incur will be proportionately more significant than for larger investors where you can easily make up for a £2,000 loss. A balanced spread of interests, with units of several shares reduces the risk of clients losing all round but the units have to be large enough to make gains worth having.

Jazz Musician/Singer

At a Glance

Qualifications/Training	Recommended	*Income bracket*	Mostly low
Licence	No	*Town/Country*	Town
Experience/Springboard	No	*Travel*	Lots
Mid-career entry	Possible	*Exit sale*	No
Entry costs	£1,000	*Work at home*	No

Mix and match Yes. You could think about: Orchestral musician, Music teacher, Typesetter, Chemical engineering consultant, Solicitor . . .

Enquiries Jazz musicians, Musicians Union

For someone who sings or plays in jazz style, and the jazz repertoire in concerts, groups, clubs, on the radio and TV etc., music college is not essential but dedication and perseverance are required. Even with really good 'ears', you need instruction to focus on good instrumental or vocal technique and listening. This is the way to develop your own individual style. Listen to records, go to concerts, memorise songs, solos and chord sequences. You must have the rare ability to communicate musically, to forget yourself and give way spontaneously to other musicians when playing.

You will need a room for practising without disturbance and without wrecking your relationship with your neighbours. You also need a record player, telephone and answering machine or service. An amplifier is often provided or you can borrow or hire one, or buy one for £250.

Go to clubs in your local city (such as the Bass Clef or 606 in London), meet musicians and if you admire one, ask for a lesson. The democratic tradition in the jazz world is for even the most famous to be willing to chat. There you will meet fellow enthusiasts and can arrange to play together informally. Or enrol at a summer school eg J DANKWORTH or GUILDHALL SCHOOL.

Join the MUSICIANS' UNION though it has little control over fees. Financial reward for a jazz performer is minimal: £10 per gig, up to £50–£70 for an experienced group leader. An internationally known leader can get £500 per gig, which is exceptional; his musicians may only receive £40 each. You therefore need another job, in a dance band or show, teaching or doing sessions.

You must be sociable, prepared to work long hours for little pay and be at the mercy of other musicians' private lives and moods. Jazzers are frequently neurotic and many try and overcome inhibitions by indulging in drink or drugs. Eventually these can destroy the musician and the music.

Successful groups may tour and you can travel if you also work in a show or dance band as a commercial musician. Electronic synthesisers like the Sampler may mean less commercial work for musicians in the future. But this has great possibilities in jazz because of its endless variations of tone and colour.

Useful magazines are the *Musician*, *Jazz Journal International* and *Crescendo International*. Get any books on jazz theory and improvisation from a library with a jazz section.

Jobbing Printer

At a Glance

Qualifications/Training	Recommended	*Income bracket*	Low–Medium
Licence	Union card recommended	*Town/Country*	Town
Experience/Springboard	Necessary	*Travel*	Local
Mid-career entry	Possible	*Exit sale*	Yes
Entry costs	£25,000+	*Work at home*	No

Mix and match   Yes.   You could think about: Typesetter, Printmaker, Man with a van, Contemporary art gallery owner . . .

Enquiries   British Printing Industries Federation, Institute of Printing

Printing is in the top ten UK manufacturing industries. New technology has savagely depleted its workforce but there are still some 200,000 people working in approximately 6,000 firms. Having said that, forget about the giants of the industry. There is plenty of room for small, specialised suppliers: printers work for all businesses throughout the UK at some time or another. Printing is not concentrated but is located throughout the UK. However, financial printing is largely in London, books mainly in East Anglia and the West Country and cartons and packaging mainly in the Midlands and the North.

Because of the enormous amount of work available, many printers set up on their own. The majority of small printers work with perhaps only one or two of the five main printing processes: lithography (most widely used), letterpress, flexography, gravure and screen printing. The connected finishing processes (collating, binding, guillotining, punching, stitching, folding) and the connected trades (retailing, stationery manufacture, distribution delivery) can either be handled directly by jobbing printers or, where more profitable, sub-contracted.

Jobbing printers often employ no staff and act as their own sales team, quality controller , estimator, accountant and machine minder; not to mention being their own collator and supervisor of the print-run. It is very hard work, made more stressful by customers always wanting their print in a hurry. You have to work late nights and over weekends, while somehow finding the time to seek your next orders.

You can compete on price, on quality, on delivery dates or on credit. If you can compete in these four ways and, most important, be reliable, you will get repeat orders. Once you have successfully completed your first order you have the beginning of a portfolio to show potential new clients and something of a reputation to build on.

Work comes mostly through recommendation, but contacts can be made at business and social gatherings and trade fairs (eg IPEX, the major printing fair at Birmingham every four years) and packaging fairs. There are endless sources of printing orders: local freebie newspapers, magazine and book publishers, advertisers, products requiring packaging or labelling, posters, stationery, information bulletins.

New printing machinery is very expensive but there is a big second hand market (particularly in offset litho machines) because the technology is changing rapidly and the big firms often get rid of perfectly adequate models to keep competitive at their own level. As a jobbing printer you should find second hand machinery holds its value in a way that, for instance, computers do not. A good second hand offset litho machine with a single colour press might cost £15,000–£20,000; two, three and four colour presses will cost progressively more. Your work space has to allow for large machines and somewhere to collate the print-run.

There are established courses for both beginners and professionals. Qualification is based on achievement of nationally-agreed standards laid down by the BRITISH PRINTING INDUSTRIES FEDERATION BPIF (the employers' organisation) in conjunction with the two printing unions: the NATIONAL GRAPHICAL ASSOCIATION and the SOCIETY OF GRAPHICAL AND ALLIED TRADES (SOGAT). The BPIF also acts as a training Clearing House. Apprenticeship has been replaced by mutually signed training agreements so you can get an employer to train you and subsequently set up on your own. The printing industry is still largely unionised, but there are many firms which are not closed shops, and you do not need a union card for many forms of printing although it can help to have one.

The best college for the jobbing printer is the LONDON COLLEGE OF PRINTING. It offers courses in typography, graphic design, pre-printing and print finishing processes, graphic reproduction techniques, machine operation and maintenance, compositing, typesetting, quotations, packaging, plate-making, colour separation and print management. Contract printing is often considered more secure than jobbing but if you lose your contract you may find you have no work at all. Hedge your bets; do not get too high a proportion of your work from any one customer. Diversification, cash flow management, confidence and credibility are important. Never call in materials until you really need them.

Read the weeklies – *Litho Week* and *Printing World* for their recruitment ads, classified ads and the second-hand machinery on offer. Also read the *British Printer*. The INSTITUTE OF PRINTING is worth contacting for its courses and technical papers.

Journalist

At a Glance

Qualifications/Training	Recommended	*Income bracket*	Low–High
Licence	No	*Town/Country*	Town
Experience/Springboard	Recommended	*Travel*	Yes
Mid-career entry	Possible	*Exit sale*	No
Entry costs	Nil	*Work at home*	Partly

Mix and match Yes. You could think about: Foreign correspondent, UK correspondent for overseas media, Football commentator, Newsletter publisher, Radio reporter and presenter, Novelist . . .

Enquiries National Union of Journalists

Newspaper journalists usually start in staff jobs on a local paper. The normal training involves a course in newspaper editing and design: the NATIONAL COUNCIL FOR THE TRAINING OF JOURNALISTS awards Proficiency Certificates which involve full-time or sandwich courses: the two specialist colleges are the LONDON COLLEGE OF PRINTING and NAPIER POLY in Edinburgh. There are postgraduate courses at UNIVERSITY COLLEGE, CARDIFF and CITY UNIVERSITY. A period of training on a local paper is usually involved, where hours are long, subject matter is often tedious (weddings, fetes etc) and pay is paltry.

To become a freelance journalist you need a vast number of contacts, both to give you the commissions you need, and to provide the background information to the story. However, with the growth of cheque book journalism, if you are in the right place at the right time, the sky is the limit when it comes to selling a story. But that 'if' is a big one, so you can expect to earn a few hundred, rather than a few thousand, pounds per week.

The day-to-day routine depends on the field of specialisation. For example, freelance reporters on national papers have to do a lot of footwork, and be prepared to dash off all over the country (or the world, if they specialise in foreign news), so it is not ideal for a family person. Then they have to write up the story, accurately, interestingly and fast, and be prepared to have it rejected, rewritten or cut to shreds by the editor and subeditors.

On the other hand, a journalist specialising in, say, medical subjects or interior design is likely to be London based, and have a more regular time-table (attending press conferences, interviewing specialists and so on). Other areas of specialisation include theatre criticism, book reviewing, or acting as foreign correspondent – either in Britain for a foreign paper, or abroad for a British paper.

Getting a commission as a freelance journalist on a national newspaper requires energy, dedication, accuracy, a flair for writing. However, there are plenty of other openings on magazines, trade journals and so on. At a national level, most newspapers are now set electronically, which means that the reporter, rather than typing his copy, which is then circulated to editors and subeditors for necessary

HOLD PAGE SEVENTYSEVEN!

JOURNALIST

revisions, actually puts his copy straight on to a disk. This has made little difference to the job content of the journalist – it is the printer whose job has changed (or been lost).

Journalists are traditionally members of the NATIONAL UNION OF JOURNALISTS which produces a free leaflet *Careers in Journalism*. Jobs are advertised in the publication itself (for national and local papers). *UK Press Gazette*, *Campaign*, media pages in the *Guardian* and the *Independent*.

Kennel/Cattery Owner

At a Glance

Qualifications/Training	Available	Income bracket	Low–Medium
Licence	Yes for quarantine	Town/Country	Country
Experience/Springboard	Recommended	Travel	No
Mid-career entry	Likely	Exit sale	Yes
Entry costs	£10,000+	Work at home	Yes

Mix and match Possible. You could think about: Greyhound trainer, Vet, Farmer, Tree surgeon, Taxidermist . . .

Enquiries Kennel Agency, Feline Advisory Board, Local kennels and catteries

Kennels and catteries look after dogs and cats whose owners are temporarily unable to do so themselves, usually because they are on holiday. Some also offer a longer term service for animals returning from overseas who must, by law, be kept in quarantine for 6 months. The job involves feeding, watering and exercising the animals, providing them with living quarters and arranging for any necessary veterinary attention. Another, though more unusual, way of being self employed in this area is by offering your services as a freelance, temporary kennelmaid.

There are no necessary, formal qualifications for this but you'll need an unsentimental love of animals and some idea of what you're doing. Kennel work is hard and attention to detail is essential; you can't be a clock watcher. You also have to remember that you're providing a service and to be prepared to put yourself out for others from time to time. Various residential kennelmaid courses are available (eg from BELLMEAD KENNELS) and the CANINE STUDIES INSTITUTE offers a correspondence course in Kennel Management. If you want a taste of what you're letting yourself in for you can do a working weekend as a kennelmaid. It helps if you enjoy being outdoors in all weather, and can cope with mucking out kennels and the incessant noise and smell of dogs/cats. Contact also the FELINE ADVISORY BUREAU.

You'll need specially designed premises. You can buy an existing establishment (see the KENNEL AGENCY) or build your own. This will require consent from your local authority who issues stringent guidelines and will want to see detailed plans. Contact the RSPCA or get *Guidelines for the Inspection of Animal Boarding Establishments* for indications of the sort of building required. Location is important, not only for the sake of the animals but also because objections may be raised about noise, smell, hygiene, increase in traffic and general nuisance. In general you won't be able to set up business in town, but you will have to be accessible for your clients.

If you're proposing to take animals in quarantine, you'll need to apply to the MINISTRY OF AGRICULTURE and to nominate a veterinary superintendent who can be an owning partner or someone who lives nearby and is prepared to be on 24 hour standby.

Set up costs vary widely depending on the number of kennels, size of house and grounds etc. You will need an animals' food preparation room with refrigeration, supplies of food from wholesalers, bedding etc. Again, depending on the size, you may want to employ help with the work. Charges depend a lot on what sort of service you're offering, how much attention you give to each animal and what clientele you are aiming for. You can, for example, specialise by boarding only small dogs, big breeds, dogs recovering from surgery or aged and infirm dogs, bitches in season or dogs all of one particular breed. About £3 per animal per day is reasonable. Your clients are liable for any vet bills incurred by their pets, so insist that the animals in your care are insured and sell policies to those who aren't.

Advertise in local (or as near to local as possible) shops and vets' surgeries for business. A lot should come via word of mouth as long as pets go home in good condition and happy (some grooming and attention helps). Pet owners who travel a lot are worth cultivating, as are vets for both their professional expertise and for their contact with animal owners. It's worth cossetting your regulars.

During a working day you'll have to feed the animals, clean them out and keep an eye on them. Dogs in particular need exercise, ideally a chance to run free for a while. There is also administration, taking bookings, dealing with arrivals and departures and, of course, bookkeeping, invoicing etc. Your busy times will be at weekends and

---

holiday seasons so time off may be difficult unless you've either got reliable staff to take over in your absence, or are willing to close the business for a few days. Above all, you need to be physically fit; it's hard, continual slog – but an outdoor life is also both refreshing and rewarding.

Further reading, *Running Your Own Boarding Kennels* and *Holiday Retreats for Cats and Dogs in England*, also the *Dog Business*.

Keyboard Hire

At a Glance

Qualifications/Training	No	Income bracket	Low–High
Licence	No	Town/Country	Town
Experience/Springboard	Useful	Travel	Lots
Mid-career entry	Possible	Exit sale	Possible
Entry costs	£5,000+	Work at home	Possible

Mix and match   Yes.   You could think about: Man with a van, Musician, Music teacher, Hi-fi shop owner, Piano tuner, Music/instrument retailer . . .

Enquiries   Musicians Union

This involves hiring out any form of keyboard instrument – piano, harpsichord, organ or synthesiser – transporting it to the performance or recording venue and tuning it to the pitch required. A good knowledge of the mechanics of keyboard instruments is useful but not essential; a really accurate sense of pitch and the ability to play are. You will also need to be physically strong, have a clean driving licence and own an electronic tuner. It's helpful to have good business sense and an accountant.

You can run your business from home in a large ground floor room or garage. These should be dry but not centrally heated. It is possible to start with a small harpsichord and synthesiser; these will cost £4,000 or you can buy them second hand. You will also need a telephone, answering machine or service and a small light piano trolley. Hire a van to start with, but buy a second hand one as soon as possible. There will be a lot of travelling so a basic knowledge of motor mechanics is useful should you break down in the middle of the night.

You will have to arrive before rehearsal, tune the instrument for the performer, kill time all day returning in the breaks, before the concert and in the interval to retune. Always talk to the performer: their recommendation can get you the next engagement. Porters at concert halls and theatres are generally reluctant to help and need tipping so stamina is necessary for loading the van after an evening engagement and driving off early in the morning.

Allow at least £500 to get cards or brochures printed and distributed to music shops, recording studios, music societies, festivals, arts centres and dance halls. If using postal services, there is a very good value first time small business delivery.

This is an energetic life. The bias tends to be towards men because of the physical requirements; a woman can organise, take bookings, and employ men to lift and transport. To succeed, you and your instrument must be reliable, punctual, in tune and of the best quality available. If you need to employ others, choose them with care and ensure they do not damage the instruments. Get good insurance cover. If you are accepted by a prestigious venue, musical show, orchestra or opera company you can make up to £80,000.

Union membership is not required but if you play and hire out yourself with your instrument you must join the MUSICIANS' UNION.

Knitwear Designer

At a Glance

Qualifications/Training	Recommended	Income bracket	Low–High
Licence	No	Town/Country	Either
Experience/Springboard	No	Travel	Possible
Mid-career entry	Unlikely	Exit sale	No
Entry costs	£1,500+	Work at home	Possible
Mix and match	Possible.	You could think about: Fashion clothes/hat designer, Photographer, Illustrator . . .	
Enquiries	Art colleges		

Designer knitwear is highly fashionable with good markets for successful designers to sell ready made clothes; kits that give customers the instructions and materials needed to knit your designs themselves, and ideas for designs that can be sold to other manufacturers (if you do this, make sure that you have an agreement which will allow you to benefit if your designs really take off). Increased use of cotton yarns means that this is an all year round business with most designers presenting two collections a year.

There are several routes into the business, but most start with a college training in fashion or textiles. (See *Design Courses in Britain*). Although at the upper end of the market, some designer knitting is done on needles, most hand made knits are made on small (hand operated), knitting machines. You have to know how to use these and being able to do a few, simple repairs on your machine will cut down on bills. As with any small manufacturing business you need: creativity and the ability to come up with attractive, workable designs; an efficient business-like approach; knowledge of the market; and the ability to set and work to realistic deadlines.

As well as a small studio (which can be a spare room at home) you need two knitting machines and a couple of domestic sewing machines for finishing off. Second hand machines cost about £250 and are often advertised in general knitwear magazines. Surviving your first year is difficult because of cash flow problems brought on by your having to buy yarn several weeks before you'll be paid for the finished product; it's a labour intensive craft and you'll probably have to use and pay outworkers to knit up your designs which reduces your profits. If you're selling through retailers, they will double your price to them, which reduces the size of your market. (Hand knits retail for about £150, machine knits are about £80–100).

You can sell directly to customers or through shops. College fashion shows are visited by the trade so you may get some commissions there; or you can take samples of your collection around shops and to trade shows. If you want to sell directly to the customer you'll have to open your own shop, rent a stall in a craft market or arrange mail order selling. You get much better profits by selling overseas, as long as you sell direct and cut out the middlemen. Selling kits is more profitable than ready made knits because you avoid the costs of having your designs knitted up.

The BRITISH KNITTING AND CLOTHING EXPORT COUNCIL, provides information on export marketing exhibitions and sales promotional events.

Landlord

At a Glance

Qualifications/Training	No	*Income bracket*	Low–High
Licence	No	*Town/Country*	Either
Experience/Springboard	No	*Travel*	Between properties
Mid-career entry	Yes	*Exit sale*	Excellent
Entry costs	£50,000++	*Work at home*	Yes

Mix and match　Yes.　You could think about: Almost anything . . .

Enquiries　Landlords

If you've got enough money to buy a flat or house outright you can let it to tenants and become a landlord. Alternatively, if you already own property (especially in an expensive and desirable area) you could let it and go and live somewhere cheaper and/or more exciting. For anyone with several tens of thousands to spare, it's an excellent way of earning an income from an investment which should give you capital growth as well. Laws affecting the leasing of property are set to change during 1989. In particular, rent fixing by rent assessment officers called in by tenants or housing benefit departments, is changing for new tenants which will remove the risk of an uncommercially low rent being set for your property. Being a landlord needn't be a very time consuming job so is ideal for mixing and matching.

There are no essential formal qualifications but you must know what you're doing or you risk being caught out by unscrupulous (or over-scrupulous) tenants using a variety of legal loopholes. Arm yourself with a good solicitor to check all contracts and tenancy agreements. The more house maintenance you can do yourself the better – this saves the money you'd otherwise be paying to someone else and allows you to keep in touch with the property and its condition. Even better, if you have experience in construction buy unconverted or rundown property and convert it yourself into several letting units cheaply.

Setting up from scratch costs masses. On the whole, letting property on a small scale is only worth doing if you can buy somewhere outright; once you're personally involved in repaying a new mortgage it'll be difficult to raise enough rent to cover your expenses and make a decent profit. Apart from buying the property, you also need to furnish, decorate and equip it. Basically, the more you spend in the early stages, the more you stand to make from rent in the future, ie, you can charge more for a well decorated and equipped flat in an expensive area than for a grotty shack in a rundown area furnished only with a mattress and a broken chair. You'll also save on maintenance costs if you make sure the place is in good nick when you first let it. Other expenses include repairs and redecoration, solicitor's fees and the cost of advertising for new tenants. Telephone, electricity and gas bills are virtually always paid by tenants but, unless electricity and gas are supplied on a coin meter, the landlord may be responsible for tenants' unpaid bills. Many landlords make tenants responsible for rates and water rates and again this may be left to you to pay if your tenants do a bunk; check with your local council. Always inform British Telecom, the Gas, Electricity and Water Boards and local council of the names of new tenants and, when possible, give forwarding addresses of outgoing ones. Rents vary considerably across the country and also depend on what you're providing. Letting bedsits may maximise the income you can get from a property but you'll have to spend more time finding tenants and the property will suffer more wear and tear. It's normal to take a deposit from incoming tenants as some sort of surety against non-payment of rent or bills and against minor damage and breakages (allowing for reasonable wear and tear) – not always successful as tenants who leave without paying rent often owe money on bills and may have caused damage as well. Deposits are usually a month's rent, occasionally three months'.

Outgoing tenants may not give you much notice before you leave – contracts usually stipulate a month but that doesn't give you much time to find someone else, especially if you don't live in the area. You'll have to check the property over too, finding someone else to take on the lease as soon as possible usually means advertising in the local paper. Then it's up to you to show prospective tenants the property and decide who should have it. Be prepared for some prospective tenants to fail to show up at the time you've arranged.

It's pretty well up to you what restrictions you put into the contract (eg no pets, no noise after 11pm). It's normal for landlords to be responsible for external decoration and most prefer to maintain control over interior decoration (liaising with tenants) to avoid having to completely re-decorate over someone else's dubious taste in interior design before you can re-let. Once you've found someone, check references from their bank or building society, employer and previous landlord. This may take a couple of weeks to clear but is important.

To minimise the risk of having a sitting tenant, draw up a shorthold lease (this is usually for a year or more); it also makes it easier to get rid of tenants who aren't paying the rent. If both you and the tenant are happy, shortlease contracts can be renewed. Long term non-payment of rent doesn't often arise but when it does, it's a great nuisance. You may have to get an eviction order from the local magistrate's court – this can mean that tenants are allowed some time to pay up or move out; they're given longer if they've got children (a situation which forces many landlords to refuse to let to families) and the period can sometimes be extended under other extenuating circumstances. In the meantime, you'll have no income from your property and the rent that you're owed could be paid by the tenant in small weekly instalments over several months. Moral: keep in touch with tenants on a fairly formal level. Although bad tenants are very bad, good tenants are more common and very good. They'll pay rent and bills regularly, let you know when anything needs to be done and leave the place as they found it allowing you to live in peace.

Landscape Designer

At a Glance			
Qualifications/Training	Yes	*Income bracket*	Low–High
Licence	No	*Town/Country*	Either
Experience/Springboard	Essential	*Travel*	Yes
Mid-career entry	Unlikely	*Exit sale*	No
Entry costs	£2,000	*Work at home*	Possible

Mix and match   Yes. You could think about: Gardener/garden designer, Property manager, Timeshare holiday accommodation owner, Garden gnome maker . . .

Enquiries   Landscape Institute

There is a steady demand for landscape professionals, both at home and overseas, many of whom work as consultants receiving commissions from public authorities or private clients. The work is varied in type, scale and geographical range, as is the amount of time spent in office or on site. It ranges from wide questions of environmental impact and general ecology to urban and rural landscaping. Urban landscaping covers projects like housing, roadworks, parks, play areas and regeneration; rural landscaping covers agriculture, forests and tourist areas. Larger projects include industrial buildings, oil refineries, nuclear problems and so on.

You are the client's agent and your job includes the co-ordination of your designs' implementation. You nearly always work as part of a team involving planners, architects and contractors or various combinations of these. You have to be able to get on with people, and be prepared to tackle a certain amount of bureaucracy, for example when dealing with local councils. You need some talent for drawing, visual perception, imagination, an interest in the history of art and landscape design, architecture and building design, and in ecology and allied subjects such as horticulture and geology. You also need some knowledge of surveying, planning and contract law. All of these are covered in a degree course in Landscape Architecture. For information about courses apply to the LANDSCAPE INSTITUTE. To qualify for Associateship of the Landscape Insitute (ALI) you must then work for 1½–2 years for a landscape business of some sort, then do a 1-year postgraduate diploma in Landscape Architecture, after which you can take the professional exams. The terms 'landscape designer' and 'landscape architect' have been borrowed by many people who appear in the Yellow Pages, but ALI is the only recognised professional qualification for landscape architects. Read *Landscape Design*.

The best thing about this career is the variety of choice: if you feel committed to the third world you can work there; if you feel passionately about urban renewal you can do something about it; if your heart is in the countryside, you can live and work there; if you are

LANDSCAPE DESIGNER

against nuclear power, you can avoid designing power stations; or you can just work on small garden projects.

To set up as a consultant you have to be certain that you have secured the commissions and will be able to secure more. You will need to be employed for a while in order to gain experience. You can set up an office with a telephone and drawing board; the rest is reputation and persuading new clients to use your services rather than anybody else's. It is important to have a good working relationship with the contractors you choose and the planners and architects with whom you deal.

Light Music Composer

At a Glance

Qualifications/Training	Recommended	Income bracket	Low–High
Licence	No	Town/Country	Either
Experience/Springboard	No	Travel	Possible
Mid-career entry	Possible	Exit sale	Yes
Entry costs	£3,500	Work at home	Yes

Mix and match   Essential.   You could think about: Impresario, Festival director, Conductor, Repetiteur/accompanist/coach . . .

Enquiries   Performing Right Society

This person writes music mostly in a style which is lighter or swing style, suitable for the media, films, radio and television. Going to music college is not essential but useful for making contacts and learning to play keyboards. It is vital to be able to write easily in folk, jazz, pop, classical styles; look at other composers' scores (in public libraries) and try to copy them. Time is money in the commercial music world. You must be flexible and able to work fast and to change and accommodate producers, directors and performers during rehearsals. To succeed, you need talent, persistence and a lot of luck. It is not necessary to join a union, but do join the PERFORMING RIGHT SOCIETY.

Do another job which leaves you time and energy to write or arrange; persuade musicians and friends to perform your work. You can form your own group, give concerts and hope that TV, radio or commercial fixers will come and hear your work. Send out scores and tapes to TV, Radio 2 and theatrical producers. One success may encourage you to set up on your own.

You will need a telephone and answering machine or service; and about £3,000 to purchase a synthesiser, multi-track tape recorder for demonstration cassettes, small upright piano and special calculator which transfers the metronome speed to the timing of the film track. When successful you will need a publisher and an agent to get you work and negotiate fees.

To start with you are paid either by the bar or the number of minutes in the music, at very variable rates. If you hit the jackpot and write a television theme, you can probably live off the proceeds. Top income is around £100,000, with recording royalties and performing rights. Improvements in electronics are making recording easier and more accurate; but to avoid getting stale do not concentrate solely on TV work. Accept less lucrative but more challenging commissions from impoverished classical musicians to keep your creative process going.

You can usually work from home; the job keeps you on your toes, pays well and you meet interesting people who are good at their jobs.

A useful book is Cecil Forsyth's *Orchestration*; study scores by Tchaikovsky and Ravel.

List Broker

At a Glance

Qualifications/Training	No	Income bracket	Low–High
Licence	No	Town/Country	Town
Experience/Springboard	No	Travel	Local
Mid-career entry	Good	Exit sale	Yes
Entry costs	£500+	Work at home	Possible

Mix and match   Yes.   You could think about: Direct marketing agent, Book seller, Opening to the public, Garden gnome maker, Newsletter publisher . . .

Enquiries   British List Brokers' Association, British Direct Marketing Association

Classified lists of names and addresses are a valuable commodity used in direct marketing and mailing campaigns. List brokers rent out lists (at about 20% commission) on behalf of client companies. Customers who want to rent a list approach a list broker who will know which manager has the most appropriate list. To prevent the same list from being used more than once, the list owner will seed it with the names of friends (users should be advised of such seeding); pressure can then be applied on customers who infringe (litigation is costly and time consuming). The direct mail industry has doubled in the last five years; about £5 million is spent on it per annum and it looks set to grow. List broking is a fast moving business; in its early days it was a good way of making a fast buck and cowboy list brokers gave the industry a bad name. The BRITISH LIST BROKERS ASSOCIATION has stepped in to regulate and tighten up on this.

There are no formal qualifications but you'll have to prove an ability to handle lists, and make good recommendations to potential list users. It's illegal to make money from other people's lists (yellow pages, professional directories etc) but difficult to make a prosecution case stick. List poaching is a hazard for established brokers. Successful list brokers need the self discipline to work to their own deadlines. They also need to be good at selling and capable of inspiring confidence in their own judgment and ability in others.

Lists come from many sources. Specialising helps; the owner of one list may be interested in renting another in a related field. You'll get feedback from the lists you rent out which helps maintain their accuracy. Clients have lists based on magazine subscriptions, insurance policies, market research results etc. 10 company lists or a classified list of 200,000 can make your living. A good list lasts for about a year before it needs to be updated.

Set up costs needn't be great. You can start up with £500 for a typewriter and printer but you'll need a computer once you've expanded. Basic lists are presented on sticky labels but customers who want to send personalised letters need lists on magnetic tape – the machinery for this costs about £8–10,000 or you can subcontract the conversion to a special bureau. Each list must be registered under the Data Protection Act – this costs £15–20 for simple name and address lists but increases in price and complexity the more information you hold.

For a straightforward list (eg of local solicitors) expect to get about £15 per thousand names. For a good, response generated list you can get up to £500 per 1,000 names. People to talk to are the BRITISH LIST BROKERS' ASSOCIATION, the BRITISH DIRECT MARKETING ASSOCIATION and the DIRECT MAIL SERVICES STANDARDS BOARD (a regulatory body). Also the MAILING PREFERENCE SERVICE who will remove any name from a mailing list on request.

Literary Agent

At a Glance

Qualifications/Training	No	*Income bracket*	Low–High
Licence	No	*Town/Country*	Town
Experience/Springboard	Recommended	*Travel*	Yes
Mid-career entry	Probably essential	*Exit sale*	Yes
Entry costs	£3,500	*Work at home*	Possible

Mix and match   Limited.   You could think about: Book publisher, Novelist . . .
Enquiries   Association of Authors' Agents

Literary agents negotiate, sell, promote and protect the interests of authors. Most agencies are small businesses and are owned and run by one or two people who have been in the publishing industry for some time and have a lot of contacts. They operate by negotiating with publishers to get the best deal for their clients and making sure that agreements are kept, mistakes (conscious or unconscious) can be made easily. New technology, such as computers and fax machines, has streamlined a lot of the work involved and means that agents need to employ fewer assistants than before.

Getting into the network is essential. Your success depends on getting people (especially publishers) to listen to you in the first place and they're far more likely to do so if they know who you are. Best ways of building your networks are through working for a publisher or a literary agent – a difficult area to get into. Many people start as secretaries (increasingly men as well as women), graduate trainees, etc and work their way up, moving from company to company. This takes a long time but will get you contacts. Get as broad a view as possible of the different areas. You'll need to know about copyright, rights and contracts, (editing, production, marketing, sales etc are also useful).

Literary agents have to be sociable, self-starters and self-sufficient with an eye for detail. You won't have time to get lonely but neither (unless you've got a partner) will you have anyone with whom to discuss decisions. Life is a mixture of appointments and trying to fit in necessary follow through with constant interruptions as things develop.

To start up, 2 telephone lines are essential (you'll lose business if people can't get hold of you) and an answering machine as well as the usual office files, desk, typewriter, etc. You may also want a computer and a photocopier, a telex and ultimately a fax – getting documents to arrive quickly is valuable. Regular expenses include letterheads, service agreements (heavily recommended) for your equipment, telephone bills and lunching publishers (a far more efficient way of finding out what they want and what's going on than telephone conversations).

You'll need some money to tide you over the first few months. Once you've got a client with a book to sell it will take at least 3 months (for an established author) and up to about a year (for a new one) before you'll see any money for it. You retain commission (usually about 10%) on whatever you manage to negotiate for your clients. This includes an advance against royalties as well as royalties which are paid twice a year (once the advance has been earned) and any additional rights agreements such as translation, film, USA or serial. That means you'll need a turnover of £100,000 just to realise £10,000 for your own income and expenses. (The average author earns about £5,000 per annum). You'll need an accountant and an understanding bank manager.

Clients will come through word of mouth, from other authors or even from publishers (seldom the ones who actually publish their books though). You can hunt authors via reviews or the grapevine but you are not allowed to poach from other agents and must, when you approach a potential client, tell them to ignore you if they are already represented. You may find a few clients through your own slush file of unsolicited and unintroduced manuscripts. Handling the lists of foreign (especially American) publishers and agents for British editions is another source of revenue. There is growing use of contracts between agent and client which clarify the general agreement that agents should handle their clients' subsequent work. The material you handle depends on your experience (what you know how to sell) and interests, you can specialise if you want. There's little point trying to sell a book that you're not enthusiastic about but you may have to make exceptions for a regular, usually satisfactory author who turns out an aberration. Using the same publisher for an author's subsequent work will have a worthwhile knock-on effect – previous books by that author being re-released – the sales force will know something about what they're selling. You can continue to represent and reap profit from your clients' estates for up to fifty years after they have died, until the client's work is out of copyright.

Read *Bluff Your Way in Publishing, Writers' Handbook* and contact the ASSOCIATION OF AUTHORS' AGENTS.

Local Trader

At a Glance

Qualifications/Training	No	Income bracket	High
Licence	Yes	Town/Country	Town
Experience/Springboard	Essential	Travel	No
Mid-career entry	Yes	Exit sale	No
Entry costs	£30,000++	Work at home	No
Mix and match Limited.	You could think about: Property developer, Sculptor,
Landlord, Farmer . . .	
Enquiries AFBD	

Locals are self employed floor traders on the Futures and Options Markets who derive their income from successful trading on their own behalf, and by taking commissions from other brokers who do not employ their own floor traders. They do not trade directly for the public, or producers/purchasers of the commodities.

Organised Futures Markets, often called terminal markets grew out of the trade in agriculture commodities. With the expansion in world trade in the 19th century producers, merchants, manufacturers and consumers found it necessary to incur obligations forward for increasing periods. Futures and Options contracts are derived from the commodity markets as a way for the producers and purchasers of commodities (metals, grains, sugar, coffee, cocoa etc) to hedge against price fluctuations when buying or selling several months before delivery. Futures are contracts to buy or sell, on a pre-determined day, a set amount of a commodity at the trading price of the day on which the future was issued. Options are similar, although by buying an option you buy the *right* rather than the obligation, to buy or sell on that day. To increase liquidity of the markets futures and options can be traded by speculators as well as producers or purchasers of commodities; locals are one of the ways in which the markets are kept liquid.

A very small percentage of the trade on the market floors actually results in the buying or selling of a commodity – most trade is in the transfer of futures and options paper contracts. Futures contracts can be bought or sold to counterbalance the trader's physical position. Normally the futures contract is not used to achieve delivery. The 'hedge' will be lifted by entering into an offsetting sale on purchase of futures contracts when the trader is no longer exposed.

There are no formal qualifications for Locals but each exchange will have its own requirements regarding trading abilities or floor examinations which must be taken. Locals must be sponsored by a clearing member of the exchange on which they are going to trade; that is a member of the International Commodites Clearing House. The financial security of the futures contract is safe-guarded by the INTERNATIONAL COMMODITIES CLEARING HOUSE LIMITED (ICCH). The ICCH acts as an intermediary between all clearing member companies on exchange future market transactions, guaranteeing that should one default, it will undertake the financial obligations of that member. Although this rarely happens, this financial safeguard is an undeniable benefit to the business user. To provide this service it maintains strict financial controls on the overall positions of clearing member companies in the markets. Under current rules Local floor members are required to be authorised under the Financial Services Act (1986). This will be acquired by membership of the ASSOCIATION OF FUTURES BROKERS AND DEALERS (AFBD) or directly from the SECURITIES INVESTMENT BOARD (SIB). There are some Local traders who are chartists and base their forecasts on charts of market movement as well as using expert knowledge of the market.

Locals can make money by making, often very short term, sales or purchases of futures or options at the right time. To do this successfully you need an active mind, to be good with figures, quick to make decisions, methodical (you must know exactly how you stand financially all the time), be disciplined and patient enough to wait for the right time to make a deal. Each deal must be registered and all the day's trading to be recorded as required by the Exchange regulations.

Set up costs to become a Local vary from exchange to exchange. Membership of the AFBD can cost more than £1,800 (£500 initial membership fee, £500 for a licence and in 1988 £875 per annum membership fees). On top of that you also need to buy a Local seat on the exchange and this will vary depending on which exchange you are going to. In addition, your sponsor clearing member will require a deposit which can depend on your experience and reputation and also on the amount of trading you are going to be allowed to do. Sponsor and Local settle at the end of each day – one paying the other so that the deposit remains the same. The Locals are monitored by their sponsors to make sure they are not overtrading.

The markets are very volatile and a violent move in the market price can result very quickly in losses being made which are close to, or even above the value of the investors deposit. If you are not able to be on the floor throughout the trading hours you can have an alternate to stand in for you. Alternates are representing you and you are responsible for their actions, so one has to get the agreement of the sponsor and also of the AFBD. If you enjoy speculating and have the nerve to do it well, to be a local is an exciting and rewarding way to make (or lose!) a lot of money!

Magazine Designer

At a Glance

Qualifications/Training	Recommended	Income bracket	Low–Medium
Licence	No	Town/Country	Town
Experience/Springboard	Recommended	Travel	Local
Mid-career entry	No	Exit sale	No
Entry costs	£3,500	Work at home	Possible

Mix and match   Yes.   You could think about: Book designer, Illustrator, Magazine publisher, Book packager, Wine merchant, Motorcycle racer . . .

Enquiries   Chartered Society of Designers

Although most magazine designers work on the staff of the magazine, there are openings for freelance designers – and the work can be well paid. On the staff of a magazine, a designer will earn £10–£15,000 a year. A freelance designer will earn £60–£100 per day. A top designer will become an art editor or art director in a publishing company: a top freelance may become a design consultant, producing dummy layouts for publishers who are re-vamping existing magazines or developing new ones.

Most magazine designers start with a foundation course at art school, followed by a vocational course which will include options in magazine layout, printing and so on. There are few specialist courses: the LONDON COLLEGE OF PRINTING and NAPIER COLLEGE in Edinburgh are the two colleges best oriented towards the publishing trade. The first job is traditionally as a paste-up artist (on a small publication, where finished copy and illustrations are mounted on a board ready for the printing process) or as a junior layout artist on larger publications, devising a layout to suit the copy and illustrations available. The advent of 'desk-top' publishing, where all preparation is done on computer, has altered the nature of paste-up work: layout artists in many companies now need to be conversant with the new technology. If you intend to branch out and set up on your own, you may choose to work 'in-house' for different companies. If you want to work from home, designing house magazines for small companies or local interest magazines for estate agents, for example, you will need to equip a small studio (a room in a house is adequate). The equipment you need includes a drawing board (if you like to work at one), a light box (for studying transparencies and checking colour, and black and white proofs), a Grant machine (a type of projector which you use to blow-up transparencies, to trace on to the layout), plus stationery, storage space and work surfaces. You will also have to learn how to cost a job, including an allowance for materials and typesetting where necessary. You may also find that you take on book design work to fill gaps between jobs, or you may combine the job with illustration work. On the other hand, if you are used to working to tight deadlines, you may diversify into the more lucrative field of newspaper layout (which involves working unsocial hours). You will have to build up a portfolio of work to show to prospective employers. Good contacts are vital, and it is useful to consult the *Writers' and Artists' Year Book* and the *Writers' Handbook* or *Willings Press Guide* to keep up to date with the names of editors of publications you intend to work for. You will also have to buy (or at least read) a wide range of magazines, including foreign ones, to keep up to date with style and design. Many designers are members of the CHARTERED SOCIETY OF DESIGNERS and subscribe to its magazine, the *Designer*. You can also advertise your services in *Publishing News*. *Creative Review* is the journal of the closely allied advertising world.

Most designers are members of either the NATIONAL UNION OF JOURNALISTS or the NATIONAL GRAPHICAL ASSOCIATION who run a call office where members can register themselves as available for freelance work.

Magazine Publisher

At a Glance

Qualifications/Training	No	Income bracket	Low–High
Licence	No	Town/Country	Town
Experience/Springboard	Recommended	Travel	Yes
Mid-career entry	Likely	Exit sale	Excellent
Entry costs	£5,000++	Work at home	Possible

Mix and match   Yes.   You could think about: Book publisher, Book packager, Space sales agent, Direct marketing agent, Nanny and babysitting agent . . .

Enquiries   Periodical Publishers' Association

This is a vast area, covering a wide range of products from Country Life to soft porn; from free magazines deposited through your letter box to highly specialist targeted products. Magazine publishing is fundamentally a commercial business, but is a high risk activity with only a 40% success rate. Big companies that can survive in spite of these high mortality rates dominate the industry. There is room for independent magazine publishers so long as they avoid competing head on with the giants of the industry and concentrate on producing a unique product. This means filling a gap in the market that you have found or created. Money is usually made primarily from advertising; circulation sales are secondary. Good circulation figures often boost advertising revenue. Once you have an established, successful product it might be bought out by one of the giant publishing houses. Alternatively the giants can wreck your profit or even force you to close down by launching a directly competitive product and achieving their circulation through promotional expenditure so enormous that you can't match it. If you sell, (one free, local magazine was recently bought for £¾ million after three years) you can use the money to set up a new magazine or retire. The current trend in magazine publishing is towards narrower and narrower specialisation.

Although no formal qualifications are necessary to produce a magazine, any experience of the field, including working on an undergraduate magazine is useful. What you need is a target market, (defined by age, socio-economic group, special interests, sex etc) and an idea to hit it with. You'll also have to decide how to distribute the magazine. You can do this in one of three ways. Firstly, from newstands; for this you'll need wholesalers who will ensure that you get your target distribution through the retail trade, (the wholesale trade and, to an extent, the retail trade is dominated by John Menzies and W H Smith, although there are thousands of outlets that may be better geared to your magazine). Secondly, you can operate a subscription list, which will save you the costs of retail distribution but will involve you in the time-consuming and equally expensive administration of the mailing list, although you can get the money up front. (Some magazines are distributed through a mixture of these ways). Finally, you can hand it out or send it out free, deriving your income from advertisements alone.

Before you launch your magazine you have to get as good an idea as possible about how viable it may be. Major magazine distributors will help and may even try a regional test. By careful monitoring of the test, you might determine whether you have a success or not, but remember that the settle down circulation is usually only about 50–60% of the initial sampling. Before you get this far you must have worked out production costs (paper, printing, quality etc) and revenue (from advertisers and/or cover price). Base your revenue calculations on the assumptions that you will penetrate only a small part of your target market; for newstand sales you should expect to receive 45–50% of the cover price per issue sold; the trade regards sales of 85% of an issue to be a 'technical' sell out. Of the 2,500 newstrade consumer magazines in Britain, only about 100 have circulations of more than 70,000. For subscription magazines, which are usually more specialised and with equally specialised advertisements, the market is more clearly defined and can be approached via list brokers. In any case, you have to get it right from day one. You'll soon find out if it's wrong; if you aren't reaching your objective sales figures within 4–5 issues for newstand distributed magazines (longer perhaps for subscriptions where there is a certain amount of buyer inertia), then you've probably failed. Advertisers will be monitoring the response that they get from your magazine and will stop using you if it isn't worthwhile. The success of free magazines is judged on advertising response.

Set up costs include financing all of this research plus producing a mock up edition for distributors and advertisers, before you even start to think about revenue. You probably should register as a company and you'll certainly need libel insurance and insurance against other disasters (floods, fires, etc). The absolute minimum of equipment is a telephone, a typewriter and some printed stationery. A bank manager who understands the needs of new enterprises is essential; if your one doesn't – find one who does. Planning your cash flow is critical.

Printers and paper merchants might give 60 days credit on bills (more if they know you). Advertisers are usually good at paying new

---

companies quickly especially if they've had some direct contact with you and your magazine is small. Base cover price and rates card for advertisers on the research you've done and by referring to the competition.

Some people find having a partner with a different outlook useful for bouncing ideas off – not a friend though ('friendships never survive partnership'). Others find a partner only leads to clashes of ideas. Contacts are useful. You may want some freelance writers, editors and designers (try also the *Publishers' Freelance Directory*). You'll also probably want to employ help with ad sales, office administration etc. Young inexperienced staff are easy to find, enthusiastic and not blinkered by anybody else's training; they will need supervision though and employing some more experienced and expensive staff will give you more time to develop the business.

In the early days you have to establish confidence in your product. Get as much coverage in the media and in other magazines as possible. Make changes with caution and keep an eye on all competitors. Using established writers for regular features or columns helps to boost circulation as does satisfying any specific interest that you can identify in your market. As you expand you'll have to get used to spending an increasing amount of time managing staff, budgets etc.

Go to the PERIODICAL PUBLISHERS' ASSOCIATION for further information and read industry magazines like the *Publisher*.

Makeup Artist

At a Glance

Qualifications/Training	Recommended	Income bracket	Low–High
Licence	No	Town/Country	Town
Experience/Springboard	Not necessary	Travel	Yes
Mid-career entry	Possible	Exit sale	No
Entry costs	£500	Work at home	No

Mix and match Possible. You could think about: Beauty consultant, Hairdresser, Yoga teacher...
Enquiries Art colleges, model agencies, magazines

It's every little girl's dream to earn her living by painting faces and that's exactly what a makeup artist does. It's a glamorous life involving a lot of variety – creating a fantasy makeup for a pop video one day and in a photographic studio making up models for the fashion shots in a magazine the next. But don't be misled by the glamour – it's also hard work, demanding a great deal of dedication and determination, particularly in the early days, and competition is stiff.

Most makeup artists are female, though there is no reason why men can't enter the field too. Most are self-employed and work on a freelance basis. A good eye for colour and interest in makeup are essential. You need to enjoy working with people and to be tactful, tolerant, discreet, outgoing and inventive. You also need to be able to work as part of a team.

Some cosmetic houses have trainee schemes for potential makeup artists but these tend to be short and invariably use only their own products. Art school is a good start, and beauty consultants, hairdressers and models often move on to become makeup artists. Television companies, such as the BBC and THAMES TELEVISION, run training courses but these are for employees only and there is fierce competition. The LONDON COLLEGE OF FASHION runs courses in London, and there are City and Guilds courses throughout the country. The many private schools can be expensive – a makeup course at COMPLECTIONS INTERNATIONAL, for example, will set you back a cool £4,295.

Alternatively, you can simply enlist the help of a few photogenic guinea pigs, find a good photographer and then tout your portfolio around as many outlets – magazines, photographic studios, advertising agencies, etc – as possible. If you've got the talent, someone will recognise it.

The initial costs and the money you can earn vary greatly, depending on how you go about it and how successful you are. Earnings can be very high (£80,000 is not unheard of) but not everyone scores so high. You could even progress to opening your own beauty school, but you will really know you've made it when you're in constant demand for all the top magazines. Most good artists have an agent who will do all their bookings for them and send their portfolio to prospective clients. Many of the model agencies also have makeup artists on their books.

Man with a Van

At a Glance

Qualifications/Training	No	*Income bracket*	Low–Medium
Licence	Driving licence	*Town/Country*	Usually town
Experience/Springboard	No	*Travel*	Yes
Mid-career entry	Yes	*Exit sale*	No
Entry costs	£5,000	*Work at home*	No

Mix and match Excellent. You could think about: Mini-cab driver, Disco owner, Painter/decorator, Events organiser, Hire shop owner, Musician . . .

Enquiries Local removals companies, studios etc

A man with a van who knows his way about town can earn something in the region of £100 per day if he plays his cards right. Of course, there are overheads: tax, insurance, maintenance, parking tickets, a telephone paging account, not to mention the cost of the van itself, but if you enjoy driving, and want to be free to work when and as you please, this is the ideal job.

There are several different ways of setting up in the business – it depends on the type of people you are going to fetch and carry for. Many van drivers start off with minicab companies, breaking away to work on their own when they find that they are repeatedly working for

MAN WITH A VAN

three or four major clients: the clients may be in advertising, in media, small manufacturing companies who have to distribute products, and so on. You can also build up a reputation independently, if you know one or two people who need stuff moved at short notice. Another approach is to set yourself up as a small, local removals company; this tends to be less lucrative as you will need to be able to employ casual labour to help with hefty pieces of furniture.

One of the best ways to get yourself known is to have business cards printed to hand to anyone you do a small job for, send to office managers and leave pinned to noticeboards at offices, studios, warehouses and so on. If you are setting up as a small removals firm, a notice in the local paper is the best way to advertise yourself, plus an entry in the yellow pages.

You will have to keep careful accounts – some people will pay cash, but others will have to put your invoices through the system, which may cause cash flow problems. Some of the most successful van drivers specialise in moving props for film or photo sessions. By working in one field like this, the job becomes easier as you gain experience: you will get to know the suppliers and the studios, and as you get to know them better, you build up a reputation among the people who hire you so that you become more popular. The problem comes when you are in such demand that you have to start turning work down. If you turn down a couple of jobs in succession, the hirer may not come to you again – so you have to find a balance between guaranteed, reliable delivery and an ability to take on any job at short notice.

Market Research Interviewer

		At a Glance		
Qualifications/Training	Yes	Income bracket		Low–Medium
Licence	No	Town/Country		Either
Experience/Springboard	No	Travel		Yes
Mid-career entry	Yes	Exit sale		No
Entry costs	Nil	Work at home		No
Mix and match	Excellent. You could think about: Actor, Musician, Novelist, House converter, Tourist guide, Dealer in antiques . . .			
Enquiries	Market Research Society			

Interviewing some 300 randomly selected people can, surprisingly, give an accurate idea of the characteristics, preferences, behaviour and opinions of the whole of a population. Market researchers exploit this on behalf of clients with specific commercial or political interests. Their results are then interpreted and used by the clients who can profit by pleasing the public (manufacturers, broadcasters, politicians etc). Market research findings have wide commercial value: for example, list brokers use research findings for direct mail and marketing.

There are different areas of field market research: consumer research where a sample of the general public is asked what it thinks of eg washing powder or magazines; executive researchers collect information and statistics from people in business and industry by appointment. Others may specialise in eg medicine or farming; others test new questionnaires to make sure they produce valid results. There are no formal qualifications but you do need credentials to encourage people to commission you. There are short courses run by the MARKET RESEARCH SOCIETY or you can be trained on the job by a market research company in what to ask and how to ask it. For telephone research, in particular, you need excellent interviewing skills so you can keep the interviewee's interest while you fill in your questionnaire. For consumer research you will have to stand on street corners, or in supermarkets, interviewing passers-by; or visit people in their houses – either preselected addresses or a 'random walk'. This may be great in fine weather but you may not enjoy it when it's raining. You'll have to cope with a lot of walking the streets, finding nobody at home and willing to talk to you. Your clients won't always have done much research themselves and may send you on wild goose chases (researching opinions of the gas service in areas with no gas). You'll have to work at weekends and evenings especially if you're trying to reach heads of households. Executive research is cushier but you will usually need to have consumer research experience first. Executive research interviews can take several hours and one of the hardest parts of the job is getting people to agree to talk to you. A lot of research has been undertaken in the last 5–10 years and respondents, especially in London, are getting tired of giving up the time. You'll need stamina to cope with this and with periods of disheartening lack of progress. Statistics or maths qualifications are useful when you're interpreting what you've found. You have to be methodical and know your questionnaire before letting loose on the public.

Fees for market research are usually negotiated with clients who own the findings. Base your charges on the amount of time you expect to take; clients are unlikely to know much about the field and some of the

findings you come up with have a high resale value so you can charge quite a lot.

You can get clients through contracts, companies you've already done research for whilst working at another research company, or perhaps you can do some research and hawk it around companies who may be interested.

It is a good job if you want to mix and match with another one, to keep the cash flow positive while you are building up. It is also a good job for parents of young families, as you can make your own interviewing schedules to suit your own constraints.

Market Stall Holder

At a Glance

Qualifications/Training	No	*Income bracket*	Low–Medium
Licence	Yes	*Town/Country*	Town
Experience/Springboard	No	*Travel*	Local
Mid-career entry	Yes	*Exit sale*	No
Entry costs	£300++	*Work at home*	No

Mix and match   Yes.   You could think about: Dealer in antiques, Caterer, Street entertainer . . .

Enquiries   Local markets or local authority

Market stalls need lower overheads than shops. They are an alternative small outlet for low value goods (collectables, costume jewellery, food, cheap clothes), but unsatisfactory for larger, more expensive things because they aren't secure. Although it is possible to use a market stall as a way into shop owning (more likely with antiques than with food) the vast difference in scale makes it a slow way in. Many towns have covered markets especially for antiques and crafts, some of these are privately owned; other markets are a collection of stalls on a street managed by the local council. It is illegal to sell from anywhere other than a licensed pitch in a market.

The only qualifications are having something to sell which suits the market and, in local authority markets, getting a licence from the local council. For a permanent licence, entitling you to a pitch on all market days (usually Monday–Saturday; sometimes only until Friday) you have to register with the council. There is usually a long waiting list (often 2 years or more) before you'll be offered a vacancy, subject to your commodity suiting the available pitch in the opinion of the council: eg no antiques in Smithfield. Licences can be passed on but only to a relation, some pitches stay in one family for generations.

Alternatively, get a casual licence, these are issued within a few days. With this you turn up early on market day, present yourself to the market inspector and are issued with any available pitch on either a first come or lottery system. There is no guarantee that you'll get a pitch when you want one but you can get a casual licence while on the waiting list for a permanent one; it's also useful for a one off shot.

Costs of a pitch vary: up to £30 per week in a permanent market and about £10 per day for a casual licence holder. Additional set up costs include about £5 registration fee to get a licence, your stock and something to sell it from that will protect both you and it from the rain (build your own stall or rent one), somewhere nearby (garage or shed) to store it in when the market is closed or a van. You'll also need something to carry the stock to market in.

The type of customer depends on the market. Food markets attract a high proportion of local shoppers while antiques and crafts have a less regular clientele of tourists, browsers, collectors and the trade. If you're selling your own craft work a market stall may lead to special commissions or interest from shops in stocking your goods. For some things reduced overheads may allow you to undercut shop prices and increase turnover.

It helps to have a partner or assistant, this will require your profits to support two but will allow you some time off. If you can't manage this, cultivate the friendship of neighbouring stall holders who will watch your stall while you have breaks during the day. You also need to find a stand-in to man the stall while you go on holiday. Market days are long, especially if you're selling food that has to be bought before you set up, this means starting work at about 5 am. Stalls have to be erected and displays set up before you open at about 9.00 or 10.00 and you'll have to pack up every night. Hours are even stranger for the specialist meat, fish and vegetable markets which serve the trade and are open all night. You have to work outside in all weathers, bad weather may keep people away but getting known at the market is important and your regular clientele will expect you to be there.

Marketing Consultant

At a Glance

Qualifications/Training	Recommended	Income bracket	High
Licence	No	Town/Country	Either
Experience/Springboard	A must	Travel	Lots
Mid-career entry	Essential	Exit sale	Possible
Entry costs	£5,000	Work at home	Yes

Mix and match Possible. You could think about: Public relations consultant, Farmer, Timeshare holiday accommodation owner . . .

Enquiries Institute of Marketing

Marketing consultants sell one principal resource – their own skilled time. Businessmen buy this resource because they have confidence in the skill of the consultant to bring solutions to their particular businesses.

Marketing is an approach to business which holds that customers buy benefits or solutions to needs, rather than just products or services. It is concerned with the needs and attitudes of the customers and how to influence them in favour of given products, and with identifying market gaps to exploit competitors' weaknesses. Marketing is restless and dynamic; always trying to do things better, to improve market share and long term profits. Market information gathered by a plethora of research methods underpins it.

Marketing is used in advertising to identify the best audiences and the most relevant benefits, in new product development, in sales promotion, in corporate design, in package design, and in multinational business – to explain how overseas markets are structured and work, and whether to enter them by means of joint ventures, by, say, starting from scratch or by acquisition. It is used in planning and executing mergers; in hiring and managing distributors; in building and running a sales force.

Marketing consultants must be able to persuade businessmen that they have some distinctive and sellable functional knowhow, or industry knowledge, or other personal attribute. It is – theoretically – possible to obtain such skills from outside industry (eg as a business studies professor or industrial journalist) but in practice this is rare. The purchasers are businessmen used to demanding solid reasons to justify purchase decisions. The best reasons are the consultant's track record both as manager and consultant. Consultants must be seen to be able to deliver the goods.

The best way to start is to possess a CV which includes as many as possible of the following: good university degree, any subject; possibly an MBA – overrated unless from top institutions like Harvard, Columbia or Insead; basic marketing training in a highly regarded marketing and training company – eg Unilever, IBM, Proctor & Gamble; progressive career development, ideally to director level, in highly regarded companies; international experience; some language capabilities; marketing consultancy work with a leading consultancy such as McKinsey, Boston Consulting Group; demonstrable marketing record in a major industry sector such as retailing, liquor, banking, where many firms already value and understand your record; high visibility – eg marketing writer, marketing media person, lecturer, public person; age at least 30. Paragons who boast all these CV attributes will already have sleek company cars and even sleeker salaries.

Starting out as a marketing consultant with a good CV is easy. You will already have a pool of potential buyers, ideally your first customers, waiting for you to begin. So start selling. You will need minimal capital since consultancy offers a generally positive cash flow, but budget to survive without income for the first six months. Keep down initial overheads, forego the chauffeur, dispense with expensive trappings, at least until you are solidly established. The only essential start-up kit is top quality communications and top quality presentation, and much of this can be bought in.

The sort of people you sell to (their levels and their companies) will depend on what you are selling, what your skills are and whom you know. Do not try to sell acquisition studies to assistant brand managers, or sales promotion to the chairman. If the services you are selling fall within functional areas such as market research, PR, training, sales promotion, there will already be budgets you can feed on and specialists in the firm with a professional appreciation of your worth. But if you are selling solutions to ad hoc needs (such as acquisition searches, sales force re-organisations), no regular budget will exist. Unbudgeted projects are only approved at top level. Be persistent. The daily ratio of contacts to sales may be low but all contacts you make help prepare them for the time when they need you.

Firms engage consultants for a number of reasons: an overflow of work requiring your help temporarily; a young and untrained department needing to be galvanised by your new thinking; the specialist help which you can offer them. Firms often believe they already know the answer but want a second opinion, or face decisions laden with political and status risks to the managers who therefore need outsiders to identify solutions, take responsibility, and shoulder blame.

Marketing consultants come in all sizes: big-name consultancy companies and a host of smaller and one-man operators. Big companies charge the highest fees and often land the client when price is no object, or where the purchasers want to cover their backs by showing that they have used a top firm. But the key selection criterion is the confidence that the consultant can deliver and this confidence comes best from direct personal experience which leaves much scope for you to sell to people who know that you are good.

The amount of consultancy work is never just right for long. All projects are innovative (no problem, no consultancy project), and the work is demand-dedicated. Hence one more client may be one too many; but clients imagine they are your sole benefactors and if you prevaricate they will not come back. Uncomfortable as this can become, it does mean that life is seldom boring.

Demand for your services will vary between industry sectors, companies, management levels and problem areas. No two consultants will have identical experience. Projects handled by one marketing consultant in his first year of operation included: assessment of the 'brown ale' phenomenon in the UK beer market, for a French brewing group; review of the marketing plans for a new branded wine concept, to be launched in Belgium; sales force re-organisation and retraining, for a UK food manufacturer; development of incentive programmes for pharmaceutical reps, detailing to doctors in the UK; warehousing and distribution study for a cigarette company newly arrived in the UK market.

Whatever your stock in trade, it will be a wasting asset. The more you succeed in promoting and practising your skills, the more you will breed imitators. Imitators will compete by improving your product and undercutting your price. You must therefore invest in keeping your products modern and superior, and in placing them continuously before your audience. Never rest on your laurels. If successful, rewards are outstanding.

Read *Offensive Marketing*. Use the INSTITUTE OF MARKETING for its library and courses; and the Business Information Section of the British Library, located in the SCIENCE REFERENCE LIBRARY.

Media Convertor

At a Glance

Qualifications/Training	Not essential	*Income bracket*	Medium–High
Licence	No	*Town/Country*	Town
Experience/Springboard	Essential	*Travel*	Local
Mid-career entry	Yes	*Exit sale*	No
Entry costs	£60,000	*Work at home*	Possible

Mix and match Yes. You could think about: Computer software author, Computer consultant, Newsletter publisher, Jazz musician . . .
Enquiries British Computer Society

Media convertors are not hidden persuaders but computer specialists supplying a tailor-made client service to computer users. They convert a client's existing medium of data to a form compatible with new hardware, or combinations of previously incompatible hardware. Most of the work involves transferring information from floppy disk to floppy disk.

No formal training or qualification is needed although courses run by the BRITISH COMPUTER SOCIETY may start you off. It is more important to be in the right place at the right time and to be able to sell. Experience in selling, computing and business management are essential for success. The vast majority of necessary knowledge can be built up on the job, most importantly how to deal with clients and the applications to which systems can be put. Personal qualities required have been described as 'bloody-mindedness, conceit and arrogance'. Clients must be kept happy with personal service; patience may be tested.

At least £60,000 is helpful for equipment necessary for setting up (but not essential as more equipment can be bought along the way) and for funding premises suitable to convince clients you know what you are doing. As with any small business, getting off the ground involves hard work and holidays are difficult to fit in. This job need not follow you home as conversions are carried out quickly and usually in business hours and a conventional working week is possible.

Media conversion is new, fast-expanding and highly specialised. This is as a result of a rapidly changing computer market and the increased use by non-specialists. A good deal of money can be made – tens of thousands after a couple of years. You deal largely with those who have no specialised computer staff themselves, so you meet a wide variety of people. However it is a specialised and inaccessible occupation. Getting established is a matter of building a reputation. It is probably a good idea to start in the computer world in a less-specialised field.

Mini-Cab Driver

At a Glance

Qualifications/Training	No	Income bracket	Low–Medium
Licence	Driving licence	Town/Country	Mostly town
Experience/Springboard	No	Travel	Local
Mid-career entry	Excellent	Exit sale	No
Entry costs	£3,500	Work at home	No

Mix and match Excellent. You could think about: Almost anything . . .
Enquiries Local mini-cab companies

Mini-cab drivers use their own cars as taxis; legislation governing them is less stringent than for licensed cabs. They are self-employed and operate through companies who liaise between passengers and drivers. By and large cab drivers choose their own hours subject to the basic requirements of the company being fulfilled. This makes it a good job if you've got other commitments or want to mix and match with another job, or simply augment your income. There are more men than women mini-cab drivers due to the greater risks for women taking strangers in their cars. There is a market for all women cab companies, to take women passengers only, which is not often tapped.

Anyone with a four door car and a clean driving licence can become a cab driver. You pay rent to the controlling company which also provides (on payment of a rent of about £2 pw) a radio phone which will keep you in touch with them while you're driving. Companies also arrange for advertising. By law mini-cab drivers may only carry passengers who have contacted the company (usually by phone) in advance – you cannot ply for hire on the streets without being a licensed cab driver. On the other hand there are no laws saying you must agree to carry passengers for certain distances and you can refuse to pick up any passengers you don't like the look of. The local police station will support you if any passenger refuses to compensate you for loss of income incurred by your having to clean up after they've been sick. Your insurance will probably stipulate the maximum number of passengers you can carry – usually four.

As well as a car and deposit for the radio phone, you will need hire and reward insurance which costs at least twice as much as standard motor insurance. The amount you earn depends on how many fares you can get which can depend on traffic conditions. Passengers are usually fairly local but, when they want to go for long distances, you may have an empty car on the way back. The cab company sets a rough fare scale (including a minimum charge for very short journeys, usually around £1.50, and extra charges for carrying baggage, animals etc). Mini-cabs don't have metres, fares and tips are paid in cash.

There are obvious risks. It helps if you're a good driver and also if you're careful about who you pick up (within reason). It's easy to get into; local mini-cab companies are often delighted to take on more drivers. Although there may be some routine work from regular customers (more likely during the day when local businesses or hospital out-patients may use you) most of this is unscheduled.

Trade press; *Cab Trade News*.

Motorcycle Messenger

At a Glance

Qualifications/Training	No	*Income bracket*	Low
Licence	Driving licence	*Town/Country*	Town
Experience/Springboard	No	*Travel*	Local
Mid-career entry	Yes	*Exit sale*	No
Entry costs	£1,000+	*Work at home*	No

Mix and match Excellent. You could think about: Almost anything . . .
Enquiries Local courier services

If you can ride well and have a good knowledge of a large city, the potential earnings may outweigh the thought of periods off work due to injury. Very few despatch services provide much more than an agency for booking the services of their riders, so expect to take care of your own bike and other necessities (although a few agencies do provide bikes). Fees are on a piecework basis, with the agency taking a cut of the job. If you want to keep in business you will need a reliable bike and expect it to be worn out very rapidly – budget up to £1000 or more. Find out what the agency provides in the way of insurance, an ordinary policy is likely to be invalidated by working as a messenger. A good agency will have plenty of work, so earnings depend entirely on how fast you are and how well you can find your way around but £7 an hour is easily possible. Many companies offer 'guaranteed' minimum earnings (in London commonly of £200 or £250 per week). Some specify minimum capacity bikes. Some charge a fee for the circuit and for the radio. There are also openings for bicycle messengers. Hours are basically the same as the businesses who use the service. *Despatch Rider* is a useful magazine.

Motorcycle Racer

At a Glance

Qualifications/Training	No	Income bracket	Low
Licence	Yes	Town/Country	Either
Experience/Springboard	No	Travel	Yes
Mid-career entry	Possible	Exit sale	No
Entry costs	£1,000+	Work at home	No

Mix and match Yes. You could think about: Motorcycle messenger, Pop group sound engineer, Garage owner, Sex therapist . . .

Enquiries Auto Cycle Union, Amateur Motor Cycle Association

Very few riders ever make it to a level where they can earn a living, but if you're good enough and lucky enough, you might land a 'works' contract from a major manufacturer or sponsor.

There are two organising bodies for motorcycle sport. The AUTO CYCLE UNION (ACU) covers all branches, while the AMATEUR MOTOR CYCLE ASSOCIATION (AMCA) caters only for off-road riding (such as moto-cross and trials).

You'll need to buy or borrow a suitable bike for the class of riding which interests you, then join a club affiliated to one of the organised bodies (they will supply lists). You need to apply for a competition licence – the fee of £10 includes compulsory Personal Accident Insurance. Expect to spend a year as a Novice (you have to qualify at 10 events over at least 3 circuits) before obtaining a full licence which costs £15 for National or £62 for International. For details buy a copy of the *ACU Handbook* which costs £1.50 by mail order.

Trade magazines abound but the most useful are *Motor Cycle News*, *Road Racer* and *Dirt Bike Rider*.

MP

At a Glance

Qualifications/Training	No	Income bracket	High
Licence	No	Town/Country	Town
Experience/Springboard	No	Travel	Yes
Mid-career entry	Excellent	Exit sale	No
Entry costs	£500+	Work at home	No

Mix and match Excellent. You could think about: Barrister, Novelist, Public relations consultant, Journalist, Farmer . . .

Enquiries   Political parties

The job of a Member of Parliament is several rolled into one. The demands of your electorate, your constituency party, the whips' office and public life are all different and if you are unlucky, they conflict. Conflict with family life is certain and the divorce rate is one of the highest. If you join a front bench, things only get worse. To be successful, you will need to be articulate, with a good line in 'flannel', the ability to think on your feet and excellent personal organisation. Life will be less gruelling too if you get on well with people, have plenty of self-assurance (critics call it conceit) and resilience to insult and rotting fruit. Strong political convictions probably come next.

'Members of Parliament are selected not elected'. You can be bold, pay a depost of £500 and stand as an independent. But the more usual route is to be adopted by one of the major parties, whose selection practices vary. Find out more by contacting the head office of the CONSERVATIVE, LABOUR, SOCIAL AND LIBERAL DEMOCRATIC or SDP party. Conservatives first attend the regular selection course (discussion followed by dinner to check on your table manners!). If you pass this stage, your name is placed on the list of candidates. When a vacancy occurs in a local constituency, you will be notified and you can apply if you wish. The local party committee will make a final shortlist after another interview. Those on the final list are invited (with spouses) to a selection conference composed of around 200 paid-up constituency association members who take a secret ballot on the outcome. The losers are free to try their luck for the next vacancy.

In the Labour party, every local branch of the Party, and affiliated organisations like trade unions, can put forward a name to the constituency general mangement committee which selects the winner. This means that potential candidates canvass support in the constituency to achieve nomination.

How you finally get adopted as a candidate is largely a matter of chemistry, your face fitting in the locality and your political views matching any idiosyncracies of the local party. Labour hopefuls tend to polish up working class credentials; Conservatives their devotion to cutting costs etc. There is an unofficial system whereby you cut your teeth in a no-hope constituency before getting the prize of a safe seat. But you can serve your 'apprenticeship' in other ways, working for the party HQ, local government, trade unions etc.

Your election campaign will be run by your election agent, who may be distinct from your full-time agent. Your choice of election agent is important – the job requires someone who is efficient and who you can get along with under stress.

Once elected, many suffer from culture shock. You are exhausted, the rituals unfamiliar, you will start with no office and your support system may be a long way away. If you represent a constituency outside London, you have to decide how much of both your political and domestic operation to move to London. The hours are punishing. Parliamentary holidays are long, allowing you to devote some time to your constituency. You should either be single or be married to a saint. It's not a life recommended for single parents. Women generally are almost accepted; blacks and handicapped are novelties.

Some MPs are sponsored (mostly Labour, arranged before election) or use their position as an MP to gain eg consultancies outside

MP.

parliament. All interests are expected to be declared in the parliamentary register of interests. Some MPs develop specialisms early, particularly if they are politically ambitious. Membership of select committees may then follow and maybe the front bench. If you don't mind not being re-elected, you can do nothing at all. Representing all but the safest constituency is a precarious business and political fortunes are made or lost very quickly. A second career is an asset, particularly if you can keep it going while you are an MP – law is a popular one.

The salary is not excessive but you can claim additional costs – to stay in London if the constituency is distant; free rail warrants; and up to £21,000 pa for secretarial and office support. You can use your position to get some freelance work eg writing and on television but you'll never get rich being an MP alone.

Useful reading is profuse; try the *House Magazine* and *Hansard*. Also, *Westminster Blues*; *Careers in Politics*; *Parliament and the Public*; *Westminster Man*; *A Tribal Anthropology of the Commons People*; *Honourable Member*; *Parliament in the 1980s*; *How Parliament Works*.

Musical Instrument Maker

At a Glance

Qualifications/Training	Recommended	*Income bracket*	Low–Medium
Licence	No	*Town/Country*	Town
Experience/Springboard	Recommended	*Travel*	No
Mid-career entry	Possible	*Exit sale*	Unlikely
Entry costs	£2,000+	*Work at home*	Yes

Mix and match Possible. You could think about: Cabinet maker, Musical instrument repairer, Music/instrument retailer, Counsellor . . .
Enquiries Other musical instrument makers

The degree of expertise needed for this means that most musical instrument makers specialise in one particular instrument and nearly all specialise to the degree of making only, eg string, brass, woodwind. Some basic knowledge is needed of the principles of engineering, design draughtsmanship, and a gift for working with wood or other natural materials, is essential. It's very useful to be able to play the instrument – failing that you must have very close contact with

MUSICAL INSTRUMENT MAKER

someone who does and who can tell you what's good or bad about the instruments you make.

Courses at the LONDON COLLEGE OF FURNITURE, NEWARK or MERTON COLLEGE are a very good way of developing contacts and your own specialisations. If you want to go further afield you could try the NATIONAL SCHOOL OF VIOLIN MAKING in Mittenwald in West Germany or the Italian equivalent in Cremona. There are very few traditional apprenticeships still available, but another good way of making contacts and gaining experience is by working for someone else after you've done a course and gradually starting to make your own instruments. When you have sold one to a professional who likes it, then you can think about working part of the time for yourself. You must be able to empathise with your customers who tend to identify with their instruments to the point of neurosis. Makers need to be sympathetic, tactful, have physical stamina and an ability to trust their own judgment. Making an instrument involves the sensitivity of an artist which is why there are so few successful makers in the UK. The profession is overcrowded and the fall-out rate colossal.

To set up on your own you need either capital or a working partner to keep you for the first 2 years when there will be no income. The CRAFTS COUNCIL gives very few grants. Approach NATIONAL FEDERATION OF SELF-EMPLOYED AND SMALL BUSINESSES for information and advice. Allow about £2,000 to purchase a workbench, band saw, circular saw, small drill and special wood etc. You can make your tools while in employment. Get accommodation of your own *before* you start; think about disturbance to the neighbours – musicians playing at all hours, the noise of electric tools etc. You can set up anywhere within reach of deliveries. Get a good accountant. After 10 years you can earn up to

£20,000 pa. Charge by the hour plus materials; unlike furniture makers who quote for a job in advance and have to stick to what they've quoted, you can charge more if the job takes longer than usual. Enter competitions but contacts are best made within the profession.

Avoid becoming a workaholic by working from 9–5. Try to develop a sporting hobby to compensate for the enormous concentration which this exacting craft demands. But the job brings great personal satisfaction in the freedom to experiment with design and the pleasure of hearing your instruments played well.

Musical Instrument Repairer

At a Glance

Qualifications/Training	Recommended	*Income bracket*	Low–Medium
Licence	No	*Town/Country*	Town
Experience/Springboard	Recommended	*Travel*	Possibly local
Mid-career entry	Possible	*Exit sale*	Unlikely
Entry costs	£2,000+	*Work at home*	Possible

Mix and match Possible. You could think about: Musical instrument maker, Music/instrument retailer, Piano tuner, Musician, Direct marketing agent . . .
Enquiries Other musical instrument repairers

This is someone who repairs and restores musical instruments. You must have a natural interest in mechanics and be good with your hands. You should be able to play the instruments you repair or to know someone who does and who is able to advise you on any additional modifications that would improve the instruments. Learn the basic principles of engineering and bookkeeping, either through the public library or at adult education classes. It is not necessary to go to a college such as MERTON or NEWARK (wind and brass) or the LONDON COLLEGE OF FURNITURE (which has specialist courses in a wide range of instruments) but colleges are a good source of contacts and work – musicians often ask colleges to recommend repairers. You can learn to make your own tools by going to an evening class. You should have a good ear for fine tuning and understand dynamics (playing loudly or softly). If you are accepted as an apprentice by an experienced instrument builder or repairer you will have to work under pressure. This helps you to get on with the job quickly and efficiently; a professional musician may need an emergency repair just before a concert. You alone will be responsible for professional musicians' instruments, so must be able to do the repair quickly.

It is important to socialise and listen to musicians' problems: sometimes it is the musician that needs repair rather than the instrument.

When you feel confident and have made enough contacts, work from home (with family consent) or hire a small industrial unit through one of the government's small business aid schemes. This must be located centrally with good public transport and parking; because musicians travel in their work they are unwilling to do so to have their instruments repaired. This means that there are more opportunities in places like London than in small towns.

Most publicity comes by word of mouth. If you have a reputation for speed and accuracy, career prospects are good. Specialise in one particular instrument and corner the market. Advertise your service in the local press, *The Musician* and *Classical Music* magazines. Have business cards printed. Contact the local education office so that you can repair school instruments. Big, well established orchestras tend to have their own repairers but smaller ones may not have.

You will need £2,000 to buy a good drill, a lathe, pads for woodwind and wood for stringed instruments. Better machinery is improving the quality and efficiency of the job. You can expect to start earning at a rate of about £14 per week up to £15,000–£20,000 pa once you're established. Base charges on time taken plus materials; this may have to be modified, some fairly straightforward repairs may take hours, while you can charge more for a quick job which requires a lot of expertise. You can also take into account the value of the instrument being repaired. A car is not essential, but may be useful for returning a large number of school instruments to an education authority some distance away. Make sure clients insure their instruments while they're with you.

Running a mail order business on the side, eg making reeds, reed boxes, tools etc, can help financially. To prevent interference with your repairing work, this and the packing must be done in the evenings. You can also sell instruments. If you can do so without interruption, working at home can be enjoyable. To complete a job on time, plan a schedule; but you must be prepared for rush jobs late at night if players want their instruments next morning. Be prepared to work up to 12 hours a day. Work is sporadic. Build up a network of musicians and other repairers who may pass work to you when they're busy and take on some of yours when you are. Read any books on light engineering from your local library.

Music Copyist

At a Glance

Qualifications/Training	No	*Income bracket*	Low–Medium
Licence	No	*Town/Country*	Either
Experience/Springboard	No	*Travel*	Local
Mid-career entry	Yes	*Exit sale*	No
Entry costs	Nil	*Work at home*	Yes

Mix and match Probably essential. You could think about: Orchestral musician, Repetiteur/accompanist/coach, Computer software author, Social worker . . .

Enquiries Musicians' Union

This is someone who copies individual instrumental parts from original scores so that the music can be performed by bands/groups/orchestras. You need to be able to play and read music, have a good ear and knowledge of harmony. You should be able to write neatly and quickly, and know when to leave spaces so the player can turn the page without stopping in mid phrase. The job requires patience, and an ability to work accurately and under pressure – possibly through the night, ready for an early morning recording session.

You can work from home with good light, a decent pen and a telephone. You can combine it with another job, which may be necessary as the pay is bad: £1.20 per page; £8 per hour for a publisher, up to £15 per hour for 10-stave work. Working flat out, and if you can stand the strain and loneliness, you can earn up to £2,000 a week for

TV, but you're likely to end up having a nervous breakdown. If you own a motorbike you can earn more by delivering your work and charging the customer. No computer is faster or more accurate than the human hand, but job prospects are poor. Join the MUSICIANS' UNION so that your name appears in the section on copyists in their directory. Send out cards advertising your services to music publishers, and recording, film and TV companies. Try to get in with TV, films, a successful conductor, composer or group who commission or are involved in new music.

There should be a new book called the *Essentials of Music Copying* out in 1988.

Music Critic

At a Glance

Qualifications/Training	No	Income bracket	Low–Medium
Licence	No	Town/Country	Town
Experience/Springboard	No	Travel	Yes
Mid-career entry	Possible	Exit sale	No
Entry costs	£500+	Work at home	Partly

Mix and match Excellent. You could think about: Script writer, Journalist, Festival director, Novelist . . .

Enquiries Local papers or music critics

A real love of music is essential and it will help you to read a score if you can play an instrument, preferably the piano. Take a degree course, not necessarily in music, which will provide training in writing creatively, organising, selecting and expressing your thoughts clearly. Perhaps most important, perform in an amateur way which will not only refresh you but prevent your using up your musical 'capital' – by continually listening to music with a critical ear. The danger is that you will lose enthusiasm and get stale. It also reminds you what it's like being a performing artist.

You must be aware of your subjectivity. If a production or perform-ance is bad, take the trouble to find out whether this was due to the conductor or soloist suffering from 'flu, or there were deputies in the orchestra. If you want to be devastatingly critical of some performer, composer or organisation, make sure they are the high and mighty – it is cruel and pointless to attack unknown beginners.

For the first few years it's wise to have other employment eg freelance journalism on another subject, a steady job in advertising, teaching or anything that leaves you enough energy to listen to concerts or records in the evening. All you need to start with is a room with a good record player and a telephone. Get to know as many journalists and musicians as possible. Write some sample programme notes or record reviews, submit them to an art editor or record magazine. Use a lot of bluff to persuade them to try you out. There is now a wide range of magazines and newspapers which include music criticism: see them in your public library. Travelling to provincial productions in the UK is unrewarding, but going abroad to festivals is a bonus.

This job is bad for your social life. If you enjoy doing background research and find pleasure in expressing yourself in writing, you should be able to endure enforced loneliness for the greater part of each day including weekends. If you use a computer terminal at home and type your article straight on to the page in the newsroom, this will increase your isolation.

To start with, you can earn the odd £30 per article, up to £20,000 as a full-time critic.

You need access to *Grove's Dictionary of Music* and you should read *Classical Music* and the *Musical Times*.

Musician

At a Glance

Qualifications/Training	Recommended	*Income bracket*	Low–High
Licence	No	*Town/Country*	Town
Experience/Springboard	No	*Travel*	Yes
Mid-career entry	Unlikely	*Exit sale*	No
Entry costs	£1,000+	*Work at home*	No

Mix and match Probably essential. You could think about: Music teacher, Music critic, Musicians' answering and booking service, Orchestral fixer, Specialist food manufacturer, Counsellor, Wine merchant . . .
Enquiries Musicians' Union

Work as a professional musician, whether in traditional, classical, pop or commercial music, is insecure, highly competitive, corrupt and has a very high stress rating. Only consider it as a career if you are so highly

MUSICIAN

motivated that you cannot bear to do anything else. Working as a professional musician looks glamorous, seductive and romantic from a distance, but it is a tough business where resilience is essential. You need energy, excellent health, iron determination, and a belief in yourself. Life must be seen as a professional challenge with little hope of adequate reward. Being able to prove and express yourself must count for more than financial security.

All musicians require patience, tact and an ability to get on with people. It is a small world where everyone either knows or has heard of everyone else. The bush telegraph functions speedily and efficiently: your reputation will precede you. Contacts are essential and you need good friends.

The number of jobs is shrinking. This has forced musicians to seek commercial sponsorship. British musicians have outpriced themselves in the international market. While the MUSICIANS' UNION works at creating more opportunities for musicians to perform live, the rates it sets for film and TV recordings have led to commercial work nearly disappearing. Electronic synthesisers, like the Sampler, can reproduce any sound, making it possible to produce a perfect copy and dispensing with the commercial need for live musicians. However, there are still 2,000+ recording studios in London alone and it's worth making and keeping contact with them in case they need any extra musicians.

Although there are now more provincial opera companies, cuts have affected amateur choral and music societies all over the country. These used to employ professional artists for their concerts and now make do with music students whether performing as soloists, in chamber music or accompanying on the piano. Peripatetic teachers have been axed in many areas and the market for their services is shrinking.

It is absolutely essential to have a good accountant: disaster will strike without one. Professional musicians are constantly suspected by tax inspectors of fiddling their books. It is therefore important to keep copies of invoices, and receipts for all money earned. Being on tax schedule D you can claim relief for the room where you work, heating, lighting, telephone, costs of transport and printing, clothes, hairdressing, instruments, repairs and tools. Before starting out it is wise to have a financial plan which includes a partner who has capital or a steady income. Don't plan a family or take out a heavy mortgage until you are on a sound financial footing or you may find yourself sacrificing your art for money to pay the household bills.

Many professional musicians' jobs are bad for social life and marriage, especially when they involve long working hours and continual travelling. It helps to have a partner who believes in you and supports your ambition to succeed. Plan ahead. Many professional musicians' jobs, particularly in the pop scene, are for the young. By middle-age, if you have not already made a fortune so you can live off the income, you should be prepared to change jobs.

Read *The Musician*.

Music/Instrument Retailer

At a Glance

Qualifications/Training	No	Income bracket	Low–Medium
Licence	No	Town/Country	Town
Experience/Springboard	Recommended	Travel	No
Mid-career entry	Excellent	Exit sale	Yes
Entry costs	£8,000+	Work at home	No

Mix and match   Limited.   You could think about: Jazz musician, Music publisher, Musical instrument repairer . . .

Enquiries   Music Retailers' Association

This is someone who owns a shop which sells music and musical instruments. The only qualifications needed for this job are a knowledge of music and the ability to play an instrument. You must be resilient, be able to spot a good business prospect, have charm, tact and an eye for making attractive window displays. With these qualities the potential is limitless, but you need a good accountant.

You need a large amount of capital. If you have a partner, friend or relation with their own business who will act as your guarantor, this helps. Remember that accepting investment from outsiders takes away your independence, even though initially it might be useful financially. Borrow as much as possible from your bank, having sold your idea to the sympathetic manager. Find a suitable shop, possibly in a secondary trading position, making sure it is accessible and convenient for public transport and parking. The rent will depend on the area or region of the country. Allow at least £1,000 for buying second-hand display cabinets and counters or having them made by a friendly carpenter. Advertise in the local press, circularise musicians, music teachers; get addresses from the INCORPORATED SOCIETY OF MUSICIANS and the County Music Adviser. You will need good insurance cover for the instruments and music you are selling. Engage intelligent, reliable and cheerful staff, possibly on a part-time or job-share basis.

Working hours will probably be 10.00–5.30 but evenings will be spent pricing, checking deliveries, window displays, invoicing, doing accounts and chasing bad debts. When you can afford to, research the market for a computer to suit your particular needs. After 6 months you may be able to combine this with another job such as teaching or playing part-time. You are vulnerable to political moves such as school staff going on strike, so no extra-curricular lunchtime activities and thus no sale of music or instruments to schools for many months.

If you survive the first 2 years you will be lucky to have made £8,000. You will find music publishers are often out of date and out of touch; instrument makers on the whole are businesslike. You can join the MUSIC RETAILERS ASSOCIATION. It's an enjoyable job if you like meeting interesting people, learning more about music and creating your own business.

Music Publisher

	At a Glance		
Qualifications/Training	No	Income bracket	Low–usually
Licence	No	Town/Country	Town
Experience/Springboard	No	Travel	Yes
Mid-career entry	Yes	Exit sale	Yes
Entry costs	£2,500	Work at home	Possible
Mix and match Usually. You could think about: Musician, Music/instrument retailer, Music critic, Recording studio owner . . .			
Enquiries Music Publishers' Association			

This is nothing to do with book publishing. It is a business venture in which the publisher searches for composers, procures their unpublished music, edits it and arranges for its printing and distribution to retailers under the publishing firm's own brand name. It is an area of endeavour paved with financial disasters. The few small independent publishers who succeed make little money and specialise in compositions of a well-defined historical period of music or for a particular instrument. You should be able to play an instrument, read music and like gambling. You also need enthusiasm, perseverance and a good accountant; a business management course is useful.

You can work from home preferably with £1,000 capital (a bank loan is not a good idea), telephone, typewriter, filing cabinet and storage space for stock awaiting distribution. A computer will help. Carry out careful market research to establish the most profitable area, it's best to go either for the top of the market or the bottom. Educational music (in book or sheet form) must be durable and therefore cost more to produce; books which always look good are also more expensive. At the other end of the market, the turnover of pop sheet music is quicker.

Maintain the goodwill of the composers and retailers; and, if you're publishing educational music, the teachers. Keep in touch with musicians or pupils to test the products and read musical magazines on your subject area; you will have to travel to keep in touch with the retailers who handle your list. With most music publishing it will be a year before you see a return on your mcney and your income will depend on how many works are published in a year. Find a good reliable printer and establish a good working relationship. You can sub-contract to sole selling agents but use only one to start with: they can deliberately suppress work to avoid competition. Membership of the IPG is useful for seminars on publishing information and advice; and join the MUSIC PUBLISHERS' ASSOCIATION when you are successful. You can do another job at the same time; if you are full-time, avoid becoming a workaholic by providing recreation periods during the day.

You must enjoy your work as you won't make any money unless you are very lucky in pop music.

Music Teacher

At a Glance

Qualifications/Training	Recommended	Income bracket	Low–Medium
Licence	No	Town/Country	Either
Experience/Springboard	No	Travel	Local
Mid-career entry	Possible	Exit sale	No
Entry costs	£2,000	Work at home	Yes

Mix and match   Probably essential.   You could think about: Musician, Orchestral fixer, Instrumental soloist, Classical/operatic singer, Counsellor, Hi-fi shop owner, Music therapist . . .

Enquiries   Incorporated Society of Musicians

This is someone who either teaches people how to sing or play an instrument, or the history/theory of music, either privately or in a school or college.

If you want to have private pupils and teach an instrument from home it is useful first to get a practical teaching qualification: LRAM (ROYAL ACADEMY OF MUSIC) or the equivalent LRCM, LGSM or LTCM from one of the other colleges. Contact the INCORPORATED SOCIETY OF MUSICIANS (ISM) for the name of a really good local private teacher although this will be expensive. Going to music college or university will help to make contacts within the profession and get a wider musical education.

You need to enjoy communicating with people, especially children, be patient, understanding, enthusiastic and encouraging with your pupils. If you live in an area where parents can afford private lessons for their children, you can build up a practice quite quickly. Personal recommendation is the most effective way, but you can advertise in local shops and newspapers, the *Music Teacher* or *Classical Music*. The ISM fixes a minimum rate, (£10 per hour in 1987) for private teaching. Join them to benefit from legal advice, workshops and conferences. The life can be isolated so ISM provides some social contact and stimulation.

This is not the quickest way to the pot of gold at the end of the rainbow, but with a good reputation and pupils who go on to music college, participate and do well in competitions and local festivals, you can raise your income to as high as £15–£20,000 pa. Private lessons tend to be after school hours or in the evenings which eats into your weekday social life. If you want to get some peripatetic teaching during school hours, write to the local county or borough Music Adviser offering your services (make sure they know you are paying schedule D tax).

If you also want to teach music theory and harmony etc in schools or colleges of education, it is useful to get a Diploma of Education. This involves attending a suitable 1-year course at poly, university or teacher training college, possibly one day a week over 2 years.

For private teaching you need a room, £1,000 to buy a secondhand or reconditioned piano, a telephone and neighbours who are tolerant of your pupils' musical efforts. You can work as a freelance performer so long as this does not interfere with your pupils, and they and their parents do not mind constantly changing lesson times. Allow another £1,000 for a car, particularly if you are in the country and doing peripatetic work. You may be able to earn a bit more by teaching the organ, playing for the church or amateur choirs and musical societies.

You have freedom to organise your life in this job and it's useful for those with young families who need to work from home.

Music Therapist

At a Glance

Qualifications/Training	Essential	Income bracket	Low–Medium
Licence	No	Town/Country	Town
Experience/Springboard	Recommended	Travel	Local
Mid-career entry	Recommended	Exit sale	No
Entry costs	£500+	Work at home	Possible

Mix and match   Yes.   You could think about: Music teacher, Musician, China restorer, Word processor . . .

Enquiries   British Society for Music Therapy, Association of Professional Music Therapists

This is someone who uses a mixture of music and psychology to help people change both physically and psychologically. First you will need a diploma from a music college or a degree in music. Then apply for a one-year diploma at eg the GUILDHALL SCHOOL, the ROEHAMPTON INSTITUTE or the NORDOFF ROBBINS course. All courses are in London. A PGCE is useful if you want to work in a school.

Primarily, you need the rare ability to move others emotionally through your performance. You should be able to play an instrument well in all styles and have good keyboard skills, sight-reading and improvisation. You must be born with intuition and an awareness of others' feelings. You should enjoy working with other therapists, doctors or teachers in a team. Self esteem and hope are advantageous; good results do not come quickly. Do-gooders don't make good music therapists, but happy accepting people do.

Try to get experience working with a therapist in a local hospital or school before applying for a course. It can be an isolated job so keep in touch with others through the BRITISH SOCIETY FOR MUSIC THERAPY or the ASSOCIATION OF PROFESSIONAL MUSIC THERAPISTS workshops and journals. You can work in hospitals, special schools or clinics, with the deaf, mentally or physically handicapped, psychiatric, geriatric or the terminally ill.

You can work on your own from a large room at home with a telephone, tape recorder and, if you feel rich, a video. If you have to travel to visit your clients you will need a car, and £2,000 to purchase a good piano or synthesiser as well as various percussion and tonal instruments. You can negotiate your fees to match your clients' means.

Working in private practice, you can mix work in a school or hospital, take private clients, and can teach music at the same time. There will not be a great deal of travelling. You should preferably be over 25 before starting training. You may find it useful to contact the DISABLED LIVING FOUNDATION (music advisory service) and to join the MUSICIANS' UNION or the INCORPORATED SOCIETY OF MUSICIANS.

Those in the music therapy field are sometimes looked upon as 'brown rice and sandals' do-gooders, not always understood or taken seriously by medics or teachers. It is a young and growing profession; practitioners see themselves as pioneers needing to 'spread the gospel' so you should be able to speak confidently about your work.

Musicians' Answering and Booking Service

At a Glance

Qualifications/Training	No	Income bracket	Low
Licence	No (Musicians' Union membership vital	Town/Country	Town
		Travel	No
Experience/Springboard	No	Exit sale	Possible
Mid-career entry	Yes	Work at home	Possible
Entry costs	2,000++		

Mix and match Possible. You could think about: Musician, Concert agent, Music/instrument retailer . . .
Enquiries Musicians' Union

This is someone who arranges for phone calls to be answered for absent musicians and is responsible for communicating the information to them. You need to be a performing musician, or have a partner who is, and know every fixer in town. You must be known and trusted by your clients as you must guarantee them total confidentiality – after all, you handle their private diaries. Your qualities should include calmness in a crisis – of which there will be many – diplomacy, patience and the ability to accept the judgment of a fixer or conductor whose opinion about who is a good musician may differ from yours – this is known as 'ghost fixing'. You will need some £2,000 to set up your service in a room, garage or shed with several telephone lines and a photocopier (second hand will do). You also need a computer and a good accountant. It is useful to buy the yellow pages for the whole country, have a telex book and the specialist directory for whatever line you specialise in. Your staff should be intelligent and willing to work till the early hours; international telephone calls may come at any hour of day or night, so you must be able to cope with interrupted sleep and have an understanding partner. Musicians are notoriously unreliable about checking regularly and after a night on the tiles may forget to collect urgent messages from their answerphone left by the service the previous evening. When fully developed, the new voice messaging computer will enable messages left with the service to be played back to the client. It is not possible to combine this with another job so for the first 3 years you must live on your savings, the dole, or your partner's income. After that you can expect around £10,000 pa depending on your investment in equipment.

Your service can be blamed if a player does not perform well and players will blame you if they do not get enough work. The job is bad for your social life, but you will meet interesting people and can evolve ways of exploiting your equipment. You will not have to travel but it is vital that you join the MUSICIANS' UNION.

Nanny and Babysitting Agent

At a Glance

Qualifications/Training .	No	*Income bracket*	Low–Medium
Licence	Yes	*Town/Country*	Town
Experience/Springboard	Recommended	*Travel*	No
Mid-career entry	Yes	*Exit sale*	Yes
Entry costs	£1,000	*Work at home*	Yes

Mix and match Yes. You could think about: Journalist, Childminder, Holiday accommodation owner . . .
Enquiries Employment Agency Licensing Office

You don't have to be a City head-hunter to make a living from finding staff for other people. There is an increasing demand, especially in the South East, for nannies and mother's helps and many people would rather have a nanny agency send them one or two likely candidates than wade through masses of applications resulting from advertising. There is also a great demand for people who can supply good, reliable babysitters at short notice; once you, as a nanny agency, have placed a few nannies you'll have a pool of reliable, vetted, nannies to choose from. Nanny and babysitting agents can easily work from home so this is an option for people wanting to spend time with their own young children or who want to mix and match.

Nanny and babysitting agents are subject to the Employment Agencies Act, which stipulates that they must have a licence from the Department of Employment's EMPLOYMENT AGENCY LICENSING OFFICE. For this you'll have to give details of your past five years' employment history; you'll need 2 personal references; and you'll have to put notices in the local press and at your proposed place of business for 21 days in advance; you also have to have the terms and conditions of your business checked, these then have to be displayed in your office. Once you've done that you'll get a licence number to go on your stationery. Without one, nobody will accept or publish your adverts. After that, your premises will be inspected by, for example, planning and health authorities and you have to reapply for this licence every year.

There are no formal qualifications for nanny agents. Very useful previous experience is selecting and appointing nannies for your own children. You have to be able to spot good nannies and a lot of this is a case of using your instinct. There are nanny qualifications eg, NNEB (NATIONAL NURSERY EXAMINATION BOARD) which requires full time attendance for two years at college. These give a good indication of proficiency but many excellent nannies with experience don't have them while some of those with impressive qualifications may prove to be useless when confronted by real children. Some clients will insist on formally qualified nannies only. Back up your instinct by checking nannies' references – do this by telephone – a glowing reference could have been written by one of the nanny's friends or an employer eager to get the nanny out of the home. You'll have to have good communication skills, to like people and to be good at summing them up – much of your success depends on being able to match nannies and clients.

To set up you need a telephone, a typewriter and some stationery (with your licence number). An answering machine is useful, especially if you're organising babysitting and people want to get hold of you in a hurry; a lot of people won't talk to machines so don't depend on it too much. Ultimately, you may want to instal a second telephone line as a lot of this work is done by telephone. Advertising is probably your biggest expense. Use any suitable local press, free magazines etc and the *Lady*. Finding clients may well be less of a problem than finding suitable nannies and babysitters, bear that in mind when you're deciding where to put adverts.

As an agent you are paid a fee by the client for successfully introducing a nanny to them. You can decide to charge a set amount or to base the charge on how much the nanny is to be paid by the client (the drawback with this is that you'll have to do just as much work to find a nanny for £40 a week as you would to find one for £200). You won't get paid until the nanny has actually started the job – this may not always be immediately, so you can expect some cash flow problems. If you don't find a nanny you don't get paid; many agents charge clients a nominal registration fee (say £5–10) to help cover time and expenses. For babysitting you may prefer to charge clients an annual fee rather than fiddly little amounts every time you get them a babysitter. You never charge the nanny or babysitter for finding work. As an agent you don't set the rates your clients should pay; you can, however, suggest guidelines and should be able to advise nannies on how much they can reasonably expect to earn given their experience. You should also suggest babysitting rates; you'll find you need a lot of babysitters so it's worth making sure that they're happy.

On the whole, this job is fairly desk bound and you'll spend a lot of time interviewing and checking references but its a good idea to visit clients to get a better idea of the sort of person they're looking for. The telephone rings a lot; clients and nannies often have problems they want to discuss with you; you may be asked to find a babysitter in the afternoon for that same evening. You'll also want to keep in touch with your babysitters so you know who you can call on at short notice. Ultimately you have to keep everyone happy. Make sure that employers are very clear about what they expect their nanny to do and if it seems more than normal check that they let the nanny know before the appointment's made. Is the appointment to be sole charge or not? Does the nanny know how much time off is allowed? Insist on letters of appointment – you're the one they'll turn to if anything goes wrong. Although you could be a part-time nanny agent by using an answer phone for several hours a day, it's difficult to take a whole day away; you're likely to have to deal with last minute emergencies, which is when a second (emergency only) telephone comes in. If you do go away you'll have to make sure that everybody knows and books their babysitters in advance. Ideally you should have someone else around just to keep the business going if you can't be on call yourself.

New House Builder

At a Glance

Qualifications/Training	Recommended	*Income bracket*	Low–High
Licence	No	*Town/Country*	Either
Experience/Springboard	Essential	*Travel*	Local
Mid-career entry	Yes	*Exit sale*	Possible
Entry costs	£30,000+++	*Work at home*	No

Mix and match Yes. You could think about: House converter, property developer, Surveyor, Farmer, Toy maker . . .

Enquiries Building Employers Confederation

Businesses which build homes for sale come in all shapes and sizes. Unless you have access to vast amounts of capital (£ millions) you will probably start in a small way, building (or organising sub-contractors to build) individual houses or small developments. Many firms are still family concerns. If it's a trade you want to get into you may find it best to join a major firm, where you can find out about buying land, employing architects and surveyors, negotiating planning permission, the actual building work and selling the finished product.

Then it's a question of raising the capital for the first project – you can try your own bank, but you may need to go to a merchant bank or go into partnership with a property developer.

If you're starting in a small way, you can buy house plans – or even complete house kits, which will save on architects' fees. You will have to find reliable tradesmen to do the donkey work from clearing the site to applying the final skim of plaster.

There are plenty of willing hands in the summer months: the problem is finding skilled tradesmen who are available and prepared to work to your schedules – whatever the weather. And the weather can be a great enemy, there are some jobs which can't be done in heavy rain, high wind or sub-zero temperatures.

The income from building can be unpredictable: it is very dependent on the state of the property market. You must find sites which are in the right place at the right time, and know that you can sell the finished product before you start. There's always a danger that a change in local government policy, a new road scheme or an apparently unrelated market force (eg a shift in oil prices or the closure of a local car factory) will affect the demand for finished property. So many builders will diversify, and work on some projects for the local authority or for a major industrial firm, or work on two or three sites in different parts of the country. Once your business is established, you can employ managers with different skills to run different aspects of the business.

You will certainly need a skilled accountant, and to reassure customers and employees you should be a member of the BUILDING EMPLOYERS' CONFEDERATION – if you can get round the Catch 22: you can't get the contracts unless you're a member, and you can't become a member unless you are recommended by other members and you can satisfy the Confederation that your work is up to standard.

Newsletter Publisher

At a Glance

Qualifications/Training	No	*Income bracket*	Low–High
Licence	No	*Town/Country*	Either
Experience/Springboard	No	*Travel*	No
Mid-career entry	Likely	*Exit sale*	Good
Entry costs	£1,000+	*Work at home*	Yes

Mix and match Yes. You could think about: Journalist, UK correspondent for overseas media, Book packager, Snail farmer, Contemporary art gallery owner, Estate agent . . .

Enquiries Newsletter publishers

Roughly speaking, newsletters are periodical publications which seldom carry advertising and are neither large nor smart enough to call themselves magazines. Unlike Great Aunt Felicia's Christmas newsletter or Suckem & Sockem's give-away to clients, newsletters as a means of earning a living, are normally based on one of two assumptions. The first is that there's always one per cent of the population barmy enough to buy anything (a standard direct marketing assumption). Enterprising newsletter publishers have made fortunes in the USA with newsletters for nutcases, like 'Stocking Your Cellar Against Nuclear War'. The second, more conventional assumption is that there are often small audiences who will pay well for highly-qualified information on subjects of insufficient general interest to sustain magazines. *Euromoney* and the *Financial Times*, for example, publish a wide range of newsletters for select sub-sections of the financial markets. Although some of them have subscription lists of only a few hundred, their prices are high so they still make good money. Big newsletter publishers are always searching for acquisitions so you can usually get out by selling a successful newsletter once its got a track record.

It's not that difficult to start up. In general anything of narrow yet intense interest could work. As a rule of thumb, your subscribers will have to be prepared to pay about £300 pa in advance for what you're going to tell them. They could be all sorts of people: expats, for example, might subscribe to a UK educational newsletter if they are interested in schools for ex-pat brats or to a UK pensions newsletter if interested in good pensions for themselves; or, as one newsletter which went well for years, you could try a monthly sheet for non-English speaking business men on how to write correct English. Newsletters can be influential. Marshall McLuhan, of 'the medium is the message' fame, used this medium with some success to spread the message. All that's needed to start is a bright idea in an area where you have enough knowledge, experience and contacts to allow you to produce regular, up to date, specialist information. Capital requirements are low – as low as a typewriter, although a word processor and printer/copier are preferable, and you'd need access to a photocopier. The cash is up front – your subscribers are expected to pay at the beginning of the year – so your publication should be self-financing from day 2 (on day 1 you had to pay for your own stamps). You need to get enough subscriptions to make it worth your while. But, at £300 each, 200 subscribers will bring you in £60,000, from which you must then deduct costs, including production and postage.

Having dreamed up a bright idea, first identify your market, then catch it. Make a dummy edition (or, if you can afford it, make a complete first edition) and mail it, free, as widely as you can. This operation requires the names and addresses of potential subscribers. Advertising is normally too expensive and too diffuse a means of reaching your potential newsletter audience. You may have to create your own mailing list if your chosen market is not already served by ready-made lists (obtainable from list brokers at a cost, unless you can extract them free of charge by excercising charm). Beware. Once your mailing succeeds and you have banked your subscriptions, you must make sure you are able to come up with the year's worth of newsletters your subscribers paid for. Otherwise you'll risk being charged with embezzlement.

Novelist

At a Glance

Qualifications/Training	No	*Income bracket*	Mostly low
Licence	No	*Town/Country*	Either
Experience/Springboard	No	*Travel*	No
Mid-career entry	Likely	*Exit sale*	Possible
Entry costs	£5+	*Work at home*	Yes

Mix and match   Probably essential.   You could think about: Journalist, Script-writer, Radio reporter and presenter, Barrister, MP, Window cleaner, Shop-keeper . . .

Enquiries   Society of Authors, Local writers' clubs

If you are a well disciplined self-starter, with a real craving to write, you may succeed. Most novelists have always written – letters to the press, short stories in notebooks. It can become a time-consuming hobby and, if you are lucky, become a full-time job.

To start with, you will be lucky to get an advance of £500 for a book. You will normally get a royalty of approximately 10% of hardback sales

NOVELIST

and 7.5% of paperbacks. If you hit the jackpot, you end up as a tax exile; most reckon they are lucky if they are able to make a living from writing.

When you are unknown, it is extremely difficult to get published. First novels are a high publishing risk. Unsolicited manuscripts sent to publishers often get overlooked for several months before being returned to you with a cursory rejection. The way to get publishers to take notice is to get an agent to submit your manuscript. But Catch 22 – agents do not warm to first novels either because they are difficult to sell to publishers and 10% of your advance makes it hardly worth their while. So, it's not easy to get an agent – but even more difficult to get published without one.

Obviously the fastest way to fame and fortune is to win the Whitbread prize for a first novel but inevitably this eludes the majority. Most fit writing round another job for many years (and some never break the habit of writing at night). Take a course in journalism or a degree in a subject that will help you develop your writing style. Join your local Writers Club, where you can read out your work for criticism. Once you are a published author, you can join the SOCIETY OF AUTHORS (and receive the *Author* and guides for authors) and the WRITERS GUILD. If you specialise appropriately you can also join the CRIME WRITERS ASSOCIATION, the ROMANTIC NOVELISTS ASSOCIATION etc. The latter also takes probationary members and will provide professional criticism and a prize for a first novel which they will then submit and recommend for publication.

Outlay on equipment is minimal. All you need is some paper, pens or pencils and inspiration. Buy a secondhand typewriter when you can afford it and a word processor when you grow rich. A good dictionary, *Roget's Thesaurus* and the *Writers' and Artists' Yearbook* or the *Writer's Handbook* will be useful.

What starts off an idea for a novel is very individual. Some are prompted by a particular place; some a situation; some by commercial considerations, the inclusion of money/sex/power. Many authors find a book will take about a year, including a period of research and gestation; others take as much as 10 years; conversely, Barbara Cartland writes over 20 a year.

Writing is an isolated activity, in which you draw deeply on your own resources. Nevertheless your ability to cope with this must be combined with a strong understanding of and involvement with people. You need a fierce drive, great resilience, endless imagination and an unquenchable need to write.

Nurse

At a Glance

Qualifications/Training	Essential	*Income bracket*	Low–Medium
Licence	Yes	*Town/Country*	Either
Experience/Springboard	No	*Travel*	Local
Mid-career entry	Unlikely	*Exit sale*	No
Entry costs	Nil	*Work at home*	No

Mix and match   Yes.   You could think about: Nursing Home owner, Property manager, Gardener/garden designer, Photographer . . .

Enquiries   Royal College of Nursing

Freelance nurses get their work through an employment agency by the day or week. They are available for every kind of situation for which they may be qualified in either the NHS or private hospitals or homes.

You need to train at a school of nursing, usually in a teaching hospital. It takes 3 years to become a State Registered Nurse (SRN) usually followed by a year's experience as a staff nurse. You can then go on to take specialist training in orthopaedics, psychiatry, paediatrics (there is a shortage in this area), become a midwife or health visitor.

This is a tough and underpaid job so you need lots of dedication, good health and energy, a cheerful temperament, empathy, a liking for people, and a sense of humour. You will have to cope with difficult physical and emotional situations therefore you cannot be squeamish, faint at the sight of blood, or run away when someone has hysterics. If you have any problems dealing with authority, don't be a nurse, as the job structure is one of doing what you are told; responsibility can be considerable, but you must always answer to your superiors.

You can go freelance as soon as you are qualified; you don't need any special equipment. Having a car of your own makes travelling, usually at unusual and unsociable hours, much easier, especially when your job venue is always changing and no-one pays your fares. Don't expect to earn much more than £10,000 per annum.

The advantage of this kind of job is the freedom you have to choose where and when you work; the disadvantages are that you are usually treated as an outsider by the permanent staff and have no holiday or sick pay. It's difficult to do another job at the same time as this work is very exhausting.

On the whole there are more women in this profession, and it's more difficult to get training as a really mature student for physical reasons – unless you are very fit. You can get more information from the ROYAL COLLEGE OF NURSING. Read the *Nursing Times* and *Nursing Standard*.

Nursing Home Owner/Manager

At a Glance

Qualifications/Training	Essential	*Income bracket*	Medium
Licence	Yes	*Town/Country*	Either
Experience/Springboard	Yes	*Travel*	No
Mid-career entry	Likely	*Exit sale*	Yes
Entry costs	£10,000+++	*Work at home*	Possible

Mix and match   Limited.   You could think about: Nanny and babysitting agent, Dealer in small antiques . . .

Enquiries   Royal College of Nursing, UK Central Council for Nursing, Midwifery and Health Visiting

To run a nursing home for the elderly you need to train as a qualified State Registered Nurse, and preferably spend another year gaining a specialised qualification in eg orthopaedics. Having been the Cinderella of the medical world, now with the increasing numbers of older people in society, geriatrics has become acceptable. There are excellent part time courses in geriatrics at London and Keele universities, and you will need these if you want to be really up to date with medical and psychological methods.

Then you can, if you have sufficient capital, start to run your own little nursing home. You can set up with just 2 beds in your own home, but you must first register with and be inspected by the UK CENTRAL COUNCIL FOR NURSING. The ROYAL COLLEGE OF NURSING has a really good reference library for members, and will provide legal advice, and information about relevant training courses. You must also be inspected and licensed by your local environmental health dept, the NHS, and regularly inspected by drug, fire, and health and safety officers. You must make sure you have a good public liability insurance and an excellent accountant.

Costs vary through the country according to the price of property. Allow also for buying beds, linen, disposable dressing pads, uribags, cradles, oxygen, suckers, dripstands etc, kitchen equipment and staff uniforms. There is also the cost of decorating, carpets and curtains. A nursing home with 30 patients should be modernised every 7 years. Usually the patients like to bring some of their own furniture with them to make them feel at home and preserve their identities.

There are very strict rules regarding the ratio of patients to each SRN; GPs or consultants usually visit their own patients. If patients are strong enough, outings to local sporting and cultural events or an occasional meal out is considered important to stimulate their interest.

It's best not to use agency nurses as elderly patients are naturally happier with familiar faces.

This is a satisfying job but you are prone to backache. You must have the tact and ability to settle new patients, as the first months can be traumatic – this can be difficult for everyone. You need personal qualities of tact, tolerance, patience and a genuine interest and affection for the elderly. You need to be able to adapt your nursing to the particular needs of each individual patient: they are too old to adapt to you. You also need to be very healthy, have plenty of energy and good feet. The prospects for those working with geriatrics are excellent as the older population increases; there will be 10 million people over 65 in 1990. Although it's very expensive to live in a nursing home as a patient, many get some financial help eg BUPA will pay for acute illness; the pension funds of larger banks and industrial organisations will contribute to costs, and some charities will top up the NHS contribution if the individual's circumstances qualify them.

Useful books are *Geriatric Medicine and Gerontology*, *Laing's Review of Private Health Care*, you will also need to read the *Nursing Times*.

Opening to the Public

At a Glance

Qualifications/Training	No	*Income bracket*	Low–High
Licence	No	*Town/Country*	Either
Experience/Springboard	No	*Travel*	No
Mid-career entry	Likely	*Exit sale*	Excellent
Entry costs	Highly variable	*Work at home*	Yes

Mix and match   Yes.   You could think about: Farmer, Winegrower, Zookeeper, Contemporary art gallery owner, Goldsmith/silversmith/jeweller, Landscape designer, Accountant . . .

Enquiries   Historic Houses Association, Local Tourist Board

This assumes you have something that the Great British Public (GBP) will pay to come and see. You may have inherited or bought a house, garden or area which is of historical or natural significance (eg Windsor Castle, Lands End); or you may have developed a model railway or built up a unique collection of Georgian thimbles.

You must clearly identify the sort of visitors you want to attract. Do you want families, coach parties, Volvo Estate drivers or the Aldeburgh Festival set? Some owners ban coaches; others are into the mass market. Location is important – there is probably no point in having the best doll collection in the world on the north-east coast of Scotland – though fishing nets do well. Your price will be linked to location and what you're offering – more in London than outside; more for something good that will take at least an hour to see as opposed to something mediocre that a bored child will skip through in 10 minutes. One crude rule of thumb is to charge £1.50 for each hour the average visitor takes to go round. Tourist boards are usually a great help – both with advice and promotional literature (you pay but they produce it). Join any local association of tourist attractions. If you are selling entry to an historic house and/or garden, join the HISTORIC HOUSES ASSOCIATION. It provides seminars and information on topics such as broadcasting rights; also advice on the appropriate price and the best arrangements

THE ♡ FAMILY SEAT

OPENING
TO THE
PUBLIC

to make. Make sure you get on all local lists (and national, if you're big enough) of houses/gardens/museums open to the public.

You can increase the 'spend-per-head' by having a cafeteria or a shop stocked with postcards and a range of branded goods – teatowels, coasters etc – all good on the gifts market. Then, in addition to their admission fee, visitors will hopefully buy postcards and gifts as well as tea and cakes. If you are into this on a large scale, you will need to employ people to help so this will drastically increase your costs.

Before you open, you will need to ensure that the place is well presented, clean and tidy (particularly the loos) and properly decorated. Think also about security and GBP's sticky fingers (Sissinghurst lost all but the stump of a rare plant that was planted close to a path because GBP took cuttings). You must be tolerant of GBP and its rubbish – although by and large if your presentation is smart and tidy, GBP will also leave it tidy. You need no special licence to open to the public but you are foolish not to have public liability insurance. Keep your opening hours simple so as not to confuse the public – if you can, stay open 7 days a week.

You have to do this well to succeed. GBP is becoming much more sophisticated and will judge you against what is seen on television and what they experienced on trips to Disneyland. If you are not worth visiting, or are overpriced, you will be rumbled very quickly; even if you still attract the odd passer by, you will not get the coach parties and others directed to you by the local tourist board, so will never make your fortune. If you are successful, you should not expect to get rich though you may get your return on capital. It can combine well with another job.

Opera Producer/Director

At a Glance

Qualifications/Training	No	*Income bracket*	Low–High
Licence	No	*Town/Country*	Town
Experience/Springboard	Good idea	*Travel*	A must
Mid-career entry	Yes	*Exit sale*	No
Entry costs	£500+	*Work at home*	No

Mix and match   Possible.   You could think about: Film director, Music critic, Festival director, Classical composer, Book editor . . .

Enquiries   Opera directors

This is the person who directs the singers on how to act, move and present themselves on stage. You co-operate with the conductor and designer to interpret the opera. The best way to enter this highly competitive field is to attend a university where there are ample opportunities for producing student operas, such as Cambridge. An opera producer should be a kind of renaissance person, with a wide knowledge of all the arts – music, painting, architecture, dance, literature and history. You also need the practical skills of basic human psychology and acting stage management. You should be able to read a vocal score and have a knowledge of French, German and Italian for international work.

You need to sell yourself and to communicate easily. Persuading a number of volatile personalities to realise your artistic ideas requires patience and sensitivity. Anxiety neurosis will help you pre-empt things going wrong; you need a vivid imagination and to know about everyone else's job in the production team – lighting, designing and conducting an orchestra. (You can learn a lot by taking a job as an assistant stage manager somewhere.)

While at university, get introductions to as many influential people as possible. Write to directors or obtain good introductions to them. It's important to have done at least one production you can describe and if possible get them to come and watch. If you are lucky you may be taken on as an unpaid assistant for a production. Jobs become available at short notice, so you need a fixed address, telephone and answering machine or service. You must be free to travel. There are not many female or coloured directors but the numbers are increasing.

Spend 6–8 weeks on research in libraries and art galleries and listening to the opera on disc before meeting the designer and the conductor; rehearsals will then last 4–6 weeks. It is possible to do an average of 6 productions per year with proper thought and preparation.

There is no time for another job if you are successful and your earnings can amount to £100,000 pa. However, throughout your career you risk long periods out of work which is depressing and a production may be jeopardised by bad notices from the critics. But on the good side are the opportunities for self expression and, with a new opera, actually creating an interpretation of the composer's ideas yourself.

Optician

At a Glance

Qualifications/Training	Essential	Income bracket	Medium
Licence	Yes	Town/Country	Town
Experience/Springboard	Useful	Travel	No
Mid-career entry	Unlikely	Exit sale	Yes
Entry costs	£25,000+	Work at home	No

Mix and match   Possible. You could think about: Shopkeeper, Goldsmith/silversmith/jeweller, Jazz musician . . .

Enquiries   General Optical Council, Association of British Dispensing Opticians

Ophthalmic opticians (properly called optometrists), examine and test eyes, prescribe, fit and supply spectacles (and other optical appliances) and sometimes, if the practice is large enough to warrant a workshop, make up the lenses for prescription. The important part of this job is eye examination and care; some serious illnesses are first diagnosed by opticians who then refer the patient to a GP, also some symptom-free conditions (such as glaucoma) can lead to blindness if not treated in time. However, most optometrists have to subsidise their incomes by selling spectacles and other optical appliances. (Since the NHS stopped issuing spectacles this aspect of the job operates much like a shop although your patients may need some specific specialist advice.) There has also been deregulation of the selling of spectacles. This means that you will have competition from the new eye shops staffed by unqualified people. Eye tests are no longer free for most people on the NHS, so you recover most of your money from your patients.

Before practising on your own you need to register with the GENERAL OPTICAL COUNCIL. This involves completing a three year degree course in optometry followed by a year's paid, pre-registration experience.

You can also practice as a dispensing optician, fitting and supplying spectacles but not testing eyes; for this you need a shorter training (details from the ASSOCIATION OF BRITISH DISPENSING OPTICIANS ABDO). Opticians need a certain amount of manual dexterity, attention to detail and to be methodical. It also helps if you like people and enjoy being of service to them.

You need premises, including a consulting room as well as a showroom with space for display of spectacle frames. You'll also need the equipment for testing eyes which costs about £20,000 new, although you can pick up bits and pieces secondhand. You can set up at home to begin with, perhaps keeping on a part time job with another practice until you've built up your own. Stocks of spectacle frames come from travelling reps and wholesalers. Lenses made up to the required prescription come from prescription houses; they charge you and you charge the patient. Usually these are made to order but eye shops keep stocks of some ready made-up prescriptions and supply them over the counter. You need an assistant to arrange appointments, look after the practice while you're testing eyes and help with administration.

People usually go to their nearest optician (bear this in mind when you're finding premises). They don't have to be referred by their GP, so make your presence obvious; advertising may not increase business but word of mouth probably will. Many optometrists find working in a hospital for one or two days a week is a good way of increasing their experience and of keeping abreast with the profession. Read the *Optician* and *Optometry Today* and contact the WORSHIPFUL COMPANY OF SPECTACLE MAKERS.

Options Dealer

At a Glance

Qualifications/Training	Not essential	*Income bracket*	High
Licence	Yes	*Town/Country*	Town
Experience/Springboard	Essential	*Travel*	No
Mid-career entry	Unlikely	*Exit sale*	No
Entry costs	£100,000++	*Work at home*	No

Mix and match Limited. You could think about: Holiday accommodation owner, Potter, Farmer, Opening to the public, Racehorse owner . . .

Enquiries Stock Exchange (Membership Department), LIFFE

Options are a way of hedging on the stock exchange. Buying an option gives you the right to buy (or sell) a specified number of shares on a fixed date in the future. Options can themselves be bought and sold and are a speculative way of investing. The options market is new (established 1978) and aggressive. You can make or lose a lot of money very quickly by dealing in options.

Being self-employed is only possible if you have sufficient capital/ cash reserves in order to be allowed to trade by the stock exchange or the futures exchange (in case you lose money). Although you may have access to this capital it is highly unlikely that you will be successful trading on your own account unless you have had at least three and probably nearer five years' experience. The options and futures markets are both open outcry markets – that is, traders stand on an exchange floor or in a pit (designated trading area) and shout orders at each other. Telephone dealing is not permitted – all trade has to be transacted on the floor. That is not to say that you can't telephone down your order but if you do, a broker will still go into the pit to transact the business.

Those seeking a career in this business should call either the STOCK EXCHANGE or LIFFE for the list of names and telephone numbers of different brokers. It is still possible to start without formal qualifications (although they help to get you the first job these days). You must, however, be registered with the AFBD (The Association of Futures Brokers and Dealers) or TSA (The Securities Association) which means proving your fitness and properness. The atmosphere is tough and can be brutal. It suits very aggressive people. It is not for the shrinking violets. It is also chauvinist and vulgar and that might upset women who are in the least bit sensitive.

The route to self-employment is through a career with one of the brokers where you can learn a trade and then, provided you have the capital, you can give it a go. Salaries for successful traders are very high so self-employment is often unappealing with its additional stresses and strains. If you do want to be self-employed you will have to realise that you are risking a lot of money on any position you take in the market. Risk is what brings reward but it can also bring large losses. If you can live with risks then this might be a career worth considering, but remember, it is tough and few traders last beyond 35–40 at the most. There are probably easier ways to earn a living.

Orchestral Fixer

At a Glance

Qualifications/Training	Useful	*Income bracket*	Low–Medium
Licence	Musicians' Union	*Town/Country*	Town
Experience/Springboard	Recommended	*Travel*	Yes
Mid-career entry	Yes	*Exit sale*	No
Entry costs	£3,000	*Work at home*	Yes

Mix and match   Possible.   You could think about: Festival director, Orchestral musician, Mini-cab driver . . .

Enquiries   Musicians' Union

This person procures engagements for an orchestra, arranges terms and engages players and conductors. No knowledge of music is necessary. You will be dealing with other people's money so it is essential to understand a balance sheet, bookkeeping and filing, and be able to type and use a word processor. You need to be organised, methodical, logical and a perfectionist; to be able to run an office, negotiate with tough artists' agents, demanding promoters, sponsors or public bodies; and ensure the booking of reliable and good musicians. Sympathy, warmth and diplomacy will enable you to see and understand the wider long-term implications of a complicated situation; you will require a steely determination when taking unpleasant or tough decisions about personnel or policy.

Get to know as many people as possible in the profession – performers, agents, organisers and back-stage staff. To learn how to deal with musicians, it is best to work in orchestral management or arts administration. After a couple of years, when you feel really confident and have about £3,000 you can work from home. You will need a telephone with 2 lines, answering machine or service, typewriter or word processor, and about £1,000 worth of good stationery. Fax, telex and mailbox computer systems will make the job more efficient. Register with the MUSICIANS' UNION as a contractor.

On concert days, you may have to work at least 18 hours; try not to become a workaholic and eat sensibly. Your social life will be virtually non-existent; travelling is constant. You must remain cool, smart, in control and patient even after days spent touring with unreliable artists, sorting out hotel arrangements and transport crises.

Grants to the arts are currently being drastically cut by government and the future of music is becoming dependent on the whims of fickle sponsors. However, if you like achieving your own goals and you don't mind starting with a low income (5% or 10% fee per concert), after several years' success your income can rise to £19,000.

Orchestral Musician

At a Glance

Qualifications/Training	Necessary	Income bracket	Low–Medium
Licence	Union card	Town/Country	Town
Experience/Springboard	No	Travel	Lots
Mid-career entry	No	Exit sale	No
Entry costs	£1,000+	Work at home	No

Mix and match   Probably essential.   You could think about: Music teacher, Chamber group director, Instrumental soloist, Orchestral fixer, Dealer in small antiques, Counsellor . . .

Enquiries   Musicians' Union

These people earn their living playing in orchestras; it is not a job for you unless you cannot bear to do anything else. The use of synthesisers mean that this is a contracting area of work. Persevere if you are optimistic, outstandingly confident and talented and have good nerves. Only a small percentage of music students become successful performers: string players should find more work than those playing woodwind or brass. To receive really good tuition and make contacts, it's useful and necessary to go to music college. You must join the MUSICIANS' UNION.

ORCHESTRAL MUSICIAN

The stress level is high; you must have enormous resources of stamina and energy to withstand endless travelling in all forms of transport, all over the UK and abroad.

You will be living and working in a group so need to be calm and good-humoured, sociable and able to put up with other people's eccentricities and problems. Getting on with other musicians is as important as playing well.

To gain experience of the orchestral/operatic repertoire, it's useful to work abroad. Jobs in Europe are advertised in international music magazines. Having worked in a provincial or foreign orchestra for 2 or 3 years, use your capital to rent or buy a flat. You will find it difficult to get a mortgage without a steady part-time job, either teaching or something else which allows you time and energy to practise. It is important to have flexible hours as freelance work can come at short notice. You need a good accountant, telephone and answering machine; also an answering/diary service to deal with enquiries as to whether you are available to play. Jobs are advertised in *Classical Music* magazine and the *Daily Telegraph*, usually on Saturdays.

Getting work probably means being in London. Telephone or write to orchestral managers, including opera and ballet, and the freelance fixers who manage the small chamber orchestras boasting and telling them of your experience. Let all your musical friends know that you need work and then you may be able to deputise for them in musical shows, dance bands or hotels. If you can play several instruments you will be more employable. Commercial TV and film recording sessions are mostly male-dominated; only the excellence of your playing or influential friends will help you get into this small but lucrative area.

Earnings in this overcrowded scene are unpredictable. If you like teaching, carry on as it will provide security. It is likely to take at least 5 years to become established. There is a bias towards youth. If you become number three 'cello in an orchestra in your twenties, 10 years later you may have moved sideways but rarely upwards; there's not far to go!

Frequent travelling and appalling hours will disrupt your marriage and social life. Having returned home well after midnight, you dare not plan ahead in case another job comes up. A car is useful but other musicians will give you lifts. Read or have a hobby to keep you sane and relieve the anxiety about whether or not you are playing well, not getting enough gigs or whether the fixers like you.

Osteopath

At a Glance

Qualifications/Training	Essential	*Income bracket*	Low–High
Licence	Professional register	*Town/Country*	Town
Experience/Springboard	Recommended	*Travel*	No
Mid-career entry	Possible	*Exit sale*	Possible
Entry costs	£2,000+	*Work at home*	Possible

Mix and match Possible. You could think about: Doctor, Nursing Home owner, Holiday accommodation owner . . .

Enquiries Osteopathic Association

This is someone who treats all mechanical problems of the body, bones and muscles, which can affect the nervous and circulatory systems as well as other organs. They use joint and soft tissue manipulation to restore normal function. You normally need 3 A-level passes, preferably in science subjects, to enter the BRITISH SCHOOL OF OSTEOPATHY or the EUROPEAN SCHOOL OF OSTEOPATHY. It takes four years of intensive study to qualify as a registered osteopath. If you are a qualified medical doctor, you only need 18 months at the LONDON COLLEGE OF OSTEOPATHY. You need to be really interested in people, have stamina and dedication. You should also be dextrous and physically fit as this is an energetic occupation.

It is sensible to gain experience by working as an assistant, either at the School of Osteopathy or with an established practitioner, for at least three years. This will allow you to make useful professional contacts as well as gain experience. The OSTEOPATHIC ASSOCIATION is the professional body to which registered osteopaths belong, with its own journal. It arranges lectures and conferences and gives careers advice on where a new practice may be set up.

When you start your own practice you will probably make no more than £5,000 the first year. In a fashionable area you could make £30,000 upwards per annum. You first need to get known – circularise the local doctors and any other people who might send you referrals, such as the local orthopaedic surgeon. At present, you must work privately – only osteopaths who are already doctors or physiotherapists can treat patients on the NHS.

Your consulting room should be on the ground floor and near public transport as many of your patients will be old or disabled. You must apply to the local planning office for permission to use your room as a clinic. You need running hot and cold water in the room and a loo nearby. Allow £2,000, apart from premises, to cover equipment such as treatment plinth, chair, desk, filing cabinet, phone and answerphone as well as stethoscope etc. CAT and TT scans will help diagnosis in the future though they are expensive to buy. As soon as you can afford it, it is worth employing a practice manager to answer the door, the phone, and deal with payment. You also need good malpractice insurance in case a patient sues you, and also a good accountant.

You can work normal office hours but you need to have a flexible lunch hour to accommodate patients who cannot come during working hours. It is also worth having flexible working arrangements on Fridays, to avoid patients being ill or in pain over the weekend and then to be available to cope with emergencies.

This is a very rewarding job with instant feedback – you actually see the results of your labours. But it is hard on the feet and tiring both physically and mentally. You can't possibly do another job at the same time unless you work sessional hours in a clinic, with others such as psychotherapists and acupuncturists.

Apart from the OSTEOPATHIC ASSOCIATION, get information from the BRITISH HOLISTIC MEDICAL ASSOCIATION; and read *Clinical Biomechanics* and *Osteopathy*.

Oyster Farmer

At a Glance

Qualifications/Training	Necessary	*Income bracket*	Low–High
Licence	No	*Town/Country*	Country
Experience/Springboard	Essential	*Travel*	Local
Mid-career entry	Likely	*Exit sale*	Excellent
Entry costs	£70,000	*Work at home*	Yes

Mix and match Recommended. You could think about: Holiday accommodation owner, Sailing school owner, Tree surgeon . . .
Enquiries Shell Fish Association of Great Britain

Oyster farmers breed, grow and market oysters. You need to attend a specialist course in fish farming at INVERNESS COLLEGE, or at the AGRICULTURAL COLLEGE at Barony in Dumfries or Sparsholt in Hampshire. You must then have at least 2 or 3 years' experience working on

OYSTER FARMER

different farms before starting on your own. You must have some mechanical skills, be able to swim and, if you run a hatchery, be neat, tidy and clean. You should enjoy a country open air life with irregular hours. Oyster farming is not a full time occupation and it is possible to do another job at the same time. But the process of establishing an oyster farm is a slow one.

You can set up by finding a mixed sea/fresh water site and negotiate Crown lease for foreshore rights – this will cost you anything up to £2,500 per annum. You can either buy oyster seed and keep and grow it over 3 years (this will cost about £14,000) or buy them half grown (£40,000) and sell after one year. You will need about £70,000 to start – apart from the oysters themselves, you need to spend £4,000 on the special bags which float on trestles; a pick-up truck and a shed.

You can sell locally; join a communal marketing association; and also sell for smoking.

It's worth getting on the mailing list of the SEA FISH INDUSTRY AUTHORITY, to join the SHELL FISH ASSOCIATION OF GREAT BRITAIN and to take the *Sea Food International* magazine.

Painter/Decorator

At a Glance

Qualifications/Training	No	*Income bracket*	Low
Licence	No	*Town/Country*	Town
Experience/Springboard	Useful	*Travel*	Local
Mid-career entry	Yes	*Exit sale*	No
Entry costs	£1,000	*Work at home*	No

Mix and match   Yes. You could think about: Plumber, Electrician, House converter, Glazier, Man with a van, Actor, Musician . . .

Enquiries   Construction Industry Training Board, Local builders

Painting and decorating is regarded as a semi-skilled trade, and it is an area where there is plenty of scope to set up in a small way. You will need to have some idea of how to cost a job (calculate how much time and what materials you will need for a particular room) but you can get sufficient experience to do a convincing job just through doing your own decorating work on a DIY basis. However, if you do have the opportunity to do a basic course you will learn some of the tricks of the trade, and be able to do a more professional job.

Most decorators, however, do have some other skills (such as plastering or carpentry) so that they can offer extra services to those employing them. A rapidly expanding field of specialisation is in special paint finishes: scumbling, sponging, dragging, rag-rolling are the catchwords. These are skills you will have to be taught by an old hand, and practise so that you can produce an effective finish as quickly as possible. (Also read *Paint Magic*). If you can also offer a convincing colour-scheming service, you will be able to work in more up-market areas – and charge higher prices.

As well as brushes, wallpapering equipment and other special tools, you will need a van – both to get you to the job and store the materials in while you are working on a job. Good overalls and plenty of dust sheets are also essential. You may work in partnership with someone, or employ assistants on a casual basis. Your income will depend on the area and the type of service you can offer.

Larger companies may join the NATIONAL FEDERATION OF PAINTING AND DECORATING CONTRACTORS (NFPDC), which is involved in administering the rules of the industry and sets safety and other standards.

Photographer

At a Glance

Qualifications/Training	Recommended	*Income bracket*	Low–High
Licence	No	*Town/Country*	Either
Experience/Springboard	No	*Travel*	Probable
Mid-career entry	Possible	*Exit sale*	No
Entry costs	£2,000+	*Work at home*	Yes

Mix and match   Yes.   You could think about: Contemporary art gallery owner, Picture framer, Sculptor, Advertising photographer . . .

Enquiries   British Institute of Professional Photography

Photography requires visual and technical talents. If you want to sell pictures as art, you will have to be prepared for long hours and a lot of foot slogging. There is much more money in specialising in editorial photography for magazines/books or, better still, in advertising. Even most of Lord Snowdon's work is for glossy magazines in the first place.

Most photographers train at art school – foundation course followed by a vocational course at a college recognised by the BRITISH INSTITUTE OF PROFESSIONAL PHOTOGRAPHY. They produce a publication called the *Photographer*, which is a useful source of small ads for equipment and jobs. The *British Journal of Photography* is another publication in the field, but the design magazines, such as *Blueprint* and *Creative Review* are more fashion conscious.

PHOTOGRAPHER

If you have talent, and want to pursue a career as an art photographer, your most secure option is to look for sponsorship: some colleges and museums employ a 'photographer in residence'. Salary will be low, and you may be expected to lecture or run seminars, as well as organising exhibitions of your own work from time to time.

Another source of income may be from books, so cultivate relationships with people in publishing who could have helpful contacts. You can also place pictures with picture agencies, who sell rights on pictures for publication, but their needs are usually a bit commercial, and your style may not suit them.

You should also develop good relationships with small, private gallery owners, and persuade them to hold exhibitions (and sales) of your work – this helps to get your name known, as well as providing a small income.

Obviously your main capital outlay will be on cameras and lenses: you will need upwards of a couple of thousand pounds worth of hardware, but the chances are you will start your collection while you are at college and build up from there. If you want to process your own film, you will also need darkroom equipment, unless you have access to a dark room at an art college.

Your main overheads will be film, processing and framing pictures for exhibition. You may also need a studio, depending on the type of work you do. Income may be low for a long time, but if you do make the big time you can expect a very comfortable income.

Photographic Assistant

At a Glance

Qualifications/Training	Recommended	Income bracket	Low
Licence	No	Town/Country	Town
Experience/Springboard	No	Travel	Maybe
Mid-career entry	Unlikely	Exit sale	No
Entry costs	Nil	Work at home	No

Mix and match   Yes.   You could think about: High street photographer, Advertising photographer, Stage technician carpenter, Mini-cab driver . . .

Enquiries   Association of Fashion, Advertising and Editorial Photographers

As well as being a career in itself, photographic assistants often go on to become top photographers. A thorough understanding of the mechanics of photography (how cameras work, and basic knowledge of lighting) is essential, and this is generally gained at a foundation course followed by a vocational (BTEC) course at art school. The next step is the most difficult, finding a photographer who needs an assistant with no experience. As an assistant, your job will be to carry equipment, connect lights, check light readings, develop polaroids, label and arrange for processing of film, make the coffee and pour the wine. You may also have to organise invoicing, order background paper and film when necessary, get equipment serviced, arrange for the hire of extra lighting, keep the studio clean, and go out for last minute props (if there isn't a photographic stylist).

For all this, you will be paid as little as £100 per week, usually on a freelance basis. Some photographers will only employ you on a daily basis, but if you prove to be good at the job, and are based in London, you can make a fair living by working for several photographers, though the amount of work you get will be erratic and unpredictable.

One area of specialisation which can be fairly lucrative is in set building. Many photographers need a specialist assistant who can help to design and then build room sets (or outdoor scenes) in the studio – sometimes working from no more than a rough sketch, at other times following a brief to the last detail.

You do not usually need any equipment when you start, but most assistants build up a tool kit (electric screwdriver, hammer, scissors, handyman's knife, Blu-tac, Superglue, pliers, a selection of adhesive tapes, pins and so on). Obviously, if you specialise in set building the tool kit must be extensive.

Photographic assistants should be aware of the activities of the BRITISH INSTITUTE OF PROFESSIONAL PHOTOGRAPHY, and their magazine, the *Photographer* may be a useful source of advertising for jobs. The ASSOCIATION OF FASHION, ADVERTISING AND EDITORIAL PHOTOGRAPHERS (AFAEP) is a professional association of photographers and will enter your name on a list which members can consult.

Photographic Stylist

At a Glance

Qualifications/Training	Useful	Income bracket	Low–High
Licence	No	Town/Country	Town
Experience/Springboard	Essential	Travel	Yes
Mid-career entry	Possible	Exit sale	No
Entry costs	£300+	Work at home	Partly

Mix and match   Yes. You could think about: Magazine designer, Graphic designer, Illustrator, Wine merchant . . .

Enquiries   Association of Fashion, Advertising and Editorial Photography

For all but true photo-journalism, every photograph has to be styled (or arranged) to some extent. Often, the photographers themselves will do the work, but with more elaborate pictures, a stylist is involved, collecting necessary props together, and arranging them, or helping to arrange them, to create the desired effect.

On major home interest and fashion magazines, for example, a stylist will be employed to check that all the necessary accessories (flowers, clothes etc) are borrowed from manufacturers or agencies, hired or bought when necessary, and brought to the studio or location where the photography will take place, so that the photographer's valuable time is not wasted. They are usually employed by the magazine but there are openings for good freelance stylists – to help with rush jobs, take over when in-house stylists are not well, or fill in if there is a gap between one stylist leaving a magazine and a new member of staff being found.

When it comes to photography for advertising, the advertising agents will dictate a style, and it will be up to the stylist, usually in conjunction with the photographer, to select appropriate props. Some are hired, others have to be bought. So for an advertising shot for, say, wine, involving a glamorous lady lying back on a chaise longue in a stately home, the stylist may have to find and hire a location, hire any furniture that is needed, book a model, hire or buy a suitable outfit, choose the right style of glass for the drink, and hire a make-up artist. And be ready to change everything at the drop of a hat if the model turns up with a boil on her nose, the chosen glass is dropped half way through the session, or the owner of the location refuses to let the photographer run his electric cables across the hallway.

Most stylists start by working on magazines as full time employees, as layout artists, editorial assistants or sub editors, depending on the structure of the magazine. They may also come from the advertising side, moving on from copywriting or designing. Some design qualifications are useful, but not essential. It is helpful to get to know plenty of photographers, photographic editors of magazines, and art directors of advertising agencies. Being in the right place at the right time is all important. ASSOCIATION OF FASHION, ADVERTISING AND EDITORIAL PHOTOGRAPHY (AFAEP) is an association of professional photographers, and will enter your name on a list which members can consult.

Stylists are usually paid on a daily rate: from about £60 for editorial work to £300 for top notch advertising work. The only essential equipment is an answerphone and a huge contacts (address) book. It is also useful to have your own business cards. Which you can pin up on noticeboards in photographers' studios close to the phone, to keep your name in front of as many of the right people as possible. You can usually work from home, or use the studio where the photo session is to be.

A cheerful disposition, wit, and an ability to manipulate people who are too big for their boots are essential qualifications.

Photojournalist

At a Glance

Qualifications/Training	Recommended	*Income bracket*	Low–Medium
Licence	Union card	*Town/Country*	Town
Experience/Springboard	Useful	*Travel*	Endless
Mid-career entry	Unlikely	*Exit sale*	No
Entry costs	£1,000+	*Work at home*	No
Mix and match	Possible.	You could think about: Advertising photographer, Cabaret performer, Motorcycle messenger . . .	
Enquiries	National Union of Journalists		

Every picture tells a story. That could be the motto of every photojournalist, whose job it is to take still photographs for magazines and newspapers. This can be done either on spec or, once you are known and if the event is a scheduled one – Tory Party Conference, for example – you may be commissioned to cover it.

It's a hectic, unpredictable life, dominated by men aged between 24 and 40. After that, most move into other sorts of photography that offer more stability if less excitement. It's difficult to get started because you probably won't be given any money up front until you get that all-important break. There's a high drop-out rate and only the most determined – and the luckiest – make it to the top.

New technology is set to change things, as the process of taking still photographs off video and TV footage is perfected. Thus the freelance stills photographer will increasingly compete with big news agencies who can afford the technology and get pictures out fast.

The first step is to take a BA or Diploma course both to gain a basic training and to sample the various directions in which you can go. However, more important than qualifications is your portfolio. If it shows a lot of potential, some agencies – such as REFLEX PICTURES LTD – will take you on and give you some training and a lot of encouragement, as well as selling your pictures for you. Some may even pay you a minimal retainer fee while you find your feet. The best training of all, of course, is working alongside someone who knows what they're doing so, if you can, become an apprentice to an established photojournalist. Another good way is to establish a rapport with some magazines and newspapers. Start at the bottom with the low-budget mags, charity papers, local rags and political tracts – any that can't afford to send their own staff photographer.

The most important personal qualities are initiative, determination, dedication, and an ability to elbow your way in and go for it. The downfall of a lot of would-be photojournalists is that they lack the ability to sell their work, which is an essential asset.

You can start with basic camera equipment costing around £500 and then add to it as you make money. You have to be prepared for a high wear and tear bill, especially if you cover stormy events like major demos, industrial disputes and wars. Insurance can be difficult and some insurance companies will quickly cancel your policy if you claim against it, so it's best not to claim for every minor mishap but to wait for the big ones.

If you work from home, an answering machine and bleeper are a must. Other options include working for an agency or hiring your own agent, which is obviously the most expensive choice.

You might start by earning peanuts – as little as £25 a week. An average income after ten years is around £12,000, though some people obviously do a lot better. You can't count on a regular income, at least to start with, because you simply don't get paid unless you produce pictures that sell. Camera equipment and film are expensive, as are rail and air fares. You really need to have some degree of financial security – your own savings, another source of income or an understanding bank manager – before you set off on spec for eg Iraq. But there is money to be made if you hit the right spots: just one brilliant picture that no one else got eg in the Falklands war could have earned you £30,000.

You need a NATIONAL UNION OF JOURNALISTS (NUJ) press card and, if you plan to work abroad, an international press card. You also need a Metropolitan Police card, available from the METROPOLITAN POLICE PRESS BUREAU, if you intend to cover anything remotely connected with the law (including any major political event involving the security forces) in London and the equivalent from police forces outside London.

Useful books include *Making Waves*, *Freelance Photographer's Market Handbook*, *Photojournalism* and *Pictures on a Page – Photo-journalism, Graphics and Picture Editing*.

A good place to buy books, see exhibitions, keep up to date, meet people and generally hang out is the PHOTOGRAPHERS' GALLERY in London.

Physiotherapist

At a Glance

Qualifications/Training	Essential	Income bracket	Low–High
Licence	Yes	Town/Country	Town
Experience/Springboard	Recommended	Travel	No
Mid-career entry	Unlikely	Exit sale	No
Entry costs	£7,500+	Work at home	Possible

Mix and match Possible. You could think about: Counsellor, Specialist sports retailer, Dealer in small antiques . . .

Enquiries Chartered Society of Physiotherapy

Chartered physiotherapists are skilled in massage, manipulation, movement and exercise techniques, as well as electrotherapy, heat, high frequency currents or ultrasonics to aid recovery from various ills. They now also work in the preventative field as well as post-operative rehabilitation, chest complaints, physical handicap, pregnant women, teaching relaxation in psychiatric departments and sports and dance injuries.

If you want to gain a diploma or degree as a state registered physiotherapist you'll need to do a 3 year course at a teaching hospital or polytechnic. (The partially sighted can train at the NORTH LONDON SCHOOL OF PHYSIOTHERAPY FOR THE VISUALLY HANDICAPPED). You should join the CHARTERED SOCIETY OF PHYSIOTHERAPY which has useful lectures and seminars and keeps you in touch with latest developments. You'll need to have a healthy constitution and the ability to communicate with others. Physios have to spend much of their life encouraging, persuading and explaining. Tolerance, empathy, patience, a sense of humour and initiative plus emotional stability are vital. The body affects the mind and vice versa so it's necessary to always take the holistic view of the patient. The career prospects are excellent as this profession is expanding rapidly in many new directions, and the demand for physios in private practice is enormous.

It's advisable to work and gain experience for at least 5 years in as many different fields as possible in the NHS. This is also a way of making contacts and building a good network of specialists in all fields to whom to make referrals. You can start a part time practice and you can practice from a ground floor room in your own house. You'll need £5–10,000 to set up with a treatment bed, an ultrasound machine, a phone, answer machine, and filing cabinet. You also need hot and cold running water, to be near public transport and to have car parking. Average charges are about £15 per hour, good physiotherapists earn up to about £50,000 a year.

PHYSIOTHERAPIST

Your day can be as long or as short as you want it to be, but early morning and evenings are busy seeing patients before or after their working day. When starting out, never refuse a patient referred at short notice by a local GP, as good relations with doctors are vital. This job is very satisfying as nearly everyone gets better, and you're always learning new things. But it is isolated (unless you employ assistants). It's impossible to escape the clerical work, even with a good secretary. It takes careful organisation to allow time to give or attend lectures or teach, both of which are interesting. Advances in medicine are putting more and more pressure on physios.

You can get more information from the *Chartered Society of Physiotherapy Careers Handbook*.

Piano Tuner

At a Glance

Qualifications/Training	Recommended	*Income bracket*	Low–Medium
Licence	No	*Town/Country*	Mostly town
Experience/Springboard	Recommended	*Travel*	Local
Mid-career entry	Yes	*Exit sale*	No
Entry costs	£1,000+	*Work at home*	No

Mix and match   Possible.   You could think about: Musical instrument repairer, Keyboard hire, Cabinet maker, Jazz musician . . .
Enquiries   Piano Tuners' Association

This is someone who restores, repairs and tunes keyboard instruments. Take a full-time course at eg LONDON COLLEGE OF FURNITURE. Evening classes do not have the same prestige. To detect absolutely accurate intonation and to be able to play the instrument you need a really good ear. You should also learn bookkeeping, possess endless patience and a desire for meticulous accuracy. Work as an assistant to a tuner for at least 2 years. To go it alone you will need at least £1,000 to buy tools, a room or outhouse where you can do restoration work, telephone, answering machine or service and stationery.

Find your customers by passing the word around the local choir, and sending printed cards about your service to County Music Advisers and local piano teachers (names from the INCORPORATED SOCIETY OF MUSICIANS). Join the PIANO TUNERS' ASSOCIATION and the GUILD OF MASTER CRAFTSMEN. Develop contacts at recording studios; pianos which are being recorded need to be absolutely in tune. It is possible to do without a car; you can ask your clients to employ a piano remover if you need to take away an instrument for repair. It is dangerous both for you and the piano to try and do this yourself. You can find yourself working long hours – 12–18 a day if you have the energy – so it is unlikely that you can do another job at the same time. To start with, you can charge £20 per tuning; the number you can do in a day depends on the age and condition of the piano, and how quickly you work. There is no age, race or sex bias except that it is a tradition to prefer old, blind men. Modern electronic tuning devices speed up the work but are only as good as the ears that use them. Old pianos are likely to be affected by central heating; new pianos are seasoned to eliminate these problems.

The advantages of this job are that it is one of the few in music that's expanding, and you can earn up to £25,000 pa if you establish your reputation with a concert hall. Hours are flexible but you may find yourself working at weekends and it's easy to become a workaholic. There is usually plenty of local work so it is unlikely you will have to travel far.

Picture Agent

At a Glance

Qualifications/Training	Useful	Income bracket	Low–High
Licence	No	Town/Country	Usually town
Experience/Springboard	Recommended	Travel	No
Mid-career entry	Yes	Exit sale	Yes
Entry costs	£2,500+	Work at home	Possible

Mix and match Possible. You could think about: List broker, Newsletter publisher . . .

Enquiries   Existing picture libraries

A picture agency (or picture library) holds pictures (transparencies, negatives and prints) ready for use in newspapers, magazines, books, brochures and advertising material. The pictures may be bought direct from photographers, or they may come from magazines and books which have already been published. For example, a magazine like Ideal Home will commission photographers (at vast expense) to take shots of interiors, set up and photograph room sets, or do still life shots. Once the magazine has been published, the rights to reproduce these photographs will be handled by a picture agency. (In some cases, the agency will also syndicate the story that goes with the pictures). The agency files and records all the original material, and sells rights to other publications or agencies for the re-use of the material.

Picture agents may have trained in librarianship or in art and design. It is important to keep meticulous records, and be prepared for long delays in payment. The usual pattern is that a picture researcher contacts you asking for particular types of pictures (eg colour photographs of a specific plant, atmospheric pictures of happy, healthy families walking in the country, unusual pictures of construction workers climbing scaffolding – you name it!). You then go through your files (or make an appointment for the picture researcher to come in and look at what you've got), and then you send out the pictures (usually 'dupes' or duplicates). A picture researcher on a weekly magazine will probably make a selection within days and return pictures which are not wanted. But a picture researcher on a book may hold on to the pictures for several months while editorial and design decisions are made (and changed and re-thought). Payment is usually withheld until the picture has actually been published – which may be over a year in the case of a book (you may be able to demand a holding fee to help cover your expenses).

If you live fairly centrally, and depending on the subject area you specialise in, you can set up the agency in your own home. Agencies specialising in a subject area such as plants, where researchers' needs are fairly precise (eg 'We want a picture of a buddleia with a butterfly on it' or 'a close up of a hydrangea petiolaris in flower') can usually manage very well working out of town. Indeed, some of these agencies are actually owned by photographers who specialise in plants and gardens, and their spouses or partners run the agency. However, if you specialise in news photographs, where pictures may have to be delivered to the picture researcher or picture editor on a magazine in a matter of hours (or even minutes) or an area like home interiors, where researchers have a feeling for what they are looking for, but don't know exactly what they want until they see it, you will have to set up your office in London.

The main requirements for the office are plenty of space to set up your library system, good light box facilities, and a computer to keep tabs on the whereabouts of all your pictures and to send and chase invoices. Most agencies have specialised stationery with multiple copy invoices to help both themselves and the picture researchers they deal with to keep records of payments, rights and so on.

Picture Framer

At a Glance

Qualifications/Training	Recommended	*Income bracket*	Low–Medium
Licence	No	*Town/Country*	Town
Experience/Springboard	Recommended	*Travel*	No
Mid-career entry	Yes	*Exit sale*	Yes
Entry costs	£100–£5,000	*Work at home*	Yes

Mix and match Yes. You could think about: Contemporary art gallery owner, Picture restorer, Antique furniture restorer, Art historian/critic, Healer, Sculptor . . .

Enquiries Local picture framers

Picture framing seems to have been one of the growth industries of the eighties; most high streets have at least one framer. It's a good career to mix and match with something else (and often necessary as the chains of high street framers are often able to undercut smaller framers). Framing combines especially well with picture and any other art dealing.

You can buy a franchise which will provide you with a shop, equipment and training. Otherwise you can start off by doing a course in commercial picture framing. Frame suppliers have details of local courses or contact your local adult education centre. Working for someone else for a year or so, is a good way of developing your own technique. You need to be good at doing fiddly jobs; this isn't something you can hurry (the machinery can be dangerous and frames are fragile) so you'll need to be patient; it's essential that you're artistic enough to be able to advise on good ways of framing pictures – clients often don't know what they want. As with anything that brings you into contact with a buying public, you'll have to be fairly long suffering and, at times, diplomatic.

You need a lot of space for picture framing. You can work from home if you've got a spare room or garage but, if you can afford it, a shop front will help to attract more business. Whichever you choose, aim to be as close to a town centre as possible, your customers will have to make two trips (one to deliver and one to collect) and the less they have to travel, the better; but make sure that there's enough parking nearby. Apart from a telephone, you don't need much equipment. You can start in a very small way with a mitre saw (£80) and a hand held cutter (£5) but this will mean spending more time on each frame. It costs up to £5,000+ to equip yourself fully with: two large benches (one of which will get covered in glass splinters so don't use it for anything else); a mount cutter; a special saw or guillotine for cutting 45° angles in mouldings; a glass cutter and wooden measure; special pens; an under pinner which holds the various bits of the frame together; various rules and saws; a glazier's gun and points to fix it all in the frame. You're advised always to buy the best equipment available. You'll need supplies of glass and card for mountings; cord; wedges (to hold the corners of the frame together); rings, screws and clips, not to mention stretchers for oil paintings etc. Mouldings (the stuff that does the actual framing of the picture) have fashions – sometimes you'll sell a lot of metal ones, other times wood; keep a stock of about 50 different ones that your clients can choose from and make sure that you know a good, fast supplier so that you can get hold of other ones at short notice if needed. Framing with perspex is very similar to framing with glass although it costs more, weighs less and is more difficult to cut; it's difficult getting large bits of perspex too. Another alternative is acrylic glass which is thinner than perspex. You'll need all risks insurance cover for client's pictures while they're in your charge. Most framers calculate their charges on the dimensions or area of the frame, ie so much per square foot or inch. Charges have to cover glass, moulding, mount and other bits and pieces as well as your time. Most of the work you do will fall into the £6–90 bracket; to customers it may seem a lot especially since high street shops have devised a way of framing quickly and cheaply. You can speed up your own production by working a sort of mini-production line, mounting several pictures at once, then framing them then cutting glass etc. This means that you have to collect work in advance, customers are usually happy to wait about 2 weeks for a frame and you can always do a special, quick job if someone wants theirs before that. You really need to be doing at least 40–50 frames a week to survive but you can augment your income by selling framed and unframed prints or posters either in your shop, if you've got one, or at fairs and markets.

Good sources of work and outlets for ready framed pictures are interior designers, antique shops which sell old prints, and gift shops. Much work comes by word of mouth. You can start off by going around antiques shows with a selection of framed prints for sale (see the *Antiques Trade Gazette*). Get yourself known at art suppliers who may be able to push some customers your way. If you can cope with bulk orders art galleries generate great volumes of work but will probably want some sort of reduction; hotels and offices may also be interested in buying a set of inexpensive framed prints from you.

If you've got a shop you're tied to shop hours but, on the whole you're free to frame when you like. Christmas is a busy season. Occasionally you'll have to start a job from scratch again because frames are very easily broken during the last stages of their production.

Picture Researcher

At a Glance

Qualifications/Training	No	Income bracket	Low–Medium
Licence	No	Town/Country	Town
Experience/Springboard	Usually	Travel	Yes
Mid-career entry	Yes	Exit sale	No
Entry costs	£1,000	Work at home	Yes

Mix and match   Possible.   You could think about: Magazine designer, Photographic assistant, Motorcycle messenger . . .

Enquiries   Society of Picture Researchers and Editors (SPRED)

Picture researchers are responsible for finding pictures and handling the rights to use pictures in a range of publications. They usually start by working on the staff of a newspaper, magazine or for a book publishing company before setting up alone. They may come straight from art school, they may have started as the office secretary, or they may drift into picture research from editing or design work. As a freelance picture researcher you tend to either work in-house on a newspaper or magazine, filling in while staff are off sick or while a new appointment is being made, or you work from home, researching pictures for a range of books.

The most common source of pictures is picture agencies, where you should have no problems in negotiating fees and rights, since these are set by the agency. However, good researchers will be ingenious and look for other sources – manufacturers (who often provide pictures free if they are given an editorial credit), historical archives (which may only charge a nominal fee for use of their material), private individuals who may be so excited that one of their pictures is likely to be published that they want to pay *you*, or may have such a limited knowledge of the system that they want to charge ten times the going rate.

One of the advantages of working freelance on several projects is that you can 'double up' when you visit agencies – researching pictures on a range of topics for different clients at the same time.

Picture researchers will charge by the hour or day, and expect to earn £150–400 per week as a freelance. They must keep meticulous records, as the pictures they handle may each be worth up to £1,000. Working from home, a telephone and address book are the main pieces of equipment needed.

There is a professional association, SPRED (SOCIETY OF PICTURE RESEARCHERS AND EDITORS) which keeps a register of experienced, *bona fide* picture researchers who work on a freelance basis, so that editors and art directors can contact them.

Picture Restorer

At a Glance

Qualifications/Training	Recommended	*Income bracket*	Low–Medium
Licence	No	*Town/Country*	Either
Experience/Springboard	No	*Travel*	Yes
Mid-career entry	Possible	*Exit sale*	No
Entry costs	£2,000	*Work at home*	Yes

Mix and match   Yes.   You could think about: Antique furniture restorer, Picture framer, Contemporary art gallery owner, Artist . . .

Enquiries   Museums Association

Picture restorers mend damaged paintings and clean dirty ones. Paintings often change a lot after they've been cleaned – not only are the colours clearer and brighter but cleaning also shows up any modern additions that are not part of the original painting. It is very intricate work, and sometimes controversial; there can be outrage if the authenticity of works of art is seen as being under threat.

There are very few studentships or apprenticeships for picture restorers in this country at museums or art institutes. A few colleges offer training places: the COURTAULD INSTITUTE for oil painting restoration; GATESHEAD COLLEGE for prints and CAMBERWELL for prints and paper restoration. There are more training places in America.

You'll need a bit of capital to start with and may need to augment your income for a while. You are paid per job, not per hour, so you need to have a good idea of how long each job will take before you're ready to start quoting prices.

With training, there is quite a lot of freelance work available. Contacts and word of mouth are the normal ways to get work. Museums use freelance restorers (contact the MUSEUMS ASSOCIATION). They also keep lists of restorers and their particular specialism so that they can refer members of the public. Otherwise, finding work is just a matter of traipsing around likely clients like antique dealers. Once you've established a good reputation you'll get more and more work through referrals and clients coming back to you.

Plasterer

At a Glance

Qualifications/Training	Available	Income bracket	Low
Licence	No	Town/Country	Either
Experience/Springboard	Yes	Travel	Local
Mid-career entry	Possible	Exit sale	No
Entry costs	£700+	Work at home	No

Mix and match   Possible. You could think about: Painter/decorator, House converter, Interior designer, Man with a van, Garden gnome maker . . .

Enquiries   Local building firms

Plastering involves applying a finishing coat to walls and ceilings. It is hard work, but there is plenty of scope for working for yourself.

Most plasterers acquire their skill by serving a type of apprenticeship, learning the skills from an old hand, possibly taking courses leading to City and Guilds certificates. Plasterers work in teams, one preparing, mixing and clearing up, the other applying the plaster. In traditional homes, a smooth finish is usually called for, but there are also textured finishes. Artex, the major manufacturer of plastic finish 'plaster' run 5-day courses (often with a waiting list), which is a useful way to acquire the skill and know-how. Artex also license the use of their name to those who have completed the course satisfactorily.

Another aspect of plastering is the production (usually off site) and application of traditional fibrous plaster mouldings – friezes and ceiling roses. This is a lucrative area to get into, since it is the up-market householders who are likely to want your services.

To set up your own business, you must be reliable and hard working. You will need a van, and a few tools (trowel, float, spirit level, etc) and a supply of materials. A few hundred pounds should be enough and you can probably charge £50 plus a day. You will probably have to employ a semi-skilled assistant, possibly on a casual basis. On the other hand, you could set yourself up with several teams of plasterers, providing each with vans and equipment. Then you become a manager rather than a plasterer, although a thorough knowledge of the work is helpful in ensuring things run smoothly.

Plumber/Heating Engineer

At a Glance

Qualifications/Training	Recommended	Income bracket	Low
Licence	No	Town/Country	Either
Experience/Springboard	Recommended	Travel	Local
Mid-career entry	Possible	Exit sale	No
Entry costs	£800	Work at home	No
Mix and match	Possible.	You could think about: Electrician, Glazier, Disco owner . . .	
Enquiries	CORGI, Institute of Plumbing		

The two are linked because both tend to involve water and the installation of pipes. Being a plumber may not be the most glamorous of jobs but there is nearly always a demand for good, reliable plumbers who know what they're doing. As long as you don't mind seeing what one plumber describes as the more unsavoury side of life floating past, you should be able to make a good living from plumbing. It's a good job for mix and match.

You can learn the basics by doing a course at your local college of further education. There's no substitute, however, for learning on the job so find someone who'll employ you for a few years. Try to get wide experience of the various jobs involved and of the different types of fitting you're likely to come across. It's helpful if you have some grounding in other trades like bricklaying and plastering which are especially useful when you're installing new fitments. Plumbers need to be practical and enthusiastic; being able to get on with a job quickly and effectively is very important. Clients don't like waiting without their water supply while you potter around. You need also to be reasonably affable to cope with clients many of whom will want your

PLUMBER

services at very short notice. Build a network of builders, electricians, carpenters etc who can give you their specialist advice and can refer clients to you.

Set up costs include some specialist tools, a good van and an answering machine. You'll certainly want some special work clothes for days spent repairing drains. You should also have public liability insurance and health insurance against loss of income. Set up accounts with reliable suppliers who will give you credit, usuually of 28 days. This allows you to collect the money for materials from clients before paying for them. Estimate for each job before you do it and try not to exceed your estimates by more than a small amount. Make sure that clients know how much you're charging before you start and keep them aware of any complications that may slow you down or increase their final bill. On large jobs you should take a down payment, to cover the cost of some of the materials, and to ensure that your cash flow is positive. For the smallest jobs, establish a minimum charge eg £16–18. Once you're established and your turnover is up to the VAT threshold, make sure that you register.

Clients come through advertisements in the press and Yellow Pages and by word of mouth. This means getting on well with your clients, listening to their point of view in any disputes and always doing as good a job as you possibly can. It will probably take about 5 years to establish a large enough clientele to keep you fully occupied. As long as you've got the time to do it, never turn down small jobs as they often lead to larger ones in the future. You should be prepared to answer the phone at any time and be ready to be called out at unsociable hours, especially during cold winters when pipes freeze. Clients may sometimes be cross when they call you out but are invariably pleased to see you. Keep an appointment book but be flexible enough to take on unscheduled jobs. If you have to work particularly arduous hours for a few weeks, you'll be able to take some time off when it's quieter.

Pop Group Sound Engineer

At a Glance

Qualifications/Training	Not necessary	Income bracket	Low
Licence	Driving licence	Town/Country	Town
Experience/Springboard	Recommended	Travel	Lots
Mid-career entry	Unlikely	Exit sale	No
Entry costs	£250	Work at home	No

Mix and match   Limited.   You could think about: Landlord, Mini-cab driver, Bartender . . .

Enquiries   Recording studios

This is someone who transports, sets up and balances the sound equipment for a pop group. No formal qualifications are needed, but it is vital you understand how the equipment works so you can maintain and repair it, often quickly and under very difficult conditions. Youth, energy, strength, a good ear, and luck are all useful. You have to drive the van/car to gigs and on tours, so must have a clean driving licence.

Work in an equipment company, or as a gofer in a recording studio for a couple of years. You can meet groups there and do odd gigs with them. If they become successful, join them on tour. You will earn peanuts unless they are given a contract by a recording company, when your income can rise to £12,000 pa.

It's a good idea to buy a house or flat with a mortgage and instal a lodger when you are off on tour. You will need a telephone and answering machine or services. Transport should be provided by the group. Working hours are likely to be 19 hours a day, 7 days a week, so say good-bye to your private life.

A tour can last for up to 3 months and the group lives at close quarters so be able to 'bend with the wind' and keep cool. The job can involve driving hundreds of miles to a gig, setting up heavy gear and doing a sound test before the concert; then loading up and possibly driving again. This is why the bias is towards fit young males.

Study the adverts in pop trade magazines, get the names of public address systems companies from yellow pages and apply for anything that sounds likely.

This job is a way of acquiring electronic and organisational skills. It's exciting and fun to travel around, but don't expect to enjoy it over the age of 30.

Potter

At a Glance

Qualifications/Training	Recommended	Income bracket	Low–High
Licence	No	Town/Country	Either
Experience/Springboard	Possible	Travel	Local
Mid-career entry	Possible	Exit sale	No
Entry costs	£10,000	Work at home	Yes

Mix and match Possible. You could think about: Photographer, Holiday accommodation owner, Book publisher, Opening to the public . . .
Enquiries Society of Designer–Craftsmen, Crafts Council

Decorative ceramics are now in demand in Britain (Scandinavia vigorously promoted it some 100 years ago) and the old image of beards and open-toed sandals has given way to a close co-operation between contemporary artist and craftsman. You can get advice on courses from the SOCIETY OF DESIGNER-CRAFTSMEN, the CRAFTS COUNCIL or ADAR. Or you can take recreational classes or do some odd-jobbing for a successful ceramicist if you have enough flair. You can work from home or share costs in a workshop or studio (advice on setting up a workshop from the CRAFTS COUNCIL).

Setting up costs (tools, material, publicity) are expensive – expect to pay approx £10,000 plus cost of premises or rent. Look out for second hand equipment in trade magazines (*Ceramic Review, Crafts, Tiles & Tiling*). Use college friends to design your publicity and take photographs: it all helps to reduce costs. Teaching can augment your income.

Contacts are invaluable; enter as many trade fairs as possible for publicity, trade and overseas buyers (World Ceramics Fair, Tilex, International Gift Show, Interior Design International). The DESIGN COUNCIL has lists of exhibitions/fairs and their costs; see also *Exhibition Bulletin*. Get yourself on the CRAFTS COUNCIL register – they also have one for the 'elite', those craftsmen who they consider are high-flyers. Forge links with as many interior designers as possible. Advertise in local newspapers and 'freebies'. Price your wares realistically. Most retailers want a mass-produced, yet specialised product. You have to be very good to sell a £400 plate to a discriminating customer. Make sure that you are capable of meeting all potential orders (as many as 500) before showing at a large fair – you risk 'sudden death' if you get a name for unreliability. The larger manufacturers use out-workers, but they want skills rather than designs. Specialist outlets (interior design, tiles) use designer craftsmen (on retainers) to supply ceramics to requirements – tiles reflecting a fabric design. There is a substantial shift towards selling to department stores taking limited editions or one-offs. Hawk your work around these outlets and use your imagination: would your product sell in designer giftware shops, garden centres? Supply samples and colour charts.

Potters must keep up with fashion (tiles, ornaments etc) and the times – for example, making dinner services which can go in dishwashers.

Prep School Owner

At a Glance

Qualifications/Training	Necessary	Income bracket	Medium–High
Licence	Yes	Town/Country	Either
Experience/Springboard	Essential	Travel	No
Mid-career entry	Likely	Exit sale	Excellent
Entry costs	£175,000+	Work at home	No

Mix and match Possible. You could think about: Events organiser, Holiday accommodation owner, Sailing school owner, Music teacher . . .

Enquiries   Independent Schools Information Service

There is a growing demand for good, reliable independent schools. Currently some 444,000 (about 7%) of school children in the UK are being educated independently; this number increases by about 1% (approximately 4,440 children) per annum. Many independent schools are heavily oversubscribed and there is certainly room for more independent primary and secondary schools. On the whole, the added complications of providing GCSE and A-level syllabuses and facilities make a primary or prep school a more viable proposition for anyone thinking of starting from scratch. There's more to opening a school than buying a blackboard and a couple of reading books before sitting back and waiting for enrolments. It's big business (the annual turnover of a large school can be around £1 million or more) and needs a lot of financial backing and know how if you're to succeed.

For help and advice while you're setting up and getting going, contact ISIS, the INDEPENDENT SCHOOLS INFORMATION SERVICE. Any school providing full time education for 5 or more children of school age must be registered with the DES. You can register provisionally as soon as you open; you'll then be visited by the local fire officer to check that the buildings are safe and comply with *Fire and Design of Schools*, and by HMI (HER MAJESTY'S INSPECTORS OF SCHOOLS) who want to ensure that you are equipped to provide a useful education, ie 'the opportunity to acquire a broad and balanced range of knowledge and skills . . . appropriate and effective teaching . . . develop the personal qualities of each pupil . . . (tuition) appropriate to age, ability and aptitude'. Although independent schools can employ teachers without formal qualifications, the DES will want to see some experienced and qualified staff. If it's a boarding school you'll need some child care staff as well. Always check staff references before making appointments. You risk legal action if you employ staff deemed unsuitable to have access to children (usually because of a criminal record); *List 99* from the DES gives the names of banned teaching staff and the DES TEACHERS PAY AND GENERAL branch will help check anyone not on the list. It will take between several weeks and several terms to become fully registered; after that schools must keep daily attendance records of pupils and are subject to occasional HMI inspections. These are more in the nature of constructive visits and should be used by you as such. If you're failing to keep up to standard you'll be told how to improve or forced to close. There's a slightly different procedure in Scotland, details in *Notes of Guidance for Proprietors on the Registration of Independent Schools*.

Essential qualifications are teaching experience; good business sense /knowledge; contacts who may provide some of the financial backing or who'll help you recruit teaching and administrative staff; and, above all, enjoyment of working with children. You'll also need to present the right image; parents aren't going to hand their children into your care unless you're smart, obviously bright, businesslike and sympathetic; crisp rather than brusque. You're unlikely to have enough of any of this without several years teaching experience and it's worth planning a combination of experience at a famous school (for credentials with parents) with working in a smaller school, closer to the size of the one you're likely to be opening (where you'll learn more about the overall school management). In addition, experience in business or finance is valuable; you'll need a very good idea of how businesses, as well as schools, are run and financed.

You can buy an existing school from about £175,000 from a school broker (eg SCHOOL TRANSFER CONSULTANTS or LADBURY SHENTON). If you're starting from scratch you'll need planning permission and must ensure that you build in all the facilities required by the DES. You'll obviously need money for equipment and salaries. Start with a well defined business plan. Appoint a board of governors. (Their role is to ensure the school is run in such a way as to be a success by suggesting policy on all aspects of running the school, including PR and fundraising.) Contacts, the higher profile the better, are useful for this. When it's your school you appoint the governors yourself, something that many heads of established independent schools (most of whom are appointed by the governors) wish that they could do. Choose governors who share your aspirations for the school and what it should provide; the same goes for the staff you appoint.

Governors seldom put up money for the school; banks can be difficult. You can appoint a board of directors as a way of raising investment capital, they will be involved less in what goes on in the school than in how much money it's making. You'll have to draw up a full business proposal based on the initial plan and can offer shareholders incentives such as reduced fees for children they nominate. The current climate indicates that there are a lot of people willing to invest in education as a financial proposition and the government's Business Expansion Scheme allows investors tax relief on shareholdings in new or expanding companies. If you're operating as an educational trust you may qualify for charitable status, contact the CHARITY COMMISSION for further details. Once you're operating you'll probably find that parents are a good source of development finance if you want to expand.

Choose your location carefully. You can do your own market research by going around a chosen area and calling on people in their houses to find out how many are interested and likely to let you educate their children; the same people will also probably help to lobby for planning permission. This means selecting a rich area with insufficient independent prep schools, which doesn't always mean being the only independent school for miles. Once the school is opened, children will probably come from further afield. Premises must be big enough for the number of pupils; in a quiet area that's safe for children and easily accessible for parents but won't disrupt local residents too much with increased traffic at the beginning and end of the school day, *Good Communications Guide* gives advice on how to publicise and market schools. Make sure that you can safely charge the fees you need to make the business profitable. Find out how much other schools charge; demand for places at independent schools is such that in many areas you'll be able to get into the top range, as long as your school's good. In London day schools, you can reckon on getting about £950+ per pupil per term.

For the first year calculate on operating at no more than 50% of capacity, and probably making a loss. Once the school's opened, it should get up to capacity very quickly.

Schools have high profiles and are the subject of much dinner and cocktail party conversation; you'll need to keep an ear open for rumours about your school and make sure that the damaging ones aren't allowed to spread. Success depends on giving parents what they want; providing children with a good, useful education and offering something that parents feel is lacking at state schools. For many parents, at the moment, that means providing fairly traditional and disciplined education. Selling points include an emphasis on reading, writing, grammar, and arithmetic; a smart (but readily available) uniform and encouragement of parental involvement. Keep up with what's going on in education by reading the *Times Educational Supplement* and there are organisations like the INDEPENDENT PREP SCHOOLS ASSOCIATION which help their members through meetings with other independent school heads, and grant automatic membership to the INDEPENDENT SCHOOLS INFORMATION SERVICE (ISIS). Details on how and what to join from the INDEPENDENT SCHOOLS JOINT COUNCIL. Best of all, if you want to know about the wide range of independent secondary schools, consult the *Schools Book*.

Printmaker

At a Glance

Qualifications/Training	Necessary	*Income bracket*	Low–Medium
Licence	No	*Town/Country*	Town
Experience/Springboard	Recommended	*Travel*	No
Mid-career entry	Possible	*Exit sale*	No
Entry costs	£200+	*Work at home*	Yes

Mix and match   Possible.   You could think about: Photographer, Contemporary art gallery owner, Graphic designer, Interior designer, Artist . . .

Enquiries   Print Makers' Council

Printmaking uses some of the same techniques as graphics but differs in that while graphics tend to be directly involved with the commercial world, printmaking is more of an art for its own sake. It can, however, be very lucrative.

After doing a course in printmaking which covers techniques such as etching, lithography, screen printing and relief painting, choose whether you want to specialise in fabric printing, collage design, art prints, posters, fine art or a combination. Useful experience is working as a technician and reproducing other people's work at a studio; this will give you an idea of what's going on in the field and may lead to contacts. It helps if you've got some idea of what people want to hang on their walls; this is obviously more important when you need to sell a lot of prints (eg posters) than if you're specialising in limited editions.

Screen printing is the cheapest form of printing to set up; all you need is the screen, inks and a table top. Etching is more complicated: you need a press, acids and an acid bath. For photographic reproduction you'll need to have access to a dark room. See *Artists Newsletter* for advertisements for equipment. Screen printing is at the commercial end of 'art for art's sake'; the market for prints is larger than for many other art forms because they tend to cost a lot less.

Once you've got a design for a print, you can sell several copies of it. Galleries charge 30–50% mark up on anything they sell and sometimes need to be chased for payment. Many screenprinters augment their incomes with some part time teaching – this has the added advantage of getting you access to college facilities. There is a vast choice of small companies whom you can tap for work, perhaps via an interior designer, who may want prints for a client's boardroom or restaurant. Getting your work up in public places is a good advertisement, although large companies tend to be rather slow at paying. Exhibitions, especially national ones are a good source of commissions – the PRINT MAKERS' COUNCIL hold 2 or 3 a year.

Private Investigator

At a Glance

Qualifications/Training	Useful	*Income bracket*	Medium–High
Licence	No	*Town/Country*	Town
Experience/Springboard	Recommended	*Travel*	Some
Mid-career entry	Likely	*Exit sale*	Possible
Entry costs	£5,000++	*Work at home*	Partly

Mix and match   Possible.   You could think about: List broker, UK correspondent for overseas media, Conveyancer, Cabaret performer . . .

Enquiries   National Association of Private Investigators

Private investigators do a lot of civil law work, tracing people to serve writs and deliver affidavits – described by one as the faith healers of the legal world, as they get called in to handle cases that the police can't or won't deal with (matrimonial, industrial espionage and counter espionage, missing persons etc). You may be asked to do work which is illegal (often under the Official Secrets Act); to take on such work carries obvious risks and should be avoided.

There are no formal qualifications or legal requirements. However, it may be useful to join the NATIONAL ASSOCIATION OF PRIVATE INVESTIGATORS which involves taking a correspondence course (costs £200). Any

PRIVATE INVESTIGATOR

sort of research experience (eg for a degree) is useful. Even more useful is a police (or army) background and this is the most usual route in. It gives you not only a training in the law and tracking down law breakers, but a network you can build up and call upon when you want specific information and advice. The INTERNATIONAL PROFESSIONAL SECURITY ASSOCIATION runs correspondence courses in general security but these are geared more towards those working for large investigating firms than for those setting up alone.

To cultivate local police confidence and co-operation make sure you inform your local senior police officer before setting up – you'll then be checked over by the crime prevention officer (rumour has it that every private investigator merits a Special Branch file).

Necessary equipment is a car, a telephone, an answering machine, a typewriter and business cards. If you branch into industrial espionage you'll need some specialist, expensive equipment (anti-bugging devices, etc). Private clients may want to come to visit you so have somewhere suitable for this. Operate in an area with plenty of solicitors as, initially, they will provide most of your work, having people traced etc. You can approach them in person and with business cards. You may be required to write affidavits (for how to do this and other basics of the law see the *Penguin Guide to the Law*). If local solicitors do not provide enough work, advertise in the local press and yellow pages for private clients. It may also be worth approaching the larger investigating agencies who sometimes subcontract some of their leg work when they are busy. Charging is by the hour, £10 is a competitive starting rate, up to about £25.

Contrary to the popular image, private investigators do not do a lot of dashing around the countryside in pursuit of criminals. Most of it is routine and can be done from home by telephoning your network and following up with some legwork at the end. This means you'll probably work office hours. You may occasionally have to meet a deadline (a missing witness required in court on a specific day) and sometimes you'll have nothing to show for the bill you present to your client. You can decide how hard you work but obviously your reputation will benefit from a few efficient successes.

Property Developer

At a Glance

Qualifications/Training	No	*Income bracket*	Low–High
Licence	No	*Town/Country*	Either
Experience/Springboard	Useful	*Travel*	Local
Mid-career entry	Likely	*Exit sale*	Yes
Entry costs	£50,000+++	*Work at home*	Possible

Mix and match   Yes.   You could think about: Architect, Estate agent, Surveyor, Opening to the public, Landlord, MP...

Enquiries   Local estate agents, banks etc

Property development companies come in all sizes – and are often not the most popular people in town. At one end of the scale there are large public companies, who buy up land and run-down commercial buildings to re-develop as shops and offices; at the other end of the scale are DIY enthusiasts, who buy (and sometimes live in) run-down property, do it up, sell it at a profit, and move on to the next project.

Capital or large loans are required, but there are no formal qualifications. Some developers just run a single project, and then let the finished units to bring in an income, others will sell and plough back their profits in a new development. Most developers have experience of some aspect of the business, either as estate agents or builders. An understanding of building construction, land law, planning and building regulations are essential; professional advice, from architects, solicitors and surveyors is usually taken.

To get started, approach local estate agents, study newspapers and ask around to find a suitable site to develop. To raise the finance you may be able to get a mortgage, but you will probably have to borrow from a bank, or go into partnership with an established businessman who has finance, or a property owner who is willing for you to do the work and share the profits. Bank managers may be cautious about lending such large sums of money, so when you approach them, make sure you have thought out every aspect of the project. On a larger scale, the *Directory of Property Developers, Investors and Financiers* is a useful source of contacts.

The day-to-day work will depend on the role you play in the company: if you are developing individual homes or converting houses into flats, for example, you may find you are actually working on the site, or you may limit your activity to organising the subcontractors (bricklayers, roofers, plasterers, electricians, plumbers, carpenters, glaziers, painters and decorators and so on).

However you decide to proceed, you will need determination and entrepreneurial ability. And the possibility of over-borrowing and going bankrupt will always be hanging over you.

Property Manager

	At a Glance		
Qualifications/Training	No	*Income bracket*	Low–Medium
Licence	No	*Town/Country*	Either
Experience/Springboard	Recommended	*Travel*	Local
Mid-career entry	Likely	*Exit sale*	No
Entry costs	£1,000+	*Work at home*	Yes
Mix and match	Possible.	You could think about: Estate agent, Landlord, Holiday accommodation owner, Tourist guide . . .	
Enquiries	Estate agents, Solicitors, International companies		

Property managers are responsible for looking after the houses and flats of absentee clients who may only spend a few weeks or months in their house but who may not want to rent it out. What you do depends to a large extent on what you are prepared to do; you should expect to provide at least a caretaker service, keeping an eye on empty houses, arranging for necessary work and the payment of regular bills and rates. In effect you act as the landlord without actually owning the property. In addition, while your clients are in residence, you may be called on to procure domestic staff, theatre tickets, chauffeurs, and catering services. Nearly all of the opportunities for this sort of work are in London and the South East or in holiday resorts, as caretaker for holiday homes.

Essential qualifications are the ability to organise and a network of contacts which will grow as you develop. It helps to have experience of organising other people's lives: personal assistant, conference manager etc.

Many of your clients come from abroad – the ability to speak foreign languages is useful. You'll also have to be able to rise to the occasion, for instance, deal pleasantly with clients who ring at 5 in the morning because their pipes have burst.

Set up costs are minimal; you'll need a phone and answering machine and a car is useful. Make sure you have a good solicitor and accountant. You're well advised to register as a limited company (thus reducing your personal liability) and to take out professional indemnity insurance and cover for any accidental damage caused by your contractors. Cash flow is less of a problem than for many other new businesses because your clients lodge money for your fees and expenses when they open an account with you (your solicitor will help to set this up).

You'll find clients are prepared to pay quite highly for good service in this area – not everyone wants to derive income from their property. Charge an annual rate for the basic caretaking service, based on the value of the property (£1,500 or so for London) and 15% commission, on any job that you subcontract and on domestic staff salaries. You can also charge your contractors commission on the work you provide for them.

Getting into the network of overseas property owners is done through personal contacts and recommendation. Try large firms who are often the nominal owners of your clients' property – for tax purposes. Other essential networks are reliable domestic staff, gardeners, plumbers, etc whom you can call on at short notice. Build up trust by paying promptly, making sure that you're there to let them in and that they know what to expect. You'll find yourself tapping into more and more networks as you cope with various client requests.

During the day you'll do a lot of running around, letting plumbers into empty properties, recruiting casual staff etc, and you'll have to work at anti-social hours, meeting clients in the evening and coping with night-time emergencies. As a service industry you may find it difficult to reach the level of security to take on a full-time assistant so holidays can be difficult because you need to maintain a perpetual, comforting contact with your clients.

Psychoanalyst

At a Glance

Qualifications/Training	Essential	*Income bracket*	Low–High
Licence	No	*Town/Country*	Town
Experience/Springboard	No	*Travel*	No
Mid-career entry	Essential	*Exit sale*	No
Entry costs	£500	*Work at home*	Yes

Mix and match   Possible.   You could think about: Gardener/garden designer, Cabaret performer, Potter . . .

Enquiries   Institute of Psychoanalysis, Institute of Group Analysis

Psychoanalysts are trained to listen, observe and speak to their patients in such a way that they are able to analyse their patients' past, present and future life and problems. They meet and treat their patients once, twice or even five times a week over a period – one or many years depending on the patient's problems and financial means.

You need a degree, as wide an experience of life as possible, and to be at least 30. Then you can apply for the 3–5 year course at the INSTITUTE OF PSYCHOANALYSIS or the INSTITUTE OF GROUP ANALYSIS. It is necessary to receive analysis for at least a year (preferably more) before you begin. You will not get a grant and so you will need at least £16,000 to cover the costs of the course and the analysis, which will continue. You need good concentration, an interest in people, an ability to listen and observe them carefully and a constitution which will allow you to work long hours without tiring. The number of patients you receive is dependent on contacts and the impression you make on those who teach you and those who learn with you, as it is they who will refer patients to you after you are qualified.

You need a consulting room which can be in your own house, preferably near public transport, with 2 comfortable chairs, a couch, filing cabinet, phone and answerphone. A lavatory with a washbasin is an asset but not essential. Make sure that you are covered by insurance in case a patient sues you for malpractice.

Many patients can only come before or after work so you may have to begin early and work late. It's wise to make several breaks in a day as long as this, so go swimming or jogging to keep fit, as sitting in a chair is bad for your body if not your mind.

Try and have a really interesting hobby, preferably physical, either an art/craft or gardening, to balance the intellectual and emotional stress of the job. A lively supportive family and circle of friends are very important and be careful you don't start analysing them from habit – they won't appreciate it!

This is an isolated job, you can't share your successes or failure or discuss your work with others as it's confidential. If you like people you will rarely be bored.

Most analysts belong to the INSTITUTE OF PSYCHOANALYSIS, the INSTITUTE OF GROUP ANALYSIS or the SOCIETY OF ANALYTICAL PSYCHOLOGY, which is a professional association. All these will provide further useful information. Read anything you can find on Freud, Klein or Jūng in the local library.

Psychologist

At a Glance

Qualifications/Training	Essential	Income bracket	Medium–High
Licence	Recommended	Town/Country	Town
Experience/Springboard	Recommended	Travel	Local
Mid-career entry	Yes	Exit sale	Possible
Entry costs	£1,000+	Work at home	Unlikely

Mix and match   Possible.   You could think about: Musician, Football commentator, Landlord, Radio reporter/presenter . . .

Enquiries   British Psychological Society

Psychologists fall into several categories, but they are all people who through their knowledge and understanding of the human mind and human behaviour can solve psychological problems. Clinical psychologists if working with psychiatrists, and doctors in hospitals, assess and work therapeutically with individuals and groups who have personality and emotional problems. Educational psychologists concentrate on problems to do with learning such as dyslexia, physical and mental handicap and children's emotional difficulties in learning. Consultant, industrial or occupational psychologists use their expertise to solve problems in working situations, organisations and in industry and advertising.

You will need to do a degree in psychology and to become a member of the BRITISH PSYCHOLOGICAL SOCIETY (BPS). A consultant occupational psychologist may find it useful to have a qualification in management. Read the *Psychologist*.

Clinical psychologists need perception, to be observant, reflective and have the capacity to sit and listen for long periods. A wide life experience, an appreciation of pain and an endless curiosity about people are essential. There are good prospects in private practice.

An educational psychologist (see job profile on child/educational psychologist) must share the same personal qualities but must also enjoy children and be able to relate easily to those who are mentally or physically handicapped; a sense of humour is useful. With educational cuts, this area is not very encouraging as a career, and to work freelance you must have a good research record or show that your theories are effective in the private sector.

Industrial or consultant psychologists have excellent prospects if they have the ability to deal with complex data, to stand back and view their position in a complicated or difficult organisational situation, and can take the high level of anxiety in a very competitive field. You are employed on contract to solve a problem, or show where it lies, and if you can do this scientifically in the shortest possible time, your reputation will increase accordingly.

It's best to do regular work in your chosen area for at least 3 years, with good supervision to gain contacts and experience. You can devote part of your time to your private work while still doing sessions for the NHS or education authority, or an industrial job. You can start by charging £15–30 an hour for clinical or educational work. For consultative work the rate is £200 per day rising to £500 or even £1,000 if you are very successful. You can work from your home and only need a phone, answerphone, typewriter and filing cabinet.

Your working days are as long as you make them while you are on contract, usually for a designated number of weeks. In educational work your day can be long, as you tend to see problem children after school or have meetings when parents, teachers and administrators are available. This also applies to clinical work when you tend to see clients outside office hours.

Being a clinical or educational psychologist is stimulating if you like working with people; if you are analytically minded, consultancy or industrial work is interesting and challenging. Clinical and educational psychologists have the disadvantage of long hours which interfere with family life and consultative work which can involve a lot of travelling and a high level of anxiety. It is possible with good organisation to do another job at the same time. Video, fax and the word processor make this job much easier.

Psychotherapist

At a Glance

Qualifications/Training	Essential	Income bracket	Low–High
Licence	No	Town/Country	Town
Experience/Springboard	Useful	Travel	No
Mid-career entry	Essential	Exit sale	No
Entry costs	£15,000	Work at home	Yes

Mix and match   Possible.   You could think about: Cabinet maker, Book editor, Holiday accommodation owner . . .

Enquiries   British Association of Psychotherapists, Tavistock Institute of Human Relations

A psychotherapist is someone who is trained to sit and listen confidentially to the personal or relationship problems presented by the patient. The patient is seen at an agreed regular time, usually once a week for 50 minutes. Through this professional relationship, psychotherapists are able to facilitate psychological growth and understanding in the patient through their warmth, patience and expert observation both of the conscious and unconscious.

You need a degree (the most useful is psychology), to be over 30 years old and to have received psychotherapy for at least 18 months. Then you can apply for a 3 year part time course at a reputable organisation (there are many disreputable ones) such as the BRITISH ASSOCIATION OF PSYCHOTHERAPISTS or the TAVISTOCK INSTITUTE OF HUMAN RELATIONS. There are others, which follow different theoretical beliefs and practices; and some starting in the provinces which are still in their early days. You will get no grant so, with the ongoing psychotherapy throughout your training, you should expect to spend about £15,000. The most usual route is via a background in psychology, social work or medicine but this is not essential – a varied life experience is helpful. You need a good constitution; an interest in people; patience; warmth;

good listening, concentrating, and observing skills; and a sense of humour. A full rich personal life is vital to keep you balanced and to preserve a sense of proportion.

If you are shown to be good and will have patients while you are training, other psychotherapists will refer patients to you – so it's important to start building contacts while you are learning. Make sure you have a good insurance in case a patient sues you.

It's possible to start a private practice as soon as you qualify. Depending on your contacts and rate of successful and satisfied patients you can expect to make about £3,000 pa to begin with but this can rise to £40,000.

You can use a room in your house or flat as long as it's fairly quiet and those you live with are well disciplined. It must contain two comfortable chairs, a couch and a filing cabinet. Patients usually pay at the end of each session which saves sending invoices. You also need a phone and an answerphone; a loo with washbasin nearby is useful. If you can be near public transport this makes you available to more patients.

As a lot of patients can only attend before or after working hours you must be prepared to start work early and finish late. However it's sensible to have a long lunch with another activity – sport or jogging – as sitting in a chair all day is very unhealthy. Many psychotherapists prefer a 3-day weekend to keep really fit. It's possible to work part time, combining it with teaching or doing research or a completely different job.

This is a relentlessly isolated and tiring occupation as you can't cancel a patient when you don't feel like seeing them. The plus is that you can work from home and it's always fascinating, rewarding work. It's very important that it doesn't interrupt your family and social life.

Useful sources of information are the various associations such as the BRITISH ASSOCIATION OF PSYCHOTHERAPISTS. Wendy Dryden's book *Individual Therapy in Britain* or Anthony Storr's *Art of Psychotherapy* can be found in public libraries.

Public Relations Consultant

At a Glance

Qualifications/Training	Recommended	*Income bracket*	Medium–High
Licence	No	*Town/Country*	Town
Experience/Springboard	Essential	*Travel*	Yes
Mid-career entry	Likely	*Exit sale*	Possible
Entry costs	£7,500	*Work at home*	Not recommended

Mix and match Yes. You could think about: Direct marketing agent, Events organiser, MP, Advertising Agent, Exhibition designer . . .

Enquiries Institute of Public Relations

Public relations is the practice of helping to build and sustain a good relationship between a company, an organisation or a brand (the client) and its public. In this case public means virtually everyone and anyone who directly or indirectly is used by the client to achieve an objective – usually profit. Public relations works alongside, but should not be confused with advertising and sales promotion. PR can be directed at the factory floor, at politicians, at the financial community, at businesses or directly at the consumer. It might involve lunch with a government minister; a press conference; a sponsored event; a company newsletter; a radio or television interview. All of these and more are simply a means to an end, and the end is the communication of the right message to the right audience. Small consultancies with good client lists are very attractive to large PR and advertising agencies – make a success of this and you could sell out for a massive amount in a few years' time.

There are numerous courses available for would be PR executives and the INSTITUTE OF PUBLIC RELATIONS will help you to locate them. These give a basic background. However, there's no substitute for learning at first hand and your initial step should be to join a large consultancy as a trainee. This is not always an easy task as most don't have a formal training programme. A traditional route is to join as a secretary and move on from there. For those with no secretarial experience the way in is through persistence and using and developing contacts. Some PR consultants come from marketing, journalism or the media. The essential qualities for anyone entering public relations are common sense, enthusiasm, good writing skills and the ability to get on with others.

When you feel you have sufficient knowledge and have decided on your area of operation, you can set up on your own. Different areas of

PR (financial, corporate and consumer) operate at different paces and in different markets so, for small consultancies particularly, specialisation is important. You can do some direct advertising or sales promotion as part of a PR campaign; some consultants specialise in getting sponsorship for sporting or cultural events, others in one area of consumer marketing, fashion, travel or health for example.

Set up costs include an office with a word processor and printer, fax, telex and a photocopier. You will need a good secretary/PA. Cash flow has two elements; your fees which are based on the amount of time you expect the job to take and calculated as a monthly charge payable in advance. Then there are out of pocket or operation expenses incurred by you on the client's behalf; these are usually charged a month in arrears with commission; alternatively you can try to get them in advance and avoid having to charge clients commission.

Good contacts with journalists, photographers, printers and graphic designers are essential. Get hold of a good media contact directory such as *PIMS Media Directory*. This lists the names of media contacts according to category – the same company also handle mailing and distribution of press releases if you need it. Above all you need clients. Public relations is a part of marketing so get yourself known to potential clients through adverts or, better still, good editorial in the trade publications such as *Campaign* and *Marketing Week*. Other clients come through the network and through word of mouth. (Get into the trade press for your particular specialisation, that way you'll catch new businesses as they set up and established ones as they need new PR.

Clients provide you with a brief which may or may not include their budget. From this you draw up a proposal for a recommended PR programme, including how much it's going to cost. At this stage you may be in competition with other agencies. Each job needs a slightly differently structured campaign. This may involve large scale media relations (press releases and launches) or very small scale wooing of opinion formers, eg members of a pressure group. It may also involve boosting your client's media profile by encouraging them to set up a spokesperson who can be contacted to give a trade reaction to relevant new legislation. On the whole campaigns can be planned well in advance and emergency PR is rare although clients may want extra work done quickly from time to time.

PR Week is suggested reading, also *Offensive Marketing*.

Publican

At a Glance

Qualifications/Training	Recommended	*Income bracket*	Low–High
Licence	Essential	*Town/Country*	Either
Experience/Springboard	Recommended	*Travel*	Local
Mid-career entry	Likely	*Exit sale*	Excellent
Entry costs	£15,000+++	*Work at home*	Yes

Mix and match   Possible.   You could think about: Caterer, Restaurateur, Wine-bar owner, Wine merchant, Hotel keeper, Caravan site owner, Holiday accommodation owner, Musician . . .

Enquiries   British Institute of Innkeeping

To run a pub, you will need a strong liver, sound business sense and physical stamina. It has the advantage of being a career you can move into later in life but it is a full time job and more, so be sure it's what you want before you take the plunge. There are two self-employed options: to buy your own pub (leasehold or freehold); or be a tenant, where you own the licence but the brewery owns the pub. It is a highly regulated area of work. You have to be licensed personally by the local magistrate every year as being fit and respectable; and to comply with all sorts of government regulations such as control of opening hours, age of your customers, hygiene etc.

You will need to know something about the business. Many breweries run short training courses for their tenants; there are useful short and part-time courses on the licensed trade run by FE Colleges and by the BRITISH INSTITUTE OF INNKEEPING, who also will give advice. It is then generally best to get some practical experience before investing, either behind a bar or as a relief manager learning the ropes at someone else's expense.

Tenancies are advertised in the *Morning Advertiser*, as are Public House Brokers who specialise in matching pubs with potential publicans. They will vet your qualifications, check that you have got the money and that you comply with any brewery requirements for that pub (most are predisposed to husband and wife teams unless, for example, they are keen to get a gay pub in the area). Once over that hurdle, the broker will introduce you to the pub and the brewery. Getting this far probably means you are on a small shortlist. The brewery will want some surety before finalising the contract. If you are after a freehold, you can also use Licensed Property Agents, both national and local, (see the property pages of the *Morning Advertiser*). If you want to run a 'real ale' pub, look in CAMRA's monthly publication *What's Brewing*.

A *tenancy* costs relatively little capital. You buy the fixtures and fittings (even if they're not to your taste or clapped out which is likely) and current stock (in a well run pub, about 10 days trade) from the outgoing tenant. The price is normally fixed by a broker. For a middling sized pub you might expect to pay £15,000 (brewery deposit, £3,000; fixture and fittings, £10,000; stock, £2,000). An annual rent to the brewery will be £10,000 and upwards (peppercorn rents are a thing of the past), depending on annual beer sales, called barrelage. Look for a pub selling at least 4 barrels a week; below that level you will find it difficult to make a living. The brewery will tie you to buying much of your stock from it exclusively – at least your beer – and this can have a major effect on your profits. This tie is being considered by the EEC and may be reduced sometime, but don't bank on it. The brewery will expect a cut on takings from the fruit machine (but not bed and breakfast, if you've the energy to organise that) and increasingly they want to dictate the style of operation. You will be expected to live in the pub.

Few *leaseholds* are available now. Without the freehold, you are still tied to the brewery to some extent – and the lease agreements can vary enormously. Some will try and insist you buy their beer – one lease even included a clause allowing the brewery to de-licence and develop the site if the whim took it! Most allow the leaseholder independence – take legal advice, read the lease carefully yourself and negotiate.

Freeholds or *Free Houses* are easier to find since the breweries stopped buying and wrecking every pub in sight and started selling pubs they didn't want. You don't have to convince the brewery that you are a suitable publican but you still need to convince the magistrates who award your licence. You will need to buy the building as well as the stock. The building will cost at least £150,000 in the south, less in the north depending on the size and turnover; the sky is the limit in Central London – pools winners only. If a brewery is selling a cheap pub, it probably means it's falling down or in the middle of nowhere – good if you like a quiet life but no good for business. Don't skimp on the structural survey and, if a lot needs doing, think carefully before planning to shut a pub for alterations; it has been fatal. You may be able to borrow the money from the bank or sometimes from the brewery – perhaps in exchange for selling its beer. Other than that, the pub is yours and there's no-one else you can blame if it doesn't work out.

Most pubs need something other than booze these days – games, music, fruit machines, cigarette machines, and almost always food. There's now a market for providing office services in some areas, if you stay open all day; or you can try pub theatre. You will need to think strategically about how to place your pub in your local market, eg whether to offer your locals chip butties or Sole Veronique, darts or the telly.

Running a pub is a way of life – 7 days a week, 364½ days a year (most shut on Christmas night). And now you may find yourself under pressure to extend your opening hours beyond the traditional. Holidays are difficult – a relief manager will mean total stock-taking before and after. 'There is no such thing as an honest stand-in; if they don't help themselves to the cash, they regard themselves as totally honest'. Conviviality is an asset but it doesn't pay to get too matey with your customers. At the end of the day, what counts is a sound business sense (good management of cash, stock and staff – and no 'slates'), stamina, patience to listen to the 'pub bore' and the ability to stay sober until closing time.

Read also *Caterer & Hotel Keeper*, *Pub Caterer*, *Publican* and *Licensee*.

Puppeteer

At a Glance

Qualifications/Training	Available	*Income bracket*	Low
Licence	No	*Town/Country*	Either
Experience/Springboard	Not essential	*Travel*	Constant
Mid-career entry	Yes	*Exit sale*	No
Entry costs	£2,000+	*Work at home*	No

Mix and match Yes. You could think about: Street entertainer, Cabaret performer, Actor, Stockbroker, Radio reporter and presenter . . .

Enquiries   Puppet Centre

Puppeteering covers a vast range of styles and methods; from formalised, traditional story telling where each life sized figure is manipulated by several operators using rods and strings; to shows where one person is responsible for the actions of several puppets. Whichever branch you choose, it isn't easy to make a living on puppetry alone. Although there are possibilites in alternative or community theatre funding for these is spasmodic (many local authorities have been forced to cut their arts funding and the few permanent puppet theatres there are don't provide a lot of work for many puppeteers). If you're prepared to persevere, perhaps combining puppetry with another part-time occupation, there is work in cabarets or at children's theatres, schools and (at weekends) parties and fetes.

There aren't many courses in puppetry; formal qualifications are less useful than the imagination to create stories or satire (eg Spitting Image) and a combination of acting ability and dexterity to present them with puppets. The PUPPET CENTRE can advise on any puppetry or puppet making courses you may be interested in, they also provide information on resources and funding. You can work for one of the permanent theatres such as NORWICH PUPPET THEATRE, LITTLE ANGEL or the POLKA THEATRE for initial experience, but most theatres are very small (about 2–5 performers), financially insecure and difficult to get into. You could try to join one of the big companies like PLAYBOARD or HANSON ORGANISATION, who do a lot of TV work. The best way of starting out is to get a show together and go for it. You'll need to be co-ordinated, versatile, adaptable and capable of living with an erratic source of income. If you're looking for cabaret work you'll probably have to travel on the circuit. Anyone working with children, especially children who are being entertained, should like them a lot. It helps if you can respond to their interruptions other than by telling them to shut up and sit down but you may have to discourage the noisier ones so that they don't spoil the show for the others. If you are going to specialise in children's entertainment it is useful to have experience of working, for instance, at a playscheme. Involving children in the show with singing or holding props is often successful and some puppeteers offer a full party package with games and other entertainment.

The best puppeteers are those who have a real knowledge of how children (and sometimes adults) respond to puppets. They must understand what themes and stories work best using puppets (go and see other shows and talk to the puppeteers and read some books on the subject); have a wide range of craft skills; can play one or more musical instruments; and above all have good dramatic skills. Puppetry is a difficult and demanding art but the rewards are good for those who set their standards high and are committed to producing good quality theatre for children.

You don't need a lot of money to start up. You can make your own puppets, props and theatre which needn't cost much. Add more expensive equipment, a cassette player for background music for example, as you expand. A car is vital and a telephone answering machine will ensure that you don't lose too much business by not being at home. You may want to have cards printed to hand out at engagements, drop through letter boxes or put in local shops.

A lot of work comes via word of mouth especially for children's party entertainment. To get started you'll need to be seen; some local communities arrange showcases for performers, these often take place in parks or community centres during the holidays; build up a network of other puppeteers and offer to stand in for them when they can't keep an engagement (useful too for if you can't make one of your own because you're ill – once you've got an engagement it's essential that you keep it one way or the other). Contact local schools for end of term puppet shows; the organisers of local fetes; managers of cabaret theatres and clubs. Once you're established you may be able to get some stand in or regular work on television shows like Spitting Image. An entry in the *Yellow Pages* costs about £130 or try your local *Thomson's Directory*. Other directories worth investigating are the *Directory of Puppeteers*, the *British Alternative Theatre Directory*, the *Special Needs Drama Directory* and the *British Performing Arts Yearbook*. Charges are up to you. Some regular cabaret spots have fixed fees for performers and these vary. Otherwise base your charges on what you need to make; take local competition into consideration and any extras that you provide. In London an hour's slot at a children's party costs about

£35–40, hourly rates may be less than that if you're providing a full party's worth of entertainment. You may also want to charge travel expenses on top of that.

As with any entertainment, the audience can be the greatest hazard; you'll earn from experience how to gauge the amount of audience participation that works best and how to adapt the show to various contingencies without losing control all together. Co-ordination is essential and you may occasionally drop something or forget your lines while you're concentrating on something else. Whatever area of puppetry you choose the chances are that you'll have some quiet patches which you can use for making and repairing puppets, looking for new sources of work and working on ideas for new shows. According to one, all puppeteers are prima donnas and, although you may not make a fortune, you'll certainly have plenty of chance to be in the limelight as a puppeteer.

Race Horse Owner

At a Glance			
Qualifications/Training	No	*Income bracket*	Nil–High
Licence	No	*Town/Country*	Country
Experience/Springboard	No	*Travel*	Yes
Mid-career entry	Likely	*Exit sale*	Possible
Entry costs	£10,000+	*Work at home*	No
Mix and match Yes. You could think about: Almost anything . . .			
Enquiries Jockey Club, Federation of British Bloodstock Agents			

Racehorse owners buy horses, pay for them to be trained, stabled and ridden by others, then pocket most of the prize money that their horses win in races. It's not so much a way of earning a living as a way of disposing of some of the money you've made at other things. Horses cost a lot to buy and keep and only about 20% of those that pass through the sales ever win a race. There is the potential for massive gains, however, if your stallion is a successful enough winner for you to put him out to stud, charging hefty fees from breeders. The capital value of stud horses can reach £15 million, or more.

Essential qualifications are money and either lots of knowledge of horses and trainers or access to it. Horses are first sold when they are

RACEHORSE OWNER

yearlings. There are annual sales of yearlings in September and October at Doncaster and Newmarket. Although you may be lucky and a sound enough judge to pick up a winner for less than £10,000, the average price of a yearling with winning potential is around £100,000 with some horses fetching 7 or 8 times that amount. On top of this you have to pay for stabling and training at around £150 per week. A successful year's winnings is around £30,000 although you stand to make a lot less or more (£300,000 for a Derby winner) than this. The better your horse's track record, the better its stud value. You can reduce your financial outlay (and potential gains or losses) by joining a race horse owning syndicate or partnership. This is known as owning a leg and allows people to buy shares in one or more horses. Trainers or syndicate managers set them up and will be able to help you if you want to find out more. If you want to set up your own syndicate, contact the JOCKEY CLUB.

Horses bred to be flat racers are either sprinters or stayers; sprinters are best at short distances, they need shorter time in training and are often ready to race the spring after you bought them. Stayers need more stamina and are usually at least 2 years old before they should be raced. Yearlings are valued on the strength of their pedigrees and unless you're an expert on bloodstock, it's worth seeking advice from a bloodstock agent, they usually charge 5% commission. Contact the FEDERATION OF BRITISH BLOODSTOCK AGENTS for help with this. Horses with form (ie those that have raced and have a track record of wins or failures) are valued according to this form. Finding a good trainer who is close enough to allow you to visit your horse regularly, is equally important; bloodstock agents can help here as well. The most fashionable trainers are at Newmarket and Lambourne but there are plenty of others especially in the south east and near racing courses. If your horse is successful it will race in the Classics (the Derby, the Queen Elizabeth Diamond Stakes etc). There are other regular races at Newmarket, Cheltenham, Chester, Windsor, Goodwood, Ascot . . . It's usually the trainer who decides whether or not your horse should race and, if so, which jockey should ride it. Jockeys race in your colours. There is little point in owning a racehorse if you don't like going to races or don't have the time to travel around the UK and Europe watching your horses race. And even less if you can't afford the occasional lean year while you wait to race a winner.

Read almost any novel by Dick Francis.

Radio Reporter/Presenter

At a Glance			
Qualifications/Training	Available	Income bracket	Low–Medium
Licence	No	Town/Country	Town
Experience/Springboard	Essential	Travel	Yes
Mid-career entry	Yes	Exit sale	No
Entry costs	£2,000+	Work at home	No

Mix and match   Yes.   You could think about: Journalist, UK correspondent for overseas media, Snail farmer, Dealer in antiques, Book publisher . . .

Enquiries   BBC, Local radio stations

As a radio reporter you create the package that is broadcast; that means collecting a lot of material (interviews, readings, music, linking script) on tape and editing it down to the length needed. A presenter sits in the studio while the material is being broadcast and provides linking scripts between each report. Presenters tend to be well established radio people; it takes a long time to build up a good enough reputation to be asked to present radio shows as a freelance.

Very few people make a living from freelance radio reporting and presenting alone. It's badly paid and there aren't many sources of work. However, if you're reasonably flexible, it can tie in quite well with other careers, for example there are radio reporters who are also magazine journalists, writers, conference organisers or public relations consultants. Although some very successful radio reporters manage to cope with having young families, it's a lot easier if you're free to travel at short notice, visit people at any hour of the day or put in long hours editing your material.

There are no essential formal qualifications. Most of what you need to know – how to edit tape, where to put your microphone when you're interviewing, how to use various machines – can be picked up easily; see the *Technique of Radio Production*. The BBC run courses for reporters to help them develop their skills and which you'll get free if you're doing work for them. A journalism degree or course is useful; in particular the post graduate degree in journalism at CARDIFF UNIVERSITY. This course includes a placement in your chosen specialisation – an excellent way of picking up some experience and contacts. Otherwise, hang around your local radio station and pester. You may be allowed to make tea and answer the telephone for a pittance but you'll be able to learn a lot from being there. Local stations may broadcast one of your reports if you don't ask them for anything in return. Once you've got some experience you've got some hope of getting a short term research contract on national radio; these are few and far between but are an excellent way of getting contacts and a track record. You may be able to use any other qualification you've got as a way of building a reputation for a specific type of programme eg, a zoology degree for wildlife programmes. To succeed as a radio reporter you must be creative; you don't necessarily have to have any particular accent although there seem to be slight fashions when one regional accent is particularly prevalent on the radio. You have to get on with people and be good at getting people to talk; to be curious enough to want to investigate whatever you're reporting on fully; flexible enough to be able to put in long hours at other people's convenience; confident and able to put up with inevitable criticism.

You need a car to carry recording equipment, and a telephone. You don't need to buy any equipment – you can borrow a tape recorder from the radio station, this has to be an extremely good machine or your reports won't broadcast well, (they cost about £1,000 new). You can edit at the studio using their editing machine to cut and splice the tape (a second hand machine costs about £100). The radio stations you're working for decide what you'll get paid; virtually nothing if you're working for local radio, not much more for others. You're paid per minute on the air regardless of the hours of background research and work that you put into that minute. BBC network radio rates start at around £40 for up to six minutes of straightforward interview; £120 for up to seven minutes of report. You can regard yourself as doing pretty well if you manage to make about £11,000 pa from freelance radio work. However if a programme repeats any of your material, you may get about 75% of the original fee – depending on your initial contract. There are spin offs from radio work; you may be able to get some voice over work for adverts or company training videos (you'll need contacts for these); to run or teach courses for people who want to be trained in how to speak on radio. You'll have to persevere to get work. Theoretically, you can operate from anywhere. Most work for freelance radio reporters comes from Radio Four (*Woman's Hour, You and Yours, Today*) who are based in London. Wherever you are you're bound to have to do some travelling to find interesting material and interviewees. It takes a long time to establish a reputation and get onto the grapevine. Get to know the programmes you think you may be able to work for so that you're clear about the sort of material the producer wants; length, might they want some music or dramatised readings rather than a straightforward interview? What sort of audience do they seem to aim at? In the early days you'll have to come up with all the ideas for reports. Later on you'll sometimes be approached by a producer as someone suitable for a particular report. Get to know producers, hang around radio stations as much as possible so that you're on the spot when a job comes up. Keep an eye open for new material, pressure groups and self help groups are useful; they often have press releases which are a good source of stories. Build up as wide a contact file as possible so that you can easily get hold of the sort of people you want for a particular programme.

Roughly speaking, about 50% of your time will be spent interviewing and travelling to interviews. It's usually more successful to talk on your interviewee's own territory (people are more relaxed and you may get some appropriate background noises). For the rest of the time you'll be doing background research, writing linking scripts and editing interviews. There are hazards – people who were garrulous on the telephone may dry up completely when you put a microphone in front of them; learn how to encourage people to speak – 'without putting words into your mouth . . .' is a useful phrase. You may fall foul of the law if, for example, one of your in-depth reports goes too far. If you're working for the BBC you'll have access to legal experts and advisers. On local radio you are less well protected, read *Essential Law for Journalists* and seek legal advice if you're in doubt. Legally a recorded interview is the property of you and the radio station but you may want to agree to making some cuts if the interviewee wants; occasionally people will say things that they regret later. Interviewing can be harrowing, you may be talking to people who have suffered a lot and must be able to remain detached enough not to burst into tears in mid question; have someone you can unload on – the producer of the programme is the most obvious and make sure that you don't leave your interviewee in a state of distress – it's worth getting some counselling skills to help with this.

Making a radio report is very much a solo effort – it can be immensely satisfying. You are, however, very much at others' convenience – producers, the people you want to interview, or you may have trouble getting off on holiday or having a lot of time to yourself. The time you have for each assignment varies tremendously – sometimes you may be commissioned to do an item weeks in advance, at other times you'll be expected to turn the piece round within a day. Generally, the faster you can work without compromising accuracy or standards the more cost effective it is. Whatever happens, you can never miss a deadline!

Record Company Owner

At a Glance

Qualifications/Training	No	*Income bracket*	Low–High
Licence	No	*Town/Country*	Town
Experience/Springboard	Recommended	*Travel*	Local
Mid-career entry	Possible	*Exit sale*	Good
Entry costs	£15,000++	*Work at home*	Possible
Mix and match	Essential to start. You could think about: Mini-cab driver, Bartender, Market research interviewer . . .		
Enquiries	Record shops, recording studios, musicians		

This is an overcrowded, tough and unglamorous job. 'You must be really stupid to do what I did' said Ted Perry of Hyperion, 'but you also need real knowledge and love of music'. It involves owning and taking financial responsibility for a record label. You decide the content of the record, organise the engagement of artists, recording studios, engineers and arrange distribution of the product. You need good business sense; an ability to manipulate and co-ordinate people and their skills to create a special kind of record; enthusiasm, diplomacy, an accurate prediction of what people will buy and enjoy, and lots of luck. You must be highly motivated to succeed, have faith in your own judgment, be sociable and have endless energy. Don't leave your current employment until you have found another where you can learn the mechanics of selling records. Get a job in a leading record shop, read every kind of catalogue you can find, go to lots of concerts and read about composers in the public library. Learn about public relations, printing, pressing records, distribution. Start saving until you have about £15,000; you will need another job for the first few years, eg driving a minicab at night, and a friendly accountant or someone to handle your books.

Find a small room with a typewriter, telephone and answerphone, then start setting up a record. You will need £5,000 to book a studio and artists, £2,000 to cover costs of recording, printing sleeves etc and £5,000 for a minimum run of compact discs. Rigid discs are dying out since the advent of CDs, and the cost of making discs has doubled.

The work is obsessive and you can find yourself working 18 hours every day – very bad for your social and family life. It's exciting, full of variety and you meet interesting people, but if you're inclined to worry, don't do it: the risks are high and you will make no profit for the first 3 years. If you're successful, the sky's the limit financially.

Recording Studio Owner

At a Glance

Qualifications/Training	Recommended	*Income bracket*	Low–Medium
Licence	No	*Town/Country*	Town
Experience/Springboard	Recommended	*Travel*	Some
Mid-career entry	Unlikely	*Exit sale*	Yes
Entry costs	Highly variable	*Work at home*	Possible

Mix and match Essential to start. You could think about: Record company owner, Disco owner, Electrician, Mini-cab driver, Bartender . . .

Enquiries Association of Professional Recording Studios

This is someone who owns their own recording studio; who not only makes the equipment work but also has the musical expertise to help the musicians create a good artistic product. To be a good recording engineer it is useful but not essential to have BMus from either SURREY UNIVERSITY or the UNIVERSITY OF EAST ANGLIA. You do need a real knowledge of electronics (how the equipment works so you can use it properly and repair it) and sound general knowledge about all types of music.

You need a discriminating ear, a calm personality to deal with stressed musicians, stamina for the very long hours, tact, organisational skills and the ability to keep your accounts properly (evening classes help). It's best to be a gofer in a studio for 2 years so that you learn to work under pressure, gain experience and make contacts. To set up on your own, you will need a lot of luck and ideally about £500,000 to buy a studio or mobile van containing your equipment; you can make one yourself in a sound-proofed garage but you will need planning permission. You can work from home if others can stand the noise and nuisance of people tramping in and out at all times of the day and night. The golden rule is to spend as much as you can on really good equipment; you will need savings or another job for the first few years as there will be little income.

Advertise in the pop and classical press (*New Musical Express, Classical Music* etc), make contact with publishers and advertising companies, national and local. Record local choir(s) and orchestra(s), make demo tapes for aspiring pop groups or young classical musicians.

This job is not glamorous. The hours are appalling: you may have to record/edit for up to 24 hours non-stop. You shouldn't expect to earn more than £15,000 to £20,000 pa. The advantages are endless variety in the work and the sense of enjoyment of helping in an artistic enterprise. It is both possible and necessary to have some other form of employment, eg teaching your skills or using them in other ways. There are few coloured or female recording engineers. You will have to travel to record classical music, but not to pop recordings. The only organisation you need to join is the ASSOCIATION OF PROFESSIONAL RECORDING STUDIOS (APRS). You will need to update your equipment periodically. Consult *Studio Sound and Broadcast Engineering* or *Sound Engineer and Producer*.

Reflexologist

At a Glance

Qualifications/Training	Necessary	Income bracket	Medium
Licence	No	Town/Country	Town
Experience/Springboard	No	Travel	Local, perhaps
Mid-career entry	Yes	Exit sale	No
Entry costs	£1,000	Work at home	Possible

Mix and match   Limited.   You could think about: Greyhound trainer, Musical instrument repairer, Novelist . . .

Enquiries   College of Reflexology

Reflexology works on the principle that if certain specific points on the feet or hands are pressed in a certain way, this pressure creates a reflex action in another part of the body, stimulating that part to improve its functioning. Thus reflexology facilitates the body to use its own resources to heal itself.

No formal academic qualifications are needed to enter the COLLEGE OF REFLEXOLOGY. To be really well qualified, students must attend weekend courses over a period of 3–5 years at a total cost of £500. This covers human physiology and anatomy, and how to recognise what diseases must be referred to conventional medical practitioners. Reflexologists cannot diagnose or prescribe drugs. After the course, students become members of the College of Reflexology, the highest qualifications being Fellow and Teacher. You can do the course at any age – in your seventies if you will.

You need to be interested in people and be naturally dextrous. Career prospects are limitless and the demand far exceeds the number of qualified people. Reflexologists often have patients with chronic degenerative disease which conventional medicine cannot improve further.

Most students begin their own private practice within a year of starting training but are always supervised by their teachers. By the time they are qualified they will have enough patients but will continue to consult with other reflexologists on difficult cases. Make sure you are insured first. It's best to have a consulting room on the ground floor, near public transport, either at home or in a clinic shared with other complementary medics. Depending on the part of the country you live in, the fee for a ½ hr session can be £4–5. For an experienced reflexologist in London, the average is £20 an hour and £45 for a 'call out' visit to a patient.

The only equipment you need is a comfortable reclining chair for the patient, a stool for the practitioner (second hand cost about £50), telephone, answerphone, filing cabinet, running hot and cold water and a loo. A receptionist is essential if you are working a long day. It's normal to treat patients before or after work and in the lunch hour so surgery times are flexible; this means the job can impinge on your private life. The advantages are seeing people improve and learning new techniques.

Useful reading includes *Reflexology*, *Advanced Reflexology* and *Here's Health* magazine.

Repetiteur/Accompanist/Coach

At a Glance

Qualifications/Training	Essential	*Income bracket*	Low
Licence	Union membership	*Town/Country*	Town
Experience/Springboard	No	*Travel*	Yes
Mid-career entry	Highly unlikely	*Exit sale*	No
Entry costs	£2,000+	*Work at home*	No

Mix and match   Yes.   You could think about: Music teacher, Music copyist, Conductor, Mini-cab driver . . .

Enquiries   Musicians' Union, Incorporated Society of Musicians, BBC, Royal Society of Musicians

An accompanist accompanies other musicians by playing the piano; teaching singers their music by coaching them, or in an opera company they are known as repetiteurs or coaches. It is important to go to music college or university, preferably both, as high musical and technical standards, and good contact with your peers and in the profession, are essential. You should have excellent sight-reading, transposition and a basic knowledge of voice production and instrument playing, and be able to play all kinds of keyboard instruments in the correct style, from early music to modern jazz and pop.

You must possess an excellent ear, be sensitive and tactful with other artistes, and when accompanying them be prepared to adapt your own musical ideas in favour of theirs. An outstanding accompanist should be able to arrange music, speak foreign languages and empathise with the soloist's thoughts and feelings.

Before starting it is imperative that you join the MUSICIANS' UNION; if you are doing chamber music, the INCORPORATED SOCIETY OF MUSICIANS is useful as it has a good contract, and can provide legal back-up. It runs the Young Artists' series at the Wigmore Hall which may help gain favourable notices in the national press. Standing in for friends playing the musical shows, accompanying choirs or ballet classes, deputising in an orchestra, coaching or accompanying young singers for competitions, auditions and recitals are all ways to gain work. It is possible to audition for the BBC accompanists' list, or to apply for work as a repetiteur in an opera company. Also contact the ROYAL SOCIETY OF MUSICIANS.

Your income will be very low to start with and you will need either to teach, copy/arrange music, or develop another skill, as this is a highly competitive career. Luck and availability have a lot to do with success so a telephone and answering machine/service are vital. There tends to be a bias towards the young male although there are a few successful females. The need to travel constantly, both in the UK and abroad, may deter those with families. To start with, you only need a piano tuned to concert pitch, and a room in which you can practise all day without the neighbours objecting. Later on you will need a car. Stamina is needed to practise every day and, when you can afford your own synthesiser or harpsichord, to move that about.

To be taken on to the books of a concert agency is useful for getting work, but to be known by orchestral fixers and other musicians is just as good. Read the *Unashamed Accompanist*.

The music profession is shrinking owing to government cuts and the disappearance of commercial film and television jingles; the British have outpriced everyone in the world market. The introduction of the 'Sampler' synthesiser (which reproduces the sound of all instruments perfectly) does not bode well for the future.

Restaurateur

At a Glance

Qualifications/Training	Recommended	Income bracket	Low–High
Licence	Alcohol – yes	Town/Country	Usually town
Experience/Springboard	Recommended	Travel	Local
Mid-career entry	Likely	Exit sale	Excellent
Entry costs	£20,000+++	Work at home	No

Mix and match Possible. You could think about: Caterer, Winebar owner, Publican, Hotel keeper, Wine merchant, Winegrower, Franchisee . . .

Enquiries Hotel and Catering Training Board, British Hotel Restaurants and Caterers' Association

Sandwich bar or 3 star Michelin, hamburger joint or Chinese restaurant, there are as many different styles of catering operation as there are people running them. Fifty new ones open every month in London alone. Lots go bust quite quickly (50% of those opened in 1985 had ceased trading by the end of 1987). Success depends on a mixture of good food, atmosphere, planning and successful cash flow. Decide on a style that suits you; do you want just to make a living or do you search for self-expression, to indulge in fantasy, to create a lifestyle? Why should customers visit you? Once you move beyond sandwich bars and fast food joints, clients are also looking for entertainment, novelty, ambiance or simply want to impress their guests. Catering is part of show biz ('20% food, 40% atmosphere and 40% bullshit'). If your customers are only with you because they're hungry, you have to be well placed for passing trade eg town centre, next to an office block or factory. On the other hand clients will travel for something new and individual.

Get experience, if possible, by working in a show similar to what you have in mind. Cooks can hone up their skills at various courses eg LEITHS or CORDON BLEU. Most polytechnics run HND courses but these are mainly for people who want to be employed and are rather slow moving but the HOTEL AND CATERING TRAINING BOARD runs courses for people wanting to open their own restaurant. At the upper end of the scale, many years of training and experience are needed as well as large capital, lower down the scale, motivation counts for a lot, many restaurants are successfully run by very young people, particularly outside London.

As well as a cook, you need someone for the front with sound business sense and the tact and patience to deal with the general public. Swot up on hygiene, the local Environmental Health Officer will take a keen interest in your activities. Health regulations allow considerable latitude in interpretation and EHOs can often appear opinionated and even capricious; even so it's best to have a good working relationship with them. Consult them early in any plans for alterations to kitchens and bars. You will also have the attentions of the fire officer and consumer protection officer from time to time and, if licensed, magistrates and police. Nowadays there is little obstruction to granting Restaurant Licences which permit the sale of alcohol only with food. The BRITISH HOTEL, RESTAURANTS AND CATERERS' ASSOCIATION gives expert advice on catering law, contracts, licensing, hygiene, fire precautions, planning, insurance etc. Be prepared for contradictory advice; what pleases one lot won't necessarily satisfy them all.

Set up costs include premises either rented or owned. Look for low overheads, prestigious surroundings are for the big boys. It's easy to start catering in a pub; if you buy an existing operation, you avoid planning problems for change of use (but find out why it was for sale). You'll also need equipment for the kitchen, furniture for the front and an opening stock of cooking supplies, wine, drinks etc. It helps if you've got contacts in the trade who'll give credit for this. Otherwise raise a bank loan and a mortgage for the premises (you'll need some collateral for that – your own house for example). It's worth paying for service and maintenance contracts for your equipment so that you are guaranteed quick service should anything go wrong. Unless your operation is very small, you'll need to employ some help in the kitchen and with waiting and cleaning. Profit margins need to be quite high; a common formula is – materials × 3 + VAT, giving 66% gross on selling. But percentages don't always work satisfactorily and many operators work on a cash mark-up. Thus, decide on the cash profit needed, and the formula becomes – materials + cash amount + VAT. This has the effect of making cheap dishes relatively more expensive and expensive dishes, less so, which can be a good marketing ploy.

Making your own restaurant succeed is hard work and involves long hours, much more than meets the eye – one ex-Savoy restaurant manager returned to the Savoy after trying to go it alone for a while. You're dependent on having a reliable staff and it may take time to establish one – they won't necessarily be as committed to your operation as you are. Husband and wife teams often work well, but remember, fatigue is endemic and you could find domestic fracas on the menu.

Roofer

At a Glance

Qualifications/Training	Recommended	Income bracket	Low
Licence	No	Town/Country	Either
Experience/Springboard	Recommended	Travel	Local
Mid-career entry	Possible	Exit sale	Possible
Entry costs	£2,000	Work at home	No

Mix and match   Possible.   You could think about: Plumber, Thatcher, Man with a van, Tree surgeon . . .
Enquiries   Construction Industry Training Board

Roofers may be sub-contracted by builders, or find work repairing roofs, working directly for private householders.

Training is usually 'on-the-job', working on building sites or working for a small contractor. The best qualification is plenty of experience of the different problems involved. There are also CITB (CONSTRUCTION INDUSTRY TRAINING BOARD) courses.

Most roofers specialise in a particular type of roofing; felt (for flat roofs), tiling or slate. So if you live in an area with a lot of old slate roofs, it is obviously sensible to specialise in this field.

Promote yourself by putting an entry in the Yellow Pages, and by advertising in local papers. Most people agree that the best way to find a reliable roofer is through personal recommendation: so bear this in mind with every job you do – if the roof remains watertight, and your fees were not exorbitant, home owners will recommend you to others. It is also worth keeping in touch with local building firms, so that you can offer your services when new sites are developed.

You will need a bit of capital to buy a van, ladders and tools, but you can often get an advance on the work to cover materials. You may also find that you need to employ an assistant to help fetch and carry.

You must be fit and have a head for heights. Working hours will depend on the weather, as well as your energy. Roofing work must be done in daylight; but in the evenings you will often have to visit private houses to do estimates, and keep up with paperwork.

As a self-employed roofer you can expect to earn several times the £100 per week, which is the minimum for your colleagues in employment.

Small contractors often do other work as well as roofing: for example houses with leaking roofs may also have defective guttering, crumbling drains and badly deteriorated pointing, so it may be worth learning these jobs as well, so that you can offer a complete package.

Saddler/Leatherworker

At a Glance

Qualifications/Training	Recommended	Income bracket	Low–Medium
Licence	No	Town/Country	Either
Experience/Springboard	Recommended	Travel	Local
Mid-career entry	Possible	Exit sale	Unlikely
Entry costs	£2,000+	Work at home	Yes

Mix and match Yes. You could think about: Fashion shoe maker, Fashion clothes designer, Farrier/blacksmith, Taxidermist . . .

Enquiries Saddlers Company, British Leather Confederation

A lot of saddles on the market are cheap imports. As a British saddle maker, your commissions will come from people who want to have a saddle made to fit a particular horse; you'll also have some repairs and alterations. This is a small market and many saddle makers have to combine saddlery with making other leather goods or selling riding equipment; others go in for livery, providing stabling for and at times looking after other people's horses. You can set up a workshop in the country or in town. The number of riding stables is increasing all over the country and more horses are owned now than were before World War I.

LEATHERWORK

You can learn how to make saddles through a course in leatherwork at, for example, CORDWAINERS TECHNICAL COLLEGE. Unless you are very good, you will then need work experience with a small company. Alternatively you can serve an apprenticeship with a master saddler (contact the SADDLERS COMPANY for further details). The BRITISH LEATHER CONFEDERATION runs courses in selling, judging leather quality etc. You need technical and design expertise for leatherworking together with business acumen for your own business. Most of the work is done by hand so you'll need strong fingers.

For saddlery, you need a very small shop with enough space for a heavy grade sewing machine, a bench, a 'horse' or two to hold the finished saddles and somewhere to store leather. You may also want attached shop premises if you're going to sell other riding equipment. Excluding rent/mortgage for premises this will cost about £2,000. For general leatherwork you'll need to spend a bit more on a sewing machine (£800 second hand, £1,000–1,500 new); a skiving machine for trimming the edges (£700–800 second hand, £1,200 new); and a press (£1,000–2,000). These can be rented or bought through *Fashion Extras* or *Shoe and Leather News*. Saddles sell for about £180–500 each, averaging around £300.

You can get your first clients by going around local riding stables, offering to repair broken saddles and tack. Small leather goods such as purses, wallets, luggage, handbags and belts can be sold to small shops and boutiques. Exclusive stores may be interested in commissioning you to provide them with their own line of belts or filofaxes. You can seek more clients by taking samples of your work around potentially interested shops. There is also a big market for leather clothing.

The main trade exhibition is the International Leathergoods Exhibition in Birmingham in February.

Sailing School Owner

At a Glance

Qualifications/Training	Yes	*Income bracket*	Low–Medium
Licence	RYA	*Town/Country*	Either
Experience/Springboard	No	*Travel*	No
Mid-career entry	Likely	*Exit sale*	Yes
Entry costs	£8,000+	*Work at home*	No

Mix and match Yes. You could think about: Holiday accommodation owner, Windsurfing school owner, Shopkeeper, Garlic farmer, Potter . . .

Enquiries Royal Yachting Association

This is something that you can start on a small scale, with just one boat, and build up until you have several boats.

You'll have to pass the ROYAL YACHTING ASSOCIATION'S (RYA) yacht master exams before you can teach. The RYA has a list of training establishments which it has approved in conjunction with the Department of Trade and Industry. Most people who go in for running a sailing school have been interested in sailing for a long time; but you need to be good at teaching as well as being good at sailing.

Your most expensive initial outlay is for the boat; you'll also need life jackets and distress flares, charts and navigating equipment. You'll need some sort of office, with a telephone, from which to operate and take bookings. You'll need to arrange to have access to water, either on the sea or an inland lake.

You can run daily, weekly or fortnightly courses, and can combine teaching with day trips and cruises. If your school is in a holiday resort, you will increase your trade when the tourists arrive. Safety is very important at sea and your boats have to be checked regularly for seaworthiness, and quite a lot of time will be spent in the winter on maintenance and repairs.

You can advertise in *Yachting*, *Yachts and Yachting* or *Practical Boat Owner*.

Sales Agent

At a Glance

Qualifications/Training	No	Income bracket	Low–High
Licence	No	Town/Country	Either
Experience/Springboard	Essential	Travel	Essential
Mid-career entry	Yes	Exit sale	Possible
Entry costs	£3,000	Work at home	Partly

Mix and match   Possible.   You could think about: Direct marketing agent, List broker, Photographer, Motorcycle racer . . .

Enquiries   Sales agents

Sales agents, reps or representatives, sell their clients' products to retail outlets, by visiting them and taking orders. The client arranges delivery, payment and, almost always, debt collection. Sales agents work for commission on behalf of the manufacturers and producers of almost anything; for example, books, toys, cigarettes, whisky, chocolate, cleaning stuff and sex aids. Sometimes freelance sales agents handle all the sales for smaller clients; otherwise they may be used to promote a particular product or range or to reach remote places that don't fall within the client's usual sales area. Sometimes they can join 'drive teams' and work for a set time promoting one (usually new) product with demonstrations and leaflets. Drive teams are usually paid a set fee based on the services that they are providing and the amount of time it takes them.

There aren't any formal qualifications but you'll need selling experience; firstly so that you have some idea of what's involved in selling whatever it is you're selling, and, secondly, so that you have some proof of selling ability for potential clients. The best experience is in the sales team of a company in the field that you're going into or for another agency (one that is expanding or taking on extra help over a busy time). You'll usually be trained by either of these. Selling encyclopaedias, brushes etc is another way of finding out what it's like travelling and selling, even though, of course, in these cases you're selling directly to the customer rather than to a shop. Successful sales agents have to inspire their clients' and customers' confidence and trust. You have to put up with long hours in a car and with the possibility of being phoned at unreasonable times by demanding clients who are used to employing a sales force who will do exactly what it's told; although you need to give satisfactory service to your clients, you don't have to agree to all their requests.

To set up you need a car and if you can't arrange to have somebody there to answer your phone a telephone answering machine (preferably one that will play back your messages to you when you phone in during the day). You don't need to buy any stock, clients supply samples and specifications. You're paid commission on net invoice so you lose out if customers return goods to your client. Be prepared for about 6 months with very little income; some companies have very slow accounts departments and it's worth having a contract with them laying down how often you are to be paid (monthly, quarterly, etc) otherwise you may have to wait for years with no easy legal recourse. In any case, many orders are taken several months before the product is available which adds to the time you have to wait for payment. Another useful contract clause is one about termination. This avoids the possibility of your losing clients over night because they've decided to set up their own sales force or have been bought by somebody else. Your clients will tell you what they want you to sell; this may sometimes mean taking on products that you or your customers don't like and you have to decide whether or not that's worthwhile.

You can find clients through contacts and your experience in the trade. More come through word of mouth and you'll develop a network of regular customers in the same way. You look for more all the time. Some products are suitable for outlets other than the ones you usually use and any additional sales that you make earn more money. You can also find clients through adverts, trade shows and local magazines. Read *Campaign*. Before visiting a potential client, make sure that you know a lot about them (this is good interview technique) and you also need to know that they're reliable, liquid etc before you want to represent them. Although sales agents usually have several clients, they tend to stick to one area of products so that they can represent most of their clients at each customer they visit. It's better and fairer, however, not to take on two products that are in direct competition. If you expand, you may want to take on other agents, you can recruit these through contacts in the trade, from reps you know who want a change or by taking on and training novices. You can join in partnership with others, each taking a territory and ensuring national distribution.

It can be a 24 hour job. Most days you're on the road, visiting all the customers in one area; they all need to be regularly visited and occasional lunches, drinks etc can be useful. You may well be the customer's most direct contact with the manufacturer and so will have at least to act as go-between with some of their problems if you can't sort them out yourself. On top of this there is the necessary paperwork and follow up, making sure that orders reach your clients and that appropriate action is taken.

Salmon Farmer

At a Glance

Qualifications/Training	Necessary	*Income bracket*	Low–Medium
Licence	No	*Town/Country*	Country
Experience/Springboard	Essential	*Travel*	No
Mid-career entry	Good	*Exit sale*	Yes
Entry costs	£150,000	*Work at home*	Yes

Mix and match   Yes.   You could think about: Fish curer and smoker, Sailing school owner, Holiday accommodation owner, Novelist . . .

Enquiries   National Farmers Union, Scottish Salmon Growers Association, Sea Fish Industry Authority

This is someone who breeds, grows and markets salmon. It is essential to attend a specialist one or two year course in fish farming at INVERNESS COLLEGE or the AGRICULTURAL COLLEGE at either Dumfries or Sparsholt in Hampshire. At least 2 or 3 years experience working on different farms is important.

As wild fish become scarce, there are good prospects for the fish farmer. You must thoroughly learn the business, and particularly the marketing side, of farming before going alone. When you do, you will succeed if you either stay small or become very very large. You will need a really good accountant. There is no need to join a union although the fish farming committee of the NATIONAL FARMERS UNION can be helpful.

You will start by making somewhere between nothing and £5,000; but a successful one-man business will make £10,000–12,000 a year. You need a total of £150,000 working capital – for the site, a car, a shed with a phone in it, £50,000–60,000 for 20 floating cages to hold the fish, a motor boat and electric pick-up truck and the smelts (young salmon). The Crown lease rights for use of the foreshore cost about £2,500 per annum; your site should be in an estuary for salmon so you have salt and fresh water.

SALMON FARMER

You need to be practical and able to swim. It is a good life if you dislike fixed hours but it is difficult to get away. There should always be a babysitter to feed the fish every day and guard them against thieves, storms, ice, ravenous seals and cormorants. As well as feeding the fish, you must remove any that are dead and establish the cause of death; look for damage or pests; take out the smaller fish and put into a separate pen; and maintain the automatic feeders. You also have to kill those ready for market, gut and pack in ice and send off to market or customers. This can be made easier by communal marketing with other farmers for freezer transport.

No travelling is necessary except to attend the annual fish farm conference, keep up to date with equipment and visit customers. There are always new machines to count and grade fish. Useful organisations are SCOTTISH SALMON GROWERS ASSOCIATION and the SEA FISH INDUSTRY AUTHORITY (useful to get onto their mailing list). Read the *Sea Food International* magazine.

Scriptwriter

At a Glance

Qualifications/Training	No	*Income bracket*	Low–High
Licence	No	*Town/Country*	Either
Experience/Springboard	Work in TV	*Travel*	No
Mid-career entry	Yes	*Exit sale*	No
Entry costs	£10+	*Work at home*	Yes

Mix and match   Essential, to start.   You could think about: Actor, Novelist, Book editor, Film director, Market research interviewer, Bartender, Mini-cab driver . . .

Enquiries   Writers' Guild

Not an easy thing to get into, but if you make it, there are 3 main areas: complete one-off plays written for TV; long running series for which you may write one or more episodes; and serialisations of novels and stories. There is some overlap between these but TV companies tend to have different departments for different areas and are more likely to accept a script that will fit neatly into one of these. There's a lot of re-writing and working of scripts for TV but this has been made far easier with the advent of word processors.

Knowledge of how TV works is essential. You need to be able to set scenes and suggest shots which means knowing about shooting both on location and in front of a live audience as well as having a vague understanding of the techniques involved. Although you don't have many of the physical restrictions of writing for the stage, you will have to contend with a fairly unadventurous market. Learning how to write for TV is a bit like learning a new language. Reading a TV script helps to see what is involved but they are not often published – however, see *Adventures in the Screen Trade*. Once you've got a foot in the door, you can get valuable experience of the discipline of TV writing by working on the scriptwriting team of a long running soap opera – this is not easy to get into though, producers don't want to take risks and tend to use only writers they know something about.

Any work you can do at a TV company, from scene-shifting to acting, is useful. It will put you in contact with the script editors and producers who decide what is going to be produced. On the whole, people are pretty cautious about what goes on to TV and the bigger the name, and therefore influence, the more useful the contact. If you can't get the producer's or script editor's ear, try a well known actor who may like one of the roles in your script enough to push for its being produced.

Whatever you do, find an agent (try *Contacts* if you don't know any) who can advise and cope with the complexities of TV writers' contracts; these include international rights, syndication rights, repeat fees (100% of original fee), royalties and rights to write subsequent episodes of series. Agents can also tell you about which TV companies are worth trying. Once you've had a script produced you can join the WRITERS' GUILD. Radio is one of the greatest users of new writers' work and, although the cross over from radio to TV scriptwriting is difficult, it can be done. Radio is a good starting point for anyone who wants to derive an income from writing (eg Alan Ayckbourn). Set up costs are virtually nil, but it will take a long time to derive income from TV scriptwriting and you'll need another source of income in the meantime. Scripts can take from 6 months to 10 years from conception to broadcast – average probably 2 years. You are paid 50% on commission (whether for your own idea or for something you have been commissioned to do) and the rest on acceptance (about 2–3 months later by the time you have reworked the script to the necessary style and length and the company have decided that they definitely want it).

Present your ideas attractively and succinctly. Producers don't have much time for reading but a straightforward precis will be rather dry. Illustrate with quotations, background information, even pictures if it helps to capture the flavour of your idea. If you want to serialise a novel, you are well advised to buy the rights to it, subsequent scriptwriting is then a case of adapting the existing text. Presentation of your ideas is also important when you have been approached to write an episode for a series. Some scriptwriters find it helpful to work with a partner with whom they can thrash out ideas and who can help to produce an acceptable and polished script. No play exists until it has been produced. A lot of other people are involved in interpreting the script and you may find that the final broadcast doesn't appear as you expect.

Sculptor

At a Glance

Qualifications/Training	Essential	Income bracket	Low–High
Licence	No	Town/Country	Either
Experience/Springboard	Useful	Travel	No
Mid-career entry	Unlikely	Exit sale	No
Entry costs	£1,000++	Work at home	Possible

Mix and match   Good.   You could think about: Photographer, Caterer, Man with a van, Dealer in antiques . . .

Enquiries   Art colleges, Sculptors

The aim of the sculptor is pure art. Any money you make will either be from commissions (eg busts for private clients; perhaps large pieces for businesses) or by finding a buyer for non-commissioned work. You can choose to sculpt from almost anthing including fibreglass, terracotta, wood, stone and cast metal.

You'll have to be artistic and creative but also to know how to handle your medium, how it reacts to different treatments and what you can do with it. Most sculptors take a degree or diploma course at art college; see the *Student Book*. This is essential not only in order to learn the techniques but to have access to the prohibitively expensive materials/ foundries etc without which you will not be able to experiment. Working at a casting foundry for a while after your course is useful experience and you may pick up good contacts.

Sculptors need to derive a great deal of satisfaction from sculpting and not to mind periods of poverty. The enterprise allowance scheme is a must; mixing and matching is important and temporary work of any kind useful until you've got enough work to show for sale.

When you're setting up your studio, you need a space big enough to house the size of sculpture you are going for, also electricity and maybe heating. You could operate in an old barn or shed. If you're using fibreglass, you'll need to have special ventilation because the fumes are dangerous. You will have to spend money to get going. The more you can spend on publicity, the better. It's worth paying hundreds of pounds for some decent photographs of your work if you can't use a photographer friend from college. Most galleries like to have slides of your work so you need to get lots of duplicates of the same slide. You'll also have to pay for materials long before you get paid for the finished work; it's worth becoming acquainted with cheap processes like welding or woodcarving. Making a living comes more quickly and cash flow problems are less if you specialise in small pieces, which need less financial outlay on materials, can be churned out more quickly and, on the whole, have a larger market. It will cost £500 for a life size head in bronze at a foundry; it will also take you a minimum of 10 hours to model a portrait head out of clay or wax before you take it to the foundry. That means you have to charge at least £600 for each head in bronze.

Publicity is important. A good art college makes sure the right people in the art world are invited to your degree show. You may be able to pick up some orders there. Look out for competitions in the local and national press. The more contacts you have, the better, especially art gallery contacts, but you might find that your work has to sit around for some time before it finds a buyer. Just keep sending out slides to galleries, businesses and agents. The biggest money comes from modern art collectors but classical sculptures like life-sized portrait heads are the main work for which you get commissions. There is also an expanding market in garden sculpture, which has its more technical problems – it must be waterproof.

To keep up with what's going on in the art world, read *Artists News Letter* and *Arts Review*.

Sex Therapist

At a Glance

Qualifications/Training	Necessary	*Income bracket*	Low–High
Licence	No	*Town/Country*	Town
Experience/Springboard	No	*Travel*	No
Mid-career entry	Recommended	*Exit sale*	No
Entry costs	£400	*Work at home*	Yes

Mix and match Yes. You could think about: Doctor, Journalist, Bespoke furniture maker . . .

Enquiries Medical schools

No job in the world is right for everyone – this one is less right than most. Sex therapists counsel people to help them overcome sexual problems or disfunctions that can result from physical, mental or emotional causes or from pure ignorance. To be taken seriously – especially by the medical profession and the NHS – you have to take one of the 3 or 4 recognised courses in Britain, eg the medical schools at

Edinburgh or London University (normally part-time). If you don't already have a medical or counselling background it may take some work to persuade them of your bona fides. You need a broad knowledge of anatomy and of everything that might affect sexuality from hormone production to behavioural psychology. Sex therapists need to be able to deal with other people's problems, this means having self confidence and sanity. Deeply held religious or moral principles of acceptable sexual practice don't help.

You'll need to have suitable premises, on your own or as part of a group practice with other medical specialists. Some of your clients may prefer home visits. You can charge from about £10 per hour to about £100 (if you're on Harley Street). Most people who try to live exclusively from ST fail – not least because of people's reluctance to admit to sexual shortcomings and inadequacies.

Most work comes through contacts and networks. Visit local doctors and try to get referrals from them. This can be difficult because doctors tend to be happier advising marriage guidance rather than assistance with specifically sexual problems; this means that there is a great need for your services if you can manage to tap it. Advertising isn't very successful, it goes against the medical tradition and so people tend to be suspicious of those who do.

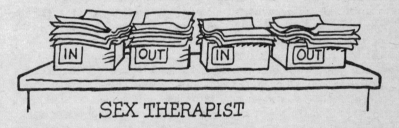

SEX THERAPIST

Like VAT men or prison officers, you don't always want to tell people at parties what you do. Your own relationships can suffer – even the most cool partner will tend to overreact to your casual comments about your sex life and you may get very involved with your subject and your clients (it's difficult not to take work home with you). Your clients may resent having to come to you and won't always thank you for the help that you've given them. However it can be very fulfilling because the results are often quick; you can see someone for 4 hours and clear up a problem they've had for 15 years – 'so that's what a clitoris is'. Once you know what you're talking about most problems are easy to solve.

Shepherd/Shepherdess

At a Glance

Qualifications/Training	Useful	*Income bracket*	Low
Licence	No	*Town/Country*	Country
Experience/Springboard	Essential	*Travel*	Between jobs
Mid-career entry	Possible	*Exit sale*	No
Entry costs	£2,000	*Work at home*	No

Mix and match   Yes.   You could think about: Tree surgeon, Man with a van, Book editor, Holiday accommodation owner . . .

Enquiries   National Sheep Association, National Farmers' Union

This is someone involved in lambing, foster mothering, clipping and dipping sheep, gathering them off the hills and taking them to sales. Farmers are using fewer full time shepherds so if you are prepared to travel around, there is plenty of work.

Work on a farm in the school holidays to make sure you like the work. Formal qualifications are not necessary but you can take a course, including some animal husbandry, at an agricultural college. You must work on a farm for at least one year assisting an experienced shepherd. Look for jobs in the farming press or ring up your local agricultural college who may have block release work contracts. It may be useful to learn to ride a three-wheeled motorbike as on many farms these are replacing the shepherd and his dog for gathering and checking. It is not necessary to join a union but the local branch of the Young Farmers is good for contacts and a social life.

You will start by only earning £20 a week, rising to £160/£200 for a really experienced shepherd, though accommodation is usually provided. If it isn't you will need a cheap base with a phone to work from (parents' home?). Invest in a secondhand van (£1,000), warm waterproof clothing (£200) and a good sheep dog (£600). A crook is not vital and other shepherds will make and give them to you. It is usually a 40 hour week except during lambing when it can be 18 hours a day. The lambing season can last from December till May if you are prepared to move jobs frequently. It is hard work but with lots of variety. It is possible to combine it with forestry work in the autumn after weaning the lambs.

You must have considerable physical stamina and not mind working in cold, wet and windy conditions. You must be able to cope with long hours alone taking responsibility and using your own initiative especially during the lambing season. On the other hand, you will have to work in a team when clipping, dipping etc. An understanding of animals and lots of patience are essential as sheep are inclined to suicide.

Young experienced men are preferred to women on the whole – although many farmers find girls are better for lambing as they have small hands and are more understanding.

Useful information can be gained from the NATIONAL FARMERS' UNION, the NATIONAL SHEEP ASSOCIATION, the AGRICULTURAL TRAINING BOARD, the MINISTRY OF AGRICULTURE, the YOUNG FARMERS' CLUBS and the agricultural colleges. Read *Farmers Weekly*, the *Scottish Farmer* and the magazines of all the different sheep breeders' societies.

Shipbroker

At a Glance

Qualifications/Training	Not necessary	*Income bracket*	Medium–High
Licence	No	*Town/Country*	Town
Experience/Springboard	Essential	*Travel*	Yes
Mid-career entry	Yes	*Exit sale*	Possible
Entry costs	£2,500	*Work at home*	Possible

Mix and match Possible. You could think about: Import/export broker, Jazz musician, Landlord . . .

Enquiries Baltic Exchange, Institute of Chartered Shipbrokers

Shipbrokers work in a market place where principals interested in transporting cargoes (eg exporters, importers, governments, oil companies, mining companies and grain traders), interact with those who own or control ships. The broking, or negotiating, is essentially a case of locating suitable vessels to match available cargoes and to agree costs for carriage of the goods. Negotiations are between the brokers representing each side in the transaction whose aims are the opposite; the one to minimise the cost of transport of goods, the other to make profits for the shipowner. These brokers are known as chartering brokers; as distinct from sale and purchase brokers who are normally solely concerned with buying and selling ships. Broking companies are concentrated in the major European capitals, Hong Kong, New York and Tokyo, although there are a number of provincial brokers who continue to succeed in this business.

The advent of improved communications has affected the shipbroking industry as it has the stockbroking. The role of the traditional trading floor, which was the BALTIC EXCHANGE, is being eroded and the majority of transactions are being concluded by fax/phone/telex. Face to face contact is still considered important, however, at home and abroad and there is an element of foreign travel.

It's unlikely that you'll be able to set up as an independent shipbroker straight from school or university. You don't need any formal qualifications, unless you want to join the INSTITUTE OF CHARTERED SHIPBROKERS which sets a membership exam (traditionally, tanker brokers dealing in oil cargoes have not been members either of the Institute of Chartered Shipbrokers or the BALTIC EXCHANGE).

You do need a lot of commercial experience and some specific knowledge of ships, import and export laws, commercial geography, the conditions under which cargoes need to be transported etc. You can get this from a variety of sources, working for a government trade or export department or the shipping departments of banks or other shipbroking firms; there is a continuous spinoff from the larger companies, individuals or groups setting up smaller units specialising in some aspect of the industry. Graduates are more likely to be recruited into these, but there are openings for non-graduates with negotiating flair. The more extensive your experience the better because you also need a lot of contacts and to be well known in the market before anybody is likely to use you. Build up a network of other brokers, ship owners and charterers and of contacts at financial institutions (banks, insurance companies etc). Shipbrokers have to be skilful negotiators to get the best deal for their clients from ship owners and charterers who have their own interests (eg having full holds all the time) to consider. You'll need a lot of tenacity to conclude some deals.

You'll need a telephone, a fax and a telex (this is a competitive business and it's important for you to contact people quickly). You may want some secretarial help but most business is done immediately over the phone so you don't need a massive staff. You will have to work long hours yourself. Because of global time differences this is not a 9 to 5 job. You may be on 24 hour call to cope with any problems your clients, subcontractors or colleagues meet on the other side of the world – you may also have to travel at very short notice. While they aren't transacting, shipbrokers carry out research and surveys on behalf of clients or to extend their own knowledge. They also make arrangements for loading and unloading of the cargoes, customs clearance etc.

You are paid commission on successful transactions only or a fee for any other services.

Shopkeeper

At a Glance

Qualifications/Training	Available	*Income bracket*	Low–High
Licence	No	*Town/Country*	Mostly town
Experience/Springboard	Recommended	*Travel*	Local
Mid-career entry	Likely	*Exit sale*	Excellent
Entry costs	Highly variable	*Work at home*	No

Mix and match   Possible.   You could think about: Franchisee, Sub postmaster, Wine merchant, Wine bar owner, Novelist . . .

Enquiries   College of the Distributive Trades, National Association of Shop-keepers

If you are thinking of opening a shop some considerations will depend on what you are going to sell (whether you need refrigeration, how much storage etc). However, some things apply to nearly all shop owners. You'll almost certainly have to work long hours; being open 6 days a week with extra time needed for accounts, buying and ordering of stock, stocktaking, maintaining and cleaning of premises etc. Even with a partner or employee to help, holidays and time off may be difficult especially to begin with. Some shop owners are subject to legislation affecting, for example, who they can sell to, storage provision, opening hours, health and safety provisions. You must be aware of these before setting up rather than risk the expense and inconvenience of being caught breaking the law. New technology (especially in computerised equipment) can make stocktaking, accounting and ordering easier. Legal Sunday opening (already widespread in Scotland) is sporadically under discussion for England and Wales. This would have obvious repercussions for shop owners.

No qualifications are necessary unless you are offering a specialist service such as dispensing prescriptions for which you will need special training and/or registration in a profession. It is extremely useful to have had some relevant experience so that you have some idea of what working in a shop can be like and are aware of some of the potential pitfalls. Knowledge of running your own business is useful, try local colleges and institutes or the COLLEGE FOR THE DISTRIBUTIVE TRADES who run a course on 'Your Own Shop'. The NATIONAL ASSOCIATION OF SHOPKEEPERS helps its members with advice and resources. You'll have to be organised and patient enough to cope with customers.

The amount of money you need varies. Budget for suitable premises, storage and display, cash registers, heating and lighting, transport if necessary (eg to get your fish from market), enough stock to open with, security for valuables, advertising and insurance. Choose premises carefully and consider: do you need to provide parking or will most of your customers be local? How much storage space do you need? Do you need changing rooms? Are you too close to the competition or, alternatively, too isolated? Two bookshops on the same road may be too many while three or four expensive dress shops may actually do better than one on its own because it's worthwhile for customers to travel. Do you need passing trade? As well as doing as much initial market research as possible, you should follow up by keeping abreast of developments in your particular section of the market (there are fashions in virtually everything from meat to spectacle frames) and also by getting to know your own customers so that you can gather some idea of the sort of things that they want. You'll also find it helpful to cultivate suppliers. Your success will depend upon your suppliers, what you are selling, the profit margins that you can charge, overheads including staff and your own ability to experiment successfully.

Snail Farmer

At a Glance

Qualifications/Training	Useful	Income bracket	Medium
Licence	No	Town/Country	Country
Experience/Springboard	Recommended	Travel	No
Mid-career entry	Yes	Exit sale	Excellent
Entry costs	£10,000++	Work at home	Yes

Mix and match Possible. You could think about: Restaurateur, Fish smoker and curer, Sculptor, Holiday accommodation owner, Opening to the public . . .

Enquiries   Snail Centre, British Snail Farmers' Association

Heliculturists breed, purge and usually kill edible snails for sale to restaurants and processing plants (a lot of snails are tinned or frozen before being sold to be eaten). It is a potentially expanding market; while protein rich snails are becoming an increasingly popular food in Britain, France consumes about 2,000–3,200 million snails every year and produces only 20% of what it eats; snail eggs are a new delicacy in parts of France where they are regarded as a sort of caviar; there is also an, as yet largely untapped potential for using snails in pharmaceuticals where their blood coagulating properties are useful. At the same time, the Chernobyl disaster of 1986 has prevented Eastern Europe from supplying the snails it used to provide. Those bred in Taiwan are generally regarded as inferior to the helix pomatia or helix aspera (petit gris) that can be bred here. It's been claimed by snail farming enthusiasts that snails may yield up to £6,000 per acre.

There are no UK qualifications for snail farmers. The WELSH OFFICE, AGRICULTURE DEPARTMENT produces an introductory information folder on snail farming. Working at a French snail farm is still the best way of learning. This also puts you in touch with the suppliers of your first breeding snails and will make acceptance of your ability to raise snails from the Maitres Escargoties de France (essential for serious snail farmers) easier to get. Other useful organisations are the SNAIL CENTRE (for advice and stock) and the BRITISH SNAIL FARMERS ASSOCIATION a supplier and franchise contractor, membership of which costs £1,800 for which you get advice and support in your venture including a guarantee to sell all the stock you produce. You need contacts in the food and wine world so experience as a chef, wine merchant or in another branch of specialist farming or food production is useful. Snail farming is not yet recognised as a normal form of agriculture in the UK and you'll have to be patient to build up the business into a profitable concern.

To start off you need about 20+ acres of water meadow planted with radishes, thistles, nettles and dock leaves and about 4,000 reproductuers (three year old breeding snails – snails are hermaphrodite) costing about £3–4,000. They need the right soil and dampness; in the UK the West Country is one of the best snail producing areas. The snails are free to roam in this area which can be fenced by a 6 volt electric wire to prevent them from escaping. For breeding, hibernating and purging they need to be kept under cover (plastic sheeted sheds will do). In addition you have to provide them with special, large, long-legged, wire mesh boxes in which to hibernate. (Under the 1947 Agricultural Act, you don't need planning permission if you're breeding animals for food, fur or skin.) An area of this size will support 4 million snails. They take at least 15 months to reach edible maturity and are at their best at

2–3 years; they usually die at about 5. Bulk snail selling is best done through the French or British snail market co-operative (BRITSNAIL); snails will reach about £4,000–4,500 a tonne – (approximately 65,000 snails). Some can be sold locally (restaurants, specialist food shops), when they reach up to £8,000 a tonne.

The work is seasonal in so far as snails hibernate from October to April and are harvestable for the rest of the year (September and October being the best months). Rounding them up takes several hours of waiting for them to climb onto the plastic sheeting you cover them with before putting them into their hibernation boxes or purging tanks. For the rest of the time you must make sure that they have enough live or very fresh plants to eat. Preparing snails for sale isn't a job for animal lovers. They must first be purged by feeding them on bran for a day and then on nothing for six days cleans them out so they can be eaten safely and comfortably. Unless you're selling them live (some restaurants prefer this as proof of freshness), you kill them by immersing them in brine for 24–36 hours then boiling and simmering them for five before removing them from their shells, getting rid of their galls, cleaning them and putting them back into their shells with some butter before freezing. Snails are quiet, relatively inactive animals; very peaceful if you can tolerate them and protect them from moles and fieldmice (who eat them unpurged) and from ants who steal their eggs.

Social Worker

At a Glance

Qualifications/Training	Essential	*Income bracket*	Low–Medium
Licence	No	*Town/Country*	Either
Experience/Springboard	Essential	*Travel*	Local
Mid-career entry	Usual	*Exit sale*	No
Entry costs	Nil	*Work at home*	No

Mix and match Yes. You could think about: Counsellor, Guardian ad Litem, Nursing Home owner, Light music composer, Potter . . .
Enquiries Central Council for Education and Training in Social Work

While the vast majority of social workers are employed by local authorities and the voluntary organisations, there is a small proportion that is freelance. But you need a good range of reliable contacts and proven skills that can only be gained by first being in conventional employment. People will need to know and trust you personally to give you freelance work.

You will need to be properly trained – a course leading to the Certificate of Qualification in Social Work (CQSW) can be taken with a degree or when you are older (get information from the CENTRAL COUNCIL FOR EDUCATION AND TRAINING IN SOCIAL WORK). Then you need a good deal of experience – and probably specialise – before you can think of going solo.

Working without the support of a team can be isolated and lonely. You need the qualities routinely required of social workers, including compassion and toughness. Read *Community Care* and *Social Work Today*.

Some social workers go freelance in order to continue their social work part time while changing direction to eg counselling. But there is a full time living to be made as an independent – so long as you are working in an area of the country where people will pay for your services and particularly if you have specialised in eg psychiatric, geriatric or family work. Most freelancers have specialised in children and work as guardians ad litem. Others get work from eg local solicitors and doctors. It may involve regular visiting of the elderly, writing reports on conditions in which children are being kept, some family therapy, maybe some teaching, social work and consultancy work for local authorities. The latter will depend upon your credibility with the social workers in your local authority – by and large they don't smile upon their independent colleagues.

Solicitor

At a Glance

Qualifications/Training	Essential	*Income bracket*	Medium–High
Licence	Yes	*Town/Country*	Town
Experience/Springboard	Essential	*Travel*	Local
Mid-career entry	Possible	*Exit sale*	Excellent
Entry costs	£20,000+	*Work at home*	No

Mix and match Possible. You could think about: Property developer, Landlord, Estate agent, MP, Sailing school owner, Jazz musician . . .
Enquiries Law Society

Solicitors give their clients appropriate legal advice on anything from buying a house to what to do if they are arrested on a murder charge; increasing specialisation means it is unlikely the same solicitor will be called upon to do both. Most solicitors (nearly ¾ of the 42,000) are in private practice; 19,000 are partners and 4,000 are sole principals. The trend is away from setting up entirely alone and towards either staying in established partnerships, or a small group of partners from an established partnership setting up together. This is partly for financial reasons (it costs a lot to set up a solicitor's office) and for practical reasons, for example allowing the responsibility and administration to be shared and ensuring the partnership is never left unattended. Practices are broadly on three levels of profitability: some take rich pickings from the financial services revolution, largely London based with corporate clients; most are the steady local solicitors; the least profitable are the legal aid practices in large cities.

All new legislation has some effect on the legal profession. Recent examples include the loss of the conveyancing monopoly and the increased use of other professions for tax advice. There is now talk of solicitors joining mixed professional practices to allow a sort of 'one-stop shopping'.

You must be a graduate to become a solicitor and then take professional exams (fewer if the degree is in law) before becoming an articled clerk for two years. As an articled clerk you will get a taste of most of the departments in the partnership (see *Roset* for details of available clerkships). Articled clerks do a lot of fairly routine jobs but you only have to stick it for two years and most firms try not to make it too boring. After that you will need to work for an existing practice for at least three years before the LAW SOCIETY allows you to run your own office. (This and other regulations are explained in the Law Society pamphlet, *Professional Conduct of Solicitors*). About ⅓ newly qualified solicitors are women. It is possible (if you can stand being an articled clerk) to come to the profession later in life. Training is slightly different in Scotland, where law graduates or non-graduates who have a three year training contract with an employer, do a year's full time course leading to a diploma in legal practice followed by 2 years' post diploma training with a firm before qualifying. Details from the LAW SOCIETY OF SCOTLAND.

It takes between 5 and 10 years to become a full partner in an existing firm, often following a stint as a salaried partner (it can take longer, the older and larger the firm). You may have to accept established practices – scales of profit-sharing, office management – but you avoid some of the headaches of a new practice. It can be a good thing to change jobs until you find the firm in which you want to stay and become a partner. It is best to do this straight after qualifying or after two or three years. But don't change too often.

If you are setting up a new partnership, raising the necessary capital (although important) is less of a problem than building up your clientele. Some have set up practices where the partners are all ethnic minorities or women, obviously with a particular clientele in mind. The number of clients you can take with you when you set up will depend on the prestige of the firm you are leaving and, more importantly, there are likely to be restrictive covenants. It is wise to consider how long the clients will be with you – you may set up as a divorce specialist with 50 clients, whose cases may all have settled within a year, by which time you must have made your reputation. You can now advertise. Location is also important. Clients, in general, don't like travelling to see their solicitors; nor do they like them to change address too often so find somewhere with room to expand. You may have covenanted not to set up a new partnership within a certain radius of the one you are leaving, which can force you into an area where your particular specialisation is less likely to flourish. If you want to move right out of the area, the Law Society provides lists of members, with date of qualification, and location of practice. You can therefore identify a town where many solicitors are near retiring.

Apart from premises, office equipment and an extensive library, you will need an absolute minimum of one member of staff who is prepared to act as secretary, receptionist, telephonist etc. Such people are difficult to find and before you have established a reputation, you may have difficulty finding articled clerks and assistants. Banks are quite helpful to professionals setting up on their own.

SOLICITOR

Office procedure is important for solicitors – it is not a job for people who can't stand filling in forms. There is a lot of paperwork so it helps if you're methodical. However the days when solicitors acknowledge acknowledgements seem to be over. Much of your time is spent talking and writing to people. You need to be able to maintain a detached judgement but to inspire the trust of your clients by being patient, sympathetic and capable of understanding what their needs are.

Some firms have produced videos for universities and polytechnics. The LAW SOCIETY publish pamphlets on *Education and Training of Entrants to the Solicitors' Profession*, *Becoming a Solicitor*, and *About Solicitors*.

Space Sales Agent

At a Glance

Qualifications/Training	No	Income bracket	Low–High
Licence	No	Town/Country	Either
Experience/Springboard	Essential	Travel	Some
Mid-career entry	Yes	Exit sale	Possible
Entry costs	£500	Work at home	Yes

Mix and match   Yes.   You could think about: Direct marketing agent, Advertising agent, Magazine publisher, Motorcycle racer . . .

Enquiries   Space sales agents, Magazine and Newspaper publishers

Media space sales people are responsible for getting advertisements into books, magazines and newspapers. They do this by contacting potential advertisers (or their advertising agencies) and encouraging them to book advertising space in the publication. Their client is the publisher. Publishers may also want advice on charges, target advertising revenue and so on. Space salesmen sell to people who already have advertising budgets, many of them running to literally millions of pounds, so the emphasis is on advertising in the client's product rather than on having to sell the idea of advertising itself. It's a fast moving, competitive business, you work under pressure to meet deadlines and have to keep up momentum and enthusiasm for what can be a fairly thankless job, by being constantly on the move, phoning, writing and visiting.

There are no formal qualifications but you'll need some experience. National newspapers are always recruiting space salesmen; there is a fast turnover because people soon get bored with a product and want to try selling on another publication. Many newspapers and magazines train their sales staff and, as long as you've got a reasonable telephone manner and are suitably persuasive, you shouldn't have any trouble getting in. Appropriate experience on an undergraduate magazine or any magazine/book production experience is also useful.

You can operate from anywhere with a telephone so set up costs are minimal. You may find, especially as you expand, that you want to be closer to your clients and to media buyers. If your client is productive enough, you'll only need one. You can get this client through contacts or by approaching one and suggesting that you sell space for them. You'll have to have a reasonable idea about the sort of advertiser your client will attract. You have a rate card, describing the publication (competitors' rates are easily established from BRAD – British Rates and

Data), its value to advertisers, cost per thousand readers and so on. The price on the rate card is often calculated to allow you to cut some of the margins for some advertisers. You'll usually get between 15 and 30% commission on your client's yield from advertising. Advertisers pay the publisher; you are paid by the publisher after you've sold the space. Sometimes you may be given an advance for outgoings; these include arranging the printing of a rate card. For magazines, newspapers and journals you want to book as many series as possible – ie a space regularly filled by the same advertiser. Rates vary according to size and positions of the advertisement and whether it's colour or black and white.

You'll spend a lot of time on the phone, but you may need to entertain major media buyers from time to time. There's a certain amount of cajoling involved but when you are dealing with advertising agencies you'll find that many are delighted to buy space on behalf of their clients. If you decide to expand the operation and take on your own staff you can pay them a small flat rate and a percentage of the commission that you're getting. It's a competitive business in which clients often move their accounts. You can't rest on your laurels for long.

Specialist Food Manufacturer

At a Glance

Qualifications/Training	Available	*Income bracket*	Low–High
Licence	No	*Town/Country*	Either
Experience/Springboard	Useful	*Travel*	Some
Mid-career entry	Possible	*Exit sale*	Possible
Entry costs	£1,000+++	*Work at home*	Possible

Mix and match Yes. You could think about: Snail farmer, Fish curer and smoker, Restaurateur, Psychotherapist, Shopkeeper . . .

Enquiries Specialist food manufacturers

Current interest in healthy eating and real food, which has fewer preservatives and more taste than some mass produced foods, means that you can make a living by producing and selling pies, mustards, preserves, cakes, biscuits, pizzas, filled rolls . . . as long as you're prepared to persevere. It can take a long time to turn a very small scale cottage industry into a business with a reasonable turnover. For the less independently minded, one alternative would be to sell out to one of the larger food manufacturers and to exchange total autonomy for a seat on the board and what may be a lot of money; or to sell out completely and start doing something else. As long as you're relatively accessible to suppliers and for deliveries you can set up a food manufacturing business anywhere in the country.

To start up you need to have a product that you can make well, try it out on your friends to begin with, then you may be able to interest a local shop in testing how sellable it is. Find out, also, how long the shelf life of your product is – put some on one of your own shelves and see how long it lasts. Before going into production check which bits of consumer protection legislation affect you. This will vary depending on what you're making but the two most likely things to consider will be the labelling of foods act (which stipulates that your product must have a legible list of ingredients in descending order of weight or volume on every jar or packet) and the Weights and Measures Act (which subjects your weighing and measuring equipment to periodic checks). Both of these fall under the jurisdiction of the county council and some councils are more stringent than others. On the whole though, the approval of your own council is usually enough to satisfy the councils of any other county in which you sell your products so it pays to co-operate. You will also have to have your premises inspected by the environmental health office of your district council. They will continue to give regular checks which may become less frequent as you establish a reputation for being hygenic. Experience in the food industry is useful, there are a lot of factors that make the manufacture and distribution of food very different than that of, say, shoes.

Set up costs needn't be great. You can start production on a very small scale, baking a few cakes for a local baker every day or making a tray of sandwiches for an office. As you expand you can buy bigger and better equipment and premises; machinery for sticking on labels, measuring equipment. Most ingredients are readily available from wholesalers, if you're going to import from abroad check customs and import laws and make sure that you aren't going to end up with a load of rotting food because it was stuck on the quayside while you went through the necessary procedures. You will need a telephone and a van, a supply of stationery and labels and some packaging (some suppliers of jars are reluctant to supply the small quantities you may need in the early days). Base your charges on how much it costs to produce and how much you want to make per sale; people will pay more for specialist food but base your charges on the competition in the retail outlets you use – remember that the retailer will make a mark up.

Because food doesn't last forever, your busiest times may be dictated by, for example, the lead up to busy selling times or during certain seasons – these depend on what you're making (Christmas puddings or strawberry jam). As well as manufacturing you'll have to take orders and make sure that they're delivered, design promotional material and packaging and experiment with new lines. You also have to deliver to retailers, this can be handed over to a specialist distributor, who may help to extend your market field but the attention they pay to your range may be erratic – depending on what else they've got to distribute. Otherwise you can find your own retail outlets by driving around the country, using contacts and going to trade and food shows and exhibitions. This also means that you can, if you want, decide exactly which market you're aiming for (delicatessens, health food shops etc). If your product is good, retailers will approach you. Although you can have a very wide and varied range of retail clients you have to be very big before you can supply supermarkets and once you're doing that you may have to drop your smaller specialist outlets who won't be able to compete with supermarket pricing. Another alternative is to market under someone else's label; small retailers often don't have the facilities to manufacture their own products.

Specialist Sports Retailer

At a Glance

Qualifications/Training	No	Income bracket	Low–High
Licence	No	Town/Country	Town
Experience/Springboard	Essential	Travel	No
Mid-career entry	Likely	Exit sale	Excellent
Entry costs	Highly variable	Work at home	No

Mix and match   Possible.   You could think about: Sailing school owner, Windsurfing school owner, Football commentator, Physiotherapist, Holiday accommodation owner . . .

Enquiries   Sports associations and local sports shops

General sports shops tend not to be able to offer the expert advice that is needed by people buying specialist equipment, eg riding or watersports. This means that there is little point in opening a specialist sports shop without having a lot of experience and enthusiasm for the sports involved. If you combine two sports, pick eg windsurfing and ski-ing whose seasons complement one another.

Shop experience is essential so you'll know how the business is run. It's particularly useful if you've worked for another specialist sports shop and so have a better idea of what you're getting into. As well as the usual attributes of a shopkeeper, you'll have to have the patience and stamina to spend a lot of time with each customer (allow about an hour to sell a set of ski-ing kit for example). They need individual attention so you should have at least one partner or employee with the necessary expertise to man the shop.

You'll need to rent or buy a shop with suitable storage space. Location is important, customers will travel up to about 35 miles but most will be local; don't open up too close to competition unless you think you can take over and survive on half its clientele. Most sports gear is bulky so you should try and have parking facilities.

Initially you have to get dealership of the brands you want to use – this means convincing them that you are a creditable outlet for their goods and are not too close to a rival stockist. For some reason, although people only use sports equipment seasonally, many people buy bits and pieces (for tennis etc) throughout the year. Aim to turn round your stock about 4 or 5 times a year. Ski buying is different – about 90% of the year's stock is delivered in September and October having been ordered the previous spring via trade fairs and visits to dealers. The equipment that you stock will be made to order by companies in France, Switzerland, Austria etc. This means that your requirements will have to be carefully predicted (not made easier by dependence on the weather and changing fashions in ski-wear and equipment). You may be able to make a few negotiations during the season but not many. You can pay for ski stock under various instalment schemes from the supplier. You'll build up a regular clientele, who will return to you every year to add or replace equipment and you can stock bits and pieces of more general equipment to keep people coming in regularly.

You can hire out ski equipment. Unless you're near one of the Scottish centres, most of your equipment will be used abroad (people don't like using new kit on dry slopes) so you won't have a demand for ski hire. But you may be able to hire out basic ski-ing outfits several times a season, which pays for them very quickly. Windsurf hire is totally dependent on access to water and good weather. You'll have to keep abreast of what's going on in the sport via the press – *Watersports Trade News, Ski Survey, Equestrian Trade News* etc. Contact the relevant body – eg SKI CLUB OF GREAT BRITAIN or PROFESSIONAL BOARD SAILERS ASSOCIATION.

Stage Designer

At a Glance

Qualifications/Training	Necessary	*Income bracket*	Low–Medium
Licence	No	*Town/Country*	Town
Experience/Springboard	Recommended	*Travel*	Local
Mid-career entry	Possible	*Exit sale*	No
Entry costs	£50	*Work at home*	Partly

Mix and match   Yes.   You could think about: Illustrator, Artist, Stage technician carpenter, Book packager, Yoga teacher . . .

Enquiries   Theatrical agents

Stage designers design and build sets appropriate both for the production and the stage. They usually work from scale models, making sure that the lighting works and that a special scenic effect isn't going to block the audience's view. Commercial theatre is the most lucrative, but there are also openings in repertory, fringe and youth theatre, ballet and opera. Stage design is also used in film and TV, creating special effects, models of monsters and fantasy worlds, costumes and interiors. There are other openings in industrial theatre, eg for large promotional conventions which have to be produced, stage managed and publicised in much the same way as a piece of theatre. Most opportunities are in London but there is scope anywhere with a theatre – Edinburgh, Glasgow, Birmingham, Stratford etc.

As a designer, you don't have to be a member of EQUITY but it's advisable; they lay down minimum rates of pay but if you are sought after you get better rates. A course in theatre production and design is the starting point for anyone who wants to work in the theatre. As well as set design and construction you'll need to have a background knowledge of theatre, scene painting, props, lighting, management, publicity, special effects, costume cutting and making, construction and model making, technical drawing etc. Most freelance designers have been assistant stage hands at theatres before setting up on their own. Other good sources of experience and contacts are annual festivals, Glyndebourne etc, where freelance stage builders and painters are needed for the season. You'll need contacts (your college may have some initial contacts with commercial, youth, repertory or fringe theatre); and it helps if you can offer some impressive experience (helping with designs for a West End show etc). Once you have established a reputation people will come to you, so you have to make a splash with your first designs. Read the *Stage*.

To find your first job you have to show people your portfolio and go to theatrical agents; you'll have to pay them commission for any work they get you, but they have contacts and will push for somebody they think is worth promoting. It is a competitive world and is often pressured. The theatre has tight deadlines to meet.

Stage Technician Carpenter

At a Glance

Qualifications/Training	Available	*Income bracket*	Low–Medium
Licence	No	*Town/Country*	Town
Experience/Springboard	Essential	*Travel*	Maybe
Mid-career entry	Possible	*Exit sale*	No
Entry costs	£250	*Work at home*	No

Mix and match Possible. You could think about: Stage designer, Bespoke furniture maker/designer, Cabinet maker, Mini-cab driver, Photographer . . .
Enquiries FE and drama colleges or local theatres

This is someone who builds, repairs, sets up and takes down stage scenery, in the theatre, or for TV or films.

Experience in the building trade is useful if you are lucky enough to get a rare apprenticeship. You can take a carpentry course at a further education college or a theatre technicians' course at a drama college. You need to be physically strong, and have practical skills, intelligence and quick reactions for striking or setting up a set at speed. You must be able to get on well with other people; not only to work in a team but, if you work as a master carpenter eventually, to organise and direct others. Punctuality is vital. It's essential to join the BROADCASTING ENTERTAINMENT TRADES ALLIANCE if you do TV and film work but not necessary in the theatre. To set up, you can get part-time work as a flyman (who pulls scenery up and down) with a panto or musical where there are many scene changes. If reliable you can find a job as a full-time assistant carpenter. You will start by getting £90 a week plus overtime as a flyman (£40–50 part-time) rising to £200+ a week as a master carpenter. Film and TV companies will pay £100 a day.

Setting up you will need to outlay a minimum of £80–100 on tools. However, a proper tool kit is £600. You need a base with a phone, and someone or an answerphone to answer it.

There is a shortage of carpenters. Once it is known that you are good at your job, everyone wants you. You can work in the theatre; freelance with commercial TV and film companies, where there is a lot of money; or you can work for large set-building companies. It is possible to set up your own set-building business if you have good contacts and a good accountant.

The advantages of the job are the lack of routine and the interesting people you mix with. These make up for the lack of social life outside the theatre. In film and TV the work is irregular – it's possible to work 24 hours a day. This can also happen when you are changing complicated sets in opera, particularly if you are working on tour. You must be prepared to travel to find work unless you have plenty of contacts in a large city but it's possible to do other jobs between assignments. There are few women in this job because of the heavy lifting. New fly technology and developments such as rechargeable drills improve the job all the time. Useful magazines are the *Stage*, *TV Today* (for jobs), *Spotlight*.

Stockbroker

At a Glance

Qualifications/Training	Essential	Income bracket	Medium–High
Licence	Yes	Town/Country	Town
Experience/Springboard	Essential	Travel	No
Mid-career entry	Possible	Exit sale	Possible
Entry costs	£50,000+	Work at home	No

Mix and match   Possible.   You could think about: Options dealer, Farmer, MP, Cabaret performer . . .

Enquiries   Stock Exchange

Stockbrokers give advice to private clients, companies and institutions on investments. They also buy and sell these investments on behalf of clients. Private clients may be: discretionary – where the stockbroker has the power to buy/sell investments without reference each time to the client; or execution only – where the stockbroker merely does what he is asked to do. There are many different types of investment, but those considered for a private client's portfolio might include: government stocks, debentures, loan stocks, preference or ordinary shares, warrants, unit trusts, options (traded options – which are only dealt in by a few brokers and the conventional option, which most, if not all brokers deal in). There is no guarantee that the value of securities will go up and successful stockbroking depends on knowing the market well enough to be able to predict with some accuracy which investments are likely to realise the maximum profits, and to decide on a suitable strategy within each client's own investment needs – whether primarily income, capital growth or a combination of the two.

Almost all trading in shares in public companies and government stocks is carried out by registered dealers or representatives through the STOCK EXCHANGE (SE) to which stockbroking firms must belong. London is one of the major world markets and dominates trading in the European time zone.

Since Big Bang, many City partnerships have been bought by financial institutions, some of them gigantic American, French, Japanese and Swiss banks. The trend has been for these to shed private investors. This means there are good opportunities for independent stockbrokers, especially outside London, who live amongst their clients and get to know them. Big Bang has also meant that all stockbrokers can deal directly by computer (the Stock Exchange Automated Quotation System – SEAQS). Recent government policy aimed at wider share ownership, combined with Big Bang, has led to greater public aware-ness of the SE and to larger numbers of small investors using the services of stockbrokers – often through their own clearing bank.

First, become a trainee with a member firm. There are no formal requirements – trainees are taken on as graduates, straight from school or from some other related field. Your firm will provide training to help you pass the formal SE exams (details of SE examination from the STOCK EXCHANGE Examinations Department). After that you need £1,000 to pay to the SE and you're a member.

Before a new firm can trade it has to be registered under the Financial Services Act (as a member of a self regulatory organisation or an exempted or 'Europerson'). A new firm must also become a corporate member of the SE which means conforming to its rule book on, eg, activities of directors and minimum liquidity margins (usually 25% of annual trading budget). Entry to the SE costs £10,000–50,000, with a subscription of £1,000 pa thereafter. On top of this come the costs of running an office, secretarial and administrative back up. Stockbrokers are paid commission on their transactions. Commission rates are no longer set by the Stock Exchange and are usually around 1.5% of the value of the shares bought or sold, with a minimum charge rather like a cover charge in restaurants to protect the stockbroker against the cost of executing very many tiny transactions.

You'll need a good understanding of how investment works in general and to keep up with what's going on in various sectors. There are over 7,000 different securities traded on the Stock Exchange so most stockbrokers specialise in one sector (retail, heavy industry etc), keep-ing an eye on any changes or developments likely to affect long or short term investment prospects. Firms tend to have partners with com-plementary specialisations. A network of City and financial analyst contacts is useful for keeping up with what's going on. You will certainly need to read the *Financial Times* and *Investors Chronicle*.

By the time you're a partner/director in a new or existing firm, clients will come via personal and professional referrals. Small investors are likely to enthuse about their stockbrokers (as long as you're good) and provincial stockbrokers can provide a more personal service. You are likely to concentrate on the UK market when trading securities; diversify overseas through unit trusts if you want to develop a private client's portfolio into, say, Japan, rather than attempt to be expert in overseas securities yourself. There are opportunities for working an 18 or 20 hour day by dealing on foreign markets, but most stockbrokers manage not to. It's a stressful life especially in a bear market.

Street Entertainer

At a Glance

Qualifications/Training	Useful	Income bracket	Low
Licence	Usually	Town/Country	Town
Experience/Springboard	No	Travel	Local
Mid-career entry	Possible	Exit sale	No
Entry costs	Nil	Work at home	No

Mix and match Essential. You could think about: Cabaret performer, Puppeteer, Actor, Musician, Accountant . . .

Enquiries   Street entertainers, Equity

You can earn money, if not a particularly secure living, from entertaining passers by in the street. Sometimes called buskers, street entertainers want to distinguish themselves from the image of tired old men shuffling through a few tap dance steps. The hours are flexible, so it's a very good way of making extra money, especially for musicians, children's entertainers, actors or cabaret performers who may have stretches of free time during the day or evening while they aren't fulfilling conventional appointments. You aren't necessarily going to be picked up by a talent scout but you will be able to develop your skills while keeping the wolf from the door. Some prefer to limit outside performances to the summer; others find it a good way of helping to finance overseas travel. The street entertaining network is worldwide.

There are no formal qualifications. However, laws govern where and when you may perform on the street and (although arrests are rare) these are often rigorously enforced by the police and local traders who will send you off no matter how big an, as yet unpaying, crowd you may have attracted. It's advisable to work only in legally defined patches (and that means no straying even by a few yards) and for that you'll often need to get a licence. For this you have to pass an audition and your performance has to be unoffensive, socially and politically sound in the view of the licensers. In London the main centre for street performers is at Covent Garden (licences are controlled by the COVENT GARDEN MARKET MANAGEMENT; out of London performers are often allowed in market towns or at festivals and carnivals like Edinburgh and Glastonbury. For some of these you'll have to book in advance so check with the organisers. Street entertainers are encouraged in many countries, especially in tourist centres, like Paris, Amsterdam and Copenhagen. Some street entertainers happen to be members of EQUITY but this is useful only when you're mixing and matching this with other professional performing.

Success is largely a matter of trial and error. Unlike conventional theatre where the audience shells out for a ticket in advance, street audiences only pay after they've seen the show – if they weren't amused or impressed they won't pay. You must be able to make people stop, stay, watch and pay. Everyone has their own ways of doing this; planting generous stooges who will ostentatiously give you fivers, borrowing money from a member of the audience, getting the audience involved, playing music, leaving open violin cases in the path of passers by, bullying the crowd to get them to pay and ridiculing anyone who doesn't. You can pick up some basic skills at a part- or full-time performance course and then develop your own show and extra skills such as magic tricks. No matter how well you may perform in front of the mirror or your admiring parents, there's no substitute for an audience. Good starting experience is in children's entertainment or for cabaret audiences; neither is likely to sit in polite silence if you haven't grabbed their attention. Street entertainers need to be outgoing, self-confident, sensitive to audience response and quick thinking enough to be able to capitalise on audience reaction and involvement. You have to please the audience which may mean being subtly patronising. Apart from props, there are no set up costs for street entertainers, but in general anyone who makes a living from entertaining or performing is likely to have to pay more for things like insurance (house insurance can carry as much as 50% loading) and pension plans. For a half hour show at somewhere like Covent Garden, you can expect to make anything from about £3 (occasionally very good performers may collect £100) and for that you'll have had to do a lot of hanging around waiting for your pitch.

The network is extremely active. Read *Cascade* the juggling monthly which has details of what's going on including the addresses of jugglers all over the world who will put up any visiting colleagues. You may be able to pick up some ideas from other performers especially if you're prepared to hand over any of your own which you can't use yourself (eg time sensitive jokes about current events). The downbeat of this is plagiarism; don't discuss the material you're developing for future use unless you want to see it being used by someone else.

Sub Postmaster

At a Glance

Qualifications/Training	Yes	Income bracket	Low–High
Licence	Yes	Town/Country	Town/Village
Experience/Springboard	No	Travel	No
Mid-career entry	Excellent	Exit sale	Yes
Entry costs	£1,000++	Work at home	No

Mix and match   Yes.   You could think about: Shopkeeper, Publican, Kennel/cattery owner, Calligrapher . . .

Enquiries   District postmaster

Sub-post offices are a popular escape from the rat race because they offer a secure way of running your own business; sub postmasters are paid by the post office, which they can combine with another business (village shop, chemist, newsagent, pub etc) from the same premises. The post office brings in trade for this.

You can apply to the Head Postmaster of the district to start a sub-post office, but as (in the Post Office's view) there are too many already this is unlikely to prove successful. Alternatively you find one up for sale in Dalton's Weekly (price ranges from about £40,000–100,000). In either case you apply to the district Head Postmaster and are called for an interview. The two main planks of the interview are reliability and cash/collateral, so that you are unlikely to be caught with your fingers in the till.

If accepted you get 4 weeks free tuition with someone from Head Office sitting beside you. There is always a drop in income of up to £3,000 pa when someone new takes over, this is negotiated back as results are seen. Income is based on units which in turn are based on varying percentages on all transactions including pensions, stamps, Giro, National Savings, Leicester Alliance Building Society etc. There is a range of about 140 different items for an average sub-post office to select from. Income ranges from about £1,100 to about £60,000. If you're working alone you should be able to cope with enough PO work to earn you about £12,500 pa.

It is recommended that a first-timer buys a post office without mails (ie no vans, postmen's pay, deliveries etc) which includes most sub-post offices in towns and cities.

Head Office carries out an audit about twice a year, although this tends to be irregular. The business can be built up by applying for more transactions such as Motor Vehicle Tax, normally carried out by GPOs, so increasing your units and so your income.

Losses in a sub-post office come out of the sub postmaster's pocket, so accuracy is of prime importance. The principal requirements for the job, other than reliability and cash are a basic knowledge of mathematics and the ability to be polite and friendly to infuriating customers who don't know what they want and become abusive because you haven't got it.

Surveyor

At a Glance

Qualifications/Training	Essential	*Income bracket*	Medium–High
Licence	For financial advice	*Town/Country*	Town
Experience/Springboard	Recommended	*Travel*	Local
Mid-career entry	Possible	*Exit sale*	Possible
Entry costs	£7,500++	*Work at home*	Partly

Mix and match Possible. You could think about: Estate agent, Property developer, House converter, Landlord . . .

Enquiries Royal Institution of Chartered Surveyors

There are several branches of surveying. Roughly speaking surveyors are concerned with measuring, developing and managing buildings and those natural resources which can belong to people. Some of this overlaps estate agency but chartered surveyors are qualified to do more. Chartered surveyors can set up as general practitioners, or they can specialise in building or quantity surveying; others are valuers, agricultural surveyors, auctioneers, and land surveyors. The ROYAL INSTITUTION OF CHARTERED SURVEYORS (RICS) issues rules and codes of practice and news of any relevant new technology or legislation.

Before establishing a practice as a chartered surveyor you will need to be either an associate or a fellow of the RICS. For this you need a degree and 2–3 years' probationary experience culminating in a professional exam. You may also need a licence (eg, if you're going to give mortgage advice). Surveyors need to be meticulous and painstaking; able to alternate between working from an office and scrambling around on roofs. You have to work under pressure and are often involved with other professions (solicitors, etc) which can entail conflicts of schedule.

Get as much experience as possible (public authorites can provide good varied work, if you can stand it). Once you feel ready to set up on your own, you'll need to decide whether to be a sole practitioner or whether to set up or join a partnership or a company. Consult an accountant and solicitor before entering into partnership. You can buy into an existing partnership, usually one where you have done your probation or associateship. Set up costs (or the costs of buying into an existing partnership) can be advanced from banks, merchant banks, and insurance companies. You don't need much equipment to set up; apart from professional apparatus, theodolites etc which varies depending on your branch. You need a telephone and a desk. Keep overheads down by using typing services, making your own coffee etc. Your main expense is insurance; as well as public liability, you should insure against loss of fees and have personal insurance. An RICS leaflet *Insurance* outlines rules which stipulate that you have professional indemnity insurance which costs around £50 per week.

The RICS has a recommended scale of charges for quantity and certain building surveying services. Otherwise charges are made on an ad valorem scale, a time charge or a fixed sum. You'll need a nucleus of customers to start out with. Send your present clients a carefully worded letter telling them about your new practice; the RICS actually provide the wording in their pack *Setting Up In Practice*). RICS also help chartered surveyors to recruit professional staff.

Tailor

At a Glance

Qualifications/Training	Available	*Income bracket*	Low–Medium
Licence	No	*Town/Country*	Town
Experience/Springboard	Recommended	*Travel*	No
Mid-career entry	Possible	*Exit sale*	Possible
Entry costs	£2,000	*Work at home*	Not recommended

Mix and match Possible. You could think about: Fashion retailer, Wedding shop owner, Costume designer, Import/export broker, Graphologist . . .
Enquiries Tailors

In spite of the ready availability of off-the-peg suits from chain stores there is a demand for independent tailors who will make suits to their clients' measurements and carry out repairs on their own and other suits. Although from time to time you may be asked to fit and make suits for women, most of your clients will be men who want suits of traditional design with a few modifications according to current fashions (size of lapel, cut of trousers etc). Most tailors' clients tend not to be interested in innovative suit design.

The traditional way in involves years of hard and badly paid apprenticeship. It takes 3 years to learn the basics of the trade. After that you need another 2 years at least specialising in cutting, trouser-making, jacket-making, or fitting. If you don't want to do it this way, you'll have to be very good at fitting and making suits, have some contacts who will use you and have some experience of working in a tailor's shop so that you can give your customers the sort of service they expect. Each tailor has a slightly different style and uses slightly different methods so, the more you see, the more variety you will have from which to develop your own style. As well as being good at sewing, you'll have to keep full records of customers' details.

To set up you need a sewing machine, needles, scissors, tape measure etc and also a work room. Ideally, premises should be fairly central to attract passing trade and also near offices so that customers can visit you easily for fittings. This means that it costs a lot to rent or buy a suitable shop and some tailors visit their customers at home or the office for fittings.

You can charge a deposit when you take an order but the bulk of what you're paid comes once the suit has been finished to the customer's satisfaction. Customers select the fabric from samples that you have from the suppliers. Fabric comes from the mills in Scotland, Yorkshire etc. You may have to shop around until you find one that will supply the comparatively small quantities that independent tailors need. Initially clients come from contacts; people you have fitted at previous employers; clients spread the word and the suits themselves are a walking advertisement. New clients are attracted by competitive prices, and good cuts and fits. Once you're off the ground, you'll have to employ assistance or subcontract some of the work.

It is important not to rest on your laurels once you start being successful. You have to keep in with your clients and not neglect your old customers. A lot of success depends on your ability to get on with your clients. You also have to be very exacting with those who work for you and be prepared to work long hours yourself.

Tattooist 513

Tattooist

At a Glance

Qualifications/Training	No	*Income bracket*	Low–Medium
Licence	No	*Town/Country*	Town
Experience/Springboard	No	*Travel*	No
Mid-career entry	Possible	*Exit sale*	No
Entry costs	£5,000	*Work at home*	Possible

Mix and match Possible. You could think about: Make up artist, Private investigator, Dealer in antiques, Taxidermist . . .

Enquiries European Tattoo Artists Federation

Unless you have a lot of contacts in the trade or have been born into it, there is little point in attempting to set up a new tattooing business. There are more men than women but this matters less than who you are and where you come from. Shortage of money among traditional customers along with recent AIDS and hepatitis scares have reduced demand for tattoos – although the risks are reduced by the health and safety regulations.

No formal qualifications or training courses are available. Tattooists learn through practice on family and friends until they feel confident enough to start charging. By law, you must be registered by your local Health Authority who will inspect the premises and check up on you from time to time to make sure that your practice is hygienic. Tattooists have to be able to make their own designs and to reproduce them on human skin so there is no room for error. Some also do ear-piercing or removal of old tattoos, and there is some cosmetic work on scars etc. A few work on animals for identification purposes but a completely different set of equipment is needed for this. You need a very steady hand. The hours you work are up to you and depend on the amount of business you get.

As well as premises you will need needles, sterilising equipment, colours etc. Most of this is handed on from other tattooists, but to buy it new would probably cost about £5,000. Tattooists mix their own colours from natural lead and zinc-free pigments. This is a very secret operation because there are certain tricks to mixing colours that will keep under the skin. What you charge varies, probably from about £1.50 for a name to £30 for a large tattoo. A good tattooist can expect to do a large tattoo eg back sized in about 2 hours as long as the client can bear it.

Much work comes from regular customers who know and trust you. Contacts are all important because the existing tattooing business has a

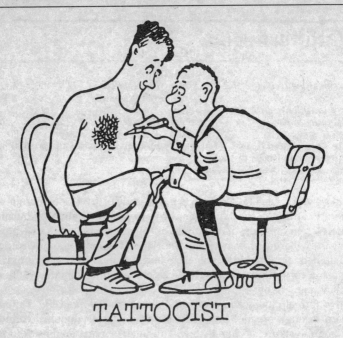

TATTOOIST

strong hold over suppliers etc and without their co-operation you probably won't be able to open. The EUROPEAN TATTOO ARTISTS FEDERATION is a self-regulating body. Tattooists see an unusual view of life. They have to cope with a great many of their clients passing out and should know how to cope with that. It also helps to be fairly tough (black belt in karate perhaps) because you will have to deal with some fairly strange people and may not want to have to comply with their requests.

Taxidermist

At a Glance

Qualifications/Training	Available	*Income bracket*	Low
Licence	No	*Town/Country*	Either
Experience/Springboard	Recommended	*Travel*	Local
Mid-career entry	Yes	*Exit sale*	No
Entry costs	£100+	*Work at home*	Yes

Mix and match   Yes.   You could think about: Artist, Book packager, Embalmer, Accountant . . .

Enquiries   Guild of Taxidermists

Taxidermists stuff and preserve dead animals. Popular taste and legislation aimed at protecting endangered species has lessened the demand for stuffing pets or big game trophies so one of the most successful ways of making a living from taxidermy is by building up a collection of stuffed animals and hiring them for films, theatres, displays and private parties. Most of the stuffing you'll do will be of fish, legal game birds and deer. There's no need to work regular hours so you could mix and match taxidermy with another job. The way to learn is to find a commercial taxidermist who is willing to teach you; the GUILD OF TAXIDERMISTS may be able to help. CROWCRAFT arrange short courses in specialist areas such as bird mounting, modelling rocks and mounts and there's a range of books from the general *Taxidermy* to specialist works like *Symmetric System of Big Game Head Mounting*. If you want job experience, try museums. You'll need a fairly strong stomach, to be dexterous and artistic enough to finish up with something that looks very like a living animal.

Basic equipment costs about £50–100. You need fleshing knives, scalpels and forceps, scissors, hooks to hold down bits of the animal you're skinning and supplies of syringes, pins, wire, thread, needles, tape and glue. In addition you need supplies of preserving chemicals, stuffing materials (tow and wood pulp) and putty. Once you've got a commission you have to select imitation eyes and noses, mounts, and an animal form which act as a skeleton for the animal you're stuffing. Base your charges on materials plus time. If you're hiring stuffed animals, charge a percentage of their value; remember they may need to be cleaned when you get them back and make sure clients know they're responsible for damages. Repairs are difficult because of having to match, for example, legs or beaks. Stuffed animals must be kept in a dry cool place and be treated carefully. Replacement, especially of endangered species, can be very difficult unless you have an arrangement with a zoo.

Taxidermy isn't a glamorous career, many lay people find it funny in spite of the skill required. There is a small market for pet stuffing. Always make sure you know how the client wants the animal to be presented – this is especially important for pets whose owners will expect you to reproduce the animal's personality as well as its appearance. Most work comes by getting yourself known at any local hotel or house which runs shooting and fishing parties whose clients may want souvenirs of their successful kills. Never handle an endangered or protected species unless you're sure and can prove that it died of natural causes. Under the Wildlife and Countryside Act you risk heavy fines even if it's someone else's illegal catch you've stuffed, big auction houses have been known to suffer heavy penalties for handling illegally shot, stuffed eagles.

Taxi Driver

At a Glance

Qualifications/Training	Yes	Income bracket	Low–High
Licence	Yes	Town/Country	Either
Experience/Springboard	No	Travel	Yes
Mid-career entry	Yes	Exit sale	No
Entry costs	£500++	Work at home	No

Mix and match   Possible.   You could think about: Garage owner, Street entertainer, Bookie, Plumber . . .

Enquiries   Licensed Taxi Drivers Association

As a licensed cab driver you can ply for hire in the streets and taxi ranks which mini-cab drivers can't. You can also take passengers who contact the taxi company. The vehicles cabbies drive tend to be of a standard design, to carry up to five passengers and baggage. In major cities they are often built to a special design with diesel engines, still often referred to as black cabs although the colour can vary.

To get a licence you will have to pass various tests which vary depending on the local authority that governs them. These are especially stringent in London where after registering at the PUBLIC CARRIAGE OFFICE you will go through medical and police vetting before going on to 'The Knowledge' which is details of all routes and street names within six miles of Charing Cross. You learn this by driving around on a motor bike teaching yourself the routes from specially provided maps; alternatively some garages run schools. This culminates in a driving test in a taxi; it usually takes about 1½–2 years to pass.

Once through all of that you can work. Taxi drivers are self-employed and operate through companies (rather like co-operatives). You can hire a cab from the company for either a weekly rent or a cut of your takings but to make proper money you really need your own cab – they cost up to £16,000 new and will need to be well maintained. The local authority which awards licences controls maximum fares and taxis have meters which indicate how much to charge on each journey. Tips are always in cash.

Licensed cab drivers are subject to certain rules (depending on where they are). For instance, once you've stopped to pick up a passenger you must carry them anywhere within a six mile radius; but you don't have to stop for anyone. There is no legal limit on the number of hours you can work. The busy times are usually in mornings and evenings. You can expect to cover about 30,000 miles each year – more if you work at night, which avoids the stress of driving in traffic jams all day.

Further information from the LICENSED TAXI DRIVERS ASSOCIATION which also publishes *Taxi*.

Textile Designer

At a Glance

Qualifications/Training	Recommended	Income bracket	Low–High
Licence	No	Town/Country	Either
Experience/Springboard	Not necessary	Travel	Yes
Mid-career entry	Possible	Exit sale	No
Entry costs	£100+	Work at home	Yes

Mix and match   Yes.   You could think about: Interior designer, Fashion clothes designer, Market stall holder, Print maker . . .
Enquiries   Design Council

For the individual designer, selling to the British market is extremely difficult and many designs go overseas to more receptive markets. Selling is then largely through overseas trade fairs and buyers. Formal training is usual, but on the smaller scale (printing) occasional classes or similar can be adequate. There are opportunities to specialise in many fields (scarves, buttons, printed ribbons). Contacts are invaluable. A large amount of hard sell and publicity will be required involving long hours. A flamboyant nature is an asset.

Numerous degree and diploma courses are available (details from ADAR). These cover some commercial aspects of the textile trade and often offer opportunities to be placed short-term with experienced designers, colour consultants etc. Colleges exhibit students' work in their own shows and abroad (enter as many as possible). This provides good experience in presentation (which is 50% of the ingredients of success), recognition and contacts.

Set up costs are minimal (paint, brushes, boards, paper). Producing material from your own designs can be low (batik) or high cost (screen printing). Colleges will rent out use of equipment and you can operate from home. The alternative is to set up a small concern and print your own and others' designs. Take a market stall for one or two days a week, in eg Covent Garden.

Use all contacts, wear your own designs made up, and go out and sell. Trade fairs and shows are vital (see *Exhibition Bulletin* in reference libraries; DESIGN COUNCIL for lists and costs); but they are expensive, especially abroad (£500–1,000). Get an agent (they go to all the shows) who will take your portfolio to the fairs for you, for 30–40% commission. Personal contact is better. Sell designs to suitable retailers (Next; Designers' Guild). If you have an interest in interior design, approach individuals and outlets to supply designs, to order or original. This is an under-exploited area but it can be extremely satisfying and lucrative.

Textile design has a large fashion turnover, so make the most of opportunities and success can be achieved. Follow current trends through fashion and interior design magazines eg *Craft, Designer's Journal*. Seasonal colour forecasts, part of a style and design package, are available from the INTERNATIONAL INSTITUTE FOR COTTON, and the INTERNATIONAL WOOL SECRETARIAT at £40 per annum.

Thatcher

At a Glance

Qualifications/Training	Essential	*Income bracket*	Low–Medium
Licence	No	*Town/Country*	Mostly country
Experience/Springboard	No	*Travel*	Yes
Mid-career entry	Good	*Exit sale*	No
Entry costs	£5,000+	*Work at home*	No

Mix and match   Possible.   You could think about: Roofer, House converter, Import/export broker, Man with a van, Gardener/garden designer, MP . . .

Enquiries   Thatching Advisory Service

This is a traditional craft that is attracting refugees from the rat race. Thatchers spend most of their time rethatching houses or barns either from scratch or by building on an existing foundation of thatch. Thatched roofs are fashionable and are sometimes put on new houses or to replace tiles; thatching is also used for garden sheds etc. Most work comes from private house owners but there are opportunities for thatch building in film and TV sets, for exhibitions and occasionally on showpiece factories. A thatch should last anything from about 15 years to more than 50. Although repairs are sometimes needed, you should only expect to spend about 3 weeks a year repairing. So you'll need to travel and work away from home. Traditionally a men only job, there are now some women around, but they are regarded as exceptional.

You can learn how to thatch by serving a 5 year trade apprenticeship with an established thatcher, this includes some courses on day and block release at local FE colleges. Alternatively the THATCHING ADVISORY SERVICE (TAS) runs a franchise system where for a fee of £12,000 (get a bank loan) you will be given a 6 month training (and paid £600 a month while you do it) before becoming a franchise holder with them. This scheme is over subscribed and only about 2% of applicants can be accepted. The TAS offer continuing guidance through their magazine *Thatch*; (their managing director has written the authoritative book on the subject, also called *Thatch*). Either of these ways of learning gives you the qualification to thatch and will have taught you enough to be able to work for yourself.

Obviously thatchers have to enjoy being outside, have good balance and a degree of physical strength. You can decide how long you work and when. Some thatchers choose not to work during the winter, while others are prepared to work whenever they can. You'll probably get more work in the summer and can use longer daylight hours. Rain

THATCHER

needn't stop you from thatching, but may make the job less agreeable; winds can be a hindrance.

You will have collected the necessary tools and equipment during training – hammers, leggat, ladders, needles, mallet, knives and shearing hooks. In addition you'll need insurance to cover damage to your clients' houses and contents for which you are liable while thatching (£1½–2 million worth of cover). You'll need to buy the reed for your first commission in advance. It will cost about £3,000 (bank loan) and is usually brought from the South of France, Hungary or Poland by lorry. Importing direct from the supplier cuts out the reed dealer, saving about £700 a load, and giving you a sideline to thatching. The average charge for a cottage (about 3 week's work) is between £8,000 and £10,000. Rather than work alone you may prefer to employ assistants which means you'll get jobs done more quickly but your profits will be less, so it depends on how much local work there is. The TAS recommend a minimum monthly turnover of £4,000 during the first year (about £1,450 of that goes on salaries and profit). They also suggest that you should wait until your 3rd or 4th year before gauging profitability.

Thatched roofs are usually a luxury, so clients may be demanding and will want some say about what you do. You can opt to specialise in certain designs, eg for the ridge (often decorated and a job you may be called upon to do on its own), and you will have to give expert advice on which sort of reed to use and the basic structure of the roof. Reputation counts for a lot so it's a good idea to keep your clients as happy as possible.

Further information from COSIRA and TAS.

Theatrical Agent

At a Glance

Qualifications/Training	No	Income bracket	Low–Medium
Licence	No	Town/Country	Town
Experience/Springboard	Yes	Travel	Some
Mid-career entry	Possible	Exit sale	Possible
Entry costs	£2,000+	Work at home	Possible

Mix and match   Limited.   You could think about: Scriptwriter, Calligrapher, Potter . . .

Enquiries   Spotlight, Theatrical agents

Theatrical agents help actors to find work and make sure that they are fairly treated, (given reasonable contracts, pay etc) when they are working. Particularly for young actors who don't always know the ropes and who are vulnerable to unscrupulous directors and producers, agents are very important to their clients; helping them to cope with problems and crises in their private lives as well as sorting out their professional affairs. Agents can also be managers for well known and established clients, actively promoting actors both on the stage and off – arranging for them to write books, open village fetes etc, and becoming more involved in all aspects of their client's life that could have a bearing on their career.

There are no formal qualifications but you'll need to have had some experience of working in a theatrical agency so that you have some idea of what's involved and, more importantly, have a grounding in actors' contracts and how they work. You have to balance being businesslike, efficient and tough, with being prepared to listen sympathetically to your clients at times when they are having difficulty in coping with the problems of long rests or difficult working conditions. Acting experience

THEATRICAL AGENT

gives you useful insights into actors' problems. It's a good idea to set up with a partner – having someone to consult often helps you to make decisions. You may find that one of you is better suited to concentrating on the business/legal side of the agency while the other spends more time with clients and work hunting. The more you know about plays and drama the better for when you're looking for suitable parts for which your clients can audition.

Set up equipment includes typewriter, stationery, an efficient filing system and perhaps a computer. Later it may be worth investing in a fax machine; this is a very visual business and casting directors like to see what you're sending them. You'll spend so much time on the phone that you need at least a second line for incoming calls and somebody to answer it as well as to help with administrative and secretarial back up. Once you get busy a secretary is essential to cope with the paperwork and invoicing and a book-keeper for the accounts. You're paid commission on the fees that your clients get – actors are not often paid a lot. Exactly what commission you get is negotiated between you and the client; usually around 10% for theatre work and about 12½–15% for films, TV and voice overs (these are the disembodied voices on advertisements – usually very well paid and often well known). Managers get up to about 20% commission.

Actors can have several agents (eg one for theatre work, another for voice overs). You aren't allowed to try and poach another agent's clients, although big agents often do successfully grab up and coming actors. You can, however, take on anybody who approaches you because they want a different agent and you'll probably be able to take quite a few of your clients from wherever you were before you opened on your own. (Remember this when you start to employ assistants in your own agency). Otherwise, contact SPOTLIGHT, and send them details of your agency. SPOTLIGHT helps actors to find agents and will tell them about you if you seem to be right for the actor. After that, new clients come via word of mouth and reputation.

When you're choosing clients you have to select those you can get work for, this will usually mean having one or two examples of each of a wide range of age and appearance. There is a lot of work for very young actors, but also a lot of them around and when your clients are resting (ie not earning any money from acting), you are not earning commission. Some agents have different partners to handle different areas (theatre, TV etc), other split the work load by sharing out clients. You need a network of contacts who will listen to you when you're trying to promote your clients. That means getting to know producers and casting directors; you won't necessarily meet them very often but you'll spend a lot of time talking to them on the phone when you're finding out what they're casting so that you can promote your clients. You may not have a lot of time to yourself during the week. You spend days on the phone, meeting clients and casting directors; then you have to visit the theatre several times a week, watching how your clients are doing and looking out for parts that may suit them (especially in productions that are about to go on tour which are often recast). Some agents choose to spend their weekends touring around the country watching other companies or their own clients on tour.

Timeshare Holiday Accommodation Owner

At a Glance

Qualifications/Training	No	*Income bracket*	Low–High
Licence	No	*Town/Country*	Either
Experience/Springboard	No	*Travel*	Between sites
Mid-career entry	Likely	*Exit sale*	Yes
Entry costs	£100,000++	*Work at home*	No

Mix and match Yes. You could think about: Holiday accommodation owner, Landlord, Direct marketing agent, List broker, Estate agent, Import/export broker . . .

Enquiries Timeshare Developers' Association

You can sell and manage units of holiday accommodation on a timeshare basis – either refurbishing property you already own or, if you are brave, building it specifically for the purpose. But if you can't sell quickly once you've started investing the money, you will follow many others and go bust. This is a business with high capital risks but is also the fastest growing area of tourism in the 1980s.

You need at least 10 units of accommodation which must be furnished to luxury standard and on a good site. There is no point trying to run this alongside the letting of standard holiday accommodation, except in the short term, since the standard of the amenities must be excellent and cannot be justified by ordinary holiday rents. Amenities not provided locally you will need to provide on site – shops, swimming, videos, good play facilities etc.

Before you start, you are wise to commission a feasibility study from a reputable timeshare consultant. Once you have started renovation and have sample accommodation to show, you can apply to an international timeshare organisation, such as RESORT CONDOMINIUMS INTERNATIONAL (RCI) for affiliation. This allows those who buy your units to exchange their holiday for another within the organisation (in the case of RCI, this gives the possibility of exchanging for a holiday in any one of 1350 resorts, from China to the United States). So you can make buying your timeshare attractive to British buyers, even to people who live fairly locally, but have the place full of Yanks and Swedes.

A professional selling operation is essential and it is worth employing specialists. You will probably need several people selling in peak season to get it right, as well as any on-site management. You are, after all, persuading people to make a capital investment. Your buyers will usually be over 40, largely with kids off their hands. Once they have committed themselves to buy, you are expected to give them five days in which to change their minds again. They will need to be satisfied as to the security of their investment and the proper running of the operation – so you need to have thought all that out before you start. A sound legal framework is essential, so you should find a solicitor who is familiar with timeshare. A trust company will also have to be formed to protect buyers. You may want to join the new TIMESHARE DEVELOPERS' ASSOCIATION.

Banks are extremely cautious because they cannot repossess the accommodation once time has been sold on it. 50% is the maximum you should expect to be able to borrow. You may find others who are more adventurous but beware of interest rates. If you do not sell a basic minimum quickly, to service the initial loan, the whole operation will abort. You need a cool business head.

To be successful, you should also have a good selling technique, sound management skills, and the ability to design the accommodation with flair or to select others who will. It's worth reading a study on timeshare produced by RCI.

Tourist Guide

At a Glance

Qualifications/Training	Necessary	Income bracket	Medium
Licence	In some cases	Town/Country	Either
Experience/Springboard	No	Travel	Yes
Mid-career entry	Yes	Exit sale	No
Entry costs	£1,000	Work at home	No

Mix and match Yes. You could think about: Mini-cab driver, Interpreter, Costume designer, Opening to the public . . .

Enquiries Local tourist boards

With tourism in the UK becoming a leading industry, tourist guides play an important part in entertaining visitors from home and abroad, by sharing their knowledge about places, people and life in the most imaginative and informative way possible. Tourist guides en masse are a disturbing force with each endeavouring to out-face the other, but no 2 tourist guides are alike when it comes to leading a group of visitors through our national heritage, and it is the individual's love of his or her own subject that makes one guide different from another. Tourist guiding is open to all creeds and races, but beware, there is an unhealthy majority of the retired headmistress type. Young blood of both sexes is desperately needed to swell the ranks, and graduates are coming into the industry in their twenties. Training is through one of the Blue Badge courses operated by tourist boards in conjunction with local authorities and tourism related businesses. Courses vary in length and entry qualifications. THE LONDON TOURIST BOARD trains guides over six months, involving a considerable amount of on-site training, and successful candidates are then registered and qualify to work in and near London. Other regions run shorter courses. Courses include local history lectures and core knowledge covering law, religion, geography, etc. Languages are of immense help in winning a place on a course which might be over-subscribed. Less well-known languages such as Chinese, Japanese or Arabic will assist and in time, bring financial reward. Tourist guides come from all walks of life: road-sweepers, bus drivers, housewives, air stewards, nurses and publicans to name a few. All have to be good listeners. Academics, whilst knowing their subject, do not necessarily have the expertise to put it across in the world outside the classroom. You must keep up to date with developments such as excavations or the opening of new attractions. Other Blue

Badges and endorsements should be sought out and thereby increase your chances of employment.

Most tourist guides run an office from home. Along with a telephone, you'll need a reliable answering machine, and given time, even a telex. Suitable letter headings for your stationery, and business cards to match; beware of how you advertise yourself in travel trade publications until you can justify the expense and have sufficient expertise as a guide. Having drafted suggested itineraries, mail shot tour operators, travel agencies, tourist boards, ... informing them of your services which could complement theirs in your neck of the woods. Tourist guides often put packages together by co-ordinating travel, a meal stop and places of interest through a knowledge of the area. Given time, most business comes direct through personal recommendation. Tourist guides are well known for passing business amongst themselves, but as you develop your own standards, you soon learn who to pass work on to and who not. Income in the first year or so will not be that forthcoming. It takes time to establish your own niche, especially in the major tourist destination centres where so many guiding organisations ply for a living. It takes just one hi-jacking of a North American aircraft to put you out of business. If you've got another job, hang on to it until you can afford to concentrate on tour guiding. It's a good thing to mix and match with others, especially in the depths of winter when supplies of tourists dry up.

There's no such thing as an average day; no 2 tourists are the same, and no question is ever stupid even though the enquirer thinks so. When you get to the point of having to explain the purpose of a flying buttress in driving rain, just remember how far some of your visitors have flown to listen to you.

The season is usually for six months or so. Few work all year round, but with earnings for some in excess of £15,000 per year, you can forget your summer holidays, and spend Christmas in the Bahamas (at the cost of not having a day off for weeks or even months on end).

Avoid ruts! Doing the same old tour day in day out becomes stale, so keep extending your areas of interest. For example, driver-guiding is a specialist form of touring small groups in the tourist guide's own car, often setting up complete itineraries to include accommodation. Some guides lecture on cruise ships, others join forces with tourist boards and work on promotions overseas. Some painstakingly develop tours for the handicapped. As long as you can combine tact, diplomacy and have the ability to bring history alive through public speaking, along with the odd story or two, you're well on the way to becoming a tourist guide.

Useful organisations for courses:

Contact the local tourist information centres, local authorities/regions tourist boards and regional colleges.

Read *Please Follow Me* and contact the GUILD OF GUIDE LECTURERS.

Toymaker

At a Glance

Qualifications/Training	Available	*Income bracket*	Low–Medium
Licence	No	*Town/Country*	Either
Experience/Springboard	No	*Travel*	No
Mid-career entry	Yes	*Exit sale*	No
Entry costs	£500+	*Work at home*	Yes

Mix and match   Yes.   You could think about: Wood carver, New house builder, Dealer in antiques, Farmer . . .

Enquiries   British Toy Makers Guild, Guild of Master Craftsmen, British Toy and Hobby Manufacturers Association

A lot of modern toys are mass produced in factories. However, there is a market for traditional hand made toys – rocking horses, porcelain dolls, soft toys, dolls houses etc and collectors' pieces (for adults rather than children), such as toy soldiers and mechanical toys. You can sell directly to the customer or to a retailer. If you don't want to or can't make the toys yourself, with or without assistance, you can sell new designs for toys to other manufacturers; make sure that any agreement you enter into with the manufacturer will let you benefit if your idea really takes off. You don't need any special qualifications. There are various courses in toymaking (evening classes in puppet making for example). But, if formally trained at all, toymakers are more likely to have done a course in woodwork, pottery etc. Toys have to satisfy certain safety rules (no lead paint, nylon hair to be only a certain length etc) before they can be sold for children. The BRITISH STANDARDS INSTITUTION will send you a list of these rules. Toymakers have to be consistently good craftsmen; innovative in their ideas for new toys and market places; business like and reliable, clients aren't impressed by unexplained late delivery or ignored customer enquiries. Initially you'll need a lot of confidence and determination to make your ideas succeed.

As well as the tools and equipment you need to make the toys, set up costs include a workshop. Small toys can be made in a spare room at home, otherwise a garage, shed or barn if you don't want to buy a workshop straightaway. You can change premises as you grow. As long as you're relatively accessible, so that materials can get in to and toys out from your workshop, you don't have to be particularly close to big towns. Banks aren't always helpful but are more likely to listen if you present them with coherent and realistic business plans and proposals. You'll need some capital to keep you going until your business takes off. Charges are based on costs of equipment and time. Keep an eye on competition but make sure that you're earning enough to make the business worthwhile.

Your first few orders will probably come from friends and then, if your work is good, your reputation will spread by word of mouth. Sell to a prestigious name like Harrods, it helps with further orders. Publicity is important. Advertising is expensive so try and get some write ups (which are free) in the local and national press. Try and get onto children's TV (not easy) if your products are particularly appealing and you're comparatively charismatic. Develop your contacts all the time.

For publicity purposes, it looks good to be a member of the BRITISH TOY MAKERS GUILD or the GUILD OF MASTER CRAFTSMEN; they also give advice to their members. The BRITISH TOY AND HOBBY MANUFACTURERS ASSOCIATION has useful information although it caters for mass producers rather more than craftsmen.

You can find useful facts about toy marketing and trade associations in the *British Toy Industry Fact Book* and from *British Toy and Hobby Briefing*.

Travel Agent

At a Glance

Qualifications/Training	Recommended	*Income bracket*	Medium
Licence	Recommended	*Town/Country*	Town
Experience/Springboard	Essential	*Travel*	No
Mid-career entry	Good	*Exit sale*	Yes
Entry costs	£40,000	*Work at home*	No
Mix and match	Limited.	You could think about: List broker, Specialist sports retailer, Novelist . . .	
Enquiries	Association of British Travel Agents		

Travel agents reserve, issue and sell tickets for air, rail, sea and coach travel. They also sell package holidays offered by tour operators, give advice and help with passports, visas, foreign currency and insurance, arrange reservations for hotels and car hire and compile tailor made packages.

To open your own travel agency approved by the ASSOCIATION OF BRITISH TRAVEL AGENTS (ABTA), you must lodge a bond of £7,500 (this goes towards the rescue of any stranded customers if a member goes bankrupt). ABTA also requires you to have capital of at least £10,000 and to have 2 people working full time, one with 2 years ABTA experience. If you want to issue, rather than merely reserve, air tickets you have to be a member of the INTERNATIONAL AIR TRANSPORT ASSOCIATION having lodged a bond equal to 50% of a month's air turnover (based on the reservations you have made) and to have a year's air ticket selling experience. Although no additional qualifications are formally necessary, there are ABTA approved courses which you are well-advised to investigate. See also *Travel Trade Gazette, Travel News* and *Airline World* for help with getting the necessary travel agent experience.

Travel agents have to be methodical and meticulous (a mistake on an air ticket is serious), long-suffering enough to cope with long hours on the telephone and patient enough to do all of this in spite of constant interruptions from customers. You'll need some sort of office; theoretically, the only equipment you need is a desk and a telephone but it's useful to have a computer link with airlines (Travicom) and/or tour operators (Prestel) which give quicker access to details of availability. Altogether, allow about £40,000 to open. You will be paid on commission, ranging from 7–15%, by the companies whose tickets you sell (including British Rail and National Express coaches). Turnover will seem vast, £½ million per month isn't unusual for air sales alone. But commission is paid on profits only so don't get too excited.

People use their local travel agent, so set up in an area which will provide enough business and check out local competition. Nearby offices will buy tickets for business travel, residential areas may want more package holidays (but not always the same ones). In either case, your customers will have some idea of where they want to go and when; the bulk of your job is finding out how to get them there, which may mean offering them compromises. Make your presence obvious, and advertise the services you offer, the companies you are agent for, and any special offers (cut-price late bookings etc) that are available. Tour operators and travel lines do a lot of their own advertising on TV and in the press.

Holidays are sold all year round but there are seasonal variations in clientele; some stick to school holidays, some off season; sun lovers and skiers. Cultivating contacts in the trade is useful for speeding up enquiries and getting hold of unobtainable tickets; a spot of ostentatious use of contacts is impressive for customers.

Tree Surgeon

At a Glance

Qualifications/Training	Recommended	*Income bracket*	Low–Medium
Licence	No	*Town/Country*	Mostly country
Experience/Springboard	No	*Travel*	Yes
Mid-career entry	Possible	*Exit sale*	No
Entry costs	£2,000+	*Work at home*	No

Mix and match   Yes. You could think about: Gardener/garden designer, Man with a van, Farmer, Roofer . . .

Enquiries   Forestry Training Council

Tree surgery (aboriculture) is mainly concerned with the health of trees which are usually, though not necessarily, large or mature. This work is carried out for private and public customers whose trees are diseased or wind damaged, or which have grown too large. There is a need for people trained in the science and technology of trees, from their planting to their felling, and also to supply wood and wood products.

The FORESTRY TRAINING COUNCIL provides courses for the private sector – employees, self-employed contractors and specialist advisers – in a wide range of skills and technical management. This is a relatively new industry and training programmes are still being developed. MERRIST WOOD AGRICULTURAL COLLEGE offers a one-year course and you can do short courses in safety, including chain saw handling and tree climbing.

Professional tree surgeons, apart from their specialist knowledge of tree identification, tree disease and solving problems, are also concerned with felling. The problems of felling say a chestnut tree over 100ft tall are considerable. You'll need to be good at climbing trees, have a good head for heights and love trees in the way that vets love animals – ie recognise when they need to be destroyed.

To set up you need ropes, harnesses, a chain saw, a ladder and a hard hat. A vehicle that can cope with rough terrain is useful. You could cause a lot of damage if you miscalculated and allowed a tree to fall in the wrong direction, so substantial risk insurance is essential. Like most professions, the charges are based on the amount of time taken on the assignment; any timber resulting from your work belongs to the client. You need to operate in an area where people have big gardens. This is a dangerous job. The rate of serious personal injury is probably higher among tree surgeons and fellers than any other group of horticultural workers. However if the risks are high so are the rewards – tree-felling like steeplejacking and other high risk solitary occupations has a great appeal and satisfaction for a certain type of person.

TREE SURGEON

Trout Farmer

At a Glance

Qualifications/Training	Necessary	Income bracket	Low
Licence	No	Town/Country	Country
Experience/Springboard	Essential	Travel	Local
Mid-career entry	Good	Exit sale	Excellent
Entry costs	£50,000	Work at home	Yes

Mix and match   Yes. You could think about: Holiday accommodation owner, Restaurateur, Fish curer and smoker, Wind surfing school owner . . .

Enquiries   British Trout Association, National Farmers' Union

Trout farmers breed, grow and market trout. Start by taking a specialist fish farming course at INVERNESS COLLEGE or the AGRICULTURAL COLLEGE in Dumfries or Sparsholt in Hampshire. Then get some good experience working on several farms over 2 or 3 years to build up good contacts and learn the business thoroughly. Join the NATIONAL FARMERS UNION fish farming section and the BRITISH TROUT ASSOCIATION. You will make somewhere between nothing and £5,000 in the first few years, rising to £12,000 per annum. Trout farming has a quicker turnover than salmon farming and the small fish or eggs are cheaper. You need around £50,000, depending on the cost of your site. You also need to negotiate with the local water authority and the DEPARTMENT OF THE ENVIRONMENT to remove and replace water from the river. This will involve you with a lot of bureaucracy.

You will have less babysitting to do than your salmon counterparts, as there are fewer marauding animals or birds and you are more protected from the extremes of the weather and force of the elements. It is essential that you can take part in communal marketing with other fish farmers in your area which will cut costs. Get a good accountant.

As well as feeding your fish, you must also remove any that are dead and diagnose the cause; look for damage or pests; take out the smaller fish into separate cages to allow growth and prevent them getting attacked by the others; kill, gut and pack in ice for transport those that are ready for market.

You must be practical and able to swim. If you run a hatchery, you should be clean and tidy. Only go in for this if you enjoy the open air and irregular hours. Attend the annual fish farm conference and visit customers and watch new developments in equipment. Read *Fish Farming International* magazine.

Typesetter

At a Glance

Qualifications/Training	Recommended	*Income bracket*	Low–Medium
Licence	No	*Town/Country*	Town
Experience/Springboard	Useful	*Travel*	Local
Mid-career entry	Yes	*Exit sale*	Possible
Entry costs	£5,000+	*Work at home*	Yes

Mix and match Yes. You could think about: Word processor, Computer software author, Shopkeeper, Book editor, Book packager . . .

Enquiries Typesetters, National Graphical Association

This has nothing to do with the old printer's craft of setting type. It is still part of the printing process but is much closer to word processing, indeed it follows on from that. New technology has changed printing probably more than any other 'traditional' industry.

You must be able to type accurately and quickly and you must understand the process of taking a manuscript, converting the author's words into machine-readable form, visualising the finished book and inserting the necessary codes to control the photosetter. Membership of the NATIONAL GRAPHICAL ASSOCIATION used to be essential; that is no longer the case but you are unlikely to be able to work for any of the established publishing houses which has union agreement without NGA membership. That could limit your market. You need an eye for detail and an ability to remember all the codes (and sometimes these can be fairly complex) if you are not to waste time (and money) by having whole paragraphs in the wrong typeface. You need to understand all the old terms – fount, measure, typeface, etc if you are to produce a 'book' which conforms to the book designer's specification; also in order to suggest changes to that specification which can drastically affect efficiency or cost of production of the finished job.

The only equipment you need is a desk, a computer, a supply of disks. You will be subcontracting the photosetting and (if required) preparation of artwork to other specialists. But you are responsible for the final product so it is essential that you understand all the processes and can prepare an accurate quotation that is likely to be accepted by the publisher. Luck will play a great part in your eventual success but you will almost certainly need to know somebody in publishing to get your first job. No-one is likely to give you work unless you can prove that you are capable of producing the goods. Initially your earnings will be nil, and you are unlikely to get paid for any job until it is completed, so cash flow will be a real problem – the bigger the job the greater your cash problems.

The work involves liaising with the publisher (and possibly the author) to understand their requirements, keying the manuscript, transferring data to the photosetter of your choice and supervising the output. You will find the most satisfactory arrangement is to deal with one or two photosetting specialists who understand you and your requirements and who, at the same time, offer you the best financial terms. Mistakes can be expensive and, as sub-contracting forms such a large part of the work you need to be confident that those who are working for you (and who represent a large part of the overall costs in your calculations) do not eat up your profit. Before the whole job goes to the photosetter get a large enough sample set to bring to light any problems before they become catastrophes. You need to be able to understand the needs of the writer, the publisher, the designer and the machine operator. Before beginning work spend time with the publisher so that you are absolutely clear about what is required. Do a good job at the right price and you will be able to hope for more work from the publisher but don't expect any favours. There are too many people around offering the same services as you for you to be able to rely on loyalty for the future. On the other hand you must be prepared to pester publishers to allow you to quote for more jobs – emphasise any areas in your favour – preliminary mailings of questionnaires to collect data, fast efficient updating for second and subsequent editions, sub-editing ability etc. Remember that the data on your disk is not your data and the publisher may well require you to supply copies of any disks on completion of a job.

Typist

At a Glance

Qualifications/Training	Recommended	Income bracket	Low–Medium
Licence	No	Town/Country	Town mostly
Experience/Springboard	Yes	Travel	Local
Mid-career entry	Yes	Exit sale	No
Entry costs	£5+++	Work at home	Yes

Mix and match   Yes.   You could think about: Word processor, Typesetter, List broker, Book editor, Bookkeeper, Novelist, Sculptor . . .

Enquiries   Secretarial agencies

It is easy to learn to type if you have time to practise. But to be convincing when looking for work it is useful to have certificates to show you have reached good speeds and are competent. You can pick up the skills at evening classes, private secretarial schools, further education colleges (some are tailored for graduates) or from a book. Some offer courses leading to their own certificates; others to qualifications such as RSA (ROYAL SOCIETY OF ARTS). Like learning to ride a bike, touch-typing may seem impossible at first, but once you've mastered it you'll never forget it. Straight typing is being replaced in more and more offices by word processing – a closely related job.

Typists can specialise – in shorthand and typing, audio typing (where the material has been dictated on to a special tape recorder) or copy typing (where the material is handwritten or a revision of something that has been typed or printed before). If you don't want to work for a company, you can find work typing at home (eg students' theses, book manuscripts) or do temp work, getting jobs through an agency.

Either way, you can usually work the hours or days that suit you. It is a useful job to fall back on if, for example, you are trying to get into another career but the work is not coming in as regularly as you would like.

If you want to do more than be a typist you can go on to use a word processor or become a secretary or a personal assistant. Working as a temp is a good way of getting a taste of different types of business – you can pick up information on office management and see exactly what people do in a range of different offices – before making a final decision on your career. You can also temp while you travel around if you choose.

If you get fed up with working for an agency, who take a cut of the money paid out by your temporary employer, you can try volunteering yourself as a freelance typist with companies who know you; they can call on you when their own staff are on holiday or off sick. If you are working from home, advertise your services with local businesses, university, colleges etc.

As a typist you may be paid by the hour (£5+) or by the page if you work at home (so you need good speeds to make a living). You will need a supply of stationery and your own electric typewriter if you are working at home, and should also consider developing skills in computing (or at least word processing), as much of this work can now be done at home and transmitted to the appropriate destination via the telephone.

UK Correspondent for Overseas Media

At a Glance

Qualifications/Training	Available	Income bracket	Low–Medium
Licence	No	Town/Country	Town
Experience/Springboard	Essential	Travel	Yes
Mid-career entry	Yes	Exit sale	No
Entry costs	£2,500	Work at home	Partly

Mix and match   Good.   You could think about: English language school owner, Journalist, Interpreter, Insurance broker, Book editor, Wig maker . . .

Enquiries   International news agencies, Overseas media

You can make money as a freelance journalist working for overseas newspapers, magazines, radio and TV companies. The amount of work you can get depends largely on who and what you know but it's an excellent thing to mix and match with virtually anything else and you may be able to make it pay for some overseas travel.

There are no formal qualifications but you must be fluent in the language you're working in and familiar with the culture of the country you're reporting to. It helps also if you're an expert in an area that people are likely to be interested in reading about: art, theatre, food, economics, pop-music . . . and you need to have a supply of good ideas for material as well as being in touch with current events in the UK and the one you're writing for. You need good writing skills, imagination and the ability to work quickly. You also need contacts who can help with research; journalists and others, both in your field of speciality and in other areas which may be of interest to your overseas audience or readership. Unless you're working for a very large publication or broadcasting company which uses a wide range of special correspondents in the UK, you should be prepared to cover stories on virtually anything including current events and special features tailored to your overseas audience/readership.

Set up equipment is minimal, you need a phone and a typewriter or word processor. Depending on the work you're doing and the sophistication of your client, you may also need a tape recorder, a fax and/or a modem. The amount you're paid varies a lot but is usually calculated on the final number of words or air-time minutes you produce. You definitely need to be pushy to get into this job. Write to, telephone and visit international news agencies. Get the names of people to contact at overseas publications and broadcasting companies. This is best done while you're in the country you want to write for. Talk to anyone you know who's already involved in the area: journalists, researchers, producers, editors. Then send out your CV and visit as many people as you can see. It's easier if you're a national of the country you're hoping to report to, if not, you should have spent some time there and have family or friends living there. If you aren't a national, you'll improve your chances by having good credentials; these can be either in doing similar work in the UK or by having a lot of experience or expertise in a sexy area. Once you've found someone who's interested in what you've got to offer, you can work out between you how much work you do for them. Some correspondents have a regular slot, reporting on current events in the UK or on subjects of general interest when events aren't exciting. Others do occasional work or do series on, for example, British painters, from time to time. You can work for as many people as you like as long as you're careful about copyright ownership when you use the same material for more than one.

What you write about is largely up to you as long as you know your audience. Virtually everywhere is interested in hearing about the Royal Family so following them around can be lucrative. In many ways it's up to you how much time you spend on being a correspondent. You may have to do some intensive research for a story, alternatively you could use your own experience in the UK or abroad and turn it into publishable or broadcastable material at the drop of a hat.

Upholsterer

At a Glance

Qualifications/Training	Recommended	Income bracket	Low
Licence	No	Town/Country	Town
Experience/Springboard	Recommended	Travel	Local
Mid-career entry	Possible	Exit sale	Possible
Entry costs	£1,500+	Work at home	Possible

Mix and match Possible. You could think about: Bespoke furniture maker/ designer, Man with a van, Dealer in large antiques . . .

Enquiries   Local upholsterers, Guild of Master Craftsmen

In spite of an increase in throw-away furniture, there is a demand for upholsterers especially to refurbish antiques. The work you do is meant to last up to 50 years and requires extensive knowledge of fabrics, stuffing, wood and the best ways of using them; an appreciation of antiques and their value is essential. Women may encounter a certain amount of sexism from more old fashioned practitioners of the trade; ('a woman just can't do some of this work') but clients are usually broader minded. You need skill to set up a new business and the more experience you have the better.

You can learn the trade by taking a course leading to a City and Guilds certificate. This will give you the rudiments but not the vast range of experience and practice that is regarded as essential. Traditionally upholsterers serve a 5-year apprenticeship including time at a technical college before they are let loose on commercial work. During this time you will earn very little and if you're a woman, may find you are expected to be more interested in curtains and soft furnishings than in stuffing, caning etc. Some people drift into upholstery mid-career, without this training or experience. There are obvious exceptions but, by and large, they have neither the skill nor the speed to make a living – usually doing this as a side line to something else. Experience and practice are essential; you will have to have attained a certain degree of speediness before it is worthwhile operating as an upholsterer. You can charge around £25 for the seat of a dining chair, £600 for refurbishing a 3 seater sofa, so if you can't work fast enough, you won't make money.

You need large premises, to work in and to store both the materials (stuffing, springs, buttons, braid, hair etc) and the pieces you are working on. You also need tools, hammers, needles, shears etc. A very basic kit costs a minimum of £20, but you will want to build on that (heavy-duty sewing machine, web stretcher), and to replace tools with better quality (shears range from £7–£150 for a pair). Covering fabrics are usually bought to client specification. A van is useful so that you can collect from and deliver to your clients. Insurance is essential especially if you are going to work on valuable antiques.

Upholsterers have to be painstaking, dexterous and able to work to deadlines. Clients believe they are paying a great deal (although you may disagree) for their upholstery service so it is important to get everything right as business comes from word of mouth.

There are no definitive texts on upholstery. However, *Upholstery* and *Practical Upholstering and the Cutting of Loose Covers* give a good introduction and you will find the GUILD OF MASTER CRAFTSMEN helpful.

Venue Manager

At a Glance			
Qualifications/Training	No	Income bracket	Low–Medium
Licence	No	Town/Country	Town
Experience/Springboard	Recommended	Travel	No
Mid-career entry	No	Exit sale	Yes
Entry costs	£5,000++	Work at home	No
Mix and match	Very limited. You could think about: Disco owner/DJ, Race-horse owner, Landlord . . .		
Enquiries	Local venues, booking agents		

Venue managers are businessmen who provide the 'theatre' in which bands and groups perform to their audiences. It is a young person's job and the secret of success is to get in at an early age. Often the most successful people are graduates and ex-students who managed to cut their teeth arranging concerts and events while still at university or polytechnic. Many social secretaries leave without their degrees because they've spent all their time arranging gigs (eg Harvey Goldsmith). At college there is a ready-made structure for arranging events with an eager audience but without the economic pressure of the real world.

The first step is to join the Ents society at your college. Get to know everyone and work your way to becoming the Ents secretary. Normally these are sabbatical posts that you can take up during or at the end of your course.

Take an interest in the music industry and what's being written up in the music newspapers; follow local bands. The newspapers give you some idea of who's up-and-coming across the country from which you can identify possible candidates for college bookings. Contacts you make at this early stage can prove invaluable to you later when you start up on your own.

Having got some experience at college and made initial contact with some of the people established in the industry, your next move must be to London if you aren't already there. Nearly all the major booking agents are London-based, as is the music industry itself, so there's really no alternative. Start by working for a booking agent. They are the lynch pin between bands and promoters, choosing and arranging venues throughout the country and therefore ideal people to work for in order to find your feet. But beware, the music business is not for slackers. It's a ruthless business and the only way you can justify yourself is by earning your booking agent money. The experience should be good – you'll learn all about contracts and the organisation of the business – but the salary is likely to be bad, perhaps £7,500 or £8,000 if you're lucky.

From here, you can springboard into venue management. It is important to have some idea of the sort of place you would like to run and the types of band or music you want to put on. The next step is to find a suitable, available venue and a financial backer. If all this is forthcoming, you can concentrate on the job in hand which, apart from a lot of hard graft, largely boils down to PR. The best approach is to try and build a reputation for an individual or specialist type of music that will distinguish your venue from others. The work is very tiring and demands your complete attention; a six day week is normal; working fourteen days on the trot, twelve or thirteen hours each day, is not uncommon. You'll need good man-management skills, as there'll be a high staff turnover. You'll have to be willing to get your hands dirty since much of the work will involve you in shifting heavy equipment.

Financial rewards may not be high – probably no more than £13,500. However, you could have the satisfaction of turning an empty space into a successful venue and the kudos that goes with it.

Vet

		At a Glance	
Qualifications/Training	Essential	*Income bracket*	Medium–High
Licence	Yes	*Town/Country*	Either
Experience/Springboard	Yes	*Travel*	Local
Mid-career entry	Unlikely	*Exit sale*	Excellent
Entry costs	£15,000+	*Work at home*	No
Mix and match Yes. You could think about: Farmer, Novelist, Property developer . . .			
Enquiries Royal College of Veterinary Surgeons			

A large number of vets work in private practice; some are in towns dealing with small animals; there are also openings in rural practices (farm animals, horses etc). Variety can be achieved if you have a small zoo in your area.

Before being allowed to practice vets must, by law, become members of the ROYAL COLLEGE OF VETERINARY SURGEONS (RCVS). To do this you face very fierce competition for a 5 or 6 year degree course (about 300 places for 1200+ applicants – you will need 3 As in science A-levels).

The trend now is for newly qualified vets to set up in partnership as soon as possible after gaining experience as an assistant or locum. This is partly due to the poor pay and conditions normally offered to assistants. If you are setting up your own practice, it is important to have had experience of as many different practices as possible so you see the work vets do at first hand and also the business aspects. (The BRITISH VETERINARY ASSOCIATION has started to run courses on the business aspects of running a practice). Students can always visit practices but, once you are qualified, the best way of doing this is by working as a locum for a while.

Vets sometimes share the responsiblity of their practice with one or more partners – this involves a very great commitment ('more difficult to get out of than marriage'). A male/female combination allows you to pander to any client preference. On the whole, sexism is no longer rife although farmers may expect to see a man doing things like calving or trimming cows' feet. You are dependent on good nurses and lay staff to help run the practice and establish good client relations. You can buy yourself into an existing practice but you will usually need to be known first because of the amount of financial and professional dependence between partners. These opportunities arise from contacts or by working as an assistant in the practice for a year or so (look for jobs 'with prospects' in the *Veterinary Record*). To set up a new practice you need planning permission. This can take 3–6 months and involves providing eg sound-proofing, an efficient waste disposal system and agreeing to run an appointments system. Then you can apply for a mortgage – 100% available from some such as the Royal Trust Company of Canada. People tend to use their nearest vet so choose your site carefully and know your competition (animal hospitals etc). You will need about £8–10,000 worth of equipment (although secondhand can be bought from hospitals etc) and about £4–5,000 stock of drugs. A good relationship with your bank is essential for loans and because you will probably not make any profit for several years.

Theoretically you can charge what you like but the NHS has made people unaware of the real cost of treatment. You can expect to make up to £20–30,000 as a partner. You will put about 25% of what you charge back into the practice. Specialism is restricted by the fact that the RCVS insists that all practices treat any sick animal that is brought in. So you cannot advertise yourself as being a specialist for any particular type of animal or problem, although other vets will get to know and refer particular problems to you if you have a specialist knowledge or experience. You have to provide 24 hour emergency cover every day of the year.

You need to be able to cope with people who may be anxious or distressed about their animal and it helps to have some business sense. It is important to keep abreast of medical and veterinary developments through journals, books, continuing education courses and contact with local hospitals, dentists etc. You should have a strong liking for animals, lots of stamina to cope with the physically and mentally demanding work and sometimes long hours. You should not be squeamish.

Village Shopkeeper

At a Glance

Qualifications/Training	Available	*Income bracket*	Low–Medium
Licence	No (but alcohol licence)	*Town/Country*	Village
Experience/Springboard	Recommended	*Travel*	No
Mid-career entry	Good	*Exit sale*	Excellent
Entry costs	£20,000++	*Work at home*	No

Mix and match Limited. You could think about: Sub postmaster, Holiday accommodation owner, Scriptwriter . . .

Enquiries National Association of Shopkeepers

Supermarkets pose a severe threat to traditional small shops. Survival depends on adapting; rather than being a main stop for your customers, you'll depend on having a large clientele who buy a few essentials.

If you're opening a shop in residential premises, you apply for planning permission to change the use of the property. Objectors will most likely be the next door neighbours and the nearest competition. Alternatively you purchase an existing shop for a given sum plus the valuer's assessment of the value of the stock at takeover.

You can do a course at the COLLEGE FOR THE DISTRIBUTIVE TRADES or, as most people do, use their common sense and buy a book on VAT. Keep what your predecessors stock until you find it wrong. The stock value from scratch is approx £15,000 to £20,000. Join the NATIONAL ASSOCIATION OF SHOPKEEPERS.

Get yourself onto a wholesaler's books and/or get a card from the best local cash and carry. Once a week, check what is left of each item and re-order or dash down to the cash and carry. Some items, such as milk, bread and fresh vegetables, need daily deliveries from the local milkman, baker etc.

If you're going to sell newspapers, you'll find that all areas are currently covered by franchise; unless you buy the newspaper round with your shop, you will not get any newspapers or magazines from the wholesalers.

If you wish to stock alcohol you must apply to the magistrates and appear before them for a licence. If it is granted, you have to put your name over the door and keep your alcohol in a secure way. Find out the law about selling alcohol to youngsters before you appear before the magistrate. A friendly police sergeant appears in your shop about once a year to see if all is well with the sale of alcohol. It is unclear what this achieves but it happens.

To run a successful village/corner shop you need to know your customers, be willing to vary your stock according to their wants, ensure your staff are polite and courteous and be prepared to stay open for long hours to fit in with customer demand – this will mean that you'll probably be at your busiest when other people are on holiday, coming home from work etc.

Wedding Shop Owner

At a Glance

Qualifications/Training	None	Income bracket	Low–Medium
Licence	No	Town/Country	Town
Experience/Springboard	Recommended	Travel	None
Mid-career entry	Yes	Exit sale	Yes
Entry costs	£500+	Work at home	No

Mix and match   Yes.   You could think about: Fashion clothes/hat designer, Fashion retailer, Photographer, Caterer . . .
Enquiries   Local bridal retailers

There are nearly 350,000 weddings a year; a lot of these are traditional church weddings for which the bride and her attendant bridesmaids want to wear special dresses and accessories. For these they will pay anything from about £80–1,500+. That means that there is a demand for shops which make, sell and alter wedding dresses, artificial floral headdresses and bouquets and sell wedding accessories.

You could start off in a very small way, making dresses for friends and contacts to your own or their designs; from this you may be able to build up a good enough reputation to make a living. On the whole though, if you want to make a commercial success from outfitting brides and bridesmaids, you'll have to have a shop and to do more than making dresses. For this it's very useful to have experience of bridal retail quite different from selling other clothes. Customers want a lot of attention, they'll probably expect this to be a once in a lifetime occasion; remember this when you're putting up with yet another panic stricken phone call about whether or not the flowers will match the bridesmaids' dresses. You need to advise on what to wear with what; to know how to alter dresses; and it helps if you can think ahead and predict when an apparently calm bride is going to start worrying. Expect to have to put in some long hours from time to time, making sure that everything's ready in time. This is one job where you can't miss a deadline. You'll need, at the very least, a sewing machine, some scissors, tape measure and other sewing kit. Once you've got a shop you'll have to spend something on making it suitably pretty – buy some chairs and little tables and have flowers around, this puts people into the right mood. As well, you need enough space to store dresses before customers pick them up. Premises needn't be on the High Street, people are willing to travel some distance to the right wedding dress shop.

There's a vast range of ready made wedding dresses available; for these you'll have to know your market. Hold a supply of samples of each style and order the right size as customers want them; for most you'll have to make some alterations. You should always have a supply of bridal accessories. Base your charges on what you're providing and on the time you expect to take making everything ready; you may need to employ some extra help during busy times so don't undervalue this. Customers pay half of their bill when they place an order and the rest when you deliver. Other sources of income include altering wedding dresses under contract with larger shops and department stores; making headdresses and bouquets (if you limit this to artificial flowers you'll avoid having to work frantically on the morning of the wedding with live ones and will be able to sell them to other retail outlets); your sample dresses can also generate income if you hire them out – it's normal to charge about half the retail price for this but hire customers will probably expect just as much attention as buying ones. You can also make money by making special wedding dresses to order.

You won't have many regular customers; most come through word of mouth; getting some good editorial in a local paper helps in the early days. Otherwise use leaflets, ads in the local press (you may get lost in the national press or in specialist magazines). Customers approach you about six months before the wedding and may want to make evening appointments to see you and often use you as an agony aunt as the day approaches and they are finding their bridesmaids unobliging about dress fittings. The busiest season is from April to September so you can forget summer holidays; the only truly quiet time is over Christmas. During the quiet times you can build up your stock and keep an eye on slow moving wedding fashions by reading *Brides*.

Wigmaker

At a Glance

Qualifications/Training	Available	*Income bracket*	Low–Medium
Licence	No	*Town/Country*	Town
Experience/Springboard	Usual	*Travel*	Local
Mid-career entry	Possible	*Exit sale*	No
Entry costs	£2,000+	*Work at home*	Possible

Mix and match Possible. You could think about: Hairdresser, Beauty consultant, Costume designer . . .
Enquiries Wigmakers

Wigmaking has been a dying trade for a while. There are a few specialist companies left, who carry out commissions for theatre, television or film companies. Large opera and theatre houses have their own wig-makers but there are openings for self employed wig-makers on other shows. Special wigs were needed, for example, for 'Starlight Express' and 'Cats'; and wigs are in demand for private use (called streetwear) toupees etc for those naturally losing their hair, chemotherapy patients and so on. Wig-making involves making the mount or foundation for the wig, knotting the hair into the mount, and dressing the finished wig into a style.

You learn the trade either through the theatre or by working with a wig company. Another route in is via a normal hair-dressing course. A wig-maker has to combine creative design with practicality and realism; to have ideas for style and colours that suit the client or are appropriate to the production. They have to be dexterous and (especially for theatrical wig making where production schedules are often tight) capable of working under pressure.

You'll need a workshop, tools and equipment. You don't have to have a consulting room for clients if you are prepared to travel to them. Wigs can be made from hair (usually human) or, rarely, nylon. It takes a full week to put the hair into just one wig, which is why they are expensive. A wig with waist length hair costs £500, and a streetwear toupee can cost £1,000 (preying on the psychology of balding men). Legal wigs are very expensive because they are made in the original way from horsehair and take a long time to make and style. There is a two year waiting list for a legal wig.

Maintenance of wigs is always needed. A national health wig is cleaned and dressed once a month; a private wig probably more often. But film and television wigs may need to be dressed every day while shooting is going on. Running repairs also have to be done.

Once you become known as a good wig-maker the word gets around and you are in demand. You can get to a position of using outworkers and helpers to do the actual making of the wigs, and do more advising and designing and running a wig company.

WIGMAKER

Window Cleaner

At a Glance

Qualifications/Training	No	*Income bracket*	Low
Licence	No	*Town/Country*	Either
Experience/Springboard	No	*Travel*	Local
Mid-career entry	Possible	*Exit sale*	No
Entry costs	£300+	*Work at home*	No

Mix and match Yes. You could think about: Painter/decorator, Thatcher, Man with a van, Novelist . . .

Enquiries Window cleaners

Window cleaners are very rare birds in many places – all you have to do is choose the right area. You need a ladder, a bucket, cloths and some sort of transport, also preferably a telephone number and business cards. Start off with a bit of practice at home; make sure that your balance is good and heights don't make you dizzy.

To begin with you'll have to establish a clientele – once you've established a reputation people will start to search you out rather than vice versa. Put cards through lots of letter boxes and wait to find out which areas give the best response. Even in London people don't want to have their windows cleaned more than once a month or 6 weeks so build up enough customers to keep you going. Charge from about £3 for a flat to about £12–15 for a large house; more to clean inside as well as out. Most of it is outside work so there may be times when you won't be able to do as much as usual.

Phone your customers to make an appointment beforehand; if they're going to be out you'll have to make special arrangements. It also shows that you're reliable – worth doing because window cleaning is a well known cover for house-breaking.

Windsurfing School Owner

At a Glance

Qualifications/Training	Necessary	*Income bracket*	Low–Medium
Licence	No	*Town/Country*	Country
Experience/Springboard	Useful	*Travel*	No
Mid-career entry	Good	*Exit sale*	Good
Entry costs	£5,000+	*Work at home*	No

Mix and match Yes. You could think about: Specialist sports retailer, Sailing school owner, Motorcycle racer, Magazine publisher . . .

Enquiries Royal Yachting Association, Professional Board Sailers Association, British Fun Board Association

The popularity of this relatively new (10 years old) sport has led to a demand for windsurf instruction. This is usually done by windsurfing schools – on man-made lakes or gravel pits – only the most advanced part of the ROYAL YACHTING ASSOCIATION (RYA) scheme is taught on the sea. Running a school is a risky business (many fail) with little chance of a long term future unless you run it alongside another business (a specialist sports shop for example) which allows cross fertilisation between your 2 businesses (pupils will buy equipment and customers will take courses).

The RYA has a windsurfing training scheme which allows you to award RYA certificates to successful pupils. If you want to use this scheme (which also gives credibility to your school) you will have to pass the RYA Instructors' course. This costs about £100 and can be full time or part time. You'll also need a first aid certificate and life saving training. It's helpful to have had some previous instructing experience – not all good windsurfers make good teachers. As well as enjoying water sports (especially windsurfing) you'll need to have some organisational and business skills to run the school or the wherewithal to delegate.

Rent a lake to teach on. These are not easy to come by and usually cost at least £1,000 (and sometimes up to £5,000) per annum in rent with rates and any bills on top of that. On the whole motor and sail water sports can't operate on the same lake unless you time-share. You'll be paying for the lake all year round even though the windsurfing season only lasts from about April to September. Find a lake that is accessible, (pupils won't want to travel too far) with adequate parking. Get the owner's agreement before you open the windsurfing school. If you're teaching on the sea you will need the permission of the local authority.

Basic equipment includes boards and sails, wet suits, buoyancy aids, marker buoys and a first aid kit. Also a rescue boat with outboard motor (£500–1,000). In addition to boat and motor it costs about £1,000–1,500 to equip a windsurfing school. You'll probably want to have at least a storage shed on the lake, and will need planning permission for it. This can grow and double up as a club house for regular lake users. You will need third party and liability insurance, also cover for the equipment. Build up a network of qualified freelance instructors. You'll need to have someone there all the time to stop people from using your lake without paying for it and to generally keep an eye on it. You may also need office staff to take bookings, deal with correspondence etc. You can enlist enthusiastic school leavers to help issue pupils with boards and getting them water bound.

Advertise in local sports shops and newspapers. You may also get groups from local schools, clubs and businesses. Courses are usually 1 or 2 days long (costing about £25–40 per person) and groups are ideally of about 3–6 pupils. (The RYA will tell you which aspects of the sport you should cover at each level.) Get your pupils to pay in advance and make sure that they sign a responsibility disclaimer. Cancelled lessons, eg due to the weather, lose money because you have to fit them in at another time without charging. Business will also come from ex-pupils who hire boards, and use the lake for practice (charge about £5 per hour for hire and the same for access to the lake, with own board, per day) and taking additional courses. Many schools have clubs attached allowing use of the lake for an annual fee. Clubs also work as a way of keeping in touch with lake users over the winter so that they'll remember to come back again for the new season.

Useful publications include *Watersport Trade News*, *Boards*, *On Board Windsurfing Magazine* and *Windsurf and Boardsailing*. You may also want to contact the BRITISH FUN BOARD ASSOCIATION and the PROFESSIONAL BOARD SAILERS ASSOCIATION.

Wine Bar Owner

At a Glance

Qualifications/Training	Recommended	Income bracket	Medium
Licence	Yes	Town/Country	Town
Experience/Springboard	Essential	Travel	Local
Mid-career entry	Good	Exit sale	Excellent
Entry costs	£25,000+	Work at home	No

Mix and match   Possible.   You could think about: Wine merchant, Wine grower, Restaurateur, Dealer in Antiques, Contemporary art gallery owner, Opening to the public . . .

Enquiries   Wine and Spirit Education Trust, Wine bar owners

Although wine bars are opening all the time, a great many of them go bust very quickly so it's worth doing some research before deciding where to open. Thanks to breathalysers and health consciousness, food is becoming increasingly important in wine bars. A good cook is essential as is some idea of local tastes. Changes expected soon in the licensing laws are likely to give wine bars greater flexibility over opening hours. It's a full time job, certainly to begin with, and it helps if you have a partner to share eg book-keeping, front of house, planning menus and buying supplies; that way you may be able to take a few hours off without having to close.

No formal qualifications are necessary, but some experience working in a wine bar (at least a few months) is essential and is a good way of establishing contacts in the trade. You should know something about wine or have a dealer you trust. A catering or business training is useful. To survive, you'll have to be sociable and diplomatic and to balance friendliness with the ability to run a successful and profitable business.

Before opening, you'll need to have a licence obtained by applying to the magistrates' court. Brewers may put up opposition to this on behalf of local pubs especially if you're applying to sell draught beer or spirits. But on the whole, a wine only licence is quite straightforward unless you have any sort of criminal record in which case your chances are slim. Unless you're taking over an existing wine bar premises you'll need permission for change of use from the local planning department. They will make stringent checks on fire, safety and health as well as considering objections from local residents. Choose premises that are not too small (seating for at least 40–50) in a mainly residential area ideally with some local business too for lunchtime trade.

The costs of setting up, apart from premises, vary. It will cost about £20,000 to equip from scratch, with ovens, storage, fridges, loos etc, and you will need about £2–3,000 worth of stock (trade contacts are useful for credit for this). Apply for a mortgage or bank loan but expect to have to put up about 50% of the opening costs yourself. On top of any staff costs, you also need to budget for heating, lighting, accountant and solicitor, a good laundry service, and maintenance back up prepared to answer any emergency calls. You can charge approximately three times cost price, plus VAT. The obvious hazard is the ease with which you can become an alcoholic; you also have to deal with occasional drunks and under-age drinkers, listen to bores, act as confessor and put up with patronising customers. If you come from a non-catering background and are used to being treated with some deference, you may be surprised by the churlish attitude of some customers; wine-bar owners in Britain report on a national disdain for the catering profession. It's easy to fall foul of the finer details of health and safety regulations so it's important to be familiar with them all. The WINE AND SPIRITS EDUCATION TRUST courses vary from the most elementary to the most sophisticated. *Decanter* is the bible of the trade. For someone who enjoys socialising and doesn't mind working very hard it's rewarding.

Wine Grower

At a Glance

Qualifications/Training	Recommended	Income bracket	Low–Medium
Licence	Yes	Town/Country	Country
Experience/Springboard	Useful	Travel	No
Mid-career entry	Good	Exit sale	Excellent
Entry costs	£90,000+	Work at home	Yes

Mix and match   Essential to start. You could think about: Wine bar owner, Opening to the public, Holiday accommodation owner, Gardener/garden designer . . .

Enquiries   English Vineyard Association

A vineyard – what a marvellous idea! This is the normal reaction to the thought of being a winegrower, as the imagination conjures up a picture of sunny days spent lovingly tending the vines – which have plentiful bunches of juicy, disease-free grapes, swelling magnificently just ready for picking. Reality is of course entirely different.

To start, you will need access to plenty of money and a willingness to put up with a negative cash flow (ie no income) for the first five years and the subsequent risk that the enterprise fails and you lose the lot. You will need a well-sheltered site in the south of England, south facing, with free-draining soil, not in a frost pocket nor too high. If tourism is a consideration, it needs to be well placed for that too. The smallest viable vineyard is about 10 acres. Once you have the site, it will cost about £35,000 to establish the vineyard, plus at least £20,000 for a tractor and related machinery and equipment. You should expect to harvest 5,000 bottles from 10 acres in your third year (for sale in your fourth), building up to 30,000 bottles after 5–6 years – so you will need a second income to live on at least in the short term. You ought to know how you are going to sell your wine at the outset. There are a remarkable number of vineyards with bonded stores full of unsold wine and it is difficult to establish an unknown brand – especially through the wine trade which is, not unnaturally, able to be choosy as to whose wines it will stock. English wine is a premium product but many people still confuse it with the totally different British Wine.

It makes sense to open a tourist related enterprise too. You can then promote your wine direct to the public and sell at full retail prices. You need to be near where tourists go or be able to offer something pretty special if you are to persuade them off the beaten track. To do it properly you will need further capital to build a car park, winebar or tasting room, interpretation facilities – and loos, of course. Selling a premium product needs to be done properly; it's hard work convincing someone to spend £4 on a bottle of wine when you're selling it out of a tin shed!

To succeed you will need to be able to grow what is a high value and very demanding crop – diseases and disorders need to be recognised and acted on swiftly or they can write off your whole crop. A formal horticultural or agricultural qualification is desirable. If you are going to make your own wine, then a science and mathematics background is useful as winemaking is much more science based than it used to be. Many growers send their grapes away to another vineyard or a contract winemaker who comes back a few months later with their (usually well made) wine in bottles – and a bill. You will need to be able to cope with interference from the Trading Standards Officer (they check how full your bottles are), the Wine Standards Board (who administer all the EEC regulations on wine), and of course Customs and Excise (who license you to make wine and collect the duty). This means careful record keeping. But you are allowed four bottles a day, duty free, if you can drink that much.

If you send a large SAE to the ENGLISH VINEYARD ASSOCIATION they will send you a list of vineyards open to the public and membership details. They also produce a useful quarterly magazine, the *Grape Press*. Read also the *New English Vineyard, Vinegrowing in Britain*, or *A Tradition of English Wine*. Visit as many vineyards as you can – most growers are gregarious and friendly, if a little odd.

You will be watching for diseases during the summer and picking grapes in October so you should have an enthusiasm for winter holidays. It is a very pleasant way of life, if not wildly profitable. But it is possible to succeed, with a good dose of realism injected into initial plans. It's too easy to get carried away and nothing would be worse than to find ten years later that it doesn't work after all and the best years of your life have gone.

Wine Merchant

At a Glance

Qualifications/Training	Recommended	*Income bracket*	Low–High
Licence	Yes, if you sell single bottles	*Town/Country*	Either
Experience/Springboard	No	*Travel*	Yes
Mid-career entry	Good	*Exit sale*	Yes
Entry costs	£5,000++	*Work at home*	Yes

Mix and match   Essential to start.   You could think about: Wine bar owner, Restaurateur, Direct marketing agent, List broker, Events organiser . . .

Enquiries   Wine and Spirit Educational Trust, Wine merchants

Don't become an independent wine merchant if you have to make money to start with; there are too many people at it, margins are too low, and big customers are surprisingly loyal to existing suppliers. But, if you are looking for a means of earning whilst following your wine tasting hobby or giving some commercial purpose to your wine tasting holidays then maybe you are on to something. There are many merchants operating successfully who started by bringing a few cases back from holiday and selling to friends. But bear in mind that the wine trade generally tends to suffer from chronic cash flow problems and fierce competition, although the rivalry is friendly.

You will need to take the courses run by the WINE AND SPIRIT EDUCATION TRUST (they are short and part-time). If, like many aspiring merchants, you are an enthusiastic amateur (member of a wine tasting club and reader of eg *Wine Magazine* or *Decanter*), you can probably skip the first certificate course. But you will need to take the Higher Certificate and Diploma courses to know enough about wines (regions, labels, tasting etc) in order to be able to speak reasonably knowledgeably to your customers. (A very few progress to Master of Wine and it is not really necessary). It is possible, though not advisable, to take the courses at home. Expect to take about three years to get the Diploma. Languages are useful, especially if you want to use small suppliers who may not speak English.

The traditional structure of the trade is – producer – shipper – wholesaler – retailer – consumer. Though still discernible, this is crumbling as wholesalers sell direct to the public and shippers direct to retailers. And, of course, supermarkets and wine warehouses ship many of their products direct from producers to the final consumer. This has the effect of shattering margins on wines coming through the old set-up, making some of them quite uncompetitive. But the big chains require large volumes of totally consistent wine so they have to buy from the large producers, co-operatives and negociants or shippers.

Most wine regions still have plenty of independent growers whose production is nowhere near the size to interest the big buyers, so here is an opportunity for the small specialist. (Small providers often have less modern equipment so quality could be less consistent though.) As wine consumption increases, so will the sophistication of the consumer and a market exists for those looking for wines with individuality in the middle and upper price range. Here the independent can give personal attention and advice unlikely to be found in a supermarket.

Buying from producers is not difficult and can be great fun. Shipment is generally easy; 25 cases can be viable, using groupage through freight-forwarders, but rates reduce dramatically as quantity rises. However, the more prestigious proprietors will already have UK customers or agents they will expect you to use and, though there are plenty of others, you cannot always be certain that the wine they send will be the same as tasted in the cellar. If you are exporting, you should be able to reclaim the VAT but will have to pay excise duty when you import it to this country.

If you buy from producers you will get the best prices but have to carry stock which requires capital. If you buy from shippers they will have a minimum order of 5 or 6 cases, perhaps with a discount structure for larger quantities, so you need only modest stocks. If you buy from wholesalers they will sell you a single case (at a higher price, of course) but your stocks are minimal. The same rules apply as in any business – a quick turnover can be done at a low margin; a slow turnover needs a margin to cover the capital involved.

Restaurants are often interested in lesser-known wines but they may take extended credit, can be quite demanding about delivery and may want contributions towards printing the wine list; cash from the general public is best. Mail order is a ripe market for some specialist wines; national advertising is needed and delivery costs can be very high (less significant with more expensive wine). No licence is required to sell by the case but don't get caught selling single bottles. Or you can buy an off-licence as a base so you can display and sell single bottles. If you want to sell specialist wines, there is no need to get involved in cut price spirits and beers but choose your site carefully. Here you would need magistrates' approval of yourself and your activities but there should be no problem with an existing off-licence. To get permission to convert a property to an off-licence is much more difficult, requiring planning consent and probably attracting objection from other off-licence holders and probably the local residents.

WINE MERCHANT

Wood Carver

At a Glance

Qualifications/Training	Recommended	*Income bracket*	Low–Medium
Licence	No	*Town/Country*	Either
Experience/Springboard	No	*Travel*	No
Mid-career entry	Possible	*Exit sale*	No
Entry costs	£2,500	*Work at home*	Yes

Mix and match   Yes. You could think about: Cabinet maker, Psychoanalyst, Sculptor, Carpenter . . .

Enquiries   Guild of Master Craftsmen

Much of this work involves commissions for clients who want pieces custom-built to their own specifications. In addition to an expert knowledge of wood and how to treat it, you will therefore need tact, patience and determination. Within reason you can set your own deadlines but these must be met so if things go wrong, you may have to do some quick thinking.

You will need to rent or buy somewhere to work (possibly a converted garage), £700–£1,000 worth of equipment and tools (these can be bought secondhand), publicity material and a ready source of wood. Some form of transport is useful for larger jobs away from your workshop. Setting up on your own as a craftsman is difficult but you can survive by producing small items for local craft shops/markets and the tourist trade.

To learn the trade you can become an apprentice for several years before qualifying. This will provide regular employment but restrict your artistic freedom; and apprenticeship tends to be available only to those of school-leaving age. Or you can take a degree course in three-dimensional design (find one specialising in wood; or apply to ADAR). The CITY & GUILDS OF LONDON ART SCHOOL and the JOHN MAKEPEACE SCHOOL are the only places in the UK offering courses specifically for craftsmen wood carvers; but even with this qualification you will need perseverance.

Contacts are all-important. Most work will come via interior designers and those who desire those extra touches, eg special carving, panelling, plinths etc, for their dream homes, so you should cultivate an artistic aura. Try approaching the specialists direct (see local Yellow Pages), get some cards printed – design them yourself. The most likely route is to pool resources with others, invest in a workshop or join an established group of fellow craftsmen.

A newly-qualified wood carver can expect to earn about £50 per day by calculating the cost of each piece produced plus a charge for time and materials, not forgetting any special effects or finishes but you are almost bound to have slack periods. Having become established, commissions are likely to come through word of mouth so get as much exposure for your work as possible. Arrange joint exhibitions with other craftworkers. The local press may be interested in writing a short article, with photographs, about an especially decorative or outrageous item (but check with the owner first), particularly if it's for a local celebrity. Some shops, galleries or restaurants may be willing to exhibit samples of work, or display your cards.

If you are working with others, this can be a sociable, relaxed job but you are likely to have to devote a lot of time to repetitive jobs, eg friezes, panelling. Your clients may not share your taste, but if you find that some of your ideas are commercial, you may have to spend more time on them than being creative.

Useful books about wood carving include *Practical Woodworking*, the *Craftsman's Handbook*. Join the GUILD OF MASTER CRAFTSMEN.

Word Processor

At a Glance

Qualifications/Training	Useful	*Income bracket*	Low–Medium
Licence	No	*Town/Country*	Mostly town
Experience/Springboard	Recommended	*Travel*	Local maybe
Mid-career entry	Yes	*Exit sale*	No
Entry costs	£4,000	*Work at home*	Yes

Mix and match Yes. You could think about: Typist, Typesetter, Shopkeeper, Book editor, Jazz musician . . .

Enquiries Word processing agencies

Almost all offices are now equipped with micro computers and use word processors and their secretarial staff are expected to have word processing skills. To make a career as your own boss in word processing you have to be able to offer something not otherwise available, or in short supply, to clients who already have offices equipped with micros. If you can offer specific skills like languages, mathematical or engineering knowledge for example, you may be able to carve out a specialist niche for yourself.

You don't need any formal skills to become a word processor. What you do need is intelligence, good spelling, common-sense, a capacity for working accurately for hours at a time, often on a boring job. Computers are marvellous machines (if you are afraid of them don't become a word processor) but they don't correct your mistakes. The fewer mistakes you make at the initial keying stage, the more time you have to take on more work. Word processing is a competitive business (just look at the Yellow Pages) and the rates you charge are generally restricted by the competition. But do a good job once, and however small it is put something into it that your competition doesn't offer (often sensible comments before you start) and your client will undoubtedly come back to you next time.

You need at least one computer (preferably two identical ones in case one goes wrong), a reliable and high quality printer, computer stationery (disks, labels, paper), a telephone and electricity. You will need to advertise your service (not in newspapers or other short life publications) but this will not bring you an immediate response. Your first source of work will probably be through a carefully selected mailing of possible clients in your region. In general it isn't worth looking for work outside a radius of more than thirty or forty miles.

You are very unlikely to make a fortune (unless you can afford to branch out into related fields, such as translation, recruitment, publishing) but you should expect to make a living after four or five years – if you don't, try something else.

A good computer will cost approx £1,000 (including cables and word processing programs), a printer £2,000–3,000; allow at least £100 for floppy disks and £100 for stationery. If you are starting with a bank loan or HP be warned that you will probably only be offered a three year agreement, although if you have enough clout you may get this extended to five. You will find that all machines you buy will outlive the technology they represent so it is important to get advice before committing yourself to ensure that data will be transferable to future generations of equipment.

You must be prepared to work 7 days a week. Anybody who wants you to do a job for them wants it very quickly – that is why they come to you. It is worth trying to get some sort of arrangement with another word processing office, or having a network of outside contacts (ideally with their own machines and certainly able to produce compatible disks) so that you never need to turn a job away because it is too large.

You must be interested in every job that you do – typing a list of names and addresses is very boring but you have got to find something in it that interests you. If you don't you will make silly mistakes and lose that client. All word processing work has three parts: 1) keying in data. Typing skills are essential for this. 2) Correcting data. Here you need an ability to read quickly and accurately and a thorough knowledge of your word processing program. 3) Printing, This is a mechanical process but it is surprising how much time you can save by knowing how to ensure that machines are set up correctly for each job. By and large clients will bring their work to you (often they want to see what your equipment is like) but you may well need to deliver proofs and final copy. You should always insist that your client reads and corrects a proof: resist as far as you can any pressure to take a job through to final output without your client seeing it. Always expect copy to be a mess (and quote on that basis) and never believe anyone who says they won't need to make changes to the manuscript. Your clients will vary enormously, from academics writing books on abstract technical subjects to the local builder who wants you to type a quotation for building a public urinal. Each has its own challenge and each must be equally important to you. Before you take on any work satisfy yourself that you have considered all the possible problems before you give a quotation and make sure you allow for subsequent 'extras'. You must have a schedule of rates for all types of work (keying, correcting, printing) even if you depart from these rates for any reason. It is all too easy to give a figure for a job and then forget how you worked it out!

You will need Yellow Pages, any local trade directory or Chamber of Commerce directory to find potential clients.

Yoga Teacher

At a Glance

Qualifications/Training	Yes	_Income bracket_	Low
Licence	No	_Town/Country_	Either
Experience/Springboard	No	_Travel_	Local
Mid-career entry	Yes	_Exit sale_	No
Entry costs	£100+	_Work at home_	Possible

Mix and match   Yes.   You could think about: Healthfood shopkeeper, Bee-keeper, Healer, Bespoke furniture maker/designer . . .

Enquiries   Iyengar Institute, Yoga teachers

The very essence of yoga is that it is for most people strictly non-competitive, so the concept of 'making it to the top' is not an appropriate one. Having said that, only very few yoga teachers do more than scrape a living.

Most yoga teaching in this country is by the method practised by the IYENGAR INSTITUTE. To qualify as a teacher you need to have done a minimum of two years' regular Iyengar yoga (most people do more); then take and pass the teacher's training course (one class a week for a minimum of two years). The most important qualities required to succeed as a yoga teacher are maturity, sensitivity and acute observation.

Expenses to set up depend on where you intend to teach. If you use a suitable room in your own house, costs will be minimal; you may be able to teach in other people's houses, in which case you'll find it useful to have a car; some companies organise yoga classes for their employees at their offices; or you can hire premises, such as a church hall, which is obviously more expensive. Start by spending just a few pounds on a mat for yourself and some belts. You can progress to spending up to £1,000 on various items of equipment such as wooden and foam blocks, blankets, back stretchers, ropes and bolsters.

How much you earn will depend on the number of pupils you teach and how much time you are prepared to spend. Some people do not feel able to teach for longer than three hours a day because they find it too exhausting, though some manage to do perhaps six hours. Few teachers earn enough to be able to live off their earnings. You can start by taking two classes a day, say, which would earn you a maximum of £25. Even if you did this for five days a week, it's obvious that we're not talking big money. An established teacher hiring a hall and teaching yoga weekends can charge students £40 for the weekend. A few internationally known teachers earn more and spend considerable amounts of money on travel. By being very organised about advertising you can do better too; though for most people word of mouth is the best way of getting work. Few people are in it for the money.

It's not an easy option, demanding a great deal of personal practice. It's also important to keep up to date with new developments and ways of thinking. Two magazines which will help you do this are *Yoga and Health* and *Yoga Journal*. Three good books to read are *Light on Yoga* and *Light on Pranayama*, and *Yoga a Gem for Women*.

Zookeeper

At a Glance

Qualifications/Training	Recommended	*Income bracket*	Medium
Licence	Yes	*Town/Country*	Either
Experience/Springboard	Essential	*Travel*	Yes
Mid-career entry	Likely	*Exit sale*	Excellent
Entry costs	£1 million+	*Work at home*	No

Mix and match Possible. You could think about: Opening to the public, Vet, Restaurateur, Novelist . . .

Enquiries Zoological Society of London, Association of British Wild Animal Keepers

Britain has lots of zoos – over 250 – so you should be quite certain this is what you want to do before you think of starting up another. If you want to make money, do something else. If you have a strong commitment to animals and their preservation, and can stand people as well as animals, then it's worth considering. By law you must have a licence.

Zoos see themselves as being in the conservation business. They are keen to scotch the myth that zoos are full of animals snatched from the wild. A tiny proportion of zoo animals in this country have ever caught sight of the wild (mostly the geriatrics) and many are bred in captivity with a policy of then returning them to the wild.

You can start with a small number of animals if you choose to be very specialised and have say just a few great apes. Once you are established and have started a breeding programme, you probably won't have to buy animals because there is strong co-operation between zoos in the

UK and abroad. But to start up, you should expect to spend sums in the order of £400 for a marmoset, £250,000 for an okapi. And this is only the beginning. To start up a zoo is wildly expensive – millions to start a reasonable sized one. The animals must be satisfactorily housed, cared for and fed – so you will need to obtain planning consent and staff and be able to foot substantial food bills. In addition, your visitors will need facilities – perhaps somewhere to park, loos, food, a shop or play area – all of which have to be built and then staffed. You must have a good head for business and be able to manage staff.

ZOO KEEPER

As well as the financial considerations you must have worked in a zoo, to get to know the business, and have a good theoretical and practical knowledge of animals. Most take a City and Guilds Diploma (you can take it by correspondence) or some other animal husbandry course. You must also have a sound concept of the wider issues of conservation. Approach the ZOOLOGICAL SOCIETY OF LONDON and the ASSOCIATION OF BRITISH WILD ANIMAL KEEPERS.

Understandably, this area is much governed by regulations. To open at all you must be licensed. This involves being inspected by the local authority together with two specialised inspectors (a zoo curator and a zoo vet), appointed by the DEPARTMENT OF THE ENVIRONMENT. You are also controlled by the animal health regulations administered by the MINISTRY OF AGRICULTURE. Britain is a signatory to the Convention on International Trade in Endangered Species and this is administered in this country by the DEPARTMENT OF THE ENVIRONMENT. Imported animals are covered by the usual constraints – blood tests on zebras, specialist dockside quarantine for antelopes, 6 months rabies quarantine on cats, primates and most other species.

Your visitors will be seasonal – you'll get more winter visitors in an urban zoo. But Easter and the school summer holidays are the favourite zoo visiting times. You will need good insurance cover, including a large public liability insurance. However, most of your claims are likely to be for people falling over, rather than being savaged by a tiger – a well run zoo has a safety record comparable with a farm. One zoo owner believed the biggest danger on his zoo was visitors parking their cars.

Job
Spotter

Job Spotter

Accommodation
Animals
Art
Books and Magazines
Business Services
Cars, Bikes and Driving
Children
Clothes
Construction
Cottage Industries
Country
Crafts
Design
Finance
Grooming
Health
House and Garden

Land Use
Law
Lifelines
Marketing, Advertising, Sales
    and Promotion
Music
Outdoors
People
Performing
Photography and Film
Plants
Possible Investments '
Shops
Sports
TV, Radio and Press
Wine and Food
Writing

Accommodation

How about looking up:
caravan site owner; holiday accommodation owner; hotel keeper; landlord; property manager; publican; timeshare holiday accommodation owner?

Animals

How about looking up:
bee keeper; farmer; farrier and blacksmith; greyhound trainer; kennel/cattery owner; oyster farmer; racehorse owner; salmon farmer; shepherd/shepherdess; snail farmer; taxidermist; trout farmer; vet; zookeeper?

Art

How about looking up:
art historian/critic; artist; artist's agent; calligrapher; china restorer; contemporary art gallery owner; illustrator; picture agent; picture framer; picture researcher; printmaker; sculptor; tattooist; textile designer?

Books and Magazines

How about looking up:
book designer; book editor; book packager; book publisher; bookseller; editorial photographer; graphic designer; illustrator; jobbing printer; literary agent; magazine designer; magazine publisher; music publisher; newsletter publisher; novelist; picture agent; picture researcher; space sales agent; typesetter; UK correspondent for overseas media?

Business Services

How about looking up:
accountant; actuary; advertising agent; bookkeeper; caterer; cleaner; cleaning contractor; company doctor; computer consultant; computer hardware engineer; computer software author; conference organiser; courier service; direct marketing agent; events organiser; graphic designer; graphologist; haulier; headhunter; hire shop owner; import/ export broker; in-company trainer; insurance broker; interior designer; interpreter; jobbing printer; list broker; man with a van; market research interviewer; marketing consultant; media convertor; motorcycle messenger; picture agent; public relations consultant; sales agent; shipbroker; solicitor; space sales agent; typesetter; typist; word processor?

Cars, Bikes and Driving

How about looking up:
courier service; driving instructor; garage owner; haulier; man with a van; mini-cab driver; motorcycle messenger; motorcycle racer; taxi driver?

Children

How about looking up:
careers adviser; childminder; child/educational psychologist; dance teacher; English language school owner; guardian ad litem; music teacher; nanny/babysitting agent; prep school owner; puppeteer; social worker?

Clothes

How about looking up:
costume designer; dress agent; fashion clothes/hat designer; fashion retailer; fashion shoe maker; knitwear designer; tailor; wedding shop owner?

Construction

How about looking up:
architect; carpenter; electrician; glazier; ground worker; hire shop owner; house convertor; landscape designer; new house builder; painter/decorator; plasterer; plumber/heating engineer; property developer; roofer; surveyor; thatcher?

Cottage Industries

How about looking up:
antique furniture restorer; beekeeper; book editor; caterer; childminder; china restorer; fish curer and smoker; garden gnome maker; graphologist; inventor; kennel/cattery owner; newsletter publisher; novelist; opening to the public; taxidermist; toymaker; typist; upholsterer; word processor?

Country

How about looking up:
beekeeper; caravan site owner; farmer; farrier and blacksmith;

fish curer and smoker; garage owner; garlic farmer; greyhound trainer; haulier; holiday accommodation owner; kennel/cattery owner; landscape designer; opening to the public; oyster farmer; publican; racehorse owner; sailing school owner; salmon farmer; shepherd/shepherdess; snail farmer; sub postmaster; thatcher; tourist guide; trout farmer; vet; village shopkeeper; windsurfing school owner; winegrower?

Crafts

How about looking up:
antique furniture restorer; bespoke furniture maker; cabinet maker; calligrapher; carpenter; china restorer; dental technician; farrier and blacksmith; fashion shoe maker; garden gnome maker; glass designer/maker; goldsmith/silversmith/jeweller; knitwear designer; musical instrument maker; muscial instrument repairer; piano tuner; picture maker; potter; printmaker; puppeteer; saddler/leatherworker; stage technician carpenter; tailor; taxidermist; textile designer; thatcher; toymaker; upholsterer; wig maker; wood carver?

Design

How about looking up:
architect; bespoke furniture maker; book designer; contemporary art gallery owner; costume designer; editorial photographer; exhibition designer; fashion clothes/hat designer; gardener/garden designer; graphic designer; interior designer; inventor; knitwear designer; landscape designer; magazine designer; photographic stylist; stage designer; textile designer; wedding shop owner?

Finance

How about looking up:
accountant; actuary; bookkeeper; company doctor; futures broker; independent financial adviser; insurance broker; investment manager; local trader; options dealer; shipbroker; stockbroker?

Grooming

How about looking up:
beauty consultant; dental technician; embalmer; hairdresser; make up artist; photographic stylist; tattooist; wig maker?

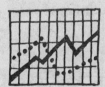

Health

How about looking up:
acupuncturist; Alexander technique teacher; child/educational psychologist; chiropodist; chiropractor; counsellor; dentist; dietary therapist; dispensing chemist; doctor; healer; healthfood shop keeper; homeopath; hypnotherapist; music therapist; nurse; nursing home owner/manager; optician; osteopath; physiotherapist; psychoanalyst; psychologist; psychotherapist; reflexologist; sex therapist; vet?

House and Garden

How about looking up:
antique furniture restorer; caterer; childminder; china restorer; cleaner; cleaning contractor; coal merchant; electrician; gardener/garden designer; garden gnome maker; glazier; hire shop owner; interior designer; nanny/babysitting agent; painter/decorator; piano tuner; plasterer; plumber; property manager; tree surgeon; upholsterer; window cleaner?

Land Use

How about looking up:
beekeeper; caravan site owner; farmer; gardener/garden designer; garlic farmer; ground worker; landscape designer; new house builder; opening to the public; oyster farmer; sailing school owner; salmon farmer; snail farmer; trout farmer; windsurfing school owner; wine-grower; zookeeper?

Law

How about looking up:
accountant; barrister/advocate; conveyancer; criminal; guardian ad litem; private investigator; solicitor?

Lifelines

How about looking up:
bartender; bookkeeper; book editor; cabaret performer; caterer; market research interviewer; mini cab driver; motorcycle messenger; painter/decorator; street entertainer; typist; window cleaner?

Marketing, Advertising, Sales and Promotion

How about looking up:
advertising agent; advertising photographer; conference organiser; direct marketing agent; events organiser; exhibition designer; graphic designer; list broker; market research interviewer; marketing consultant; public relations consultant; sales agent; sales promoter; space sales agent?

Music

How about looking up:
cabaret performer; chamber group director; classical composer; classical/operatic singer; concert agent; conductor; disco owner/DJ; festival director; impresario; instrumental soloist; jazz musician/singer; keyboard hire; light music composer; music copyist; music critic; music/instrument retailer; music publisher; music teacher; music

therapist; musical instrument maker; musical instrument repairer, musician; musicians' answering and booking service; opera producer/director; orchestral fixer; orchestral musician; piano tuner; pop group sound engineer; record company owner; recording studio owner; repetiteur/accompanist/coach; street entertainer?

Outdoors

How about looking up:
beekeeper; farmer; farrier and blacksmith; football commentator; gardener/garden designer; garlic farmer; glazier; greyhound trainer; ground worker; kennel/cattery owner; landscape designer; market stall holder; motorcycle messenger; motorcycle racer; new house builder; oyster farmer; roofer; sailing school owner; salmon farmer; shepherd/shepherdess; snail farmer; street entertainer; surveyor; thatcher; tourist guide; tree surgeon; trout farmer; window cleaner; windsurfing school owner; winegrower; zookeeper?

People

How about looking up:
artists' agent; careers adviser; child/educational psychologist; childminder; cleaning contractor; conductor; counsellor; dietary therapist; doctor; events organiser; film director; guardian ad litem; headhunter; healer; homeopath; hotel keeper; hypnotherapist; in-company trainer; independent financial adviser; literary agent; MP; music therapist; nanny/babysitting agent; nurse; nursing home owner/manager; opera producer/director; prep school owner; private investigator; psychoanalyst; psychologist; psychotherapist; publican; restaurateur;

sex therapist; social worker; theatrical agent; tourist guide; wine bar owner; yoga teacher?

Performing

How about looking up:
actor; cabaret performer; classical/operatic singer; conductor; dancer; disco owner/DJ; instrumental soloist; jazz musician/singer; motorcycle racer; musician; orchestral musician; puppeteer; repetiteur/accompanist/coach; street entertainer; tourist guide?

Photography and Film

How about looking up:
advertising photographer; assistant film director; camera person; continuity person; editorial photographer; film director; film production person; high street photographer; photographer; photographic assistant; photographic stylist; photojournalist?

Plants

How about looking up:
farmer; gardener/garden designer; garlic farmer; market stall holder; specialist food manufacturer; thatcher; tree surgeon; winegrower?

Possible Investments

How about looking up:
brewer; caravan site owner; English language school owner; farmer; franchisee; garage owner; garlic farmer; holiday accommodation owner; hotel keeper; house convertor; impresario; landlord; new house builder; nursing home owner/manager; opening to the public; oyster farmer; picture agent; prep school owner; property developer; publican; race horse owner; record company owner; recording studio owner; restaurateur; sailing school owner; salmon farmer; timeshare holiday accommodation owner; trout farmer; windsurfing school owner; wine bar owner; winegrower; zookeeper?

Shops

How about looking up:
bookseller; butcher; coal merchant; contemporary art gallery dealer; dealer in large antiques; dealer in small antiques; dispensing chemist; dress agent; estate agent; fashion retailer; franchisee; goldsmith/silversmith/jeweller; healthfood shop keeper; hi-fi shop owner; high street photographer; hire shop owner; market stall holder; motorcycle dealer; music/instrument retailer; picture framer; shopkeeper; specialist sports retailer; sub postmaster; village shopkeeper; wedding shop owner?

Sports

How about looking up:
bookie; events organiser; football commentator; greyhound trainer; motor cycle racer; physiotherapist; race horse owner; sailing school owner; specialist sports retailer; windsurfing school owner?

TV, Radio and Press

How about looking up:
advertising photographer; assistant film director; camera person; continuity person; editorial photographer; film production person; football commentator; foreign correspondent; graphic designer; jobbing printer; journalist; magazine designer; magazine publisher; newsletter publisher; photographer; photographic stylist; photojournalist; picture agent; picture researcher; radio reporter/presenter; recording studio owner; script writer; space sales agent; theatrical agent; typesetter; UK correspondent for overseas media; word processor?

Wine and Food

How about looking up:
bartender; brewer; caterer; fish curer and smoker; franchisee; healthfood shopkeeper; publican; restaurateur; specialist food manufacturer; wine bar owner; wine grower; wine merchant?

Writing

How about looking up:
art historian; book editor; book packager; classical composer; foreign correspondent; journalist; music critic; newsletter publisher; novelist; scriptwriter; UK correspondent for overseas media; word processor?

Special
Features
Index

Job	Qualifications/ Training	Licence	Experience/ Springboard	Mid-career entry	Entry costs	Income bracket	Town/ Country	Travel	Exit sale	Mix and match	Work at home
Accountant	Yes	Yes, to audit	Necessary	Possible	£20,000	Medium–High	Town	Local	Yes	Possible	Possible
Actor	Recommended	Union card essential	No	Unlikely	£100	Low	Town	Yes	No	Often essential	No
Actuary	Essential	Yes	Essential	Possible	£2,000+	High	Town	Yes	Possible	Possible	Yes
Acupuncturist	Yes	Recommended	Yes	Possible	£1,000	Low–Medium	Town	No	No	Yes	Yes
Advertising Agent	Useful	No	Essential	Unlikely	£5,000	Medium	Town	Possible	Yes	Yes	Unlikely
Advertising Photographer	Recommended	No	Recommended	Possible	£6,000	Medium–High	Town	Yes	No	Yes	No
Alexander Technique Teacher	Yes	No	Recommended	Possible	£500	Low–Medium	Town	None	No	Possible	Yes
Antique Furniture Restorer	Recommended	No	Recommended	Yes	£5,000	Low–Medium	Either	Local	No	Yes	Possible
Architect	Essential	Yes	Yes	Unlikely	£2,000+	Medium–High	Town	Yes	Yes	Possible	Possible
Art Historian/Critic	Recommended	No	Essential	Yes	Nil	Low–Medium	Either	Yes	No	Yes	Yes
Artist	Recommended	No	No	Yes	£500	Low	Either	Possible	No	Yes	Yes
Artists' Agent	No	No	Helpful	Yes	£5,000	Low	Town	Local	Possible	Yes	Not recommended
Assistant Film Director	No	Union card	Yes	No	£500	Low–Medium	Town	Yes	No	Limited	No

Job	Qualifications/Training	Licence	Experience/Springboard	Mid-career entry	Entry costs	Income bracket	Town/Country	Travel	Exit sale	Mix and match	Work at home
Barrister/Advocate	Essential	Yes	No	Unlikely	£1,000+	Medium–High	Town	Yes	No	Possible	No
Bartender	No	No	No	Yes	Nil	Low	Either	No	No	Yes	No
Beauty Consultant	Recommended	No	Recommended	Possible	£2,000	Low–Medium	Town	Local	No	Possible	Possible
Beekeeper	Available	No	Useful	Yes	£5,000	Low	Country	Local	Yes	Yes	Yes
Bespoke Furniture Maker/Designer	Recommended	No	Recommended	Yes	£10,000+	Low–Medium	Either	Local	No	Yes	Yes
Book Designer	Recommended	No	Recommended	Doubtful	£1,000+	Low–Medium	Town preferably	Local	No	Yes	Yes
Book Editor	Available	No	Almost essential	Possible	£1,000	Low–Medium	Town preferably	No	No	Yes	Yes
Bookkeeper	Available	No	Recommended	Yes	£2,000	Low–Medium	Either	Some	No	Excellent	Yes
Book Packager	Available	No	Essential	Likely	£5–10,000	Medium	Either	Possible	Yes	Yes	Possible
Book Publisher	Available	No	Essential	Possible	£20,000	Low–High	Town	Yes	Yes	Possible	Yes
Bookie	Available	Yes	Essential	Yes	£1,000 (on-course)	Highly variable	Town or on-course	Yes (on-course)	Possible	Possible	No
Bookseller	Available	Booksellers Association	Recommended	Yes	£20,000	Medium	Town	None	Yes	Possible	No
Brewer	Available	Yes	Essential	Likely	£60,000 +++	Low–High	Either	No	Excellent	Possible	Yes
Butcher	Available	No	Essential	Possible	£20,000	Medium	Town/Village	Local	Yes	Limited	No

Job	Qualifications/Training	Licence	Experience/Springboard	Mid-career entry	Entry costs	Income bracket	Town/Country	Travel	Exit sale	Mix and match	Work at home
Cabaret Performer	Recommended	No	No	Possible	£2,000	Low–High	Town	Yes	No	Probably essential	No
Cabinet Maker	Recommended	No	Recommended	Yes	£500+	Low	Either	No	No	Yes	Yes
Calligrapher	Necessary	No	Good idea	Possible	£200	Low	Town preferably	No	No	Yes	Yes
Camera Person	Recommended	Union card necessary	No	Unlikely	£500+	Low–Medium	Town	Lots	No	Limited	No
Caravan Site Owner	No	No	No	Good	£125,000	Medium	Country	No	Yes	Excellent	Yes
Careers Adviser	Recommended	No	Usual	Yes	£2,000	Medium–High	Town	Local	Possible	Yes	Possible
Carpenter	Recommended	No	Recommended	Possible	£2,000	Low	Either	Local	No	Possible	No
Caterer	Useful	No	Useful	Yes	£2,500+	Low–Medium	Town or nearby	Local	Possible	Yes	Yes
Chamber Group Director	Essential	Union card necessary	Vital	Yes	£5,000	Low	Town	Lots	No	Yes	No
Chemical Engineering Consultant	Essential	No	Essential	Yes	£8,000+	Medium–High	Town	Yes	Possible	Yes	Not recommended
Child/Educational Psychologist	Essential	Recommended	Essential	Possible	£1,500	Medium–High	Town	Local	Possible	Possible	Yes
Child Minder	No	Yes	Yes	Yes	Nil	Low	Town/Village	None	No	Limited	Yes
China Restorer	Recommended	No	Recommended	Possible	£1,000	Low	Town preferably	Local	No	Good	Yes

Job	Qualifications/Training	Licence	Experience/Springboard	Mid-career entry	Entry costs	Income bracket	Town/Country	Travel	Exit sale	Mix and match	Work at home
Chiropodist	Vital	Yes	Recommended	Possible	£5,000	Medium–High	Town	Local, possibly	No	Possible	Possible
Chiropractor	Essential	No	Yes	Unlikely	£9,000	Medium–High	Town	No	No	Limited	Possible
Classical Composer	Recommended	No	Recommended	Possible	£1,000	Low	Either	Possible	Yes	Essential	Yes
Classical/Operatic Singer	Recommended	Equity for opera chorus	No	Unlikely	£500+	Low	Town	Yes	No	Essential	No
Cleaner	No	No	No	Yes	Nil	Low	Town/Village	Local	No	Yes	No
Cleaning Contractor	No	No	No	Yes	£3,000+	Medium	Town	Local	Possible	Possible	Not recommended
Coal Merchant	Recommended	Yes, if new	Recommended	Possible	£5,000	Low–Medium	Either	Local	Yes	Possible	Possible
Company Doctor	No	No	Essential	Essential	Nil	Low–High	Town	Yes	No	Yes	No
Computer Consultant	Available	No	Vital	Usual	£8,000+	Medium–High	Town	Local	No	Yes	Yes
Computer Hardware Engineer	Necessary	No	Recommended	Yes	£5,000+	Medium	Town	Local	No	Possible	Possible
Computer Software Author	Usual	No	Recommended	Possible	£2,000+	Medium	Town or nearby	Local	No	Possible	Possible
Concert Agent	Recommended	Yes	Essential	Possible	£5,000	Low–Medium	Town	Yes	Possible	Possible	Yes
Conductor	Recommended	No	Yes	Possible	£2,000	Low–High	Town	Endless	No	Yes	No

Job	Qualifications/ Training	Licence	Experience/ Springboard	Mid-career entry	Entry costs	Income bracket	Town/ Country	Travel	Exit sale	Mix and match	Work at home
Conference Organiser	No	No	Essential	Yes	£5,000++	Medium–High	Town	Yes	Possible	Yes	Yes
Contemporary Art Gallery Owner	No	No	Recommended	Yes	£20,000+	Medium	Town	No	Yes	Yes	No
Continuity Person	No	No	Yes	Yes	£100	Medium	Town	Yes	No	Limited	No
Conveyancer	Essential	Yes	Essential	Yes	£5,000	Medium	Town	Local	Possible	Yes	Possible
Corporate Video Producer	Recommended	No	Recommended	Possible	£2,000	Low–High	Town	Essential	Possible	Yes	No
Costume Designer	Yes	No	Recommended	Difficult	£100	Low–Medium	Town	Yes	No	Limited	No
Counsellor	Essential	No	No	Essential	£500	Medium	Town	None	No	Excellent	Yes
Courier Service	No	No	No	Excellent	£1,000+	Low–High	Town	No	Possible	Limited	No
Criminal	No	No	No	Yes	Nil	Low–High	Either	Maybe	No	Yes	Possible
Dancer	Necessary	No	No	No	£200	Low	Town	Lots	No	Yes	Limited
Dance Teacher	Essential	No	Recommended	Possible	£200	Low	Town	Local	No	Yes	No
Dealer in Large Antiques	Available	No	Recommended	Excellent	£10,000+++	Low–High	Town/ Village	Essential	Yes	Yes	Possible
Dealer in Small Antiques and Collectibles	Available	No	Recommended	Excellent	£500++	Low–High	Town/ Village	Yes	Possible	Yes	No
Dental Practice Broker	Recommended	No	Useful	Yes	£5,000	Medium	Town preferably	Yes	Possible	Yes	Possible

Job	Qualifications/ Training	Licence	Experience/ Springboard	Mid-career entry	Entry costs	Income bracket	Town/ Country	Travel	Exit sale	Mix and match	Work at home
Dental Technician	Recommended	Not yet	Essential	Unlikely	£65,000	Medium	Town	Local	Yes	Limited	Unlikely
Dentist	Essential	Yes	No	Highly unlikely	Highly variable	Medium–High	Town	None	Yes	Yes	Possible
Dietary Therapist	Essential	Yes from 1992	No	Possible	£1,000	Low–Medium	Town	Local	No	Yes	Yes
Direct Marketing Agent	Useful	No	Essential	Yes	£1,000+	Medium–High	Town	Yes	Possible	Yes	Possible
Disco Owner/DJ	No	No	No	Highly unlikely	£4,000	Medium–High	Town	Lots	Possible	Yes	No
Dispensing Chemist	Essential	Yes	Yes	Unlikely	£20,000	Medium	Town	None	Yes	Limited	No
Doctor (GP in the NHS)	Essential	Yes	Recommended	Limited	Highly variable	High	Town/ Village	Local	Possible	Yes	Possible
Doctor (Private GP)	Essential	Yes	Recommended	Highly unlikely	Highly variable	High	Town	Local	Yes	Yes	Possible
Dress Agent	No	No	Useful	Ideal	£2,000	Low	Town	None	Yes	Limited	No
Driving Instructor	Essential	Yes	Recommended	Good	£10,000	Medium	Town	Local	Possible	Yes	No
Editorial Photographer	Recommended	No	Recommended	Possible	£1,000+	Medium–High	Town	Yes	No	Yes	Possible
Electrician	Essential	Yes	Good idea	Possible	£2,000	Medium	Either	Local	No	Yes	No
Embalmer	Recommended	No	Recommended	Yes	£300	Low–Medium	Either	Local	No	Yes	No
English Language School Owner	Recommended	Recommended	Recommended	Yes	£8,000	Medium	Town	No	Yes	Yes	No

Job	Qualifications/ Training	Licence	Experience/ Springboard	Mid-career entry	Entry costs	Income bracket	Town/ Country	Travel	Exit sale	Mix and match	Work at home
Estate Agent	No	No	Essential	Yes	£10,000+	Low–High	Town	Local	Yes	Yes	No
Events Organiser	No	No	Recommended	Likely	£3,000	Medium–High	Town	Yes	Possible	Possible	Partly
Exhibition Designer	Yes	No	No	Unlikely	£2,000	Medium	Town	Yes	No	Yes	No
Farmer	Recommended	No	Useful	Yes	£100,000+++	Low–High	Country	Local	Yes	Excellent	Essential
Farrier/Blacksmith	Yes	Farriers	Essential	Possible	£100–£30,000	Low–Medium	Country	Local	Possible	Possible	No
Fashion Clothes/Hat Designer	Advisable	No	Yes	Unlikely	£500	Low–High	Town	Probably	No	Yes	Possible
Fashion Retailer	Not necessary	No	Recommended	Yes	£8,000+	Low–High	Town	Some	Excellent	Limited	No
Fashion Shoe Maker	Necessary	No	No	Unlikely	£500	Low–High	Either	Yes	No	Yes	Possible
Festival Director	Available	No	Essential	Good	£500	Low–High	Town	Yes	No	Essential	No
Film Director	Available	Union card	Not necessary	Good	£250	Medium–High	Town	Lots	No	Yes	No
Film Production Person	Recommended	Union card	Recommended	Yes	£500	Medium–High	Town	Lots	No	Limited	No
Fish Curer and Smoker	Recommended	No	Essential	Possible	£10,000	Low–Medium	Country	Local	Yes	Possible	Yes
Football Commentator	Available	No	Essential	Yes	£100+	High	Town	Essential	No	Good	No
Foreign Correspondent	Available	No	Recommended	Yes	£1,000	Low–High	Town	Yes	No	Excellent	Partly

Job	Qualifications/ Training	Licence	Experience/ Springboard	Mid-career entry	Entry costs	Income bracket	Town/ Country	Travel	Exit sale	Mix and match	Work at home
Franchisee	Franchisor's	No	Useful	Good	£5,000 +++	Low–High	Town usually	Varies	Yes	Depends on business	No
Funeral Director	Recommended	No	Useful	Good idea	£50,000+++	Low–Medium	Town	Local	Yes	Limited	No
Futures Broker	No	Yes	Essential	Yes	£20,000	High	Town	No	Possible	Yes	Possible
Garage Owner	Recommended	Yes, (MOT)	Yes	Yes	£1,000 +++	Low–Medium	Town/ Village	No	Yes	Limited	No
Garden Gnome Maker	No	No	No	Yes	£500	Low	Either	Local	No	Essential	Yes
Gardener/Garden Designer	Recommended	No	Useful	Yes	£600+	Low	Either	Local	No	Yes	No
Garlic Farmer	Useful	No	Useful	Yes	£50,000+	Medium	Country	Some	Excellent	Yes	Yes
Glass Designer and Maker	Recommended	No	Useful	Possible	£50,000	Low	Either	Some	No	Limited	Possible
Glazier	Recommended	No	Essential	Possible	£5,000+	Low	Town	Local	Possible	Yes	No
Goldsmith/ Silversmith/Jeweller	Recommended	No	No	Possible	£2,500	Low–Medium	Town	Yes	No	Yes	Yes
Graphic Designer	Recommended	No	No	Unlikely	£1,000	Low–High	Town	Local	No	Yes	Possible
Graphologist	Recommended	No	Essential	Possible	£1,000	Low–Medium	Either	Possible	No	Yes	Yes
Greyhound Trainer	No	Yes	Recommended	Possible	£5,000	Low	Country	Yes	No	Yes	Yes
Ground Worker	No	No	Recommended	Possible	£5,000+	Low	Either	Local	No	Yes	No

Job	Qualifications/ Training	Licence	Experience/ Springboard	Mid-career entry	Entry costs	Income bracket	Town/ Country	Travel	Exit sale	Mix and match	Work at home
Guardian ad Litem	Essential	No	Essential	Vital	Nil	Low–Medium	Either	Local	No	Yes	Partly
Hairdresser	Recommended	No	Recommended	Possible	£8,000+	Low–Medium	Town	Maybe local	Yes	Possible	No
Haulier	Recommended	Yes	Not necessary	Possible	£40,000+	Low–High	Either	Yes	Yes	Yes	Partly
Headhunter	Yes	No	Essential	Likely	£10,000+	Medium–High	Town	Yes	Possible	Possible	Unlikely
Healer	No	No	No	Yes	£2,000	Low–Medium	Town	Local	No	Yes	Possible
Healthfood Shopkeeper	No	No	Useful	Good	£5,000+	Low–Medium	Town	No	Good	Possible	No
Hi-Fi Shop Owner	No	Yes, for HP	Essential	Yes	£12,000	Low–High	Town	No	Excellent	Possible	No
High Street Photographer	Recommended	No	Yes	Possible	£10,000	Medium	Town	Local	Yes	Possible	No
Hire Shop Owner	No	No	Useful	Yes	Highly variable	Low–Medium	Town	No	Yes	Limited	No
Holiday Accommodation Owner	No	No	Not necessary	Good	Highly variable	Low–High	Either	Possible	Excellent	Yes	No
Homeopath	Essential	Yes from 1992	Recommended	Yes	£5,000	Medium	Town	No	No	Yes	Yes
Hotel Keeper	Recommended	Yes for alcohol	Recommended	Ideal	£150,000++	Low–High	Either	Local	Excellent	Possible	Yes
House Converter	Available	No	Essential	Yes	£30,000++	Low–High	Either	Local	Possible	Yes	Possible

Job	Qualifications/ Training	Licence	Experience/ Springboard	Mid-career entry	Entry costs	Income bracket	Town/ Country	Travel	Exit sale	Mix and match	Work at home
Hypnotherapist	Yes	No	No	Recommended	£1,000	Low–Medium	Town	No	No	Excellent	Possible
Illustrator	Recommended	No	No	Unlikely	£50	Low–Medium	Town	Some	No	Good	Yes
Import/Export Broker	No	No	Essential	Excellent	Bank credit	Medium–High	Either	Possible	Yes	Yes	Possible
Impresario	No	No	Essential	Possible	£7,500++	Low–High	Town	Yes	Possible	Yes	Yes
In-Company Trainer	Recommended	No	Essential	Essential	£20,000+	Medium–High	Town	Yes	Possible	Yes	Not recommended
Independent Financial Adviser	Not yet	Yes	Essential	Yes	£12,000+	Medium–High	Town	Local	Possible	Yes	No
Instrumental Soloist	Essential	No	No	Unlikely	£2,000+	Low–High	Town	Lots	No	Probably essential	No
Insurance Broker	Essential	Yes	Essential	Good	£1,000	Low–High	Town	Local	Yes	Possible	Possible
Interior Designer	Recommended	No	No	Yes	£5,000++	Low–High	Mostly town	Local	No	Yes	Possible
Interpreter	Essential	Recommended	Necessary	Yes	£500+	Medium–High	Town	Yes	No	Yes	No
Inventor	No	No	Probably	Probably	Highly variable	Low–High	Either	Yes	Yes	Probably essential	Possible
Investment Manager	Recommended	Yes	Yes	Yes	£50,000+	Medium–High	Town	No	Yes	Possible	No
Jazz Musician/Singer	Recommended	No	No	Possible	£1,000	Mostly low	Town	Lots	No	Yes	No

Job	Qualifications/Training	Licence	Experience/Springboard	Mid-career entry	Entry costs	Income bracket	Town/Country	Travel	Exit sale	Mix and match	Work at home
Jobbing Printer	Recommended	Union card recommended	Necessary	Possible	£25,000+	Low-Medium	Town	Local	Yes	Yes	No
Journalist	Recommended	No	Recommended	Possible	Nil	Low-High	Town	Yes	No	Yes	Partly
Kennel/Cattery Owner	Available	Yes, for quarantine	Recommended	Likely	£10,000+	Low-Medium	Country	No	Yes	Possible	Yes
Keyboard Hire	No	No	Useful	Possible	£5,000+	Low-High	Town	Lots	Possible	Yes	Possible
Knitwear Designer	Recommended	No	No	Unlikely	£1,500+	Low-High	Either	Possible	No	Possible	Possible
Landlord	No	No	No	Yes	£50,000++	Low-High	Either	Between properties	Excellent	Yes	Yes
Landscape Designer	Yes	No	Essential	Unlikely	£2,000	Low-High	Either	Yes	No	Yes	Possible
Light Music Composer	Recommended	No	No	Possible	£3,500	Low-High	Either	Possible	Yes	Essential	Yes
List Broker	No	No	No	Good	£500+	Low-High	Town	Local	Yes	Yes	Possible
Literary Agent	No	No	Recommended	Probably essential	£3,500	Low-High	Town	Yes	Yes	Limited	Possible
Local Trader	No	Yes	Essential	Yes	£30,000++	High	Town	No	No	Limited	No
Magazine Designer	Recommended	No	Recommended	No	£3,500	Low-Medium	Town	Local	No	Yes	Possible
Magazine Publisher	No	No	Recommended	Likely	£5,000++	Low-High	Town	Yes	Excellent	Yes	Possible
Make Up Artist	Recommended	No	Not necessary	Possible	£500	Low-High	Town	Yes	No	Possible	No

Job	Qualifications/ Training	Licence	Experience/ Springboard	Mid-career entry	Entry costs	Income bracket	Town/ Country	Travel	Exit sale	Mix and match	Work at home
Man with a Van	No	Driving licence	No	Yes	£5,000	Low– Medium	Usually town	Yes	No	Excellent	No
Market Research Interviewer	Yes	No	No	Yes	Nil	Low– Medium	Either	Yes	No	Excellent	No
Market Stall Holder	No	Yes	No	Yes	£300++	Low– Medium	Town	Local	No	Yes	No
Marketing Consultant	Recommended	No	A must	Essential	£5,000	High	Either	Lots	Possible	Possible	Yes
Media Converter	Not essential	No	Essential	Yes	£60,000	Medium– High	Town	Local	No	Yes	Possible
Mini-Cab Driver	No	Driving licence	No	Excellent	£3,500	Low– Medium	Mostly town	Local	No	Excellent	No
Motorcycle Messenger	No	Driving licence	No	Yes	£1,000+	Low	Town	Local	No	Excellent	No
Motorcycle Racer	No	Yes	No	Possible	£1,000+	Low	Either	Yes	No	Yes	No
MP	No	No	No	Excellent	£500+	High	Town	Yes	No	Excellent	No
Musical Instrument Maker	Recommended	No	Recommended	Possible	£2,000+	Low– Medium	Town	No	Unlikely	Possible	Yes
Musical Instrument Repairer	Recommended	No	Recommended	Possible	£2,000+	Low– Medium	Town	Possibly local	Unlikely	Possible	Possible
Music Copyist	No	No	No	Yes	Nil	Low– Medium	Either	Local	No	Probably essential	Yes
Music Critic	No	No	No	Possible	£500+	Low– Medium	Town	Yes	No	Excellent	Partly

Job	Qualifications/Training	Licence	Experience/Springboard	Mid-career entry	Entry costs	Income bracket	Town/Country	Travel	Exit sale	Mix and match	Work at home
Musician	Recommended	No	No	Unlikely	£1,000+	Low–High	Town	Yes	No	Probably essential	No
Music/Instrument Retailer	No	No	Recommended	Excellent	£8,000+	Low–Medium	Town	No	Yes	Limited	No
Music Publisher	No	No	No	Yes	£2,500	Low–usually	Town	Yes	Yes	Usually	Possible
Music Teacher	Recommended	No	No	Possible	£2,000	Low–Medium	Either	Local	No	Probably essential	Yes
Music Therapist	Essential	No	Recommended	Recommended	£500+	Low–Medium	Town	Local	No	Yes	Possible
Musicians' Answering and Booking Service	No	Union membership	No	Yes	£2,000 ++	Low	Town	No	Possible	Possible	Possible
Nanny and Babysitting Agent	No	Yes	Recommended	Yes	£1,000	Low–Medium	Town	No	Yes	Yes	Yes
New House Builder	Recommended	No	Essential	Yes	£30,000 +++	Low–High	Town	Local	Possible	Yes	No
Newsletter Publisher	No	No	No	Likely	£1,000+	Low–High	Either	No	Good	Yes	Yes
Novelist	No	No	No	Likely	£5+	Mostly low	Either	No	Possible	Probably essential	Yes
Nurse	Essential	Yes	No	Unlikely	Nil	Low–Medium	Either	Local	No	Yes	No
Nursing Home Owner/Manager	Essential	Yes	Yes	Likely	£10,000 +++	Medium	Either	No	Yes	Limited	Possible

Job	Qualifications/ Training	Licence	Experience/ Springboard	Mid-career entry	Entry costs	Income bracket	Town/ Country	Travel	Exit sale	Mix and match	Work at home
Opening to the Public	No	No	No	Likely	Highly variable	Low–High	Either	No	Excellent	Yes	Yes
Opera Producer/ Director	No	No	Good idea	Yes	£500+	Low–High	Town	A must	No	Possible	No
Optician	Essential	Yes	Useful	Unlikely	£25,000+	Medium	Town	No	Yes	Possible	No
Options Dealer	Not essential	Yes	Essential	Unlikely	£100,000 ++	High	Town	No	No	Limited	No
Orchestral Fixer	Useful	Musicians Union	Recommended	Yes	£3,000	Low– Medium	Town	Yes	No	Possible	Yes
Orchestral Musician	Necessary	Union card	No	No	£1,000+	Low– Medium	Town	Lots	No	Probably essential	No
Osteopath	Essential	Professional register	Recommended	Possible	£2,000+	Low–High	Town	No	Possible	Possible	Possible
Oyster Farmer	Necessary	No	Essential	Likely	£70,000	Low–High	Country	Local	Excellent	Recommen- ded	Yes
Painter/Decorator	No	No	Useful	Yes	£1,000	Low	Town	Local	No	Yes	No
Photographer	Recommended	No	No	Possible	£2,000+	Low–High	Either	Probable	No	Yes	Yes
Photographic Assistant	Recommended	No	No	Unlikely	Nil	Low	Town	Maybe	No	Yes	No
Photographic Stylist	Useful	No	Essential	Possible	£300+	Low–High	Town	Yes	No	Yes	Partly
Photojournalist	Recommended	Union card	Useful	Unlikely	£1,000+	Low– Medium	Town	Endless	No	Possible	No
Physiotherapist	Essential	Yes	Recommended	Unlikely	£7,500+	Low–High	Town	No	No	Possible	Possible

Job	Qualifications/Training	Licence	Experience/Springboard	Mid-career entry	Entry costs	Income bracket	Town/Country	Travel	Exit sale	Mix and match	Work at home
Piano Tuner	Recommended	No	Recommended	Yes	£1,000+	Low–Medium	Mostly town	Local	No	Possible	No
Picture Agent	Useful	No	Recommended	Yes	£2,500+	Low–High	Usually town	No	Yes	Possible	Possible
Picture Framer	Recommended	No	Recommended	Yes	£100–£5,000	Low–Medium	Town	No	Yes	Yes	Yes
Picture Researcher	No	No	Usually	Yes	£1,000	Low–Medium	Town	Yes	Yes	Possible	Yes
Picture Restorer	Recommended	No	No	Possible	£2,000	Low–Medium	Either	Yes	No	Yes	Yes
Plasterer	Available	No	Yes	Possible	£700+	Low	Either	Local	No	Possible	No
Plumber/Heating Engineer	Recommended	No	Recommended	Possible	£800	Low	Either	Local	No	Possible	No
Pop Group Sound Engineer	Not necessary	Driving licence	Recommended	Unlikely	£250	Low	Town	Lots	No	Limited	No
Potter	Recommended	No	Possible	Possible	£10,000	Low–High	Either	Local	No	Possible	Yes
Prep School Owner	Necessary	Yes	Essential	Likely	£175,000+	Medium–High	Either	No	Excellent	Possible	No
Print Maker	Necessary	No	Recommended	Possible	£200+	Low–Medium	Town	No	No	Possible	Yes
Private Investigator	Useful	No	Recommended	Likely	£5,000++	Medium–High	Town	Some	Possible	Possible	Partly
Property Developer	No	No	Useful	Likely	£50,000+++	Low–High	Either	Local	Yes	Yes	Possible

Job	Qualifications/Training	Licence	Experience/Springboard	Mid-career entry	Entry costs	Income bracket	Town/Country	Travel	Exit sale	Mix and match	Work at home
Property Manager	No	No	Recommended	Likely	£1,000+	Low–Medium	Either	Local	No	Possible	Yes
Psychoanalyst	Essential	No	No	Essential	£500	Low–High	Town	No	No	Possible	Yes
Psychologist	Essential	Recommended	Recommended	Yes	£1,000+	Medium–High	Town	Local	Possible	Possible	Unlikely
Psychotherapist	Essential	No	Useful	Essential	£15,000	Low–High	Town	No	No	Possible	Yes
Public Relations Consultant	Recommended	No	Essential	Likely	£7,500	Medium–High	Town	Yes	Possible	Yes	Not recommended
Publican	Recommended	Essential	Recommended	Likely	£15,000+++	Low–High	Either	Local	Excellent	Possible	Yes
Puppeteer	Available	No	Not essential	Yes	£2,000+	Low	Either	Constant	No	Yes	No
Race Horse Owner	No	No	No	Likely	£10,000+	Nil–High	Country	Yes	Possible	Yes	No
Radio Reporter/Presenter	Available	No	Essential	Yes	£2,000+	Low–Medium	Town	Yes	No	Yes	No
Record Company Owner	No	No	Recommended	Possible	£15,000++	Low–High	Town	Local	Good	Essential to start	Possible
Recording Studio Owner	Recommended	No	Recommended	Unlikely	Highly variable	Low–Medium	Town	Some	Yes	Essential to start	Possible
Reflexologist	Necessary	No	No	Yes	£1,000	Medium	Town	Local, perhaps	No	Limited	Possible
Repetiteur/Accompanist/Coach	Essential	Union membership	No	Highly unlikely	£2,000+	Low	Town	Yes	No	Yes	No

Job	Qualifications/Training	Licence	Experience/Springboard	Mid-career entry	Entry costs	Income bracket	Town/Country	Travel	Exit sale	Mix and match	Work at home
Restaurateur	Recommended	Alcohol – yes	Recommended	Likely	£20,000+++	Low–High	Usually town	Local	Excellent	Possible	No
Roofer	Recommended	No	Recommended	Possible	£2,000	Low	Either	Local	Possible	Possible	No
Saddler/Leatherworker	Recommended	No	Recommended	Possible	£2,000+	Low–Medium	Either	Local	Unlikely	Yes	Yes
Sailing School Owner	Yes	RYA	No	Likely	£8,000+	Low–Medium	Either	No	Yes	Yes	No
Sales Agent	No	No	Essential	Yes	£3,000	Low–High	Either	Essential	Possible	Possible	Partly
Salmon Farmer	Necessary	No	Essential	Good	£150,000	Low–Medium	Country	No	Yes	Yes	Yes
Scriptwriter	No	No	Work in TV	Yes	£10+	Low–High	Either	No	No	Essential, to start	Yes
Sculptor	Essential	No	Useful	Unlikely	£1,000++	Low–High	Either	No	No	Good	Possible
Sex Therapist	Necessary	No	No	Recommended	£400	Low–High	Town	No	No	Yes	Yes
Shepherd/Shepherdess	Useful	No	Essential	Possible	£2,000	Low	Country	Between jobs	No	Yes	No
Shipbroker	Not necessary	No	Essential	Yes	£2,500	Medium–High	Town	Yes	Possible	Possible	Possible
Shopkeeper	Available	No	Recommended	Likely	Highly variable	Low–High	Mostly town	Local	Excellent	Possible	No
Snail Farmer	Useful	No	Recommended	Yes	£10,000++	Medium	Country	No	Excellent	Possible	Yes

Job	Qualifications/Training	Licence	Experience/Springboard	Mid-career entry	Entry costs	Income bracket	Town/Country	Travel	Exit sale	Mix and match	Work at home
Social Worker	Essential	No	Essential	Usual	Nil	Low–Medium	Either	Local	No	Yes	No
Solicitor	Essential	Yes	Essential	Possible	£20,000+	Medium–High	Town	Local	Excellent	Possible	No
Space Sales Agent	No	No	Essential	Yes	£500	Low–High	Either	Some	Possible	Yes	Yes
Specialist Food Manufacturer	Available	No	Useful	Possible	£1,000++	Low–High	Either	Some	Possible	Yes	Possible
Specialist Sports Retailer	No	No	Essential	Likely	Highly variable	Low–High	Town	No	Excellent	Possible	No
Stage Designer	Necessary	No	Recommended	Possible	£50	Low–Medium	Town	Local	No	Yes	Partly
Stage Technician Carpenter	Available	No	Essential	Possible	£250	Low–Medium	Town	Maybe	No	Possible	No
Stock Broker	Essential	Yes	Essential	Possible	£50,000+	Medium–High	Town	No	Possible	Possible	No
Street Entertainer	Useful	Usually	No	Possible	Nil	Low	Town	Local	No	Essential	No
Sub Postmaster	Yes	Yes	No	Excellent	£1,000++	Low–High	Town/Village	No	Yes	Yes	No
Surveyor	Essential	For financial advice	Recommended	Possible	£7,500++	Medium–High	Town	Local	Possible	Possible	Partly
Tailor	Available	No	Recommended	Possible	£2,000	Low–Medium	Town	No	Possible	Possible	Not recommended
Tattooist	No	No	No	Possible	£5,000	Low–Medium	Town	No	No	Possible	Possible

Job	Qualifications/Training	Licence	Experience/Springboard	Mid-career entry	Entry costs	Income bracket	Town/Country	Travel	Exit sale	Mix and match	Work at home
Taxidermist	Available	No	Recommended	Yes	£100+	Low	Either	Local	No	Yes	Yes
Taxi Driver	Yes	Yes	No	Yes	£500++	Low–High	Either	Yes	No	Possible	No
Textile Designer	Recommended	No	Not necessary	Possible	£100+	Low–High	Either	Yes	No	Yes	Yes
Thatcher	Essential	No	No	Good	£5,000+	Low–Medium	Mostly country	Yes	No	Possible	No
Theatrical Agent	No	No	Yes	Possible	£2,000+	Low–Medium	Either	Some	Possible	Limited	Possible
Timeshare Holiday Accommodation Owner	No	No	No	Likely	£100,000++	Low–High	Either	Between sites	Yes	Yes	No
Tourist Guide	Necessary	In some cases	No	Yes	£1,000	Medium	Either	Yes	No	Yes	No
Toymaker	Available	No	No	Yes	£500+	Low–Medium	Either	No	No	Yes	Yes
Travel Agent	Recommended	Recommended	Essential	Good	£40,000	Medium	Town	Yes	Yes	Limited	No
Tree Surgeon	Recommended	No	No	Possible	£2,000+	Low–Medium	Mostly country	Yes	No	Yes	No
Trout Farmer	Necessary	No	Essential	Good	£50,000	Low	Country	Local	Excellent	Yes	Yes
Typesetter	Recommended	No	Useful	Yes	£5,000+	Low–Medium	Town	Local	Possible	Yes	Yes
Typist	Recommended	No	Yes	Yes	£5+++	Low–Medium	Town mostly	Local	No	Yes	Yes
UK Correspondent for Overseas Media	Available	No	Essential	Yes	£2,500	Low–Medium	Town	Yes	No	Good	Partly
Upholsterer	Recommended	No	Recommended	Possible	£1,500+	Low	Town	Local	Possible	Possible	Possible

Addresses

Addresses

ACTT (Association of Cinematograph Television and Allied Technicians)
111 Wardour Street,
London W1
tel 01-437 8506

Acupuncture Association
34 Alderney Street,
London SW1
tel 01-834 1012

ADAR (Art and Design Admissions Registry)
Penn House,
9 Broad Street,
Hereford HR4 9AP
tel 0432 266653

AFBD (Association of Futures Brokers and Dealers Ltd)
Plantation House,
Mincing Lane,
London EC3
tel 01-626 9763

AGCAS (Association of Graduate Careers Advisory Services)
Central Services Unit,
Crawford House,
Precinct Centre,
Oxford Road,
Manchester M13 9EP
tel 061-273 4233

Agricultural Colleges
Hampshire –
Hampshire College of Agriculture,
Sparsholt,
Winchester SO21 2NF
tel 096 272 441
Dumfries and Galloway –
Barony Agricultural College,
Parkgate,
Dumfries DG1 3NE
tel 038 786 251

Agricultural Training Board
Summit House,
Glebe Way,
West Wickham,
Kent BR4 0RF
tel 01-777 9003

Allied Brewery Traders' Association
85 Tettenhall Road,
Wolverhampton WV3 9NF
tel 0902 22303

Amateur Motor Cycle Association (AMCA)
Darlaston Road,
Pleck, Walsall WS2 9SL
tel 0922 39517

Anglo-European College of Chiropractic
13–15 Parkwood Road,
Bournemouth,
Dorset BH5 2DF
tel 0202 431021

Approved Coal Merchants' Scheme
Victoria House,
Southampton Row,
London WC1B 4DH
tel 01-405 1601

**Architects Registration Council
of the UK**
73 Hallam Street,
London W1N 6EE
tel 01-580 5861

**Arels-Felco Ltd (Association of
Recognised English Language
Schools and Federation of
English Language Course
Organisers)**
2 Pontypool Place,
Valentine Place,
London SE1 8QF
tel 01-242 3136

Arts Council (of Great Britain)
105 Piccadilly,
London W1
tel 01-629 9495

Associated Press
12 Norwich Street,
London EC4
tel 01-353 1515

**Association Internationale des
Interpretes de Conferences
(AIIC)**
14 rue de l'Ancien Port,
CH 1201,
Geneve, Switzerland

Association of Authors' Agents
c/o 20 John Street,
London WC1N 2DR
tel 01-405 6774

**Association of British Dispensing
Opticians**
22 Nottingham Place,
London W1
tel 01-935 7411

**Association of British Travel
Agents (ABTA)**
55–57 Newman Street,
London W1P 4AH
tel 01-637 2444

**Association of British Wild
Animal Keepers (The)**
12 Tackley Road,
Eastville,
Bristol BS5 6UQ

**Association of Certified
Accountants**
29 Lincoln's Inn Fields,
London WC2A 3EE
tel 01-242 6855

**Association of Consulting
Actuaries**
Rolls House,
7 Rolls Buildings,
Fetter Lane,
London EC4A 1NH

**Association of Educational
Psychologists**
The Secretary,
3 Sunderland Road,
Durham DH1 2LH
tel 091-384 95112

**Association of Fashion,
Advertising and Editorial
Photographers (AFAEP)**
9–10 Domingo Street,
London EC1Y 0TA
tel 01-608 1441

Association of Pension Trustees
417 Midsomer Boulevard,
Saxon Gate West,

Central Milton Keynes MK9 3BN
tel 0908 662288

**Association of Professional
Composers**
34 Hanway Street,
London W1
tel 01-436 0919

**Association of Professional
Music Therapists**
Amelia Oldfield,
1 Station Road,
Fulbourn,
Cambridge CB7 5ES

**Association of Professional
Recording Studios**
163a High Street,
Rickmansworth,
Herts
tel 0923 772907

Autocycle Union (ACU)
Millbuck House,
Corporation Street,
Rugby,
Warwicks CV21 2DN
tel 0788 540519

Baltic Exchange
24 St Mary Axe,
London EC3A 8DE
tel 01-623 5501

Bass Riley Creative Consultants
14 Culford Gardens,
Chelsea,
London SW3 2ST
tel 01-589 8718

BBC
Broadcasting House,
Portland Place,
London W1
tel 01-580 4468

BBC Publications
35 Marylebone High Street,
London W1
tel 01-580 5577

Bee Farmers Association
Sec: K.A.J. Ellis,
22 York Gardens,
Clifton,
Bristol BS8 4LN

Bellmead Kennels
Priest Hill,
Old Windsor,
Berks
tel 0784 32929

**BMA (British Medical
Association)**
BMA House,
Tavistock Square,
London WC1
tel 01-387 4499

Book House Training Centre
45 East Hill,
Wandsworth,
London SW18 2QZ
tel 01-874 2718/4608

Booksellers Association
154 Buckingham Palace Road,
London SW1W 9TZ
tel 01-730 8214

Bootstrap Co Ltd
18 Ashwin Street,
London E8 3DL
tel 01-254 0775

Brewers Society, The
42 Portman Square,
London W1
tel 01-486 4831

**British Antique Furniture
Restorers' Association**
37 Upper Addison Gardens,
Holland Park,
London W14 8AJ
tel 01-603 5643

**British Artist Blacksmiths'
Association**
c/o Alan Evans,
Hon Sec,
2 Police House,
Cheltenham Road,
Bisley,
Glos

**British Association of Concert
Agents**
c/o 12 Penzance Place,
London W11 4TA

**British Association of
Counsellors**
37a Sheep Street,
Rugby, Warwickshire
tel 0788 78328

**British Association of
Psychotherapists**
121 Hendon Lane,
London N3
tel 01-346 1747

British Chiropractic Association
Premier House,
10 Greycoat Place,
London SW1P 1SB
tel 01-222 8866

**British Clothing Industries'
Association**
7 Swallow Place,
London W1R 7AA
tel 01-408 0020

British Coal Enterprise Ltd
14–15 Lower Grosvenor Place,
London SW1W 0EX
tel 01-630 5304

British College of Acupuncture
8 Hunter Street,
London WC1N 1BN
tel 01-833 8164

**British College of Ophthalmic
Opticians**
10 Knaresborough Place,
London SW5 0TG
tel 01-373 7765

British Council
10 Spring Gardens,
London SW1
tel 01-930 8466

British Dental Association
63 Wimpole Street,
London W1M 8AL
tel 01-935 0875/3963

**British Direct Marketing
Association**
Grosvenor Gardens House,

Grosvenor Gardens,
London SW1
tel 01-630 0361

**British Footwear Manufacturers'
Federation**
Royalty House,
72 Dean Street,
London W1V 5HB
tel 01-437 5573

British Computer Society
13 Mansfield Street,
London W1
tel 01-637 0471

British Franchise Association
Franchise Chambers,
75a Bell Street,
Henley on Thames,
Oxon RG9 2BD
tel 0491 578049/50

British Funboard Association
163 West Lane,
Hayling Island,
Hants PO11 0JW
tel 0705 463595

**British Holidays and Home Parks
Association**
Chichester House,
31 Park Road,
Gloucester GL1 1LH
tel 0452 411574

**British Holistic Medical
Association**
179 Gloucester Place,
London NW1
tel 01-262 5299

**British Hotels, Restaurants and
Caterers' Association**
40 Duke Street,
London W1M 6HR
tel 01-499 6641

British Institute of Embalmers
21c Station Road,
Knowle,
Solihull,
West Midlands B91 3TG
tel 5674 778991

British Institute of Innkeeping
121 London Road,
Camberley,
Surrey GU15 3LF
tel 0276 684449

British Institute of Management
Africa House,
Kingsway,
London WC2
tel 01-405 3456

**British Institute of Professional
Photography**
2 Amwell End,
Ware,
Herts SG12 9HN
tel 0920 4011

**British Insurance Brokers
Association**
14 Bevis Marks,
London EC3A 7NT
tel 01-623 9043

**British Knitting and Clothing
Export Council**
7 Swallow Place,

London W1R 7AA
tel 01-493 6622

British Leather Federation
Leather Trade House,
Kings Park Road,
Moulton Park,
Northampton NN3 1JD
tel 0604 494131

**British Library, Business
Information Service**
Reference and Information
Service,
25 Southampton Buildings,
London WC2
tel 01-323 7979

**British Library, Official
Publications Library**
Official Publications and Social
Sciences Service,
Great Russell Street,
London WC1
tel 01-323 7536

British List Brokers' Association
Springfield House,
Princess Street,
Bedminster,
Bristol BS3 4EF
tel 0272 666900

British Overseas Trade Board
1 Victoria Street,
London SW1
tel 01-215 7877

**British Printing Industries
Federation**
11 Bedford Row,

London WC1R 4DX
tel 01-242 6904

British Psychological Society
St Andrews House,
48 Princess Road East,
Leicester LE1 7DR
tel 0533 549568

British Refugee Council
Bondway House,
3 Bondway,
London SW8 1SJ
tel 01-582 6922

British School at Rome
Inner Circle,
Regents Park,
London NW1
tel 01-487 7403

British School of Osteopathy
1 Suffolk Street,
London SW1
tel 01-930 9254

**British Snail Farmers'
Association, The**
Mr Jacques Aubree,
Barrow Farm,
Rode Hill,
Frome,
Somerset
tel 0373 830621

British Society for Music Therapy
c/o Mrs Denise Christophers,
69 Avondale Avenue,
East Barnet,
Herts EN4 8NB
tel 01-368 8879

British Standards Institution
2 Park Street,
London W1
tel 01-629 9000

**British Toy and Hobby
Manufacturers' Association Ltd**
80 Camberwell Road,
London SE5
tel 01-701 7271

British Toymakers' Guild
c/o 240 The Broadway,
Wimbledon,
London SW19
tel 01-878 9055

British Trout Association
Fishfarmers Trade Association,
136 Bishops Mansions,
Bishops Park Road,
London SW6
tel 01-736 1659

British Veterinary Association
7 Mansfield Street,
London W1A 0AT
tel 01-636 6541

Britsnail
Mr Charles Wells,
6 Stoughton Avenue,
Leicester LE2 2DA
tel 0533 706794

**Broadcasting and Entertainment
Trades Alliance (BETA)**
181–185 Wardour Street,
London W1
tel 01-439 7585

BSC Industry
Ground Floor,
Canterbury House,
2–6 Sydenham Road,
Croydon CR9 2LJ
tel 01-686 2311

**Building Employers
Confederation**
82 New Cavendish Street,
London W1
tel 01-580 5588

Business in the Community
227a City Road,
London EC1V 1LX
tel 01-253 3716

Camberwell (School of Art)
Peckham Road,
London SE5 8UF
tel 01-703 0987

**Cambridge Venture Management
Ltd**
Cambridge Science Park,
Milton Road,
Cambridge CB4 4GG
tel 0223 862618

**CAMRA (The Campaign for Real
Ale)**
321 Alma Road,
St Albans,
Herts AL1 3BW
tel 0727 67201

Canine Studies Institute
c/o David Cavill
tel 0344 420898

Cardiff University
University College,
Cardiff,
PO Box 78,
Cardiff CF1 1XL
tel 0222 874000

Central Clearing House
International Commodities
Clearing House Ltd,
Roman Wall House,
1–2 Crutched Friars,
London EC3N 2AN
tel 01-488 3200

**Central Council for Education
and Training in Social Work**
Derbyshire House,
St Chad's Street,
London WC1
tel 01-278 2455

**Centre for Alternative
Technology**
Machynlleth,
Powys,
North Wales
tel 0654 2400

Charity Commission
St Alban's House,
57–60 Haymarket,
London SW1
tel 01-210 3000

**Chartered Association of
Certified Accountants**
29 Lincoln's Inn Fields,
London WC2A 3EE
tel 01-242 6855

**Chartered Institute of Patent
Agents**
Staple Inn Buildings,
335 High Holborn,
London WC1V 7PZ
tel 01-405 9450

Chartered Insurance Institute
20 Aldermanbury,
London EC2V 7HY
tel 01-606 3835

Chartered Society of Designers
29 Bedford Square,
London WC1
tel 01-631 1510

**Chartered Society of
Physiotherapy**
14 Bedford Row,
London WC1
tel 01-242 1941

Children's Legal Centre
20 Compton Terrace,
London N1
tel 01-359 6251

**Church Commissioners for
England**
1 Millbank,
London SW1
tel 01-222 7010

**City and Guilds of London Art
School**
124 Kennington Park Road,
London SE11
tel 01-735 2306

City Business Library
106 Fenchurch Street,
London EC3
tel 01-638 8215

City University
Northampton Square,
London EC1V 0HB
tel 01-253 4399

Clothing and Footwear Institute
71 Brushfield Street,
London E1 6AA
tel 01-247 1696

Coal Merchants' Federation
Victoria House,
Southampton Row,
London WC1B 4DH
tel 01-405 8218

College for the Distributive Trades
30 Leicester Square,
London WC2H 7LE
tel 01-839 1547

College of Dietary Therapy
Hillsborough House,
Ashley,
Tiverton,
Devon
tel 0884 255879

College of Psychic Studies
16 Queensberry Place,
London SW7
tel 01-589 3292/3

College of Reflexology
9 Mead Road,

Shenley,
Radlett,
Herts WD7 9DA
tel 0923 857192

College of Traditional Chinese Acupuncture
Tao House,
Queensway,
Royal Leamington Spa,
Warwicks
tel 0926 22121

Comedy Store, The
28a Leicester Square,
London WC2
tel 01-839 6665

Communications, Advertising and Marketing Foundation
Abford House,
15 Wilton Road,
London SW1V 1NJ
tel 01-828 7506

Companies Registration Office
Companies House,
55 City Road,
London EC1
tel 01-253 9393
and Companies House,
Crown Way,
Cardiff CF4 3UZ
tel 0222 388588

Complection International (London School of Makeup)
47 Lamb's Conduit Street,
London WC1N 3LE
tel 01-242 0778

Composers' Guild
34 Hanway Street,
London W1
tel 01-436 0007

Conservative Party
32 Smith Square,
London SW1P 3HH
tel 01-222 9000

Construction Industry Training Board (CITB)
Careers Advisory Service,
Bircham Newton,
King's Lynn,
Norfolk PE31 6RH
tel 0553 776677

Consultant Chemical Engineers Bureau
c/o College of Petroleum Studies,
Sun Alliance House,
New Inn Hall Street,
Oxford OX1 2QD
tel 0865 250521

Co-Operative Development Agency
Broadmead House,
21 Panton Street,
London SW1Y 4DR
tel 01-839 2985

Cordon Bleu Cookery School (London) Ltd
114 Marylebone Lane,
London W1
tel 01-935 3503

Cordwainers' Technical College
182 Mare Street,

London E8
tel 01-985 0273

CORGI (Confederation for the Registration of Gas Installers)
See local telephone directory

CoSIRA (Council of Small Industries in Rural Areas)
141 Castle Street,
Salisbury
tel 0722 336255

Council for Dance Education and Training
5 Tavistock Place,
London WC1
tel 01-388 5770

Council for Licensed Conveyancers
Golden Cross House,
Duncannon Street,
London WC2N 4JF
tel 01-210 4604

Council of Legal Education
The Inns of Court School of Law,
4 Gray's Inn Place,
London WC1R 5DX
tel 01-404 5787

Courtauld Institute (of Art)
20 Portman Square,
London W1H 0BE
tel 01-935 9292

Covent Garden Market Management
Guardian Royal Exchange,
41 Central Avenue,

The Market,
Covent Garden,
London WC2E
tel 01-836 9136

CRAC
Careers Research and Advisory
Centre
Bateman Street,
Cambridge CB2 1LZ
tel 0223 3146640

Crafts Council
1 Oxendon Street,
London SW1Y 4AT
tel 01-930 4811

Crimewriters' Association
PO Box 172,
Tring,
Herts HP23 5LP

Crowcraft
Orchard Farm,
Escrick Road,
Wheldrake,
York YO4 6BQ
tel 0904 89727

**Customs and Excise,
Department of**
New Kings Beam House,
22 Upper Ground,
London SE1
tel 01-620 1313

Dance Forum
8 Ingestre Place,
London W1R 3LQ
tel 01-439 0988

J. Dankworth Summer School
The Stables,
Wavendon,
Bucks (Attn Miss Billy Watkins)
tel 0908 582522

**Department of Employment's
Loan Guarantee Unit**
Room 221,
Steel House,
11 Tothill Street,
London SW1H 9NF
tel 01-273 3000

Department of the Environment
2 Marsham Street,
London SW1
tel 01-276 0990

**Department of the Environment
(Endangered Species)**
Room 308,
Tollgate House,
Houghton Street,
Bristol
tel 0272 218811

**Department of Trade and
Industry**
1–19 Victoria Street,
London SW1
tel 01-215 7877

**DES (Department of Education
and Science)**
Elizabeth House,
York Road,
London SE1 7PH
tel 01-9334 9000

Department of Transport
2 Marsham Street,
London SW1
tel 01-276 3000

Design Council
28 Haymarket,
London SW1
tel 01-839 8000

Dietary Therapy Society
210 Tufnell Park Road,
London N7 0PZ

Direct Mail Producers Association
34 Grand Avenue,
London N10
tel 01-883 7229

Direct Mail Services Standards Board
26 Eccleston Street,
London SW1W 9PY
tel 01-824 8651

Directors' Guild of Great Britain
125 Tottenham Court Road,
London W1P 9HN
tel 01-387 7131

Disabled Living Foundation
380 Harrow Road,
London W9
tel 01-289 6111

Driving Instructors Association
Lion Green Road,
Coulsdon,
Surrey CR3 2NL
Hotline: 01-660 3333

Edinburgh Fringe Festival
180 High Street,
Edinburgh
tel 031-226 5247

Employment Agency Licensing Office
2 Church Road,
Stanmore,
Middlesex
tel 01-954 76777

Employment Consultants Institute
Institute of Employment
Consultants,
55 Charterhouse Street,
London EC1
tel 01-251 4559

Employment Service, Department of Employment
200 Great Dover Street,
London SE1
tel 01-357 7110

English Tourist Board
Thames Tower,
Blacks Road,
London W6
tel 01-846 9000

English Vineyard Association
38 West Park,
London SE9 4RH
tel 01-857 0452

Equity (British Actors Equity Association)
8 Harley Street, London W1
tel 01-636 6367/9311
    01-631 0327

European School of Osteopathy
104 Tonbridge Road,
Maidstone, Kent ME16 8SL

European Tattoo Artists Federation
2a Canada Road,
Deal,
Kent

Faculty of Actuaries
23 St Andrew Square,
Edinburgh EH2 1AQ
tel 031-557 1575

Faculty of Advocates
Advocates Library,
Parliament House,
Edinburgh
tel 031-226 5071

Faculty of Homeopathy
Royal London Homeopathic Hospital,
Great Ormond Street,
London WC1N 3HR
tel 01-837 3091

Farriers' Registration Council
PO Box 49,
East of England Show Ground,
Peterborough PE2 0GU
tel 0733 234451

Federation of British Bloodstock Agents
c/o The Old Brewery,
Hampton Street,
Tetbury,
Glos
tel 0666 53595

Federation of International Competitions
12 rue de l'Hotel de Ville,
CH 1204,
Geneva,
Switzerland

Feline Advisory Bureau
(Boarding Cattery Officer),
Stonehenge Cats' Hotel,
Orcheston,
Nr Salisbury,
Wilts
tel 0980 620251

Ferrary Publications Ltd
Ground Floor,
Boundary House,
91–93 Charterhouse Street,
London EC1N 6HR
tel 01-250 0646/01-253 2724

FIMBRA (Financial Intermediaries and Brokers Regulatory Association)
22 Great Tower Street,
London EC3
tel 01-929 2711

Forestry Training Council
Forestry Commission,
231 Corstorphine Road,
Edinburgh EH12 7AT
tel 031-334 8083

Franchise Development Services
Castle House,
Castle Meadow,
Norwich NR2 1PG
tel 0603 620301

Freight Transport Association
Hermes House,
St John's Road,
Tunbridge Wells,
Kent TN4 9UZ
tel 0892 26171

Gaming Board of Great Britain
Berkshire House,
168–173 High Holborn,
London WC1V 7AA
tel 01-240 0821

Gateshead College
Durham Road,
Gateshead NE9 5BN
tel 091-477 0524

**Gemmological Association
(of Great Britain)**
2 Carey Lane,
London EC2
tel 01-726 4374

General Council of the Bar
11 South Square,
London WC1
tel 01-242 0934

General Dental Council
37 Wimpole Street,
London W1M 8DQ
tel 01-486 2171

General Medical Council
44 Hallam Street,
London W1N 6AE
tel 01-580 7642

General Optical Council
41 Harley Street,
London W1N 2DJ
tel 01-580 3898

Glass Manufacturers' Federation
19 Portland Place,
London W1N 4BH
tel 01-580 6952

Glasshouse
65 Long Acre,
London WC2
tel 01-836 9785

Glastonbury (Festival)
Enquiries to Michael Eavis,
Worthy Farm,
Pilton,
Shepton Mallet,
Somerset BA4 4BY
tel 074989 254

**Goldsmiths' Company
(Worshipful Company of
Goldsmiths)**
Goldsmiths Hall,
Foster Lane,
London EC2
tel 01-606 7010

Graduate Enterprise in Wales
Dr D.A. Kirby,
St David's University College,
University of Wales,
Lampeter,
Dyfed SA48 7ED
tel 0570 422351

Graduate Enterprise Programme
Michelle Kent,
Cranfield School of Management,
Cranfield,
Beds MK43 0AL
tel 0234 751122

Graphology Centre, The
tel 01-262 0198 (telephone
enquiries only)

Greyhound Stud Book
16 Clocktower Mews,
Newmarket,
Suffolk
tel 0638 667381

**Guildhall School (Guildhall
School of Music and Drama)**
Silk Street,
Barbican,
London EC2Y 8DT
tel 01-628 2571

**Guild of Air Pilots and
Navigators**
30 Eccleston Street,
London SW1
tel 01-730 3525

Guild of Guide Lecturers
2 Bridge Street,
London SW1
tel 01-839 7438/5314

Guild of Master Craftsmen
166 High Street,
Lewes,
East Sussex BN7 1YE
tel 0273 478449

Guild of Taxidermists
c/o Duncan Ferguson,
Membership Secretary,
Guild of Taxidermists,
Glasgow Museum and Art
Gallery,
Kelvingrove,
Glasgow G3 8AG
tel 041-357 3929

Hambros
Hambros Bank Ltd,
51 Bishopsgate,
London EC2
tel 01-588 2851

Hanson Organisation
1 Grosvenor Place,
London SW1
tel 01-245 1245

Herb Society (The)
77 Great Peter Street,
London SW1P 2EZ
tel 01-222 3634

Herefordshire Technical College
Folly Lane,
Hereford HR1 1LS
tel 0432 267311

Hippodrome
Cranbourn Street,
London WC2
tel 01-437 4311/4837

Historic Houses Association
38 Ebury Street,
London SW1
tel 01-730 9419

HMSO Bookshop
49 High Holborn,
London WC1
tel 01-211 5656

Horserace Totalisator Board
Tote House,
74 Upper Richmond Road,
London SW15
tel 01-874 6411

**Hotel and Catering Training
Board**
International House,
High Street,
London W5
tel 01-579 2400

**IFCA (International Foreign
Correspondents Association)**
Dominion House,
101 Southwark Street,
London SE1 0JF
tel 01-401 3177

**IMRO (Investment Mangers'
Regulatory Organisation)**
Centre Point,
New Oxford Street,
London W1
tel 01-379 0601

**Incorporated Society of
Musicians**
10 Stratford Place,
London W1
tel 01-629 4413

**Incorporated Society of Valuers
and Auctioneers**
3 Cadogan Gate,

London SW1X 0AS
tel 01-235 2282

**Independent Film, Video and
Photography Association**
79 Wardour Street,
London W1V 3PH
tel 01-439 0460

**Independent Prep Schools
Association**
Incorporated Association of
Preparatory Schools,
138 Kensington Church Street,
London W8
tel 01-727 2316

**Independent Schools
Information Service (ISIS)**
56 Buckingham Gate,
London SW1
tel 01-630 8793

**Independent Schools Joint
Council**
25 Victoria Street,
London SW1
tel 01-222 4957

Institute of Actuaries
Staple Inn Hall,
High Holborn,
London WC1
tel 01-242 0106

**Institute of Chartered
Accountants in England and
Wales**
Chartered Accountants' Hall,
Moorgate Place,
London EC2P 2BJ
tel 01-628 7060

**Insitute of Chartered
Accountants in Scotland**
27 Queen Street,
Edinburgh EH2 1LA
tel 031-225 5673

**Institute of Chartered
Shipbrokers**
24 St Mary Axe,
London EC3A 8DE
tel 01-283 1361

Institute of Group Analysis
1 Daleham Gardens,
London NW3
tel 01-431 2693

Institute of Horticulture
80 Vincent Square,
London SW1
tel 01-834 4333

Institute of Inventors
19 Fosse Way,
London W13
tel 01-998 3540

Institute of Linguists
24a Highbury Grove,
London N5 2EA
tel 01-359 7445

Institute of Marketing
Moor Hall,
Cookham,
Berks
tel 06285 24922

**Institute of Patentees and
Inventors**
505a Triumph House,

Regent Street,
London W1
tel 01-242 7812

Institute of Plumbing
64 Station Lane,
Hornchurch,
Essex
tel 04024 72791

Institute of Printing
8 Lonsdale Gardens,
Tunbridge Wells,
Kent TN1 1NU
tel 0892 38118

Institute of Psychoanalysis
63 New Cavendish Street,
London W1
tel 01-580 4952

Institute of Public Relations
Gate House,
1 St John's Square,
London EC1 4DM
tel 01-253 5151

Institution of Chemical Engineers
13 Gayfere Street,
London SW1
tel 01-222 2681

Institution of Electrical Engineers
Savoy Place,
London WC2
tel 01-240 1871

**Insurance Brokers Registration
Council**
15 St Helens Place,
London EC3
tel 01-588 4387

Intermediate Technology Development Group
103 Southampton Row,
London WC1
tel 01-436 9761

International Air Transport Association (IATA)
Greener House,
66 Haymarket,
London W1
tel 01-930 1625

International Institute for Cotton
21 Cavendish Place,
London W1
tel 01-636 7676

International Professional Security Association
c/o Mr Rabbitts,
292a Torquay Road,
Paignton,
Devon TQ3 2EZ

International Register of Oriental Medicine
Greenhedges House,
Greenhedges Avenue,
East Grinstead,
Sussex RH19 1DZ
tel 0342 313106/7

International Wool Secretariat
6 Carlton Gardens,
London SW1
tel 01-930 7300

Inventalink
28 Lexington Street,
London W1
tel 01-439 8427

Inverness College (of Higher and Further Education)
3 Longman Road,
Longman South,
Inverness IV1 1SA
tel 0463 236681

Investors in Industry (plc)
91 Waterloo Road,
London SE1
tel 01-928 7822

IPG (Independent Publishers Guild)
147–149 Gloucester Terrace,
London W2 6DX
tel 01-723 7328

IRCHIN (Independent Representation of Children in Need)
Lingmel,
Thurstaston Road,
Heswall,
Merseyside
tel 051-342 2836

ITV (Independent Broadcasting Authority)
70 Brompton Road,
London SW3
tel 01-584 7011

Iyengar Institute
223a Randolph Avenue,
London W9 1NL
tel 01-624 3080

Jockey Club, The
42 Portman Square,
London W1
tel 01-486 4921

John Makepeace School for Craftsmen in Wood
Parnham House,
Beaminster,
Dorset
tel 0308 862204

Kennel Agency
Animal Boarding Advisory
Bureau
c/o Blue Grass Animal Hotel,
Little Leigh,
Northwich,
Cheshire CW8 4RJ
tel 0606 891303

Labour Party
150 Walworth Road,
London SE17
tel 01-703 0833

Ladbury Shenton
28 Glenferness Avenue,
Bournemouth BH4 9NQ
tel 0202 761478

Landscape Institute
12 Carlton House Terrace,
London SW1Y 5AH
tel 01-839 4044

LAUTRO (Life Assurance and Unit Trust Regulatory Organisation) Ltd
Centre Point,
103 New Oxford Street,
London WC1A 1QH
tel 01-379 0444

Law Society
113 Chancery Lane,

London WC2
tel 01-242 1222

Law Society of Scotland
26–27 Drumsheugh Gardens,
Edinburgh EH3 7YB
tel 031-226 7411

Legal and General Young Entrepreneurs' Scheme
Legal and General Group plc,
Temple Court,
11 Queen Victoria Street,
London EC4N 4TP
tel 01-248 9678

Leith's (School of Food and Wine)
21 St Alban's Grove,
London W8
tel 01-229 0177

Licensed Taxi Drivers' Association
9–11 Woodfield Road,
London W9 2BA
tel 01-286 1046

LIFFE (London International Financial Futures Exchange, The)
Royal Exchange,
Cornhill,
London EC3
tel 01-623 0444

Little Angel, The
Marionette Theatre,
14 Dagmar Passage,
London N1
tel 01-226 1787

Livewire
60 Grainger Street,
Newcastle upon Tyne NE1 5JG
tel 091-261 5584

**London and Provincial Antique
Dealers Association**
3 Cheval Place,
London SW7
tel 01-584 7911

London College of Fashion
20 John Prince's Street,
Oxford Street,
London W1R 0BJ
tel 01-629 9401

London College of Furniture
41 Commercial Road,
London E1
tel 01-247 1953

London College of Osteopathy
8 Boston Place,
London NW1
tel 01-262 5250

London College of Printing
Elephant and Castle,
London SE1 6SB
tel 01-735 9100

London Enterprise Agency
4 Snow Hill,
London EC1A 2DL
tel 01-236 3000

London Foot Hospital
33 Fitzroy Square,
London W1
tel 01-636 0602

London FOX
1 Commodity Quay,
St Katharine's Dock,
London E1 9AX
tel 01-481 2080

**London Retail Meat Traders
Association**
27 Central Markets,
London EC1
tel 01-248 0732

Mailing Preference Service
Freepost 22,
London W1E 7EZ
tel 01-734 0058

**Management Consultants
Association Ltd**
11 West Halkin Street,
London SW1
tel 01-235 3897

Market Research Society
175 Oxford Street,
London W1
tel 01-439 2585

Marriage Guidance Council
Herbert Gray College,
Little Church Street,
Rugby,
Warwicks CV21 3AP
tel 0788 73241

Mecca (Leisure) Ltd
76 Southwark Street,
London SE1
tel 01-928 2323

Merrist Wood Agricultural College
Worplesdon,
Guildford,
Surrey
tel 0483 232424

Merton College
Morden Park,
London Road,
Morden,
Surrey SM4 5QX
tel 01-640 3001

Metropolitan Police Press Bureau
New Scotland Yard,
Broadway,
London SW1H 0BG
tel 01-230 1212

MI Group
Centrepoint,
New Oxford Street,
London WC1
tel 01-379 5995

Ministry of Agriculture (Fisheries and Food)
Whitehall Place,
London SW1A 2HH
tel 01-270 8492

Ministry of Agriculture (Veterinary Division)
Government Buildings,
Hook Rise,
Tolworth,
Surrey
tel 01-330 4411

Ministry of Transport (MOT)
Department of Transport,
2 Marsham Street,
London SW1
tel 01-276 3000

Motor Agents' Association Ltd, The
201 Great Portland Street,
London W1
tel 01-580 9122

Motor Cycle Association
Stanley House,
Eaton Road,
Coventry CV1 2FH
tel 0203 27427

Museums Association
34 Bloomsbury Way,
London WC1
tel 01-404 4767

Music Publishers' Association
103 Kingsway,
London WC2
tel 01-831 7591

Music Retailers Association
PO Box 249,
London W4
tel 01-994 7592

Musicians Union
60 Clapham Road,
London SW9
tel 01-582 5566

**NACRO (National Association
for the Care and Resettlement of
Offenders)**
169 Clapham Road,
London SW9
tel 01-582 6500

Napier Polytechnic
Colinton Road,
Edinburgh EH10 5DT
tel 031-447 7070

**National Association of
Bookmakers**
Sabian House,
26 Cowcross Street,
London EC1
tel 01-390 8222

**National Association of Estate
Agents**
21 Jury Street,
Warwick
tel 0926 496800

**National Association of Funeral
Directors**
57 Doughty Street,
London WC1N 2NE
tel 01-242 9388

**National Association of Private
Investigators**
27a High Street,
Andover,
Hants
tel 0264 332323

**National Association of
Shopkeepers**
Lynch House,

91 Mansfield Road,
Nottingham NG1 5FN
tel 0602 475046

**National Association of Trade
Protection Societies**
8 New Street,
Leicester LE1 5NF
tel 0533 531951

**National Childminding
Association**
8 Mason's Hill,
Bromley,
Kent BR2 9EY
tel 01-464 6164

**National Council for Drama
Training**
5 Tavistock Place,
London WC1H 9SS
tel 01-387 3650

**National Council for the Training
of Journalists**
Carlton House,
Henwall Street,
Epping CM16 4NL
tel 0378 72395

**National Council for Vocational
Qualifications**
222 Euston Road,
London NW1 2BZ
tel 01-387 9898

National Farmers Union
Agriculture House,
Knightsbridge,
London SW1
tel 01-235 5077

National Federation of Fishmongers
Pisces,
London Road,
Feering,
Colchester,
Essex CO5 9ED
tel 0376 71391

National Federation of Music Societies
Francis House,
Francis Street,
London SW1
tel 01-828 7320

National Federation of Painting and Decorating Contractors (NFPDC)
82 New Cavendish Street,
London W1
tel 01-580 5588

National Federation of Self-Employed and Small Businesses Ltd
32 St Anne's Road West,
Lytham St Annes,
Lancs FY8 1NY
tel 0253 720911

National Graphical Association (NGA)
Graphic House,
63–67 Bromham Road,
Bedford MK40 2AG
tel 0234 51521

National Greyhound Racing Club
Shipton House,
Oval Road,
London NW1
tel 01-267 9256

National Inspection Council for Electrical Installation Contracting
Vintage House,
36 Albert Embankment,
London SE1
tel 01-582 7746

National Joint Council for the Craft of Dental Technicians
64 Wimpole Street,
London W1M 8AL
tel 01-935 0875

National Joint Council for the Motor Vehicle and Repair Industry
201 Great Portland Street,
London W1
tel 01-580 9122

National Joint Council of Driving Instructors
c/o John Milne,
121 Marshalwick Lane,
St Albans,
Herts AL1 4UX

National Master Farriers', Blacksmiths' & Agricultural Engineering Association (NMFB&AEA)
Avenue R,
7th Street,
National Agricultural Centre,
Stoneleigh,
Kenilworth,
Warwickshire CV8 2LG
tel 0203 20870

**National Nursery Examination
Board**
Argyle House,
Euston Road,
London NW1
tel 01-837 5458

**National Schools of Violin
Making**
Istituto per L'Artigianato,
Lintario e del Legno,
Piazza Marconi 5,
261000,
Cremona,
Italy

Staatliche Berufsfach und
Fachschule für Giegenbau,
Parten Kirchener Str. 24,
8102 Mittenwald,
West Germany

National Sheep Association
The Sheep Centre,
Malvern, Worcester WR13 6PH
tel 0684 892661

**National Union of Journalists
(NUJ)**
Acorn House,
314 Gray's Inn Road,
London WC1X 8DP
tel 01-278 7916

Newark College
Chauntry Park,
Newark-on-Trent NG24 1PB
tel 0636 705921

**Nordoff-Robins (Music Therapy
Centre Ltd)**
3 Leighton Place,

London NW5
tel 01-267 6296

**North London School of
Physiotherapy for the Visually
Handicapped**
10 Highgate Hill,
London N19 5ND
tel 01-272 1659

Norwich Puppet Theatre
St James,
Whitefriars,
Norwich,
Norfolk NR3 1TN
tel 0603 615564

Office of Fair Trading
Field House,
Breams Buildings,
London EC4
tel 01-242 2858

**Office of Population Censuses
and Surveys**
St Catherine's House,
10 Kingsway,
London WC2
tel 01-242 0262

Open University
Open University,
Walton Hall,
Milton Keynes MK7 6AA
tel 0908 74066

**Osteopathic Association (British
Naturopathic and Osteopathic
Association)**
6 Netherhall Gardens,
London NW3 5RR
tel 01-435 8728

Oxford Polytechnic
Headington,
Oxford OX3 0BP
tel 0865 64777

Patent Office
State House,
66–71 High Holborn,
London WC1R 4TP
tel 01-829 6910

Pensions Management Institute, The
124 Middlesex Street,
London SE1
tel 01-247 1452/4348

PER (Professional and Executive Recruitment)
Rex House,
4 Regent Street,
London SW1
tel 01-930 3484

Performing Right Society Ltd
29 Berners Street,
London W1
tel 01-580 5544

Periodical Publishers' Association
Imperial House,
15–19 Kingsway,
London WC2B 6UN
tel 01-379 6268

Pharmaceutical Society of Great Britain
1 Lambeth High Street,
London SE1 7JN
tel 01-735 9141

Photographers' Gallery
5 Great Newport Street,
London WC2
tel 01-831 1772

Piano Tuners' Association
The Secretary,
10 Reculver Road,
Herne Bay,
Kent CT6 6LD
tel 0227 368808

Playboard
Playboard Puppets,
94 Ockendon Road,
London N1
tel 01-226 5911

Polka Theatre, The
240 The Broadway,
London SW19
tel 01-542 4258
   01-543 3741

Polytechnic of Central London School of Languages
309 Regent Street,
London W1R 8AL
tel 01-580 2020

Prince's Trust
8 Bedford Row,
London WC1R 4BA
tel 01-430 0521/2

Printmakers' Council
31 Clerkenwell Close,
London EC1
tel 01-250 1927

Professional Board Sailers Association
British Funboard Association

163 West Lane,
Hayling Island,
Hants PO11 0JW
tel 0705 463595

Public Carriage Office
15 Penton Street,
London N1
tel 01–278 1744

Puppet Centre
Battersea Arts Centre,
Lavender Hill,
London SW11 5TJ
tel 01-228 5335

Reflex Pictures Ltd
83 Clerkenwell Road,
London EC1 5BX
tel 01-405 8545

Registrar of Companies
Companies Registration Office
Crown Way,
Maindy,
Cardiff CF4 3UZ
tel 0222 388588

**Resort Condominiums
International (RCI)**
Parnell Street,
Victoria Street,
London SW1
tel 01-821 6622

Reuters (Ltd)
85 Fleet Street,
London EC4
tel 01-250 1122

Riverside Studios
Crisp Road,

Hammersmith,
London W6
tel 01-741 2251

Road Haulage Association, Ltd
104 New King's Road,
London SW6
tel 01-736 1183

**Road Transport Industry
Training Board**
Capitol House,
Empire Way,
Wembley,
Middlesex HA9 0NG
tel 01-902 8880

Roehampton Institute
Roehampton Lane,
London SW15 5PU
tel 01-878 5751

Romantic Novelists' Association
Hon Sec Mrs Dorothy Entwistle,
20 First Avenue,
Amersham,
Bucks HP7 9BJ

Royal Academy of Dancing
48 Vicarage Crescent,
London SW11
tel 01-223 0091

Royal Academy of Music
Marylebone Road,
London NW1 5HT
tel 01-935 5461

**Royal College of General
Practitioners**
14 Princes Gate,

London SW7
tel 01-581 3232

Royal College of Music
Prince Consort Road,
London SW7 2BS
tel 01-589 3643

Royal College of Nursing
20 Cavendish Square,
London W1H 0AB
tel 01-409 3333

**Royal College of Veterinary
Surgeons**
32 Belgrave Square,
London SW1X 8QP
tel 01-235 4971

**Royal Horticultural Society
(RHS)**
Horticultural Hall,
Vincent Square,
London SW1
tel 01-834 4333

**Royal Institute of British
Architects (RIBA)**
66 Portland Place,
London W1N 4AD
tel 01-580 5533

**Royal Institution of Chartered
Surveyors**
12 Great George Street,
London SW1P 3AD
tel 01-222 7000

Royal Northern College of Music
124 Oxford Road,
Manchester M13 9RD
tel 061-273 6283

Royal Society of Arts (RSA)
8 John Adam Street,
London WC2
tel 01-930 5115

Royal Society of Arts (RSA)
Murray Road,
Orpington,
Kent BR5 3RB
tel 0689 32421

Royal Society of Medicine
1 Wimpole Street,
London W1
tel 01-408 2119

Royal Society of Musicians
10 Stratford Place,
London W1
tel 01-629 6137

**Royal Society of Painter-Etchers
& Engravers**
Bankside Gallery,
48 Hopton Street,
London SE1
tel 01-928 7521

**Royal Society of Painters in
Watercolours**
Bankside Gallery,
48 Hopton Street,
London SE1
tel 01-928 7521

**Royal Yachting Association
(RYA)**
RYA House,
Romsey Road,
Eastleigh,
Hants SO5 4YA
tel 0703 629962

RSPCA (Royal Society for the Prevention of Cruelty to Animals)
Causeway,
Horsham,
West Sussex RH12 1HG
tel 0403 64181

Rural Development Commission
11 Cowley Street,
London SW1P 3NA
tel 01-222 9134

Rycotewood College
Priest End,
Thame,
Oxon OX9 2BR
tel 084 421 2501

Saddlers Company (Worshipful Company of)
Saddlers Hall,
Gutter Lane,
London EC2
tel 01-726 8661

School Transfer Consultants
55 Cleveland Street,
London W1P 1PQ
tel 01-636 2956

Science Reference Library
25 Southampton Buildings,
London WC2A 1AW
tel 01-636 1544

Scottish Development Agency
120 Bothwell Street,
Glasgow G2 7JP
tel 041-248 2700

Scottish Enterprise Foundation
University of Stirling,
Stirling FK9 4LA
tel 0786 73171

Scottish Salmon Growers Association
Drummond House,
Scott Street,
Perth PH1 5EJ
tel 0738 35420

Scottish Smoked Salmon Association
21 Longman Drive,
Inverness IV1 1SU
tel 0463 225959

Sea Fish Industry Authority
142–144 Cromwell Road,
London SW7
tel 01-373 8495

Shell Enterprise Loan Fund
Shell-Mex House,
Strand,
London WC2R 0DX
tel 01-257 3185

Shellfish Association of Great Britain
Fishmongers Hall,
London Bridge,
London EC4
tel 01-283 8305

Ski Club of Great Britain
118 Eaton Square,
London SW1
tel 01-245 1033

Snail Centre, The
Mr Roy Groves,
Plaas Newydd,
90 Dinerth Road,
Colwyn Bay,
Clwydd LL28 4YH
tel 0492 48253

Social and Liberal Democrats
4 Cowley Street,
London SW1
tel 01-222 7999

Social Democratic Party (SDP)
2nd Floor,
25–28 Buckingham Gate,
London SW1E 6LD
tel 01-821 9661

Society for the Promotion of New Music
10 Stratford Place,
London W1
tel 01-491 8111

Society of Analytical Psychology
1 Daleham Gardens,
London NW3
tel 01-435 7696

Society of Apothecaries
Apothecaries Hall,
Blackfriars Lane,
Queen Victoria Street,
London EC4V 6EJ
tel 01-236 1189

Society of Authors
84 Drayton Gardens,
London SW10 9SB
tel 01-373 6642

Society of Chiropodists
53 Welbeck Street,
London W1M 7HE
tel 01-486 3381

Society of Designer-Craftsmen
24 Rivington Street,
London EC2
tel 01-739 3663

Society of Graphical and Allied Trades (SOGAT)
Sogat House,
London Road,
Hadleigh,
Southend on Sea,
Essex
tel 0702 554111

Society of Homeopaths
2 Artizan Road,
Northampton NN1 4HU
tel 00604 21400

Society of Licensed Conveyancers
32 Craignish Avenue,
Norbury,
London SW16 4RN
tel 01-679 1619

Society of Picture Researchers and Editors (SPRED)
BM Box 259,
London WC1N 3XX
tel 01-404 5011

Society of Scribes and Illuminators
54 Boileau Road,
London SW13 9BL
tel 01-748 9951

Society of Teachers of Alexander Technique
10 London House,
266 Fulham Road,
London SW10 9EL
tel 01-351 0828

Solid Fuel Advisory Service
Hobart House,
Grosvenor Place,
London SW1
tel 01-235 2020

Southfields College (of Further Education)
Aylestone Road,
Leicester LE2 7LW
tel 0533 541818

Stock Exchange (International Stock Exchange of the United Kingdom & the Republic of Ireland Ltd)
London EC2N 1HB
tel 01-588 2355

Surrey University
Guildford,
Surrey GU2 5XH
tel 0483 571281

Tavistock Institute of Human Relations
120 Belsize Lane,
London NW3
tel 01-435 7111

Teachers Pay and General Branch Division A
Department of Education and Science,

Elizabeth House,
York Road,
London SE1 7PH
tel 01-934 9000

Thames Television
Thames Studios,
Teddington Lock,
Teddington,
Middlesex TW11 9NT
tel 01-977 3252

Thatching Advisory Service Ltd
Rose Tree Farm,
29 Nine Mile Ride,
Finchampstead,
Wokingham,
Berks RG11 4QD
tel 0734 734203

Timeshare Developers' Association
23 Buckingham Gate,
London SW1E 6LB
tel 01-821 8845

Trinity College of Music
Mandeville Place,
London W1M 6AQ
tel 01-935 5773

TSA (The Securities Association)
Stock Exchange Tower,
Old Broad Street,
London EC2
tel 01-256 9000

UK Central Council for Nursing, Midwifery and Health Visiting
23 Portland Place,
London W1N 3AS
tel 01-637 7181

UK Training College of Hypnotherapy and Counselling
10 Alexander Street,
London W2 5NT
tel 01-727 0255/01-221 1796

Unit Trust Association
65 Kingsway,
London WC2
tel 01-831 0898

University of London, Department of Extramural Studies
25 Russell Square,
London WC1
tel 01-636 8000

University College Cardiff
PO Box 78,
Cardiff CF1 1XL
tel 0222 874000

University of East Anglia
Norwich,
Norfolk NR4 7TJ
tel 0603 56161

Urban Centre for Alternative Technology
101 Philip Street,
Bedminster,
Bristol BS3 4DR
tel 0272 662008

Victoria and Albert Museum
South Kensington,
London SW7 2RL
tel 01-938 8500

Victorian Society
1 Priory Gardens,
London W4
tel 01-994 1019

Watford College
Hempstead Road,
Watford,
Herts WD1 3EZ
tel 0923 57500

Welsh Development Agency
Pearl Assurance House,
Greyfriars Road,
Cardiff CF1 3XX
tel 0222 222666

Welsh Office, Agriculture Department
Station Road,
Ruthin,
Clwydd LL15 1BP
tel 08242 2611

West Dean (College of Arts)
West Dean,
Chichester,
West Sussex
tel 0243 63301

Westminster Central Reference Library
Business and Official Publications Section,
St Martin's Street,
London WC2
tel 01-798 2034

Wine and Spirit Education Trust (Ltd)
Five Kings House,

Kennet Wharf Lane,
Upper Thames Street,
London EC4V 3AJ
tel 01-236 3551

**Worshipful Company of
Spectacle Makers**
Apothecaries Hall,
Blackfriars Lane,
London EC4V 6EL
tel 01-236 2932

Writers' Guild (of Great Britain)
430 Edgware Road,
London W2
tel 01-723 8074

Young Disco Centre
20 Malden Road,
London NW5

Young Enterprise
Robert Hyde House,
Bryanston Square,
London W1
tel 01-724 7641

**Young Farmers' Clubs (The
National Federation of)**
National Agricultural Centre,
Stoneleigh,
Kenilworth,
Warwickshire CV8 2LG
tel 0203 696544

Zoological Society of London
Regent's Park,
London NW1 4RY
tel 01-722 3333

Bibliography

Bibliography

AA Guides
Automobile Association
(London)
Annually

About Solicitors
Law Society
113 Chancery Lane,
London W2A 1PL

Accountancy
The Institute of Chartered
Accountants in England & Wales,
40 Bernard Street,
London WC1N 1LD
£20 Monthly

Accountancy Age
VNU Business Publications,
32–34 Broadwick Street,
London W1A 2HG
£70 pa Weekly

Actor's Handbook
Barry Turner
Bloomsbury Publishers
£9.99

ACU Handbook
Autocycle Union,
Corporation Street,
Rugby,
Warwicks CV21 2DN
£1.50 (mail order)

Adoption and Fostering
British Agencies for Adoption and
Fostering,
11 Southwark Street,

London SE1 1RQ
£3 Quarterly

Advanced Reflexology
R Dalamore
Cockatrice Press

Adventures in the Screen Trade
William Goldman
Future (London) 1985

**Agriculture, Horticulture and
Forestry (Choose Your Course)**
DES
Elizabeth House,
London SE1

Airline World
Travel Weekly Publications Ltd,
23 Dering Street,
London W1R 9AA
Free Weekly

Alexander Principle
Wilfred Barlow
Arrow Books (London)

Alexander Technique
Chris Stevens
Macdonald Optima (London)

American Way of Death (The)
Jessica Mitford
Penguin (Harmondsworth)

Annual Careers Guide
COIC,
Manpower Services Commission,
Moorfoot,
Sheffield S1 4PQ

Antique Collector (The)
National Magazine Co Ltd,
72 Broadwick Street,
London W1V 2BP
£2 Monthly

Antique Dealer and Collectors Guide
IPC Magazines Ltd,
Kings Reach Tower,
Stamford Street,
London SE1 9LS
£1.60 Monthly

Antiques Trade Gazette
Metropress Ltd,
17 Whitcomb Street,
London WC2H 7PL
£30 pa Weekly

Apollo
22 Davies Street,
London W1Y 1LH
£4 Monthly

Art & Artists (see The Artist)

Art of Psychotherapy (The)
Anthony Storr
Penguin (Harmondsworth)

Artist (The) (formerly Art and Artists)
The Artist Publishing Co Ltd,
Caxton House,
63–65 High Street,
Tenterden,
Kent TN30 6BD
£1.20 Monthly

Artists Newsletter
Artic Producers,
PO Box 23,
Sunderland,
Tyne and Wear SR1 1EJ
75p Monthly

Arts Review
Star City Ltd,
69 Faroe Road,
London W14 0EL
£1.80 (single copy); £35 pa (post free) Fortnightly

Ashley Courtenay Guides
A Courtenay
Annual

Author (The)
Society of Authors,
84 Drayton Gardens,
London SW10 9SB
£3 Quarterly

Autotrade
Morgan-Grampian (Publishers) Ltd,
Morgan-Grampian House,
Calderwood Street,
London SE18 6QH
Monthly

Basic Facts About Patents for Inventions in the UK
Patent Office (Marketing & Publicity),
State House,
High Holborn,
London WC1R 4TP

BBC Index
BBC Publications,
35 Marylebone High Street,
London W1 4AA

BBC Small Business Guide
Colin Barrow
BBC Publications (London) 1982

Becoming a Solicitor
Law Society
113 Chancery Lane,
London W2A 1PL

Beecraft
Beecraft Ltd,
15 West Way,
Copthorne Bank,
Crawley,
West Sussex RH10 3QS
£5.76 pa Monthly

Be Your Own Boss at 16
A Watts
Kogan Page (London) 1986

Be Your Own Boss – Starter Kit
National Extension College,
18 Brooklands Avenue,
Cambridge CB2 2HN

Bit on the Side (A)
Christine Brady
William Collins (London) 1983

Blueprint
26 Cramer Street,
London W1M 3HE
£2 Monthly

Bluff Your Way in Publishing
Anne Tauté
Bluffers' Guides, Ravette
(Horsham) 1987

Boards
Yachting Press Ltd,
196 Eastern Esplanade,
Southend-on-Sea,
Essex
£1.35 Nine issues pa

Body Learning
Michael Gelb
Aurum Press

Bone and Joint Surgery (Journal of)
British Editorial Society of Bone &
Joint Surgery; ads to: Ad Medica,
Stevenson,
Haddington,
East Lothian EG41 4PU
£20 pa Five times per year

Book Retailing in the 1990s
Booksellers Association,
154 Buckingham Palace Road,
London SW1W 9TZ
£2.25 pa (members); £40 pa (non-members)

Bookseller (The)
J Whitaker & Sons Ltd,
12 Dyott Street,
London WC1A 1DF
£7 pa Weekly

BRAD
British Rates and Data,

Maclean Hunter Limited,
Maclean Hunter House,
Chalk Lane,
Cockfosters Road,
Barnet,
Herts EN4 0BU
£205 pa Monthly

Breakthrough
Andrew Ferguson
Duncan Publishing
£19.95 inc p&p; available from the
author,
The Breakthrough Centre,
7 Poplar Mews,
Uxbridge Road,
London W12 7JS

Brides (and Setting Up Home)
The Conde Nast Publications Ltd,
Vogue House,
Hanover Square,
London W1R 0AD
Alternate months

**British Alternative Theatre
Directory**
Conway & McGillivray,
The Conway & McGillivray
  Publishing House Ltd,
22a Birchington Road
London NW6

**British Association of Concert
Agents' List of Artists**
British Association of Concert
Agents,
12 Penzance Place,
London W11 4TA

British Bee Journal
ed C Tousley,
46 Queen Street,
Geddington,
Nr Kettering,
Northants NN14 1AZ
Monthly

British Blacksmith
NMFB & AEA,
Avenue R,
7th Street,
National Agricultural Centre,
Stoneleigh,
Kenilworth,
Warwickshire CV8 2LG

British Dental Journal
Professional & Scientific
Publications,
BMA House,
Tavistock Square,
London WC1H 9JR
£71 pa Twice monthly

British Jeweller
Official Journal of the British
Jewellery and Giftware
Federation,
St Dunstan's House,
Carey Lane,
London EC2V 8AA
£2.60 Monthly

British Journal of Photography
Henry Greenwood & Co Ltd,
234 Temple Chambers,
Temple Avenue,
London EC4Y 0DT
60p Weekly

British Medical Journal
BMA House,
Tavistock Square,
London WC1H 9JR
£142 pa Weekly

British Music Year Book
ed Marianne Barton
Rhinegold Publishing Ltd,
239–241 Shaftesbury Avenue,
London WC2H 8EH

British Performing Arts Yearbook
Rhinegold Publishers 1988

British Printer
Maclean Hunter Ltd,
Maclean Hunter House,
Chalk Lane,
Cockfosters Road,
Barnet,
Herts EN4 0BU
£35 pa Monthly

British Toy and Hobby Briefing
British Toy and Hobby
Manufacturers Association
80 Camberwell Road,
London SE5 0EG

British Toy Industry Fact Book
British Toy and Hobby
Manufacturers' Assoc,
80 Camberwell Road,
London SW19

Broadcast
International Thompson
Publishing Ltd
100 Avenue Road,

London NW3 3TP
£1.10 Weekly

Build Your Own Rainbow
Barrie Hopson and Mike Scally
Life Skills Associates, 1984

Burlington Magazine (The)
The Burlington Magazine
Publications Ltd,
6 Bloomsbury Square,
London WC1A 2LP
£6.50 (single copy); £8 inc
postage; £87 pa (UK); £96
(overseas) Monthly

Cab Trade News
Cab Trade News Co-operative
Society Ltd,
203–209 North Gower Street,
London NW1
15p Monthly

Cabinetmakers' Notebook
James Krenov
Van Nostrand Reinhold, 1983

Campaign
Marketing Publications Ltd,
22 Lancaster Gate,
London W2 3LY
£1 (single copy); £65 pa Weekly

Car and Accessory Trader
Haymarket Publishing Ltd,
38–42 Hampton Road,
Teddington,
Middlesex TW11 0JE
Monthly

Career Change
Ruth Lancashire and RF
Holdsworth
Hobsons Press (Cambridge) 1976

**Career Guide for Young
American Singers**
Central Opera Service

Careers Encyclopaedia
ed Audrey Segal
Cassell (London) 1984

Careers in Journalism
Leaflet pub free by National
Union of Journalists,
Acorn House,
314 Gray's Inn Road,
London WC1X 8DP

Careers in Music
Incorporated Society of
Musicians,
10 Stratford Place,
London W1

Careers in Politics
George Cunningham
Kogan Page (London) 1984

Careers in Psychology
Kogan Page Ltd,
120 Pentonville Road,
London N1 9JN

Cascade
Paul and Gabi Keasc,
Aubastrasse 7,
D-6200 Kriesbadau,
W Germany
£1 (single copy) Quarterly

Caterer and Hotel Keeper
Reed Business Publishing,
Quadrant House,
The Quadrant,
Sutton,
Surrey SM2 5AS
85p Weekly

Ceramic Review
21 Carnaby Street,
London W1V 1PH
£2.70 Alt months

Certified Accountant
Chapter Three Publications Ltd,
8a Hythe Street,
Dartford,
Kent DA1 1BX
£1.20 Monthly

Changing Your Job
Godfrey Golzen and Philip
Plumbley
Kogan Page Ltd (London)

**Chartered Society of
Physiotherapy Careers
Handbook**
14 Bedford Row,
London WC1

Check Your Own IQ
HJ Eysenk
Penguin (Harmondsworth)

Chemical Engineer (The)
Institution of Chemical Engineers,
George E Davis Building,
165 Railway Terrace,
Rugby CV21 3HQ
£32 pa Monthly

Chemist & Druggist
Benn Publications Ltd,
Sovereign Way,
Tonbridge,
Kent TN9 1RW
£1.45 Weekly

Childright
Children's Legal Centre,
20 Compton Terrace,
London N1

Chiropodist (The)
The Society of Chiropodists,
53 Welbeck Street,
London W1M 7HE
£2.50 Monthly

Classical Music
241 Shaftesbury Avenue,
London WC2H 8EH
£1 Fortnightly

Cleaning
RJ Dodd Publishing,
Fairway House,
Dartmouth Road,
Forest Hill,
London SE23 3HN
Monthly

Cleaning Business News
RJ Dodd Publishing,
Fairway House,
Dartmouth Road,
Forest Hill,
London SE23 3HN
Fortnightly

Clinical Biomechanics (formerly British Osteopathic Journal)
Butterworth Scientific Ltd,
PO Box 63,
Westbury House,
Bury Street,
Guildford GU2 5BH
Quarterly

Clothing Industry Yearbook
British Clothing Industry Assoc,
7 Swallow Place,
London W1R 7AA

Commercial Motor
Reed Business Publishing,
Quadrant House,
The Quadrant,
Sutton,
Surrey SM2 5AS
80p (single copy); £40 pa Weekly

Community Care
Reed Business Publishing Ltd,
Carew House, Wallington,
Surrey SM6 0DX
70p Weekly

Community Pharmacy
Joint Marketing & Publishing
Services Ltd,
8th Floor,
Newcombe House,
45 Notting Hill Gate,
London W11 3LQ
£25.50 pa Monthly except Dec

Competitions for Singers
Arts Council of Great Britain,
105 Piccadilly,
London W1

Complete Guide to Executive Manners
L Baldridge

Complete Guide to Total Fitness (The)
Jan Percival, Lloyd Percival and Joe Taylor
EP Publishing (London) 1982

Computing
VNU Business Publications,
VNU House,
32–34 Broadwick Street,
London W1A 2HG
Free to UK registrants, otherwise £32 Weekly

Contact (Journal of British Chiropractic Assoc)
ed Peter Dixon,
207 London Road East,
Batheaston,
Bath,
Avon

Conference Blue Book
Spectrum Communications Group,
16–18 Acton Park Estate,
Stanley Gardens,
London W3
£35

Contacts
Available from The Spotlight Casting Directory & Contacts,
42 Cranbourn Street,
London WC2

Controlling Interest Rate Risk
Platt
Wiley 1986

Conveyancer and Property Lawyer, The
Ads: DA Goodall Ltd,
New Bridge Street House,
30–34 New Bridge Street,
London EC4V 6BJ
£8.75 (single copy); £36 pa (post free) Alt months

Counsel
Butterworth Law Publishers Ltd,
9–12 Bell Yard,
Temple Bar,
London WC2A 2JR
£1.50 Alt months

Country Life
IPC Magazines Ltd,
Kings Reach Tower,
Stamford Street,
London SE1 9LS
£1.10 Weekly

Crafts
Crafts Council,
8 Waterloo Place,
London SW1Y 4AT
£2.50 Alt months

Craftsman's Directory
ed S and J Lance
S and J Lance, 1987

Craftsman's Handbook
Cennini
Dover Publications,
London

Crawford's Directory (of City Connections)
Economist Publications (London)
Annual

Creating Your Own Work
Micheline Mason
Gresham Books (Henley-on-Thames)

Creative Handbook
British Media Publications (East Grinstead)

Creative Review
Centaur Communications Ltd,
St Giles House,
50 Poland Street,
London W1V 4AX
£2 Monthly

Crescendo International
Whitehall Press Ltd,
230 Vauxhall Bridge Road,
London SW1V 1AL
£1.75 Monthly

Daily Telegraph
The Daily Telegraph plc,
Peterborough Court,
South Quay,
181 Marsh Wall,
London E14 9SR
25p Daily

Dance and Dancers
Plus Publications,
248 High Street,
Croydon,
Surrey CR0 1TN
£1.50 Monthly

Dance News
Dance News Ltd,
Hamble House,
Meadrow,
Godalming,
Surrey GU7 3HJ
50p Weekly

Dance Theatre Journal
Laban Centre,
Laurie Grove,
New Cross,
London SE14
£1.50 Quarterly

Dancing Times (The)
Clerkenwell House,
45–47 Clerkenwell Green,
London EC1R 0BE
£1 Monthly

Decanter
Decanter Magazine Ltd,
St John's Chambers,
2–10 St John's Road,
London SW11 1PN
£1.80 Monthly

Dental Practice
AE Morgan Publications Ltd,
Stanley House,
9 West Street,
Epsom,
Surrey KT18 7RL
Twice monthly

Dentist (The)
Update-Siebert Publications,
Friary Court,
13–21 High Street,

Guildford,
Surrey GU1 3DX
£1.25 Eleven times pa

Design
Design Magazine,
The Design Council,
28 Haymarket, London SW1Y 4SU
£25 pa Monthly

Design Courses in Britain
The Design Council,
28 Haymarket,
London SW1Y 4SV

Design Week
Centaur Communications Ltd,
St Giles House,
50 Poland Street,
London W1V 4AX
80p Weekly

Designer (The)
29 Bedford Square,
London WC1B 3EG
Alt months

Designer's Journal
The Architectural Press Ltd,
9 Queen Anne's Gate,
London SW1H 9BY
£2 Ten issues pa

Despatch Rider
PO Box 398,
London SE13 5RW

Direct Mail Handbook
Exley
£19.95

Direct Mail Magazine
Ferrary Publications Ltd,
Ground Floor,
Boundary House,
91–93 Charterhouse Street,
London EC1N 6HR
£50 pa inc Direct Mail News Alt
months from Feb

Direction
Marketing Publications Ltd,
30 Lancaster Gate,
London W2 3LP
£1.80 Monthly

**Directory of Enterprise Agencies
and Community Action
Programmes**
Business in the Community,
227A City Road,
London EC1V 1JU and
25 St Andrew's Square,
Edinburgh EH1 2AF
Free

**Directory of Property
Developers, Investors and
Financiers**
Building Economics Bureau,
Carlton Chambers,
Station Road,
Shortlands,
Bromley,
Kent BR2 0EY

**Directory of Professional
Puppeteers**
The Puppet Centre Trust,
Battersea Arts Centre,
Lavender Hill,
London SW11

Dirt Bike Rider
EMAP National Publications Ltd,
Bushfield House,
Orton Centre,
Peterborough PE28 0UW
£1.10 Monthly

Disco International (Disco and Club Trade International)
Mountain Lion Productions Ltd,
410 St John Street,
London EC1V 4NJ
£1.50 Monthly

DOG (Directory of Opportunities for Graduates)
New Opportunity Press Ltd,
London

Dog Business (The)
Douglas Appleton
Popular Dogs (London) 1960

Drapers Record
International Thomson
Publishing Ltd,
100 Avenue Road,
London NW3
90p Weekly

Driving
Driving Instructors' Association,
Lion Green Road,
Coulsdon
Surrey CR3 2NL
£15 pa (subscription) Alt months

Driving Instructor's Handbook
Kogan Page (London)

Economist (The)
25 St James's Street,
London SW1A 1HG
£1.30 Weekly

Editing and Design. (A) 5-volume manual of English Typography and Layout
Harold Evans
William Heinemann (London)
1972–76

Education and Training of Entrants to the Solicitors Profession
Law Society
113 Chancery Lane,
London W2A 1PL

Egon Ronay
Greencoat House,
Francis Street,
London SW1
Annual

Embalmer (The)
British Institute of Embalmers,
21c Station Road,
Knowle,
Solihull,
West Midlands B93 0HL
Free to members only Six times a year

Employing Jobsharers, Part-time and Temporary Staff
Michael Syrett, 1983
Institute of Personnel
Management,
35 Camp Road,
London SW19

Employment for Disabled People
Mary Thompson
Kogan Page (London)

Equal Opportunities, A Career Guide (for Women and Men)
Ruth Miller and Anna Alston
Penguin (Harmondsworth) 1987

Equestrian Trade News (Journal of British Equestrian Industry)
Wothersome Grange,
Bramham,
Nr Wetherby,
Yorks LS23 6LY
Monthly

Essential Law for Journalists
Macrae
Butterworth 1988

Essentials of Music Copying
Colin Matthews and
Susan Homewood
Music Publishers Association,
103 Kingsway,
London WC2B 6QX, 1988

Estate Agent
National Association of Estate
Agents,
21 Jury Street,
Warwick

Estates Gazette
Estates Gazette Ltd (The),
151 Wardour Street,
London W1V 4BN
90p Weekly

Euromoney
Euromoney (Publications) plc,
London
£72 pa (UK); £92 pa (Europe) –
subscription only Monthly

Executive Post
available from Fitzwilliam House,
2 Fitzwilliam Gate,
Sheffield S1 4JH
Single copy free to PER
registrants; £10 pa to others
Weekly

Exhibition Bulletin
The London Bureau,
266–272 Kirkdale,
Sydenham,
London SE26 4RZ

Export
Institute of Export,
64 Clifton Street,
London EC2A 4HB
£1.60 (single copy); £16 pa (UK);
£20 pa (Europe); £35 pa (overseas
airmail) Monthly

Farmers Weekly
The Farmers Publishing Group,
Reed Business Publishing,
Carew House,
Wallington,
Surrey SM6 0DX
60p Weekly

Fashion Extras
Reflex Publishing Ltd,
86 Clarendon Road,
Croydon,
Surrey CR0 3SG
£28 pa Monthly

Fashion Weekly
Minot Ltd,
172–174 Tottenham Court Road,
London W1P 9LG
Weekly

Financial Decisions
VNU Business Publications,
VNU House,
32–34 Broadwick Street,
London W1A 2HG
£25 pa Monthly

Financial Times
The Financial Times Ltd,
Bracken House,
10 Cannon Street,
London EC4P 4BY
45p Daily

Finding Job Vacancies
Mary Munroe and John Yates
CRAC Publications,
Hobsons Ltd,
Bateman Street,
Cambridge CB2 1LZ

**Fire and Design of Schools
(Bulletin No. 7)**
DES (Department of Education
and Science)
£2.50

First Voice
Magazine of the National
Federation of Self-Employed and
Small Businesses Ltd,
YCG,
17a Monckton Road,
Wakefield,
West Yorkshire WF2 7AL
Free to members only Alt months

Fish Farming International
AGB Heighway Ltd,
Cloister Court,
22–26 Farringdon Lane,
London EC1R 3AU
£1.75 Monthly

**Five Day Course in Thinking
(The)**
Edward de Bono
Pelican (Harmondsworth)

**Forge 88 (Formerly Farriers'
Journal)**
Avenue R,
7th Street,
National Agricultural Centre,
Stoneleigh,
Kenilworth,
Warwickshire CV8 2LG
Alt months

Franchise Magazine (The)
Franchise Development Services
Ltd,
Castle House,
Castle Meadow,
Norwich,
Norfolk NR2 1PJ
£15 pa Quarterly

Franchise World
James House,
37 Nottingham Road,
London SW17 7EA
£35 pa Alt months

Freelance Alternative
Marianne Gray
Piatkus Books (London) 1987

Freelance Photographer's Market Handbook
ed John Tracy and Stewart Gibson
Bureau of Freelance
Photographers,
Focus House,
Green Lanes,
London N13

Fundamentals of Advertising (The)
John Wilmshurst
William Heinemann (London) 1985

Galleries
Barrington Publications,
London
75p (single copy); £11.50 pa (UK);
£18 pa (Europe); £25 pa (USA and elsewhere) Monthly

Garage Equipment (Garage and Automotive Retailer)
AGB Hulton Ltd,
Warwick House,
Azalea Drive,
Swanley,
Kent BR8 8JF
Monthly

Garage and Transport (Group Selector)
AGB Hulton Ltd,
Warwick House,
Swanley,
Kent BR8 8JF
Quarterly

Garden (The)
Journal of the Royal Horticultural Society
Home and Law Publishing Ltd,
Great London House,
Hamstead Road,
London NW1 7QQ
Free to members Monthly

Geriatric Medicine and Gerontology
Brockelhurst

Going for it! How to Succeed as an Entrepreneur
V Kiam
Fontana (London) 1986

GNI Guide to Traded Options
Macmillan Press,
London

Going Freelance
Godfrey Golzen
Riverside Books (London) 1985

Goldsmiths Gazette
Goldsmiths Company,
Goldsmiths Hall,
Foster Lane,
London EC2

Good Communications Guide
National ISIS,
56 Buckingham Gate,
London SW1E 6AG
£2.50 inc p & p

Good Food Guide
Hodder and Stoughton
(Sevenoaks) London
Annual

Good Hotel Guide
Hodder and Stoughton
(Sevenoaks) London
Annual

Graduate Post
Newpoint Publishing Co Ltd,
Newpoint House,
St James's Lane,
London N10 3DF
Fortnightly

Grape Press (The)
English Vineyards Association,
38 West Park,
London SE9 4RH
Quarterly

Greatest Little Business Book, (The)
Peter Hingston
Hingston
£5.75

Grove's Dictionary of Music (New)
ed Stanley Sadie
Macmillan, London,1980

Guardian (The)
119 Farringdon Road,
London EC1R 3ER
25p Daily

Guide for Guardians Ad Litem in Adoption Proceedings
Available from Dept of Health
and Social Services

Guide for Guardians Ad Litem in Juvenile Courts
Available from Department of
Health and Social Services

Guidelines for Inspection of Boarding Establishments
British Veterinary Association,
7 Mansfield Street,
London W1A 0AT

Hairdressers' Journal International
Reed Business Publishing,
Quadrant House,
The Quadrant,
Sutton,
Surrey SM2 5AS
60p Weekly

Handbook Royal College of General Practitioners
14 Princes Gate,
London SW7

Hansard
HMSO,
St Crispins,
Duke Street,
Norwich NR3 1PD

£4.35 inc p & p (dependent on the issue required)

Here's Health
Argus Health Publications Ltd,
Victory House,
Leicester Place,
London WC2H 7NB
95p (single copy); £14 pa (UK); £18 pa (overseas, surface mail inc postage) Monthly

Hi-Fi Choice
Dennis Publishing,
14 Rathbone Place,
London W1P 1DE
£2.95 (single copy); £40 pa (inc p & p) Monthly

Hi-Fi News and Record Review
Link House Magazines Ltd,
Dingwall Avenue,
Croydon CR9 2TA
£1.40 pa (single copy); £16.80 pa (UK); £24.80 (overseas surface); £42.50 (airmail) Monthly

Hireman
Hireman Publishing Ltd,
174 Park Road,
Peterborough PE1 2UF
Monthly

Hire News
Response Publishing Ltd,
Wentworth House,
Wentworth Street,
Peterborough PE1 1DS
Monthly

Holiday Retreats for Cats and Dogs in England
Scarlet Tipping
The Book Guild Ltd,
Temple House,
25–26 High Street,
Lewes,
East Sussex BN7 2LU

Hollis (Press and PR Annual)
Contact House,
Sunbury-on-Thames,
Middlesex TW16 5HG

Homeopathy; Medicine for the 21st century
Ullman
North Atlantic Books 1987

Honourable Member
Richard Needham
Patrick Stephens
(Wellingborough) 1983

Horticulture Week
Haymarket Publishing
38–42 Hampton Road,
Teddington,
Middx TW11 0JE
65p Weekly

House Magazine
Parliamentary Communications Ltd,
12–13 Clerkenwell Green,
London EC1R 0DP
£2.50 Weekly

How Parliament Works
Paul Silk
Longman (London) 1987

How to Choose Business Premises
Kogan Page

How to evaluate a Franchise
Martin Mendelsohn
Available from Franchise World,
James House,
37 Nottingham Road,
London SW17 7EA

How to Get Control of Your Time and Your Life
Alan Laikein
Signe, 1973

How to Start and Run Your Own Business
M Mogano
Graham and Trotman (London)
1985

How to win customers
Heinz Goldman
Pan, London
£3.50

Hypnosis
Ursula Markham
Macdonald Optima (London)
1987

Hypnosis: A Gateway to Better Health
Dr Brian Roet
Weidenfeld & Nicolson (London)

Hypnosis: Guide for Patients and Practitioners
David Waxman
Unwin (London)

Ideas for Self-Employment and Part-Time Work
T Crawley
Careers Consultants (Richmond)
1983

Incorporated Society of Musicians' Arts Festival Book
Incorporated Society of Musicians,
10 Stratford Place,
London W1

Independent (The)
Newspaper Publishing plc,
40 City Road,,
London EC1Y 2DB
30p Daily

Individual Therapy in Britain
Wendy Dryden
Harper and Row (London) 1984

Inside the Technical Consultancy Business
H Kaye
John Wiley (Chichester) 1986

Insurance
RICS Insurance Services Ltd,
Plantation House,
31–35 Fenchurch Street,
London EC3M 3DX

Insurance Journal
Chartered Insurance Institute,
20 Aldermanbury,
London EC2V 7HY

Introducing Patents: A Guide for Inventors
Patent Office (Marketing & Publicity),
State House,
High Holborn,
London WC1R 4TP

Investors' Chronicle
Financial Times Business
Information Ltd,
Greystoke Place,
Fetter Lane,
London EC4A 1ND
£1.20 Weekly

Jazz Journal International
Jazz Journal Ltd,
35 Great Russell Street,
London WC1B 3PP
£1.50 Monthly

Job Ideas
COIC (Careers and Occupational
Information Centre),
Manpower Services
Commission,
Moorfoot,
Sheffield S1 4PQ

Job Sharing
Atkinson
Institute of Manpower Studies,
Mansell Building,
University of Sussex,
Falmer,
Brighton,
Sussex

Jocks
Spotlight Publications Ltd,
Greater London House,
Hampstead Road,
London NW1 7QZ
£1.25 Monthly

Journal of Alternative and Complementary Medicine
Argus Health Publications Ltd,
Victory House,
Leicester Place,
London WC2H 7NB
£1.50 (single copy), £18.50 pa
Monthly

Know Your Own IQ
HJ Eysenk
Penguin (Harmondsworth)

Lady (The)
39–40 Bedford Street,
London WC2E 9ER
45p Weekly

Laing's Review of Private Health Care
Laing and Buisson Ltd,
1 Perrin Street,
London NW5

Lancet (The)
The Lancet Ltd,
46 Bedford Square,
London WC1B 3SL
£2.75 Weekly

Landscape Design
5a West Street,
Reigate,
Surrey RH2 9BL
£12 pa Alt months from Feb

Law of Burial, Cremation and Exhumation (The)
MR Russell Davis
Shaw and Sons Ltd,
Shaway House,
Lower Sydenham,
London SE26 5AE

Licensee
National Licensed Victuallers'
Association,
Boardman House,
2 Downing Street,
Farnham,
Surrey GU9 7NX
Monthly

Light on Pranayama
BKS Iyengar
George Allen & Unwin (London)

Light on Yoga
BKS Iyengar
George Allen & Unwin (London)

List 99
DES,
London

Litho Week
Haymarket Publishing Ltd,
38–42 Hampton Road,
Teddington,
Middlesex TW11 0JE
Weekly

Look After Yourself
Health Education Council,
78 New Oxford Street,
London WC1A 1AH

Making Waves
ed David Butler
Artic Producers Publishing
Company

Managing Negotiations
G Kennedy, J Benson and
J McMillan
Business Books (London) 1986

Marketing
Marketing Publications Ltd,
22 Lancaster Gate,
London W2 3LY
Weekly

Marketing
Eddie Martin
Mitchell Beazley
£2.95

Marketing for the small firm
Rick Brown
Cassell,
London
£6.95

Marketing Week
Centaur Communications Ltd,
St Giles House,
50 Poland Street,
London W1V 4AX
£1 (single copy), £55 pa Weekly

Match Weekly
EMAP Pursuit Publishing Ltd,
Bretton Court,
Peterborough,
Cambs PE3 8DZ
45p Weekly

Media Week
Media Week Ltd,
20–22 Wellington Street,
London WC2E 7DD
90p Weekly

Megatrends
John Naisbitt
Futura,
London
£2.50

Michelin Guides
Michelin,
France

Micro Decision
VNU Business Publications,
VNU House,
32–34 Broadwick Street,
London W1A 2HG
£1.50 Monthly

Microscope
Dennis Publishing,
14 Rathbone Place,
London W1P 2HB
£2 Weekly

**Miller's Professional Antique
Price Guide**
Miller's Publications (Cranbrook)
Annual

Money for Business
Bank of England
£3

Money into Light
John Boorman
Faber (London) 1985

Money Magazine
Money Magazine Ltd,
Thames House,
18 Park Street,
London SE1 9ER

Money Management
Financial Times Business
Information,
Greystoke Place,
Fetter Lane,
London EC4A 1ND
£2.85 Monthly

Morning Advertiser
13–27 Brunswick Place,
London N1 6DX
22p Daily

Motor Cycle News
8 Herbal Hill,
London EC1R 5JB
48p Weekly

Music Teacher (The)
Rhinegold Publishing Ltd,
241 Shaftesbury Avenue,
London WC2H 8EH
£1.25 Monthly

Musical Times (The)
Novello & Co Ltd,
8 Lower James Street,
London W1R 4DN
£1.20 Monthly

Musician (The)
Rhinegold Publishing Ltd,
241 Shaftesbury Avenue,
London WC2H 8EH
Free to members of Musicians'
Union Quarterly

Musicians Handbook
Rhinegold Publishing Ltd,
239–241 Shaftesbury Avenue,
London WC2H 8EH

National Federation of Music Societies' Handbook
National Federation of Music Societies,
Francis House,
Francis Street,
London SW1

National Trust Magazine
The Publishing Consultancy Ltd
15 Adeline Place,
London WC1B 3AJ
50p, free to Trust members Tri-anually

Negotiator
FB Corporate Image Ltd,
Fotoscript House,
Jubilee Close,
Townsend Lane,
Kingsbury,
London NW9 8TR
Single copy free to estate agents;
£32.60 pa Fortnightly

Neues Glas
Obtainable from Verlagsanstalt
Handwerk Gmbh,
AUFM Tetleberg 7,
4000 Dusseldorf 1,
W Germany
DM14 (£5.25 single copy) from
Crafts Council Bookshop,
12 Waterloo Place,
London SW1Y 4AU

New English Vineyard (The)
Joanna Smith
Sidgwick & Jackson Ltd (London)
1979

New Musical Express
Holborn Publishing Group,
IPC Magazines Ltd,
Room 330,
Commonwealth House,
1–19 New Oxford Street,
London WC1A 1NG
50p Weekly

Notes of Guidance for Proprietors on the Registration of Independent Schools
Registrar of Independent Schools,
Scottish Education Department,
New St Andrew's House,
Edinburgh EH1 3SY

Nursing Standard
Scutari Publications,
17–19 Peterborough Road
Harrow-on-the-Hill,
Middlesex HA1 2AX
55p Weekly

Nursing Times
Macmillan Magazines Ltd,
4 Little Essex Street,
London WC2R 3LF
60p Weekly

Occupation – Self-Employed
Rosemary Pettit
Wildwood House Ltd (Aldershot)
1981

Occupations 88 (COIC Annual Careers Guide)
Careers and Occupational Centre
Annual (Sheffield)

Offensive Marketing (and how to make your competitors followers)
Hugh Davidson
Penguin (Harmondsworth)
£5.95

Ogilvy on Advertising
David Ogilvy
Pan (London)

Old Bike Mart
PO Box 7,
Poynton,
Stockport,
Cheshire

On Being a Counsellor
E Kennedy
Macmillan,
London

On Board Windsurfing Magazine
The DRG Building,
Longmoor Lane,
Breaston,
Derby DE7 3BQ
£1.35 Monthly

One Minute Manager, The
Kenneth Blanchard and Spencer
Johnson
Fontana,
London
£2.95

One Minute Sales Person, The
Spencer Johnson
Fontana,
London
£3.50

Optician (The)
Reed Business Publishing Ltd,
Quadrant House,
The Quadrant,
Sutton
Surrey SM2 5AS
70p Weekly

Optometry Today
Bridge House,
233–4 Blackfriars Road,
London SE1 8NW
£30 pa

Orchestration
Walter Piston
Gollancz (London)

Orchestration
Cecil Forsyth
Dover (London) 1986

Osteopathy
Stephen Sandler
Pan (London) 1987

Paint Magic
Jocasta Innes
Windward and Berger Paints
(Leicester)

Parliament and the Public
Edmund Marshall
Macmillan (London) 1982

Parliament in the 1980s
Philip Norton
Basil Blackwell (Oxford) 1985

Pathfinders: How to achieve happiness by conquering life's crises
Gail Sheehy
Sidgwick and Jackson
£5.95

PC User
EMAP Business and Computer Publications,
155 Farringdon Road,
London EC1R 3AD
£1.75 Fortnightly

PC Week
VNU Business Publications,
VNU House,
32–34 Broadwick Street,
London W1A 2HG
Single copy free Weekly

PC Yearbook
VNU Business Publications,
VNU House,
32–34 Broadwick Street,
London W1A 2HG
£51.50 Annual

Penguin Guide to the Law
Penguin (Harmondsworth)

Pharmaceutical Journal (The)
The Pharmaceutical Society of Great Britain,
1 Lambeth High Street,
London SE1 7JN
£4 + postage Weekly

Photographer (The)
Penblade Publishers Ltd,
1 Gayford Road,
London W12 9BY
Monthly

Photo Journalism
Arthur Rothstein
American Photographic Book Publishing Co

Pictures on a Page; Photojournalism, Graphics and Picture Editing
Harold Evans
Heinemann Professional Publishing (London)

PIMS Media Directory
PIMS (London) Ltd,
4 St John's Place,
London EC1
£57 monthly

Please Follow Me
Don Cross,
available from Wessexplore,
20 Coldharbour Lane,
Salisbury,
Wilts SP2 8BY
£2

Practical Boat Owner
IPC Magazines Ltd,
Westover House,
West Quay Road,
Poole,
Dorset BH15 1JG
£1.50 Monthly

Practical Guide to Making at Home (A)
Olga Franklin
Macdonald (London) 1981

Practical Upholstering and the Cutting of Loose Covers
Frederick Palmer

Practical Woodworking
IPC Magazines Ltd,
Kings Reach Tower,
Stamford Street,
London SE1 9LS
£1.30 Monthly

Principles and Practice of Embalming
Strub and Frederick
Lawrence G Frederick,
1827 Maryvale Drive,
Dallas,
Texas 75208,
USA

Printing World
Benn Publications Ltd,
Sovereign Way,
Tonbridge,
Kent TN9 1RW
£1.40 + postage Weekly

Professional Partnerships – Facing the Future
Spicer and Pegler,
65 Crutched Friars,
London EC3N 2NI

PR Week
Rangenine Ltd,
100 Fleet Street,
London EC4Y 1DE
£40 pa Weekly

Psychology of Interpersonal Behaviour
M Argyle
Penguin (Harmondsworth) 1984

Psychologist (The)
British Psychological Society
St Andrew's House,
48 Princes Road East,
Leicester LE1 7DR

Pub Caterer
Reed Business Publishing,
Quadrant House,
The Quadrant,
Sutton,
Surrey SM2 5AS
£1 Ten times/year

Publican
Maclaren Publishers Ltd,
PO Box 109,
Maclaren House,
Scarbrook Road,
Croydon CR9 1QH
Twice monthly

Publisher (The)
Macro Publishing Ltd,
Conbar House,
Mead Lane,
Hertford,
Herts SG13 7AS
Monthly

Publishers' Freelance Directory
Elvendon Press,
The Old Surgery,
High Street,
Goring-on-Thames,
Reading,
Berks RG8 9AW

Publishing News
Gradegate Ltd,
43 Museum Street,
London WC1A 1LY
80p (single copy); £45 pa
(subscription) Weekly

RAC Guides
RAC Publications (London)
Annual

Record Mirror
Spotlight Publications Ltd,
Greater London House,
Hampstead Road,
London NW1 7QZ
65p Weekly

Reflexology
T Unwin and JM Foulkes
Cockatrice Press

Resurgence
Ford House,
Harland,
Bideford,
Devon
£1.80 Bi-monthly

Retail Jeweller
International Thomson Business
Publishing,
100 Avenue Road,

Swiss Cottage,
London NW3 3TP
Fortnightly

Road Racer
Road Racer Ltd,
Myatt McFarlane Publishing,
PO Box 28,
Altrincham,
Cheshire WA15 8SH
£1.25 Alt months

**ROGET (Register of Graduate
Employment and Training)**
AGCAS,
Central Services Unit,
Crawford House,
Precinct Centre,
Oxford Road,
Manchester M13 9EP

Roget's Thesaurus
Longman (London)

Royal Doulton Figures
Desmond Eyles, Richard Dennis,
   Louise Irving
Royal Doulton and Richard
   Dennis
£35

**Running Your Own Boarding
Kennels**
Sheila Zabawa
Kogan Page (London)

**Running Your Own Driving
School**
Kogan Page (London)

Savoy Cocktail Book
Muller, Blond & White Ltd,
55–57 Great Ormond Street,
London WC1N 3HZ

Schools Book, The
Papermac,
London
£10.99

Science of Homeopathy, The
George Vithoukas
Dawson Publications
£6.99

Scottish Farmer (The)
Holmes McDougall (Magazine
Division),
The Plaza Tower,
The Plaza,
East Kilbride,
Glasgow G74 1LW
65p Weekly

Scribe: Journal of the Society of Scribes and Illuminators
54 Boileau Road,
London SW13 9BL

Seafood International
AGB Heighway Ltd,
Cloister Court,
22–26 Farringdon Lane,
London EC1R 3AU
£1.50 Monthly

Secret Self, The: A Comprehensive Guide to Handwriting Analysis
Anna Koren

Adama Books
£14.95

Self Sufficiency 16–25
R Bourne and J Gould
Kogan Page (London) 1983

Setting Up in Practice
Leaflet from RICS Publications
Department,
Norden House,
Basing View,
Basingstoke RG21 2HN

Shoe and Leather News
84–88 Great Eastern Street,
London EC2A 3ED
60p Weekly

Shoe Trade Directory
84–88 Great Eastern Street,
London EC2A 3ED
£35 pa Annual

Shoot
IPC Magazines Ltd,
Berkshire House,
168–173 High Holborn,
London WC1 7AU
42p Weekly

Skills of Negotiating
B Scott
Gower (Aldershot) 1981

Ski Survey
The Ski Club of Great Britain
Publications,
Advertisement Dept,
Jackson, Rudd & Associates Ltd,

Oldebourne House,
46–47 Chancery Lane,
London WC2A 1JB
£1.40 Five times a year
(September, October, November,
December, February)

Small Business Guide, The
Colin Barrow
BBC
£6.50

Social Work Today
Ads: Macmillan Magazines Ltd,
4 Little Essex Street,
London WC2R 3LF
£30 pa post free Weekly

Sound Engineer and Producer
International Thomson
Publishing Ltd,
100 Avenue Road,
London NW3 3TP
£1.50 Monthly

Spare-Time Income
Peter Farrell
Kogan Page (London)

Special Needs Drama Directory
ILEA Cockpit Theatre and Arts
    Workshop

Spending Advertising Money
Simon Broadbent
Business Books Ltd (London)
1975

**Spotlight (Casting Directory)
(The)**
42 Cranbourn Street,
London WC2

Stage (The)
Carson & Comerford Ltd,
47 Bermondsey Street,
London SE1 3XT
60p Weekly

**Standard Handbook of
Consulting Engineering Practice**
Hicks and Mueller
McGraw-Hill (Maidenhead) 1985

Starting up in Practice
Susan Hay
Royal Institute of British
Architects,
66 Portland Place,
London W1N 4AD

Starting Your Own Business
Consumers Association (London)

Stress Check
Cary Cooper
Pentice Hall International,
66 Wood Lane End,
Hemel Hempstead,
Herts, 1975

Student Book (The)
Macmillan (London)
£8.95 Annual

Studio Sound
Link House Magazines Ltd,
Link House,

Dingwall Avenue,
Croydon CR9 2TA
£1.50 Monthly

Symmetric System of Big Game Head Hunting
Fred Crandall,
available from Crowcraft,
Orchard Farm,
Escrick Road,
Wheldrake,
York YO4 6BQ
£13.60

Systems International
Reed Business Publishing,
Quadrant House,
The Quadrant,
Sutton,
Surrey SM2 5AS
£35 pa Monthly

Taking Stock
Charles Handy
BBC Publications (London) 1983

Taxidermy
J Metcalf
Duckworth 1981
£14.60

Tax Intelligence
Simmons
Butterworth (London)

Taxi
Licensed Taxi Drivers'
Association,
9–11 Woodfield Road,
London W9 2BA
30p Fortnightly

Teach Yourself Bookkeeping
A T Piper
Hodder and Stoughton
£2.95

Technique of Radio Production
Robert MacLeish
Focal Press 1978

Thatch
Bob West
David and Charles (London) 1987

Thatch (Newsmagazine)
Thatching Advisory Service Ltd,
Rose Tree Farm,
29 Nine Mile Ride,
Finchampstead,
Wokingham,
Berks RG11 4QD

Think and Grow Rich
Napoleon Hill
Wilshire

Third Wave, The
Alvin Toffler
Pan, London
£5.99

Thomson Local Directories
Thomson Directories,
Thomson House,
296 Farnborough Road,
Farnborough,
Hants GU14 7NU
Additional copies (price on
application)

Tiles and Tiling
Hyperion Publishing Company
Ltd,

Vale House,
32 Vale Road,
Bushey,
Watford,
Herts
8 times a year

Time Magazine
Time-Life International BV,
5 Ottho Heldingstraat,
1066 AZ,
Amsterdam,
The Netherlands
(UK Office Time & Life Building,
New Bond Street,
London W1)
£1.30 (UK) Weekly

Times (The)
Times Newspapers Ltd,
PO Box 496,
Virginia Street,
London E1 9XJ
30p Daily

**Times Educational Supplement,
The**
Priory House,
St John's Lane,
London EC1M 4BX
60p Weekly

Trading in Oil Futures
Clubley
Woodhead-Faulkner 1980

Tradition of English Wine (A)
Hugh Barty-King
Oxford Illustrated Press,
Oxford, 1977

Travel News
ABC Travel Publications Ltd,
242 Vauxhall Bridge Road,
London SW1V 1AU
Weekly

Travel Trade Gazette
Morgan Grampian House,
Calderwood Street,
London SE18 6QH
£42.50 pa Weekly

Truth About Publishing (The)
Sir Stanley Unwin
Penguin (Harmondsworth)

TV Today (Television Today)
47 Bermondsey Street,
London SE1

UK Press Gazette
Bouverie Publishing Co Ltd,
Rooms 244–249 Temple
Chambers,
Temple Avenue,
London EC4Y 0DT
80p Weekly

Unashamed Accompanist (The)
Gerald Moore
Methuen (London) 1943

Understand Your Accounts
H Price
Kogan Page (London)

Upholstery
Desmond Gaston
William Collins (London) 1982

Use of Self
FM Alexander
Gollancz (London)

Willings Press Guide
British Media Publications (East Grinstead)

Veterinary Record
British Veterinary Association,
7 Mansfield Street,
London W1M 0AT
£1.65; £80 pa (post free) Weekly

Vinegrowing in Britain
Gillian Pearkes
JM Dent (London) 1982

Watersport Trade News
Underwater World Publications Ltd,
40 Gray's Inn Road,
London WC1X 8LR
Single copy free Quarterly

Westminster Blues
Julian Critchley
Hamish Hamilton (London) 1985

Westminster Man: A Tribal Anthropology of the Commons People
Austin Mitchell
Methuen (London) 1982

What Colour is your Parachute?
Richard Bolles
Ten Speed Press, 1983

What Hi-Fi?
Haymarket Publishing Ltd,
London
£1.40 (single copy); £19 pa
Monthly

What to do when Someone Dies
Consumers Association,
14 Buckingham Street,
London WC2

What's Brewing
The Campaign for Real Ale (CAMRA),
34 Alma Road,
St Albans,
Herts AL1 3BW
Monthly

Where to Study
Compiled by Edward Martin
BIPP,
Henry Greenwood & Co Ltd,
20 Great James Street,
London WC1N 3HL

Windsurf and Boardsailing
Ocean Publications,
34 Buckingham Palace Road,
London SW1W 0QP
£1.10 Nine issues/year

Wine
The EVRO Publishing Co Ltd,
5–6 Church Street,
Twickenham,
Middlesex TW1 3NJ
£1.50; £18 pa Monthly

Woman in your own Right (A)
Anne Dickson
Quartet Books (London) 1982

Woman's Wear Resources
Woman's Wear Resources Ltd,
25–26 Poland Street,
London W1V 3DB
£54 pa Monthly

Work for Yourself
Paddy Hall
National Extension College,
18 Brooklands Avenue,
Cambridge CB2 2HN

Woodworker
Argus Specialist Publications Ltd,
No. 1 Golden Square,
London W1R 3AB
£1.10 Monthly

World Soccer
Websters Publications Ltd,
Onslow House,
60–66 Saffron Hill,
London EC1N 8AY
£1.10 Monthly

Working for Yourself
Godfrey Golzen
Kogan Page (London)

Working Mother – A Practical Handbook
Litvinoff and M Velmans
Corgi Books (London)

Writers' and Artists' Yearbook
A & C Black Ltd (London)
Annual

Writer's Handbook
Barry Turner
Macmillan (London) 1988
£6.95

Yachting (Monthly)
IPC Magazines Ltd,
Room 2215,
King's Reach Tower,
Stamford Street,
London SE1 9LS
£1.50 Monthly

Yachts and Yachting
Yachting Press Ltd,
196 Eastern Esplanade,
Southend-on-Sea
£1.20 Fortnightly

Yellow Pages
British Telecom

Yoga – A Gem for Women
Geeta S Iyengar
Allied Publishers Private Ltd

Yoga Journal – The Magazine for Conscious Living
PO Box 6076,
Syracuse,
NY 13217,
USA

Yoga and Health
Surgery Advertising,
64 High Street,
Lewes,
East Sussex
BN7 1XG
£1.10 Monthly

Index